The

COMPLETE WORKS

of

MRS. HEMANS,

Reprinted entire from the last

English Edition

Edited By Her Sister

In Two Volumes

VOL. L

New York
D. Appleton & Company, 200 Broadway

1853

TO

COLONEL SIR HENRY BROWNE, K. C. H.

THESE PAGES,

WRITTEN UNDER HIS ROOF,

WHICH HAS ALWAYS BEEN A REFUGE FOR THE SORROWFUL

ARE DEDICATED,

BY HIS SURVIVING SISTER,

IN REMEMBRANCE OF HER,

WHO, DURING MANY YEARS OF TRIAL,

FOUND HER BEST EARTHLY SOLACE,

IN HIS CARE AND AFFECTION.

CONTENTS.

ENGLAND AND SPAIN: OR VALOR AND PATRIOTISM,	11
WALLACE'S INVOCATION TO BRUCE,	24
TALES AND HISTORIC SCENES,	
The Abencerrage,	32
Notes to ditto,	66
The Widow of Crescentius,	73
Notes to ditto,	87
The Last Banquet of Antony and Cleopatra	91
Notes to ditto,	95
Alaric in Italy,	96
Notes to ditto,	101
The Wife of Asdrubal,	102
Heliodorus in the Temple,	104
Night-Scene in Genoa,	107
The Troubadour and Richard Cœur de Lion,	112
Notes to ditto,	116
The Death of Conradin,	117
Notes to ditto,	122
RESTORATION OF THE WORKS OF ART TO ITALY:	123
Notes to ditto,	135
MODERN GREECE,	136
Notes to ditto,	160
Critical Annotation on "Tales and Historic Scenes,"	166
Do. on " Restoration of the Works of Art to Italy," and on "Modern Greece,"	167
TRANSLATIONS FROM CAMOENS AND OTHER POETS,	169
MISCELLANEOUS POEMS:—	
Lines written in a Hermitage	191
Dirge of a Child,	192
Invocation,	193
To the Memory of Gen. Sir E—d P—k—m,	194
To the Memory of Sir H—y E—li—s,	195
Guerilla Song,	196
The Aged Indian,	ib.
Evening among the Alps,	197
Dirge of the Highland Chief in "Waverly,"	198
The Crusader's War-Song,	199
The Death of Clanronald,	200
To the Eye,	ib.
The Hero's Death,	201
Stanzas on the Death of the Princess Charlotte,	202
ITALIAN LITERATURE:—	
The Basvigliana of Monti,	209
The Alcestis of Alfieri,	213
Il Conte di Carmagnola, by Manzoni,	220
Caius Gracchus, by Monti,	236
Patriotic Effusions of the Italian Poets,	243
THE SCEPTIC,	247
A TALE OF THE SECRET TRIBUNAL,	262
SUPERSTITION & REVELATON,	296
CARAVAN IN THE DESERTS,	303
MARIUS AMONGST THE RUINS OF CARTHAGE.	307
SONG, FOUNDED ON AN ARABIAN ANECDOTE,	310
ALP-HORN SONG,	311
TRANSLATIONS FROM HORACE,	312
THE CROSS OF THE SOUTH,	314
THE SLEEPER OF MARATHON,	315
TO MISS F. A. L., ON HER BIRTHDAY,	316
WRITTEN IN THE FIRST LEAF OF THE ALBUM OF THE SAME,	317
TO THE SAME, ON THE DEATH OF HER MOTHER,	ib.
FROM THE ITALIAN OF GARCILASSO DE LA VEGA,	318
FROM THE ITALIAN OF SANNAZARO,	319
APPEARANCE OF THE SPIRIT OF THE CAPE TO VASCO DE GAMA,	ib.
A DIRGE,	322
THE MAREMMA,	323
TO THE MEMORY OF GEO. III.	329
A TALE OF THE 14th CENTURY,	335
BELSHAZZAR'S FEAST,	347
THE LAST CONSTANTINE,	351
GREEK SONGS,	377
ELYSIUM,	383
THE FUNERAL GENIUS,	386
THE TOMBS OF PLATÆA,	387
THE VIEW FROM CASTRI,	389
THE FESTAL HOUR,	390
SONG OF THE BATTLE OF MORGARTEN,	392
SEBASTIAN OF PORTUGAL,	396
ODE ON THE DEFEAT OF SEBASTIAN OF PORTUGAL.	408
THE SIEGE OF VALENCIA,	411
THE FOREST SANCTUARY,	472
Notes to ditto,	506
Critical Annotations,	511
LAYS OF MANY LANDS:	
Moorish Bridal Song,	512
The Bird's Release,	513
The Sword of the Tomb,	514
Valkyriur Song,	517
Cavern of the Three Tells,	519
Swiss Song,	520
The Messenger Bird,	522
The Stranger in Louisiana,	523
The Isle of Founts,	524
The Bended Bow,	527

A*

CONTENTS.

He Never Smiled Again,	852	The Green Isles of Ocean,	591
Cœur de Lion at the Bier		The Sea-Song of Gafran,	592
of his Father,	529	The Hirlas Horn,	ib.
The Vassal's Lament for		The Hall of Cynddylan,	593
the Fallen Tree,	531	Lament of Llywarch Hen,	594
The Wild Huntsman,	532	Grufydd's Feast,	595
Brandenburg Harvest-Song,	533	The Cambrian in America,	596
The Shade of Theseus,	534	The Monarchy of Britain,	ib.
Ancient Greek Song of Exile,	535	Taliesin's Prophecy,	597
Greek Funeral Chant,	ib.	Owen Glyndwr's War Song,	598
The Parting Song,	538	Prince Madoc's Farewell,	599
The Suliote Mother,	540	Caswallon's Triumph,	600
The Farewell to the Dead,	541	Howel's Song,	ib.
MISCELLANEOUS PIECES:		The Mountain Fires,	601
The Treasures of the Deep,	542	Eryri Wen,	602
Bring Flowers,	543	Chant of the Bards,	603
The Crusader's Return,	544	The Dying Bard's Prophecy,	604
Thekla's Song,	546	The Fair Isle,	605
The Revellers,	ib.	The Rock of Cader Idris,	ib.
The Conqueror's Sleep,	548	HYMNS FOR CHILDHOOD;—	
Our Lady's Well,	549	Introductory Verses,	606
The Parting of Summer,	550	The Rainbow,	607
The Songs of Our Fathers,	551	The Sun,	608
The World in the Open Air,	552	The Rivers,	ib.
Kindred Hearts,	553	The Stars,	609
The Traveller at the		The Ocean,	610
Source of the Nile,	554	The Thunder-Storm,	611
Casabianca,	556	The Birds,	612
The Dial of Flowers,	557	The Sky-lark,	613
Our Daily Paths,	ib.	The Nightingale,	614
The Cross in the Wilderness	559	The Northern Spring,	615
Last Rites,	561	Paraphrase of Ps. cxlviii.,	ib.
The Hebrew Mother,	562	DE CHATILLON, or the Crusaders, a Tragedy,	616
The Wreck,	564		
The Trumpet,	565	Annotation on ditto,	644
Evening Prayer at a		MISCELLANEOUS PIECES;—	
Girl's School,	566	I go, Sweet Friends,	645
The Hour of Death,	567	Angel Visits,	646
The Lost Pleiad,	568	Ivy Song,	647
The Cliffs of Dover,	ib.	To one of the Author's Children, on his Birthday,	648
The Graves of Martyrs,	569		
The Hour of Prayer,	570	On a Similar Occasion,	ib.
The Voice of Home		Christ Stilling the Tempest,	649
to the Prodigal.	571	Epitaph over the Grave of Two Brothers.	ib.
The Wakening,	572		
The Breeze from Shore,	573	Monumental Inscription,	650
The Dying Improvisatore,	574	The Sound of the Sea,	ib.
Music of Yesterday,	575	The Child and Dove,	651
The Forsaken Hearth,	476	A Dirge,	ib.
The Dreamer,	577	Scene in a Dalecarlian Mine,	652
The Wings of the Dove,	578	English Soldier's Song of Memory,	653
Psyche borne to the Isle of Pleasure,	579		
		Haunted Ground,	654
The Boon of Memory,	580	The Child of the Forests,	655
DARTMOOR, (a Prize Poem,)	582	To the Memory of * * *.	656
Notes to ditto,	589	The Vaudois Valleys,	ib.
WELSH MELODIES:—		Song of the Spanish Wanderer,	658
Introductory Stanzas—			
The Harp of Wales,	590	The Contadina,	659
Druid Chorus on the Landing of the Romans,	591	Troubadour Song,	ib

ENGLAND AND SPAIN;*

OR,

VALOR AND PATRIOTISM.

"His sword the brave man draws
And asks no omen but his country's cause."—*Pope.*

Too long have Tyranny and Power combined,
To sway, with iron sceptre, o'er mankind;
Long has Oppression worn th' imperial robe,
And Rapine's sword has wasted half the globe!
O'er Europe's cultured realms, and climes afar,
Triumphant Gaul has pour'd the tide of war:
To her fair Austria veil'd the standard bright;
Ausonia's lovely plains have own'd her might;
While Prussia's eagle, never taught to yield,
Forsook her tow'ring height on Jena's field!

Oh! gallant Frederic! could thy parted shade
Have seen thy country vanquish'd and betray'd;
How had thy soul indignant mourn'd her shame,
Her sullied trophies, and her tarnish'd fame!
When Valor wept lamented BRUNSWICK's doom,
And nursed with tears the laurels on his tomb;
When Prussia, drooping o'er her hero's grave,
Invoked his spirit to descend and save;
Then set her glories—then expir'd her sun,
And fraud achieved e'en more than conquest won!

O'er peaceful realms, that smiled with plenty gay,
Has desolation spread her ample sway;
Thy blast, oh Ruin! on tremendous wings,
Has proudly swept o'er empires, nations, kings!
Thus the wild hurricane's impetuous force,
With dark destruction marks its whelming course,
Despoils the woodland's pomp, the blooming plain,
Death on its pinion, vengeance in its train!

Rise, Freedom, rise! and, breaking from thy trance,
Wave the dread banner, seize the glitt'ring lance!
With arm of might assert thy sacred cause,
And call thy champions to defend thy laws!

* Written at the age of fourteen.

How long shall tyrant power her throne maintain?
How long shall despots and usurpers reign?
Is honor's lofty soul for ever fled?
Is virtue lost? is martial ardor dead?
Is there no heart where worth and valor dwell,
No patriot WALLACE, no undaunted TELL?
Yes, Freedom, yes! thy sons, a noble band,
Around thy banner, firm, exulting stand;
Once more, 'tis thine, invincible, to wield
The beamy spear and adamantine shield!
Again thy cheek with proud resentment glows,
Again thy lion-glance appals thy foes;
Thy kindling eye-beam darts unconquer'd fires,
Thy look sublime the warrior's heart inspires;
And, while to guard thy standard and thy right
Castilians rush, intrepid, to the fight,
Lo! Britain's gen'rous host their aid supply,
Resolved for thee to triumph or to die!
And Glory smiles to see Iberia's name
Enroll'd with Albion's in the book of fame!

Illustrious names! still, still united beam,
Be still the hero's boast, the poet's theme:
So, when two radiant gems together shine,
And in one wreath their lucid light combine
Each, as it sparkles with transcendant rays,
Adds to the lustre of its kindred blaze.

Descend, oh Genius! from thy orb descend
Thy glowing thought, thy kindling spirit lend
As Memnon's harp (so ancient fables say)
With sweet vibration meets the morning ray,
So let the chords thy heavenly presence own,
And swell a louder note, a nobler tone;
Call from the sun, her burning throne on high,
The seraph Ecstasy, with lightning eye;
Steal from the source of day empyreal fire,
And breath the soul of rapture o'er the lyre!

Hail, Albion! hail, thou land of freedom's birth
Pride of the main, and Phœnix of the earth!
Thou second Rome, where mercy, justice, dwell,
Whose sons in wisdom as in arms excel!
Thine are the dauntless bands, like Spartans brave
Bold in the field, triumphant on the wave;
In classic elegance, and arts divine,
To rival Athens' fairest palm is thine;
For taste and fancy from Hymettus, fly,
And richer bloom beneath thy varying sky,
Where science mounts in radiant car sublime,
To other worlds beyond the sphere of time!

ENGLAND AND SPAIN.

Hail, Albion, hail! to thee has fate denied
Peruvian mines and rich Hindostan's pride;
The gems that Ormuz and Golconda boast,
And all the wealth of Montezuma's coast:
For thee no Parian marbles brightly shine;
No glowing suns mature the blushing vine;
No light Arabian gales their wings expand,
To waft Sabæan incense o'er the land;
No graceful cedars crown thy lofty hills,
No trickling myrrh for thee its balm distils;
Not from thy trees the lucid amber flows,
And far from thee the scented cassia blows;
Yet fearless Commerce, pillar of thy throne,
Makes all the wealth of foreign climes thy own;
From Lapland's shore to Afric's ferved reign,
She bids thy ensigns float above the main;
Unfurls her streamers to the fav'ring gale,
And shows to other worlds her daring sail:
Then wafts their gold, their varied stores to thee,
Queen of the trident! empress of the sea!

For this thy noble sons have spread alarms,
And bade the zones resound with Britain's arms!
Calpé's proud rock, and Syra's palmy shore,
Have heard and trembled at their battle's roar;
The sacred waves of fertilizing Nile
Have seen the triumphs of the conquering isle;
For this, for this, the Samiel-blast of war
Has roll'd o'er Vincent's cape and Trafalgar!
Victorious RODNEY spread thy thunder's sound,
And NELSON fell, with fame immortal crown'd;
Blest if their perils and their blood could gain,
To grace thy hand—the sceptre of the main!
The milder emblems of the virtues calm,
The poet's verdant bay, the sage's palm;
These in thy laurel's blooming foliage twine,
And round thy brows a deathless wreath combine:
Not Mincio's banks, nor Meles' classic tide,
Are hal'ow'd more than Avon's haunted side;
Nor is thy Thames a less inspiring theme,
Than pure Ilissus, or than Tiber's stream.

Bright in the annals of th' impartial page,
Britannia's heroes live from age to age!
From ancient days, when dwelt her savage race,
Her painted natives, formost in the chase,
Free from all cares for luxury or gain,
Lords of the wood and monarchs of the plain;
To these Augustan days, when social arts,
Refine and meliorate her manly hearts;
From doubtful Arthur, hero of romance,
King of the circled board, the spear, the lance;

To those whose recent trophies grace her shield,
The gallant victors of Vimiera's field ;
Still have her warriors borne th' unfading crown,
And made the British flag the ensign of renown.

   Spirit of ALFRED ! patriot soul sublime !
Thou morning-star of error's darkest time !
Prince of the lion-heart ! whose arm in fight,
On Syria's plains repell'd Saladin's might !
EDWARD ! for bright heroic deeds revered,
By Cressy's fame to Britain still endear'd !
Triumphant HENRY ! thou, whose valor proud,
The lofty plume of crested Gallia bow'd !
Look down, look down, exalted shades ! and view
Your Albion still to freedom's banner true !
Behold the land, ennobled by your fame,
Supreme in glory, and of spotless name ;
And, as the pyramid indignant rears
Its awful head, and mocks the waste of years ;
See her secure in pride of virtue tower,
While prostrate nations kiss the rod of power !

   Lo ! where her pennons, waving high, aspire,
Bold Victory hovers near, " with eyes of fire !"
While Lusitania hails, with just applause,
The brave defenders of her injured cause ;
Bids the full song, the note of triumph rise,
And swells th' exulting pæan to the skies !

   And they, who late with anguish, hard to tell,
Breathed to their cherish'd realms a sad farewell !
Who, as the vessel bore them o'er the tide,
Still fondly linger'd on its deck, and sigh'd ;
Gazed on the shore, till tears obscured their sight,
And the blue distance melted into light ;
The Royal exiles, forced by Gallia's hate
To fly for refuge in a foreign state :
They, soon returning o'er the western main,
Ere long may view their clime beloved again ;
And, as the blazing pillar led the host
Of faithful Israel, o'er the desert coast ;
So may Britannia guide the noble band,
O'er the the wild ocean, to their native land.
Oh, glorious isle !—oh sov'reign of the waves !
Thine are the sons who " never will be slaves !"
See them once more, with ardent hearts advance,
And rend the laurels of insulting France ;
To brave Castile their potent aid supply,
And wave, O Freedom ! wave thy sword on high !

   Is there no bard of heavenly power possess'd,
To thrill, to rouse, to animate the breast ?

Like Shakspeare o'er the secret mind to sway,
And call each wayward passion to obey?
Is there no bard, imbued with hallow'd fire,
To wake the chords of Ossian's magic lyre;
Whose numbers breathing all his flame divine,
The patriot's name to ages might consign?
Rise! Inspiration! rise, be this thy theme,
And mount, like Uriel, on the golden beam!

Oh, could my muse on seraph pinion spring,
And sweep with rapture's hand the trembling string!
Could she the bosom energies control,
And pour impassion'd fervor o'er the soul!
Oh, could she strike the harp to Milton given,
Brought by a cherub from th' empyrean heaven!
Ah, fruitless wish! ah, prayer preferr'd in vain,
For her—the humblest of the woodland train;
Yet shall her feeble voice essay to raise
The hymn of liberty, the song of praise!

Iberian bands! whose noble ardor glows,
To pour confusion on oppressive foes;
Intrepid spirits, hail! 'tis yours to feel
The hero's fire, the freeman's godlike zeal!
Not to secure dominion's boundless reign,
Ye wave the flag of conquest o'er the slain;
No cruel rapine leads you to the war,
Nor mad ambition, whirl'd in crimson car;
No, brave Castilians! yours a nobler end,
Your land, your laws, your monarch to defend!
For these, for these, your valiant legions rear
The floating standard, and the lofty spear!
The fearless lover wields the conquering sword,
Fired by the image of the maid adored!
His best beloved, his fondest ties, to aid,
The father's hand unsheaths the glitt'ring blade!
For each, for all, for ev'ry sacred right,
The daring patriot mingles in the fight!
And e'en if love or friendship fail to warm,
His country's name alone can nerve his dauntless arm!

He bleeds! he falls! his death-bed is the field!
His dirge the trumpet, and his bier the shield!
His closing eyes the beam of valor speak,
The flush of ardor lingers on his cheek;
Serene he lifts to heaven those closing eyes,
Then for his country breaths a prayer—and dies
Oh! ever hallow'd be his verdant grave,
There let the laurel spread, the cypress wave!
Thou, lovely Spring! bestow, to grace his tomb,
Thy sweetest fragrance, and thy earliest bloom;

There let the tears of heaven descend in balm,
There let the poet consecrate his palm!
Let honor, pity, bless the holy ground,
And shades of sainted heroes watch around!
'Twas thus, while Glory rung his thrilling knell,
Thy chief, oh Thebes! at Mantinea fell;
Smiled undismay'd within the arms of death,
While Victory, weeping nigh, received his breath!

Oh! thou, the sovereign of the noble soul!
Thou source of energies beyond control!
Queen of the lofty thought, the gen'rous deed,
Whose sons unconquer'd fight, undaunted bleed,—
Inspiring Liberty! thy worship'd name
The warm enthusiast kindles to a flame;
Thy charms inspire him to achievements high,
Thy look of heaven, thy voice of harmony;
More blest, with thee to tread perennial snows,
Where ne'er a flower expands, a zephys blows;
Where Winter, binding nature in his chain,
In frost-work palace holds perpetual reign;
Than, far from thee, with frolic step to rove
The green savannas and the spicy grove;
Scent the rich balm of India's perfumed gales,
In citron-woods and aromatic vales:
For, oh! fair Liberty, when thou art near,
Elysium blossoms in the desert drear!

Where'er thy smile its magic power bestows,
There arts and taste expand, there fancy glows;
The sacred lyre its wild enchantment gives,
And every chord to swelling transport lives;
There ardent Genius bids the pencil trace
The soul of beauty, and the lines of grace;
With bold Promethean hand, the canvas warms,
And calls from stone expression's breathing forms.
Thus, where the fruitful Nile o'erflows its bound,
Its genial waves diffuse abundance round,
Bid Ceres laugh o'er waste and sterile sands,
And rich profusion clothe deserted lands.

Immortal Freedom! daughter of the skies!
To thee shall Britain's grateful incense rise.
Ne'er, goddess! ne'er forsake thy fav'rite isle,
Still be thy Albion brighten'd with thy smile!
Long had thy spirit slept in dead repose,
While proudly triumph'd thine insulting foes;
Yet, though a cloud may veil Apollo's light,
Soon, with celestial beam, he breaks to sight:
Once more we see thy kindling soul return,
Thy vestal-flame with added radiance burn;

ENGLAND AND SPAIN.

Lo! in Iberian hearts thine ardor lives,
Lo! in Iberian hearts thy spark revives!

Proceed, proceed, ye firm undaunted band!
Still sure to conquer, if combined ye stand:
Though myriads flashing in the eye of day,
Stream'd o'er the smiling land in long array;
Though tyrant Asia pour'd unnumber'd foes,
Triumphant still the arm of Greece arose:
For ev'ry state in sacred union stood,
Strong to repel invasion's whelming flood;
Each heart was glowing in the gen'ral cause,
Each hand prepared to guard their hallow'd laws;
Athenian valor join'd Laconia's might,
And but contended to be first in fight;
From rank to rank the warm contagion ran,
And Hope and Freedom led the flaming van:
Then Persia's monarch mourn'd his glories lost,
As wild confusion wing'd his flying host;
Then Attic bards the hymn of victory sung,
The Grecian harp to notes exulting rung!
Then Sculpture bade the Parian stone record
The high achievements of the conquering sword.
Thus, brave Castilians! thus may bright renown
And fair success your valiant efforts crown!

Genius of chivalry! whose early days
Tradition still recounts in artless lays;
Whose faded splendors fancy oft recalls,
The floating banners, and the lofty halls;
The gallant feats thy festivals display'd,
The tilt, the tournament, the long crusade;
Whose ancient pride Romance delights to hail,
In fabling numbers, or heroic tale:
Those times are fled, when stern thy castles frown'd,
Their stately towers with feudal grandeur crown'd;
Those times are fled, when fair Iberia's clime
Beheld thy Gothic reign, thy pomp sublime;
And all thy glories, all thy deeds of yore,
Live but in legends wild, and poet's lore.
Lo! where thy silent harp neglected lies,
Light o'er its chords the murm'ring zephyr sighs;
Thy solemn courts, where once the minstrel sung,
The choral voice of mirth and music rung;
Now, with the ivy clad, forsaken, lone,
Hear but the breeze and echo to its moan:
Thy lonely tow'rs deserted fall away,
Thy broken shield is mould'ring in decay.
Yet though thy trancient pageantries are gone,
Like fairy visions, bright, yet swiftly flown;
Genius of chivalry! thy noble train,
Thy firm, exalted virtues yet remain!

Fair truth, array'd in robes of spotless white,
Her eye a sunbeam, and her zone of light;
Warm emulation, with aspiring aim,
Still darting forward to the wreath of fame;
And purest love, that waves his torch divine,
At awful honor's consecrated shrine;
Ardor, with eagle-wing and fiery glance;
And gen'rous courage, resting on his lance;
And loyalty, by perils unsubdued;
Untainted faith, unshaken fortitude;
And patriot energy, with heart of flame—
These, in Iberia's sons are yet the same!
These from remotest days their souls have fired.
"Nerved ev'ry arm," and ev'ry breast inspired!
When Moorish bands their suffering land possess'd,
And fierce oppression rear'd her giant crest;
The wealthy caliphs on Cordova's throne,
In eastern gems and purple splendor shone,
Theirs was the proud magnificence that vied
With stately Bagdat's oriental pride;
Theirs were the courts in regal pomp array'd,
Where arts and luxury their charms display'd;
'Twas theirs to rear the Zehrar's costly towers,
Its fairy-palace and enchanted bowers;
There all Arabian fiction e'er could tell,
Of potent genii or of wizard spell;
All that a poet's dream could picture bright,
One sweet Elysium, charm'd the wond'ring sight!
Too fair, too rich, for work of mortal hand,
It seem'd an Eden from Armida's wand!

Yet vain their pride, their wealth, and radiant state,
When freedom waved on high the sword of fate!
When brave Ramiro bade the despots fear,
Stern retribution frowning on his spear;
And fierce Almanzor, after many a fight,
O'erwhelmed with shame, confess'd the Christian's might.

In later times the gallant Cid arose,
Burning with zeal against his country's foes;
His victor-arm Alphonso's throne maintain'd,
His laureate brows the wreath of conquest gain'd;
And still his deeds Castilian bards rehearse,
Inspiring theme of patriotic verse!
high in the temple of recording fame,
Iberia points to great Gonsalvo's name;
Victorious chief! whose valor still defied
The arms of Gaul, and bow'd her crested pride;
With splendid trophies graced his sov'reign's throne,
And bade Granada's realms his prowess own.
Nor were his deeds thy only boast, O Spain!
In mighty FERDINAND's illustrious reign;

'Twas then thy glorious Pilot spread the sail,
Unfurl'd his flag before the eastern gale ;
Bold, sanguine, fearless, ventured to explore
Seas unexplored, and worlds unknown before.
Fair science guided o'er the liquid realm,
Sweet hope, exulting, steer'd the daring helm ;
While on the mast, with ardor-flashing eye,
Courageous enterprise still hover'd nigh :
The hoary genius of th' Atlantic main,
Saw man invade his wide majestic reign ;
His empire, yet by mortal unsubdued,
The throne, the world of awful solitude!
And e'en when shipwreck seem'd to rear his form,
And dark destruction menaced in the storm,
In ev'ry shape, when giant-peril rose,
To daunt his spirit and his course oppose ;
O'er ev'ry heart when terror sway'd alone,
And hope forsook each bosom but his own :
Moved by no dangers, by no fears repell'd,
His glorious track the gallant sailor held ;
Attentive still to mark the sea-birds lave,
Or high in air their snowy pinions wave,
Thus princely Jason, launching from the steep,
With dauntless prow explored th' untravell'd deep ;
Thus, at the helm, Ulysses' watchful sight,
View'd ev'ry star and planetary light.
Sublime COLUMBUS ! when, at length descried,
The long-sought land arose above the tide ;
How ev'ry heart with exultation glow'd,
How from each eye the tear of transport flow'd !
Not wilder joy the sons of Israel knew,
When Canaan's fertile plains appeared in view.
Then rose the choral anthem on the breeze,
Then martial music floated o'er the seas ;
Their waving streamers to the sun display'd,
In all the pride of warlike pomp array'd ;
Advancing nearer still, the ardent band
Hail'd the glad shore, and bless'd the stranger land ;
Admired its palmy groves and prospects fair,
With rapture breathed its pure ambrosial air :
Then crowded round its free and simple race,
Amazement pictured wild on ev'ry face ;
Who deem'd that beings of celestial birth,
Sprung from the sun, descended to the earth—
Then first another world, another sky,
Beheld Iberia's banner blaze on high!

Still prouder glories beam on history's page,
Imperial CHARLES ! to mark thy prosperous age :
Those golden days of arts and fancy bright,
When Science poured her mild, refulgent light ;

When Painting bade the glowing canvass breathe,
Creative Sculpture claim'd the living wreath;
When roved the Muses in Ausonian bowers,
Weaving immortal crowns of fairest flowers;
When angel-truth dispersed, with beam divine,
The clouds that veil'd religion's hallow'd shrine;
Those golden days beheld Iberia tower
High on the pyramid of fame and power;
Vain all the efforts of her numerous foes,
Her might, superior still, triumphant rose.
Thus, on proud Lebanon's exalted brow,
The cedar, frowning o'er the plains below,
Though storms assail, its regal pomp to rend,
Majestic, still aspires, disdaining e'er to bend!

When Gallia pour'd, to Pavia's trophied plain,
Her youthful knights, a bold, impetuous train;
When, after many a toil and danger past,
The fatal morn of conflict rose at last;
That morning saw her glittering host combine,
And form in close array the threat'ning line;
Fire in each eye, and force in ev'ry arm,
With hope exulting, and with ardour warm;
Saw to the gale their streaming ensigns play,
Their armor flashing to the beam of day;
Their gen'rous chargers panting, spurn the ground,
Roused by the trumpet's animating sound;
And heard in air their warlike music float,
The martial pipe, the drum's inspiring note!

Pale set the sun—the shades of evening fell,
The mournful night-wind rung their funeral knell;
And the same day beheld their warriors dead,
Their sovereign captive, and their glories fled!
Fled like the lightning's evanescent fire,
Bright, blazing, dreadful—only to expire!
Then, then, while prostrate Gaul confess'd her might,
Iberia's planet shed meridian light!
Nor less, on famed St. Quintin's deathful day,
Castilian spirit bore the prize away;
Laurels that still their verdure shall retain,
And trophies beaming high in glory's fane!
And lo! her heroes, warm with kindred flame,
Still proudly emulate their fathers' fame;
Still with the soul of patriot-valor glow,
Still rush impetuous to repel the foe;
Wave the bright faulchion, lift the beamy spear,
And bid oppressive Gallia learn to fear!
Be theirs, be theirs, unfading honor's crown,
The living amaranths of bright renown!
Be theirs th' inspiring tribute of applause,
Due to the champions of their country's cause!

Be theirs the purest bliss that virtue loves,
The joy when conscience whispers and approves!
When ev'ry heart is fired, each pulse beats high,
To fight, to bleed, to fall, for liberty;
When ev'ry hand is dauntless and prepared,
The sacred charter of mankind to guard;
When Britain's valiant sons their aid unite,
Fervent and glowing still for freedom's right,
Bid ancient enmities for ever cease,
And ancient wrongs forgotten sleep in peace;
When, firmly leagued, they join the patriot band,
Can venal slaves their conquering arms withstand?
Can fame refuse their gallant deeds to bless?
Can victory fail to crown them with success?
Look down, oh, Heaven! the righteous cause maintain,
Defend the injured, and avenge the slain!
Despot of France! destroyer of mankind!
What spectre-cares must haunt thy sleepless mind!
Oh! if at midnight round thy regal bed,
When soothing visions fly thine aching head;
When sleep denies thy anxious cares to calm,
And lull thy senses in his opiate balm;
Invoked by guilt, if airy phantoms rise,
And murder'd victims bleed before thine eyes;
Loud let them thunder in thy troubled ear,
"Tyrant! the hour, th' avenging hour is near!"
It is, it is! thy star withdraws its ray,
Soon will its parting lustre fade away;
Soon will Cimmerian shades obscure its light,
And veil thy splendors in eternal night!
Oh! when accusing conscience wakes thy soul,
With awful terrors, and with dread control,
Bids threat'ning forms, appalling, round thee stand,
And summons all her visionary band;
Calls up the parted shadows of the dead,
And whispers, peace and happiness are fled;
E'en at the time of silence and of rest,
Paints the dire poniard menacing thy breast;
Is then thy cheek with guilt and horror pale?
Then dost thou tremble, does thy spirit fail?
And wouldst thou yet by added crimes provoke
The bolt of heaven to launch the fatal stroke?
Bereave a nation of its rights revered,
Of all to mortals sacred and endear'd?
And shall they tamely liberty resign,
The soul of life, the source of bliss divine?
Can'st thou, supreme destroyer! hope to bind,
In chains of adamant, the noble mind?
Go, bid the rolling orbs thy mandate hear,
Go, stay the lightning in its wing'd career!
No, tyrant! no, thy utmost force is vain,
The patriot-arm of freedom to restrain:

Then bid thy subject-bands in armor shine,
Then bid thy legions all their power combine!
Yet could'st thou summon myriads at command,
Did boundless realms obey thy scepter'd hand,
E'en then her soul thy lawless might would spurn,
E'en then, with kindling fire, with indignation burn!

Ye sons of Albion! first in danger's field,
The sword of Britain and of truth to wield!
Still prompt the injured to defend and save,
Appal the despot, and assist the brave;
Who now intrepid lift the gen'rous blade,
The cause of Justice and Castile to aid!
Ye sons of Albion! by your country's name,
Her crown of glory, her unsullied fame;
Oh! by the shades of Cressy's martial dead,
By warrior-bands, at Agincourt who bled;
By honors gain'd on Blenheim's fatal plain,
By those in Victory's arms at Minden slain;
By the bright laurels WOLFE immortal won,
Undaunted spirit! valor's fav'rite son!
By Albion's thousand, thousand deeds sublime,
Renown'd from zone to zone, from clime to clime;
Ye British heroes! may your trophies raise
A deathless monument to future days!
Oh! may your courage still triumphant rise,
Exalt the "lion banner" to the skies!
Transcend the fairest names in hist'ry's page,
The brightest actions of a former age;
The reign of Freedom let your arms restore,
And bid oppression fall—to rise no more!
Then soon returning to your native isle,
May love and beauty hail you with their smile;
For you may conquest weave th' undying wreath,
And fame and glory's voice the song of rapture breathe!

Ah! when shall mad ambition cease to rage?
Ah! when shall war his demon-wrath assuage?
When, when, supplanting discord's iron reign,
Shall mercy wave her olive-wand again?
Not till the despot's dread career is closed,
And might restrain'd and tyranny deposed!

Return, sweet Peace, ethereal form benign!
Fair blue-ey'd seraph! balmy power divine!
Descend once more! thy hallow'd blessings bring,
Wave thy bright locks, and spread thy downy wing
Luxuriant plenty laughing in thy train,
Shall crown with glowing stores the desert-plain;
Young smiling Hope, attendant on thy way,
Shall gild thy path with mild celestial ray.

Descend once more, thou daughter of the sky!
Cheer every heart, and brighten ev'ry eye;
Justice, thy harbinger, before thee send,
Thy myrtle-sceptre o'er the globe extend:
Thy cherub-look again shall soothe mankind;
Thy cherub-hand the wounds of discord bind
Thy smile of heaven shall ev'ry muse inspire,
To thee the bard shall strike the silver lyre.
Descend once more! to bid the world rejoice—
Let nations hail thee with exulting voice;
Around thy shrine with purest incense throng,
Weave the fresh palm, and swell the choral song!
Then shall the shepherd's flute, the woodland reed,
The martial clarion and the drum succeed;
Again shall bloom Arcadia's fairest flowers,
And music warble in Idalian bowers.
Where war and carnage blew the blast of death,
The gale shall whisper with Favonian breath;
And golden Ceres bless the festive swain,
Where the wild combat redden'd o'er the plain.
These are thy blessings, fair benignant maid!
Return, return, in vest of light array'd!
Let angel-forms and floating sylphides bear
Thy car of sapphire through the realms of air,
With accents milder than Æolian lays,
When o'er the harp the fanning zephyr plays;
Be thine to charm the raging world to rest,
Diffusing round the heaven—that glows within thy breast!

Oh, Thou! whose fiat lulls the storm asleep!
Thou, at whose nod subsides the rolling deep!
Whose awful word restrains the whirlwind's force,
And stays the thunder in its vengeful course;
Fountain of life! Omnipotent Supreme!
Robed in perfection! crown'd with glory's beam!
Oh! send on earth thy consecrated dove,
To bear the sacred olive from above;
Restore again the blest, the halcyon time,
The festal harmony of nature's prime!
Bid truth and justice once again appear,
And spread their sunshine o'er this mundane sphere;
Bright in their path, let wreaths unfading bloom,
Transcendant light their hallow'd fand illume;
Bid war and anarchy for ever cease,
And kindred seraphs rear the shrine of peace;
Brothers once more, let men her empire own,
And realms and monarchs bend before the throne;
While circling rays of angel-mercy shed
Eternal haloes round her sainted head!

WALLACE'S INVOCATION TO BRUCE.

[ADVERTISEMENT.—" A Native of Edinburgh, and Member of the Highland Society of London," with a view to give popularity to the project of rearing a suitable National Monument to the Memory of Wallace, lately offered Prizes for the three best poems on the subject of—that Illustrious Patriot inviting Bruce to the Scottish Throne. The following Poem obtained the first of these prizes. It would have appeared in the same form in which it is now offered to the Public, under the direction of its proper Editor, the giver of the Prize: but his privilege has, with. pride as well as pleasure, been yielded to a Lady of the Author's own Country, who solicited permission to avail herself of this opportunity of honoring and further remunerating the genius of the Poet; and, at the same time, expressing her admiration of the theme in which she has triumphed. It is a noble feature in the character of a generous and enlightened people, that, in England, the memory of the patriots and martyrs of Scotland has long excited an interest not exceeded in strength by that which prevails in the country which boasts their birth, their deeds, and their sufferings.]

"Great patriot hero! Ill requited chief!"

THE morn rose bright on scenes renown'd,
Wild Caledonia's clasic ground,
Where the bold sons of other days
Won their high fame in Ossian's lays,
And fell—but not till Carron's tide
With Roman blood was darkly died.
The morn rose bright—and heard the cry
Sent by exulting hosts on high,
And saw the white-cross banner float
(While rung each clansman's gathering note)
O'er the dark plumes and serried spears
Of Scotland's daring mountaineers;
As all elate with hope, they stood,
To buy their freedom with their blood.

The sunset shone—to guide the flying,
And beam a farewell to the dying!
The summer moon, on Falkirk's field,
Streams upon eyes in slumber seal'd;
Deep slumber—not to pass away
When breaks another morning's ray,

WALLACE'S INVOCATION TO BRUCE.

Nor vanish, when the trumpet's voice
Bids ardent hearts again rejoice:
What sunbeam's glow, what clarion's breath,
May chase the still cold sleep of death?
Shrowded in Scotland's blood-stain'd plaid,
Low are her mountain-warriors laid;
They fell, on that proud soil whose mould
Was blent with heroes' dust of old,
And guarded by the free and brave,
Yielded the Roman—but a grave!
Nobly they fell; yet with them died
The warrior's hope, the leader's pride.
Vainly they fell—that martyr host—
All save the land's high soul, is lost.
Blest are the slain!. *they* calmly sleep,
Nor hear their bleeding country weep!
The shouts of England's triumph telling,
Reach not their dark and silent dwelling;
And those surviving to bequeath
Their sons the choice of chains or death,
May give the slumberer's lowly bier
An envying glance—but not a tear.

But thou, the fearless and the free,
Devoted Knight of Ellerslie!
No vassal-spirit, form'd to bow
When storms are gathering, clouds thy brow;
No shade of fear, or weak despair,
Blends with indignant sorrow there!
The ray which streams on yon red field,
O'er Scotland's cloven helm and shield,
Glitters not *there* alone, to shed
Its cloudless beauty o'er the dead;
But, where smooth Carron's rippling wave
Flows near that deathbed of the brave,
Illuming all the midnight scene,
Sleeps brightly on thy lofty mien.
But other beams, O Patriot! shine
In each commanding glance of thine,
And other light hath fill'd thine eye
With inspiration's majesty,
Caught from th' immortal flame divine,
Which makes thine inmost heart a shrine!
Thy voice a prophet's tone hath won,
The grandeur Freedom lends her son;
Thy bearing a resistless power,
The ruling genius of the hour!
And he, yon Chief, with mien of pride,
Whom Carron's waves from thee divide,
Whose haughty gesture fain would seek
To veil the thoughts that blanch his cheek,

Feels his reluctant mind controll'd
By thine of more heroic mould;
Though, struggling all in vain to war
With that high soul's ascendant star,
He, with a conqueror's scornful eye,
Would mock the name of Liberty.

Heard ye the Patriot's awful voice?—
"Proud Victor! in thy fame rejoice!
Hast thou not seen thy brethren slain,
The harvest of thy battle plain,
And bathed thy sword in blood, whose spot
Eternity shall cancel not?
Rejoice!—with sounds of wild lament,
O'er her dark heaths and mountains sent,
With dying moan, and dirge's wail,
Thy ravaged country bids thee hail!
Rejoice!—while yet exulting cries
From England's conquering host arise,
And strains of choral triumph tell,
Her Royal Slave hath fought too well!
Oh! dark the clouds of wo that rest,
Brooding, o'er Scotland's mountain-crest;
Her shield is cleft, her banner torn,
O'er martyr'd chiefs her daughters mourn,
And not a breeze, but wafts the sound
Of wailing through the land around.
Yet deem not thou, till life depart,
High hope shall leave the patriot's heart;
Or courage to the storm inured,
Or stern resolve by woes matured,
Oppose, to Fate's severest hour,
Less than unconquerable power!
No! though the orbs of heaven expire,
Thine, Freedom! is a quenchless fire;
And wo to him whose might would dare
The energies of *thy* despair!
No!—when thy chain, O Bruce! is cast,
O'er thy land's charter'd mountain-blast,
Then in my yeilding soul shall die
The glorious faith of Liberty!"

"Wild hopes! o'er dreamer's mind that rise!"
With haughty laugh the Conqueror cries,
(Yet his dark cheek is flush'd with shame,
And his eye fill'd with troubled flame;)
"Vain, brief illusions! doom'd to fly
England's red path of victory!
Is not her sword unmatch'd in might?
Her course, a torrent in the fight?
The terror of her name gone forth
Wide o'er the regions of the north?

Far hence, 'midst other heaths and snows,
Must freedom's footstep now repose.
And thou—in lofty dreams elate,
Enthusiast! strive no more with Fate!
'Tis vain—the land is lost and won—
Sheathed be the sword—its task is done.
Where are the chiefs that stood with thee,
First in the battles of the free?
The firm in heart, in spirit high?—
They sought yon fatal field to die.
Each step of Edward's conquering host
Hath left a grave on Scotland's coast."

" Vassal of England, yes! a grave
Where sleep the faithful and the brave;
And who the glory would resign,
Of death like theirs, for life like thine?
They slumber—and the stranger's tread
May spurn thy country's noble dead;
Yet, on the land they loved so well
Still shall their burning spirit dwell,
Their deeds shall hallow minstrel's theme,
Their image rise on warrior's dream,
Their names be inspiration's breath,
Kindling high hope and scorn of death,
Till bursts, immortal from the tomb,
The flame that shall avenge their doom!
This is no land for chains—away!
O'er softer climes let tyrants sway;
Think'st thou the mountain and the storm
Their hardy sons for bondage form?
Doth our stern wintry blast instil
Submission to a despot's will?
No! *we* were cast in other mould
Than theirs by lawless power controll'd;
The nurture of our bitter sky
Calls forth resisting energy,
And the wild fastnesses are ours,
The rocks with their eternal towers;
The soul to struggle and to dare,
Is mingled with our northern air,
And dust beneath our soil is lying
Of those who died for fame undying.
Tread'st thou that soil! and can it be,
No loftier thought is roused in thee?
Doth no high feeling proudly start
From slumber in thine inmost heart?
No secret voice thy bosom thrill,
For thine own Scotland pleading still?
Oh! wake thee yet—indignant, claim
A nobler fate, a purer fame,

And cast to earth thy fetters riven,
And take thine offer'd crown from Heaven.
Wake! in that high majestic lot
May the dark past be all forgot;
And Scotland shall forgive the field
Where, with her blood, thy shame was seal'd.
E'en I—though on that fatal plain
Lies my heart's brother with the slain;
Though reft of his heroic worth,
My spirit dwells alone on earth;
And when all other grief is past,
Must *this* be cherish'd to the last—
Will lead thy battles, guard thy throne,
With faith unspotted as his own,
Nor in thy noon of fame recall,
Whose was the guilt that wrought his fall."

Still dost thou hear in stern disdain?
Are freedom's warning accents vain?
No! royal Bruce! within thy breast
Wakes each high thought, too long suppress'd.
And thy heart's noblest feelings live,
Blent in that suppliant word—" Forgive!"
" Forgive the wrongs to Scotland done!
Wallace! thy fairest palm is won;
And, kindling at my country's shrine,
My soul hath caught a spark from thine.
Oh! deem not in the proudest hour
Of triumph and exulting power—
Deem not the light of peace could find
A home within my troubled mind.
Conflicts by mortal eye unseen,
Dark, silent, secret, there have been,
Known but to Him whose glance can trace
Thought to its deepest dwelling-place!
—'Tis past—and on my native shore
I tread, a rebel son no more.
Too blest, if yet my lot may be,
In glory's path to follow thee;
If tears, by late repentance pour'd
May lave the blood-stains from my sword!"
Far other tears, O Wallace! rise
From the heart's fountain to thine eyes;
Bright, holy, and uncheck'd they spring,
While thy voice falters, " Hail! my King!
Be ever wrong, by memory traced,
In this full tide of joy effaced:
Hail! and rejoice!—thy race shall claim
A heritage of deathless fame,
And Scotland shall arise at length,
Majestic in triumphant strength,

WALLACE'S INVOCATION TO BRUCE.

An eagle of the rock, that won
A way through tempests to the sun!
Nor scorn the visions wildly grand
The prophet-spirit of thy land:
By torrent-wave, in desert vast,
Those visions o'er my thought have pass'd;
Where mountain vapors darkly roll,
That spirit hath possess'd my soul;
And shadowy forms have met mine eye,
The beings of futurity;
And a deep voice of years to be,
Hath told that Scotland shall be free!
He comes! exult, thou Sire of Kings!
From thee the chief, th' avenger springs!
Far o'er the land he comes to save,
His banners in their glory wave,
And Albyn's thousand harps awake
On hill and heath, by stream and lake,
To swell the strains, that far around
Bid the proud name of Bruce resound!
And I—but wherefore now recall
The whisper'd omens of my fall?
They come not in mysterious gloom—
There is no bondage in the tomb!
O'er the soul's world no tyrant reigns,
And earth alone for man hath chains!
What though I perish ere the hour
When Scotland's vengeance wakes in power?
If shed for her my blood shall stain
The field or scaffold not in vain:
Its voice to efforts more sublime
Shall rouse the spirit of her clime;
And in the noontide of her lot,
My country shall forget me not!"

Art thou forgot? and hath thy worth
Without its glory pass'd from earth?
Rest with the brave, whose names belong
To the high sanctity of song,
Charter'd our reverence to control,
And traced in sunbeams on the soul,
Thine, Wallace! while the heart hath still
One pulse a generous thought can thrill—
While youth's warm tears are yet the meed
Of martyr's death, or hero's deed,
Shall brightly live from age to age,
Thy country's proudest heritage!
'Midst her green vales thy fame is dwelling,
Thy deeds her mountain winds are telling,
Thy memory speaks in torrent-wave,
Thy step hath hallow'd rock and cave,

And cold the wanderer's heart must be,
That holds no converse there with thee!
Yet, Scotland! to thy champion's shade,
Still are thy grateful rites delay'd;
From lands of old renown, o'erspread
With proud memorials of the dead,
The trophied urn, the breathing bust,
The pillar guarding noble dust,
The shrine where art and genius high
Have labored for eternity—
The stranger comes—his eye explores
The wilds of thy majestic shores,
Yet vainly seeks one votive stone,
Raised to the hero all thine own.

Land of bright deeds and minstrel-lore!
Withhold that guerdon now no more.
On some bold height of awful form,
Stern eyrie of the cloud and storm,
Sublimely mingling with the skies,
Bid the proud Cenotaph arise;
Not to *record* the name that thrills
Thy soul, the watch-word of thy hills;
Not to assert, with needless claim,
The bright *for ever* of its fame;
But in the ages yet untold,
When *ours* shall be the days of old,
To rouse high hearts and speak thy pride
In him, for thee who lived and died.

These verses were thus critically noticed at the time of publication:—

"Our readers will remember, that, about a year ago, a truly patriotic person signified his intention of giving £1000 towards the erection of a monument to Sir William Wallace At the same time he proposed a prize of £50 to the best poem on the following subject: 'The meeting of Wallace and Bruce on the Banks of the Carron.' The prize was lately adjudged to Mrs. Hemans, whose poetical genius has been for some years well known to the public * * When we mentioned in the tent, that Mrs. Hemans had authorized the judges who awarded to her the prize, to send her poem to us, it is needless to say with what enthusiasm the proposal of reading it aloud was received on all sides; and at its conclusion thunders of applause crowned the genius of the fair poet. Scotland has her Baillie—Ireland her Tighe—England her Hemans."—*Blackwood's Magazine*, vol. v., Sept. 1819.

"Mrs. Hemans so soon again!—and with a palm in her hand! We welcome her cordially, and rejoice to find the high opinion of her genius which we lately expressed so unequivocally confirmed.

"On this animating theme (the meeting of Wallace and Bruce,) several of the competitors, we understand, were of the other side of the Tweed—a circumstance, we learn, which was known from the references before the prizes were determined. Mrs. Hemans's was the first prize, against fifty-seven competitors. That a Scottish prize, for a poem on a subject purely, proudly Scottish, has been adjudged to an English candidate,* is a proof at once of the perfect fairness of the award, and of the merit of the poem. It further demonstrates the disappearance of those jealousies, which, not a hundred years ago, would have denied to such a candidate any thing like a fair chance with a native—if we can suppose any poet in the south then dreaming of making the trial, or viewing Wallace in any other light than that of an enemy, and a rebel against the paramount supremacy of England. We delight in every gleam of high feeling which warms the two nations alike, and ripens yet more that confidence and sympathy which bind them together in one great family."— *Edinburgh Monthly Review*, vol. ii.

---

* We have learned that two of the prizes were adjudged to English writers.

THE ABENCERRAGE.

[The events with which the following tale is interwoven, are related in the *Historia de las Guerras Civiles de Granada*. They occurred in the reign of Abo Abdeli, or Abdali, the last Moorish king of that city, called by the Spaniards El Rey Chico. The conquest of Granada, by Ferdinand and Isabella, is said by some historians to have been greatly facilitated by the Abencerrages, whose defection was the result of the repeated injuries they had received from the king, at the instigation of the Zegris. One of the most beautiful Halls of the Alhambra is pointed out as the scene where so many of the former celebrated tribe were massacred; and it still retains their name, being called the "Sala de los Abencerrages." Many of the most interesting old Spanish ballads relate to the events of this chivalrous and romantic period.]

"Le Maure ne se venge pas parce que sa colère dure encore, mais parce que la vengeance seule peut écarter de sa tête le poids d'infamie dont il est accablé. Il se venge, parce qu'à ses yeux il n'y a qu'une âme basse qui puisse pardonner les affronts ; et il nourrit sa rancune, parce que s'il la sentoit s'éteindre, il croiroit avec elle, avoir perdu une vertu." *Sismondi.*

LONELY and still are now thy marble halls,
   Thou fair Alhambra! there the feast is o'er;
And with the murmur of thy fountain-falls,
   Blend the wild tones of minstrelsy no more.

Hush'd are the voices, that in years gone by,
   Have mourn'd, exulted, menaced, through thy towers,
Within thy pillar'd courts the grass waves high,
   And all uncultured bloom thy fairy bowers.

Unheeded there the flowering myrtle blows,
   Through tall arcades unmark'd the sunbeam smiles,
And many a tint of soften'd brilliance throws
   O'er fretted walls and shining peristyles.

And well might Fancy deem thy fabrics lone,
   So vast, so silent, and so wildly fair,
Some charm'd abode of beings all unknown,
   Powerful and viewless, children of the air.

For there no footstep treads th' enchanted ground,
   There not a sound the deep repose pervades,

Save winds and founts, diffusing freshness round,
　Through the light domes and graceful colonnades.

Far other tones have swell'd those courts along,
　In days romance yet fondly loves to trace;
The clash of arms, the voice of choral song,
　The revels, combats, of a vanish'd race.

And yet awhile, at Fancy's potent call,
　Shall rise that race, the chivalrous, the bold;
Peopling once more each fair, forsaken hall,
　With stately forms, the knights and chiefs of old.

—The sun declines—upon Nevada's height
There dwells a mellow flush of rosy light;
Each soaring pinnacle of mountain snow
Smiles in the richness of that parting glow
And Darro's wave reflects each passing dye
That melts and mingles in th' empurpled sky.
Fragrance, exhaled from rose and citron bower,
Blends with the dewy freshness of the hour;
Hush'd are the winds, and Nature seems to sleep
In light and stillness; wood, and tower, and steep,
Are dyed with tints of glory, only given
To the rich evening of a southern heaven;
Tints of the sun, whose bright farewell is fraught
With all that art hath dreamt, but never caught.
—Yes, Nature sleeps; but not with her at rest
The fiery passions of the human breast.
Hark! from th' Alhambra's towers what stormy sound,
Each moment deepening, wildly swells around?
Those are no tumults of a festal throng,
Not the light zambra,[1] nor the choral song:
The combat rages—'tis the shout of war,
'Tis the loud clash of shield and scymitar.
Within the hall of Lions,[2] where the rays
Of eve, yet lingering, on the fountain blaze;
There, girt and guarded by his Zegri bands,
And stern in wrath, the Moorish monarch stands:
There the strife centres—swords around him wave
There bleed the fallen, there contend the brave,
While echoing domes return the battle-cry,
"Revenge and freedom! let the tyrant die!"
And onward rushing, and prevailing still,
Court, hall, and tower, the fierce avengers fill.

　But first and bravest of that gallant train,
Where foes are mightiest, charging ne'er in vain;
In his red hand the sabre glancing bright,
His dark eye flashing with a fiercer light,
Ardent, untired, scarce conscious that he bleeds,
His Aben-Zurrahs[3] there young Hamet leads;

While swells his voice that wild acclaim on high,
"Revenge and freedom! let the tyrant die!"

Yes, trace the footsteps of the warrior's wrath,
By helm and corslet shatter'd in his path;
And by the thickest harvest of the slain,
And by the marble's deepest crimson stain:
Search through the serried fight, where loudest cries
From triumph, anguish, or despair, arise;
And brightest where the shivering falchions glare,
And where the ground is reddest—he is there.
Yes, that young arm, amidst the Zegri host,
Hath well avenged a sire, a brother, lost.

They perish'd—not as heroes should have died,
On the red field, in victory's hour of pride,
In all the glow and sunshine of their fame,
And proudly smiling as the death-pang came:
Oh! had they *thus* expired, a warrior's tear
Had flowed, almost in triumph, o'er their bier.
For thus alone the brave should weep for those
Who brightly pass in glory to repose.
—Not such their fate—a tyrant's stern command
Doom'd them to fall by some ignoble hand,
As, with the flower of all their high-born race,
Summon'd Abdallah's royal feast to grace,
Fearless in heart, no dream of danger nigh,
They sought the banquet's gilded hall—to die.
Betray'd, unarm'd, they fell—the fountain wave
Flow'd crimson with the life-blood of the brave,
Till far the fearful tidings of their fate
Through the wide city rung from gate to gate,
And of that lineage each surviving son
Rush'd to the scene where vengeance might be won.

For this young Hamet mingles in the strife,
Leader of battle, prodigal of life,
Urging his followers, till their foes, beset,
Stand faint and breathless, but undaunted yet.
Brave Aben-Zurrahs, on! one effort more,
Yours is the triumph, and the conflict o'er.

But, lo! descending o'er the darken'd hall,
The twilight-shadows fast and deeply fall,
Nor yet the strife hath ceased—though scarce they know,
Through that thick gloom, the brother from the foe;
Till the moon rises with her cloudless ray,
The peaceful moon, and gives them light to slay.

Where lurks Abdallah?—'midst his yielding train,
They seek the guilty monarch, but in vain.

He lies not number'd with the valiant dead,
His champions round him have not vainly bled;
But when the twilight spread her shadowy veil,
And his last warriors found each effort fail,
In wild despair he fled—a trusted few
Kindred in crime, are still in danger true;
And o'er the scene of many a martial deed,
The Vega's[4] green expanse, his flying footsteps lead.
He pass'd th' Alhambra's calm and lovely bowers,
Where slept the glistening leaves and folded flowers
In dew and starlight—there, from grot and cave,
Gush'd, in wild music, many a sparkling wave;
There, on each breeze, the breath of fragrance rose,
And all was freshness, beauty, and repose.

But thou, dark monarch! in thy bosom reign
Storms that, once roused, shall never sleep again.
Oh! vainly bright is Nature in the course
Of him who flies from terror or remorse!
A spell is round him which obscures her bloom,
And dims her skies with shadows of the tomb;
There smiles no Paradise on earth so fair,
But guilt will raise avenging phantoms there.
Abdallah heeds not, though the light gale roves
Fraught with rich odor, stolen from orange-groves;
Hears not the sounds from wood and brook that rise,
Wild notes of Nature's vesper-melodies;
Marks not how lovely, on the mountain's head,
Moonlight and snow their mingling lustre spread;
But urges onward, till his weary band,
Worn with their toil, a moment's pause demand.
He stops, and turning, on Granada's fanes
In silence gazing, fix'd awhile remains
In stern, deep silence—o'er his feverish brow,
And burning cheek, pure breezes freshly blow,
But waft, in fitful murmurs, from afar,
Sounds, indistinctly fearful,—as of war.
What meteor bursts, with sudden blaze, on high,
O'er the blue clearness of the starry sky?
Awful it rises, like some Genie-form,
Seen 'midst the redness of the desert storm,[5]
Magnificently dread—above, below,
Spreads the wild splendor of its deepening glow.
Lo! from th' Alhambra's towers the vivid glare
Streams through the still transparence of the air,
Avenging crowds have lit the mighty pyre,
Which feeds that waving pyramid of fire;
And dome and minaret, river, wood, and height,
From dim perspective start to ruddy light.

Oh Heaven! the anguish of Abdallah's soul,
The rage, though fruitless, yet beyond control!

Yet must he cease to gaze, and raving, fly
For life—such life as makes it bliss to die!
On yon green height, the mosque, but half reveal'd
Through cypress-groves, a safe retreat may yield.
Thither his steps are bent—yet oft he turns,
Watching that fearful beacon as it burns.
But paler grow the sinking flames at last,
Flickering they fade, their crimson light is past;
And spiry vapors, rising o'er the scene,
Mark where the terrors of their wrath have been.
And now his feet have reach'd that lonely pile,
Where grief and terror may repose awhile;
Embower'd it stands, 'midst wood and cliff on high,
Through the grey rocks, a torrent sparkling nigh;
He hails the scene where every care should cease,
And all—except the heart he brings—is peace.

There is deep stillness in those halls of state
Where the loud cries of conflict rang so late;
Stillness like that, when fierce the Kamsin's blast
Hath o'er the dwellings of the desert pass'd.[6]
Fearful the calm—nor voice, nor step, nor breath,
Disturbs that scene of beauty and of death:
Those vaulted roofs re-echo not a sound,
Save the wild gush of waters—murmuring round,
In ceaseless melodies of plaintive tone,
Through chambers peopled by the dead alone.
O'er the mosaic floors, with carnage red,
Breastplate, and shield, and cloven helm are spread
In mingled fragments—glittering to the light
Of yon still moon, whose rays, yet softly bright,
Their streaming lustre tremulously shed,
And smile, in placid beauty, o'er the dead:
O'er features, where the fiery spirit's trace
E'en death itself is powerless to efface;
O'er those, who, flush'd with ardent youth, awoke,
When glowing morn in bloom and radiance broke,
Nor dreamt how near the dark and frozen sleep,
Which hears not Glory call, nor Anguish weep;
In the low silent house, the narrow spot,
Home of forgetfulness—and soon forgot.

But slowly fade the stars—the night is o'er—
Morn beams on those who hail her light no more;
Slumberers who ne'er shall wake on earth again,
Mourners, who call the loved, the lost, in vain.
Yet smiles the day—oh! not for mortal tear
Doth nature deviate from her calm career;
Nor is the earth less laughing or less fair,
Though breaking hearts her gladness may not share.
O'er the cold urn the beam of summer glows,
O'er fields of blood the zephyr freshly blows;

Bright shines the sun, though all be dark below,
And skies arch cloudless o'er a world of woe,
And flowers renew'd in spring's green pathway bloom,
Alike to grace the banquet and the tomb.

Within Granada's walls the funeral-rite
Attends that day of loveliness and light;
And many a chief, with dirges and with tears,
Is gathered to the brave of other years:
And Hamet, as beneath the cypress-shade
His martyr'd brother and his sire are laid,
Feels every deep resolve, and burning thought
Of ampler vengeance, e'en to passion wrought;
Yet is the hour afar—and he must brood
O'er those dark dreams awhile in solitude.
Tumult and rage are hush'd—another day
In still solemnity hath pass'd away,
In that deep slumber of exhausted wrath,
The calm that follows in the tempest's path.

And now Abdallah leaves yon peaceful fane,
His ravaged city traversing again.
No sound of gladness his approach precedes,
No splendid pageant the procession leads;
Where'er he moves the silent streets along,
Broods a stern quiet o'er the sullen throng.
No voice is heard—but in each alter'd eye,
Once brightly beaming when his steps were nigh;
And in each look of those, whose love hath fled
From all on earth to slumber with the dead,
Those, by his guilt made desolate, and thrown
On the bleak wilderness of life alone:
In youth's quick glance of scarce-dissembled rage,
And the pale mien of calmly-mournful age,
May well be read a dark and fearful tale
Of thought that ill th' indignant heart can veil,
And passion, like the hush'd volcano's power,
That waits in stillness its appointed hour.

No more the clarion, from Granada's walls,
Heard o'er the Vega, to the tourney calls;
No more her graceful daughters, throned on high,
Bend o'er the lists the darkly-radiant eye;
Silence and gloom her palaces o'erspread,
And song is hush'd, and pageantry is fled
—Weep, fated city! o'er thy heroes weep—
Low in the dust the sons of glory sleep!
Furl'd are their banners in the lonely hall,
Their trophied shields hang mouldering on the **wall,**
Wildly their chargers range the pastures o'er,
Their voice in battle shall be heard no more;

And they, who still thy tyrant's wrath survive,
Whom he hath wrong'd too deeply to forgive,
That race, of lineage high, of worth approved,
The chivalrous, the princely, the beloved—
Thine Aben-Zurrahs—they no more shall wield
In thy proud cause the conquering lance and shield:
Condemn'd to bid the cherish'd scenes farewell
Where the loved ashes of their fathers dwell,
And far o'er foreign plains, as exiles, roam,
Their land the desert, and the grave their home.
Yet there is one shall see that race depart,
In deep, though silent, agony of heart:
One whose dark fate must be to mourn alone,
Unseen her sorrows, and their cause unknown,
And veil her heart, and teach her cheek to wear
That smile in which the spirit hath no share;
Like the bright beams that shed their fruitless glow
O'er the cold solitude of Alpine snow.

Soft, fresh, and silent, is the midnight hour,
And the young Zayda seeks her lonely bower;
That Zegri maid, within whose gentle mind
One name is deeply, secretly enshrined.
That name in vain stern Reason would efface:
Hamet! 'tis thine, thou foe to all her race!

And yet not hers in bitterness to prove
The sleepless pangs of unrequited love;
Pangs, which the rose of wasted youth consume,
And make the heart of all delight the tomb,
Check the free spirit in its eagle-flight,
And the spring-morn of early genius blight;
Nor such her grief—though now she wakes to weep,
While tearless eyes enjoy the honey-dews of sleep.'

A step treads lightly through the citron-shade,
Lightly, but by the rustling leaves betray'd—
Doth her young hero seek that well-known spot,
Scene of past hours that ne'er may be forgot?
'Tis he—but changed that eye, whose glance of fire
Could, like a sunbeam, hope and joy inspire,
As, luminous with youth, with ardor fraught,
It spoke of glory to the inmost thought;
Thence the bright spirit's eloquence hath fled,
And in its wild expression may be read
Stern thoughts and fierce resolves—now veil'd in shade,
And now in characters of fire portray'd.
Changed e'en his voice—as thus its mournful tone
Wakes in her heart each feeling of his own.

" Zayda, my doom is fix'd—another day
And the wrong'd exile shall be far away:

Far from the scenes where still his heart must be,
His home of youth, and, more than all—from thee.
Oh! what a cloud hath gather'd o'er my lot,
Since last we met on this fair tranquil spot!
Lovely as then, the soft and silent hour,
And not a rose hath faded from thy bower;
But I—my hopes the tempest hath o'erthrown,
And changed my heart to all but thee alone.
Farewell, high thoughts! inspiring hopes of praise,
Heroic visions of my early days!
In me the glories of my race must end,
The exile hath no country to defend!
E'en in life's morn, my dreams of pride are o'er.
Youth's bouyant spirit wakes for me no more,
And one wild feeling in my alter'd breast
Broods darkly o'er the ruins of the rest.
Yet fear not thou—to thee, in good or ill,
The heart, so sternly tried, is faithful still!
But when my steps are distant, and my name
Thou hears't no longer in the song of fame,
When Time steals on, in silence to efface
Of early love each pure and sacred trace,
Causing our sorrows and our hopes to seem
But as the moonlight pictures of a dream,—
Still shall thy soul be with me, in the truth
And all the fervor of affection's youth?
If such thy love, one beam of heaven shall play
In lonely beauty, o'er thy wanderer's way."

" Ask not, if such my love! Oh! trust the mind
To grief so long, so silently resign'd!
Let the light spirit, ne'er by sorrow taught
The pure and lofty constancy of thought,
Its fleeting trials eager to forget,
Rise with elastic power o'er each regret!
Foster'd in tears, *our* young affection grew,
And I have learn'd to suffer and be true.
Deem not my love a frail, ephemeral flower,
Nursed by soft sunshine and the balmy shower;
No! 'tis the child of tempests and defies,
And meets unchanged, the anger of the skies!
Too well I feel, with grief's prophetic heart,
That ne'er to meet in happier days, we part.
We part! and e'en this agonizing hour,
When love first feels his own o'erwhelming power,
Shall soon to Memory's fixed and tearful eye
Seem almost happiness—for thou wert nigh!
Yes! when this heart in solitude shall bleed,
As days to days all wearily succeed,
When doom'd to weep in loneliness, 'twill be
Almost like rapture to have wept with thee.

"But thou, my Hamet, thou canst yet bestow
All that of joy my blighted lot can know.
Oh! be thou still the high-soul'd and the brave,
To whom my first and fondest vows I gave,
In thy proud fame's untarnished beauty still
The lofty visions of my youth fulfil,
So shall it soothe me, 'midst my heart's despair,
To hold undimm'd one glorious image there!"

"Zayda, my best-beloved! my words too well,
Too soon, thy bright illusions must dispel;
Yet must my soul to thee unveil'd be shown,
And all its dreams and all its passions known.
Thou shalt not be deceived—for pure as heaven
Is thy young love, in faith and fervor given.
I said my heart was changed—and would thy thought
Explore the ruin by thy kindred wrought,
In fancy trace the land whose towers and fanes,
Crush'd by the earthquake, strew its ravaged plains,
And such that heart—where desolation's hand
Hath blighted all that once was fair or grand!
But Vengeance, fix'd upon her burning throne,
Sits, 'midst the wreck, in silence and alone,
And I, in stern devotion at her shrine,
Each softer feeling, but my love, resign.
—Yes! they whose spirits all my thoughts control,
Who hold dread converse with my thrilling soul;
They, the betray'd, the sacrificed, the brave,
Who fill a blood-stain'd and untimely grave,
Must be avenged! and pity and remorse,
In that stern cause, are banished from my course.
Zayda, thou tremblest—and thy gentle breast
Shrinks from the passions that destroy my rest;
Yet shall thy form, in many a stormy hour,
Pass brightly o'er my soul with softening power,
And, oft recall'd, thy voice beguile my lot,
Like some sweet lay, once heard, and ne'er forgot.

"But the night wanes—the hours too swiftly fly,
The bitter moment of farewell draws nigh;
Yet, loved one! weep not thus—in joy or pain,
Oh! trust thy Hamet, we shall meet again!
Yes, we shall meet! and haply smile at last
On all the clouds and conflicts of the past.
On that fair vision teach thy thoughts to dwell,
Nor deem these mingling tears our last farewell!"

Is the voice hush'd, whose loved, expressive tone
Thrill'd to her heart—and doth she weep alone?
Alone she weeps; that hour of parting o'er,
When shall the pang it leaves be felt no more?

The gale breathes light, and fans her bosom fair,
Showering the dewy rose-leaves o'er her hair;
But ne'er for her shall dwell reviving power,
In balmy dew, soft breeze, or fragrant flower,
To wake once more that calm, serene delight,
The soul's young bloom, which passion's breath could blight;
The smiling stillness of life's morning hour,
Ere yet the day-star burns in all his power.
Mean-while, through groves of deep luxurious shade,
In the rich foliage of the South array'd,
Hamet, ere dawns the earliest blush of day,
Bends to the vale of tombs his pensive way.
Fair is that scene where palm and cypress wave
On high o'er many an Ahben-Zurrah's grave.
Lonely and fair, its fresh and glittering leaves,
With the young myrtle there the laurel weaves,
To canopy the dead—nor wanting there
Flowers to the turf, nor fragrance to the air,
Nor wood-bird's note, nor fall of plaintive stream,
Wild music, soothing to the mourner's dream.
There sleep the chiefs of old—their combats o'er,
The voice of glory thrills their hearts no more.
Unheard by them th' awakening clarion blows;
The sons of war at length in peace repose.
No martial note is in the gale that sighs,
Where proud their trophied sepulchres arise,
'Mid founts, and shade, and flowers of brightest bloom,
As, in his native vale, some shepherd's tomb.

There, where the trees their thickest foliage spread
Dark o'er that silent valley of the dead;
Where two fair pillars rise, embower'd and lone,
Not yet with ivy clad, with moss o'ergrown,
Young Hamet kneels—while thus his vows are pour'd,
The fearful vows that consecrate his sword.
—" Spirit of him, who first within my mind
Each loftier aim, each nobler thought enshrined,
And taught my steps the line of light to trace,
Left by the glorious fathers of my race,
Hear thou my voice—for thine is with me still,
In every dream its tones my bosom thrill,
In the deep calm of midnight they are near,
'Mid busy throngs they vibrate on my ear,
Still murmuring ' vengeance !'—nor in vain the call,
Few, few shall triumph in a hero's fall!
Cold as thine own to glory and to fame,
Within my heart there lives one only aim;
There, till th' oppressor for thy fate atone,
Concentring every thought, it reigns alone.
I will not weep—revenge, not grief, must be,
And blood, not tears, an offering meet for thee;

But the dark hour of stern delight will come,
And thou shalt triumph, warrior! in thy tomb.

" Thou, too, my brother! thou art pass'd away,
Without thy fame, in life's fair-dawning day,
Son of the brave! of thee no trace will shine
In the proud annals of thy lofty line;
Nor shall thy deeds be deathless in the lays
That hold communion with the after-days.
Yet, by the wreaths thou might'st have nobly won,
Hadst thou but lived till rose thy noontide sun;
By glory lost, I swear! by hope betray'd,
Thy fate shall amply, dearly, be repaid;
War with thy foes I deem a holy strife,
And, to avenge thy death, devote my life.

" Hear ye my vows, O spirits of the slain!
Hear, and be with me on the battle-plain!
At noon, at midnight, still around me bide,
Rise on my dreams, and tell me how ye died!"

CANTO II.

" Oh! ben provvide il Cielo
Ch' Uom per delitti mai lieto non sia."
Alfieri.

Fair land! of chivalry the old domain,
Land of the vine and olive, lovely Spain!
Though not for thee with classic shores to vie
In charms that fix th' enthusiast's pensive eye;
Yet hast thou scenes of beauty richly fraught
With all that wakes the glow of lofty thought;
Fountains, and vales, and rocks, whose ancient name
High deeds have raised to mingle with their fame.
Those scenes are peaceful now: the citron blows,
Wild spreads the myrtle where the brave repose.
No sound of battle swells on Douro's shore,
And banners wave on Ebro's banks no more.
But who, unmoved, unawed, shall coldly tread
Thy fields that sepulchre the mighty dead?
Blest be that soil! where England's heroes share
The grave of chiefs, for ages slumbering there;
Whose names are glorious in romantic lays,
The wild, sweet chronicles of elder days—
By goatherd lone, and rude serrano sung,
Thy cypress dells, and vine-clad rocks among.
How oft those rocks have echoed to the tale
Of knights who fell in Roncesvalles' vale;
Of him, renown'd in old heroic lore,
First of the brave, the gallant Campeador;

Of those, the famed in song, who proudly died
When "Rio Verde" roll'd a crimson tide;
Or that high name, by Garcilaso's might,
On the green Vega won in single fight.[8]

Round fair Granada, deepening from afar
O'er that Green Vega rose the din of war.
At morn or eve no more the sunbeams shone
O'er a calm scene, in pastoral beauty lone;
On helm and corslet tremulous they glanced,
On shield and spear in quivering lustre danced.
Far as the sight by clear Xenil could rove,
Tents rose around, and banners glanced above.
And steeds in gorgeous trappings, armor bright
With gold, reflecting every tint of light,
And many a floating plume, and blazon'd shield,
Diffused romantic splendor o'er the field.

There swell those sounds that bid the life-blood start
Swift to the mantling cheek, and beating heart.
The clang of echoing steel, the charger's neigh,
The measured tread of hosts in war's array;
And, oh! that music, whose exulting breath
Speaks but of glory on the road to death;
In whose wild voice there dwells inspiring power
To wake the stormy joy of danger's hour;
To nerve the arm, the spirit to sustain,
Rouse from despondence, and support in pain;
And, 'midst the deepening tumults of the strife,
Teach every pulse to thrill with more than life.

High o'er the camp, in many a broider'd fold,
Floats to the wind a standard rich with gold:
There, imaged on the cross, *his* form appears
Who drank for man the bitter cup of tears.[9]
His form, whose word recall'd the spirit fled,
Now borne by hosts to guide them o'er the dead!
O'er yon fair walls to plant the cross on high,
Spain hath sent forth her flower of chivalry.
Fired with that ardor which, in days of yore,
To Syrian plains the bold crusaders bore;
Elate with lofty hope, with martial zeal,
They come, the gallant children of Castile;
The proud, the calmly dignified:—and there
Ebro's dark sons with haughty mein repair,
And those who guide the fiery steed of war
From yon rich province of the western star.[10]

But thou, conspicuous 'midst the glitt'ring scene,
Stern grandeur stamp'd upon thy princely mien;
Known by the foreign garb, the silvery vest,
The snow-white charger, and the azure crest,[11]

Young Aben-Zurrah! 'midst that host of foes,
Why shines *thy* helm, thy Moorish lance? Disclose.
Why rise the tents, where dwell thy kindred train,
O son of Afric, 'midst the sons of Spain?
Hast thou with these thy nation's fall conspired,
Apostate chief! by hope of vengeance fired?
How art thou changed! Still first in every fight,
Hamet, the Moor! Castile's devoted knight!
There dwells a fiery lustre in thine eye,
But not the light that shone in days gone by;
There is wild ardor in thy look and tone,
But not the soul's expression once thine own,
Nor aught like peace within. Yet who shall say
What secret thoughts thine inmost heart may sway?
No eye but Heaven's may pierce that curtain'd breast,
Whose joys and griefs alike are unexpress'd.

There hath been combat on the tented plain;
The Vega's turf is red with many a stain;
And, rent and trampled, banner, crest, and shield,
Tell of a fierce and well-contested field:
But all is peaceful now—the west is bright
With the rich splendor of departing light;
Mulhacen's peak, half lost amidst the sky,
Glows like a purple evening-cloud on high,
And tints, that mock the pencil's art, o'erspread
Th' eternal snow that crowns Veleta's head;[12]
While the warm sunset o'er the landscape throws
A solemn beauty, and a deep repose.
Closed are the toils and tumults of the day,
And Hamet wanders from the camp away.
In silent musings rapt:—the slaughter'd brave
Lie thickly strewn by Darro's rippling wave.
Soft fall the dews—but other drops have dyed
The scented shrubs that fringe the river side,
Beneath whose shade, as ebbing life retired,
The wounded sought a shelter—and expired.[13]
Lonely, and lost in thoughts of other days,
By the bright windings of the stream he strays,
Till, more remote from battle's ravaged scene,
All is repose, and solitude serene.
There, 'neath an olive's ancient shade reclined,
Whose rustling foliage waves in evening's wind,
The harrass'd warrior, yielding to the power,
The mild sweet influence of the tranquil hour,
Feels, by degrees, a long-forgotten calm
Shed o'er his troubled soul unwonted balm;
His wrongs, his woes, his dark and dubious lot,
The past, the future, are awhile forgot;
And Hope, scarce own'd, yet stealing o'er his breast,
Half dares to whisper, "Thou shalt yet be blest!"

Such his vague musings—but a plaintive sound
Breaks on the deep and solemn stillness round ;
A low, half-stifled moan, that seems to rise
From life and death's contending agonies.
He turns : Who shares with him that lonely shade ?
—A youthful warrior on his death-bed laid.
All rent and stain'd his broider'd Moorish vest,
The corslet shatter'd on his bleeding breast ;
In his cold hand the broken falchion strain'd,
With life's last force convulsively retain'd ;
His plumage soil'd with dust, with crimson dyed,
And the red lance, in fragments, by his side :
He lies forsaken—pillow'd on his shield,
His helmet raised, his lineaments reveal'd.
Pale is that quivering lip, and vanish'd now
The light once throned on that comanding brow,
And o'er that fading eye, still upward cast,
The shades of death are gathering dark and fast.
Yet, as yon rising moon her light serene
Sheds the pale olive's waving bows between,
Too well can Hamet's conscious heart retrace,
Though changed thus fearfully, that pallid face,
Whose every feature to his soul conveys
Some bitter thought of long-departed days.

" Oh ! is it thus," he cries, " we meet at last ?
Friend of my soul in years for ever past !
Hath fate but led me hither to behold
The last dread struggle, ere that heart is cold,—
Receive thy latest agonizing breath,
And, with vain pity, soothe the pangs of death ?
Yet let me bear thee hence—while life remains,
E'en though thus feebly circling through thy veins,
Some healing balm thy sense may still revive,
Hope is not lost—and Osmyn yet may live !
And blest were he, whose timely care should save
A heart so noble, e'en from glory's grave."

Roused by those accents, from his lowly bed
The dying warrior faintly lifts his head ;
O'er Hamet's mien, with vague, uncertain gaze,
His doubtful glance awhile bewilder'd strays ;
Till, by degrees, a smile of proud disdain
Lights up those features late convulsed with pain ;
A quivering radiance flashes from his eye,
That seems too pure, too full of soul to die ;
And the mind's grandeur, in its parting hour,
Looks from that brow with more than wonted power.

" Away ! " he cries, in accents of command,
And proudly waves his cold and trembling hand.

"Apostate, hence! my soul shall soon be free,
E'en now it soars, disdaining aid from thee:
'Tis not for thee to close the fading eyes
Of him who faithful to his country dies;
Not for *thy* hand to raise the drooping head
Of him who sinks to rest on glory's bed.
Soon shall these pangs be closed, this conflict o'er
And worlds be mine where thou canst never soar:
Be thine existence with a blighted name,
Mine the bright death which seals a warrior's fame.

The glow hath vanish'd from his cheek—his eye
Hath lost that beam of parting energy;
Frozen and fix'd it seems—his brow is chill;
One struggle more—that noble heart is still.
Departed warrior! were thy mortal throes,
Were thy last pangs, ere Nature found repose,
More keen, more bitter, than th' envenomed dart
Thy dying words have left in Hamet's heart?
Thy pangs were transient; *his* shall sleep no more,
Till life's delirious dream itself is o'er;
But thou shalt rest in glory, and thy grave
Be the pure altar of the patriot brave.
Oh, what a change that little hour hath wrought
In the high spirit, and unbending thought!
Yet, from himself each keen regret to hide,
Still Hamet struggles with indignant pride;
While his soul rises, gathering all its force,
To meet the fearful conflict with remorse.

To thee, at length, whose artless love hath been
His own, unchanged, through many a stormy scene;
Zayda! to thee his heart for refuge flies;
Thou still art faithful to affection's ties.
Yes! let the world upbraid, let foes contemn,
Thy gentle breast the tide will firmly stem;
And soon thy smile, and soft consoling voice
Shall bid his troubled soul again rejoice.

Within Granada's walls are hearts and hands
Whose aid in secret Hamet yet commands;
Nor hard the task, at some propitious hour,
To win his silent way to Zayda's bower,
When night and peace are brooding o'er the world,
When mute the clarions, and the banners furl'd.
That hour is come—and, o'er the arms he bears,
A wandering fakir's garb the chieftain wears:
Disguise that ill from piercing eye could hide
The lofty port, and glance of martial pride;
But night befriends—through paths obscure he pass'd,
And hail'd the lone and lovely scene at last:

Young Zayda's chosen haunt, the fair alcove,
The sparkling fountain, and the orange grove;
Calm in the moonlight smiles the still retreat,
As form'd alone for happy hearts to meet.
For happy hearts?—not such as hers, who there
Bends o'er her lute, with dark, unbraided hair;
That maid of Zegri race, whose eye, whose mien,
Tell that despair her bosom's guest hath been.
So lost in thought she seems, the warrior's feet
Unheard approach her solitary seat,
Till his known accents every sense restore—
" My own loved Zayda! do we meet once more?"
She starts, she turns—the lightning of surprise,
Of sudden rapture, flashes from her eyes;
But that is fleeting—it is past—and now
Far other meaning darkens o'er his brow;
Changed is her aspect, and her tone severe—
" Hence, Aben-Zurrah! death surrounds thee here!"
" Zayda! what means that glance, unlike thine own?
What mean those words, and that unwonted tone?
I will not deem thee changed—but in thy face
It is not joy, it is not love, I trace!
It was not thus in other days we met:
Hath time, hath absence, taught thee to forget?
Oh! speak once more—these rising doubts dispel;
One smile of tenderness, and all is well!"

" Not thus we met in other days!—oh, no!
Thou wert not, warrior, then thy country's foe!
Those days are past—we ne'er shall meet again
With hearts all warmth, all confidence, as then.
But *thy* dark soul no gentler feelings sway,
Leader of hostile bands! away, away!
On in thy path of triumph and of power,
Nor pause to raise from earth a blighted flower"

" And *thou* too changed; thine early vow forgot!
This, this alone, was wanting to my lot!
Exiled and scorn'd, of every tie bereft,
Thy love, the desert's lonely fount, was left;
And thou, my soul's last hope, its lingering beam,
Thou, the good angel of each brighter dream,
Wert all the barrenness of life possest,
To wake one soft affection in my breast!
That vision ended—fate hath nought in store
Of joy or sorrow e'er to touch me more.
Go, Zegri maid! to scenes of sunshine fly,
From the stern pupil of adversity!
And now to hope, to confidence, adieu!
If thou art faithless, who shall e'er be true?"

"Hamet! oh, wrong me not!—I too could speak
Of sorrows—trace them on my faded cheek,
In the sunk eye, and in the wasted form,
That tell the heart hath nursed a canker worm!
But words were idle—read my sufferings there,
Where grief is stamp'd on all that once was fair.

" Oh, wert thou still what once I fondly deem'd,
All that thy mien express'd, thy spirit seem'd,
My love had been devotion—till in death
Thy name had trembled on my latest breath.
But not the chief who leads a lawless band,
To crush the altars of his native land;
Th' apostate son of heroes, whose disgrace
Hath stain'd the trophies of a glorious race;
Not *him* I loved—but one whose youthful name
Was pure and radiant in unsullied fame.
Hadst thou but died, ere yet dishonor's cloud
O'er that young name had gather'd as a shroud,
I then had mourn'd thee proudly, and my grief
In its own loftiness had found relief;
A noble sorrow, cherish'd to the last,
When every meaner woe had long been past.
Yes! let Affection weep—no common tear
She sheds, when bending o'er a hero's bier.
Let Nature mourn the dead—a grief like this,
To pangs that rend *my* bosom, had been bliss!"

" High-minded maid! the time admits not now
To plead my cause, to vindicate my vow.
That vow, too dread, too solemn to recall,
Hath urged me onward, haply to my fall.
Yet this believe—no meaner aim inspires
My soul, no dream of poor ambition fires.
No! every hope of power, of triumph, fled,
Behold me but th' avenger of the dead!
One whose changed heart no tie, no kindred knows,
And in thy love alone hath sought repose.
Zayda! wilt *thou* his stern accuser be?
False to his country, he is true to thee!
Oh, hear me yet!—if Hamet e'er was dear,
By our first vows, our young affection, hear!
Soon must this fair and royal city fall,
Soon shall the cross be planted on her wall;
Then who can tell what tides of blood may flow,
While her fanes echo to the shrieks of woe?
Fly, fly with me, and let me bear thee far
From horrors thronging in the path of war:
Fly! and repose in safety—till the blast
Hath made a desert in its course—and pass'd!"

" Thou that wilt triumph when the hour is come,
Hasten'd by thee, to seal thy country's doom,
With *thee* from scenes of death shall Zayda fly
To peace and safety ?—Woman, too, can die!
And die exulting, though unknown to fame,
In all the stainless beauty of her name!
Be mine, unmurmuring, undismay'd, to share
The fate my kindred and my sire must bear,
And deem thou not my feeble heart shall fail,
When the clouds gather and the blasts assail.
Thou hast but known me ere the trying hour
Call'd into life my spirit's latent power;
But I have energies that idly slept,
While withering o'er my silent woes I wept,
And now, when hope and happiness are fled,
My soul is firm—for what remains to dread?
Who shall have power to suffer and to bear,
If strength and courage dwell not with Despair?

" Hamet, farewell—retrace thy path again,
To join thy brethren on the tented plain.
There wave and wood, in mingling murmurs, tell
How, in far other cause, thy fathers fell!
Yes! on that soil hath Glory's footstep been,
Names unforgotten consecrate the scene!
Dwell not the souls of heroes round thee there,
Whose voices call thee in the whispering air?
Unheard, in vain, they call—their fallen son
Hath stain'd the name those mighty spirits won,
And to the hatred of the brave and free
Bequeath'd his own, through ages yet to be!"

Still as she spoke, th' enthusiast's kindling eye
Was lighted up with inborn majesty,
While her fair form and youthful features caught
All the proud grandeur of heroic thought,
Severely beauteous:[14] awe-struck and amazed,
In silent trance a while the warrior gazed,
As on some lofty vision—for she seem'd
One all-inspired—each look with glory beam'd,
While, brightly bursting, through its cloud of woes,
Her soul at once in all its light arose.
Oh! ne'er had Hamet deem'd there dwelt enshrined,
In form so fragile, that unconquer'd mind;
And fix'd, as by some high enchantment, there
He stood—till wonder yielded to despair.

" The dream is vanish'd—daughter of my foes!
Reft of each hope the lonely wanderer goes.
Thy words have pierced his soul—yet deem thou not
Thou couldst be once adored, and e'er forgot!

O form'd for happier love ; heroic maid !
In grief sublime, in danger undismay'd,
Farewell, and be thou blest !—all words were vain
From him who ne'er may view that form again ;
Him, whose sole thought, resembling bliss, must be,
He *hath* been loved, once fondly loved, by thee !"
And is the warrior gone?—doth Zayda hear
His parting footstep, and without a tear ?
Thou weep'st not, lofty maid !—yet who can tell
What secret pangs within thy heart may dwell ?
They feel not least, the firm, the high in soul,
Who best each feeling's agony control.
Yes, we may judge the measure of the grief
Which finds in Misery's eloquence relief ;
But who shall pierce those depths of silent woe
Whence breathes no language, whence no tears may flow ?
The pangs that many a noble breast hath proved,
Scorning itself that thus it *could* be moved ?
He, He alone, the inmost heart who knows,
Views all its weakness, pities all its throes,
He who hath mercy when mankind contemn,
Beholding anguish—all unknown to them.

Fair city ! thou that 'midst thy stately fanes
And gilded minarets, towering o'er the plains,
In eastern grandeur proudly dost arise
Beneath thy canopy of deep-blue skies ;
While streams that bear thee treasures in their wave,[1]
Thy citron-groves and myrtle-gardens lave :
Mourn, for thy doom is fixed—the days of fear,
Of chains, of wrath, of bitterness, are near !
Within, around thee, are the trophied graves
Of kings and chiefs—their children shall be slaves.
Fair are thy halls, thy domes majestic swell,
But there a race that rear'd them not shall dwell ;
For 'midst thy councils Discord still presides,
Degenerate fear thy wavering monarch guides,
Last of a line whose regal spirit flown
Hath to their offspring but bequeath'd a throne,
Without one generous thought, or feeling high,
To teach his soul how kings should live and die.

A voice resounds within Granada's wall,
The hearts of warriors echo to its call.[16]
Whose are those tones, with power electric fraught,
To reach the source of pure exalted thought ?

See, on a fortress tower, with beckoning hand,
A form, majestic as a prophet, stand !
His mien is all impassion'd—and his eye
Fill'd with a light whose fountain is on high ;

Wild on the gale his silvery tresses flow,
And inspiration beams upon his brow;
While, thronging round him, breathless thousands gaze,
As on some mighty seer of elder days.

"Saw ye the banners of Castile display'd
The helmets glittering, and the line array'd?
Heard ye the march of steel-clad hosts?" he cries;
"Children of conquerors! in your strength arise!
O high-born tribes! O names unstain'd by fear!
Azarques, Zegris, Almoradis, hear![17]
Be every feud forgotten, and your hands
Dyed with no blood but that of hostile bands.[18]
Wake, princes of the land! the hour is come,
And the red sabre must decide your doom.
Where is that spirit which prevail'd of yore,
When Tarik's bands o'erspread the western shore?[19]
When the long combat raged on Xeres' plain,[20]
And Afric's tecbir swell'd through yielding Spain?[21]
Is the lance broken, is the shield decay'd,
The warrior's arm unstrung, his heart dismay'd?
Shall no high spirit of ascendant worth
Arise to lead the sons of Islam forth?
To guard the regions where our fathers' blood
Hath bathed each plain, and mingled with each flood;
Where long their dust hath blended with the soil
Won by their swords, made fertile by their toil?

"O ye sierras of eternal snow!
Ye streams that by the tombs of heroes flow,
Woods, fountains, rocks of Spain! ye saw their might
In many a fierce and unforgotten fight—
Shall ye behold their lost, degenerate race,
Dwell 'midst your scenes in fetters and disgrace?
With each memorial of the past around,
Each mighty monument of days renown'd?
May this indignant heart ere then be cold,
This frame be gather'd to its kindred mould!
And the last life-drop circling through my veins
Have tinged a soil untainted yet by chains!

"And yet one struggle ere our doom is seal'd,
One mighty effort, one deciding field!
If vain each hope, we still have choice to be,
In life the fetter'd, or in death the free!"

Still while he speaks, each gallant heart beats high,
And ardor flashes from each kindling eye;
Youth, manhood, age, as if inspired, have caught
The glow of lofty hope and daring thought,
And all is hush'd around—as every sense
Dwelt on the tones of that wild eloquence.

But when his voice hath ceased, th' impetuous cry
Of eager thousands bursts at once on high;
Rampart, and rock, and fortress, ring around,
And fair Alhambra's inmost halls resound.
" Lead us, O chieftain! lead us to the strife,
To fame in death, or liberty in life!"
O zeal of noble hearts! in vain display'd;
Now, while the burning spirit of the brave
Is roused to energies that yet might save,
E'en now, enthusiasts! while ye rush to claim
Your glorious trial on the field of fame,
Your king hath yielded! Valor's dream is o'er;[22]
Power, wealth, and freedom, are your own no more.
And for your children's portion, *but* remains
That bitter heritage—the stranger's chains.

CANTO III.

"Fermossi al fin il cor che balzò tanto."
Hippolito Pindemonte

HEROES of elder days! untaught to yield,
Who bled for Spain on many an ancient field;
Ye, that around the oaken cross of yore[23]
Stood firm and fearless on Asturia's shore,
And with your spirit, ne'er to be subdued,
Hallow'd the wild Cantabrian solitude;
Rejoice amidst your dwellings of repose,
In the last chastening of your Moslem foes!
Rejoice!—for Spain, arising in her strength,
Hath burst the remnant of their yoke at length,
And they, in turn, the cup of woe must drain,
And bathe their fetters with their tears in vain.
And thou, the warrior *born in happy hour*,[24]
Valencia's lord, whose name alone was power,
Theme of a thousand songs in days gone by,
Conqueror of kings! exult, O Cid! on high.
For still 'twas thine to guard thy country's weal,
In life, in death, the watcher for Castile!

Thou, in that hour when Mauritania's bands
Rush'd from their palmy groves and burning lands,
E'en in the realm of spirits didst retain
A patriot's vigilance, remembering Spain![25]
Then, at deep midnight, rose the mighty sound,
By Leon heard, in shuddering awe profound,
As through her echoing streets, in dread array,
Beings, once mortal, held their viewless way:

Voices, from worlds we know not—and the tread
Of marching hosts, the armies of the dead,
Thou and thy buried chieftains—from the grave
Then did thy summons rouse a king to save,
And join thy warriors with unearthly might
To aid the rescue in Tolosa's fight.
Those days are past—the cresent on thy shore,
O realm of evening! sets, to rise no more.[26]
What banner streams afar from Vela's tower?[27]
The cross, bright ensign of Iberia's power!
What the glad shout of each exulting voice?
Castile and Aragon! rejoice, rejoice!
Yielding free entrance to victorious foes,
The Moorish city sees her gates unclose,
And Spain's proud host, with pennon, shield, and lance,
Through her long streets in knightly garb advance.

Oh! ne'er in lofty dreams hath Fancy's eye
Dwelt on a scene of statelier pageantry,
At joust or tourney, theme of poet's lore,
High masque, or solemn festival of yore.
The gilded cupolas, that proudly rise
O'erarch'd by cloudless and cerulean skies;
Tall minarets, shining mosques, barbaric towers,
Fountains, and palaces, and cypress bowers:
And they, the splendid and triumphant throng,
With helmets glittering as they move along
With broider'd scarf, and gem-bestudded mail,
And graceful plumage streaming on the gale;
Shields, gold-emboss'd, and pennons floating far,
And all the gorgeous blazonry of war,
All brighten'd by the rich transparent hues
That southern suns o'er heaven and earth diffuse;
Blend in one scene of glory, form'd to throw
O'er memory's page a never-fading glow.
And there, too, foremost 'midst the conquering brave,
Your azure plumes, O Aben-Zurrahs! wave.
There Hamet moves; the chief whose lofty port
Seems nor reproach to shun, nor praise to court;
Calm, stern, collected—yet within his breast
Is there no pang, no struggle unconfess'd?
If such there be, it still must dwell unseen,
Nor cloud a triumph with a sufferer's mien.

Hears't thou the solemn, yet exulting sound,
Of the deep anthem floating far around?
The choral voices, to the skies that raise
The full majestic harmony of praise?
Lo! where, surrounded by their princely train,
They come, the sovereigns of rejoicing Spain,
Borne on their trophied car—lo! bursting thence
A blaze of chivalrous magnificence!

Onward their slow and stately course they bend
To where th' Alhambra's ancient towers ascend,
Rear'd and adorn'd by Moorish kings of yore,
Whose lost descendants there shall dwell no more.

They reach those towers—irregularly vast
And rude they seem, in mould barbaric cast:[28]
They enter—to their wondering sight is given
A genii palace—an Arabian heaven![29]
A scene by magic raised, so strange, so fair,
Its forms and colors seem alike of air.
Here, by sweet orange-boughs, half shaded o'er,
The deep clear bath reveals its marble floor,
Its margin fringed with flowers, whose glowing hues
The calm transparence of its wave suffuse.
There, round the court, where Moorish arches bend,
Aerial columns, richly deck'd, ascend;
Unlike the models of each classic race,
Of Doric grandeur, or Corinthian grace,
But answering well each vision that portrays
Arabian splendor to the poet's gaze:
Wild, wondrous, brilliant, all—a mingling glow
Of rainbow-tints, above, around, below;
Bright streaming from the many-tinctured veins
Of precious marble, and the vivid stains
Of rich mosaics o'er the light arcade,
In gay festoons and fairy knots display'd.
On through th' enchanted realm, that only seems
Meet for the radiant creatures of our dreams,
The royal conquerors pass—while still their sight
On some new wonder dwells with fresh delight.
Here the eye roves through slender colonnades,
O'er bowery terraces and myrtle shades;
Dark olive-woods beyond, and far on high
The vast sierra mingling with the sky.
There, scattering far around their diamond spray,
Clear streams from founts of alabaster play,
Through pillar'd halls, were, exquisitely wrought,
Rich arabesques, with glittering foliage fraught,
Surmount each fretted arch, and lend the scene
A wild, romantic, oriental mien:
While many a verse, from eastern bards of old,
Borders the walls in characters of gold.[30]
Here Moslem luxury, in her own domain,
Hath held for ages her voluptuous reign
'Midst gorgeous domes, where soon shall silence brood
And all be lone—a splendid solitude.
Now wake their echoes to a thousand songs,
From mingling voices of exulting throngs;
Tambour, and flute, and atabal, are there,[31]
And joyous clarions pealing on the air;

While every hall resounds, " Granada won !
Granada ! for Castile and Aragon ! "[32]

'Tis night—from dome and tower, in dazzling maze,
The festal lamps innumerably blaze ;[33]
Through long arcades their quivering lustre gleams,
From every latice tremulously streams,
'Midst orange-gardens plays on fount and rill,
And gilds the waves of Darro and Xenil ;
Red flame the torches on each minaret's height,
And shines each street an avenue of light ;
And midnight feasts are held, and music's voice
Through the long night still summons to rejoice.

Yet there, while all would seem to heedless eye
One blaze of pomp, one burst of revelry,
Are hearts unsoothed by those delusive hours,
Gall'd by the chain, though deck'd awhile with flowers;
Stern passions working in th' indignant breast,
Deep pangs untold, high feelings unexpress'd,
Heroic spirits, unsubmitting yet—
Vengeance, and keen remorse, and vain regret.

From yon proud height, whose olive-shaded brow
Commands the wide, luxuriant plains below,
Who lingering gazes o'er the lovely scene,
Anguish and shame contending in his mien ?
He, who, of heroes and of kings the son,
Hath lived to lose whate'er his fathers won ;
Whose doubts and fears his people's fate hath seal'd,
Wavering alike in council and in field ;
Weak, timid ruler of the wise and brave,
Still a fierce tyrant or a yielding slave.

Far from these vine-clad hills and azure skies,
To Afric's wilds the royal exile flies ;[34]
Yet pauses on his way, to weep in vain
O'er all he never must behold again.
Fair spreads the scene around—for him *too* fair,
Each glowing charm but deepens his despair.
The Vega's meads, the city's glittering spires,
The old majestic palace of his sires,
The gay pavilions, and retired alcoves,
Bosom'd in citron and pomegranate groves ;
Tower-crested rocks, and streams that wind in light,
All in one moment bursting on his sight,
Speak to his soul of glory's vanished years,
And wake the source of unavailing tears.
—Weep'st thou, Abdallah ?—Thou dost well to weep
O feeble heart ! o'er all thou couldst not keep !
Well do a woman's tears befit the eye
Of him who knew not as a man to die.[35]

THE ABENCERRAGE.

The gale sighs mournfully through Zayda's bower,
The hand is gone that nursed each infant flower.
No voice, no step, is in her father's halls,
Mute are the echos of their marble walls;
No stranger enters at the chieftain's gate,
But all is hush'd, and void, and desolate

There, through each tower and solitary shade,
In vain doth Hamet seek the Zegri maid:
Her grove is silent, her pavilion lone,
Her lute forsaken, and her doom unknown;
And through the scene she loved, unheeded flows
The stream whose music lull'd her to repose.

But oh! to him, whose self-accusing thought
Whispers, 'twas *he* that desolation wrought;
He, who his country and his faith betray'd,
And lent Castile revengeful, powerful aid;
A voice of sorrow swells in every gale,
Each wave, low rippling tells a mournful tale;
And as the shrubs, untended, unconfined,
In wild exuberance rustle to the wind;
Each leaf hath language to his startled sense,
And seems to murmur—" Thou hast driven her hence '"
And well he feels to trace her flight were vain,
—Where hath lost love been once recall'd again?
In her pure breast, so long by anguish torn,
His name can rouse no feeling now—but scorn.
O bitter hour! when first the shuddering heart
Wakes to behold the void within—and start!
To feel its own abandonment, and brood
O'er the chill bosom's depth of solitude.
The stormy passions that in Hamet's breast
Have sway'd so long, so fiercely, are at rest;
Th' avenger's task is closed:[36]—he finds too late,
It hath not changed his feelings, but his fate.
He was a lofty spirit, turned aside
From its bright path by woes, and wrongs, and pride,
And onward, in its new tumultuous course,
Borne with too rapid and intense a force
To pause one moment in the dread career,
And ask—if such could be its native sphere?
Now are those days of wild delirium o'er,
Their fears and hopes excite his soul no more;
The feverish energies of passion close,
And his heart sinks in desolate repose,
Turns sickening from the world, yet shrinks not less
From its own deep and utter loneliness.

There is a sound of voices on the air,
A flash of armor to the sunbeam's glare,

'Midst the wild Alpuxarras;[37]—there, on high,
Where mountain snows are mingling with the sky,
A few brave tribes, with spirit yet unbroke,
Have fled indignant from the Spaniard's yoke.

O ye dread scenes! where Nature dwells alone,
Severely glorious on her craggy throne;
Ye citadels of rock, gigantic forms,
Veil'd by the mists, and girdled by the storms,—
Ravines and glens, and deep resounding caves,
That hold communion with the torrent-waves;
And ye, th' unstain'd and everlasting snows,
That dwell above in bright and still repose;
To you, in every clime, in every age,
Far from the tyrant's or the conqueror's rage,
Hath freedom led her sons:—untired to keep
Her fearless vigils on the barren steep.
She, like the mountain eagle, still delights
To gaze exulting from unconquer'd heights,
And build her eyrie in defiance proud,
To dare the wind, and mingle with the cloud.

Now her deep voice, the soul's awakener, swells,
Wild Alpuxarras, through your inmost dells.
There, the dark glens and lonely rocks among,
As at the clarion's call, her children throng.
She with enduring strength had nerved each frame,
And made each heart the temple of her flame,
Her own resisting spirit, which shall glow
Unquenchably, surviving all below.

There high-born maids, that moved upon the earth,
More like bright creatures of ærial birth,
Nurslings of palaces have fled to share
The fate of brothers and of sires; to bear,
All undismay'd, privation and distress,
And smile the roses of the wilderness:
And mothers with their infants there to dwell
In the deep forest or the cavern cell,
And rear their offspring midst the rocks, to be,
If now no more the mighty, still the free.

And 'midst that band are veterans, o'er whose head
Sorrows and years their mingled snow have shed:
They saw thy glory, they have wept thy fall,
O royal city! and the wreck of all
They loved and hallow'd most:—doth aught remain
For these to prove of happiness or pain?
Life's cup is drain'd—earth fades before their eye,
Their task is closing—they have but to die.
Ask ye, why fled they hither?—that their doom
Might be, to sink unfetter'd to the tomb.

And youth, in all its pride of strength, is there,
And buoyancy of spirit, form'd to dare
And suffer all things—fall'n on evil days
Yet darting o'er the world an ardent gaze,
As on th' arena, where its powers may find
Full scope to strive for glory with mankind.
Such are the tenants of the mountain-hold,
The high in heart, unconquer'd, uncontroll'd:
By day, the huntsman of the wild—by night,
Unwearied guardians of the watch-fire's light,
They from their bleak majestic home have caught,
A sterner tone of unsubmitting thought,
While all around them bids the soul arise
To blend with Nature's dread sublimities.
—But these are lofty dreams, and must not be
Where tyranny is near:—the bended knee,
The eye, whose glance no inborn grandeur fires,
And the tamed heart, are tributes she requires;
Nor must the dwellers of the rock look down
On regal conquerers, and defy their frown.
What warrior-band is toiling to explore
The mountain-pass, with pine-wood shadow'd o'er?
Startling with martial sounds each rude recess,
Where the deep echo slept in loneliness.
These are the sons of Spain! Your foes are near,
O exiles of the wild sierra! hear!
Hear! wake! arise! and from your inmost caves
Pour like the torrent in its might of waves!

Who leads the invaders on?—his features bear
The deep-worn traces of a calm despair;
Yet his dark brow is haughty—and his eye
Speaks of a soul that asks not sympathy.
'Tis he! 'tis he again! th' apostate chief;
He comes in all the sternness of his grief.
He comes, but changed in heart, no more to wield
Falchion for proud Castile in battle-field,
Against his country's children—though he leads
Castilian bands again to hostile deeds:
His hope is but from ceaseless pangs to fly,
To rush upon the Moslem spears, and die.
So shall remorse and love the heart release,
Which dares not dream of joy, but sighs for peace.
The mountain-echoes are awake—a sound
Of strife is ringing through the rocks around.
Within the steep defile that winds between
Cliffs piled on cliffs, a dark, terrific scene,
Where Moorish exile and Castilian knight
Are wildly mingling in the serried fight.
Red flows the foaming streamlet of the glen,
Whose bright transparence ne'er was stain'd till **then;**

While swell the war-note, and the clash of spears,
To the bleak dwellings of the mountaineers,
Where thy sad daughters, lost Granada! wait,
In dread suspense, the tidings of their fate.
But he—whose spirit, panting for its rest,
Would fain each sword concentrate in his breast—
Who, where a spear is pointed, or a lance
Aim'd at another's breast, would still advance—
Courts death in vain ; each weapon glances by,
As if for him 'twere bliss too great to die.
Yes, Aben-Zurrah! there are deeper woes
Reserved for thee ere Nature's last repose ;
Thou know'st not yet what vengeance fate can wreak,
Nor all the heart can suffer ere it break.
Doubtful and long the strife, and bravely fell
The sons of battle in that narrow dell ;
Youth in its light of beauty there hath past,
And age, the weary, found repose at last ;
Till, few and faint, the Moslem tribes recoil,
Born down by numbers, and o'erpower'd by toil.
Dispers'd, dishearten'd, through the pass they fly,
Pierce the deep wood, or mount the cliff on high ;
While Hamet's band in wonder gaze, nor dare
Track o'er their dizzy path the footsteps of despair.

Yet he, to whom each danger hath become
A dark delight, and every wild a home,
Still urges onward—undismay'd to tread
Where life's fond lovers would recoil with dread
But fear is for the happy—*they* may shrink
From the steep precipice, or torrent's brink ;
They to whom earth is paradise—their doom
Lends no stern courage to approach the tomb :
Not such his lot, who, school'd by fate severe,
Were but too blest if aught remain'd to fear.[38]
Up the rude crags, whose giant masses throw
Eternal shadows o'er the glen below ;
And by the fall, whose many-tinctured spray
Half in a mist of radiance veils its way,
He holds his venturous track :—supported now
By some o'erhanging pine or ilex bough ;
Now by some jutting stone that seems to dwell
Half in mid-air, as balanced by a spell :
Now hath his footstep gain'd the summit's head,
A level span, with emerald verdure spread,
A fairy circle—there the heath-flowers rise,
And the rock-rose unnoticed blooms and dies ;
And brightly plays the stream, ere yet its tide
In foam and thunder cleave the mountain side ;
But all is wild beyond—and Hamet's eye
Roves o'er a world of rude sublimity

That dell beneath, where e'en at noon of day
Earth's charter'd guest, the sunbeam scarce can stray;
Around, untrodden woods; and far above
Where mortal footstep ne'er may hope to rove,
Bare granite cliffs, whose fix'd, inherent dyes
Rival the tints that float o'er summer skies;[39]
And the pure glittering snow-realm, yet more high,
That seems a part of Heaven's eternity.

There is no track of man where Hamet stands
Pathless the scene as Lybia's desert sands;
Yet on the calm, still air, a sound is heard
Of distant voices, and the gathering-word
Of Islam's tribes, now faint and fainter grown.
Now but the lingering echo of a tone.

That sound, whose cadence dies upon his ear,
He follows, reckless if his bands are near.
On by the rushing stream his way he bends,
And through the mountain's forest zone ascends;
Piercing the still and solitary shades
Of ancient pine, and dark, luxuriant glades,
Eternal twilight's reign:—those mazes past,
The glowing sunbeams meet his eyes at last,
And the lone wanderer now hath reach'd the source
Whence the wave gushes, foaming on its course.
But there he pauses—for the lonely scene
Towers in such dread magnificence of mien,
And, mingled oft with some wild eagle's cry,
From rock-built eyrie rushing to the sky,
So deep the solemn and majestic sound
Of forests, and of waters murmuring round—
That, wrapt in wondering awe, his heart forgets
Its fleeting struggles, and its vain regrets.
—What earthly feeling, unabash'd, can dwell
In Nature's mighty presence?—'midst the swell
Of everlasting hills, the roar of floods,
And frown of rocks, and pomp of waving woods?
These their own grandeur on the soul impress,
And bid each passion feel its nothingness.

'Midst the vast marble cliffs, a lofty cave
Rears its broad arch beside the rushing wave;
Shadow'd by giant oaks, and rude, and lone,
It seems the temple of some power unknown,
Where earthly being may not dare intrude
To pierce the secrets of the solitude.
Yet thence at intervals a voice of wail
Is rising, wild and solemn on the gale.
Did thy heart thrill, O Hamet! at the tone?
Came it not o'er thee as a spirit's moan?

As some loved sound, that long from earth had fled,
The unforgotten accents of the dead?
E'en thus it rose—and springing from his trance
His eager footsteps to the sound advance.
He mounts the cliffs, he gains the cavern floor;
Its dark green moss with blood is sprinkled o'er;
He rushes on—and lo! where Zayda rends
Her locks, as o'er her slaughter'd sire she bends,
Lost in despair;—yet, as a step draws nigh,
Disturbing sorrow's lonely sanctity,
She lifts her head, and, all subdued by grief,
Views, with a wild, sad smile, the once-loved chief;
While rove her thoughts, unconscious of the past,
And every woe forgetting—but the last.

"Com'st thou to weep with me?—for I am left
Alone on earth, of every tie bereft.
Low lies the warrior on his blood-stain'd bier;
His child may call, but he no more shall hear.
He sleeps—but never shall those eyes unclose;
'Twas not my voice that lull'd him to repose,
Nor can it break his slumbers. Dost thou mourn?
And is thy heart like mine, with anguish torn?
Weep, and my soul a joy in grief shall know,
That o'er his grave my tears with Hamet's flow!"

But scarce her voice had breathed that well-known name,
When, swiftly rushing o'er her spirit, came
Each dark remembrance; by affliction's power
Awhile effaced in that o'erwhelming hour,
To wake with tenfold strength; 'twas then her eye
Resumed its light, her mien its majesty,
And o'er her wasted cheek a burning glow
Spreads, while her lips' indignant accents flow.

"Away! I dream—oh, how hath sorrow's might
Bow'd down my soul, and quench'd its native light—
That I should thus forget! and bid *thy* tear
With mine be mingled o'er a father's bier!
Did he not perish, haply by thy hand,
In the last combat with thy ruthless band?
The morn beheld that conflict of despair:—
'Twas then he fell—he fell!—and thou wert there!
Thou! who thy country's children hast pursued
To their last refuge 'midst these mountains rude.
Was it for this I loved thee? thou hast taught
My soul all grief, all bitterness of thought!
'Twill soon be past—I bow to Heaven's decree,
Which bade each pang be minister'd by thee."

"I had not deem'd that aught remain'd below
For me to prove of yet untasted woe;

But thus to meet thee, Zayda! can impart
One more, one keener agony of heart.
Oh, hear me yet!—I would have died to save
My foe, but still thy father, from the grave;
But, in the fierce confusion of the strife,
In my own stern despair, and scorn of life,
Borne wildly on, I saw not, knew not aught,
Save that to perish there in vain I sought.
And let me share thy sorows—hadst thou known
All I have felt in silence and alone,
E'en *thou* might'st then relent, and deem, at last
A grief like mine might expiate all the past.

"But oh! for thee, the loved and precious flower,
So fondly rear'd in luxury's guarded bower,
From every danger, every storm secured,
How hast *thou* suffer'd! what hast thou endured!
Daughter of palaces! and can it be
That this bleak desert is a home for thee!
These rocks *thy* dwelling! thou, who should'st have known
Of life the sunbeam and the smile alone!
Oh, yet forgive!—be all my guilt forgot,
Nor bid me leave thee to so rude a lot!"

"That lot is fix'd; 'twere fruitless to reply,
Still must a gulf divide my fate with thine.
I may forgive—but not at will the heart
Can bid its dark remembrances depart.
No, Hamet, no!—too deeply are these traced,
Yet the hour comes when all shall be effaced!
Not long on earth, not long, shall Zayda keep
Her lonely vigils o'er the grave to weep:
E'en now, prophetic of my early doom,
Speaks to my soul a presage of the tomb;
And ne'er in vain did hopeless mourner feel
That deep foreboding o'er the bosom steal!
Soon shall I slumber calmly by the side
Of him for whom I lived, and would have died;
Till then, one thought shall soothe my orphan lot,
In pain and peril—I forsook him not.

"And now, farewell!—behold the summer-day
Is passing, like the dreams of life, away.
Soon will the tribe of him who sleeps draw nigh,
With the last rites his bier to sanctify.
Oh, yet in time, away!—'twere not *my* prayer
Could move their hearts a foe like thee to spare!
This hour they come—and dost thou scorn to fly?
Save me that one last pang—to see thee die!"
E'en while she speaks is heard their echoing tread;
Onward they move, the kindred of the dead.

They reach the cave—they enter—slow their pace,
And calm, deep sadness marks each mourner's face;
And all is hush'd till he who seems to wait
In silent, stern devotedness, his fate,
Hath met their glance—then grief to fury turns;
Each mien is changed, each eye indignant burns,
And voices rise, and swords have left their sheath:
Blood must atone for blood, and death for death;
They close around him: lofty still his mien,
His cheek unalter'd, and his brow serene.
Unheard, or heard in vain, is Zayda's cry;
Fruitless her prayer, unmark'd her agony.
But as his foremost foes their weapons bend
Against the life he seeks not to defend,
Wildly she darts between—each feeling past,
Save strong affection, which prevails at last.
Oh! not in vain its daring—for the blow
Aim'd at his heart hath bade her life-blood flow;
And she hath sunk a martyr on the breast,
Where, in that hour, her head may calmly rest,
For he is saved:—behold the Zegri band
Pale with dismay and grief, around her stand:
While, every thought of hate and vengeance o'er,
They weep for her who soon shall weep no more.
She, she alone is calm:—a fading smile,
Like sunset, passes o'er her cheek the while;
And in her eye, ere yet it closes, dwell
Those last faint rays, the parting soul's farewell.

"Now is the conflict past, and I have proved
How well, how deeply, thou hast been beloved!
Yes! in an hour like this 'twere vain to hide
The heart so long and so severely tried:
Still to thy name that heart hath fondly thrill'd,
But sterner duties call'd! and were fulfill'd:
And I am blest!—To every holier tie
My life was faithful,—and for thee I die!
Nor shall the love so purified be vain;
Sever'd on earth, we yet shall meet again.
Farewell!—And ye, at Zayda's dying prayer,
Spare him, my kindred tribe! forgive and spare!
Oh! be his guilt forgotten in his woes,
While I, beside my sire, in peace repose."

Now fades her cheek, her voice hath sunk, and death
Sits in her eye, and struggles in her breath.
One pang—'tis past—her task on earth is done,
And the pure spirit to its rest hath flown.
But he for whom she died—Oh! who may paint
The grief, to which all other woes were faint?
There is no power in language to impart
The deeper pangs, the ordeals of the heart,

By the dread Searcher of the soul survey'd;
These have no words—nor are by words portray'd.

A dirge is rising on the mountain-air,
Whose fitful swells its plaintive murmurs bear
Far o'er the Alpuxarras;—wild its tone,
And rocks and caverns echo, " Thou art gone!"

Daughter of heroes! thou art gone
    To share his tomb who gave thee birth;
Peace to the lovely spirit flown!
    It was not form'd for earth.
Thou wert a sunbeam in thy race,
    Which brightly pass'd, and left no trace.

But calmly sleep!—for thou art free,
    And hands unchain'd thy tomb shall raise.
Sleep! they are closed at length for thee.
    Life's few and evil days!
Nor shalt thou watch, with tearful eye,
    The lingering death of liberty.

Flower of the desert! thou thy bloom
    Didst early to the storm resign:
We bear it still—and dark *their* doom
    Who cannot weep for thine!
For us whose every hope is fled,
    The time is past to mourn the dead.

The days have been, when o'er thy bier
    Far other strains than these had flow'd;
Now, as a home from grief and fear,
    We hail thy dark abode!
We, who but linger to bequeath
    Our sons the choice of chains or death.

Thou art with those, the free, the brave,
    The mighty of departed years:
And for the slumberers of the grave
    Our fate hath left no tears.
Though loved and lost, to weep were vain
For thee, who ne'er shalt weep again.

Have we not seen, despoil'd by foes,
    The land our fathers won of yore?
And is there yet a pang for those
    Who gaze on *this* no more?
Oh, that like them 'twere ours to rest!
Daughter of heroes! thou art blest!

A few short years, and in the lonely cave
Where sleeps the Zegri maid, is Hamet's grave.

Sever'd in life, united in the tomb—
Such, of the hearts that loved so well, the doom!
Their dirge, of woods and waves th' eternal moan;
Their sepulchre, the pine-clad rocks alone.
And oft beside the midnight watch-fire's blaze,
Amidst those rocks, in long departed days
(When freedom fled, to hold, sequester'd there,
The stern and lofty councils of despair,)
Some exiled Moor, a warrior of the wild,
Who the lone hours with mournful strains beguiled,
Hath taught his mountain-home the tale of those
Who thus have suffer'd, and who thus repose.

NOTES.

Note 1, page 33, line 30.
Not the light zambra.
Zambra, a Moorish dance.

Note 2, page 33, line 33.
Within the hall of Lions.
The hall of lions was the principal one of the Alhambra, and was so called from twelve sculptured lions which supported an alabaster basin in the centre.

Note 3, page 33, line 52.
His Aben-Zurrahs there young Hamet leads.
Aben-Zurrahs: the name thus written is taken from the translation of an Arabic MS. given in the 3d volume of Bourgoanne's Travels through Spain.

Note 4, page 35, line 8.
The Vega's green expanse.
The Vega, the plain surrounding Granada, the scene of frequent actions between the Moors and Christians.

Note 5, page 35, line 40.
Seen 'midst the redness of the desert storm.
An extreme redness in the sky is the presage of the Simoom.—See Bruce's *Travels.*

Note 6, page 36, lines 19 and 20.
Stillness like that, when fierce the Kamsin's blast
Hath o'er the dwellings of the desert pass'd.
Of the Kamsin, a hot south wind, common in Egypt, we have the following account in Volney's Travels: "These winds are known in Egypt by the general name of the winds of fifty days, because they prevail more frequently in the fifty days preceding and following the equinox. They are mentioned by travellers under the name of the poisonous winds, or hot winds of the desert: their heat is so excessive that it is difficult to form any idea of its violence without having experienced it. When they begin to blow, the sky, at other times so clear in this climate, becomes dark and heavy; the sun loses his splendor, and appears of a violet color; the air is not cloudy, but grey and thick, and is filled with a subtle dust, which penetrates every where: respiration becomes short and difficult, the skin parched and dry, the lungs are contracted and painful, and the body consumed with internal heat. In vain is coolness sought for; marble, iron, water, though the sun no longer appears, are hot the streets are deserted, and a dead silence pervades every where. The natives of towns and villages shut themselves up in their houses, and those of the desert in tents, or holes dug in the earth, where they wait the termination of this heat, which generally lasts three days. Woe to the traveller whom it surprises remote from shelter: he must suffer all its dreadful effects, which are sometimes mortal.'

NOTES.

Note 7, page 38, line 32.
While tearless eyes enjoy the honey-dews of sleep.
"Enjoy the honey-heavy-dew of slumber."—SHAKSPEARE.

Note 8, page 43, line 4.
On the green Vega won in single fight.
Garcilaso de la Vega derived his surname from a single combat (in which he was the victor) with a Moor, on the Vega of Granada.

Note 9, page 43, line 32.
Who drank for man the bitter cup of tears.
"El Rey D. Fernando bolviò à la Vega, y puso su Real à la vista de Huecar, a veyute y seys dias del mes de Abril, adonde fuè fortificado de todo lo necessario; poniendo el Christiano toda su gente en esquadron, con todas sus vanderas tendidas, y su Real Estandarte, el qual llevava por divisa un Christo crusificado."—*Historia de las Guerras Civiles de Granada.*

Note 10, page 43, line 44,
From yon rich province of the western star.
Andalusia signifies, in Arabic, the region of the evening or the west; in a word, the *Hesperia* of the Greeks.—See CASIRI. *Bibliot. Arabico-Hispana,* and GIBBON's *Decline and Fall, &c.*

Note 11, page 43, line 48.
The snow-white charger, and the azure crest.
"Los Abencerrages salieron con su acostumbrada librea azul y blanca, todos llenos de ricos texidos de plata, las plumas de la misma color; en sus adargas, su acostumbrada divisa, salvages que desquixalavan leones, y otros un mundo que lo deshazia un selvage con un baston."—*Guerras Civiles de Granada.*

Note 12, page 44, line 26.
Th' eternal snow that crowns Veleta's head.
The loftiest heights of the Sierra Nevada, are those called Mulhacen and Picacho de Veleta.

Note 13, page 44, line 36.
The wounded sought a shelter—and expired.
It is known to be a frequent circumstance in battle, that the dying and the wounded drag themselves, as it were mechanically, to the shelter which may be afforded by any bush or thicket on the field.

Note 14, page 49, line 35.
Severely beauteous.
"Severe in youthful beauty."—MILTON.

Note 15, page 50, line 27.
While streams that bear thee treasures in their wave.
Granada stands upon two hills, separated by the Darro. The Genil runs under the walls. The Darro is said to carry with its stream small particles of gold, and the Genil, of silver. When Charles V. came to Granada with the Empress Isabella, the city presented him with a crown made of gold, which had been collected from the Darro.—See BOURGOANNE's *and other travels.*

Note 16, page 50, line 42.
The hearts of warriors echo to its call.
At this period, while the inhabitants of Granada were sunk in

indolence, one of those men, whose natural and impassioned eloquence has sometimes aroused a people to deeds of heroism, raised his voice, in the midst of the city, and awakened the inhabitants from their lethargy. Twenty thousand enthusiasts, ranged under his banners, were prepared to sally forth, with the fury of desperation, to attack the besiegers, when Abo Abdeli, more afraid of his subjects than of the enemy, resolved immediately to capitulate, and made terms with the Christians, by which it was agreed that the Moors should be allowed the free exercise of their religion and laws; should be permitted, if they thought proper, to depart unmolested with their effects to Africa; and that he himself, if he remained in Spain, should retain an extensive estate, with houses and slaves, or be granted an equivalent in money if he preferred retiring to Barbary."—See JACOB's *Travels in Spain.*

Note 17, page 51, line 9.

Azarques, Zegris, Almoradis, hear!

Azarques, Zegris, Almoradis, different tribes of the Moors of Granada, all of high distinction.

Note 18, page 51, line 11.

Dyed with no blood but that of hostile bands.

The conquest of Granada was greatly facilitated by the civil dissensions which, at this period, prevailed in the city. Several of the Moorish tribes, influenced by private feuds, were fully prepared for submission to the Spaniards; others had embraced the cause of Muley el Zagal, the uncle and competitor for the throne of Abdallah (or Abo Abdeli) and all was jealousy and animosity.

Note 19, page 51, line 13.

When Tarik's bands o'erspread the western shore.

Tarik, the first leader of the Arabs and Moors into Spain. "The Saracens landed at the pillar or point of Europe. The corrupt and familiar appellation of Gibraltar (Gebel al Tarik) describes the mountain of Tarik; and the entrenchments of his camp were the first outline of those fortifications, which, in the hands of our countrymen, have resisted the art and power of the house of Bourbon. The adjacent governors informed the court of Toledo of the descent and progress of the Arabs; and the defeat of his lieutenant, Edeco, who had been commanded to seize and bind the presumptuous strangers, first admonished Roderic of the magnitude of the danger At the royal summons, the dukes and counts, the bishops and nobles, of the Gothic monarchy, assembled at the head of their followers, and the title of king of the Romans, which is employed by an Arabic historian, may be excused by the close affinity of language, religion, and manners, between the nations of Spain."—GIBBON's *Decline and Fall, &c.*, vol. ix. p. 472, 473.

Note 20, page 51, line 14.

When the long combat raged on Xeres' plain.

"In the neighborhood of Cadiz, the town of Xeres has been illustrated by the encounter which determined the fate of the kingdom; the stream of the Gaudalete, which falls into the bay, divided the two camps, and marked the advancing and retreating skirmishes of three successive days. On the fourth day, the two armies joined a more serious and decisive issue. Notwithstanding the valor of the Saracens, they fainted under the weight of multitudes, and the plain of Xeres was overspread with sixteen thousand of their dead bodies —'My brethren,' said Tarik to his surviving companions, 'the enemy is before you, the sea is behind; whither wouldyou fly? Follow your general; I am resolved either to lose my life, or to trample on the prostrate king of the Romans.'—Besides the resource of despair, he confided in the secret correspondence and nocturnal interviews of Count Julian with the sons and the brother of Witiza. The two princes, and the Archbishop of Toledo, occupied the most important post: their well-timed defection broke the ranks of the Christians; each warrior was prompted by fear or suspicion to consult his personal safety; and the remains of the Gothic army were scattered or destroyed in the flight and pursuit of the three following days."—GIBBON'S *Decline and Fall, &c.,* vol. ix. p. 473, 474.

Note 21, page 51, line 15.
And Afric's tecbir swell'd through yielding Spain.

The *tecbir*, the shout of onset used by the Saracens in battle

Note 22, page 52, line 12.
Your king hath yielded! Valor's dream is o'er.

The terrors occasioned by this sudden excitement of popular feeling seem even to have accelerated Abo Abdeli's capitulation. "Aterrado Abo Abdeli con el alboroto y temiendo no ser ya el Dueño de un pueblo amotinádo, se apresuró á concluir una capitulation, la menos dura que podia obtenir en tan urgentes circunstancias, y ofrecio entregor á Granada el dia seis de Enero."—*Paseos en Granada,* vol. i p. 298.

Note 23, page 52, line 18.
Ye, that around the oaken cross of yore.

The oaken cross, carried by Pelagius in battle.

Note 24, page 52, line 28.
And thou, the warrior born in happy hour.

See Southey's Chronicle of the Cid, in which that warrior is frequently styled, "*he who was born in happy hour.*"

Note 25, page 52, lines 36 and 37.
E'en in the realm of spirits didst retain
A patriot's vigilance, remembering Spain!

"Moreover, when the Miramamolin brought over from Africa, against King Don Alfonso, the eighth of the name, the mightiest power of the misbelievers that had ever been brought against Spain, since the destruction of the kings of the Goths, the Cid Campeador remembered his country in that great danger; for the night before the battle was fought at the Navas de Tolosa, in the dead of the night, a mighty sound was heard in the whole city of Leon, as if it were the tramp of a great army passing through; and it passed on to the royal monastery of St. Isidro, and there was a great knocking at the gate thereof, and they called to a priest who was keeping vigils in the church, and told him, that the captains of the army whom he heard were the Cid Ruydiez, and Count Ferran Gonzalez, and that they came there to call up King Don Ferrando the Great, who lay buried in that church, that he might go with them to deliver Spain. And on the morrow that great battle of the Navas de Tolosa was fought, wherein sixty thousand of the misbelievers were slain, which was one of the greatest and noblest battles ever won over the Moors."—SOUTHEY'S *Chronicle of the Cid.*

Note 26, page 53, line 8.
O realm of evening!

The name of Andalusia, the *region of evening,* or *of the west,* was applied by the Arabs not only to the province so called, but to the whole peninsula.

THE ABENCERRAGE.

Note 27, page 53, line 9.
What banner streams afar from Vela's tower.
" En este dia, para siempre memorable, los estandartes de la Cruz, de St. Jago, y el de los Reyes de Castilla se tremoláran sobre la torre mas alta, llamada de *la Vela;* y un exercito prosternado, inundandose en lagrimas de gozo y reconocimiento, assistio al mas glorioso de los espectaculos."—*Paseos en Granada,* vol. i. p. 299.

Note 28, page 54, lines 5 and 6.
*They reach those towers—irregularly vast
And rude they seem, in mould barbaric cast*
Swinburne, after describing the noble palace built by Charles V. in the precincts of the Alhambra, thus proceeds: "Adjoining (to the north) stands a huge heap of as ugly buildings as can well be seen, all huddled together, seemingly without the least intention of forming *one* habitation out of them. The walls are entirely unornamented, all gravel and pebbles, daubed over with plaster by a very coarse hand; yet this is the palace of the Moorish kings of Granada, indisputably the most curious place within that exists in Spain, perhaps in Europe. In many countries you may see excellent modern as well as ancient architecture, both entire and in ruins; but nothing to be met with any where else can convey an idea of this edifice, except you take it from the decorations of an opera, or, the tales of the genii."—Swinburne's *Travels through Spain.*

Note 29, page 54, line 8.
A genii palace—an Arabian heaven.
" Passing round the corner of the emperor's palace, you are admitted at a plain unornamented door, in a corner. On my first visit, I confess, I was struck with amazement as I stepped over the threshold, to find myself on a sudden transported into a species of fairy land. The first place you come to is the court called the Communa, or *del Mesucar,* that is, the common baths: an oblong square, with a deep bason of clear water in the middle; two flights of marble steps leading down to the bottom; on each side a parterre of flowers, and a row of orange-trees. Round the court runs a peristyle paved with marble; the arches bear upon very slight pillars, in proportions and style different from all the regular orders of architecture. The ceilings and walls are incrustated with fretwork in stucco, so minute and intricate, that the most patient draughtsman would find it difficult to follow it, unless he made himself master of the general plan."—Swinburne's *Travels in Spain.*

Note 30, page 54, line 42.
Borders the walls in characters of gold.
The walls and cornices of the Alhambra are covered with inscriptions in Arabic characters. " In examining this abode of magnificence," says Bourgoanne, " the observer is every moment astonished at the new and interesting mixture of architecture and poetry. The palace of the Alhambra may be called a collection of fugitive pieces; and whatever duration these may have, time, with which every thing passes away, has too much contributed to confirm to them that title."—See Bourgoanne's *Travels in Spain.*

Note 31, page 54, line 49.
Tambour, and flute, and atabal, are there.
Atabal, a kind of Moorish drum.

Note 32, page 55, line 2.
Granada! for Castile and Aragon!

" Y ansi entraron en la ciudad, y subieron al Alhambra, y encima de la torre de Comares tan famosa se levantò la señal de la Santa Cruz, y luego el real estandarte de los dos Christianos reyes. Y al punto los reyes de armas, à grandes bozes dizieron, ' Granada! Granada! por su magestad, y por la reyna su muger.' La serenissima reyna D. Isabel, que viò la señal de la Santa Cruz sobre la hermosa torre de Comares, y el su estandarte real con ella, se hincò de Rodillas, y diò infinitas gracias à Dios por la victoria que le avia dado contra aquella gran ciudad. La musica real de la capilla del rey luego à canto de organo cantò Te Deum laudamus. Fuè tan grande el plazer que todos lloravan. Luego del Alhambra sonaron mil instrumentos de musica de belicas trompetas. Los Moros amigos del rey, que querian ser Christianos, cuya cabeza era el valerosa Muca, tomaron mil dulzaynas y añafiles, sonando grande ruydo de atambores por toda la ciudad."—*Historia de las Guerras Civiles de Granada.*

Note 33, page 55, line 4.
The festal lamps innumerably blaze.

" Los cavalleros Moros que avemos dicho, aquella noche jugaron galanamente alcancias y cañas. Andava Granada aquella noche con tanta alegria, y con tantas luminarias, que parecia que se ardia la terra."—*Historia de las Guerras Civiles de Granada.*

Swinburne, in his Travels through Spain, in the years 1775 and 1776, mentions, that the aniversary of the surrender of Granada to Ferdinand and Isabella, was still observed in the city as a great festival and day of rejoicing; and that the populace on that occasion paid an annual visit to the Moorish palace.

Note 34, page 55, line 32.
To Afric's wilds the royal exile flies.

" Los Gomeles todos se passaron en Africa, y el Rey Chico con ellos, que no quisò estar en España, y en Africa le mataron los Moros de aquellas partes, porque perdiò à Granada."—*Guerras Civiles de Granada.*

Note 35, page 55, line 48.
Of him who knew not as a man to die.

Abo Abdeli, upon leaving Granada, after its conquest by Ferdinand and Isabella, stopped on the hill of Padul to take a last look of his city and palace. Overcome by the sight, he burst into tears, and was thus reproached by his mother, the Sultaness Ayxa,—" Thou doest well to weep, like a woman, over the loss of that kingdom which thou knewest not how to defend and die for, like a man.'

Note 36, page 56, line 33.
Th' avenger's task is closed.

" El rey mandò, que si quedavan Zegris, que no viviessen en Granada, por la maldad qui hizieron contra los Abencerrages."—*Guerras Civiles de Granada.*

Note 37, page 57, line 1.
'Midst the wild Alpuxarras.

"The Alpuxarras are so lofty, that the coast of Barbary, and the cities of Tangier and Ceuta, are discovered from their summits; they are about seventeen leagues in length, from Veles Malaga to Almeria, and eleven in breadth, and abound with fruit-trees of great beauty and prodigious size. In these mountains the wretched remains of the Moors took refuge."—BOURGOANNE's *Travels in Spain.*

Note 38, page 59, line 34.
Where but too blest if aught remain'd to fear.
"Plût à Dieu que je craignisse!"—*Andromaque.*

Note 39, page 60 line 6.
Rival the tints that float o'er summer skies.

Mrs. Radcliffe, in her journey along the banks of the Rhine, thus describes the colors of granite rocks in the mountains of the Bergstrasse. "The nearer we approached these mountains, the more we had occasion to admire the various tints of their granites. Sometimes the precipices were of a faint pink, then of a deep red, a dull purple, or a blush approaching to lilac, and sometimes gleams of a pale yellow mingled with the low shrubs that grew upon their sides. The day was cloudless and bright, and we were too near these heights to be deceived by the illusions of aërial coloring; the real hues of their features were as beautiful as their magnitude was sublime."

THE WIDOW OF CRESCENTIUS.

"In the reign of Otho III. Emperor of Germany, the Romans, excited by their Consul, Crescentius, who ardently desired to restore the ancient glory of the Republic, made a bold attempt to shake off the Saxon yoke, and the authority of the Popes, whose vices rendered them objects of universal contempt. The Consul was besieged by Otho in the Mole of Hadrian, which long afterwards continued to be called the Tower of Crescentius. Otho, after many unavailing attacks upon this fortress, at last entered into negotiations; and, pledging his imperial word to respect the life of Crescentius, and the rights of the Roman citizens, the unfortunate leader was betrayed into his power, and immediately beheaded, with many of his partisans. Stephania, his widow, concealing her affliction and her resentment for the insults to which she had been exposed, secretly resolved to revenge her husband and herself. On the return of Otho from a pilgrimage to Mount Gargano, which, perhaps, a feeling of remorse had induced him to undertake, she found means to be introduced to him, and to gain his confidence; and a poison administered by her was soon afterwards the cause of his painful death."—See Sismondi, *History of the Italian Republics*, vol. i.

"L'orage peut briser en un moment les fleurs qui tiennent encore la tête levée. *Mad. de Staël.*

'Midst Tivoli's luxuriant glades,
Bright foaming falls, and olive shades,
Where dwelt, in days departed long,
The sons of battle and of song,
No tree, no shrub its foliage rears,
But o'er the wrecks of other years,
Temples and domes, which long have been
The soil of that enchanted scene.

There the wild fig-tree and the vine
O'er Hadrian's mouldering villa twine;[1]
The cypress, in funereal grace,
Usurps the vanish'd column's place;
O'er fallen shrine, and ruin'd frieze;
The wall-flower rustles in the breeze;
Acanthus-leaves the marble hide
They once adorned, in sculptured pride,
And nature hath resumed her throne
O'er the vast works of ages flown.

Was it for this that many a pile,
Pride of Ilissus and of Nile,
To Anio's banks the image lent
Of each imperial monument?[2]
Now Athens weeps her shatter'd fanes,
Thy temples, Egypt, strew thy plains;
And the proud fabrics Hadrian rear'd
From Tibur's vale have disappear'd.
We need no prescient sibyl there
The doom of grandeur to declare;
Each stone, where weeds and ivy climb,
Reveals some oracle of Time;
Each relic utters Fate's decree,
The future as the past shall be.

Halls of the dead! in Tibur's vale,
Who now shall tell your lofty tale?
Who trace the high patrician's dome,
The bard's retreat, the hero's home?
When moss-clad wrecks alone record
There dwelt the world's departed lord.
In scenes where verdure's rich array
Still sheds young beauty o'er decay,
And sunshine on each glowing hill,
Midst ruins finds a dwelling still.

Sunk is thy palace—but thy tomb,
Hadrian! hath shared a prouder doom,[3]
Though vanish'd with the days of old
Its pillars of Corinthian mould;
And the fair forms by sculpture wrought,
Each bodying some immortal thought,
Which o'er that temple of the dead,
Serene, but solemn beauty shed,
Have found, like glory's self, a grave
In time's abyss, or Tibur's wave:[4]
Yet dreams more lofty, and more fair,
Than art's bold hand hath imaged o'er,
High thoughts of many a mighty mind,
Expanding when all else declined,
In twilight years, when only they
Recall'd the radiance pass'd away,
Have made that ancient pile their home,
Fortress of freedom and of Rome.

There he, who strove in evil days
Again to kindle glory's rays,
Whose spirit sought a path of light,
For those dim ages far too bright,—
Crescentius long maintain'd the strife
Which closed but with its martyr's life,
And left the imperial tomb a name,

A heritage of holier fame.
There closed De Brescia's mission high,
From thence the patriot came to die;[5]
And thou, Whose Roman soul the last,
Spoke with the voice of ages past,[6]
Whose thoughts so long from earth had fled,
To mingle with the glorious dead,
That midst the world's degenerate race
They vainly sought a dwelling-place,
Within that house of death didst brood
O'er visions to thy ruin woo'd.
Yet, worthy of a brighter lot,
Rienzi, be thy faults forgot!
For thou, when all around thee lay
Chain'd in the slumbers of decay;
So sunk each heart, that mortal eye
Had scarce a *tear* for liberty;
Alone, amidst the darkness there,
Could'st gaze on Rome—yet not despair![7]

'Tis morn, and Nature's richest dyes
Are floating o'er Italian skies;
Tints of transparent lustre shine
Along the snow-clad Apennine;
The clouds have left Soracte's height,
And yellow Tiber winds in light,
Where tombs and fallen fanes have strew'd
The wide Campagna's solitude,
'Tis sad amidst that scene to trace
Those relics of a vanish'd race;
Yet, o'er the ravaged path of time,—
Such glory sheds that brilliant clime,
Where Nature still, though empires fall,
Holds her triumphant festival;
E'en Desolation wears a smile,
Where skies and sunbeams laugh the while;
And Heaven's own light, Earth's richest bloom,
Array the ruin and the tomb.

But she, who from yon convent tower
Breathes the pure freshness of the hour;
She, whose rich flow of raven hair
Streams wildly on the morning air,
Heeds not how fair the scene below,
Robed in Italia's brightest glow.
Though throned 'midst Latium's classic plains
Th' Eternal City's towers and fanes
And they, the Pleiades of earth,
The seven proud hills of Empire's birth,
Lie spread beneath: not now her glance
Roves o'er that vast sublime expanse;

Inspired, and bright with hope, 'tis thrown
On Adrian's massy tomb alone:
There, from the storm, when Freedom fled,
His faithful few Crescentius led;
While she, his anxious bride, who now
Bends o'er the scene her youthful brow,
Sought refuge in the hallow'd fane,
Which then could shelter, not in vain.

But now the lofty strife is o'er,
And Liberty shall weep no more.
At length imperial Otho's voice
Bids her devoted sons rejoice;
And he, who battled to restore
The glories and the rights of yore,
Whose accents, like the clarion's sound,
Could burst the dead repose around,
Again his native Rome shall see,
The sceptred city of the free!
And young Stephania waits the hour
When leaves her lord his fortress-tower,
Her ardent heart with joy elate,
That seems beyond the reach of fate;
Her mein, like creature from above,
All vivified with hope and love.

Fair is her form, and in her eye
Lives all the soul of Italy;
A meaning lofty and inspired,
As by her native day-star fired;
Such wild and high expression, fraught
With glances of impassion'd thought,
As fancy sheds, in visions bright,
O'er priestess of the God of Light;
And the dark locks that lend her face
A youthful and luxuriant grace,
Wave o'er her cheek, whose kindling dyes
Seem from the fire within to rise;
But deepen'd by the burning heaven
To her own land of sunbeams given.
Italian art that fervid glow
Would o'er ideal beauty throw,
And with such ardent life express
Her high-wrought dreams of loveliness;—
Dreams which, surviving Empire's fall,
The shade of glory still recall.

But see,—the banner of the brave
O'er Adrian's tomb hath ceased to wave.
'Tis lower'd—and now Stephania's eye
Can well the martial train descry.

Who, issuing from that ancient dome,
Pour through the crowded streets of Rome.
Now from her watch-tower on the height,
With step as fabled wood-nymphs light,
She flies—and swift her way pursues,
Through the lone convent's avenues.
Dark cypress groves, and fields o'erspread
With records of the conquering dead,
And paths which track a glowing waste,
She traverses in breathless haste;
And by the tombs where dust is shrined,
Once tenanted by loftiest mind,
Still passing on, hath reach'd the gate
Of Rome, the proud, the desolate!
Throng'd are the streets, and, still renew'd,
Rush on the gathering multitude.

Is it their high-soul'd chief to greet,
That thus the Roman thousands meet?
With names that bid their thoughts ascend
Crescentius, thine in song to blend;
And of triumphal days gone by
Recall th' inspiring pageantry?
—There is an air of breathless dread,
An eager glance, a hurrying tread;
And now a fearful silence round,
And now a fitful murmuring sound,
'Midst the pale crowds, that almost seem
Phantoms of some tumultuous dream.
Quick is each step, and wild each mien,
Portentous of some awful scene.
Bride of Crecentius! as the throng
Bore thee with whelming force along,
How did thine anxious heart beat high,
Till rose suspense to agony!
Too brief suspense, that soon shall close,
And leave thy heart to deeper woes.

Who 'midst yon guarded precinct stands
With fearless mien, but fetter'd hands?
The ministers of death are nigh,
Yet a calm grandeur lights his eye;
And in his glance there lives a mind
Which was not form'd for chains to bind,
But cast in such heroic mould
As theirs, th' ascendant ones of old.
Crescentius! Freedom's daring son,
Is this the guerdon thou hast won?
O worthy to have lived and died
In the bright days of Latium's pride!
Thus must the beam of glory close
O'er the seven hills again that rose,

When at thy voice, to burst the yoke,
The soul of Rome indignant woke?
Vain dream! the sacred shields are gone,[8]
Sunk is the crowning city's throne:[9]
Th' illusions, that around her cast
Their guardian spells, have long been past.[10]
Thy life hath been a shot-star's ray,
Shed o'er her midnight of decay;
Thy death at Freedom's ruin'd shrine
Must rivet every chain—but thine.

Calm is his aspect, and his eye
Now fix'd upon the deep blue sky,
Now on those wrecks of ages fled,
Around in desolation spread;
Arch, temple, column, worn and grey,
Recording triumphs pass'd away;
Works of the mighty and the free,
Whose steps on earth no more shall be,
Though their bright course hath left a trace
Nor years nor sorrows can efface.
Why changes now the patriot's mien,
Erewhile so loftily serene?
Thus can approaching death control
The might of that commanding soul?
No!—Heard ye not that thrilling cry
Which told of bitterest agony?
He heard it, and at once subdued,
Hath sunk the hero's fortitude.
He heard it, and his heart too well
Whence rose that voice of woe can tell;
And 'midst the gazing throngs around
One well-known form his glance hath found;
One fondly loving and beloved,
In grief, in peril, faithful proved.
Yes, in the wildness of despair,
She, his devoted bride, is there.
Pale, breathless, through the crowd she flies,
The light of frenzy in her eyes:
But ere her arms can clasp the form,
Which life ere long must cease to warm;
Ere on his agonizing breast
Her heart can heave, her head can rest;
Check'd in her course by ruthless hands,
Mute, motionless, at once she stands;
With bloodless cheek and vacant glance,
Frozen and fix'd in horror's trance;
Spell-bound, as every sense were fled,
And thought o'erwhelm'd, and feeling dead.
And the light waving of her hair,
And veil, far floating on the air,

Alone, in that dread moment, show
She is no sculptured form of woe.

The scene of grief and death is o'er,
The patriot's heart shall throb no more:
But *hers*—so vainly form'd to prove
The pure devotedness of love,
And draw from fond affection's eye
All thought sublime, all feeling high;
When consciousness again shall wake,
Hath now no refuge—but to break.
The spirit long inured to pain
May smile at fate in calm disdain;
Survive its darkest hour, and rise
In more majestic energies.
But in the glow of vernal pride,
If each warm hope *at once* hath died,
Then sinks the mind, a blighted flower
Dead to the sunbeam and the shower;
A broken gem, whose inborn light
Is scatter'd—ne'er to re-unite.

PART II.

Hast thou a scene that is not spread
With records of thy glory fled?
A monument that doth not tell
The tale of Liberty's farewell?
Italia! thou art but a grave
Where flowers luxuriate o'er the brave
And nature gives her treasures birth
O'er all that hath been great on earth.
Yet smile thy heavens as once they smiled,
When thou wert Freedom's favor'd child:
Though fane and tomb alike are low,
Time hath not dimm'd thy sunbeam's glow:
And, robed in that exulting ray,
Thou seem'st to triumph o'er decay.
Oh, yet, though by thy sorrows bent,
In nature's pomp magnificent;
What marvel if, when all was lost,
Still on thy bright, enchanted coast,
Though many an omen warn'd him thence,
Linger'd the lord of eloquence?[11]
Still gazing on the lovely sky,
Whose radiance woo'd him—but to die:
Like him *who* would not linger there,
Where heaven, earth, ocean, all are fair?

Who 'midst thy glowing scenes could dwell,
Nor bid awhile his griefs farewell?
Hath not thy pure and genial air
Balm for all sadness but despair?[12]
No! there are pangs, whose deep-worn trace
Not all *thy* magic can efface!
Hearts by unkindness wrung may learn,
The world and all its gifts to spurn;
Time may steal on with silent tread,
And dry the tear that mourns the dead;
May change fond love, subdue regret,
And teach e'en vengeance to forget:
But thou, Remorse! there is no charm,
Thy sting, avenger, to disarm!
Vain are bright suns and laughing skies,
To soothe thy victim's agonies:
The heart once made thy burning throne,
Still, while it beats, is thine alone.

In vain for Otho's joyless eye
Smile the fair scenes of Italy,
As through her landscapes' rich array
Th' imperial pilgrim bends his way.
Thy form, Crescentius, on his sight
Rises when nature laughs in light
Glides round him at the midnight hour,
Is present in his festal bower,
With awful voice and frowning mien,
By all but him unheard, unseen.
Oh! thus to shadows of the grave
Be every tyrant still a slave!

Where through Gargano's woody dells,
O'er bending oaks the north winds swells,[13]
A sainted hermit's lowly tomb
Is bosom'd in umbrageous gloom,
In shades that saw him live and die
Beneath their waving canopy.
'Twas his, as legions tell, to share
The converse of immortals there;
Around that dweller of the wild
There " bright appearances" have smiled,[14]
And angel-wings, at eve, have been
Gleaming the shadowy boughs between.
And oft from that secluded bower
Hath breathed, at midnight's calmer hour,
A swell of viewless harps, a sound
Of warbled anthems pealing round.
Oh, none but voices of the sky
Might wake that thrilling harmony,
Whose tones, whose very echoes made
An Eden of the lonely shade!

THE WIDOW OF CRESCENTIUS.

Years have gone by; the hermit sleeps
Amidst Gargano's woods and steeps;
Ivy and flowers have half o'er grown,
And veil'd his low, sepulchral stone:
Yet still the spot is holy, still
Celestial footsteps haunt the hill;
And oft the awe-struck mountaineer
Aerial vesper-hymns may hear
Around those forest-precincts float,
Soft, solemn, clear, but still remote.
Oft will Affliction breathe her plaint
To that rude shrine's departed saint,
And deem that spirits of the blest
There shed sweet influence o'er her breast.

And thither Otho now repairs,
To soothe his soul with vows and prayers;
And if for him, on holy ground,
The lost one, Peace, may yet be found,
'Midst rocks and forests, by the bed,
Where calmly sleep the sainted dead,
She dwells, remote from heedless eye,
With Nature's lonely majesty.

Vain, vain the search—his troubled breast
Nor vow nor penance lulls to rest;
The weary pilgrimage is o'er,
The hopes that cheer'd it are no more.
Then sinks his soul, and day by day
Youth's buoyant energies decay.
The light of health his eye hath flown,
The glow that tinged his cheek is gone.
Joyless as one on whom is laid
Some baleful spell that bids him fade,
Extending its mysterious power
O'er every scene, o'er every hour;
E'en thus *he* withers; and to him
Italia's brilliant skies are dim.
He withers—in that glorious clime
Where Nature laughs in scorn of Time;
And suns, that shed on all below
Their full and vivifying glow,
From him alone their power withhold,
And leave his heart in darkness cold.
Earth blooms around him, heaven is fair,
He only seems to perish there.

Yet sometimes will a transient smile
Play o'er his faded cheek awhile,
When breaths his minstrel-boy a strain
Of power to lull all earthly pain;

So wildly sweet, its notes might seem
Th' ethereal music of a dream,
A spirit's voice from worlds unknown,
Deep thrilling power in every tone!
Sweet is that lay, and yet its flow
Hath language only given to woe;
And if at times its wakening swell
Some tale of glory seems to tell,
Soon the proud notes of triumph die,
Lost in a dirge's harmony:
Oh! many a pang the heart hath proved,
Hath deeply suffer'd, fondly loved,
Ere the sad strain could catch from thence
Such deep impassion'd eloquence!—
Yes! gaze on him, that minstrel boy—
He is no child of hope and joy!
Though few his years, yet have they been
Such as leave traces on the mein,
And o'er the roses of our prime
Breathe other blights than those of time.

Yet seems his spirit wild and proud,
By grief unsoften'd and unbow'd.
Oh! there are sorrows which impart
A sternness foreign to the heart,
And, rushing with an earthquake's power,
That makes a desert in an hour,
Rouse the dread passions in their course,
As tempests wake the billows' force!—
'Tis sad, on youthful Guido's face,
The stamp of woes like these to trace.
Oh! where can ruins awe mankind,
Dark as the ruins of the mind?

His mien is lofty, but his gaze
Too well a wand'ring soul betrays:
His full dark eye at times is bright
With strange and momentary light,
Whose quick uncertain flashes throw
O'er his pale cheek a hectic glow:
And oft his features and his air
A shade of troubled mystery wear,
A glance of hurried wildness, fraught
With some unfathomable thought.
Whate'er that thought, still, unexpress'd,
Dwells the sad secret in his breast;
The pride his haughty brow reveals,
All other passion well conceals.
He breathes each wounded feeling's tone,
In music's eloquence alone;
His soul's deep voice is only pour'd
Through his full song and swelling chord.

He seeks no friend, but shuns the train
Of courtiers with a proud disdain:
And save when Otho bids his lay
Its half unearthly power essay,
In hall or bower the heart to thrill,
His haunts are wild and lonely still.
Far distant from the heedless throng,
He roves old Tiber's banks along,
Where Empire's desolate remains
Lie scatter'd o'er the silent plains:
Or lingering midst each ruin'd shrine
That strews the desert Palatine,
With mournful, yet commanding mien,
Like the sad genius of the scene,
Entranced in awful thought appears
To commune with departed years.
Or, at the dead of night, when Rome
Seems of heroic shades the home;
When Tiber's murmuring voice recalls
The mighty to their ancient halls;
When hush'd is every meaner sound,
And the deep moonlight-calm around
Leaves to the solemn scene alone
The majesty of ages flown;
A pilgrim to each hero's tomb,
He wanders through the sacred gloom;
And, 'midst those dwellings of decay,
At times will breathe so sad a lay,
So wild a grandeur in each tone,
'Tis like a dirge for empires gone!

Awake thy pealing harp again,
But breathe a more exulting strain,
Young Guido! for awhile forgot
Be the dark secrets of thy lot,
And rouse th' inspiring soul of song
To speed the banquet's hour along!—
The feast is spread, and music's call
Is echoing through the royal hall,
And banners wave, and trophies shine,
O'er stately guests in glittering line;
And Otho seeks awhile to chase
The thoughts he never can erase,
And bid the voice, whose murmurs deep
Rise like a spirit on his sleep,
The still small voice of conscience die,
Lost in the din of revelry.
On his pale brow dejection lowers,
But that shall yield to festal hours:
A gloom is in his faded eye,
But that from music's power shall fly:

His wasted cheek is wan with care,
But mirth shall spread fresh crimson there.
Wake, Guido! wake thy numbers high,
Strike the bold chord exultingly!
And pour upon the enraptured ear
Such strains as warriors love to hear'
Let the rich mantling goblet flow,
And banish all resembling woe;
And, if a thought intrude, of power
To mar the bright convivial hour,
Still must its influence lurk unseen,
And cloud the heart—but not the mien!

Away, vain dream!—on Otho's brow,
Still darker lower the shadows now;
Changed are his features, now o'erspread
With the cold paleness of the dead;
Now crimson'd with a hectic dye,
The burning flush of agony!
His lip is quivering, and his breast
Heaves with convulsive pangs oppress'd;
Now his dim eye seems fix'd and glazed,
And now to heaven in anguish raised;
And as, with unavailing aid,
Around him throng his guests dismay'd,
He sinks—while scarce his struggling breath
Hath power to falter—" This is death!"

Then rush'd that haughty child of song,
Dark Guido, through the awe-struck throng:
Fill'd with a strange delirious light,
His kindling eye shone wildly bright:
And on the sufferer's mien awhile
Gazing with stern vindictive smile
A feverish glow of triumph dyed
His burning cheek, while thus he cried:—
" Yes! these are death-pangs—on thy brow
Is set the seal of vengeance now!
Oh! well was mix'd the deadly draught,
And long and deeply hast though quaff'd;
And bitter as thy pangs may be,
They are but guerdons meet from me!
Yet, these are but a moment's throes,
Howe'er intense, they soon shall close.
Soon shalt thou yield thy fleeting breath—
My life hath been a lingering death;
Since one dark hour of woe and crime,
A blood-spot on the page of time!

" Deem'st thou my mind of reason void?
It is not frenzied,—but destroy'd!

Aye! view the wreck with shuddering thought,—
That work of ruin thou hast wrought!
The secret of thy doom to tell,
My name alone suffices well!
Stephania!—once a hero's bride!
Otho! thou know'st the rest—*he died.*
Yes! trusting to a monarch's word,
The Roman fell, untried, unheard!
And thou, whose every pledge was vain,
How couldst *thou* trust in aught again?

" He died, and I was changed—my soul,
A lonely wanderer, spurn'd control.
From peace, and light, and glory hurl'd,
The outcast of a purer world,
I saw each brighter hope o'erthrown,
And lived for one dread task alone.
The task is closed—fulfill'd the vow,
The hand of death is on thee now.
Betrayer! in thy turn betray'd,
The debt of blood shall soon be paid!
Thine hour is come—the time hath been
My heart had shrunk from such a scene;
That feeling long is past—my fate
Hath made me stern as desolate.

" Ye that around me shuddering stand,
Ye chiefs and princes of the land!
Mourn ye a guilty monarch's doom?
Ye wept not o'er the patriot's tomb!
He sleep's unhonor'd—yet be mine
To share his low, neglected shrine.
His soul with freedom finds a home,
His grave is that of glory—Rome!
Are not the great of old with her,
That city of the sepulchre?
Lead me to death! and let me share
The slumbers of the mighty there!"

The day departs—that fearful day
Fades in calm loveliness away:
From purple heavens its lingering beam
Seems melting into Tiber's stream,
And softly tints each Roman hill
With glowing light, as clear and still
As if, unstain'd by crime or woe,
Its hours had pass'd in silent flow.
The day sets calmly—it hath been
Mark'd with a strange and awful scene:
One guilty bosom throbs no more,
And Otho's pangs and life are o'er.

And thou, ere yet another sun
His burning race hath brightly run,
Released from anguish by thy foes,
Daughter of Rome! shalt find repose.
Yes! on thy country's lovely sky
Fix yet once more thy parting eye!
A few short hours—and all shall be
The silent and the past for thee.
Oh! thus with tempests of a day
We struggle, and we pass away,
Like the wild billows as they sweep,
Leaving no vestige on the deep!
And o'er thy dark and lowly bed
The sons of future days shall tread,
The pangs, the conflicts, of thy lot
By them unknown, by thee forgot.

NOTES.

Note 1, page 73, line 10.
O'er Hadrian's mouldering villa twine.

"J'étais allé passer quelques jours seuls à Tivoli. Je parcourus les environs, et surtout celles de la Villa Adriana. Surpris par la pluie au milieu de ma course, je me réfugiai dans les Salles des *Thermes* voisins du *Pécile* (monumens de la villa,) sous un figuier qui avait renversé le pan d'un mur en s'élevant. Dans un petit salon octogone, ouvert devant moi, une vigne vierge avait percé la voûte de l'édifice, et son gros cep lisse, rouge, et tortueux, montait le long du mur comme un serpent. Autour de moi, à travers les arcades des ruines, s'ouvraient des points de vue sur la Campagne Romaine. Des buissons de sureau remplissaient les salles désertes où venaient se refugier quelques merles solitaires. Les fragmens de maçonnerie étaient tapissées de feuilles de scolopendre, dont la verdure satinée se dessinait comme un travail en mosaïque sur la blancheur des marbres : çà et là de hauts cyprès remplaçaient les colonnes tombées dans ces palais de la Mort ; l'acanthe sauvage rampait à leurs pieds, sur des débris, comme si la nature s'était plu à reproduire sur ces chefs-d'œuvre mutilés d'architecture, l'ornement de leur beauté passée."—CHATEAUBRIAND's *Souvenirs d'Italie.*

Note 2, page 74, line 4.
Of each imperial monument?

The gardens and buildings of Hadrian's villa were copies of the most celebrated scenes and edifices in his dominions ; the Lycæum, the Academia, the Prytaneum of Athens, the Temple of Serapis at Alexandria, the Vale of Tempe, &c.

Note 3, page 74, lines 25 and 26.
Sunk is thy palace, but thy tomb,
Hadrian! hath shared a prouder doom.

The mausoleum of Hadrian, now the castle of St. Angelo, was first converted into a citadel by Belisarius, in his successful defence of Rome against the Goths. "The lover of the arts," says Gibbon, "must read with a sigh that the works of Praxiteles and Lysippus were torn from their lofty pedestals, and hurled into the ditch on the heads of the besiegers." He adds, in a note, that the celebrated sleeping Faun of the Barberini palace was found, in a mutilated state, when the ditch of St. Angelo was cleansed under Urban VIII. In the middle ages, the Moles Hadriani was made a permanent fortress by the Roman government, and bastions, outworks, &c. were added to the original edifice, which had been stripped of its marble covering, its Corinthian pillars, and the brazen cone which crowned its summit.

Note 4, page 74, lines 33 and 34.
Have found, like glory's self, a grave
In time's abyss, or Tiber's wave

" Les plus beaux monumens des arts, les plus admirables statues, ont étés jetées dans le Tibre, et sont cachées sous ses flots. Qui

NOTES.

sait si, pour le chercher, on ne le détournera pas un jour de son lit ? Mais quand on songe que les chefs-d'œuvres du génie humain sont peut-être là devant nous, et qu'un œil plus perçant les verrait à travers les ondes, l'on éprouve je ne sais quelle émotion qui renaît à Rome sans cessé sous diverses formes, et fait trouver une société pour la pensée dans les objets physiques, muets partout ailleurs "—MAD. DE STAEL.

Note 5, page 75, lines 2 and 3.
There closed De Brescia's mission high;
From thence the patriot came to die.

Arnold de Brescia, the undaunted and eloquent champion of Roman liberty, after unremitting efforts to restore the ancient constitution of the republic, was put to death in the year 1155 by Adrian IV. This event is thus described by Sismondi, *Histoire des Republiques Italiennes*, vol. ii. pages 68 and 69. "Le préfect demeura dans le château Saint Ange avec son prisonnier; il le fit transporter un matin sur la place destinée aux exécutions, devant la porte du peuple. Arnaud de Brescia, élevé sur un bûcher, fut ataché à un poteau, en face du Corso. Il pouvoit mesurer des yeux les trois longues rues qui aboutissoient devant son echafaud; elles font presqu' une moitié de Rome. C'est là qu'habitoient les hommes qu'il avoit si souvent appelés à la liberté. Ils reposoient encore en paix, ignorant le danger de leur legislateur. Le tumulte de l'execution et la flamme du bûcher réveillèrent les Romains; ils s'armèrent, ils accoururent, mais trop tard; et les cohortes du pape repoussèrent, avec leurs lances, ceux qui, n'ayant pu sauver Arnaud, vouloient du moins recueillir ses cendres comme de précieuses reliques."

Note 6, page 75, line 5.
Spoke with the voice of ages past.

' Posterity will compare the virtues and failings of this extraordinary man; but in a long period of anarchy and servitude, the name of Rienzi has often been celebrated as the deliverer of his country, and the last of the Roman patriots."—GIBBON's *Decline and Fall,* &c., vol. xii. p. 362.

Note 7, page 75, line 19.
Could'st gaze on Rome—yet not despair!

"Le consul Terentius Varron avoit fui honteusement jusqu'à Venouse: cet homme de la plus basse naissance, n'avoit été élevé au consulat que pour mortifier la noblesse: mais le sénat ne voulut pas jouir de ce malheureux triomphe; il vit combien il étoit nécessaire qu'il s'attirât dans cette occasion la confiance du peuple, il alla au-devant Varron, et le remercia de ce *qu'il n'avoit pas désespéré de la republique.*—MONTESQUIEU's *Grandeur et Decadence des Romains.*

Note 8, page 78, line 3.
Vain dream! the sacred shields are gone.

Of the sacred bucklers, or *ancilia* of Rome, which were kept in the temple of Mars, Plutarch gives the following account:—" In the eighth year of Numa's reign, a pestilence prevailed in Italy; Rome also felt its ravages. While the people were greatly dejected, we are told that a brazen buckler fell from heaven into the hands of Numa. Of this he gave a very wonderful account, received from Egeria and the Muses: that the buckler was sent down for the preservation of the city, and should be kept with great care: that eleven others should be made as like it as possible in size and fashion, in order that if any person were disposed to steal it, he might not be able to distingush that which fell from heaven from the rest. He further declared that the place and the meadows about it, where he frequently conversed with the Muses, should be consecrated to those divinities; and that the spring which watered the ground should be sacred to the use of the Vestal Virgins, daily to sprinkle and purify their temple. The immediate cessation of the pestilence is said to have confirmed the truth of this account."—*Life of Numa*

Note 9, page 78, line 4

Sunk is the crowning city's throne

" Who hath taken this counsel against Tyre, the *crowning city*, whose merchants are princes, whose traffickers are the honorable of the earth?"—*Isaiah*, chap. 23.

Note 10, page 78, line 6.

Their guardian spells have long been past.

" Un mélange bizarre de grandeur d'ame, et de foiblesse entroit dès cette époque, (l'onzième siècle,) dans le caractère des Romains. Un mouvement généreux vers les grandes choses faisoit place tout-à-coup à l'abattement ; ils passoient de la liberté la plus orageuse, à la servitude la plus avilissante. On auroit dit que les ruines et les portiques déserts de la capitale du monde, entretenoient ses habitans dans le sentiment de leur impuissance ; au milieu de ces monumens de leur domination passée, les citoyens éprouvoient d'une manière trop décourageante leur propre nullité. Le nom des Romains qu'ils portoient ranimoit fréquemment leur enthousiasme, comme il le ranime encore aujourd'hui ; mas bientôt la vue de Rome, du forum désert, des sept collines de nouveau rendues au pâturage des troupeaux, des temples désolés, des monumens tombant en ruine, les ramenoit à sentir qu'ils n'etoient plus les Romains d'autrefois."—Sismondi, *Histoire des Républiques Italiennes*, vol. i., p. 172.

Note 11, page 79, line 40.

Linger'd the lord of eloquence.

" As for Cicero, he was carried to Astyra, where, finding a vessel, he immediately went on board, and coasted along to Circæum with a favorable wind. The pilots were preparing immediately to sail from thence, but whether it was that he feared the sea, or had not yet given up all his hopes in Cæsar, he disembarked, and travelled a hundred furlongs on foot, as if Rome had been the place of his destination. Repenting, however, afterwards, he left that road, and made again for the sea. He passed the night in the most perplexing and horrid thoughts; insomuch, that he was sometimes inclined to go privately into Cæsar's house, and stab himself upon the altar of his domestic gods, to bring the divine vengeance upon his betrayer. But he was deterred from this by the fear of torture. Other alternatives, equally distressful, presented themselves. At last, he put himself in the hands of his servants, and ordered them to carry him by sea to Cajeta, where he had a delightful retreat in the summer, when the Etesian winds set in. There was a temple of Apollo on that coast, from which a flight of crows came with great noise towards Cicero's vessel as it was making land. They perched on both sides the sail-yard, where some sat croaking, and others pecking the ends of the ropes. All looked upon this as an ill omen ; yet Cicero went on shore, and, entering his house, lay down to repose himself. In the meantime a number of the crows settled in the chamber window, and croaked in the most doleful manner. One of them even entered it, and, alighting on the bed, attempted, with its beak, to draw off the clothes with which he had covered his face. On sight of this, the servants began to reproach themselves. 'Shall we,' said they, 'remain to be spectators of our master's murder ; Shall we not protect him, so innocent and so great a sufferer as he is, when the brute creatures give him marks of their care and attention?' Then, partly by entreaty, partly by force, they got him into his litter, and carried him towards the sea."—PLUTARCH, *Life of Cicero*.

Note 12, page 80, line 4.
Balm for all sadness but despair.

" Now purer air
Meets his approach, and to the heart inspires,
Vernal delight and joy, able to drive
All sadness but despair."—MILTON.

Note 13, page 80, line 32.
O'er bending oaks the north wind swells.

Mount Gargano. "This ridge of mountains forms a very large promontory advancing into the Adriatic, and separated from the Apennines on the west by the plains of Lucera and San Severo. We took a ride into the heart of the mountains through shady dells and noble woods, which brought to our minds the venerable groves that in ancient times bent with the loud winds sweeping along the rugged sides of Garganus.

' Aquilonibus
Querceta Gargani laborant
Et foliis viduantur orni.'—HORACE.

" There is still a respectable forest of evergreen and common oak, pine, hornbeam, chesnut, and manna-ash. The sheltered valleys are industriously cultivated, and seem to be blest with luxuriant vegetation."—SWINBURNE's *Travels*.

Note 14, page 80, line 40.
There " bright appearances" have smiled.

In yonder nether world where shall I seek
His bright appearances, or footstep trace?"—MILTON

THE LAST BANQUET

OF

ANTONY AND CLEOPATRA

["Antony, concluding that he could not die more honorably than in battle, determined to attack Cæsar at the same time both by sea and land. The night preceding the execution of this design, he ordered his servants at supper to render him their best services that evening, and fill the wine round plentifully, for the day following they might belong to another master, whilst he lay extended on the ground, no longer of consequence either to them or to himself. His friends were affected, and wept to hear him talk thus; which, when, he perceived, he encouraged them by assurances that his expectations of a glorious victory were at least equal to those of an honorable death. At the dead of night, when universal silence reigned through the city, a silence that was deepened by the awful thought of the ensuing day, on a sudden was heard the sound of musical instruments, and a noise which resembled the exclamations of Bacchanals. This tumultuous procession seemed to pass through the whole city, and to go out at the gate which led to the enemy's camp. Those who reflected on this prodigy concluded that Bacchus, the god whom Antony affected to imitate, had then forsaken him."—LANGHORNE's *Plutarch.*]

THY foes had girt thee with their dread array,
   O stately Alexandria!—yet the sound
Of mirth and music, at the close of day,
   Swell'd from thy splendid fabrics, far around
O'er camp and wave. Within the royal hall,
   In gay magnificence the feast was spread;
And, brightly streaming from the pictured wall,
   A thousand lamps their trembling lustre shed
O'er many a column, rich with precious dyes,
That tinge the marble's vein, 'neath Afric's burning skies.

And soft and clear that wavering radiance play'd
   O'er sculptured forms, that round the pillar'd scene
Calm and majestic rose, by art array'd
   In godlike beauty, awfully serene.
Oh! how unlike the troubled guests, reclined
   Round that luxurious board!—in every face
Some shadow from the tempest of the mind,
   Rising by fits, the searching eye might trace,
Though vainly mask'd in smiles which are not mirth,
But the proud spirit's veil thrown o'er the woes of earth.

Their brows are bound with wreaths, whose transcient
   May still survive the wearers—and the rose

Perchance may scarce be wither'd, when the tomb
　　Receives the mighty to its dark repose!
The day must dawn on battle, and may set
　　In death—but fill the mantling wine-cup high!
Despair is fearless, and the Fates e'en yet
　　Lend her one hour for parting revelry.
They who the empire of the world possess'd,
Would taste its joys again, ere all exchanged for rest.

Its joys! oh, mark yon proud triumvir's mien,
　　And read their annals on that brow of care!
'Midst pleasure's lotus-bowers his steps have been;
　　Earth's brightest pathway led him to despair.
Trust not the glance that fain would yet inspire
　　The buoyant energies of days gone by;
There is delusion in its meteor-fire,
　　And all within is shame, is agony!
Away! the tear in bitterness may flow,
But there are smiles which bear a stamp of deeper woe.

Thy cheek is sunk, and faded as thy fame.
　　O lost, devoted Roman! yet thy brow
To that ascendant and undying name,
　　Pleads with stern loftiness thy right e'en now.
Thy glory is departed, but hath left
　　A lingering light around thee—in decay
Not less than kingly, though of all bereft,
　　Thou seem'st as empire had not pass'd away.
Supreme in ruin! teaching hearts elate,
A deep, prophetic dread of still mysterious fate!

But thou, enchantress-queen! whose love hath made
　　His desolation—thou art by his side,
In all thy sovereignty of charms array'd,
　　To meet the storm with still unconquer'd pride.
Imperial being! e'n though many a stain
　　Of error be upon thee, there is power
In thy commanding nature, which shall reign
　　O'er the stern genius of misfortune's hour;
And the dark beauty of thy troubled eye
E'en now is all illumed with wild sublimity.

Thine aspect, all impassion'd, wears a light
　　Inspiring and inspired—thy cheek a dye,
Which rises not from joy, but yet is bright
　　With the deep glow of feverish energy.
Proud siren of the Nile! thy glance is fraught
　　With an immortal fire—in every beam
It darts, there kindles some heroic thought,
　　But wild and awful as a sybil's dream;
For thou with death hast commun'd, to attain
Dread knowledge of the pangs that ransom from the chain.

ANTONY AND CLEOPATRA.

And the stern courage by such musings lent,
　Daughter of Afric! o'er thy beauty throws
The grandeur of a regal spirit, blent
　With all the majesty of mighty woes;
While he, so fondly, fatally adored,
　Thy fallen Roman, gazes on thee yet,
Till scarce the soul, that once exulting soar'd,
　Can deem the day-star of its glory set;
Scarce his charm'd heart believes that power can be
In sovereign fate, o'er him, thus fondly loved by thee.

But there is sadness in the eyes around,
　Which mark that ruin'd leader, and survey
His changeful mein, whence oft the gloom profound
　Strange triumph chases haughtily away.
" Quaff, ere we part, the generous nectar deep!
Ere sunset gild once more the western skies,
　Your chief, in cold forgetfulness, may sleep,
While sounds of revel float o'er shore and sea,
And the red bowl again is crown'd—but not for me.

" Yet weep not thus—the struggle is not o'er,
　O victors of Philippi! many a field
Hath yielded palms to us:—one effort more,
　By one stern conflict must our doom be seal'd!
Forget not, Romans! o'er a subject world
　How royally your eagle's wing hath spread,
Though, from his eyrie of dominion hurl'd,
　Now bursts the tempests on his crested head!
Yet sovereign still, if banish'd from the sky,
The sun's indignant bird, he must not droop—but die."

The feast is o'er. 'Tis night, the dead of night—
　Unbroken stillness broods o'er earth and deep;
From Egypt's heaven of soft and starry light
　The moon looks cloudless o'er a world of sleep:
For those who wait the morn's awakening beams.
　The battle signal to decide their doom,
Have sunk to feverish rest and troubled dreams;
　Rest, that shall soon be calmer in the tomb,
Dreams, dark and ominous, but *there* to cease,
When sleep the lords of war in solitude and peace.

Wake, slumberers, wake! Hark! heard ye not a sound
　Of gathering tumult?—Near and nearer still
Its murmur swells. Above, below, around,
　Bursts a strange chorus forth, confused and shrill.
Wake, Alexandria! through thy streets the tread
　Of steps unseen is hurrying, and the note
Of pipe, and lyre, and trumpet, wild and dread,
　Is heard upon the midnight air to float;

7*

And voices, clamorous as in frenzied mirth,
Mingle their thousand tones, which are not of the earth.

These are no mortal sounds—their thrilling strain
  Hath more mysterious power, and birth more high;
And the deep horror chilling every vein
  Owns them of stern, terrific augury.
Beings of worlds unknown! ye pass away,
  O ye invisible and awful throng!
Your echoing footsteps and resounding lay
  To Cæsar's camp exulting move along.
Thy gods forsake thee, Antony! the sky
By that dread sign reveals thy doom—" Despair and die!"²

NOTES.

Note 1, page 92, line 48.
Dread knowledge of the pangs that ransom from the chain.

Cleopatra made a collection of poisonous drugs, and being desirous to know which was least painful in the operation, she tried them on the capital convicts. Such poisons as were quick in their operation, she found to be attended with violent pain and convulsions; such as were milder were slow in their effect: she therefore applied herself to the examination of venomous creatures; and at length she found that the bite of the asp was the most eligible kind of death, for it brought on a gradual kind of lethargy.—See PLUTARCH.

Note 2, page 94, line 12.
Despair and die!

"To-morrow in the battle think on me,
And fall thy edgeless sword; despair and die!"
Richard III.

ALARIC IN ITALY.

After describing the conquest of Greece and Italy by the German and Scythian hordes united under the command of Alaric, the his-historian of *The Decline and Fall of the Roman Empire* thus proceeds:—" Whether fame, or conquest, or riches were the object of Alaric, he pursued that object with an indefatigable ardor which could neither be quelled by adversity nor satiated by success. No sooner had he reached the extreme land of Italy, than he was attracted by the neighboring prospect of a fair and peaceful island. Yet even the possession of Sicily he considered only as an intermediate step to the important expedition which he already meditated against the continent of Africa. The straits of Rhegium and Messina are twelve miles in length, and in the narrowest passage about one mile and a half broad; and the fabulous monsters of the deep, the rocks of Scylla and the whirlpool of Charybdis, could terrify none but the most timid and unskilful mariners: yet, as soon as the first division of the Goths had embarked, a sudden tempest arose, which sunk or scattered many of the transports. Their courage was daunted by the terrors of a new element; and the whole design was defeated by the premature death of Alaric, which fixed, after a short illness, the fatal term of his conquests. The ferocious character of the barbarians was displayed in the funeral of a hero, whose valor and fortune they celebrated with mournful applause. By the labor of a captive multitude, they forcibly diverted the course of the Busentinus, a small river that washes the walls of Consentia. The royal sepulchre, adorned with the splendid spoils and trophies of Rome, was constructed in the vacant bed; the waters were then restored to their natural channel, and the secret spot where the remains of Alaric had been deposited, was for ever concealed by the inhuman massacre of the prisoners who had been employed to execute the work."—See *The Decline and Fall of the Roman Empire*, vol. v. p. 329.]

HEARD ye the Gothic trumpet's blast?
The march of hosts, as Alaric pass'd?
His steps have track'd that glorious clime,
The birth-place of heroic time;
But he, in northern deserts bred,
Spared not the living for the dead,[1]
Nor heard the voice, whose pleading cries
From temple and from tomb arise.
He pass'd—the light of burning fanes
Hath been his torch o'er Grecian plains;
And woke they not—the brave, the free,
To guard their own Thermopylæ?
And left they not their silent dwelling,
When Sythia's note of war was swelling?

ALARIC IN ITALY.

No! where the bold Three Hundred slept,
Sad freedom battled not—but wept!
For nerveless then the Spartan's hand,
And Thebes could rouse no Sacred band;
Nor one high soul from slumber broke,
When Athens own'd the northern yoke.

But was there none for *thee* to dare
The conflict, scorning to despair?
O city of the seven proud hills!
Whose name e'en yet the spirit thrills,
As doth a clarion's battle-call—
Didst thou too, ancient empress, fall?
Did no Camillus from the chain
Ransom thy Capitol again?
Oh! who shall tell the days to be,
No patriot rose to bleed for thee?

Heard ye the Gothic trumpet's blast?
The march of hosts, as Alaric pass'd?
That fearful sound, at midnight deep,[2]
Burst on the eternal city's sleep:
How woke the mighty? She, whose will
So long had bid the world be still,
Her sword a sceptre, and her eye
Th' ascendant star of destiny!
She woke—to view the dread array
Of Scythians rushing to their prey,
To hear her streets resound the cries
Pour'd from a thousand agonies!
While the strange light of flames, that gave
A ruddy glow to Tiber's wave,
Bursting in that terrific hour
From fane and palace, dome and tower,
Reveal'd the throngs, for aid divine
Clinging to many a worshipp'd shrine
Fierce fitful radiance wildly shed
O'er spear and sword, with carnage red,
Shone o'er the suppliant and the flying,
And kindled pyres for Romans dying.

Weep, Italy! alas! that e'er
Should tears alone thy wrongs declare!
The time hath been when *thy* distress
Had roused up empires for redress!
Now, her long race of glory run,
Without a combat Rome is won,
And from her plunder'd temples forth
Rush the fierce children of the north,
To share beneath more genial skies
Each joy their own rude clime denies.

ALARIC IN ITALY.

Ye who on bright Campania's shore
Bade your fair villas rise of yore,
With all their graceful colonnades,
And crystal baths, and myrtle shades,
Along the blue Hesperian deep,
Whose glassy waves in sunshine sleep;
Beneath your olive and your vine
Far other inmates now recline,
And the tall plane, whose roots ye fed
With rich libations duly shed,[3]
O'er guests, unlike your vanish'd friends,
Its bowery canopy extends.
For them the southern heaven is glowing,
The bright Falernian nectar flowing;
For them the marble halls unfold,
Where nobler beings dwelt of old,
Whose children for barbarian lords
Touch the sweet lyre's resounding chords,
Or wreaths of Pæstan roses twine,
To crown the sons of Elbe and Rhine.
Yet, though luxurious they repose
Beneath Corinthian porticoes,
While round them into being start
The marvels of triumphant art;
Oh! not for them hath genius given
To parian stone the fire of heaven,
Enshrining in the forms he wrought
A bright eternity of thought.
In vain the natives of the skies
In breathing marble round them rise,
And sculptured nymphs of fount or glade
People the dark-green laurel shade;
Cold are the conqueror's heart and eye
To visions of divinity;
And rude his hand which dares deface
The models of immortal grace.

Arouse ye from your soft delights!
Chieftains! the war-note's call invites;
And other lands must yet be won,
And other deeds of havoc done.
Warriors! your flowery bondage break,
Sons of the stormy north, awake!
The barks are launching from the steep,
Soon shall the Isle of Ceres weep,[4]
And Afric's burning winds afar
Waft the shrill sounds of Alaric's war.
Where shall his race of victory close?
When shall the ravaged earth repose?
But hark! What wildly mingling cries
From Scythia's camp tumultuous rise?

ALARIC IN ITALY.

Why swells dread Alaric's name on air?
A sterner conqueror hath been there!
A conqueror—yet his paths are peace,
He comes to brings the world's release;
He of the sword that knows no sheath,
Th' avenger, the deliverer—Death!

Is then that daring spirit fled?
Doth Alaric slumber with the dead?
Tamed are the warrior's pride and strength,
And he and earth are calm at length.
The land where heaven unclouded shines,
Where sleep the sunbeams on the vines;
The land by conquest made his own,
Can yield him now—a grave alone.
But his—her lord from Alp to sea—
No common sepulchre shall be!
Oh, make his tomb where mortal eye
Its buried wealth may ne'er descry!
Where mortal foot may never tread
Above a victor-monarch's bed.
Let not his royal dust be hid
'Neath star-aspiring pyramid;
Nor bid the gather'd mound arise,
To bear his memory to the skies.
Years roll away—oblivion claims
Her triumph o'er heroic names;
And hands profane disturb the clay
That once was fired with glory's ray;
And Avarice, from their secret gloom,
Drags e'en the treasures of the tomb.
But thou, O leader of the free!
That general doom awaits not thee:
Thou, where no step may e'er intrude,
Shalt rest in regal solitude,
Till, bursting on thy sleep profound,
The' Awakener's final trumpet sound.
Turn ye the waters from their course,
Bid Nature yield to human force,
And hollow in the torrent's bed
A chamber of the mighty dead.
The work is done—the captive's hand
Hath well obey'd his lord's command.
Within that royal tomb are cast
The richest trophies of the past,
The wealth of many a stately dome,
The gold and gems of plunder'd Rome;
And when the midnight stars are beaming,
And ocean waves in stillness gleaming,
Stern in their grief, his warriors bear
The Chastener of the Nations there;

To rest at length, from victory's toil,
Alone, with all an empire's spoil!

Then the freed current's rushing wave
Rolls o'er the secret of the grave;
Then streams the martyr'd captives' blood
To crimson that sepulchral flood,
Whose conscious tide alone shall keep
The mystery in its bosom deep.
Time hath past on since then—and swept
From earth the urns where heroes slept;
Temples of gods, and domes of kings,
Are mouldering with forgotten things;
Yet shall not ages e'er molest
The viewless home of Alaric's rest:
Still rolls, like them, th' unfailing river,
The guardian of his dust for ever.

NOTES.

Note 1, page 96, line 6.
Spared not the living for the dead.

After the taking of Athens by Sylla, " though such numbers were put to the sword, there were as many who laid violent hands upon themselves in grief for their sinking country. What reduced the best men among them to this despair of finding any mercy or moderate terms for Athens, was the well-known cruelty of Sylla; yet partly by the intercession of Midias and Caliphon, and the exiles, who threw themselves at his feet, partly by the entreaties of the senators who attended him in that expedition, and being himself satiated with blood besides, he was at last prevailed upon to stop his hand, and, in compliment to the ancient Athenians, he said, ' he forgave the many for the sake of the few, the *living for the dead*.' "— PLUTARCH.

Note 2, page 97, line 19.
That fearful sound at midnight deep.

" At the hour of midnight, the Salarian gate was silently opened and the inhabitants were awakened by the tremendous sound of the Gothic trumpet. Eleven hundred and sixty-three years after the foundation of Rome, the imperial city, which had subdued and civilized so considerable a portion of mankind, was delivered to the licentious fury of the tribes of Germany and Scythia."—*Decline and Fall of the Roman Empire*, vol. v., p. 311.

Note 3. page 98, line 10.
With rich libations duly shed.

The plane-tree was much cultivated among the Romans, on account of its extraordinary shade; and they used to nourish it with wine instead of water, believing (as Sir W. Temple observes) that " this tree loved that liquor as well as those who used to drink under its shade."—*See the notes to* MELMOTH's *Pliny.*

Note 4, page 98 line 44.
Soon shall the Isle of Ceres weep

Sicily was anciently considered as the favored and peculiar dominion of Ceres.

THE WIFE OF ASDRUBAL.

"This governor, who had braved death when it was at a distance, and protested that the sun should never see him survive Carthage—this fierce Asdrubal was so mean-spirited as to come alone, and privately throw himself at the conqueror's feet. The general, pleased to see his proud rival humbled, granted his life, and kept him to grace his triumph. The Carthaginians in the citadel no sooner understood that their commander had abandoned the place, than they threw open the gates, and put the proconsul in possession of Byrsa. The Romans had now no enemy to contend with but the nine hundred deserters, who, being reduced to despair, retired into the temple of Esculapius, which was a second citadel within the first. There the proconsul attacked them; and these unhappy wretches, finding there was no way to escape, set fire to the temple. As the flames spread, they retreated from one part to another, till they got to the roof of the building. There Asdrubal's wife appeared in her best apparel, as if the day of her death had been a day of triumph; and after having uttered the most bitter imprecations against her husband, whom she saw standing below with Emilianus—'Base coward!' said she, 'the mean things thou hast done to save thy life shall not avail thee; thou shalt die this instant, at least in thy two children.' Having thus spoken, she drew out a dagger, stabbed them both, and while they were yet struggling for life, threw them from the top of the temple, and leaped down after them into the flames'"—*Ancient Universal History.*]

    THE sun sets brightly—but a ruddier glow
O'er Afric's heaven the flames of Carthage throw;
Her walls have sunk, and pyramids of fire
In lurid splendor from her domes aspire;
Sway'd by the wind, they wave—while glares the sky
As when the desert's red simoom is nigh;
The sculptured altar, and the pillar'd hall,
Shine out in dreadful brightness ere they fall;
Far o'er the seas the light of ruin streams,
Rock, wave, and isles are crimson'd by its beams;
While captive thousands, bound in Roman chains,
Gaze in mute horror on their burning fanes;
And shouts of triumph, echoing far around,
Swell from the victor's tents with ivy crown'd.*
But mark, from yon fair temple's loftiest height,
What towering form bursts wildly on the sight,
All regal in magnificent attire,
And sternly beauteous in terrific ire?

---

* It was a Roman custom to adorn the tents of victors with **ivy**

She might be deem'd a Pythia in the hour
Of dread communion and delirious power;
A being more than earthly, in whose eye
There dwells a strange and fierce ascendancy.
The flames are gathering round—intensely bright,
Full on her features glares their meteor light;
But a wild courage sits triumphant there,
The stormy grandeur of a proud despair;
A daring spirit, in its woes elate,
Mightier than death, untameable by fate.
The dark profusion of her locks unbound,
Waves like a warrior's plumage round;
Flush'd is her cheek, inspired her haughty mien,
She seems th' avenging goddess of the scene.
Are those *her* infants, that with suppliant cry,
Cling round her, shrinking as the flame draws nigh,
Clasp with their feeble hands her gorgeous vest,
And fain would rush for shelter to her breast?
Is that a mother's glance, where stern disdain
And passion, awfully vindictive, reign?

Fix'd is her eye on Asdrubal, who stands
Ignobly safe amidst the conquering bands;
On him who left her to that burning tomb,
Alone to share her children's martyrdom;
Who, when his country perish'd, fled the strife,
And knelt to win the worthless boon of life.
" Live, traitor, live!" she cries, " since dear to thee
E'en in thy fetters, can existence be!
Scorn'd and dishonor'd live!—with blasted name,
The Roman's triumph not to grace, but shame.
O slave in spirit! bitter be thy chain,
With tenfold anguish to avenge my pain!
Still may the manes of thy children rise
To chase calm slumber from thy wearied eyes;
Still may their voices on the haunted air
In fearful whispers tell thee to despair,
Till vain remorse thy wither'd heart consume,
Scourged by relentless shadows of the tomb!
E'en now my sons shall die—and thou, their sire,
In bondage safe, shalt yet in them expire.
Think'st thou I love them not?—'Twas thine to fly—
'Tis mine with these to suffer and to die.
Behold their fate!—the arms that cannot save
Have been their cradle, and shall be their grave."

Bright in her hand the lifted dagger gleams,
Swift from her children's hearts the life blood streams;
With frantic laugh she clasps them to the breast,
Whose woes and passions soon shall be at rest;
Lifts one appealing, frenzied glance on high,
Then deep 'midst rolling flames is lost to mortal eye.

HELIODORUS IN THE TEMPLE.

[From *Maccabees*, book ii. chapter 3, v. 21. "Then it would have pitied a man to see the falling down of the multitude of all sorts, and the fear of the high priest, being in such an agony.—22. They then called upon the Almighty Lord to keep the things committed of trust safe and sure, for those that had committed them.—23. Nevertheless Heliodorus executed that which was decreed.—24. Now as he was there present himself, with his guard about the treasury, the Lord of Spirits, and the Prince of all Power, caused a great apparition, so that all that presumed to come in with him were astonished at the power of God, and fainted, and were sore afraid.—25. For there appeared unto them a horse with a terrible rider upon him, and adorned with a very fair covering, and he ran fiercely, and smote at Heliodorus with his fore-feet, and it seemed that he that sat upon the horse had complete harness of gold.—26. Moreover, two other young men appeared before him, notable in strength, excellent in beauty, and comely in apparel, who stood by him on either side, and scourged him continually, and gave him many sore stripes.—27. And Heliodorus fell suddenly to the ground, and was compassed with great darkness; but they that were with him took him up, and put him into a litter.—28. Thus him that lately came with great train, and with all his guard into the said treasury, they carried out, being unable to help himself with his weapons, and manifestly they acknowledged the power of God. —29. For he by the hand of God was cast down, and lay speechless, without all hope of life."]

A SOUND of woe in Salem!—mournful cries
   Rose from her dwellings—youthful cheeks were pale,
Tears flowing fast from dim and aged eyes,
   And voices mingling in tumultuous wail;
Hands raised to heaven in agony of prayer,
And powerless wrath, and terror, and despair.

Thy daughters, Judah! weeping, laid aside
   The regal splendor of their fair array,
With the rude sackcloth girt their beauty's pride,
   And throng'd the streets in hurrying, wild dismay;
While knelt thy priests before *His* awful shrine,
Who made, of old, renown and empire thine.

But on the spoiler moves—the temple's gate,
   The bright, the beautiful, his guards unfold;
And all the scene reveals its solemn state,
   Its courts and pillars, rich with sculptured gold;
And man, with eye unhallow'd, views th' abode,
The sever'd spot, the dwelling-place of God.

HELIODORUS IN THE TEMPLE.

Where art thou, Mighty Presence! that of yore
    Wert wont between the cherubim to rest,
Veil'd in a cloud of glory, shadowing o'er
    Thy sanctuary the chosen and the blest?
Thou! that didst make fair Sion's ark thy throne,
And call the oracle's recess thine own!

Angel of God! that through the Assyrian host,
    Clothed with the darkness of the midnight-hour,
To tame the proud, to hush th' invader's boast,
    Didst pass triumphant in avenging power,
Till burst the day-spring on the silent scene,
And death alone reveal'd where thou hadst been.

Wilt thou not wake, O Chastener! in thy might,
    To guard thine ancient and majestic hill,
Where oft from heaven, the full Shechinah's light
    Hath stream'd the house of holiness to fill?
Oh! yet once more defend thy lov'd domain,
Eternal one! Deliverer! rise again!

Fearless of thee, the plunderer, undismay'd,
    Hastes on, the sacred chambers to explore
Where the bright treasures of the fane are laid,
    The orphan's portion, and the widow's store;
What recks *his* heart though age unsuccor'd die,
And want consume the cheek of infancy?

Away, intruders!—hark! a mighty sound!
    Behold, a burst of light!—away, away!
A fearful glory fills the temple round,
    A vision bright in terrible array!
And lo! a steed of no terrestrial frame,
His path a whirlwind, and his breath a flame!

His neck is clothed with thunder*—and his mane
    Seems waving fire—the kindling of his eye
Is as a meteor—ardent with disdain
    His glance—his gesture, fierce in majesty!
Instinct with light he seems, and formed to bear
Some dread archangel through the fields of air.

But who is he, in panoply of gold,
    Throned on that burning charger? bright his form.
Yet in its brightness awful to behold,
    And girt with all the terrors of the storm!
Lightning is on his helmet's crest—and fear
Shrinks from the splendor of his brow severe.

---

* "Hast thou given the horse strength? Hast thou clothed his neck with thunder?"—*Job*, chap. xxxix. v. 19.

And by his side two radiant warriors stand
   All-arm'd, and kingly in commanding grace—
Oh! more than kingly—godlike!—sternly grand
   Their port indignant, and each dazzling face
Beams with the beauty to immortals given
Magnificent in all the wrath of heaven.

Then sinks each gazer's heart—each knee is bow'd
   In trembling awe—but, as to fields of fight,
Th' unearthly war-steed rushing through the crowd,
   Bursts on their leader in terrific might;
And the stern angels of that dread abode
Pursue its plunderer with the scourge of God.

Darkness—thick darkness!—low on earth he lies,
   Rash Heliodorus—motionless and pale—
Bloodless his cheek, and o'er his shrouded eyes
   Mists, as of death, suspend their shadowy veil;
And thus th' oppressor, by his fear-struck train,
Is borne from that inviolable fane.

The light returns—the warriors of the sky
   Have pass'd, with all their dreadful pomp, away;
Then wakes the timbrel, swells the song on high
   Triumphant as in Judah's elder day;
Rejoice, O city of the sacred hill!
Salem, exult! thy God is with thee still.

NIGHT-SCENE IN GENOA.

FROM SISMONDI'S "REPUBLIQUES ITALIENNES."

" En même temps que les Génois poursuivoient avec ardeur la guerre contre Pise, ils étoient déchirés eux-mêmes par une discorde civile. Les consuls de l'anné 1169, pour rétablir la paix dans leur patrie, au milieu des factions sourdes à leur voix et plus puissantes qu'eux, furent obligés d'ourdir en quelque sorte une conspiration. Ils commencèrent par s'assurer secrètement des dispositions pacifiques de plusieurs des citoyens, qui cependant étoient entraînés dans les émeutes par leur parenté avec les chefs de faction; puis, se concertant avec le vénérable vieillard, Hugues, leur archevêque, ils firent, long-temps avant le lever du soleil, appeler au son des cloches les citoyens au parlement; ils se flattoient que la surprise et l'alarme de cette convocation inattendue, au milieu de l'obscurité de la nuit, rendroit l'assemblée et plus complète et plus docile. Les citoyens, en accourant au parlement général, virent au milieu de la place publique, le vieil archevêque, entouré de son clergé en habit de cérémonies, et portant des torches allumées, tandis que les reliques de Saint Jean Baptiste, le protecteur de Gênes, étoient exposées devant lui, et que les citoyens les plus respectables portoient à leurs mains des croix suppliantes. Dès que l'assemblée fut formée, le vieillard se leva, et de sa voix cassée il conjura les chefs de parti, au nom du Dieu de paix, au nom du salut de leurs âmes au nom de leur patrie et de la liberté, dont leurs discordes entraîneroient la ruine, de jurer sur l'évangile l'oubli de leurs querelles, et la paix à venir.

Les hérauts, dès qu'il eut fini de parler, s'avancèrent aussitôt vers Roland Avogado, le chef de l'une des factions, qui étoit présent à l'assemblée, et, secondés par les acclamations de tout le peuple, et par les prières de ses parens eux-mêmes, ils le sommèrent de se conformer au vœu des consuls et de la nation.

Roland, à leur approche, déchira ses habits, et, s'asseyant par terre en versant des larmes, il appela à haute voix les morts qu'il avoit juré de venger, et qui ne lui permettoient pas de pardonner leurs vieilles offenses. Comme on ne pouvoit le déterminer à s'avancer, les consuls eux-mêmes, l'archevêque et le clergé, s'approchèrent de lui, et, renouvelant leurs prières, ils l'entraînèrent enfin, et lui firent jurer sur l'évangile l'oubli de ses inimitiés passées.

Les chefs du parti contraire, Foulques de Castro, et Ingo de Volta, n'étoient pas présens à l'assemblée, mais le peuple et le clergé se portèrent en foule à leurs maisons; ils les trouvèrent déjà ébranlés par ce qu'ils venoient d'apprendre, et, profitant de leur émotion, ils leur firent jurer une réconciliation sincère, et donner le baiser de paix aux chefs de la faction opposée. Alors les cloches de la ville sonnèrent en témoignage d'allégresse, et l'archevêque de retour sur la place publique entonna un Te Deum avec tout le peu

ple, en honneur du Dieu de paix qui avoit sauvé leur patrie."—
Histoire des Republiques Italiennes, vol. ii. pp. 149–50.]

In Genoa, when the sunset gave
Its last warm purple to the wave,
No sound of war, no voice of fear,
Was heard, announcing danger near:
Though deadliest foes were there, whose hate
But slumber'd till its hour of fate,
Yet calmly, at the twilight's close,
Sunk the wide city to repose.

But when deep midnight reign'd around,
All sudden woke the alarm-bell's sound,
Full swelling, while the hollow breeze
Bore its dread summons o'er the seas.
Then, Genoa, from their slumber started
Thy sons, the free, the fearless-hearted;
Then mingled with th' awakening peal
Voices, and steps, and clash of steal.
Arm, warriors, arm! for danger calls,
Arise to guard your native walls!
With breathless haste the gathering throng
Hurry the echoing streets along;
Through darkness rushing to the scene
Where their bold counsels still convene.
—But there a blaze of torches bright
Pours its red radiance on the night.
O'er fane, and dome, and column playing,
With every fitful night-wind swaying:
Now floating o'er each tall arcade,
Around the pillar'd scene display'd,
In light relieved by depth of shade:
And now, with ruddy meteor-glare,
Full streaming on the silvery hair
And the bright cross of him who stands
Rearing that sign with suppliant hands,
Girt with his consecrated train,
The hallow'd servants of the fane.
Of life's past woes, the fading trace
Hath given that aged patriarch's face
Expression holy, deep, resign'd,
The calm sublimity of mind.
Years o'er his snowy head have pass'd,
And left him of his race the last;
Alone on earth—yet still his mein
Is bright with majesty serene;
And those high hopes, whose guiding star
Shines from the eternal worlds afar,
Have with that light illumed his eye,
Whose fount is immortality,

And o'er his features pour'd a ray
Of glory, not to pass away.
He seems a being who hath known
Communion with his God alone,
On earth by nought but pity's tie
Detain'd a moment from on high!
One.to sublimer worlds allied,
One, from all passion purified,
E'en now, half mingled with the sky,
And all prepared—oh! not to die—
But, like the prophet, to aspire,
In heaven's triumphal car of fire.
He speaks—and from the throngs around
Is heard not e'en a whisper'd sound;
Awe-struck each heart, and fix'd each glance,
They stand as in a spell-bound trance:
He speaks—oh! who can hear nor own
The might of each prevailing tone?

"Chieftains and warriors! ye, so long
Aroused to strife by mutual wrong,
Whose fierce and far-transmitted hate
Hath made your country desolate;
Now by the love ye bear her name,
By that pure spark of holy flame
On freedom's altar brightly burning,
But, once extinguish'd, ne'er returning;
By all your hopes of bliss to come
When burst the bondage of the tomb:
By Him, the God who bade us live
To aid each other, and forgive—
I call upon ye to resign
Your discords at your country's shrine,
Each ancient feud in peace atone,
Wield your keen swords for her alone,
And swear upon the cross, to cast
Oblivion's mantle o'er the past!"

No voice replies—the holy bands
Advance to where yon chieftain stands
With folded arms, and brow of gloom
O'ershadow'd by his floating plume.
To him they lift the cross—in vain
He turns—oh! say not with disdain,
But with a mein of haughty grief,
That seeks not, e'en from heaven, relief:
He rends his robes he sternly speaks—
Yet tears are on the warrior's cheeks.

"Father! not thus the wounds may close
Inflicted by eternal foes.

Deem'st thou *thy* mandate can efface
The dread volcano's burning trace?
Or bid the earthquake's ravaged scene
Be, smiling, as it once hath been?
No! for the deeds the sword hath done
Forgiveness is not lightly won;
The words, by hatred spoke, may not
Be, as a summer breeze, forgot!
'Tis vain—we deem the war-feud's rage
A portion of our heritage.
Leaders, now slumbering with their fame,
Bequeath'd us that undying flame;
Hearts that have long been still and cold
Yet rule us from their silent mould;
And voices, heard on earth no more,
Speak to our spirits as of yore.
Talk not of mercy—blood alone
The stain of bloodshed may atone;
Nought else can pay that mighty debt,
The dead forbid us to forget."

He pauses—from the patriarch's brow
There beams more lofty grandeur now;
His reverend form, his aged hand,
Assume a gesture of command,
His voice is awful, and his eye
Fill'd with prophetic majesty.

" The dead!—and deem'st thou *they* retain
Aught of terrestrial passion's stain?
Of guilt incurr'd in days gone by,
Aught but the fearful penalty?
And say'st thou, mortal! blood alone
For deeds of slaughter may atone?
There *hath* been blood—by him 'twas shed
To expiate every crime who bled;
Th' absolving God who died to save,
And rose in victory from the grave!
And by that stainless offering given
Alike for all on earth to heaven;
By that inevitable hour
When death shall vanquish pride and power,
And each departing passion's force
Concentrate all in late remorse;
And by the day when doom shall be
Pass'd on earth's millions, and on thee—
The doom that shall not be repeal'd,
Once utter'd, and forever seal'd—
I summon thee, O child of clay!
To cast thy darker thoughts away,
And meet thy foes in peace and love,
As thou would'st join the blest above "

NIGHT-SCENE IN GENOA.

Still as he speaks, unwonted feeling
Is o'er the chieftain's bosom stealing;
Oh! not in vain the pleading cries
Of anxious thousands round him rise;
He yields—devotion's mingled sense
Of faith, and fear, and penitence,
Pervading all his soul, he bows
To offer on the cross his vows.
And that best incense to the skies,
Each evil passion's sacrifice.

Then tears from warriors eyes were flowing
High hearts with soft emotions glowing;
Stern foes as long-loved brothers greeting,
And ardent throngs in transport meeting;
And eager footsteps forward pressing,
And accents loud in joyous blessing;
And when their first wild tumults cease,
A thousand voices echo " Peace!"

Twilight's dim mist hath roll'd away,
And the rich Orient burns with day:
Then as to greet the sunbeam's birth,
Rises the choral hymn of earth;
Th' exulting strain through Genoa swelling,
Of peace and holy rapture telling.

Far float the sounds o'er vale and steep,
The seamen hears them on the deep,
So mellow'd by the gale, they seem
As the wild music of a dream
But not on mortal ear alone
Peals the triumphant anthem's tone;
For beings of a purer sphere
Bend with celestial joy, to hear.

THE TROUBADOUR,

AND

RICHARD CŒUR DE LION.

Not only the place of Richard's confinement," (when thrown into prison by the Duke of Austria,) "if we believe the literary history of the times, but even the circumstance of his captivity, was carefully concealed by his vindictive enemies: and both might have remained unknown but for the grateful attachment of a Provançal bard, or minstrel, named Blondel, who had shared that prince's friendship and tasted his bounty. Having travelled over all the European continent to learn the destiny of his beloved patron, Blondel accidentally got intelligence of a certain castle in Germany, where a prisoner of distinction was confined, and guarded with great vigilance. Persuaded by a secret impulse that this prisoner was the King of England, the minstrel repaired to the place; but the gates of the castle were shut against him, and he could obtain no information relative to the name or quality of the unhappy person it secured. In this extremity, he bethought himself of an expedient for making the desired discovery. He chanted, with a loud voice, some verses of a song which had been composed partly by himself, partly by Richard; and to his unspeakable joy, on making a pause, he heard it re-echoed and continued by the royal captive.—(*Hist. Troubadours.*) To this discovery the English monarch is said to have eventually owed his release."—See RUSSELL'S *Modern Europe*, vol. i. p. 369.

THE Troubadour o'er many a plain
Hath roam'd unwearied, but in vain:
O'er many a rugged mountain-scene,
And forest-wild, his track hath been;
Beneath Calabria's glowing sky
He hath sung the songs of chivalry;
His voice hath swell'd on the Alpine breeze,
And rung through the snowy Pyrenees;
From Ebro's banks to Danube's wave,
He hath sought his prince, the loved, the brave,
And yet, if still on earth thou art,
Oh, monarch of the lion-heart!
The faithful spirit, which distress
But heightens to devotedness,
By toil and trial vanquish'd not,
Shall guide thy minstrel to the spot.

He hath reach'd a mountain hung with vine,
And woods that wave o'er the lovely Rhine:
The feudal towers that crest its height
Frown in unconquerable might;
Dark is their aspect of sullen state—
No helmet hangs o'er the massy gate[1]
To bid the wearied pilgrim rest,
A the chieftain's board a welcome guest;
Vainly rich evening's parting smile
Would chase the gloom of the haughty pile,
That 'midst bright sunshine lowers on high,
Like a thunder-cloud in a summer sky.

Not these the halls where a child of song
Awhile may speed the hours along;
Their echoes should repeat alone
The tyrant's mandate, the prisoner's moan,
Or the wild huntsman's bugle blast,
When his phantom-train are hurrying past.[2]
The weary minstrel paused—his eye
Roved o'er the scene despondingly:
Within the length'ning shadow, cast
By the fortress-towers and ramparts vast,
Lingering he gazed—the rocks around
Sublime in savage grandeur frown'd;
Proud guardians of the regal flood,
In giant strength the mountains stood;
By torrents cleft, by tempests riven,
Yet mingling still with the calm blue heaven.
Their peaks were bright with a sunny glow,
But the Rhine all shadowy roll'd below;
In purple tints the vineyards smiled,
But the woods beyond waved dark and wild;
Nor pastoral pipe, nor convent's bell,
Was heard on the sighing breeze to swell;
But all was lonely, silent, rude,
A stern, yet glorious solitude.

But hark! that solemn stillness **breaking**,
The Troubadour's wild song is waking.
Full oft that song, in days gone by,
Hath cheer'd the sons of chivalry;
It hath swell'd o'er Judah's mountains lone,
Hermon! thy echoes have learn'd its tone;
On the Great Plain[3] its notes have rung,
The leagued Crusaders' tents among;
'Twas loved by the Lion-heart, who won
The palm in the field of Ascalon;
And now afar o'er the rocks of Rhine
Peals the bold strain of Palestine.

THE TROUBADOUR'S SONG.

"Thine hour is come, and the stake is set,"
 The Soldan cried to the captive knight,
"And the sons of the Prophet in throngs are met
 To gaze on the fearful sight.

"But be our faith by thy lips profess'd,
 The faith of Mecca's shrine,
Cast down the red-cross that marks thy vest,
 And life shall yet be thine."

"I have seen the flow of my bosom's blood,
 And gazed with undaunted eye;
I have borne the bright cross through fire and flood,
 And think'st thou I fear to die?

"I have stood where thousands, by Salem's towers,
 Have fall'n for the name divine;
And the faith that cheer'd *their* closing hours
 Shall be the light of mine."

"Thus wilt thou die in the pride of health,
 And the glow of youth's fresh bloom?
Thou art offer'd life, and pomp, and wealth,
 Or torture and the tomb."

"I have been where the crown of thorns was twined
 For a dying Saviour's brow;
He spurn'd the treasures that lure mankind,
 And I reject them now!"

"Art thou the son of a noble line
 In a land that is fair and blest?
And doth not thy spirit, proud captive! pine.
 Again on its shores to rest?

"Thine own is the choice to hail once more
 The soil of thy father's birth,
Or to sleep, when thy lingering pangs are o'er,
 Forgotten in foreign earth."

"Oh! fair are the vine-clad hills that rise
 In the country of my love;
But yet, though cloudless my native skies,
 There's a brighter clime above!"

The bard hath paused—for another tone
Blends with the music of his own ;
And his heart beats high with hope again,
As a well-known voice prolongs the strain.

" Are there none within thy father's hall,
  Far o'er the wide blue main,
Young Christian ! left to deplore thy fall,
  With sorrow deep and vain ?"

" There are hearts that still, through all the past,
  Unchanging have loved me well ;
There are eyes whose tears were streaming fast
  When I bade my home farewell.

" Better they wept o'er the warrior's bier
  Than th' apostate's living stain ;
There's a land where those who loved when here,
  Shall meet to love again."

    'Tis he ! thy prince—long sought, long lost,
The leader of the red-cross host !
'Tis he ! to none thy joy betray,
Young Troubadour ! away, away !
Away to the island of the brave,
The gem on the bosom of the wave ;[4]
Arouse the sons of the noble soil,
To win their Lion from the toil ;
And free the wassail-cup shall flow,
Bright in each hall the hearth shall glow ;
The festal board shall be richly crown'd,
While knights and chieftains revel round,
And a thousand harps with joy shall ring,
When merry England hails her king.

NOTES.

Note 1, page 113, line 6.
No helmet hangs o'er the massy gate.

It was a custom in feudal times to hang out a helmet on a castle as a token that strangers were invited to enter, and partake of hospitality. So in the romance of "Perceforest," "ils fasoient mettre au plus hault de leur hostel un *heaulme*, en signe que tous les gentils hommes et gentilles femmes entrassent hardiment en leur hostel comme en leur proper."

Note 2, page 113, lines 17 and 18.
Or the wild huntsman's bugle blast,
When his phantom-train are hurrying past.

Popular tradition has made several mountains in Germany the haunt of the *wild Jäger*, or supernatural huntsman—the superstitious tales relating to the Unterburg are recorded in Eustace's *Classical Tour*: and it is still believed in the romantic district of the Odenwald, that the knight of Rodenstein, issuing from his ruined castle, announces the approach of war by traversing the air with a noisy armament to the opposite castle of Schnellerts.—See the "*Manuel pour les Voyageurs sur le Rhin*," and "*Autumn on the Rhine*."

Note 3, page 113, line 43.
On the Great Plain its notes have rung.

The Plain of Esdraelon, called by way of eminence the "Great Plain;" in Scripture and elsewhere, the "field of Megiddo," the "Galilæan Plain." This plain, the most fertile part of all the land of Canaan, has been the scene of many a memorable contest in the first ages of Jewish history, as well as during the Roman empire, the Crusades, and even in later times. It has been a chosen place for encampment in every contest carried on in this country, from the days of Nebuchodonosor, king of the Assyrians, until the disastrous march of Bonaparte from Egypt into Syria. Warriors out of "every nation which is under heaven" have pitched their tents upon the Plain of Esdraelon, and have beheld the various banners of their nations wet with the dews of Hermon and Thabôr.—*Dr. Clarke's Travels*.

Note 4, page 115, line 22.
The gem on the bosom of the wave.

"This precious stone set in the silver sea."
Richard II.

THE DEATH OF CONRADIN.

FROM SISMONDI'S "REPUBLIQUES ITALIENNES."

'La défaite de Conradin ne devoit mettre une terme ni à ses malheurs, ni aux vengeances du roi (Charles d' Anjou). L'amour du peuple pour l'héritier légitime du trône, avoit éclaté d'une manière effrayante ; il pouvoit causer de nouvelles révolutions, si Conradin demeuroit en vie ; et Charles, revêtant sa défiance et sa cruaute des formes del a justice, resolut de faire périr sur l'échafaud le dernier rejeton de la Maison de Souabe, l'unique espérance de son parti. Un seul juge provençal et sujet de Charles, dont les historiens n'ont pas voulu conserver le nom, osa voter pour la mort, d'autres se renfermèrent dans un timide et coupable silence ; et Charles, sur l'autorité de ce seul juge, fit prononcer, par Robert de Bari, protonotaire du royaume, la sentence de mort contre Conradin et tous ses compagnons. Cette sentence fut communiquée à Conradin, comme il jouoit aux échecs ; on lui laissa peu de temps pour se preparer à son exécution, et le 26 d'Octobre, il fut conduit, avec tous ses amis, sur la Place du Marché de Naples, le long du rivage de la mer. Charles étoit présent, avec toute sa cour, et une foule immense entouroit le roi vainqueur et le roi condamné. Conradin étoit entre les mains des bourreaux ; il détacha lui-même son manteau, et s'étant mis à genoux pour prier, il se releva en s'écriant : 'Oh, ma mère, quelle profonde douleur te causera la nouvelle qu'on va te porter de moi !' Puis il tourna les yeux sur la foule qui l'entouroit ; il vit les larmes, il entendit les sanglots de son peuple ; alors, détachant son gant, il jeta au milieu de ses sujets ce gage d'un combat de vengeance, et rendit sa tête au bourreau. Après lui, sur le même echafaud, Charles fit trancher la tête au Duc d'Autriche, aux Comtes Gualferano et Bartolommeo, Lancia, et aux Comtes Gerard et Galvano Donoratico de Pise. Par un rafinement de cruauté, Charles voulut que le premier, fils du sécond, précédât son père, et mourût entre ses bras. Les cadavres, d'après ses ordres, furent exclus d'une terre sainte, et inhumés sans pompe sur le rivage de la mer. Charles II., cependant fit dans la suite, bâtir sur le même lieu une église de Carmelites, comme pour appaiser ces ombres irritées."

No cloud to dim the splendor of the day
Which breaks o'er Naples and her lovely bay,
And lights that brilliant sea and magic shore
With every tint that charm'd the great of yore ;
Th' imperial ones of earth—who proudly bade
Their marble domes e'en Ocean's realm invade.

That race is gone—but glorious nature here
Maintains unchanged her own sublime career,
And bids these regions of the sun display
Bright hues, surviving empires pass'd away.

The beam of Heaven expands—its kindling smile
Reveals each charm of many a fairy isle,
Whose image floats, in softer coloring drest,
With all its rocks and vines, on Ocean's breast.
Misenum's cape hath caught the vivid ray,
On Roman streamers there no more to play;
Still as of old, unalterably bright,
Lovely it sleeps on Posilipo's height
With all Italia's sunshine to illume
The ilex canopy of Virgil's tomb.
Campania's plains rejoice in light, and spread
Their gay luxuriance o'er the mighty dead;
Fair glittering to thine own transparent skies,
Thy palaces, exulting Naples! rise;
While, far on high Vesuvius rears his peak,
Furrow'd and dark with many a lava streak.

Oh, ye bright shores of Circe and the Muse!
Rich with all Nature's and all fiction's hues;
Who shall explore your regions, and declare
The poet err'd to paint Elysium there?
Call up his spirit, wanderer! bid him guide
Thy steps, those siren-haunted seas beside;
And all the scene a lovelier light shall wear,
And spells more potent shall pervade the air.
What though his dust be scatter'd, and his urn
Long from its sanctuary of slumber torn,[1]
Still dwell the beings of his verse around,
Hovering in beauty o'er th' enchanted ground:
His lays are murmur'd in each breeze that roves
Soft o'er the sunny waves and orange-groves;
His memory's charm is spread o'er shore and sea,
The soul, the genius of Parthenope;
Sheding o'er myrtle shade and vine-clad hill
The purple radiance of Elysium still.

Yet that fair soil and calm resplendent sky
Have witness'd many a dark reality.
Oft o'er those bright blue seas the gale hath borne
The sighs of exiles never to return.[2]
There with the whisper of Campania's gale
Aath mingled oft affection's funeral-wail,
Mourning for buried heroes—while to her
That glowing land was but their sepulchre.[3]
And there of old, the dread mysterious moan
Swell'd from strange voices of no mortal tone;
And that wild trumpet, whose unearthly note
Was heard, at midnight, o'er the hills to float
Around the spot where Agrippina died,
Denouncing vengeance on the matricide.[4]

THE DEATH OF CONRADIN.

Pass'd are those ages—yet another crime,
Another woe, must stain th' Elysian clime.
There stands a scaffold on the sunny shore—
It must be crimson'd ere the day is o'er!
There is a throne in regal pomp array'd,—
A scene of death from thence must be survey'd,
Mark'd ye the rushing throngs?—each mien is pale,
Each hurried glance reveals a fearful tale;
But the deep workings of th' indignant breast,
Wrath, hatred, pity, must be all suppress'd,
The burning tear awhile must check its course,
Th' avenging thought concentrate all its force;
For tyranny is near, and will not brook
Aught but submission in each guarded look.

Girt with his fierce Provençals, and with mien
Austere in triumph, gazing on the scene,[5]
And in his eye a keen suspisious glance
Of jealous pride and restless vigilance,
Behold the conqueror!—vainly in his face,
Of gentler feeling hope would seek a trace:
Cold, proud, severe, the spirit which hath lent
Its haughty stamp to each dark lineament;
And pleading mercy, in the sternness there,
May read at once her sentence—to despair!

But thou, fair boy! the beautiful, the brave,
Thus passing from the dungeon to the grave,
While all is yet around thee which can give
A charm to earth, and make it bliss to live;
Thou on whose form hath dwelt a mother's eye,
Till the deep love that not with thee shall die
Hath grown too full for utterance—Can it be?
And is this pomp of death prepared for *thee?*
Young, royal Conradin! who should'st have known
Of life as yet the sunny smile alone!
Oh! who can view thee, in the pride and bloom
Of youth, array'd so richly for the tomb
Nor feel deep swelling in his inmost soul,
Emotions tyranny may ne'er control?
Bright victim! to Ambition's altar led,
Crown'd with all flowers that heaven and earth can shed.
Who, from th' oppressor towering in his pride,
May hope for mercy—if to thee denied?
There is dead silence on the breathles throng,
Dead silence all the peopled shore along,
As on the captive moves—the only sound,
To break that calm so fearfully profound,
The low, sweet murmur of the rippling wave,
Soft as it glides, the smiling shore to lave;
While on that shore, his own fair heritage,
The youthful martyr to a tyrant's rage

Is passing to his fate: the eyes are dim
Which gaze, through tears that dare not flow, on him,
He mounts the scaffold--doth his footsteps fail?
Doth his lip quiver? doth his cheek turn pale?
Oh! it may be forgiven him if a thought
Cling to that world, for him with beauty fraught,
To all the hopes that promised glory's meed,
And all th' affections that with him shall bleed!
If, in his life's young dayspring, while the rose
Of boyhood on his cheek yet freshly glows,
One human fear convulse his parting breath,
And shrink from all the bitterness of death!

But no! the spirit of his royal race
Sits brightly on his brow—that youthful face
Beams with heroic beauty, and his eye
Is eloquent with injured majesty.
He kneels—but not to man—his heart shall own
Such deep submission to his God alone!
And who can tell with what sustaining power
That God may visit him in fate's dread hour?
How the still voice, which answers every moan,
May speak of hope—when hope on earth is gone?

That solemn pause is o'er—the youth hath given
One glance of parting love to earth and heaven:
The sun rejoices in th' unclouded sky,
Life all around him glows—and he must die!
Yet 'midst his people, undismay'd, he throws
The gage of vengeance for a thousand woes;
Vengeance, that, like their own volcanoe's fire,
May sleep suppress'd awhile—but not expire.
One softer image rises o'er his breast,
One fond regret, and all shall be at rest!
" Alas, for thee, my mother! who shall bear
To thy sad heart the tidings of despair,
When thy lost child is gone?"—that thought can thrill
His soul with pangs one moment more shall still.
The lifted axe is glittering in the sun—
It falls—the race of Conradin is run!
Yet, from the blood which flows that shore to stain,
A voice shall cry to heaven—and not in vain!
Gaze thou, triumphant from thy gorgeous throne,
In proud supremacy of guilt alone,
Charles of Anjou!—but that dread voice shall be
A fearful summoner e'en yet to thee!

The scene of death is closed—the throngs depart,
A deep stern lesson graved on every heart.
No pomp, no funeral rites, no streaming eyes,
High-minded boy! may grace thine obsequies.

O, vainly royal and beloved ! thy grave,
Unsanctified, is bathed by Ocean's wave ;
Mark'd by no stone, a rude, neglected spot,
Unhonor'd, unadorn'd—but *unforgot ;*
For thy deep wrongs in tameless hearts shall live,
Now mutely suffering—never to forgive !

The sunset fades from purple heavens away—
A bark hath anchor'd in the unruffled bay ;
Thence on the beach descends a female form,[6]
Her mein with hope and tearful transport warm ;
But life hath left sad traces on her cheek,
And her soft eyes a chasten'd heart bespeak,
Inured to woes—yet what were all the past !
She sunk not feebly 'neath affliction's blast,
While one bright hope remain'd—who now shall tell
Th' uncrown'd, the widow'd, how her loved one fell ?
To clasp her child, to ransom and to save,
The mother came—and she hath found his grave !
And by that grave, transfix'd in speechless grief,
Whose deathlike trance denies a tear's relief,
Awhile she kneels—till roused at length to know,
To feel the might, the fulness of her woe,
On the still air a voice of anguish wild,
A mother's cry is heard -" My Conradin ! my child ! "

NOTES.

Note 1, page 118, line 26.
Long from its sanctuary of slumber torn.
The urn, supposed to have contained the ashes of Virgil, has long since been lost.

Note 2, page 118, line 38.
The sighs of exiles, never to return.
Many Romans of exalted rank were formerly banished to some of the small islands in the Mediterranean, on the coast of Italy. Julia, the daughter of Agustus, was confined many years in the isle of Pandataria, and her daughter, Agrippina, the widow of Germanicus, afterwards died in exile on the same desolate spot.

Note 3, page 118, line 42.
That glowing land was but their sepulchre.
"Quelques souvenirs du cœur, quelques noms de femmes, réclament aussi vos pleurs. C'est à Misène, dans le lieu même où nous sommes, que la veuve de Pompée, Cornélie, conserva jusqu'à la mort son noble deuil; Agrippine pleura long-temps Germanicus sur ces bords. Un jour, le même assassin qui lui ravit son époux la trouva digne de le suivre. L'île de Nisida fut témoin des adieux de Brutus et de Porcie."—MADAME DE STAEL—*Corinne*.

Note 4, page 118, line 48.
Denouncing vengeance on the matricide.
The sight of that coast, and those shores where the crime had been perpetrated, filled Nero with continual horrors; besides, there were some who imagined they heard horrid shrieks and cries from Agrippina's tomb, and a mournful sound of trumpets from the neighboring cliffs and hills. Nero, therefore, flying from such tragical scenes, withdrew to Naples.—See *Ancient Universal History*.

Note 5, page 119, line 16.
Austere in triumph, gazing on the scene.
"Ce Charles," dit Giovanni Villani, "fut sage et prudent dans les conseils, preux dans les armes, âpre et forte redouté de tous les rois du monde, magnanime et de hautes pensées qui l'égaloient aux plus grandes enterprises; inébranlable dans l'adversité, ferme et fidèle dans toutes ses promesses, parlant peu et agissant beaucoup, *ne riant presque jamais*, décent comme un religieux, zélé catholique, âpre à rendre justice, féroce dans ses regards. Sa taille étoit grande et nerveuse, sa couleur olivâtre, son nez fort grand. Il paroissoit plus fait qu'aucun autre chevalier pour la majesté royale. Il ne dormoit presque point. Jamais il ne prit de plaisir aux mimes, aux troubadours, et aux gens de cour."—SISMONDI, *Republiques Italiennes* vol. iii.

Note 6, page 121, line 9.
Thence on the beach descends a female form.
"The Carmine (at Naples) calls to mind the bloody catastrophe of those royal youths, Conradin and Frederick of Austria, butchered before its door. Whenever I traversed that square, my heart yearned at the idea of their premature fate, and at the deep distress of Conradin's mother, who, landing on the beach with her son's ransom, found only a lifeless trunk to redeem from the fangs of his barbarous conqueror."—SWINBURN'S *Travels in the Two Sicilies*.

THE
RESTORATION
OF THE
WORKS OF ART TO ITALY.

["THE French, who in every invasion have been the scourge of Italy, and have rivalled or rather surpassed the rapacity of the Goths and Vandals, laid their sacrilegious hands on the unparalleled collection of the Vatican, tore its masterpieces from their pedestals, and, dragging them from their temples of marble, transported them to Paris, and consigned them to the dull, sullen halls, or rather stables of the Louvre.

* * * * * * * * *

But the joy of discovery was short, and the triumph of taste transitory."—EUSTACE's *Classical Tour through Italy*, vol. ii p. 60.]

"Italia, Italia! O tu cui die la sorte
Dono infelice di bellezza, ond' hai
Funesta dote d'infiniti guai,
Che'n fronte scritte per gran doglia porte;
Deh, fossi tu men bella, o almen più forte.
FILICAJA.

LAND of departed fame! whose classic plains
Have proudly echo'd to immortal strains;
Whose hallow'd soil hath given the great and brave,
Daystars of life, a birth, place and a grave;
Home of the Arts! where glory's faded smile,
Sheds ling'ring light o'er many a mould'ring pile;
Proud wreck of vanish'd power, of splendor fled,
Majestic temple of the mighty dead!
Whose grandeur, yet contending with decay,
Gleams through the twilight of thy glorious day;
Though dimm'd thy brightness, riveted thy chain,
Yet, fallen Italy! rejoice again!
Lost, lovely realm! once more 'tis thine to gaze
On the rich relics of sublimer days.

Awake, ye Muses of Etrurian shades,
Or sacred Tivoli's romantic glades;

Wake, ye that slumber in the bowery gloom
Where the wild ivy shadows Virgil's tomb;
Or ye, whose voice, by Sorga's lonely wave,
Swell'd the deep echoes of the fountain's cave,
Or thrill'd the soul in Tasso's numbers high,
Those magic strains of love and chivalry:
If yet by classic streams ye fondly rove,
Haunting the myrtle vale, the laurel grove;
Oh! rouse once more the daring soul of song,
Seize with bold hand the harp, forgot so long,
And hail, with wonted pride, those works revered
Hallow'd by time, by absence more endear'd.

And breathe to Those the strain, whose warrior-might
Each danger stemm'd, prevail'd in every fight;
Souls of unyielding power, to storms inured,
Sublimed by peril, and by toil matured.
Sing of that Leader, whose ascendant mind
Could rouse the slumbering spirit of mankind:
Whose banners track'd the vanquish'd Eagle's flight
O'er many a plain, and dark sierra's height;
Who bade once more the wild, heroic lay,
Record the deeds of Roncesvalles' day;
Who, through each mountain-pass of rock and snow,
An Alpine huntsman chased the fear-struck foe;
Waved his proud standard to the balmy gales,
Rich Languedoc! that fan thy glowing vales,
And 'midst those scenes renew'd th' achievements high,
Bequeath'd to fame by England's ancestry;

Yet, when the storm seem'd hush'd, the conflict past,
One strife remain'd—the mightiest and the last!
Nerved for the struggle, in that fateful hour
Untamed Ambition summon'd all his power;
Vengeance and Pride, to frenzy roused, were there,
And the stern might of resolute Despair.
  Isle of the free! 'twas then thy champions stood,
  Breasting unmoved the combat's wildest flood;
  Sunbeam of battle! then thy spirit shone,
  Glow'd in each breast, and sunk with life alone.

Oh hearts devoted! whose illustrious doom
Gave there at once your triumph and your tomb,
Ye, firm and faithful, in the ordeal tried
Of that dread strife, by Freedom sanctified;
Shrined, not entomb'd, ye rest in sacred earth,
Hallow'd by deeds of more than mortal worth.
What though to mark where sleeps heroic dust,
No sculptured trophy rise, or breathing bust,
Yours, on the scene where valor's race was run.
A prouder sepulchre—the field ye won!

There every mead, each cabin's lowly name,
Shall live a watchword blended with your fame ;
And well may flowers suffice those graves to crown
That ask no urn to blazon their renown !
There shall the bard in future ages tread,
And bless each wreath that blossoms o'er the dead ;
Revere each tree whose shelt'ring branches wave
O'er the low mounds, the altars of the brave ;
Pause o'er each warrior's grass-grown bed, and hear
In every breeze some name to glory dear ;
And as the shades of twilight close around,
With martial pageants people all the ground.
Thither unborn descendants of the slain
Shall throng as pilgrims to the holy fane,
While as they trace each spot, whose records tell
Where fought their fathers, and prevail'd, and fell
Warm in their souls shall loftiest feelings glow,
Claiming proud kindred with the dust below !
And many an age shall see the brave repair,
To learn the Hero's bright devotion there.

And well, Ausonia ! may that field of fame,
From thee one song of echoing triumph claim.
Land of the lyre ! 'twas there th' avenging sword,
Won the bright treasures to thy fanes restored ;
Those precious trophies o'er thy realms that throw
A veil of radiance, hiding half thy woe,
And bid the stranger for awhile forget
How deep thy fall, and deem thee glorious yet.

Yes, fair creations ! to perfection wrought,
Embodied visions of ascending thought !
Forms of sublimity ! by Genius traced
In tints that vindicate adoring taste ;
Whose bright originals, to earth unknown,
Live in the spheres encircling glory's throne ;
Models of art, to deathless fame consign'd,
Stamp'd with the high-born majesty of mind ;
Yes, matchless works ! your presence shall restore
One beam of splendor to your native shore,
And her sad scenes of lost renown illume,
As the bright sunset gilds some hero's tomb.

Oh ! ne'er, in other climes, though many an eye
Dwelt on your charms, in beaming ecstasy;
Ne'er was it yours to bid the soul expand
With thoughts so mighty, dreams so boldly grand,
As in that realm, where each faint breeze's moan
Seems a low dirge for glorious ages gone ;
Where 'midst the ruin'd shrines of many a vale,
E'en Desolation tells a haughty tale,

And scarce a fountain flows, a rock ascends,
But its proud name with song eternal blends!

Yes! in those scenes where every ancient stream
Bids memory kindle o'er some lofty theme;
Where every marble deeds of fame records,
Each ruin tells of Earth's departed lords;
And the deep tones of inspiration swell
From each wild olive-wood, and Alpine dell;
Where heroes slumber on their battle plains,
'Midst prostrate altars and deserted fanes,
And Fancy communes, in each lonely spot,
With shades of those who ne'er shall be forgot;
There was your home, and there your power imprest,
With tenfold awe, the pilgrim's glowing breast;
And, as the wind's deep thrills and mystic sighs
Wake the wild harp to loftiest harmonies,
Thus at your influence, starting from repose,
Thought, Feeling, Fancy, into grandeur rose.

Fair Florence! queen of Arno's lovely vale!
Justice and Truth indignant heard thy tale,
And sternly smiled in retribution's hour,
To wrest thy treasures from the Spoiler's power.
Too long the spirits of thy noble dead
Mourn'd o'er the domes they rear'd in ages fled.
Those classic scenes their pride so richly graced,
Temples of genius, palaces of taste,
Too long, with sad and desolated mien,
Reveal'd where Conquest's lawless track had been;
Reft of each form with brighter light imbued,
Lonely they frown'd, a desert solitude.
Florence! th' Oppressor's noon of pride is o'er,
Rise in thy pomp again, and weep no more!

As one, who, starting at the dawn of day
From dark illusions, phantoms of dismay,
With transport heighten'd by those ills of night,
Hails the rich glories of expanding light;
E'en thus, awak'ning from thy dream of woe,
While heaven's own hues in radiance round thee glow,
With warmer ecstacy 'tis thine to trace
Each tint of beauty, and each line of grace;
More bright, more prized, more precious, since deplored,
As loved, lost relics, ne'er to be restored,
Thy grief as hopeless as the tear-drop shed
By fond affection bending o'er the dead.

Athens of Italy! once more are thine
Those matchless gems of Art's exhaustless mine.
For thee bright Genius darts his living beam,
Warm o'er thy shrines the tints of Glory stream

And forms august as natives of the sky,
Rise round each fane in faultless majesty,
So chastely perfect, so serenely grand,
They seem creations of no mortal hand.

Ye, at whose voice fair art, with eagle glance,
Burst in full splendor from her deathlike trance;
Whose rallying call bade slumb'ring nations wake,
And daring intellect his bondage break;
Beneath whose eye the lords of song arose,
And snatch'd the tuscan lyre from long repose,
And bade its pealing energies resound,
With power electric, through the realms around;
Oh! high in thought, magnificent in soul!
Born to inspire, enlighten, and control;
Cosmo, Lorenzo! view your reign once more,
The shrine where nations mingle to adore!
Again th' Enthusiast there, with ardent gaze,
Shall hail the mighty of departed days:
Those sovereign spirits, whose commanding mind
Seems in the marble's breathing mould enshrined;
Still with ascendant power the world to awe,
Still the deep homage of the heart to draw;
To breathe some spell of holiness around,
Bid all the scene be consecrated ground,
And from the stone, by Inspiration wrought,
Dart the pure lightnings of exalted thought.

There thou, fair offspring of immortal Mind!
Love's radiant goddess, idol of mankind!
Once the bright object of Devotion's vow,
Shalt claim from taste a kindred worship now.
Oh! who can tell what beams of heavenly light,
Flash'd o'er the sculptor's intellectual sight,
How many a glimpse, reveal'd to him alone,
Made brighter beings, nobler worlds, his own;
Ere, like some vision sent the earth to bless,
Burst into life thy pomp of loveliness!

Young Genius there, while dwells his kindling eye
On forms, instinct with bright divinity,
While new-born powers, dilating in his heart,
Embrace the full magnificence of Art;
From scenes, by Raphael's gifted hand array'd,
From dreams of heaven, by Angelo portray'd;
From each fair work of Grecian skill sublime,
Seal'd with perfection, "sanctified by time;"
Shall catch a kindred glow, and proudly feel
His spirit burn with emulative zeal,
Buoyant with loftier hopes, his soul shall rise,
Imbued at once with nobler energies;

O'er life's dim scenes on rapid pinions soar,
And worlds of visionary grace explore,
Till his bold hand give glory's day-dream birth,
And with new wonders charm admiring earth.

   Venice, exult! and o'er thy moonlight seas,
Swell with gay strains each Adriatic breeze!
What though long fled those years of martial fame,
That shed romantic lustre o'er thy name;
Though to the winds thy streamers idly play,
And the wild waves another Queen obey;
Though quench'd the spirit of thine ancient race,
And power and freedom scarce have left a trace;
Yet still shall Art her splendors round thee cast,
And gild the wreck of years for ever past.
Again thy fanes may boast a Titian's dyes,
Whose clear soft brilliance emulates thy skies,
And scenes that glow in coloring's richest bloom,
With life's warm flush Palladian halls illume.
From the rich dome again th' unrivall'd steed
Starts to existence, rushes into speed,
Still for Lysippus claims the wreath of fame,
Panting with ardor, vivified with flame.

   Proud Racers of the Sun! to fancy's thought
Burning with spirit, from his essence caught,
No mortal birth ye seem—but form'd to bear
Heaven's car of triumph through the realms of air:
To range uncurb'd the pathless fields of space,
The winds your rivals in the glorious race;
Traverse empyreal spheres with buoyant feet,
Free as the zephyr, as the shot-star fleet;
And waft through worlds unknown the vital ray,
The flame that wakes creations into day.
Creatures of fire and ether! wing'd with light,
To track the regions of the Infinite!
From purer elements whose life was drawn,
Sprung from the sunbeam, offspring of the dawn.
What years on years, in silence gliding by,
Have spared those forms of perfect symmetry!
Moulded by Art to dignify, alone,
Her own bright deity's resplendent throne,
Since first her skill their fiery grace bestow'd,
Meet for such lofty fate, such high abode,
How many a race, whose tales of glory seem
An echo's voice—the music of a dream,
Whose records feebly from oblivion save
A few bright traces of the wise and brave;
How many a state, whose pillar'd strength sublime,
Defied the storms of war, the waves of time,
Towering o'er earth majestic and alone,
Fortress of power—has flourish'd and is gone!

And they, from clime to clime by conquest borne,
Each fleeting triumph destined to adorn,
They that of powers and kingdoms lost and won,
Have seen the noontide and the setting sun,
Consummate still in every grace remain,
As o'er *their* heads had ages roll'd in vain!
Ages, victorious in their ceaseless flight,
O'er countless monuments of earthly might!
While she, from fair Byzantium's lost domain,
Who bore those treasures to her ocean-reign,
Midst the blue deep, who rear'd her island-throne,
And called th' infinitude of waves her own;
Venice, the proud, the Regent of the sea,
Welcomes in chains the trophies of the Free!

And thou, whose Eagle's towering plume unfurl'd,
Once cast its shadow o'er a vassal world,
Eternal city! round whose Curule throne,
The lords of nations knelt in ages flown;
Thou, whose Augustan years have left to time
Immortal records of their glorious prime;
When deathless bards, thine olive-shades among,
Swell'd the high raptures of heroic song;
Fair, fallen Empress! raise thy languid head
From the cold altars of th' illustrious dead,
And once again, with fond delight survey,
The proud memorials of thy noblest day.

Lo! where thy sons, oh Rome! a godlike train,
In imaged majesty return again!
Bards, chieftans, monarchs, tower with mien august
O'er scenes that shrine their venerable dust.
Those forms, those features, luminous with soul,
Still o'er thy children seem to claim control;
With awful grace arrest the pilgrim's glance,
Bind his rapt soul in elevating trance,
And bid the past, to fancy's ardent eyes,
From time's dim sepulchre in glory rise.

Souls of the lofty! whose undying names,
Rouse the young bosom still to noblest aims;
Oh! with your images could fate restore
Your own high spirit to your sons once more;
Patriots and heroes! could those flames return
That bade your hearts with freedom's ardors burn,
Then from the sacred ashes of the first,
Might a new Rome in phœnix grandeur burst!
With one bright glance dispel th' horizon's gloom,
With one loud call wake empire from the tomb;
Bind round her brows her own triumphal crown,
Lift her dread ægis with majestic frown,

10*

Unchain her eagle's wing, and guide his flight,
To bathe his plumage in the fount of light.

Vain dream! degraded Rome! thy noon is o'er,
Once lost, thy spirit shall revive no more.
It sleeps with those, the sons of other days,
Who fix'd on thee the world's adoring gaze ;
Those, blest to live, while yet thy star was high,
More blest, ere darkness quench'd its beam, to die !

Yet, though thy faithless tutelary powers
Have fled thy shrines, left desolate thy towers,
Still, still to thee shall nations bend their way,
Revered in ruin, sovereign in decay !
Oh! what can realms, in fame's full zenith, boast,
To match the relics of thy splendor lost !
By Tiber's waves, on each illustrious hill,
Genius and Taste shall love to wander still,
For there has Art survived an empire's doom,
And rear'd her throne o'er Latium's trophied tomb ;
She from the dust recalls the brave and free,
Peopling each scene with beings worthy thee !

Oh! ne'er again may War, with lightning stroke,
Rend its last honors from the shatter'd oak!
Long be those works, revered by ages, thine,
To lend one triumph to thy dim decline !

Bright with stern beauty, breathing wrathful fire,
In all the grandeur of celestial ire,
Once more thine own, th' immortal Archer's form
Sheds radiance round, with more than Being warm
Oh! who could view, nor deem that perfect frame,
A iving temple of ethereal flame?

Lord of the daystar! how may words portray
Of thy chaste glory one reflected ray ?
Whate'er the soul could dream, the hand could trace,
Of regal dignity and heavenly grace ;
Each purer effluence of the fair and bright,
Whose fitful gleams have broke on mortal sight ;
Each bold idea, borrow'd from the sky,
To vest th' embodied form of Deity ;
All, all in thee ennobled and refined,
Breathe and enchant, transcendently combined !
Son of Elysium ! years and ages gone
Have bow'd in speechless homage at thy throne,
And days unborn, and nations yet to be,
Shall gaze, absorb'd in ecstacy, on thee !

And thou, triumphant wreck,[1] e'en yet sublime,
Disputed trophy, claimed by Art and Time ;

Hail to that scene again, where genius caught
From thee its fervors of diviner thought!
Where He, th' inspired One, whose gigantic mind
Lived in some sphere, to him alone assign'd;
Who from the past, the future and th' unseen,
Could call up forms of more than earthly mien:
Unrivall'd Angelo on thee would gaze,
Till his full soul imbibed perfection's blaze!
And who but he, that Prince of Art, might dare
Thy sovereign greatness view without despair?
Emblem of Rome! from power's meridian hurl'd,
Yet claiming still the homage of the world.

What hadst thou been, ere barb'rous hands defaced
The work of wonder, idolized by taste?
Oh! worthy still of some divine abode,
Mould of a Conqueror! ruin of a God![2]
Still, like some broken gem, whose quenchless beam
From each bright fragment pours its vital stream,
'Tis thine, by fate unconquer'd to dispense
From every part some ray of excellence!
E'en yet, inform'd with essence from on high,
Thine is no trace of frail mortality!
Within that frame a purer being glows,
Through viewless veins a brighter current flows;
Fill'd with immortal life each muscle swells,
In every line supernal grandeur dwells.

Consummate work! the noblest and the last
Of Grecian Freedom, ere her reign was past:[3]
Nurse of the mighty, she, while ling'ring still,
Her mantle flow'd o'er many a classic hill,
Ere yet her voice its parting accents breathed,
A hero's image to the world bequeathed;
Enshrined in thee th' imperishable ray
Of high-soul'd Genius, foster'd by her sway,
And bade thee teach, to ages yet unborn,
What lofty dreams were hers—who never shall return!

And mark yon group, transfix'd with many a throe,
Seal'd with the image of eternal woe:
With fearful truth, terrific power, exprest,
Thy pangs, Laocoon, agonize the breast,
And the stern combat picture to mankind
Of suffering nature and enduring mind.
Oh, mighty conflict! though his pains intense
Distend each nerve, and dart through every sense;
Though fix'd on him, his children's suppliant eyes
Implore the aid avenging fate denies
Though with the giant snake in fruitless strife,
Heaves every muscle with convulsive life,

And in each limb existence writhes, enroll'd
'Midst the dread circles of the venom'd fold;
Yet the strong spirit lives—and not a cry
Shall own the might of Nature's agony!
That furrow'd brow unconquer'd soul reveals,
That patient eye to angry Heaven appeals,
That struggling bosom concentrates its breath,
Nor yields one moan to torture or to death."[4]

Sublimest triumph of intrepid Art!
With speechless horror to congeal the heart,
To freeze each pulse, and dart through every vein,
Cold thrills of fear, keen sympathies of pain;
Yet teach the spirit how its lofty power
May brave the pangs of fate's severest hour.

Turn from such conflicts, and enraptured gaze
On scenes where Painting all her skill displays:
Landscapes, by coloring dress'd in richer dyes,
More mellow'd sunshine, more unclouded skies,
Of dreams of bliss, to dying martyrs given,
Descending seraphs, robed in beams of heaven.

Oh! sovereign Masters of the Pencil's might,
Its depths of shadow, and its blaze of light;
Ye, whose bold thought disdaining every bound,
Explored the worlds above, below, around,
Children of Italy! who stand alone
And unapproach'd, 'midst regions all your own;
What scenes, what beings bless'd your favor'd sight,
Severely grand, unutterably bright!
Triumphant spirits! your exulting eye
Could meet the noontide of eternity,
And gaze untired, undaunted, uncontroll'd,
On all that Fancy trembles to behold.

Bright on your view such forms their splendor shed,
As burst on prophet-bards in ages fled:
Forms that to trace no hand but yours might dare,
Darkly sublime or exquisitely fair;
These o'er the walls your magic skill array'd,
Glow in rich sunshine, gleam through melting shade,
Float in light grace, in awful greatness tower,
And breathe and move, the records of your power.
Inspired of Heaven! what heighten'd pomp ye cast
O'er all the deathless trophies of the past!
Round many a marble fane and classic dome,
Asserting still the majesty of Rome;
Round many a work that bids the world believe
What Grecian Art could image and achieve;
Again, creative minds, your visions throw
Life's chasten'd warmth, and Beauty's mellowest glow,

And when the Morn's bright beams and mantling dyes,
Pour the rich lustre of Ausonian skies,
Or evening suns illume, with purple smile,
The Parian altar, and the pillar'd aisle,
Then, as the full, or soften'd radiance falls,
On angel-groups that hover o'er the walls,
Well may those Temples, where your hand has shed
Light o'er the tomb, existence round the dead,
Seem like some world, so perfect and so fair,
That nought of earth should find admittance there,
Some sphere where beings, to mankind unknown,
Dwell in the brightness of their pomp alone!

Hence, ye vain fictions! fancy's erring theme!
Gods of illusion! phantoms of a dream!
Frail, powerless idols of departed time,
Fables of song, delusive, though sublime!
To loftier tasks has Roman Art assign'd
Her matchless pencil, and her mighty mind!
From brighter streams her vast ideas flow'd,
With purer fire her ardent spirit glow'd.
To her 'twas given in fancy to explore
The land of miracles, the holiest shore;
That realm where first the light of life was sent,
The loved, the punish'd, of th' Omnipotent!
O'er Judah's hills her thoughts inspired would stray,
Through Jordan's valleys trace their lonely way;
By Siloa's brook, or Almotana's deep,[5]
Chain'd in dead silence, and unbroken sleep;
Scenes, whose cleft rocks, and blasted deserts tell,
Where pass'd th' Eternal, where his anger fell!
Where oft his voice the words of fate reveal'd.
Swell'd in the whirlwind, in the thunder peal'd,
Or heard by prophets in some palmy vale,
Breathed "still small" whispers on the midnight gale.
There dwelt her spirit—there her hand portray'd,
'Midst the lone wilderness or cedar-shade,
Ethereal forms with awful missions fraught,
Or patriarch-seers absorb'd in sacred thought,
Bards, in high converse with the world of rest,
Saints of the earth, and spirits of the blest.
But chief to Him, the Conqueror of the grave,
Who lived to guide us, and who died to save;
Him, at whose glance the powers of evil fled,
And soul return'd to animate the dead;
Whom the waves own'd—and sunk beneath his eye,
Awed by one accent of Divinity;
To Him she gave her meditative hours,
Hallow'd her thoughts, and sanctified her powers.
O'er her bright scenes sublime repose she threw,
As all around the Godhead's presence knew,

And robed the Holy One's benignant mien
In beaming mercy, majesty serene.

Oh! mark where Raphael's pure and perfect line
Portrays that form ineffably divine!
Where with transcendent skill his hand has shed
Diffusive sunbeams round the Saviour's head;[6]
Each heaven-illumined lineament imbued
With all the fullness of beautitude,
And traced the sainted group, whose mortal sight
Sinks overpower'd by that excess of light!

Gaze on that scene, and own the might of Art,
By truth inspired to elevate the heart
To bid the soul exultingly possess,
Of all her powers, a heighten'd consciousness;
And strong in hope, anticipate the day,
The last of life, the first of freedom's ray,
To realize, in some unclouded sphere,
Those pictured glories feebly imaged here!
Dim, cold reflections from her native sky,
Faint effluence of "the Day-spring from on high!"

NOTES.

Note 1, page 130, line 45.

The Belvidere Torso, the favorite study of Michael Angelo, and of many other distinguished artists.

Note 2, page 131, line 16.

"Quoique cette statue d'Hercule ait été maltraitée et mutilée d'une manière étrange, se trouvant sans tête sans bras, et sans jambes, elle est cependant encore un chef d'œuvre aux yeux des connoisseurs ; et ceux qui savent percer dans les mysteres de l'art, se la représentent dans toute sa beauté. L'Artiste, en voulant représenter Hercule, a formé un corps idéal audessus de la nature * * * Cet Hercule paroît donc ici tel qu'il dut être lorsque purifié par le feu des foiblesses de l'humanité, il obtint l'immortalité et prit place auprès des Dieux. Il est représenté sans aucun besoin de nourriture et de réparation de forces. Les veines y sont tout invisibles."—WINCKELMANN, *Historic de l'Art chez les Anciens*, tom. ii. p. 248.

Note 3, page 131, line 28.

"Le Torso d'Hercule paroît un des derniers ouvrages parfaits que l'art ait produit en Grece, avant la perte de sa liberté. Car après que la Grece fut réduite en province Romaine, l'histoire ne fait mention d'aucun artiste célebre de cette nation, jusqu'aux temps du Triumvirat Romain."—WINCKELMANN, *ibid*, tom. ii. p. 250.

Note 4, page 132, line 8.

"It is not, in the same manner, in the agonized limbs, or in the convulsed muscles of the Laocoon, that the secret grace of its composition resides ; it is in the majestic air of the head, which has not *yielded* to *suffering*, and in the deep serenity of the forehead, which seems to be still *superior* to all its *afflictions*, and significant of a mind that cannot be subdued."—ALLISON's *Essays*, vol. ii. p. 400.

"Laocoon nous offre le spectacle de la nature humaine dans la plus grande douleur dont elle soit susceptible, sous l'image d'un homme qui tâche de rassembler contre elle toute la force de l'esprit. Tandis que l'excès de la souffrance enfle les muscles, et tire violemment les nerfs, le courage se montre sur le front gonflé : la poitrine s'éleve avec peine par la nécessité de la respiration, qui est également contrainte par le silence que la force de l'ame impose à la douleur qu'elle voudroit étouffer * * * * Son air est plaintif, et non criard."—WINCKELMANN, *Histoire de l'Art chez les Anciens*, tom. ii. p. 214.

Note 5, page 133 line 27.

Almotana. The name given by the Arabs to the Dead Sea.

Note 6, page 134, line 4.

The Transfiguration, thought to be so perfect a specimen of art, that in honor of Raphael, it was carried before his body to the grave

MODERN GREECE.

> O Greece! thou sapient nurse of finer arts,
> Which to bright Science blooming Fancy bore,
> Be this thy praise, that thou, and thou alone,
> In these hast led the way, in these excell'd,
> Crown'd with the laurel of assenting Time.
> *Thompson's Liberty.*

I.

O! who hath trod thy consecrated clime,
Fair land of Phidias! theme of lofty strains!
And traced each scene, that 'midst the wrecks of time,
The print of Glory's parting step retains;
Nor for a while, in high-wrought dreams, forgot,
Musing on years gone by in brightness there,
The hopes, the fears, the sorrows of his lot,
The hues his fate hath worn, or yet may wear;
As when, from mountain-heights, his ardent eye
Of sea and heaven hath track'd the blue infinity?

II.

Is there who views with cold unalter'd mien,
His frozen heart with proud indifference fraught,
Each sacred haunt, each unforgotten scene,
Where Freedom triumph'd or where Wisdom taught?
Souls that too deeply feel, oh, envy not
The sullen calm your faith hath never known;
Through the dull twilight of that wintry lot
Genius ne'er pierced, nor Fancy's sunbeam shone,
Nor those high thoughts, that, hailing Glory's trace,
Glow with the generous flames of every age and race.

III.

But blest the wanderer, whose enthusiast mind
Each muse of ancient days hath deep imbued
With lofty lore; and all his thoughts refined
In the calm school of silent solitude;
Pour'd on his ear, 'midst groves and glens retired,
The mighty strains of each illustrious clime,
All that hath lived, while empires have expired
To float forever on the winds of Time;
And on his soul indelibly portrayed
Fair visionary forms, to fill each classic shade.

IV.

Is not his mind to meaner thoughts unknown,
A sanctuary of beauty and of light?

There he may dwell in regions all his own,
A world of dreams, where all is pure and bright.
For him the scenes of old renown possess
Romantic charms, all veil'd from other eyes;
There every form of nature's loveliness
Wakes in his breast a thousand sympathies;
As music's voice, in some lone mountain-dell,
From rocks and caves around calls forth each echo's swell

V.

For him Italia's brilliant skies illume
The bard's lone haunts, the warrior's combat-plains,
And the wild rose yet lives to breathe and bloom
Round Doric Pæstum's solitary fanes.[1]
But most, fair Greece! on thy majestic shore
He feels the fervors of his spirit rise;
Thou birth-place of the Muse! whose voice of yore
Breathed in thy groves immortal harmonies;
And lingers still around the well-known coast,
Murmuring a wild farewell to fame and freedom lost.

VI.

By seas, that flow in brightness as they lave
Thy rocks, th' enthusiast rapt in thought may stray,
While roves his eye o'er that deserted wave,
Once the proud scene of battle's dread array.
—O ye blue waters! ye, of old that bore
The free, the conquering, hymn'd by choral strains,
How sleep ye now around the silent shore,
The lonely realm of ruins and of chains!
How are the mighty vanish'd in their pride!
E'en as their barks have left no traces on your tide.

VII.

Hush'd are the Pæans whose exulting tone
Swell'd o'er that tide[2]—the sons of battle sleep—
The wind's wild sigh, the halcyon's voice alone
Blend with the plaintive murmur of the deep.
Yet when those waves have caught the splendid hues
Of morn's rich firmament, serenely bright,
Or setting suns the lovely shore suffuse
With all their purple mellowness of light,
O! who could view the scene so calmly fair,
Nor dream that peace, and joy, and liberty, were there?

VIII.

Where soft the sunbeams play, the zephyrs blow,
'Tis hard to deem that misery can be nigh;
Where the clear heavens in blue transparence glow,
Life should be calm and cloudless as the sky;
—Yet o'er the low, dark dwellings of the dead,
Verdure and flowers in summer bloom-may smile,

And ivy-boughs their graceful drapery spread
In green luxuriance o'er the ruined pile;
And mantling woodbine veil the wither'd tree,—
And thus it is, fair land! forsaken Greece, with thee.

IX.
For all the loveliness, and light, and bloom,
That yet are thine, surviving many a storm,
Are but as heaven's warm radiance on the tomb,
The rose's blush that masks the canker-worm:—
And thou art desolate—thy morn hath pass'd
So dazzling in the splendor of its way,
That the dark shades the night hath o'er thee cast,
Throw tenfold gloom around thy deep decay.
Once proud in freedom, still in ruin fair,
Thy fate hath been unmatch'd—in glory and despair.

X.
For thee, lost land! the hero's blood hath flow'd,
The high in soul have brightly lived and died;
For thee the light of soaring genius glow'd
O'er the fair arts it form'd and glorified.
Thine were the minds, whose energies sublime
So distanced ages in their lightning-race,
The task they left the sons of later time
Was but to follow their illumined trace.
—Now, bow'd to earth, thy children, to be free,
Must break each link that binds their filial hearts to thee

XI.
Lo! to the scenes of fiction's wildest tales,
Her own bright East, thy son, Morea! flies,[3]
To seek repose 'midst rich, romantic vales,
Whose incense mounts to Asia's vivid skies.
There shall he rest?—Alas! his hopes in vain
Guide to the sun-clad regions of the palm,
Peace dwells not now on oriental plain,
Though earth is fruitfulness, and air is balm;
And the sad wanderer finds but lawless foes,
Where patriarchs reign'd of old, in pastoral repose.

XII.
Where Syria's mountains rise, or Yemen's groves,
Or Tigris rolls his genii-haunted wave,
Life to his eye, as wearily it roves,
Wears but two forms—the tyrant and the slave!
There the fierce Arab leads his daring horde,
Where sweeps the sand-storm o'er the burning wild;
There stern Oppression waves the wasting sword
O'er plains that smile, as ancient Eden smiled:
And the vale's bosom, and the desert gloom,
Yield to the injured there no shelter save the tomb.

XIII.

But thou, fair world! whose fresh unsullied charms
Welcomed Columbus from the western wave,
Wilt thou receive the wanderer to thine arms,[4]
The lost descendant of the immortal brave?
Amidst the wild magnificence of shades
That o'er thy floods their twilight-grandeur cast,
In the green depth of thine untrodden glades
Shall he not rear his bower of peace at last?
Yes! thou hast many a lone, majestic scene,
Shrined in primæval woods, where despot ne'er hath been.

XIV.

There, by some lake, whose blue expansive breast
Bright from afar, an inland-ocean, gleams,
Girt with vast solitudes, profusely dress'd
In tints like those that float o'er poet's dreams;
Or where some flood from pine-clad mountain pours
Its might of waters, glittering in their foam,
'Midst the rich verdure of its wooded shores,
The exiled Greek hath fix'd his sylvan home:
So deeply lone, that round the wild retreat
Scarce have the paths been trod by Indian huntsman's feet.

XV.

The forests are around him in their pride,
The green savannas, and the mighty waves;
And isles of flowers, bright floating o'er the tide,[5]
That images the fairy worlds it laves,
And stillness, and luxuriance—o'er his head
The ancient cedars wave their peopled bowers,
On high the palms their graceful foliage spread,
Cinctured with roses the magnolia towers,
And from those green arcades a thousand tones   [moans.
Wake with each breeze, whose voice through Nature's temple

XVI.

And there, no traces left by brighter days,
For glory lost may wake a sigh of grief,
Some grassy mound, perchance, may meet his gaze,
The lone memorial of an Indian chief.
There man not yet hath mark'd the boundless plain
With marble records of his fame and power;
The forest is his everlasting fane,
The palm his monument, the rock his tower.
Th' eternal torrent and the giant tree,
Remind him but that they, like him are wildly free

XVII.

But doth the exile's heart serenely there
In sunshine dwell?—Ah! when was exile blest?

When did bright scenes, clear heavens, or summer air,
Chase from his soul the fever of unrest?
—There is a heart-sick weariness of mood,
That like slow poison wastes the vital glow,
And shrines itself in mental solitude,
An uncomplaining and a nameless woe,
  That coldly smiles 'midst pleasure's brightest ray,
As the chill glacier's peak reflects the flush of day.

XVIII.

Such grief is theirs, who, fix'd on foreign shore,
Sigh for the spirit of their native gales,
As pines the seaman, 'midst the ocean's roar,
For the green earth, with all its woods and vales.
Thus feels thy child, whose memory dwells with thee,
Loved Greece! all sunk and blighted as thou art:
Though thought and step in western wilds be free,
Yet thine are still the day-dreams of his heart:
  The desert spread between, the billows foam,
Thou, distant and in chains, are yet his spirit's home.

XIX.

In vain for him the gay liannes entwine,
Or the green fire-fly sparkles through the brakes,
Or summer-winds waft odors from the pine,
As eve's last blush is dying on the lakes.
Through thy fair vales his fancy roves the while,
Or breathes the freshness of Cithæron's height,
Or dreams how softly Athens' towers would smile.
Or Sunium's ruins in the fading light;
  On Corinth's cliff what sunset hues may sleep,
Or, at that placid hour, how calm th' Egean deep!

XX.

What scenes, what sunbeams, are to him like thine!
(The all of thine no tyrant could destroy!)
E'en to the stranger's roving eye, they shine
Soft as a vision of remember'd joy.
And he who comes, the pilgrim of a day,
A passing wanderer o'er each Attic hill,
Sighs as his footsteps turn from thy decay,
To laughing climes, where all is splendor still;
  And views with fond regret thy lessening shore,
As he would watch a star that sets to rise no more.

XXI.

Realm of sad beauty! thou art as a shrine
That Fancy visits with Devotion's zeal,
To catch high thoughts and impulses divine
And all the glow of soul enthusiasts feel
Amidst the tombs of heroes—for the brave
Whose dust, so many an age, hath been thy soil,

Foremost in honor's phalanx, died to save
The land redeem'd and hallow'd by their toil ;
And there is language in thy lightest gale.
That o'er the plains they won seems murmuring yet their tale.

XXII.
And he, whose heart is weary of the strife
Of meaner spirits, and whose mental gaze
Would shun the dull cold littleness of life,
Awhile to dwell amidst sublimer days,
Must turn to thee, whose every valley teams
With proud remembrances that cannot die.
Thy glens are peopled with inspiring dreams,
Thy winds, the voice of oracles gone by ;
And, midst thy laurel shades the wanderer hears
The sound of mighty names, the hymns of vanish'd years

XXIII.
Through that deep solitude be his to stray,
By Faun and Oread loved in ages past,
Where clear Peneus winds his rapid way
Through the cleft heights, in antique grandeur vast.
Romantic Tempe ! thou art yet the same—
Wild, as when sung by bards of elder time :[6]
Years, that have changed thy river's classic name,[7]
Have left thee still in savage pomp sublime ;
And from thine Alpine clefts, and marble caves,
In living lustre still break forth the fountain waves.

XXIV.
Beneath thy mountain battlements and towers,
Where the rich arbute's coral-berries glow,[8]
Or, midst the exuberance of thy forest bowers,
Casting deep shadow's o'er the current's flow,
Oft shall the pilgrim pause, in lone recess,
As rock and stream some glancing light have caught,
And gaze, till Nature's mighty forms impress
His soul with deep sublimity of thought ;
And linger oft, recalling many a tale,   [thy dale.
That breeze, and wave, and wood, seem whispering through

XXV.
He, thought-entranced, may wander where of old
From Delphi's chasm the mystic vapour rose,
And trembling nations heard their doom foretold
By the dread spirit throned 'midst rocks and snows.
Though its rich fanes be blended with the dust,
And silence now the hallow'd haunt possess,
Still is the scene of ancient rites august,
Magnificent in mountain lonliness ;
Still Inspiration hovers o'er the ground,
Where Greece her councils held,[9] her Pythian victors crown'd.

MODERN GREECE.

XXVI.
Or let his steps the rude grey cliffs explore
Of that wild pass, once dyed with Spartan blood,
When by the waves that break on Œta's shore,
The few, the fearless, the devoted, stood!
Or rove where, shadowing Mantinea's plain,
Bloom the wild laurels o'er the warlike dead,[10]
Or lone Platæa's ruins yet remain,
To mark the battle-field of ages fled ;
Still o'er such scenes presides a sacred power,   [bower.
Though Fiction's gods have fled from fountain, grot, and

XXVII.
Oh! still unblamed may fancy fondly deem,
That, lingering yet, benignant genii dwell
Where mortal worth has hallow'd grove or stream,
To sway the heart with some ennobling spell ;
For mightiest minds have felt their blest control,
In the wood's murmur, in the zephyr's sigh,
And these are dreams that lend a voice and soul,
And a high power, to Nature's majesty !
And who can rove o'er Grecian shores, nor feel,
Soft o'er his inmost heart, their secret magic steal?

XXVIII.
Yet many a sad reality is there,
That Fancy's bright illusions cannot veil.
Pure laughs the light and balmy breathes the air,
But Slavery's mein will tell its bitter tale ;
And there, not Peace, but Desolation, throws
Delusive quiet o'er full many a scene,
Deep as the brooding torpor of repose
That follows where the earthquake's track hath been ;
Or solemn calm, on Ocean's breast that lies,   [cries.
When sinks the storm, and death has hush'd the seaman's

XXIX.
Hast thou beheld some sovereign spirit, hurl'd
By Fate's rude tempest from its radiant sphere,
Doom'd to resign the homage of a world,
For Pity's deepest sigh, and saddest tear?
Oh! hast thou watch'd the awful wreck of mind,
That weareth still a glory in decay ?
Seen all that dazzles and delights mankind—
Thought, science, genius, to the storm a prey,
And o'er the blasted tree, the wither'd ground,
Despair's wild nightshade spread, and darkly flourish round ?

XXX.
So mayst thou gaze, in sad and awe-struck thought,
On the deep fall of that yet lovely clime:

Such there the ruin Time and Fate have wrought,
So changed the bright, the splendid, the sublime ;
There the proud monuments of Valor's name,
The mighty works Ambition piled on high,
The rich remains by Art bequeathed to Fame—
Grace, beauty, grandeur, strength, and symmetry,
Blend in decay ; while all that yet is fair
Seems only spared to tell how much hath perish'd there!

XXXI.

There, while around lie mingling in the dust,
The column's graceful shaft, with weeds o'ergrown,
The mouldering torso, the forgotten bust,
The warrior's urn, the altar's mossy stone ;
Amidst the loneliness of shatter'd fanes,
Still matchless monuments of other years,
O'er cypress groves, or solitary plains,
Its eastern form the minaret proudly rears ;
As on some captive city's ruin'd wall
The victor's banner waves, exulting o'er its fall.

XXXII.

Still, where the column of the mosque aspires,
Landmark of slavery, towering o'er the waste,
There science droops, the Muses hush their lyres,
And o'er the blooms of fancy and of taste
Spreads the chill blight—as in that orient isle,
Where the dark upas taints the gale around,[11]
Within its precincts not a flower may smile,
Nor dew nor sunshine fertilize the ground ;
Nor wild birds' music float on zephyr's breath,
But all is silence round, and solitude, and death.

XXXIII.

Far other influence pour'd the Crescent's light
O'er conquer'd realms, in ages pass'd away ;
Full, and alone it beam'd, intensely bright,
While distant climes in midnight darkness lay.
Then rose th' Alhambra, with its founts and shades,
Fair marble halls, alcoves, and orange bowers ;
Its sculptur'd lions,[12] richly wrought arcades,
Aerial pillars, and enchanted towers ;
Light, splendid, wild, as some Arabian tale
Would picture fairy domes, that fleet before the gale.

XXXIV.

Then foster'd genius lent each caliph's throne
Lustre barbaric pomp could ne'er attain ;
And stars unnumber'd o'er the orient shone,
Bright as that Pleiad, sphered in Mecca's fane.[13]
From Bagdat's palaces the choral strains
Rose and re-echoed to the desert's bound,

And Science, woo'd on Egypt's burning plains,
Rear'd her majestic head with glory crown'd:
And the wild Muses breathed romantic lore,
From Syria's palmy groves to Andalusia's shore.

XXXV.

Those years have past in radiance—they have past,
As sinks the daystar in the tropic main;
His parting beams no soft reflection cast,
They burn—are quench'd—and deepest shadows reign.
And Fame and Science have not left a trace
In the vast regions of the Moslem's power—
Regions, to intellect a desert space,
A wild without a fountain or a flower,
Where towers Oppression 'midst the deepening glooms,
As dark and lone ascends the cypress 'midst the tombs.

XXXVI.

Alas for thee, fair Greece! when Asia pour'd
Her fierce fanatics to Byzantium's wall,
When Europe sheath'd, in apathy, her sword,
And heard unmoved the fated city's call,
No bold crusaders ranged their serried line
Of spears and banners round a falling throne;
And thou, O last and noblest Constantine! [14]
Didst meet the storm unshrinking and alone.
Oh! blest to die in freedom, though in vain,
Thine Empire's proud exchange the grave, and not the chain

XXXVII.

Hush'd is Byzantium—'tis the dead of night—
The closing night of that imperial race! [15]
And all is vigil—but the eye of light
Shall soon unfold, a wilder scene to trace:
There is a murmuring stillness on the train,
Thronging the midnight streets, at morn to die;
And to the cross in fair Sophia's fane,
For the last time is raised Devotion's eye;
And, in his heart while faith's bright visions rise,
There kneels the high-soul'd prince, the summon'd of the skies

XXXVIII.

Day breaks in light and glory—'tis the hour
Of conflict and of fate—the war-note calls—
Despair hath lent a stern, delirious power
To the brave few that guard the rampart walls.
Far over Marmora's waves th' artillery's peal
Proclaims an empire's doom in every note;
Tambour and trumpet swell the clash of steel,
Round spire and dome the clouds of battle float:
From camp and wave rush on the crescent's host,
And the Seven Towers [16] are scaled, and all is won and lost.

XXXIX.

Then, Greece! the tempest rose that burst on thee,
Land of the bard, the warrior, and the sage!
Oh! where were then thy sons, the great, the free,
Whose deeds are guiding stars from age to age?
Though firm thy battlements of crags and snows,
And bright the memory of thy days of pride,
In mountain might though Corinth's fortress rose,
On, unresisted, roll'd th' invading tide!
Oh! vain the rock, the rampart, and the tower,
If Freedom guard them not with Mind's unconquer'd power.

XL.

Where were th' avengers then, whose viewless might
Preserved inviolate their awful fane,[17]
When through the steep defiles, to Delphi's height,
In martial splendor pour'd the Persian's train?
Then did those mighty and mysterious Powers,
Arm'd with the elements, to vengeance wake,
Call the dread storms to darken round their towers,
Hurl down the rocks, and bid the thunders break;
Till far around, with deep and fearful clang,
Sounds of unearthly war through wild Parnassus rang.

XLI.

Where was the spirit of the victor-throng
Whose tombs are glorious by Scamander's tide,
Whose names are bright in everlasting song,
The lords of war, the praised, the deified?
Where he, the hero of a thousand lays,
Who from the dead at Marathon arose[18]
All arm'd; and beaming on the Athenians' gaze,
A battle-meteor, guided to their foes?
Or they whose forms to Alaric's awe-struck eye,[19]
Hovering o'er Athens, blazed in airy panoply?

XLII.

Ye slept, oh heroes! chief ones of the earth![20]
High demigods of ancient days! ye slept.
There lived no spark of your ascendant worth
When o'er your land the victor Moslem swept;
No patriot then the sons of freedom led,
In mountain pass devotedly to die;
The martyr-spirit of resolve was fled,
And the high soul's unconquer'd buoyancy;
And by your graves, and on your battle-plains,
Warriors! your children knelt, to wear the stranger's chain.

XLIII.

Now have your trophies vanish'd, and your homes
Are moulder'd from the earth, while scarce remain

E'en the faint traces of the ancient tombs
That mark where sleep the slayers or the slain.
Your deeds are with the days of glory flown,
The lyres are hush'd that swell'd your fame afar,
The halls that echo'd to their sounds are gone,
Perish'd the conquering weapons of your war;[21]
And if a mossy stone your names retain,
'Tis but to tell your sons for them ye died in vain.

XLIV.

Yet, where some lone sepulchral relic stands,
That with those names tradition hallows yet,
Oft shall the wandering son of other lands
Linger in solemn thought and hush'd regret.
And still have legends mark'd the lonely spot
Where low the dust of Agamemnon lies;
And shades of kings and leaders unforgot,
Hovering around to Fancy's visions rise.
Souls of the heroes! seek your rest again,
Nor mark how changed the realms that saw your glory's reign.

XLV.

Lo, where th' Albanian spreads his despot sway
O'er Thessaly's rich vales and glowing plains,
Whose sons in sullen abjectness obey,
Nor lift the hand indignant at its chains:
Oh! doth the land that gave Achilles birth,
And many a chief of old illustrious line,
Yield not one spirit of unconquer'd worth
To kindle those that now in bondage pine?
No! on its mountain air is slavery's breath,
And terror chills the hearts whose utter'd plaints were death.

XLVI.

Yet if thy light, fair Freedom, rested there,
How rich in charms were that romantic clime,
With streams, and woods, and pastoral valleys fair,
And wall'd with mountains haughtily sublime.
Heights, that might well be deem'd the Muses' reign,
Since, claiming proud alliance with the skies,
They lose in loftier spheres their wild domain.
Meet home for those retired divinities
That love, where nought of earth may e'er intrude,
Brightly to dwell on high, in lonely sanctitude.

XLVII.

There, in rude grandeur, daringly ascends
Stern Pindus, rearing many a pine-clad height;
He with the clouds his bleak dominion blends,
Frowning o'er vales, in woodland verdure bright.
Wild and august in consecrated pride,
There through the deep-blue heaven Olympus towers,

Girdled with mists, light-floating as to hide
The rock-built palace of immortal powers;
Where far on high the sunbeam finds repose,
Amidst th' eternal pomp of forests and of snows.

XLVIII.
Those savage cliffs and solitudes might seem
The chosen haunts where Freedom's foot would roam;
She loves to dwell by glen and torrent-stream,
And make the rocky fastnesses her home.
And in the rushing of the mountain flood,
In the wild eagle's solitary cry,
In sweeping winds that peal through cave and wood,
There is a voice of stern sublimity,
That swells her spirit to a loftier mood
Of solemn joy severe, of power, of fortitude.

XLIX.
But from those hills the radiance of her smile
Hath vanish'd long, her step hath fled afar;
O'er Suli's frowning rocks she paused a while,[22]
Kindling the watch-fires of the mountain war;
And brightly glow'd her ardent spirit there,
Still brightest 'midst privation: o'er distress
It cast romantic splendor, and despair
But fann'd that beacon of the wilderness;
And rude ravine, and precipice, and dell,
Sent their deep echoes forth, her rallying voice to swell.

L.
Dark children of the hills! 'twas then ye wrought
Deeds of fierce daring, rudely, sternly grand;
As 'midst your craggy citadels ye fought,
And women mingled with your warrior band.
Then on the cliff the frantic mother stood[23]
High o'er the river's darkly rolling wave,
And hurl'd, in dread delirium, to the flood
Her free-born infant, ne'er to be a slave.
For all was lost—all, save the power to die
The wild, indignant death of savage liberty.

LI.
Now is that strife a tale of vanish'd days,
With mightier things forgotten soon to lie;
Yet oft hath minstrel sung, in lofty lays,
Deeds less adventurous, energies less high.
And the dread struggle's fearful memory still
O'er each wild rock a wilder aspect throws;
Sheds darker shadows o'er the frowning hill,
More solemn quiet o'er the glen's repose;
Lends to the rustling pines a deeper moan,
And the hoarse river's voice a murmur not its own

LII.

For stillness now—the stillness of the dead,
Hath wrapt that conflict's lone and awful scene,
And man's forsaken homes, in ruin spread,
Tell where the storming of the cliffs hath been.
And there, o'er wastes magnificently rude,
What race may rove, unconscious of the chain?
Those realms have now no desert unsubdued,
Where freedom's banner may be rear'd again
Sunk are the ancient dwellings of her fame,
The children of her sons inherit but their name

LIII.

Go, seek proud Sparta's monuments and fanes!
In scatter'd fragments o'er the vale they lie;
Of all they were not e'en enough remains
To lend their fall a mournful majesty.[24]
Birth-place of those whose names we first revered
In song and story—temple of the free!
O thou, the stern, the haughty, and the fear'd,
Are such thy relics, and can this be thee?
Thou shouldst have left a giant-wreck behind,
And e'en in ruin claim'd the wonder of mankind.

LIV.

For thine were spirits cast in other mould
Than all beside—and proved by ruder test;
They stood alone—the proud, the firm, the bold,
With the same seal indelibly imprest.
Theirs were no bright varieties of mind,
One image stamp'd the rough, colossal race,
In rugged grandeur frowning o'er mankind,
Stern, and disdainful of each milder grace.
As to the sky some mighty rock may tower,
Whose front can brave the storm, but will not rear the flower

LV.

Such were thy sons—their life a battle day!
Their youth one lesson how for thee to die!
Closed is that task, and they have pass'd away
Like softer being train'd to aims less high.
Yet bright on earth *their* fame who proudly fell,
True to their shields, the champions of thy cause,
Whose funeral column bade the stranger tell
How died the brave, obedient to thy laws![25]
O lofty mother of heroic worth,
How couldst thou live to bring a meaner offspring forth?

LVI.

Hadst thou but perish'd with the free, nor known
A second race, when Glory's noon went by,

Then had thy name in single brightness shone
A watchword on the helm of liberty!
Thou shouldst have pass'd with all the light of fame,
And proudly sunk in ruins, not in chains.
But slowly set thy star 'midst clouds of shame,
And tyrants rose amidst thy falling fanes;
  And thou surrounded by thy warriors' graves,
Hast drain'd the bitter cup once mingled for thy slaves.

LVII.
Now all is o'er—for thee alike are flown
Freedom's bright noon, and Slavery's twilight cloud;
And in thy fall, as in thy pride, alone,
Deep solitude is round thee, as a shroud.
Home of Leonidas! thy halls are low,
From their cold altars have thy Lares fled,
O'er thee unmark'd the sunbeams fade or glow,
And wild-flowers wave, unbent by human tread;
  And 'midst thy silence, as the grave's profound,
A voice, a step, would seem as some unearthly sound.

LVIII.
Taygetus still lifts his awful brow,
High o'er the mouldering city of the dead,
Sternly sublime; while o'er his robe of snow
Heaven's floating tints their warm suffusions spread.
And yet his rippling wave Eurotas leads
By tombs and ruins o'er the silent plain,
While whisp'ring there, his own wild graceful reeds
Rise as of old, when hail'd by classic strain;
  There the rose laurels still in beauty wave,[26]
And a frail shrub survives to bloom o'er Sparta's grave.

LIX.
Oh! thus it is with man—a tree, a flower,
While nations perish, still renews its race.
And o'er the fallen records of his power
Spreads in wild pomp, or smiles in fairy grace.
The laurel shoots when those have pass'd away
Once rivals for its crown, the brave, the free;
The rose is flourishing o'er beauty's clay,
The myrtle blows when love hath ceased to be;
  Green waves the bay when song and bard are fled,
And all that round us blooms, is blooming o'er the dead.

LX.
And still the olive spreads its foliage round
Morea's fallen sanctuaries and towers,
Once its green boughs Minerva's votaries crown'd,
Deem'd a meet offering for celestial powers.
The suppliant's hand its holy branches bore;[27]
They waved around the Olympic victor's head;

And, sanctified by many a rite of yore,
Its leaves the Spartan's honour'd bier o'erspread :
Those rites have vanish'd—but o'er vale and hill
Its fruitful groves arise, revered and hallow'd still.[26]

LXI.

Where now thy shrines, Eleusis ! where thy fane,
Of fearful visions, mysteries wild and high ?
The pomp of rites, the sacrificial train,
The long procession's awful pageantry ?
Quench'd is the torch of Ceres[29]—all around
Decay hath spread the stillness of her reign,
There never more shall choral hymns resound,
O'er the hush'd earth and solitary main ;
Whose wave from Salamis deserted flows,
To bathe a silent shore of desolate repose.

LXII.

And oh ! ye secret and terrific powers,
Dark oracles ! in depth of groves that dwelt,
How are they sunk, the altars of your bowers,
Where Superstition trembled as she knelt !
Ye, the unknown, the viewless ones! that made
The elements your voice, the wind and wave ;
Spirits ! whose influence darken'd many a shade,
Mysterious visitants of fount and cave !
How long your power the awe-struck nations sway'd,
How long earth dreamt of you, and shudderingly obey'd !

LXIII.

And say, what marvel, in those early days,
While yet the light of heaven-born truth was not ;
If man around him cast a fearful gaze,
Peopling with shadowy powers each dell and grot ?
Awful is nature in her savage forms,
Her solemn voice commanding in its might,
And mystery then was in the rush of storms,
The gloom of woods, the majesty of night ;
And mortals heard Fate's language in the blast,
And rear'd your forest-shrines, ye phantoms of the past !

LXIV.

Then through the foliage not a breeze might sigh
But with prophetic sound—a waving tree.
A meteor flashing o'er the summer sky,
A bird's wild flight reveal'd the things to be.
All spoke of unseen natures, and convey'd
Their inspiration ; still they hover'd round,
Hallow'd the temple, whisper'd through the shade,
Pervaded loneliness, gave soul to sound ;
Of them the fount, the forest, murmur'd still,
Their voice was in the stream, their footstep on the hill.

LXV.

Now is the train of Superstition flown,
Unearthly Beings walk on earth no more;
The deep wind swells with no portentous tone,
The rustling wood breathes no fatidic lore.
Fled are the phantoms of Livadia's cave,
There dwell no shadows, but of crag and steep;
Fount of Oblivion! in thy gushing wave,[30]
That murmurs nigh, those powers of terror sleep.
Oh! that such dreams alone had fled that clime,
But Greece is changed in all that could be changed by time!

LXVI.

Her skies are those whence many a mighty bard
Caught inspiration, glorious as their beams;
Her hills the same that heroes died to guard,
Her vales, that foster'd Art's divinest dreams!
But that bright spirit o'er the land that shone,
And all around pervading influence pour'd,
That lent the harp of Æschylus its tone,
And proudly hallow'd Lacedæmon's sword,
And guided Phidias o'er the yielding stone,
With them its ardors lived—with them its light is flown.

LXVII.

Thebes, Corinth, Argos!—ye, renown'd of old,
Where are your chiefs of high romantic name?
How soon the tale of ages may be told!
A page, a verse, records the fall of fame,
The work of centuries—we gaze on you,
Oh cities! once the glorious and the free,
The lofty tales that charm'd our youth renew,
And wondering ask, if these their scenes could be?
Search for the classic fane, the regal tomb,
And find the mosque alone—a record of their doom!

LXVIII.

How oft hath war his host of spoilers pour'd,
Fair Elis! o'er thy consecrated vales?[31]
There have the sunbeams glanced on spear and sword,
And banners floated on the balmy gales.
Once didst thou smile, secure in sanctitude,
As some enchanted isle 'mid stormy seas;
On thee no hostile footstep might intrude,
And pastoral sounds alone were on thy breeze.
Forsaken home of peace! that spell is broke,
Thou too hast heard the storm, and bow'd beneath the yoke.

LXIX.

And through Arcadia's wild and lone retreats
Far other sounds have echo'd than the strain

Of faun and dryad, from their woodland seats,
Or ancient reed of peaceful mountain-swain !
There, though at times Alpheus yet surveys,
On his green banks renew'd, the classic dance,
And nymph-like forms, and wild melodious lays,
Revive the silvan scenes of old romance ;
Yet brooding fear and dark suspicion dwell
Midst Pan's deserted haunts, by fountain, cave, and dell.

LXX.

But thou, fair Attica ! whose rocky bound
All art and nature's richest gifts enshrined,
Thou little sphere, whose soul-illumined round
Concentrated each sunbeam of the mind ;
Who, as the summit of some Alpine height
Glows earliest, latest, with the blush of day,
Didst first imbibe the splendors of the light,
And smile the longest in its lingering ray ;[32]
Oh ! let us gaze on thee, and fondly deem
The past awhile restored, the present but a dream.

LXXI.

Let Fancy's vivid hues awhile prevail—
Wake at her call—be all thou wert once more !
Hark !—hymns of triumph swell on every gale !
Lo—bright processions move along thy shore !
Again thy temples, 'midst the olive shade,
Lovely in chaste simplicity arise ;
And graceful monuments, in grove and glade,
Catch the warm tints of thy resplendent skies ;
And sculptured forms of high and heavenly mien,
In their calm beauty smile, around the sun-bright scene.

LXXII.

Again renew'd by Thought's creative spells,
In all her pomp thy city, Theseus ! towers:
Within, around, the light of glory dwells
On art's fair fabrics, wisdom's holy bowers.
There marble fanes in finish'd grace ascend,
The pencil's world of life and beauty glows ;
Shrines, pillars, porticoes, in grandeur blend,
Rich with the trophies of barbaric foes ;
And groves of platane wave, in verdant pride
The sage's blest retreats, by calm Illissus' tide.

LXXIII.

Bright as that fairy vision of the wave,
Raised by the magic of Morgana's wand,[33]
On summer seas, that undulating lave
Romantic Sicily's Arcadian strand ;
That pictured scene of airy colonnades,
Light palaces, in shadowy glory drest,

Enchanted groves, and temples, and arcades,
Gleaming and floating on the ocean's breast;
Athens! thus fair the dream of thee appears,
As Fancy's eye pervades the veiling cloud of years.

LXXIV.
Still be that cloud withdrawn—oh! mark on high,
Crowning yon hill with temples richly graced,
That fane, august in perfect symmetry,
The purest model of Athenian taste.
Fair Parthenon! thy Doric pillars rise
In simple dignity, thy marble's hue
Unsullied shines, relieved by brilliant skies,
That round thee spread their deep ethereal blue;
And art o'er all thy light proportions throws
The harmony of grace, the beauty of repose.

LXXV.
And lovely o'er thee sleeps the sunny glow,
When morn and eve in tranquil splendor reign,
And on thy sculptures, as they smile, bestow
Hues that the pencil emulates in vain.
Then the fair forms by Phidias wrought, unfold
Each latent grace, developing in light,
Catch from soft clouds of purple and of gold,
Each tint that passes, tremulously bright;
And seem indeed whate'er devotion deems,
While so suffused with heaven, so mingling with its beams.

LXXVI.
But oh! what words the vision may portray,
The form of sanctitude that guards thy shrine?
There stands thy goddess, robed in war's array,
Supremely glorious, awfully divine!
With spear and helm she stands, and flowing vest,
And sculptured ægis, to perfection wrought,
And on each heavenly lineament imprest,
Calmly sublime, the majesty of thought;
The pure intelligence, the chaste repose,—
All that a poet's dream around Minerva throws.

LXXVII.
Bright age of Pericles! let fancy still
Through time's deep shadows all thy splendor trace,
And in each work of art's consummate skill
Hail the free spirit of thy lofty race.
That spirit, roused by every proud reward
That hope could picture, glory could bestow,
Foster'd by all the sculptor and the bard
Could give of immortality below.
Thus were thy heroes form'd, and o'er their name
Thus did thy genius shed imperishable fame.

LXXVIII.
Mark in the throng'd Ceramicus, the train
Of mourners weeping o'er the martyr'd brave:
Proud be the tears devoted to the slain,
Holy the amaranth strew'd upon their grave![34]
And hark—unrivall'd eloquence proclaims
Their deeds, their trophies, with triumphant voice!
Hark—Pericles records their honor'd names![35]
Sons of the fallen, in their lot rejoice:
What hath life brighter than so bright a doom?
What power hath fate to soil the garlands of the tomb?

LXXIX.
Praise to the valiant dead! for them doth art
Exhaust her skill, their triumphs bodying forth;
Theirs are enshrined names, and every heart
Shall bear the blazon'd impress of their worth.
Bright on the dreams of youth their fame shall rise,
Their fields of fight shall epic song record;
And, when the voice of battle rends the skies,
Their name shall be their country's rallying word!
While fane and column rise august to tell
How Athens honors those for her who proudly fell.

LXXX.
City of Theseus! bursting on the mind,
Thus dost thou rise, in all thy glory fled!
Thus guarded by the mighty of mankind,
Thus hallow'd by the memory of the dead:
Alone in beauty and renown—a scene
Whose tints are drawn from freedom's loveliest ray.
'Tis but a vision now—yet thou hast been
More than the brightest vision might portray;
And every stone with but a vestige fraught
Of thee hath latent power to wake some lofty thought.

LXXXI.
Fall'n are thy fabrics, that so oft have rung
To choral melodies, and tragic lore;
Now is the lyre of Sophocles unstrung,
The song that hail'd Harmodius peals no more.
Thy proud Piræus is a desert strand,
Thy stately shrines are mould'ring on their hill,
Closed are the triumphs of the sculptor's hand,
The magic voice of eloquence is still;
Minerva's veil is rent[36]—her image gone,
Silent the sage's bower—the warrior's tomb o'erthrown.

LXXXII.
Yet in decay thine exquisite remains
Wond'ring we view, and silently revere,

As traces left on earth's forsaken plains
By vanish'd beings of a nobler sphere!
Not all the old magnificence of Rome,
All that dominion there hath left to time;
Proud Coliseum, or commanding dome,
Triumphal arch, or obelisk sublime,
Can bid such reverence o'er the spirit steal,
As aught by thee imprest with beauty's plastic seal.

LXXXIII.
Though still the empress of the sunburnt waste,
·Palmyra rises, desolately grand—
Though with rich gold[37] and massy sculpture graced,
Commanding still, Persepolis may stand
In haughty solitude—though sacred Nile
The first-born temples of the world surveys,
And many an awful and stupendous pile
Thebes of the hundred gates e'en yet displays;
City of Pericles! O who, like thee,
Can teach how fair the works of mortal hand may be?

LXXXIV
Thou led'st the way to that illumined sphere
Where sovereign beauty dwells; and thence didst bear,
Oh, still triumphant in that high career!
Bright archetypes of all the grand and fair.
And still to thee th' enlighten'd mind hath flown
As to her country;—thou hast been to earth
A cynosure;—and, e'en from victory's throne,
Imperial Rome gave homage to thy worth;
And nations, rising to their fame afar,
Still to thy model turn, as seamen to their star.

LXXXV.
Glory to those whose relics thus arrest
The gaze of ages! Glory to the free!
For they, they only, could have thus imprest
Their mighty image on the years to be!
Empires and cities in oblivion lie,
Grandeur may vanish, conquest be forgot—
To leave on earth renown that cannot die,
Of high-soul'd genius is th' unrivall'd lot.
Honor to thee, O Athens! thou hast shown
What mortals may attain, and seized the palm alone.

LXXXVI.
Oh! live there those who view with scornful eyes
All that attests the brightness of thy prime?
Yes; they who dwell beneath thy lovely skies,
And breathe th' inspiring ether of thy clime!
Their path is o'er the mightiest of the dead,
Their homes are 'midst the works of noblest arts;

LXXXVII.

Yet all around their gaze, beneath their tread,
Not one proud thrill of loftier thought imparts.
Such are the conquerors of Minerva's land,
Where Genius first reveal'd the triumphs of his hand!

LXXXVII.

For them in vain the glowing light may smile
O'er the pale marble, coloring's warmth to shed,
And in chaste beauty many a sculptured pile
Still o'er the dust of heroes lift its head.
No patriot feeling binds them to the soil,
Whose tombs and shrines their fathers have not rear'd,
Their glance is cold indifference, and their toil
But to destroy what ages have revered,
As if exulting sternly to erase
Whate'er might prove *that* land had nursed a nobler race.

LXXXVIII.

And who may grieve that, rescued from their hands,
Spoilers of excellence and foes to art,
Thy relics, Athens! borne to other lands,
Claim homage still to thee from every heart?
Though now no more th' exploring stranger's sight,
Fix'd in deep reverence on Minerva's fane,
Shall hail, beneath their native heaven of light,
All that remain'd of forms adored in vain;
A few short years—and, vanish'd from the scene,
To blend with classic dust their proudest lot had been.

LXXXIX.

Fair Parthenon! yet still must Fancy weep
For thee, thou work of nobler spirits flown.
Bright, as of old, the sunbeams o'er thee sleep
In all their beauty still—and thine is gone!
Empires have sunk since thou wert first revered,
And varying rites have sanctified thy shrine.
The dust is round thee of the race that rear'd
Thy walls; and thou—their fate must soon be thine!
But when shall earth again exult to see
Visions divine like theirs renew'd in aught like thee?

XC.

Lone are thy pillars now—each passing gale
Sighs o'er them as a spirit's voice, which moan'd
That loneliness, and told the plaintive tale
Of the bright synod once above them throned.
Mourn, graceful ruin! on thy sacred hill,
Thy gods, thy rites, a kindred fate have shared:
Yet art thou honor'd in each fragment still
That wasting years and barbarous hands had spared;
Each hallow'd stone from rapine's fury borne,
Shall wake bright dreams of thee in ages yet unborn.

XCI.

Yes; in those fragments, though by time defaced
And rude insensate conquerors, yet remains
All that may charm th' enlighten'd eye of taste,
On shores where still inspiring freedom reigns.
As vital fragrance breathes from every part
Of the crush'd myrtle, or the bruised rose,
E'en thus th' essential energy of art
There in each wreck imperishably glows![38]
The soul of Athens lives in every line,
Pervading brightly still the ruins of her shrine.

XCII.

Mark—on the storied frieze the graceful train,
The holy festival's triumphal throng,
In fair procession, to Minerva's fane,
With many a sacred symbol, move along.
There every shade of bright existence trace,
The fire of youth, the dignity of age;
The matron's calm austerity of grace,
The ardent warrior, the benignant sage;
The nymph's light symmetry, the chief's proud mien;
Each ray of beauty caught and mingled in the scene.

XCIII.

Art unobstrusive there ennobles form,[39]
Each pure chaste outline exquisitely flows;
There e'en the steed, with bold expression warm,[40]
Is clothed with majesty, with being glows.
One mighty mind hath harmonized the whole;
Those varied groups the same bright impress bear;
One beam and essence of exalting soul
Lives in the grand, the delicate, the fair;
And well that pageant of the glorious dead
Blends us with nobler days, and loftier spirits fled.

XCIV.

O, conquering Genius! that couldst thus detain
The subtle graces, fading as they rise,
Eternalize expression's fleeting reign,
Arrest warm life in all its energies,
And fix them on the stone—thy glorious lot
Might wake ambition's envy, and create
Powers half divine: while nations are forgot,
A thought, a dream of thine hath vanquish'd fate!
And when thy hand first gave its wonders birth,
The realms that hail them now scarce claim'd a name on earth

XCV.

Wert thou some spirit of a purer sphere
But once beheld, and never to return?

No—we may hail again thy bright career,
Again on earth a kindred fire shall burn!
Though thy least relics, e'en in ruin bear
A stamp of heaven, that ne'er hath been renew'd—
A light inherent—let not man despair:
Still be hope ardent, patience unsubdued;
For still is nature fair, and thought divine,
And art hath won a world in models pure as thine.[41]

XCVI.

Gaze on yon forms, corroded and defaced—
Yet there the germ of future glory lies!
Their virtual grandeur could not be erased;
It clothes them still, though veil'd from common eyes.
They once were gods and heroes[42]—and beheld
As the blest guardians of their native scene;
And hearts of warriors, sages, bards, have swell'd
With awe that owned their sovereignty of mien.
—Ages have vanish'd since those hearts were cold,
And still those shatter'd forms retain their godlike mould.

XCVII.

'Midst their bright kindred, from their marble throne
They have look'd down on thousand storms of time;
Surviving power, and fame and freedom flown,
They still remain'd, still tranquilly sublime!
Till mortal hands the heavenly conclave marr'd.
Th' Olympian groups have sunk, and are forgot;
Not e'en their dust could weeping Athens guard—
But these were destined to a nobler lot!
And they have borne, to light another land,
The quenchless ray that soon shall gloriously expand.

XCVIII.

Phidias! supreme in thought! what hand but thine,
In human works thus blending earth and heaven,
O'er nature's truth hath shed that grace divine,
To mortal form immortal grandeur given?
What soul but thine, infusing all its power,
In these last monuments of matchless days,
Could, from their ruins, bid young Genius tower,
And hope aspire to more exalted praise?
And guide deep Thought to that secluded height
Where Excellence is throned, in purity of light.

XCIX.

And who can tell how pure, how bright a flame,
Caught from these models, may illume the west?
What British Angelo may rise to fame,[43]
On the free isle what beams of art may rest?
Deem not, O England! that by climes confined,
Genius and taste diffuse a partial ray;[44]

Deem not th' eternal energies of mind
 Sway'd by that sun whose doom is but decay!
 Shall thought be foster'd but by skies serene?
No! thou hast power to be what Athens e'er hath been.

C.

But thine are treasures oft unprized, unknown,
And cold neglect hath blighted many a mind,
O'er whose young ardors had thy smile but shone,
Their soaring flight had left a world behind!
And many a gifted hand, that might have wrought
To Grecian excellence the breathing stone,
Or each pure grace of Raphael's pencil caught,
Leaving no record of its power, is gone!
 While thou hast fondly sought, on distant coast,
Gems far less rich than those, thus precious, and thus lost.

CI.

Yet rise, O land, in all but art alone,
Bid the sole wreath that is not thine be won!
Fame dwells around thee—Genius is thine own;
Call his rich blooms to life—be thou their sun!
So, should dark ages o'er thy glory sweep,
Should *thine* e'er be as now are Grecian plains,
Nations unborn shall track thine own blue deep,
To hail thy shore, to worship thy remains;
 Thy mighty monuments with reverence trace,
And cry, "This ancient soil hath nursed a glorious race!"

NOTES

Note 1, page 137, line 12.
Round Doric Pæstum's solitary fanes.

"The Pæstan rose, from its peculiar fragrance and the singularity of blowing twice a-year, is often mentioned by the classic poets. The wild rose, which now shoots up among the ruins, is of the small single damask kind, with a very high perfume; as a farmer assured me on the spot, it flowers both in spring and autumn."—SWINBURNE's *Travels in the Two Sicilies.*

Note 2, page 137, line 30.
Swell'd o'er that tide—the sons of battle sleep.

In the naval engagements of the Greeks. "it was usual for the soldiers before the fight to sing a pæan or hymn, to Mars, and after the fight another to Apollo."—See POTTER's *Antiquities of Greece,* vol. ii. p. 155

Note 3. page 138, line 26.
Her own bright East, thy son, Morea! flies.

The emigration of the natives of the Morea to different parts of Asia is thus mentioned by Chateaubriand in his *Itinéraire de Paris à Jerusalem*—"Parvenu au dernier degré du malheur, le Moraïte s'arrache de son pays, et va chercher en Asie un sort moins rigoureux Vain espoir! il retrouve des cadis et des pachas jusques dans les sables de Jourdain et dans les deserts de Palmyre."

Note 4, page 139, line 23.
Wilt thou receive the wanderer to thine arms.

In the same work, Chateaubriand also relates his having met with several Greek emigrants who had established themselves in the woods of Florida.

Note 5, page 139, line 23.
And isles of flowers, bright-floating o'er the tide.

"La grace est toujours unie à la magnificence dans les scènes de la nature: et tandis que le courant du milieu entraîne vers la mer les cadavres des pins et des chênes, on voit sur les deux courant latéraux, remontes, le long des rivages des îles flottantes de Pistia et de Nénuphar, dont les roses jaunes s'élèvent comme de petits papillons."—*Description of the Banks of the Mississippi*, CHATEAUBRIAND's *Atala.*

Note 6, page 141, line 20.
Wild, as when sung by bards of elder time.

"Looking generally at the narrowness and abruptness of this mountain-channel (Tempe,) and contrasting it with the course of the Peneus, through the plains of Thessaly, the imagination instantly recurs to the tradition that these plains were once covered with water, for which some convulsion of nature 'had subsequently opened this narrow passage. The term *vale*, in our language, is usually employed to describe scenery in which the predominant features are breadth, beauty, and repose. The reader has already perceived that the term is wholly inapplicable to the scenery at this spot, and that the phrase, *vale* of Tempe, is one that depends on poetic fiction. . . . . The real character of Tempe, though it perhaps be less beautiful, yet possesses more of magnificence than is implied in the epithet given to it. . . . . To those who have visited St. Vincent's rocks, below Bristol, I cannot convey a more sufficient idea of Tempe, than by saying that its scenery resembles, though on a much larger scale, that of the former place. The Peneus, indeed, as it flows through the valley, is not greatly wider than the Avon; and the channel between the cliffs is equally contracted in its dimensions; but these cliffs themselves are much loftier and more precipitous, and project their vast masses of rock with still more extraordinary abruptness over the hollow beneath."—HOLLAND's *Travels in Albania, &c*

Note 7, page 141, line 21.
Years, that have changed thy river's classic name.
The modern name of the Peneus is Salympria.

Note 8, page 141, line 26.
Where the rich arbute's coral-berries glow.

"Towards the lower part of Tempe, these cliffs are peaked in a very singular manner, and form projecting angles on the vast perpendicular faces of rock which they present towards the chasm; where the surface renders it possible, the summits and ledges of the rocks are for the most part covered with small wood, chiefly oak, with the arbutus and other shrubs. On the banks of the river, wherever there is a small interval between the water and the cliffs, it is covered by the rich and widely spreading foliage of the plane, the oak, and other forest trees, which in these situations have attained a remarkable size, and in various places extend their shadow far over the channel of the stream." . . . . "The rocks on each side of the vale of Tempe are evidently the same; what may be called, I believe, a coarse, bluish-grey marble with veins and portions of the rock, in which the marble is of finer quality."—HOLLAND'S *Travels in Albania, &c*.

Note 9, page 141, last line.
Where Greece her councils held, her Pythian victors crown'd.

The Amphictyonic council was convened in spring and autumn at Delphi or Thermopylæ, and presided at the Pythian games which were celebrated at Delphi every fifth year.

Note 10, page 142, line 6.
Bloom the wild laurel o'er the warlike dead.

"This spot (the field of Mantinea) on which so many brave men were laid to rest, is now covered with rosemary and laurels."—POUQUEVILLE's *Travels in the Morea.*

Note 11, page 143, line 24.
Where the dark upas taints the gale around.

For the accounts of the upas or poison-tree of Java, now generally believed to be fabulous, or greatly exaggerated, see the notes to DARWIN's *Botanic Garden.*

Note 12, page 143, line 35.
Its sculptured lions, richly wrought arcades.

"The court most to be admired of the Alhambra is that called the court of the Lions; it is ornamented with sixty elegant pillars of an architecture which bears not the least resemblance to any of the known orders, and might be called the Arabian order. . . But its principal ornament, and that from which it took its name, is an alabaster cup, six feet in diameter, supported by twelve lions, which is said to have been made in imitation of the Brazen Sea of Solomon's temple."—BOURGOANNE's *Travels in Spain.*

Note 13, page 143, line 42.

Bright as that Pleïad sphered in Mecca's fane.

"Sept des plus fameux parmi les anciens poëtes Arabiques, son designés par les ecrivains orientaux sous le nom de *Pleïade Arabique*, et leurs ouvrages etaient suspendus autour de la Caaba, ou Mosque de la Mecque."— SISMONDI *Litterature du Midi.*

Note 14, page 144, line 21.

And thou O last and noblest Constantine!

"The distress and fall of the last Constantine are more glorious than the long prosperity of the Byzantine Cæsars."—GIBBON's *Decline and Fall, &c.*, vol. xii. p. 226.

Note 15, page 144, line 26.

The closing night of that imperial race!

See the description of the night previous to the taking of Constantinople by Mahomet II.—GIBBON's *Decline and Fall, &c.*, vol. xii. p. 225.

Note 16, page 144, last line.

And the Seven Towers are scaled, and all is won and lost.

"This building (the Castle of the Seven Towers) is mentioned as early as the sixth century of the Christian era, as a spot which contributed to the defence of Constantinople, and it was the principal bulwark of the town on the coast of the Propontis, in the last periods of the empire."—POUQUEVILLE's *Travels in the Morea.*

Note 17, page 145, line 12.

Preserved inviolate their awful fane.

See the account from Herodotus of the supernatural defence of Delphi.—MITFORD's *Greece*, vol. i. p. 396–7.

Note 18, page 145, line 26.

Who from the dead at Marathon arose.

"In succeeding ages the Athenians honored Theseus as a demigod, induced to it as well by other reasons as because, when they were fighting the Medes at Marathon, a considerable part of the army thought they saw the apparition of Theseus completely armed, and bearing down before them upon the barbarians."—LANGHORNE's *Plutarch, Life of Theseus.*

Note 19, page 145, line 29.

Or they whose forms, to Alaric's awe-struck eye.

"From Thermopylæ to Sparta, the leader of the Goths (Alaric) pursued his victorious march without encountering any mortal antagonist; but one of the advocates of expiring paganism has confidently asserted that the walls of Athens were guarded by the goddess Minerva, with her formidable ægis, and by the angry phantom of Achilles, and the conqueror was dismayed by the presence of the hostile deities of Greece."—GIBBON's *Decline and Fall, &c.*, vol. v. p. 183.

Note 20, page 145, line 31.

Ye slept, oh heroes : chief ones of the earth.

"Even all the *chief ones of the earth*."—ISAIAH, chap. xiv.

Note 21, page 146, line 6.
Perish'd the conquering weapons of your war.
"How are the mighty fallen, and the weapons of war perished!"
—SAMUEL, book ii. chap. i.

Note 22, page 147, line 17.
O'er Suli's frowning rocks she paused awhile.
For several interesting particulars relative to the Suliote warfare with Ali Pasha, see HOLLAND's *Travels in Albania.*

Note 23, page 147, line 29.
Then on the cliff the frantic mother stood.
" It is related as an authentic story, that a group of Suliote women assembled on one of the precipices adjoining the modern seraglio, and threw their infants into the chasm below, that they might not become the slaves of the enemy."—HOLLAND's *Travels, &c.*

Note 24, page 148, line 14.
To lend their fall a mournful majesty.
The ruins of Sparta, near the modern town of Mistra, are very inconsiderable, and only sufficient to mark the site of the ancient city. The scenery around them is described by travellers as very striking.

Note 25, page 148, line 38.
How died the brave, obedient to thy laws.
The inscription composed by Simonides for the Spartan monument in the pass of Thermopylæ has been thus translated: "Stranger, go tell the Lacedemonians that we have obeyed their laws, and that we lie here."

Note 26, page 149, line 27.
There the rose-laurels still in beauty wave.
" In the Eurotas I observed abundance of those famous reeds which were known in the earliest ages, and all the rivers and marshes of Greece are replete with rose-laurels, while the springs and rivulets are covered with lilies, tuberoses, hyacinths, and narcissus orientalis.'—POUQUEVILLE's *Travels in the Morea.*

Note 27, page 149, line 43.
The suppliant's hand its holy branches bore.
It was usual for suppliants to carry an olive branch bound with wool.

Note 28, page 150, line 4.
Its fruitful groves arise, revered and hallow'd still.
The olive, according to Pouqueville, is still regarded with veneration by the people of the Morea.

Note 29, page 150, line 9.
Quench'd is the torch of Ceres—all around.
It was customary at Eleusis, on the fifth day of the festival, for men and women to run about with torches in their hands, and also to dedicate torches to Ceres, and to contend who should present the largest. This was done in memory of the journey of Ceres in search of Proserpine, during which she was lighted by a torch kindled in the flames of Etna.—POTTER's *Antiquities of Greece*, vol. i. p 392.

Note 30, page 151, line 7.
Fount of Oblivion! in thy gushing wave.
The fountains of Oblivion and Memory, with the Hercynian foun-

tain, are still to be seen amongst the rocks near Livadia, though the situation of the cave of Trophonius, in their vicinity, cannot be exactly ascertained.—See HOLLAND's *Travels*.

Note 31, page 151, line 32.
Fair Elis, o'er thy consecrated vales.

Elis was anciently a sacred territory, its inhabitants being considered as consecrated to the service of Jupiter. All armies marching through it delivered up their weapons, and received them again when they had passed its boundary.

Note 32, page 152, line 16.
And smile the longest in its lingering ray.

"We are assured by Thucydides that Attica was the province of Greece in which population first became settled, and where the earliest progress was made toward civilization."—MITFORD's *Greece*, vol. i. p. 35.

Note 33, page 152, line 40.
Raised by the magic of Morgana's wand.

Fata Morgana. This remarkable aërial phenomenon, which is thought by the lower order of Sicilians to be the work of a fairy, is thus described by Father Angelucci, whose account is quoted by Swinburne.

"On the 15th August, 1643, I was surprised, as I stood at my window, with a most wonderful spectacle: the sea that washes the Sicilian shore swelled up, and became, for ten miles in length, like a chain of dark mountains, while the waters near our Calabrian coast grew quite smooth, and in an instant appeared like one clear polished mirror. On this glass was depicted, in chiaro scuro, a string of several thousands of pilasters, all equal in height, distance, and degrees of light and shade. In a moment they bent into arcades, like Roman aqueducts. A long cornice was next formed at the top, and above it rose innumerable castles, all perfectly alike; these again changed into towers, which were shortly after lost in colonnades, then windows, and at last ended in pines, cypresses, and other trees."—SWINBURNE's *Travels in the Two Sicilies*.

Note 34, page 154, line 4.
Holy the amaranth strew'd upon their grave.

All sorts of purple and white flowers were supposed by the Greeks to be acceptable to the dead, and used in adorning tombs; as amaranth, with which the Thessalians decorated the tomb of Achilles.—POTTER's *Antiquities of Greece*, vol. ii. p. 232.

Note 35, page 154, line 7.
Hark! Pericles records their honor'd names.

Pericles, on his return to Athens after the reduction of Samos, celebrated, in a splendid manner, the obsequies of his countrymen who fell in that war, and pronounced himself the funeral oration usual on such occasions. This gained him great applause; and when he came down from the rostrum, the women paid their respects to him, and presented him with crowns and chaplets, like a champion just returned victorious from the lists.—LANGHORNE's *Plutarch, Life of Pericles*.

Note 36, page 154, line 39.
Minerva's veil is rent—her image gone.

The peplus, which is supposed to have been suspended as an awning over the statue of Minerva, in the Parthenon, was a principal ornament of the Panathenaic festival; and it was embroidered with various colors, representing the battle of the Gods and Titans, and the exploits of Athenian heroes. When the festival was celebrated, the peplus was brought from the Aciopolis, and suspended as a sail to the vessel, which on that day was conducted through the Ceramicus and principal streets of Athens, till it had made the circuit of the Acropolis. The peplus was then carried to the Parthenon, and consecrated to Minerva.—See CHANDLER's *Travels*, STUART's *Athens, &c.*

Note 37, page 155, line 11.
Though with rich gold and massy sculpture graced.

The gilding amidst the ruins of Persepolis is still, according to Winckelmann, in high preservation.

Note 38, page 157, line 8.
There in each wreck imperishably glows.

"In the most broken fragment, the same great principle of life can be proved to exist, as in the most perfect figure," is one of the observations of Mr. Haydon on the Elgin Marbles.

Note 39, page 157, line 21.
Art unobtrusive there ennobles form.

"Everything here breathes life, with a veracity, with an exquisite knowledge of art, but without the least ostentation or parade of it, which is concealed by consummate and masterly skill."—CANOVA's *Letter to the Earl of Elgin.*

Note 40, page 157, line 23.
There e'en the steed, with bold expression warm.

Mr. West, after expressing his admiration of the horse's head in Lord Elgin's collection of Athenian sculpture, thus proceeds :—"We feel the same when we view the young equestrian Athenians, and in observing them, we are insensibly carried on with the impression that they and their horses actually existed, as we see them, at the instant when they were converted into marble."—WEST's *Second letter to Lord Elgin.*

Note 41, page 158, line 8.
And art hath won a world in models pure as thine.

Mr. Flaxman thinks that sculpture has very greatly improved within these last twenty years, and that his opinion is not singular—because works of such prime importance as the Elgin Marbles could not remain in any country without a consequent improvement of the public taste, and the talents of the artist.—See the *Evidence given in Reply to Interrogatories from the Committee on the Elgin Marbles.*

Note 42, page 158, line 13.
They once were gods and heroes—and beheld.

The Theseus and Ilissus, which are considered by Sir T. Lawrence, Mr. Westmacott, and other distinguished artists, to be of a higher class than the Apollo Belvidere, "because there is in them a union of very grand form, with a more true and natural expression of the effect of action upon the human frame than there is in the Apollo, or any of the other more celebrated statues.—See *The Evidence, &c.*

Note 43, page 158, line 41.
What British Angelo may rise to fame.

"Let us suppose a young man at this time in London, endowed with powers such as enabled Michael Angelo to advance the arts, as he did, by the aid of one mutilated specimen of Grecian excellence in sculpture, to what an eminence might not such a genius carry art, by the opportunity of studying those sculptures, in the aggregate, which adorned the Temple of Minerva at Athens?—WEST's *Second Letter to Lord Elgin.*

Note 44, page 158, last line.
Genius and taste diffuse a partial ray.

In allusion to the theories of Du Bos, Winckelmann, Montesquieu, &c., with regard to the inherent obstacles in the climate of England to the progress of genius and the arts.—See HOARE's *Epochs of the Arts,* page 84, 85.

CRITICAL ANNOTATIONS

ON "TALES AND HISTORIC SCENES."

" *Tales and Historic Scenes* is a collection, as the title imports, of narrative poems. Perhaps it was not on consideration that Mrs Hemans passed from a poem of picture-drawing and reflection to the writing of tales; but if we were to prescribe to a young poet his *course* of practice, this would certainly be our advice. The luxuriance of a young fancy delights in description, and the quickness and inexperience of the same age, in passing judgments;—in the one richness, in the other antithesis and effect, are too often more sought after than truth: the poem is written rapidly, and correctness but little attended to. But in narration more care must be taken : if the tale be fictitious, the conception and sustainment of the characters, the disposition of the facts, the relief of the soberer parts by description, reflection, or dialogue, form so many useful studies for a growing artist. If the tale be borrowed from history, a more delicate task is added to those just mentioned, in determining how far it may be necessary, or safe, to interweave the ornaments of fiction with the groundwork of truth, and in skilfully performing that difficult task. In both cases, the mind is compelled to make a more sustained effort, and acquires thereby greater vigor, and a more practical readiness in the detail of the art.

" The principal poem in this volume is *The Abencerrage.* It commemorates the capture of Granada by Ferdinand and Isabella, and attributes it, in a great measure to the revenge of Hamet, chief of the Abencerrages, who had been induced to turn his arms against his countrymen, the Moors, in order to procure the ruin of their king, the murderer of his father and brothers. During the siege, he makes his way by night to the bower of Zayda, his beloved, the daughter of a rival and hated family. Her character is very finely drawn; and she repels with firmness all the solicitations and prayers of the traitor to his country. The following lines form part of their dialogue: they are spirited and pathetic, but perfectly free from exaggeration:—

' Oh! wert thou still what once I fondly deem'd,' " &c.

Vide pages 27—8 *Quarterly Review,* vol xxiv.

" The more we become acquainted with Mrs. Hemans as a poet, the more we are delighted with her productions, and astonished by her powers. She will, she must, take her place among eminent poets If she has a rival of her own sex, it is Joanna Baillie; but even compared with the living *masters* of the lyre, she is entitled to a very high distinction.

* * * * * * *

"Mrs. Hemans manifests, in her own fine imagination, a fund which is less supported by loan than the wealth of some very eminent poets whom we could name. We think it impossible that she can write by mere rule, more than on credit. If she did, her poetry would lose all its charms. It is by inspiration—as it is poetically called—by a fine tact of sympathy, a vivacity and fertility of imagination, that she pours forth her enchanting song, and 'builds her lofty rhyme.' The judicious propriety wherewith she bestows on each element of her composition its due share of fancy and of feeling, much increases our respect for her powers. With an exquisite airiness and spirit, with an imagery which quite sparkles, are touched her lighter delineations; with a rich and glowing pencil, her descriptions of visible nature: a sublime eloquence is the charm of her sentiments of magnanimity; while she melts into tenderness with a grace in which she has few equals.

"It appears to us that Mrs. Hemans has yielded her own to the public taste in conveying her poetry in the vehicle of tales."—*Edinburgh Monthly Review*, vol. ii.

"*The Abencerrage* is a romance, the scene of which is appropriately laid in a most romantic period, and in the country of all others in which the spirit of romance was most powerful, and lingered longest—in the kingdom of Granada, where the power of the Moors was first established, and had the greatest continuance. . . . . The leading events of the narrative are strictly historical, and with these the fate and suffering of the unfortunate lovers are very naturally interwoven. The beauty of the descriptions here is exquisite. . . . . Choice is bewildered among the many fine passages we are tempted to extract from 'The Abencerrage.'

"If any reader considers our strictures tedious, and our extracts profuse, our best apology is, that the luxury of doing justice to so much genuine talent, adorning so much private worth, does not often occur to tempt us to an excess of this nature."—Rev. ROBERT MOREHEAD, author of *Dialogues on Natural and Revealed Religion. Specimens of Translation, &c.*—*Constables Magazine*, vol. v.

CRITICAL ANNOTATIONS

ON "THE RESTORATION OF THE WORKS OF ART TO ITALY," AND ON "MODERN GREECE."

"In our reviews of poetical productions, the better efforts of genius hold out to us a task at once more useful and delightful than those of inferior merit. In the former, the beautiful predominate, and expose while they excuse the blemishes. But the public taste would receive no benefit from a detail of mediocrity, relieved only by the censure of faults uncompensated by excellencies. We have great pleasure in calling the attention of our readers to the beautiful poem before us, which we believe to be the work of the same lady who last year put her name to the second edition of another poem on a kindred subject,

The Restoration of the Works of Art to Italy—namely, Mrs. Hemans of North Wales. That the author's fame has not altogether kept pace with her merit, we are inclined to think is a reproach to the public Poetry is at present experiencing the fickleness of fashion, and may be said to have had its day. Very recently, the *reading* public, as the phrase is, was immersed in poetry, but seems to have had enough ; and, excepting always that portion of it who are found to relish genuine poetry on its own intrinsic account, and will never tire of the exquisite enjoyment which it affords, the said public seldom read poetry at all.

* * * * * * * *

"But so little is that excitement which the bulk of readers covet necessarily connected with poetry, that these readers have tired even of romances in a metrical form, and are regarding all their late rhythmical favorites alike, with that sort of ingratitude with which repletion would lead them to regard a banquet when the dishes are removing from the table. But this is no proof that these great poets have forfeited their title to be admired. They are fixed orbs, which stand just where they did, and shine just as they were wont, although they seem to decline to the world, which revolves the opposite way But if the world will turn from the poet, whatever be his merit, there is an end of his popularity, inasmuch as the most approved conductor of the latter is the multitude, as essentially as is the air, of the sound of his voice. Profit will also fail from the lack of purchasers ; and poetry, high as it may intrinsically seem, must fall, commercially speaking, to its ancient proverbially unprofitable level. Yet poetry will still be poetry, however it may cease *to pay ;* and although the acclaim of multitudes is one thing, and the still small voice of genuine taste and feeling another, the nobler incense of the latter will ever be its reward.

"Our readers will now cease to wonder, that an author like the present, who has had no higher aim than to regale the imagination with imagery, warm the heart with sentiment and feeling, and delight the ear with music, without the foreign aid of tale or fable, has hitherto written to a select few, and passed almost unnoticed by the multitude.

"With the exception of Lord Byron, who has made the theme peculiarly his own, no one has more feelingly contrasted ancient with modern Greece.

"The poem on the Restoration of the Louvre Collection, has, of course, more allusions to ancient Rome ; and nothing can be more spirited than the passages in which the author invokes for modern Rome the return of her ancient glories. In a cursory but graphic manner, some of the most celebrated of the ancient statues are described. Referring our readers, with great confidence, to the works themselves, our extracts may be limited."—*Blackwood's Magazine,* vol. i.

"The grand act of retribution—the restoration of the treasures of the Louvre—occasioned Mrs. Hemans's first publication. *Modern Greece* next appeared, and soared still higher into the regions of beauty and pathos. It is a highly promising symptom, that each new effort of her genius excels its predecessor. The present volume strikingly confirms this observation, and leads us to think that we have yet seen no more than the trials of her strength."—*Edinburgh Monthly Review,* vol. ii.

TRANSLATIONS

FROM

CAMOENS, AND OTHER POETS,

"Siamo nati veramente in un secolo in cui gl'ingegni e gli studj degli uomini sono rivolti all' utilità. L'Agricoltura, le Arti, il Commercio acquistano tutto di novi lumi dalle ricerche de' Saggi; e il voler farsi un nome *tentando di dilettare*, quand' altri v'aspira con più giustizia giovando, sembra impresa dura e difficile." *Savioli.*

SONNET 70.

"Na metade do ceo subido ardia."

High in the glowing heavens, with cloudless beam,
The sun had reach'd the zenith of his reign,
And for the living fount, the gelid stream,
Each flock forsook the herbage of the plain:

'Midst the dark foliage of the forest shade,
The birds had shelter'd from the scorching ray;
Hush'd were their melodies—and grove and glade
Resounded but the shrill cicada's lay:

When, through the grassy vale, a love-lorn swain,
To seek the maid who but despised his pain,
Breathing vain sighs of fruitless passion, roved:
"Why pine for her," the slighted wanderer cried,
"By whom thou art not loved?" and thus replied
An echo's murmuring voice—" *Thou art not loved!*

SONNET 282.

From Psalm cxxxvii.

"Na ribeira do Euprates assentado."

Wrapt in sad musings, by Euphrates' stream
I sat, retracing days for ever flown,

While rose thine image on the exile's dream,
O much-loved Salem! and thy glories gone.

When they who caused the ceaseless tears I shed,
Thus to their captive spoke,—" Why sleep thy lays?
Sing of thy treasures lost, thy splendor fled,
And all thy triumphs in departed days!

" Know'st thou not Harmony s resistless charm
Can sooth each passion, and each grief disarm?
Sing then, and tears will vanish from thine eye."
With sighs I answer'd,—When the cup of woe
Is fill'd, till misery's bitter draught o'erflow,
The mourner's cure is not to sing—but die.

PART OF ECLOGUE 15

" Se la no assento da maior alteza."

If in thy glorious home above
Thou still recallest earthly love,
If yet retain'd a thought may be
Of him, whose heart hath bled for thee;

Remember still how deeply shrined,
Thine image in his joyless mind,
Each well-known scene, each former care,
Forgotten—thou alone art there!

Remember that thine eye-beam's light
Hath fled for ever from his sight,
And, with that vanish'd sunshine lost,
Is every hope he cherish'd most.

Think that his life, from thee apart,
Is all but weariness of heart,
Each stream, whose music once was dear,
Now murmurs discord to his ear.

Through thee, the morn, whose cloudless rays
Woke him to joy in other days,
Now in the light of beauty drest,
Brings but new sorrows to his breast.

Through thee, the heavens are dark to him
The sun's meridian blaze is dim;
And harsh were e'en the bird of eve,
But that her song still loves to grieve.

All it hath been, his heart forgets,
So alter'd by its long regrets;
Each wish is changed, each hope is o'er,
And joy's light spirit wakes no more.

SONNET 271.

"A formosura desta fresca serra."

This mountain-scene, with silvan grandeur crown'd,
These chestnut-woods, in summer verdure bright;
Those founts and rivulets, whose mingling sound
Lulls every bosom to serene delight!

Soft on these hills the sun's declining ray;
This clime, where all is new; these murmuring seas;
Flocks to the fold that bend their lingering way;
Light clouds, contending with the genial breeze;

And all that Nature's lavish hands dispense,
In gay luxuriance, charming every sense,
Ne'er in thy absence, can delight my breast:
Nought, without thee, my weary soul beguiles:
And joy may beam; yet, 'midst her brightest smiles,
A secret grief is mine, that will not rest.

SONNET 186.

"Os olhos onde o casto Amor ardia."

Those eyes, whence Love diffused his purest light,
Proud in such beaming orbs his reign to show;
That face, with tints of mingling lustre bright,
Where the rose mantled o'er the living snow;

The rich redundance of that golden hair,
Brighter than sunbeams of meridian day;
That form so graceful, and that hand so fair,
Where now those treasures?—mouldering into clay!

Thus like some blossom prematurely torn,
Hath young Perfection wither'd in its morn,
Touch'd by the hand that gathers but to blight!
Oh! how could Love survive his bitter tears?
Shed, not for her, who mounts to happier spheres,
But for his own sad fate, thus wrapt in starless night!

SONNET 108.

"*Brandas aguas do Tejo que passando.*"

Fair Tajo! thou, whose calmly-flowing tide
Bathes the fresh verdure of these lovely plains,
Enlivening all where'er thy waves may glide,
Flowers, herbage, flocks, and silvan nymphs, and swains

Sweet stream! I know not when my steps again
Shall tread thy shores; and while to part I mourn,
I have no hope to meliorate my pain,
No dream that whispers—I may yet return!

My frowning destiny, whose watchful care
Forbids me blessings, and ordains despair,
Commands me thus to leave thee, and repine:
And I must vainly mourn the scenes I fly,
And breathe on other gales my plaintive sigh,
And blend my tears with other waves than thine!

SONNET 23.—TO A LADY WHO DIED AT SEA.

"*Chara minha inimiga, em cuja mao.*"

Thou, to whose power my hopes, my joys, I give,
Oh, fondly loved! my bosom's dearest care!
Earth, which denied to lend thy form a grave,
Yields not one spell to soothe my deep despair!

Yes! the wild seas entomb those charms divine,
Dark o'er thy head th' eternal billows roll;
But while one ray of life or thought is mine,
Still shalt thou live, the inmate of my soul.

And if the tones of my uncultured song
Have power the sad remembrance to prolong,
Of love so ardent, and of faith so pure;
Still shall my verse thine epitaph remain,
Still shall thy charms be deathless in my strain,
While Time, and Love, and Memory shall endure.

SONNET 19.

"*Alma minha gentil, que te partiste.*"

Spirit beloved! whose wing so soon hath flown
The joyless precincts of this earthly sphere,

How is yon Heaven eternally thine own,
Whilst I deplore thy loss, a captive here

Oh! if allow'd in thy divine abode
Of aught on earth an image to retain,
Remember still the fervent love which glow'd
In my fond bosom, pure from every stain.

And if thou deem that all my faithful grief,
Caused by thy losss, and hopeles of relief,
Can merit thee sweet native of the skies!
Oh! ask of Heaven, which call'd thee soon away,
That I may join thee in those realms of day,
Swiftly, as *thou* hast vanish'd from mine eyes.

" Que estranho caso de amor !"

How strange a fate in love is mine!
How dearly prized the pains I feel!
Pangs, that to rend my soul combine,
    With avarice I conceal;
For did the world the tale divine,
My lot would then be deeper woe,
And mine is grief that none must know.

To mortal ears I may not dare
Unfold the cause, the pain I prove;
'Twould plunge in ruin and despair
    Or me, or her I love.
My soul delights alone to bear
Her silent, unsuspected woe,
And none shall pity, none shall know.

Thus buried in my bosom's urn,
Thus in my inmost heart conceal'd,
Let me alone the secret mourn,
In pangs unsoothed and unreveal'd.
For, whether happiness or woe,
Or life or death its power bestow,
It is what none on earth must know.

SONNET 58.

" Se as penas com que Amor tao mal me trata."

SHOULD Love, the tyrant of my suffering heart,
Yet long enough protract his votary's days,

To see the lustre from those eyes depart,
The lode-stars now* that fascinate my gaze;
To see rude Time the living roses blight,
That o'er thy cheek their lovliness unfold,
And all unpitying change thy tresses bright,
To silvery whiteness, from their native gold;

Oh! then thy heart an equal change will prove,
And mourn the coldness that repell'd my love,
When tears and penitence will all be vain;
And I shall see thee weep for days gone by,
And in thy deep regret and fruitless sigh,
Find amplest vengeance for my former pain.

SONNET 178.

"Ja cantei, ja chorei a dura guerra

Oft have I sung and mourn'd the bitter woes,
Which love for years hath mingled with my fate,
While he the tale forbade me to disclose,
That taught his votaries their deluded state.

Nymphs! who dispense Castalia's living stream,
Ye, who from Death oblivion's mantle steal,
Grant me a strain in powerful tone supreme,
Each grief by love inflicted to reveal:

That those whose ardent hearts adore his sway,
May hear experience breathe a warning lay—
How false his smiles, his promises how vain!
Then, if ye deign this effort to inspire,
When the sad task is o'er, my plaintive lyre,
For ever hush'd, shall slumber in your fane.

SONNET 80.

"Como quando do mar tempestuoso"

Saved from the perils of the stormy wave,
And faint with toil, the wanderer of the main,
But just escaped from shipwreck's billowy grave,
Trembles to hear its horrors named again.

How warm his vow, that Ocean's fairest mien
No more shall lure him from the smiles of home!

---

*"Your eyes are lode-stars."—Shakspeare

Yet soon, forgetting each terrific scene,
Once more he turns, o'er boundless deeps to roam.

Lady! thus I, who vainly oft in flight
Seek refuge from the dangers of thy sight,
Make the firm vow to shun thee and be free:
But my fond heart, devoted to its chain,
Still draws me back where countless perils reign,
And grief and ruin spread their snares for me.

SONNET 239.—FROM PSALM CXXXVII.

"Em Babylonia sobre os rios, quando."

BESIDE the streams of Babylon, in tears
Of vain desire, we sat: remembering thee,
O hallow'd Sion! and the vanish'd years,
When Israel's chosen sons were blest and free:

Our harps, neglected and untuned we hung
Mute on the willows of the stranger's land;
When songs, like those that in thy fanes we sung,
Our foes demanded from their captive band.

How shall our voices, on a foreign shore
(We answer'd those whose chains the exile wore,)
The songs of God, our sacred songs, renew?
If I forget, 'midst grief and wasting toil,
Thee, O Jerusalem! my native soil!
May my right hand forget its cunning too!

SONNET 128.

"Huma admiravel herva se conhece."

THERE blooms a plant, whose gaze from hour to hour,
  Still to the sun with fond devotion turns,
Wakes, when Creation hails his dawning power,
  And most expands, when most her idol burns:

But when he seeks the bosom of the deep,
  His faithful plant's reflected charms decay;
Then fade her flowers, her leaves dsscolor'd weep,
  Still fondly pining for the vanish'd ray.

Thou whom I love, the daystar of my sight!
When thy dear presence wakes me to delight,

Joy in my soul unfolds her fairest flower:
But in thy heaven of smiles alone it blooms,
And, of their light deprived, in grief consumes,
Born but to live within thine eye-beam's power.

"Pol o meu apartamento."

AMIDST the bitter tears that fell
In anguish at my last farewell,
Oh! who would dream that joy could dwell,
　　To make that moment bright?
Yet be my judge, each heart! and say,
Which then could most my bosom sway,
　　Affliction or delight?

It was, when Hope, oppressed with woes,
Seem'd her dim eyes in death to close,
That rapture's brightest beam arose
　　In sorrow's darkest night.
Thus, if my soul survive that hour,
'Tis that my fate o'ercame the power
　　Of anguish with delight.

For oh! her love, so long unknown,
She *then* confess'd was all my own,
And in that parting hour alone
　　Reveal'd it to my sight.
And now what pangs will rend my soul,
Should fortune still, with stern control,
　　Forbid me this delight.

I know not if my bliss were vain,
For all the force of parting pain
Forbade suspicious doubts to reign,
　　When exiled from her sight:
Yet now what double woe for me,
Just at the close of eve, to see
　　The dayspring of delight.

SONNET 205.

"Quem diz que Amor he falso, o enganoso."

HE who proclaims that Love is light and vain,
Capricious, cruel, false in all his ways;
Ah! sure too well hath merited his pain,
Too justly finds him all he thus portrays.

For Love is pitying, Love is soft and kind;
Believe not him who dares the tale oppose;
Oh! deem him one whom stormy passions blind,
One to whom heaven and earth may well be foes.

If Love bring evils, view them all in me!
Here let the world his utmost rigor see,
His utmost power exerted to annoy:
But all his ire is still the ire of love;
And such delight in all his woes I prove,
I would not change their pangs for aught of other joy.

SONNET 133.

"Doces e claras aguas do Mondego."

WAVES of Mondego! brilliant and serene,
Haunts of my thought, where memory fondly strays;
Where hope allured me with perfidious mien,
Witching my soul, in long-departed days;

Yes! I forsake your banks! but still my heart
Shall bid remembrance all your charms restore,
And, suffering not one image to depart,
Find lengthening distance but endear you more.

Let Fortune's will, through many a future day,
To distant realms this mortal frame convey,
Sport of each wind, and tost on every wave;
Yet my fond soul, to pensive memory true,
On thought's light pinion still shall fly to you,
And still, bright waters, in your current lave.

SONNET 181.

"Onde acharei lugar tao apartado."

WHERE shall I find some desert scene so rude,
Where loneliness so undisturb'd may reign
That not a step shall ever there intrude
Of roving man, or nature's savage train?

Some tangled thicket, desolate and drear,
Or deep wild forest, silent as the tomb,
Boasting no verdure bright, no fountain clear,
But darkly suited to my spirit's gloom;

That there, 'midst frowning rocks, alone with grief,
Entomb'd in life, and hopeless of relief,
In lonely freedom I may breathe my woes—
For, oh! since nought my sorrows can allay,
There shall my sadness cloud no festal day,
And days of gloom shall soothe me to repose.

SONNET 278.

"Eu vivia de lagrimas isento."

EXEMPT from every grief, 'twas mine to live
In dreams so sweet, enchantments so divine,
A thousand joys propitious Love can give
Were scarcely worth one rapturous pain of mine.

Bound by soft spells, in dear illusions blest,
I breathed no sigh for fortune or for power;
No care intruding to disturb my breast,
I dwelt entranced in Love's Elysian bower:

But Fate, such transports eager to destroy,
Soon rudely woke me from the dream of joy,
And bade the phantoms of delight begone:
Bade hope and happiness at once depart,
And left but memory to distract my heart,
Retracing every hour of bliss for ever flown.

"Mi nueve y dulce querella."

No searching eye can pierce the veil
 That o'er my secret love is thrown;
No outward signs reveal its tale,
 But to my bosom known.
Thus, like the spark, whose vivid light
In the dark flint is hid from sight,
 It dwells within, alone.

METASTASIO.

"Dunque si sfoga in pianto."

IN tears, the heart oppress'd with grief
 Gives language to its woes;

In tears its fulness finds relief,
  When rapture's tide o'erflows!

Who then unclouded bliss would seek
  On this terrestrial sphere,
When e'en Delight can only speak,
  Like Sorrow—in a tear?

VINCENZO DA FILICAJA.

"Italia, Italia! O tu cui die la sorte."

Italia, oh! Italia! thou, so graced
With ill-starr'd beauty, which to thee hath been
A dower, whose fatal splendor may be traced
In the deep-graven sorrows of thy mien;

Oh! that more strength, or fewer charms were thine,
That those might fear thee more or love thee less,
Who seem to worship at thy radiant shrine,
Then pierce thee with the death-pang's bitterness!

Not *then* would foreign hosts have drain'd the tide
Of that Eridanus thy blood hath dyed;
Nor from the Alps would legions, still renew'd,
Pour down; nor wouldst thou wield an alien brand,
And fight thy battles with the stranger's hand,
Still, still a slave, victorious or subdued!

PASTORINI.

"Genova mia, se con asciutto ciglio."

If thus thy fallen grandeur I behold,
My native Genoa! with a tearless eye,
Think not thy son's ungrateful heart is cold,
But know I deem rebellious every sigh!

Thy glorious ruins proudly I survey,
Trophies of firm resolve, of patriot might!
And in each trace of devastation's way,
Thy worth, thy courage, meet my wandering sight.

Triumphs far less than suffering virtue shine;
And on the spoilers high revenge is thine,
While thy strong spirit unsubdued remains
And lo! fair Liberty rejoicing flies

To kiss each noble relic, while she cries,
"*Hail! though in ruins, thou wert ne'er in chains.*"

LOPE DE VEGA.

"Estese el cortesano."

Let the vain courtier waste his days,
Lured by the charms that wealth displays,
The couch of down, the board of costly fare ;
Be his to kiss th' ungrateful hand
That waves the sceptre of command,
And rear full many a palace in the air ;
Whilst I enjoy, all unconfined,
The glowing sun, the genial wind,
And tranquil hours, to rustic toil assign'd ;
And prize far more, in peace and health,
Contented indigence than joyless wealth.

Not mine in Fortune's fane to bend,
At Grandeur's altar to attend,
Reflect his smile, and tremble at his frown ;
Nor mine a fond aspiring thought,
A wish, a sigh, a vision, fraught
With Fame's bright phantom, Glory's deathless crown !
Nectarious draughts and viands pure,
Luxuriant nature will ensure ;
These the clear fount, and fertile field,
Still to the wearied shepherd yield ;
And when repose and visions reign,
Then we are equals all, the monarch and the swain.

FRANCISCO MANUEL.

ON ASCENDING A HILL LEADING TO A CONVENT.

"No baxes temeroso, o peregrino."

Pause not with lingering foot, O pilgrim, here ;
Pierce the deep shadows of the mountain side ;
Firm be thy step, thy heart unknown to fear,
To brighter worlds this thorny path will guide.

Soon shall thy feet approach the calm abode,
So near the mansions of supreme delight ;
Pause not—but tread this consecrated road,
'Tis the dark basis of the heavenly height.

Behold, to cheer thee on the toilsome way,
How many a fountain glitters down the hill ;
Pure gales, inviting, softly round thee play,
Bright sunshine guides—and wilt thou linger still ?
Oh! enter there, where, freed from human strife,
Hope is reality, and time is life.

DELLA CASA.

VENICE.

" Questi palazzi, equeste logge or colte."

THESE marble domes, by wealth and genius graced,
With sculptured forms, bright hues, and Parian stone,
Were once rude cabins 'midst a lonely waste,
Wild shores of solitude, and isles unknown.

Pure from each vice, 'twas here a venturous train,
Fearless, in fragile barks explored the sea ;
Not theirs a wish to conquer or to reign,
They sought these island precincts—to be free.

Ne'er in their souls ambition's flame arose,
No dream of avarice broke their calm repose,
Fraud, more than death, abhorr'd each artless breast:
Oh! now, since fortune gilds their brightening day,
Let not those virtues languish and decay,
O'erwhelm'd by luxury, and by wealth opprest!

IL MARCHESE CORNELIO BENTIVOGLIO.

" L'anima bella, che dal vero Eliso."

THE sainted spirit which, from bliss on high,
Descends, like dayspring, to my favor'd sight,
Shines in such noontide radiance of the sky,
Scarce do I know that form, intensely bright!

But, with the sweetness of her well-known smile,
That smile of peace ! she bids my doubts depart,
And takes my hand, and softly speaks the while,
And heaven's full glory pictures to my heart.

Beams of that heaven in *her* my eyes behold,
And now, e'en now, in thought my wings unfold,

To soar with her, and mingle with the blest!
But ah! so swift her buoyant pinion flies,
That I, in vain aspiring to the skies,
Fall to my native sphere, by earthly bonds deprest.

METASTASIO.

"Al furor d'avversa Sorte."

He shall not dread Misfortune's angry mien,
Nor feebly sink beneath her tempest rude,
Whose soul hath learn'd, through many a trying scene
To smile at fate, and suffer unsubdued.

In the rough school of billows, clouds, and storms,
Nursed and matured, the pilot learns his art:
Thus Fate's dread ire, by many a conflict, forms
The lofty spirit and enduring heart!

"Quella onda che ruina."

The torrent wave, that breaks with force
Impetuous down the Alpine height,
Complains and struggles in its course,
But sparkles, as the diamond bright.

The stream in shadowy valley deep,
May slumber in its narrow bed;
But silent, in unbroken sleep,
Its lustre and its life are fled.

"Leggiadra rosa, le cui pure foglie."

Sweet rose! whose tender foliage to expand
Her fostering dews, the morning lightly shed,
Whilst gales of balmy breath thy blossoms fann'd,
And o'er thy leaves the soft suffusion spread;

That hand, whose care withdrew thee from the ground
To brighter worlds thy favor'd charms hath borne;
Thy fairest buds, with grace perennial crown'd,
There breathe and bloom, released from every thorn.

Thus, far removed, and now transplanted flower!
Exposed no more to blast or tempest rude,
Shelter'd with tenderest care from frost or shower,
And each rough season's chill vicissitude,
Now may thy form in bowers of peace assume
Immortal fragrance, and unwithering bloom.

"Che speri, instabil Dea, di sassi, e spine."

FORTUNE! why thus, where'er my footsteps tread,
Obstruct each path with rocks and thorns like these?
Think'st thou that *I* thy threatening mien shall dread,
Or toil and pant thy waving locks to seize?

Reserve the frown severe, the menace rude,
For vassal-spirits that confess thy sway!
My constant soul should triumph unsubdued,
Were the wide universe destruction's prey.

Am I to conflicts new, in toils untried?
No! I have long thine utmost power defied,
And drawn fresh energies from every fight.
Thus from rude strokes of hammers and the wheel,
With each successive shock the temper'd steel
More keenly piercing proves, more dazzling bright.

"Parlagli d'un periglio."

WOULDST thou to Love of danger speak?
Veil'd are his eyes, to perils blind!
Wouldst thou from Love a reason seek?—
He is a child of wayward mind!

But with a doubt, a jealous fear,
Inspire him once—the task is o'er;
His mind is keen his sight is clear,
No more an infant, blind no more,

"Sprezza il furor del vento."

UNBENDING 'midst the wintry skies,
Rears the firm oak his vigorous form,
And stern in rugged strength, defies
   The rushing of the storm.

Then sever'd from his native shore,
O'er ocean-worlds the sail to bear,
Still with those winds he braved before,
    He proudly struggles there.

"Sol puo dir che sia contento."

Oh! those alone, whose sever'd hearts
Have mourn'd through ling'ring years in vain,
Can tell what bliss fond Love imparts,
When Fate unites them once again.

Sweet is the sigh, and blest the tear,
Whose language hails that moment bright,
When past afflictions but endear
The presence of delight!

"Ah! frenate le piante imbelle."

Ah! cease—those fruitless tears restrain,
I go misfortune to defy,
To smile at fate with proud disdain,
To triumph—not to die!

I with fresh laurels go, to crown
My closing days at last,
Securing all the bright renown
Acquired in dangers past.

QUEVEDO.

ROME BURIED IN HER OWN RUINS.

"Buscas en Roma a Roma, o peregrino!"

Amidst these scenes, O pilgrim! seek'st thou Rome?
Vain is thy search—the pomp of Rome is fled;
Her silent Aventine is glory's tomb;
Her walls, her shrines, but relics of the dead.

That hill, where Cæsars dwelt in other days,
Forsaken mourns, where once it tower'd sublime;
Each mouldering medal now far less displays
The triumphs won by Latium, than by Time.

Tiber alone survives—the passing wave
That bathed her towers, now murmurs by her grave,
Wailing, with plaintive sound, her fallen fanes.
Rome! of thine ancient grandeur all is past,
That seem'd for years eternal framed to last,
Nought but the wave, a fugitive—remains.

EL CONDE JUAN DE TARSIS.

"Tu, que la dulce vida en tiernas anos."

Thou, who has fled from life's enchanted bowers,
In youth's gay spring, in beauty's glowing morn,
Leaving thy bright array, thy path of flowers,
For the rude convent-garb, and couch of thorn;

Thou that, escaping from a world of cares,
Hast found thy haven in devotion's fane,
As to the port the fearful bark repairs,
To shun the midnight perils of the main;

Now the glad hymn, the strain of rapture pour,
While on thy soul the beams of glory rise!
For if the pilot hail the welcome shore,
With shouts of triumph swelling to the skies;
Oh! how shouldst *thou* the exulting pæan raise,
Now heaven's bright harbor opens on thy gaze!

TORQUATO TASSO.

"Negli anni acerbi tuoi, purpurea rosa."

Thou in thy morn wert like a glowing rose
To the mild sunshine only half display'd,
That shunn'd its bashful graces to disclose,
And in its vale of verdure sought a shade:

Or like Aurora did thy charms appear
(Since mortal form ne'er vied with aught so bright)—
Aurora, smiling from her tranquil sphere,
O'er vale and mountain shedding dew and light.

Now riper years have doom'd no grace to fade;
Nor youthful charms, in all their pride array'd,
Excel, or equal, thy neglected form.
Thus, full expanded, lovelier is the flower,
And the bright daystar, in its noontide hour,
More brilliant shines, in genial radiance warm.

BERNARDO TASSO.

"Quest' ombra che giammai non vide il sole."

This green recess, where through the bowery gloom
Ne'er e'en at noontide hours, the sunbeam play'd,
Where violet-beds in soft luxuriance bloom,
'Midst the cool freshness of the myrtle shade;

Where through the grass a sparkling fountain steals
Whose murmuring wave, transparent as it flows,
No more its bed of yellow sand conceals,
Than the pure crystal hides the glowing rose;

This bower of peace, thou soother of our care,
God of soft slumbers, and of visions fair!
A lowly shepherd consecrates to thee!
Then breathe around some spell of deep repose,
And charm his eyes in balmy dew to close,
Those eyes, fatigued with grief, from tear-drops never free.

PETRARCH.

"Chi vuol veder quantunque puo natura."

Thou that wouldst mark, in form of human birth,
All heaven and nature's perfect skill combined,
Come gaze on her, the daystar of the earth
Dazzling, not me alone, but all mankind:

And haste! for Death, who spares the guilty long,
First calls the brightest and the best away;
And to her home, amidst the cherub throng,
The angelic mortal flies, and will not stay!

Haste! and each outward charm, each mental grace,
In one consummate form thine eye shall trace,
Model of loveliness, for earth too fair!
Then thou shalt own how faint my votive lays,
My spirit dazzled by perfection's blaze;
But if thou still delay, for long regret prepare.

"Se lamentar augelli, o verdi fronde."

If to the sighing breeze of summer hours
Bend the green leaves; if mourns a plaintive bird

Or from some fount's cool margin, fringed with flowers,
The soothing murmur of the wave is heard;

Her, whom the heavens reveal, the earth denies,
I see and hear: though dwelling far above,
Her spirit, still responsive to my sighs,
Visits the lone retreat of pensive love.

" Why thus in grief consume each fruitless day,"
(Her gentle accents thus benignly say,)
" While from thine eyes the tear unceasing flows?
Weep not for me, who, hastening on my flight,
Died, to be deathless; and on heavenly light
Whose eyes but open'd, when they seem'd to close!"

VERSI SPAGNUOLI DI PIETRO BEMBO.

"O Muerte! que sueles ser."

Thou, the stern monarch of dismay,
 Whom nature trembles to survey,
 O Death! to me, the child of grief,
 Thy welcome power would bring relief
Changing to peaceful slumber many a care.
 And though thy stroke may thrill with pain
 Each throbbing pulse, each quivering vein;
 The pangs that bid existence close,
 Ah! sure are far less keen than those,
Which cloud its lingering moments with despair.

FRANCESCO LORENZINI.

"O Zefiretto, che movendo vai."

Sylph of the breeze! whose dewy pinions light
Wave gently round the tree I planted here,
Sacred to her, whose soul hath wing'd its flight
To the pure ether of her lofty sphere;

Be it thy care, soft spirit of the gale!
To fan its leaves in summer's noontide hour;
Be it thy care, that wintry tempests fail
To rend its honors from the silvan bower.

Then shall it spread, and rear th' aspiring form,
Pride of the wood, secure from every storm,

Graced with her name, a consecrated tree!
So may thy Lord, thy monarch of the wind,
Ne'er with rude chains thy tender pinions bind,
But grant thee still to rove, a wanderer wild and free!

GESNER.
MORNING SONG.
"Willkommen fruhe morgensonn."

Hail! morning sun, thus early bright;
Welcome, sweet dawn! thou younger day!
Through the dark woods that fringe the height,
    Beams forth, e'en now, thy ray.

Bright on the dew it sparkles clear,
Bright on the water's glittering fall,
And life, and joy, and health appear,
    Sweet morning! at thy call.

Now thy fresh breezes lightly spring
From beds of fragrance, where they lay,
And roving wild on dewy wing,
    Drive slumber far away.

Fantastic dreams, in swift retreat,
Now from each mind withdraw their spell,
While the young loves delighted meet
    On Rosa's cheek to dwell.

Speed, zephyr! kiss each opening flower,
Its fragrant spirit make thine own;
Then wing thy way to Rosa's bower,
    Ere her light sleep is flown.

There, o'er her downy pillow fly,
Wake the sweet maid to life and day;
Breathe on her balmy lip a sigh,
    And o'er her bosom play;

And whisper, when her eyes unveil,
That I, since morning's earliest call,
Have sigh'd her name to every gale
    By the lone waterfall.

GERMAN SONG.
"Madchen, lernet Amor kennen."

Listen, fair maid, my song shall tell
How Love may still be known full well,
    His looks the traitor prove.

Dost thou not see that absent smile,
That fiery glance replete with guile?
    Oh! doubt not then—'tis Love.

When varying still the sly disguise,
Child of caprice, he laughs and cries,
    Or with complaint would move;
To-day is bold, to-morrow shy,
Changing each hour, he knows not why,
    Oh! doubt not then—'tis Love.

There's magic in his every wile,
His lips, well practiced to beguile,
    Breathe roses when they move
See, now with sudden rage he burns,
Disdains, implores, commands, by turns.
    Oh! doubt not then—'tis Love.

He comes, without the bow and dart,
That spare not e'en the purest heart;
    His looks the traitor prove;
That glance is fire, that mien is guile,
Deceit is lurking in that smile,
    Oh! trust him not—'tis Love!

CHAULIEU.

"Grotte, d'ou sorte ce clair ruisseau."

Thou grot, whence flows this limpid spring,
Its margin fringed with moss and flowers.
Still bid its voice of murmurs bring
    Peace to my musing hours.

Sweet Fontenay! where first for me
The dayspring of existence rose,
Soon shall my dust return to thee,
    And midst my sires repose.

Muses, that watch'd my childhood's morn
'Midst these wild haunts, with guardian eye,
Fair trees, that here beheld me born,
    Soon shall ye see me die.

GARCILASO DE VEGA.

"Coyed de vuestra alegre primavera."

Enjoy the sweets of life's luxuriant May
Ere envious Age is hastening on his way
With snowy wreathes to crown the beauteous brow:

The rose will fade when storms assail the year,
And Time, who changeth not his swift career,
Constant in this, will change all else below!

LORENZO DE' MEDICI.

VIOLETS.

" Non di verdi giardin ornati e colti."

WE come not, fair one, to thy hand of snow,
From the soft scenes by Culture's hand array'd;
Not rear'd in bowers where gales of fragrance blow,
But in dark glens, and depths of forest shade!

There once, as Venus wander'd, lost in woe,
To seek Adonis through th' entangled wood,
Piercing her foot, a thorn that lurk'd below,
With print relentless drew celestial blood!

Then our light stems, with snowy blossoms fraught,
Bending to earth, each precious drop we caught,
Imbibing thence our bright purpureal dyes;
We were not foster'd in our shadowy vales,
By guided rivulets, or summer gales—
Our dew and air have been, Love's balmy tears and sighs!

PINDEMONTE.

ON THE HEBE OF CANOVA.

" Dove per te, celeste ancilla, or vassi?"

WHITHER, celestial maid, so fast away?
What lures thee from the banquet of the skies?
How canst thou leave thy native realms of day,
For this low sphere, this vale of clouds and sighs?

O thou, Canova! soaring high above
Italian art—with Grecian magic vying!
We knew thy marble glow'd with life and love,
But who had seen thee image footsteps flying?

Here to each eye the wind seems gently playing
With the light vest, its wavy folds arraying
  In many a line of undulating grace;
While Nature, ne'er her mighty laws suspending,
Stands, before marble thus with motion blending,
  One moment lost in thought, its hidden cause to trace.

MISCELLANEOUS POEMS.

LINES.

WRITTEN IN A HERMITAGE ON THE SEASHORE.

O wanderer! would thy heart forget
Each earthly passion and regret,
And would thy wearied spirit rise
To commune with its native skies;
Pause for a while, and deem it sweet
To linger in this calm retreat;
And give thy cares, thy griefs, a short suspense,
Amidst wild scenes of lone magnificence.

Unmix'd with aught of meaner tone,
Here nature's voice is heard alone:
When the loud storm, in wrathful hour,
Is rushing on its wing of power,
And spirits of the deep awake,
And surges foam, and billows break,
And rocks and ocean-caves around,
Reverberate each awful sound;
That mighty voice, with all its dread control,
To loftiest thought shall wake thy thrilling soul.

But when no more the sea-winds rave,
When peace is brooding on the wave,
And from earth, air, and ocean rise
No sounds but plaintive melodies;
Sooth'd by their softly mingling swell,
As daylight bids the world farewell,
The rustling wood, the dying breeze,
The faint, low rippling of the seas,
A tender calm shall steal upon thy breast,
A gleam reflected from the realms of rest.

Is thine a heart the world hath stung,
Friends have deceived, neglect hath wrung?
Hast thou some grief that none may know,
Some lonely, secret, silent woe?
Or have thy fond affections fled
From earth, to slumber with the dead?
Oh! pause awhile—the world disown,
And dwell with nature's self alone!
And though no more she bids arise
Thy soul's departed energies,

And though thy joy of life is o'er,
　Beyond her magic to restore ;
Yet shall her spells o'er every passion steal,
And soothe the wounded heart they cannot heal.

DIRGE OF A CHILD.

No bitter tears for thee be shed,
　Blossom of being ! seen and gone !
With flowers alone we strew thy bed,
　　O blest departed One !
Whose all of life, a rosy ray,
Blush'd into dawn and pass'd away.

Yes ! thou art fled, ere guilt had power
　To stain thy cherub-soul and form,
Closed is the soft ephemeral flower
　　That never felt a storm !
The sunbeam's smile, the zephyr's breath,
All that it knew from birth to death.

Thou wert so like a form of light,
　That heaven benignly call'd thee hence,
Ere yet the world could breathe one blight
　　O'er thy sweet innocence :
And thou, that brighter home to bless,
Art pass'd, with all thy loveliness !

Oh ! hadst thou still on earth remain'd,
　Vision of beauty ! fair, as brief!
How soon thy brightness had been stain'd
　　With passion or with grief!
Now not a sullying breath can rise,
To dim thy glory in the skies.

We rear no marble o'er thy tomb ;
　No sculptured image there shall mourn ;
Ah ! fitter far the vernal bloom
　　Such dwelling to adorn.
Fragrance, and flowers, and dews, must be
The only emblems meet for thee.

Thy grave shall be a blessed shrine,
　Adorn'd with Nature's brightest wreath ;
Each glowing season shall combine
　　Its incense there to breathe ;
And oft, upon the midnight air,
Shall viewless harps be murmuring there.

And oh! sometimes in visions blest,
Sweet spirit! visit our repose;
And bear, from thine own world of rest,
　　Some balm for human woes!
What form more lovely could be given
Than thine to messenger of heaven?*

INVOCATION.

Hush'd is the world in night and sleep,
Earth, Sea, and Air, are still as death;
Too rude to break a calm so deep,
　　Where music's faintest breath.
Descend, bright Visions! from ærial bowers.
Descend to gild your own soft, silent hours.

In hope or fear, in toil or pain,
The weary day have mortals past;
Now, dreams of bliss! be yours to reign,
　　And all your spells around them cast;
Steal from their hearts the pang, their eyes the tear,
And lift the veil that hides a brighter sphere.

O! bear your softest balm to those,
Who fondly, vainly, mourn the dead,
To them that world of peace disclose,
　　Where the bright soul is fled:
Where Love, immortal in his native clime,
Shall fear no pang from fate, no blight from time.

Or to his loved, his distant land,
On your light wings the exile bear
To feel once more his heart expand,
　　In his own genial mountain-air;
Hear the wild echoes' well-known strains repeat,
And bless each note, as Heaven's own music sweet.

But oh! with Fancy's brightest ray,
Blest dreams! the bard's repose illume;
Bid forms of heaven around him play,
　　And bowers of Eden bloom!
And waft *his* spirit to its native skies
Who finds no charm in life's realities.

No voice is on the air of night,
Through folded leaves no murmurs creep,

---

*Vide Annotation from *Quarterly Review* page 287.

Nor star nor moonbeam's trembling light
Falls on the placid brow of sleep.
Descend, bright visions! from your airy bower:
Dark, silent, solemn, is your favorite hour.

TO THE MEMORY OF

GENERAL SIR E—D P—K—M.

BRAVE spirit! mourn'd with fond regret,
Lost in life's pride, in valor's noon,
Oh! who could deem *thy* star should set
    So darkly and so soon!

Fatal, though bright, the fire of mind
Which mark'd and closed thy brief career,
And the fair wreath, by hope entwined,
    Lies wither'd on thy bier.

The soldier's death hath been thy doom,
The soldier's tear thy meed shall be;
Yet, son of war! a prouder tomb
    Might Fate have rear'd for thee.

Thou shouldst have died, O high-soul'd chief?
In those bright days of glory fled,
When triumph so prevail'd o'er grief,
    We scarce could mourn the dead.

Noontide of fame! each tear-drop then
Was worthy of a warrior's grave:
When shall affection weep again
    So proudly o'er the brave?

'There, on the battle-fields of Spain,
'Midst Roncesvalles' mountain-scene,
Or on Vittoria's blood-red plain,
    Meet had thy deathbed been.

We mourn not that a hero's life
Thus in its ardent prime should close;
Hadst thou but fallen in nobler strife,
    But died 'midst conquer'd foes!

Yet hast thou still (though victory's flame
In that last moment cheer'd thee not)
Left Glory's isle another name,
    That ne'er may be forgot:

And many a tale of triumph won,
Shall breath that name in Memory's ear,
And long may England mourn a son
    Without reproach or fear.

TO THE MEMORY OF

SIR H—Y E—LL—S.

WHO FELL IN THE BATTLE OF WATERLOO.

" Happy are they who die in youth when their renown is around them."
                                                                Ossian

WEEP'ST thou for him, whose doom was seal'd
On England's proudest battle-field?
For him, the lion-heart, who died
In victory's full resistless tide?
    Oh, mourn him not!
By deeds like his that field was won
And Fate could yield to Valor's son
    No brighter lot.

He heard his band's exulting cry,
He saw the vanquish'd eagles fly;
And envied be his death of fame
It shed a sunbeam o'er his name
    That nought shall dim:
No cloud obscured his glory's day,
It saw no twilight of decay—
    Weep not for him!

And breathe no dirge's plaintive moan,
A hero claims far loftier tone!
Oh! proudly should the war-song swell,
Recording how the mighty fell
    In that dread hour,
When England, 'midst the battle-storm—
Th' avenging angel—rear'd her form
    In tenfold power.

Yet, gallant heart! to swell thy praise
Vain were the minstrel's noblest lays
Since he, the soldier's guiding-star,
The Victor-chief, the lord of war,
    Has own'd thy fame;
And oh! like *his* approving word,
What trophied marble could record
    A warrior's name?

GUERILLA SONG.

FOUNDED ON THE STORY RELATED OF THE SPANISH PATRIOT MINA.

OH! forget not the hour, when through forest and vale,
We return'd with our chief to his dear native halls;
Through the woody Sierra there sigh'd not a gale,
And the moonbeam was bright on his battlement-walls;
And nature lay sleeping in calmness and light,
Round the home of the valiant, that rose on our sight.

We enter'd that home—all was loneliness round,
The stillness, the darkness, the peace of the grave;
Not a voice, not a step, bade its echoes resound,
Ah! such was the welcome that waited the brave!
For the spoilers had pass'd, like the poison-wind's breath,
And the loved of his bosom lay silent in death.

Oh! forget not that hour—let its image be near,
In the light of our mirth, in the dreams of our rest,
Let its tale awake feelings too deep for a tear,
And rouse into vengeance each arm and each breast,
Till cloudless the dayspring of liberty shine
O'er the plains of the olive, and hills of the vine.

THE AGED INDIAN.

WARRIORS! my noon of life is past,
The brightness of my spirit flown;
I crouch before the wintry blast,
Amidst my tribe I dwell alone;
The heroes of my youth are fled,
They rest among the warlike dead.

Ye slumberers of the narrow cave!
My kindred-chiefs in days of yore
Ye fill an unremember'd grave,
Your fame, your deeds, are known no more.
The records of your wars are gone,
Your names forgot by all but one.

Soon shall that one depart from earth,
To join the brethren of his prime;
Then will the memory of your birth
Sleep with the hidden things of time.
With him, ye sons of former days!
Fades the last glimmering of your praise.

His eyes, that hail'd your spirits' flame,
Still kindling in the combat's shock,

Have seen, since darkness veil'd your fame,
Sons of the desert and the rock!
Another, and another race,
Rise to the battle and the chase.

Descendants of the mighty dead!
Fearless of heart and firm of hand!
O! let me join their spirits fled,
O! send me to their shadowy land.
Age hath not tamed Ontara's heart,
He shrinks not from the friendly dart.

These feet no more can chase the deer,
The glory of this arm is flown;—
Why should the feeble linger here,
When all the pride of life is gone?
Warriors! why still the stroke deny,
Think ye Ontara fears to die?

He fear'd not in his flower of days,
When strong to stem the torrent's force,
When through the desert's pathless maze
His way was as an eagle's course!
When war was sunshine to his sight,
And the wild hurricane, delight!

Shall then the warrior tremble *now*?
Now when his envied strength is o'er?
Hung on the pine his idle bow,
His pirogue useless on the shore?
When age hath dimm'd his failing eye,
Shall he, the joyless, fear to die?

Sons of the brave! delay no more,
The spirits of my kindred call;
'Tis but one pang, and all is o'er!
Oh! bid the aged cedar fall!
To join the brethren of his prime,
The mighty of departed time.

EVENING AMONGST THE ALPS.

Soft skies of Italy! how richly drest,
Smile these wild scenes in your purpureal glow!
What glorious hues, reflected from the west,
Float o'er the dwellings of eternal snow!

Yon torrent, foaming down the granite steep,
Sparkles all brilliance in the setting beam;
Dark glens beneath in shadowy beauty sleep,
Where pipes the goatherd by his mountain-stream.

Now from yon peak departs the vivid ray,
That still at eve its lofty temple knows;
From rock and torrent fade the tints away,
And all is wrapt in twilight's deep repose:
While through the pine-wood gleams the vesper star
And roves the Alpine gale o'er solitudes afar.

DIRGE OF THE HIGHLAND CHIEF IN "WAVERLEY"

Son of the mighty and the free!
High-minded leader of the brave!
Was it for lofty chief like thee,
    To fill a nameless grave?
Oh! if amidst the valiant slain,
The warrior's bier had been thy lot,
E'en though on red Culloden's plain,
    We then had mourn'd thee not.

But darkly closed thy dawn of fame,
That dawn whose sunbeam rose so fair;
Vengeance alone may breathe thy name,
    The watchword of Despair!
Yet oh! if gallant spirit's power
Hath e'er ennobled death like thine,
Then glory mark'd *thy* parting hour,
    Last of a mighty line!

O'er thy own towers the sunshine falls,
But cannot chase their silent gloom;
Those beams that gild thy native walls
    Are sleeping on thy tomb!
Spring on thy mountains laughs the while,
Thy green woods wave in vernal air,
But the loved scenes may vainly smile:
    Not e'en thy dust is there.

On thy blue hills no bugle-sound
Is mingling with the torrent's roar,
Unmark'd, the wild deer sport around:
    Thou lead'st the chase no more!
Thy gates are closed, thy halls are still,
Those halls where peal'd the choral strain;
They hear the wind's deep murmuring thrill,
    And all is hush'd again.

No banner from the lonely tower
Shall wave its blazon'd folds on high;
There the tall grass, and summer flower,
    Unmark'd shall spring and die.

No more thy bard, for other ear,
Shall wake the harp once loved by thine—
Hush'd be the strain *thou* canst not hear,
    Last of a mighty line!

THE CRUSADERS' WAR SONG.

CHIEFTAINS, lead on! our hearts beat high,
    Lead on to Salem's towers!
Who would not deem it bliss to die,
    Slain in a cause like ours?
The brave who sleep in soil of thine,
Die not entomb'd but shrined, O Palestine!

Souls of the slain in holy war!
    Look from your sainted rest.
Tell us ye rose in Glory's car,
    To mingle with the blest;
Tell us how short the death-pang's power,
How bright the joys of your immortal bower.

Strike the loud harp, ye minstrel train!
    Pour forth your loftiest lays;
Each heart shall echo to the strain
    Breath'd in the warrior's praise.
Bid every string triumphant swell
Th' inspiring sounds that heroes love so well.

Salem! amidst the fiercest hour,
    The wildest rage of fight,
Thy name shall lend our falchions power,
    And nerve our hearts with might,
Envied be those for thee that fall,
Who find their graves beneath thy sacred wall.

For them no need that sculptured tomb
    Should chronicle their fame,
Or pyramid record their doom,
    Or deathless verse their name;
It is enough that dust of thine
Should shroud their forms, O blessed Palestine!

Chieftains, lead on! our hearts beat high
    For combat's glorious hour;
Soon shall the red-cross banner fly
On Salem's loftiest tower!
We burn to mingle in the strife,
Where *but* to die ensures eternal life.

THE DEATH OF CLANRONALD.

It was in the battle of Sheriffmoor that young Clanronald fell, leading on the Highlanders of the right wing. His death dispirited the assailants, who began to waver. But Glengary, chief of a rival branch of the Clan Colla, started from the ranks, and, waving his bonnet round his head, cried out, "To-day for revenge, and to-morrow for mourning!" The Highlanders received a new impulse from his words, and, charging with redoubled fury, bore down all before them.—See the *Quarterly Review* article of " Culloden Papers."

Oh! ne'er be Clanronald the valiant forgot!
Still fearless and first in the combat, he fell;
But we paused not one tear-drop to shed o'er the spot,
We spared not one moment to murmur " Farewell."
We heard but the battle-word given by the chief,
" To-day for revenge, and to-morrow for grief!"

And wildly, Clanronald! we echo'd the vow,
With the tear on our cheek, and the sword in our hand;
Young son of the brave! we may weep for thee now,
For well has thy death been avenged by thy band,
When they join'd, in wild chorus, the cry of the chief,
" To-day for revenge and to-morrow for grief!"

Thy dirge in that hour was the bugle's wild call,
The clash of the claymore, the shout of the brave;
But now thy own bard may lament for thy fall,
And the soft voice of melody sigh o'er thy grave—
While Albyn remembers the words, of the Chief!
" To-day for revenge, and to-morrow for grief!"

Thou art fallen, O fearless one! flower of thy race:
Descendant of heroes! thy glory is set:
But thy kindred, the sons of the battle and chase,
Have proved that thy spirit is bright in them yet!
Nor vainly have echo'd the words of the chief,
" To-day for revenge, and to-morrow for grief!"

TO THE EYE.

Throne of expression! whence the spirit's ray
Pours forth so oft the light of mental day,
Where fancy's fire, affection's melting beam,
Thought, genius, passion, reign in turn supreme,
And many a feeling, words can ne'er impart,
Finds its own language to pervade the heart;
Thy power, bright orb, what bosom has not felt,
To thrill, to rouse, to facinate, to melt!
And by some spell of undefined control,
With magnet-influence touch the secret soul!

Light of the features! in the morn of youth
Thy glance is nature, and thy language, truth;
And ere the world with all-corrupting sway,
Hath taught e'en *thee* to flatter and betray,
Th' ingenuous heart forbids thee to reveal,
Or speak one thought that interest would conceal;
While yet thou seem'st the cloudless mirror, given
But to reflect the purity of heaven;
O! then how lovely, there unveil'd, to trace
Th' unsullied brightness of each mental grace'

When Genius lends thee all his living light,
Where the full beams of intellect unite;
When love illumes thee with his varying ray,
Where trembling Hope and tearful Rapture play
Or Pity's melting cloud thy beam subdues,
Tempering its lustre with a veil of dews;
Still does thy power, whose all-commanding spell
Can pierce the mazes of the soul so well,
Bid some new feeling to existence start,
From its deep slumbers in the inmost heart.

And O! when thought, in ecstacy sublime,
That soars triumphant o'er the bounds of time,
Fires thy keen glance with inspiration's blaze,
The light of heaven, the hope of nobler days,
(As glorious dreams, for utterance far too high,
Flash through the mist of dim mortality;)
Who does not own, that through thy lightning-beams
A flame unquenchable, unearthly, streams?
That pure, though captive effluence of the sky,
The vestal-ray, the spark that cannot die!

THE HERO'S DEATH.

LIFE's parting beams were in his eye,
Life's closing accents on his tongue,
When round him, pealing to the sky,
    The shout of victory rung!

Then, ere his gallant spirit fled,
A smile so bright illumed his face—
Oh! never, of the light it shed,
    Shall memory lose a trace!

His was a death, whose rapture high
Transcended all that life could yield;
His warmest prayer was so to die,
    On the red battle-field!

And they may feel, who loved him most,
A pride so holy and so pure:
Fate hath no power o'er those who boast
A treasure thus secure!

STANZAS

ON THE LATE NATIONAL CALAMITY, THE DEATH OF THE PRINCESS CHARLOTTE.

"Hélas! nous composions son histoire de tout ce qu'on peut imaginer de plus glorieux——Le passé et le présent nous garantissoient l'avenir——Telle étoit l'agréable histoire que nous faisions; et pour achever ces nobles projets, il n'y avoit que la durée de sa vie; dont nous ne croyions pas devoir être en peine, car, qui eût pu seulement penser, que les années eussent dû manquer, à une jeunesse qui sembloit si vive?" BOSSUET.

I.

MARK'D ye the mingling of the city's throng,
Each mien, each glance, with expectation bright?
Prepare the pageant, and the choral song,
The pealing chimes, the blaze of festal light?
And hark! what rumor's gathering sound is nigh?
Is it the voice of joy, that murmur deep?
Away! be hush'd! ye sounds of revelry.
Back to your homes, ye multitudes, to weep!
Weep! for the storm hath o'er us darkly past,
And England's royal flower is broken by the blast!

II.

Was it a dream? so sudden and so dread
That awful fiat o'er our senses came!
So loved, so blest, is that young spirit fled,
Whose early grandeur promised years of fame?
Oh! when hath life posses'd, or death destroy'd
More lovely hopes, more cloudlessly that smiled?
When hath the spoiler left so dark a void?
For all is lost—the mother and her child!
Our morning-star hath vanish'd, and the tomb
Throws its deep lengthen'd shade o'er distant years to come.

III.

Angel of Death! did no presaging sign
Announce thy coming, and thy way prepare?
No warning voice, no harbinger was thine,
Danger and fear seem'd past—but thou wert there!
Prophetic sounds along the earthquake's path
Foretell the hour of nature's awful throes;

And the volcano, ere it burst in wrath,
Sends forth some herald from its dread repose :
But *thou*, dark Spirit ! swift and unforseen,
Cam'st like the lightning's flash, when heaven is all serene

IV.

And she is gone—the royal and the young,
In soul commanding, and in heart benign ;
Who, from a race of kings and heroes sprung,
Glowed with a spirit lofty as her line.
Now may the voice she loved on earth so well,
Breathe forth her name, unheeded and in vain ;
Nor can those eyes on which her own would dwell,
Wake from that breast one sympathy again :
The ardent heart, the towering mind are fled,
Yet shall undying love still linger with the dead.

V.

Oh! many a bright existence we have seen
Quench'd in the glow and fulness of its prime ;
And many a cherish'd flower ere now, hath been
Cropt, ere its leaves were breathed upon by time.
We have lost heroes in their noon of pride,
Whose fields of triumph gave them but a bier ;
And we have wept when soaring genius died,
Check'd in the glory of his mad career !
But here our hopes were center'd—all is o'er,
All thought in this absorb'd—she was—and is no more !

VI.

We watch'd her childhood from its earliest hour,
From every word and look blest omens caught ;
While that young mind developed all its power,
And rose to energies of loftiest thought.
On her was fix'd the patriot's ardent eye,
One hope still bloom'd—one vista still was fair ;
And when the tempest swept the troubled sky,
She was our dayspring—all was cloudless *there*,
And oh ! how lovely broke on England's gaze,
E'en through the mist and storm, the light of distant days.

VII.

Now hath one moment darken'd future years,
And changed the track of ages yet to be !
Yet, mortal ! 'midst the bitterness of tears,
Kneel, and adore th' inscrutable decree !
Oh ! while the clear perspective smiled in light,
Wisdom should *then* have temper'd hope's excess,
And, lost One ! when we saw thy lot so bright,
We might have trembled at its loveliness :
Joy is no earthly flower—nor framed to bear,
In its exotic bloom, life's cold, ungenial air.

VIII.

All smiled around thee—Youth, and Love, and **Praise,**
Hearts all devotion and all truth were thine!
On thee was riveted a nation's gaze,
As on some radant and unsullied shrine.
Heiress of empires! thou art pass'd away.
Like some fair vision, that arose to throw,
O'er one brief hour of life, a fleeting ray,
Then leave the rest to solitude and wo!
Oh! who shall dare to woo such-dreams again!
Who hath not wept to know, that tears for thee were vain?

IX.

Yet there is one who loved thee—and whose soul
With mild affections nature form'd to melt;
His mind hath bow'd beneath the stern control
Of many a grief—but *this* shall be unfelt!
Years have gone by—and given his honor'd head
A diadem of snow—his eye is dim—
Around him heaven a solemn cloud hath spread,
The past, the future, are a dream to him!
Yet, in the darkness of his fate alone
He dwells on earth, while thou, in life's full pride art gone;

X.

The Chastener's hand is on us—we may weep,
But not repine—for many a storm hath past,
And, pillow'd on her own majestic deep,
Hath England slept, unshaken by the blast!
And War hath raged o'er many a distant plain,
Trampling the vine and olive in his path;
While she, that regal daughter of the main,
Smiled, in serene defiance of his wrath!
As some proud summit mingling with the sky,
Hears calmly far below the thunders roll and die.

XI.

Her voice hath been th' awakener—and her name
The gathering word of nations—in her might,
And all the awful beauty of her fame,
Apart she dwelt, in solitary light.
High on her cliffs, alone and firm she stood,
Fixing the torch upon her beacon-tower;
That torch, whose flame, far streaming o'er the flood,
Hath guided Europe through her darkest hour:
Away, vain dreams of glory!—in the dust
Be humbled, ocean-queen! and own thy sentence just!

XII.

Hark! 'twas the death-bell's note! which, full and deep,
Unmix'd with aught of less majestic tone,

While all the murmurs of existence sleep,
Swell'd on the stillness of the air alone !
Silent the throngs that fill the darken'd street,
Silent the slumbering Thames, the lonely mart ;
And all is still, where countless thousands meet,
Save the full throbbing of the awe-struck heart !
All deeply, strangely, fearfully serene,
As in each ravaged home th' avenging one had been.

XIII.

The sun goes down in beauty—his farewell,
Unlike the world he leaves, is calmly bright ;
And his last mellow'd rays around us dwell,
Lingering, as if on scenes of young delight.
They smile and fade—but, when the day is o'er,
What slow procession moves, with measured tread ?—
Lo ! those who weep, with her who weeps no more
A solemn train—the mourners and the dead !
While throned on high, the moon's untroubled ray
Looks down, as earthly hopes are passing thus away

XIV.

But other light is in that holy pile,
Where, in the house of silence, kings repose ;
There, through the dim arcade, and pillar'd aisle,
The funeral torch its deep red radiance throws.
There pall, and canopy, and sacred strain,
And all around' the stamp of woe may bear ;
But Grief, to whose full heart those forms are vain,
Grief unexpress'd, unsoothed by them—is there.
No darker hour hath Fate for him who mourns,
Than when the all he loved, as dust, to dust returns.

XV.

We mourn—but not *thy* fate, departed One !
We pity—but the living, not the dead ;
A cloud hangs o'er us—* " the bright day is done,"
And with a father's hopes, a nation's fled.
And he, the chosen of thy youthful breast,
Whose soul with thine had mingled every thought ;
He, with thine early fond affections blest,
Lord of a mind with all things lovely fraught ;
What but a desert to his eye, that earth,
Which but retains of thee the memory of thy worth ?

XVI.

Oh ! there are griefs for nature too intense,
Whose first rude shock but stupifies the soul ;
Nor hath the fragile and o'erlabor'd sense
Strength e'en to *feel*, at once, their dread control.

---

* " The bright day is done,
     And we are for the dark."—SHAKESPEARE.

But when 'tis past, that still and speechless hour
Of the seal'd bosom, and the tearless eye,
Then the roused mind awakes with tenfold power
To grasp the fulness of its agony!
Its death-like torpor vanish'd—and its doom;
To cast its own dark hues o'er life and nature's bloom.

XVII.

And such *his* lot, whom thou hast loved and left,
Spirit! thus early to thy home recall'd!
So sinks the heart, of hope and thee bereft,
A warrior's heart, which danger ne'er appall'd.
Years may pass on—and, as they roll along,
Mellow those pangs which now his bosom rend;
And he once more, with life's unheeding throng,
May, though alone in soul, in seeming blend;
Yet still, the guardian-angel of his mind
Shall thy loved image dwell, in Memory's temple shrined.

XVIII.

Yet must the days be long ere time shall steal
Aught from his grief whose spirit dwells with thee;
Once deeply bruised, the heart at length may heal,
But all it was—oh! never more shall be.
The flower, the leaf, o'erwhelm'd by winter snow,
Shall spring again, when beams and showers return
The faded cheek again with health may glow,
And the dim eye with life's warm radiance burn
But the pure freshness of the mind's young bloom,
Once lost, revives alone in worlds beyond the tomb.

XIX.

But thou—thine hour of agony is o'er,
And thy brief race in brilliance hath been run,
While Faith, that bids fond nature grieve no more,
Tells that thy crown—though not on earth—is won.
Thou, of the world so early left, hast known
Nought but the bloom and sunshine—and for thee,
Child of propitious stars! for thee alone,
The course of love ran smooth,* and brightly free—
Not long such bliss to mortal could be given,
It is enough for earth to catch one glimpse of heaven.

XX.

What though, ere yet the noon-day of thy fame
Rose in its glory on thine England's eye,
The grave's deep shadows o'er thy prospect came!
Ours is that loss—and thou wert blest to die!
Thou might'st have lived to dark and evil years,
To mourn thy people changed, thy skies o'ercast;

---

* "The course of true love never did run smooth."
SHAKESPEARE.

But thy spring morn was all undimm'd by tears,
And thou wert loved and cherish'd to the last!
And thy young name, ne'er breathed in ruder tone,
Thus dying, thou hast left to love and grief alone.

XXI.

Daughter of Kings! from that high sphere look down,
Where still in hope, affection's thoughts may rise;
Where dimly shines to thee that mortal crown,
Which earth display'd to claim thee from the skies.
Look down! and if thy spirit yet retain
Memory of aught that once was fondly dear,
Soothe, though unseen, the hearts that mourn in vain,
And, in their hours of loneliness—be near!
Blest was thy lot e'en here—and one faint sigh,
Oh! tell those hearts, hath made that bliss eternity!

Nov. 23, 1817.

CRITICAL ANNOTATIONS

ON "TRANSLATIONS FROM CAMOENS AND OTHER POETS," &c.

"The next volume in order consists principally of translations. It will give our readers some idea of Mrs. Hemans's acquaintance with books, to enumerate the authors from whom she has chosen her sub jects:—they are Camoens, Metastasio, Filicaja, Pastorini, Lope de Vega, Francisco Manuel, Della Casa, Cornelio, Bentivoglio, Quevedo, Juan de Tarsis, Torquato and Bernardo Tasso, Petrarca, Pietro Bem bo, Lorenzini, Gessner, Chaulieu, Garcilaso de Vega; names embracing almost every language in which the muse has found a tongue in Europe. Many of these translations are very pretty, but it would be less interesting to select any of them for citation, as our readers might not be possessed of or acquainted with the originals. We will pass on, therefore, to the latter part of the volume, which contains much that is very pleasing and beautiful. The poem which we are about to transcribe is on a subject often treated—and no wonder; it would be hard to find another which embraces so many of the elements of poetic feeling; so soothing a mixture of pleasing melancholy and pensive hope; such an assemblage of the ideas of tender beauty, of artless playfulness, of spotless purity, of transient yet imperishable brightness, of affections wounded, but not in bitterness, of sorrows gently subdued, of eternal and undoubted happiness. We know so little of the heart of man, that when we stand by the grave of him whom we deem most excellent, the thought of death will be mingled with some awe and uncertainty; but the gracious promises of scripture leave no doubt as to the blessedness of departed infants; and when we think what they now are and what they might have been, what they now enjoy and what they might have suffered; what they have now gained and what they might have lost, we may indeed, yearn to follow them; but we must be selfish indeed, to wish them again 'constrained' to dwell in these tenements of pain and sorrow. The 'Dirge of a Child,' which follows, embodies these thoughts and feelings, but in more beautiful order and language:—

"No bitter tears for thee be shed,"—*Vide* page 192.

Quarterly Review, vol. xxiv

ITALIAN LITERATURE.

THE BASVIGLIANI OF MONTI.

FROM SISMONDI'S "LITTERATURE DU MIDI."

VINCENZO MONTI, a native of Ferrara, is acknowledged by the unanimous consent of the Italians, as the greatest of their living poets. Irritable, impassioned, variable to excess, he is always actuated by the impulse of the moment. Whatever he feels, is felt with the most enthusiastic vehemence. He sees the objects of his thoughts—they are present, and clothed with life—before him, and a flexible and harmonious language is always at his command to paint them with the richest coloring. Persuaded that poetry is only another species of painting, he makes the art of the poet consist in rendering apparent to the eyes of all the pictures created by his imagination for himself; and he permits not a verse to escape him which does not contain an image. Deeply impressed by the study of Dante, he has restored to the character of Italian poetry those severe and exalted beauties by which it was distinguished at its birth, and he proceeds from one picture to another with a grandeur and dignity peculiar to himself. It is extraordinary that, with something so lofty in his manner and style of writing, the heart of so impassioned a character should not be regulated by principles of greater consistency. In many other poets, this defect might pass unobserved : but circumstances have thrown the fullest light upon the versatility of Monti · and his glory, as a poet, is attached to works which display him in continual opposition to himself. Writing in the midst of the various Italian revolutions, he has constantly chosen political subjects for his compositions, and he has successively celebrated opposite parties in proportion to their success. Let us suppose, in his justification, that he composes as an improvisatore, and that his feelings, becoming highly excited by the given theme, he seizes the political ideas it suggests however foreign they may be to his individual sentiments.* In these political poems—the object and purport of which are so different—the invention and manner are, perhaps, but too similar. The *Basvigliana*, or poem on the death of Basville, is the most celebrated ; but since its appearance, it has been discovered that Monti, who always imitated Dante, has now also very frequently imitated himself.

Hugh Bassville was the French Envoy who was put to death at Rome by the people, for attempting, at the beginning of the Revolu-

---

* The observation of a French author (*Le Censeur du Dictionnaire des Girouettes*) on the general versatility of poets, seems so peculiarly appropriate to the character of Monti, that it might almost be supposed to have been written for the express purpose of such an application.—" Le cerveau d'un poëte est d'une cire molle et flexible, où s'imprime naturellement tout ce qui le flatte, le séduit, et l'alimente. La muse du chant n'a pas de partie ; c'est une étourdie sans consequence, qui folâtre également et sur de riches gazons et sur d'arides bruyères. Un poète en délire chante indifferement Titus et Thamask, Louis 12me et Cromwell, Christine de Suéde, et Stanchon la Vielleuse.

tion, to excite a sedition against the Pontifical government. Monti, who was then the poet of the Pope, as he has since been of the Republic, supposes that, at the moment of Basville's death, he is saved by a sudden repentance, from the condemnation which his philosophical principles had merited. But, as a punishment for his guilt, and a substitute for the pains of purgatory, he is condemned by Divine Justice to traverse France, until the crimes of that country have received their due chastisement, and doomed to contemplate the misfortunes and reverses to which he has contributed, by assisting to extend the progress of the Revolution.

An angel of heaven conducts Bassville from province to province, that he may behold the desolation of his lovely country. He then conveys him to Paris, and makes him witness the sufferings and death of Louis XVI., and afterwards shows him the Allied armies prepared to burst upon France, and avenge the blood of her king. The poem concludes before the issue of the contest is known. It is divided into four cantos of three hundred lines each, and written in *terza rima*, like the poem of Dante. Not only many expressions, epithets, and lines, are borrowed from the Divine Comedy, but the invention itself is similar. An angel conducts Basville through the suffering world; and this faithful guide, who consoles and supports the *spectator-hero* of the poem, acts precisely the same part which is performed by Virgil in Dante. Bassville himself, thinks, feels, and suffers, exactly as Dante would have done. Monti has not preserved any traces of his revolutionary character; he describes him as feeling more pity than remorse, and he seems to forget, in thus identifying himself with his hero, that he has at first represented Basville, and perhaps without foundation, as an infidel and a ferocious revolutionist. The *Basvigliana* is, perhaps, more remarkable than any other poem for the majesty of its verse, the sublimity of its expression, and the richness of its coloring. In the first canto, the spirit of Bassville thus takes leave of the body :—

Sleep, O beloved companion of my woes,
Rest thou in deep and undisturb'd repose;
Till, at the last great day, from slumber's bed,
Heaven's trumpet-summons shall awake the dead.

Be the earth light upon thee, mild the shower,
And soft the breeze's wing, till that dread hour;
Nor let the wand'rer, passing o'er thee, breathe
Words of keen insult to the dust beneath.

Sleep thou in peace! beyond the funeral pyre,
There live no flames of vengeance or of ire,
And 'midst high hearts I leave thee, on a shore,
Where mercy's home hath been from days of yore.

Thus, to its earthly form, the spirit cried,
Then turn'd to follow its celestial guide,
But with a downcast mien, a pensive sigh,
A ling'ring step, and oft reverted eye—
As when a child's reluctant feet obey
Its mother's voice, and slowly leave its play.

Night o'er the earth her dewy veil had cast,
When from th' eternal city's towers they pass'd

And rising in their flight, on that proud dome,
Whose walls enshrine the guardian saint of Rome,
Lo! where a cherub-form sublimely tower'd,
But dreadful in his glory! sternly lower'd
Wrath in his kingly aspect: One he seem'd
Of the bright seven, whose dazzling splendor beam'd
On high amidst the burning lamps of heaven,
Seen in the dread, o'erwhelming visions given.
To the rapt seer of Patmos. Wheels of fire
Seem'd his fierce eyes, all kindling in their ire,
And his loose tresses, floating as he stood,
A comet's glare, presaging woe and blood.
He waved his sword; its red, terrific light,
With fearful radiance tinged the clouds of night,
While his left hand sustain'd a shield so vast,
Far o'er the Vatican beneath was cast
Its broad, protecting shadow. As the plume
Of the strong eagle spreads in sheltering gloom
O'er its young brood, as yet untaught to soar;
And while, all trembling at the whirlwind's roar,
Each humbler bird shrinks cowering in its nest,
Beneath that wing of power, and ample breast,
They sleep unheeding; while the storm on high
Breaks not their calm and proud security.

In the Second Canto, Basville enters Paris with his angelic guide, at the moment preceding the execution of Louis XVI.

The air was heavy, and the brooding skies
Look'd fraught with omens, as to harmonize
With his pale aspect. Through the forest round
Not a leaf whisper'd—and the only sound
That broke the stillness was a streamlet's moan
Murmuring amidst the rocks with plaintive tone,
As if a storm within the woodland bowers
Were gathering. On they moved—and lo! the towers
Of a far city! Nearer now they drew;
And all reveal'd, expanding on their view,
The Babylon, the scene of crimes and woes—
Paris, the guilty, the devoted, rose!
  * * * * *
In the dark mantle of a cloud array'd,
Viewless and hush'd, the angel and the shade
Enter'd that evil city. Onward pass'd
The heavenly being first, with brow o'ercast
And troubled mien, while in his glorious eyes
Tears had obscured the splendor of the skies.
Pale with dismay, the trembling spirit saw
That alter'd aspect, and, in breathless awe,
Mark'd the strange silence round. The deep-toned swell
Of life's full tide was hush'd; the sacred bell,

The clamorous anvil, mute ; all sounds were fled
Of labor or of mirth, and in their stead
Terror and stillness, boding signs of woe,
Enquiring glances, rumors whisper'd low,
Questions half-utter'd, jealous looks that keep
A fearful watch around, and sadness deep
That weighs upon the heart ; and voices, heard
At intervals, in many a broken word—
Voices of mothers, trembling as they press'd
Th' unconscious infant closer to their breast :
Voices of wives, with fond imploring cries,
And the wild eloquence of tears and sighs,
On their own thresholds striving to detain
Their fierce, impatient lords ; but weak and vain
Affection's gentle bonds, in that dread hour
Of fate and fury—Love hath lost his power !
For evil spirits are abroad, the air
Breathes of their influence ; Druid phantoms there,
Fired by that thirst for victims, which of old
Raged in their bosoms, fierce and uncontroll'd,
Rush, in ferocious transport, to survey
The deepest crime that e'er hath dimm'd the day.
Blood, human blood, hath stain'd their vests and hair,
On the winds tossing, with a sanguine glare.
Scattering red showers around them ! flaming brands
And serpent scourges in their restless hands
Are wildly shaken ; others lift on high
The steel, th' envenom'd bowl, and hurrying by
With touch of fire, contagious fury dart
Through human veins, fast kindling to the heart.
Then comes the rush of crowds ! restrain'd no more,
Fast from each home the frenzied inmates pour ;
From every heart affrighted mercy flies,
While her soft voice amidst the tumult dies.
Then the earth trembles, as from street to street
The tramp of steeds, the press of hastening feet,
The roll of wheels, all mingling in the breeze,
Come deepening onward, as the swell of seas
Heard at the dead of midnight ; or the moan
Of distant tempests, or the hollow tone
Of the far thunder ! Then what feelings press'd,
O wretched Basville ! on thy guilty breast ;
What pangs were thine, thus fated to behold
Death's awful banner to the winds unfold !
To see the axe, the scaffold, raised on high,
The dark impatience of the murderer's eye,
Eager for crime ! And he, the great, the good,
Thy martyr-king, by men athirst for blood
Dragg'd to a felon's death ! Yet still his mien,
'Midst that wild throng, is loftily serene ;
And his step falters not. O, hearts unmoved !
Where have you borne your monarch ?—He who loved—

Loved you so well!—Behold! the sun grows pale,
Shrouding his glory in a tearful veil!
The misty air is silent, as in dread,
And the dim sky, with shadowy gloom o'erspread,
While saints and martyrs, spirits of the blest,
Look down, all weeping, from their bowers of rest.
  * * * * * * *

In that dread moment, to the fatal pile
The regal victim came; and raised the while
His patient glance, with such an aspect high,
So firm, so calm in holy majesty,
That e'en th' assassins' hearts a moment shook
Before the grandeur of that kingly look;
And a strange thrill of pity, half-renew'd,
Ran through the bosoms of the multitude.
  * * * * * * *

Like Him, who, breathing mercy till the last,
Pray'd till the bitterness of death was past:
E'en for his murderers pray'd, in that dark hour
When his soul yielded to affliction's power;
And the winds bore his dying cry abroad—
" Hast thou forsaken me, my God! my God?"
E'en thus the monarch stood; his prayer arose,
Thus calling down forgiveness on his foes—
" To Thee my spirit I commend," he cried;
" And my lost people, Father, be their guide!"
  * * * * * * *

But the sharp steel descends—the blow is given,
And answer'd by a thunder-peal from heaven;
Earth, stain'd with blood, convulsive terrors owns,
And her kings tremble on their distant thrones!

THE ALCESTIS OF ALFIERI.

The *Alcestis* of ALFIERI is said to have been the last tragedy he composed, and is distinguished to a remarkable degree by that tenderness of which his former works present so few examples. It would appear as if the pure and exalted affection by which the impetuosity of his fiery spirit was ameliorated during the latter years of his life, had impressed its whole character on this work, as a record of that domestic happiness in whose bosom his heart at length found a resting-place. Most of his earlier writings bear witness to that "fever at the core," that burning impatience of restraint, and those incessant and untamable aspirations after a wider sphere of action, by which his youth was consumed; but the poetry of *Alcestis* must find its echo in every heart which has known the power of domestic ties, or felt the bitterness of their dissolution. The interest of the piece, however, though entirely domestic, is not for a moment allowed to languish, nor does the conjugal affection, which forms the mainspring of the action, ever degenerate into the pastoral insipidity of Metastasio. The character of Alcestis herself, with all its lofty fortitude, heroic affection, and subdued anguish, powerfully recalls to our imagination the calm and tempered majesty distinguishing the masterpieces of Greek sculpture, in which the expression of mental or bodily suffering is never allowed to transgress the limits of beauty and sublimity. The union of dignity and affliction impressing more than earthly grandeur on the countenance of Niobe, would be, perhaps, the best illustration of this analogy.

The following scene, in which Alcestis announces to Pheres, the father of Admetus, the terms upon which the oracle of Delphos has declared that his son may be restored, has seldom been surpassed by the author, even in his most celebrated productions. It is, however to be feared that little of its beauty can be transfused into a translation, as the severity of a style so completely devoid of imagery must render it dependent for many incommunicable attractions upo the melody of the original language.

ACT I.—Scene II.

Alcestis, Pheres.

Alc. Weep thou no more : O ! monarch, dry thy tears,
For know, he shall not die ; not now shall Fate
Bereave thee of thy son.
  Phe. What mean thy words ?
Hath then Apollo—is there then a hope ?
  Alc. Yes ! hope for *thee*—hope, by the voice announced
From the prophetic cave. Nor would I yield
To other lips the tidings, meet alone
For thee to hear from mine.
  Phe. But say ! oh ! say,
Shall then my son be spared ?
  Alc. He shall, to *thee*.
Thus hath Apollo said—Alcestis thus
Confirms the oracle—be thou secure.
  Phe. O sounds of joy ! He lives !
  Alc. But not for this,
Think that e'en for *this* the stranger Joy
Shall yet revisit these devoted walls.
  Phe. Can there be grief when from his bed of death
Admetus rises ? What deep mystery lurks
Within thy words ? What mean'st thou ? Gracious Heaven !
Thou, whose deep love is all his own, who hear'st
The tidings of his safety, and dost bear
Transport and life in that glad oracle
To his despairing sire ; thy cheek is tinged
With death, and on thy pure ingenuous brow,
To the brief lightning of a sudden joy,
Shades dark as night succeed, and thou art wrapt
In troubled silence—speak ! oh, speak !
  Alc. The gods
Themselves have limitations to their power
Impassable, eternal—and their will
Resists not the tremendous laws of fate :
Nor small the boon they grant thee in the life
Of thy restored Admetus.

Phe. In thy looks
There is expression, more than in thy words,
Which thrills my shuddering heart. Declare, what terms
Can render fatal to thyself and us,
The rescued life of him thy soul adores?
　Alc. O father! could my silence aught avail
To keep that fearful secret from thine ear,
Still should it rest unheard, till all fulfill'd
Were the dread sacrifice. But vain the wish;
And since too soon, too well it must be known,
Hear it from me.
　Phe. Throughout my curdling veins
Runs a cold, death-like horror; and I feel
I am not all a father. In my heart
Strive many deep affections. Thee I love,
O fair and high-soul'd consort of my son!
More than a daughter; and thine infant race,
The cherish'd hope and glory of my age;
And, unimpaired by time, within my breast,
High, holy, and unalterable love
For her, the partner of my cares and joys,
Dwells pure and perfect yet. Bethink thee, then,
In what suspense, what agony of fear,
I wait thy words; for well, too, well, I see
Thy lips are fraught with fatal auguries,
To some one of my race.
　Alc. Death hath his rights,
Of which not e'en the great Supernal Powers
May hope to rob him. By his ruthless hand,
Already seized, the noble victim lay,
The heir of empire, in his glowing prime
And noonday, struck:—Admetus, the revered,
The bless'd, the loved, by all who own'd his sway—
By his illustrious parents, by the realms
Surrounding his—and oh! what need to add,
How much by his Alcestis?—Such was he,
Already in th' unspairing grasp of death
Withering a certain prey. Apollo thence
Hath snatch'd him, and another in his stead,
Though not an equal—(who can equal him?)
Must fall a voluntary sacrifice.
Another, of his lineage or to him
By closest bonds united, must descend
To the dark realm of Orcus in *his* place,
Who thus alone is saved.
　Phe. What do I hear?
Woe to us, woe!—what victim?—who shall be
Accepted in his stead?
　Alc. The dread exchange
E'en now, O father! hath been made; the prey
Is ready, nor is who'ly worthless him
For whom 'tis freely offer'd. Nor wilt thou,

O mighty goddess of th' infernal shades!
Whose image sanctifies this threshold floor,
Disdain the victim.
 Phe. All prepared the prey!
And to our blood allied! O Heaven!—and yet
Thou bad'st me weep no more!
 Alc. Yes! thus I said,
And thus again I say, thou shalt not weep
Thy son's, nor I deplore my husband's doom.
Let him be saved, and other sounds of woe
Less deep, less mournful far, shall here be heard,
Than those *his* death had caused.—With some few tears,
But grief, and mingled with a gleam of joy,
E'en while the involuntary tribute lasts,
The victim shall be honor'd who resign'd
Life for Admetus.—Would'st thou know the prey,
The vow'd, the willing, the devoted one,
Offer'd and hallow'd to th' infernal gods,
Father!—'tis I.
 Phe. What hast thou done? O Heaven!
What hast thou done?—And think'st thou he is saved
By such a compact?—Think'st thou he can live
Bereft of thee?—Of thee, his light of life,
His very soul!—Of thee, beloved far more
Than his loved parents—than his children more—
More than himself?—Oh! no, it shall not be!
Thou perish, O Alcestis! in the flower
Of thy young beauty!—perish, and destroy
Not him, not *him* alone, but us, but all,
Who as a child adore thee! Desolate
Would be the throne, the kingdom, reft of thee.
And think'st thou not of those whose tender years
Demand thy care?—thy children! think of them!
O thou, the source of each domestic joy,
Thou, in whose life alone Admetus lives,
His glory, his delight, thou shalt not die
While I can die for thee!—Me, me alone,
The oracle demands—a withered stem,
Whose task, whose duty, is for him to die.
My race is run—the fulness of my years,
The faded hopes of age, and all the love
Which hath its dwelling in a father's heart,
And the fond pity, half with wonder blent,
Inspired by thee, whose youth with heavenly gifts
So richly is endow'd; all, all unite
To grave in adamant the just decree,
That I must die. But thou, I bid the live!
Pheres commands thee O Alcestis—live!
Ne'er, ne'er shall woman's youthful love surpass
An aged sire's devotedness.
 Alc. I know
Thy lofty soul, thy fond paternal love;

Pheres, I know them well, and not in vain
Strove to anticipate their high resolves.
But if in silence I have heard thy words,
Now calmly list to mine, and thou shalt own
They may not be withstood.
 Phe. What canst thou say
Which I should hear? I go, resolved to save
Him who with thee would perish;—to the shrine
E'en now I fly.
 Alc. Stay, stay thee! 'tis too late.
Already hath consenting Proserpine,
From the remote abysses of her realms,
Heard and accepted the terrfic vow
Which binds me, with indissoluble ties,
To death. And I am firm, and well I know
None can deprive me of the awful right
That vow hath won.
 * * * * *
Yes! thou may'st weep my fate,
Mourn for me, father! but thou canst not blame
My lofty purpose. Oh! the more endear'd
My life by every tie—the more I feel
Death's bitterness, the more my sacrifice
Is worthy of Admetus. I descend
To the dim shadowy regions of the dead
A guest more honor'd.
 * * * * *
In thy presence here
Again I utter the tremendous vow,
Now more than half fulfill'd. I feel, I know
Its dread effects. Through all my burning veins
Th' insatiate fever revels. Doubt is o'er.
The Monarch of the Dead hath heard—he calls,
He summons me away—and thou art saved,
O my Admetus!

In the opening of the third act, Alcestis enters, with her son Eumeles, and her daughter, to complete the sacrifice by dying at the feet of Proserpine's statue. The following scene ensues between her and Admetus.

 Alc. Here, O my faithful handmaids! at the feet
Of Proserpine's dread image spread my couch,
For I myself e'en now must offer here
The victim she requires. And you meanwhile,
My children! seek your sire. Behold him there,
Sad, silent, and alone. But through his veins
Health's genial current flows once more, as free
As in his brightest days: and he shall live—
Shall live for you. Go, hang upon his neck,
And with your innocent encircling arms
Twine round him fondly.
 Eum. Can it be indeed,

Father, loved father! that we see thee thus
Restored? What joy is ours!
    Adm. There is no joy!
Speak not of joy! away, away! my grief
Is wild and desperate; cling to me no more!
I know not of affection, and I feel
No more a father.
    Eum. Oh! what words are these?
Are we no more thy children? Are we not
Thine own? Sweet sister! twine around his neck
More close; he must return the fond embrace.
    Adm. O children! O my children! to my soul
Your innocent words and kisses are as darts,
That pierce it to the quick. I can no more
Sustain the bitter conflict. Every sound
Of your soft accents but too well recalls
The voice which was the music of my life.
Alcestis! my Alcestis!—was she not
Of all her sex the flower? Was woman e'er
Adored like her before? Yet this is she,
The cold of heart, th' ungrateful, who hath left
Her husband and her infants! This is she,
O my deserted children! who at once
Bereaves you of your parents.
    Alc. Woe is me!
I hear the bitter and reproachful cries
Of my despairing lord. With life's last powers,
O! let me strive to soothe him still. Approach,
My handmaids, raise me, and support my steps
To the distracted mourner. Bear me hence,
That he may hear and see me.
    Adm. Is it thou?
And do I see thee still? and com'st thou thus
To comfort me, Alcestis? Must I hear
The dying accents *thus?* Alas! return
To thy sad couch, return! 'tis meet for me
There by thy side for ever to remain.
    Alc. For me thy care is vain. Though meet for thee—
    Adm. O voice! O looks of death! are these, are *these,*
Thus darkly shrouded with mortality,
The eyes that were the sunbeams and the life
Of my fond soul? Alas! how faint a ray
Falls from their faded orbs, so brilliant once,
Upon my drooping brow! How heavily
With what a weight of death thy languid voice
Sinks on my heart! too faithful far, too fond.
Alcestis! thou art dying—and for me!
    *   *   *   *

Alcestis! and thy feeble hand supports
With its last power, supports my sinking head,
E'en now, while death is on thee! Oh! the touch
Rekindles tenfold frenzy in my heart,

I rush, I fly impetuous to the shrine,
The image of yon ruthless Deity,
Impatient for her prey. Before thy death,
There, there, I too, self-sacrificed, will fall.
   * * * *
Vain is each obstacle—In vain the gods
Themselves would check my fury—I am lord
Of my own days—and thus I swear—
 Alc. Yes! swear,
Admetus! for thy children to sustain
The load of life. All other impious vows,
Which thou, a rebel to the sovereign will
Of those who rule on high, might'st dare to form
Within thy breast; thy lip, by them enchain'd,
Would vainly seek to utter.—See'st thou not,
It is from them the inspiration flows,
Which in my language breathes? They lend me power,
They bid me through thy strengthen'd soul transfuse
High courage, noble constancy. Submit,
Bow down to them thy spirit. Be thou calm;
Be near me. Aid me. In the dread extreme
To which I now approach, from whom but thee
Should comfort be derived? Afflict me not,
In such an hour, with anguish worse than death.
O faithful and beloved support me still!
   * * * *

  The choruses with which this tragedy is interspersed, are distinguished for their melody and classic beauty. The following translation will give our readers a faint idea of the one by which the third act is concluded.

 Alc. My children! all is finish'd. Now farewell!
To thy fond care, O Pheres! I commit
My widow'd lord, forsake him not.
 Eum. Alas!
Sweet mother! wilt thou leave us? from thy side
Are we for ever parted?
 Phe. Tears forbid
All utterance of our woes. Bereft of sense,
More lifeless than the dying victim, see
The desolate Admetus. Farther yet,
Still farther, let us bear him from the sight
Of his Alcestis.
 Alc. O my handmaids! still
Lend me your pious aid, and thus compose
With sacred modesty these torpid limbs
When death's last pang is o'er.
     Chorus.
  Alas! how weak
 Her struggling voice! that last keen pang **is near.**
  Peace, mourners, peace!
 Be hush'd, be silent, in this hour of dread!

Our cries would but increase
The sufferer's pangs; let tears unheard be shed,
  Cease, voice of weeping, cease!
  Sustain, O friend!
  Upon thy faithful breast,
The head that sinks with mortal pain opprest!
  And thou assistance lend
  To close the languid eye,
  Still beautiful in life's last agony.
  Alas how long a strife!
What anguish struggles in the parting breath
  Ere yet immortal life
  Be won by death!
Death! death! thy work complete!
Let thy sad hour be fleet,
Speed, in thy mercy, the releasing sigh!
  No more keen pangs impart
  To her, the high in heart,
Th' adored Alcestis, worthy ne'er to die.

Chorus of Admetus.

  'Tis not enough, oh no!
To hide the scene of anguish from his eyes,
  Still must our silent band
  Around him watchful stand,
And on the mourner ceaseless care bestow,
That his ear catch not grief's funereal cries.
  Yet, yet hope is not dead,
  All is not lost below,
While yet the gods have pity on our woe
  Oft when all joy is fled,
  Heaven lends support to those
Who on its care in pious hope repose.
  Then to the blessed skies
Let our submissive prayers in chorus rise
  Pray! bow the knee and pray!
What other task have mortals, born to tears,
  Whom fate controls with adamantine sway?
  Oh ruler of the spheres!
Jove! Jove! enthroned immortally on high,
  Our supplication hear!
  Nor plunge in bitterest woes
Him, who nor footstep moves nor lifts his eye
  But as a child, which only knows
  Its father to revere.

IL CONTE DI CARMAGNOLA.

A TRAGEDY.—BY ALESSANDRO MANZONI.

FRANCESCO BUSSONE, the son of a peasant in Carmagnola, from whence his *nom du guerre* was derived, was born in the year 1390

Whilst yet a boy, and employed in the care of flocks and herds, the lofty character of his countenance was observed by a soldier of fortune, who invited the youth to forsake his rustic occupation, and accompany him to the busier scenes of the camp. His persuasions were successful, and Francesco entered with him into the service of Facino Cane, Lord of Alessandria. At the time when Facino died, leaving fourteen cities acquired by conquest to Beatrice di Tenda, his wife, Francesco di Carmagnola was amongst the most distinguished of his captains. Beatrice afterwards marrying Philip Visconti, Duke of Milan, (who rewarded her by an ignominious death for the regal dowery she had conferred upon him,) Carmagnola entered his army at the same time, and having, by his eminent services, firmly established the tottering power of that prince, received from him the title of Count, and was placed at the head of all his forces. The natural caprice and, ingratitude of Philip's disposition, however, at length prevailed, and Carmagnola disgusted with the evident proof of his wavering friendship and doubtful faith, left his service and his territories, and after a variety of adventures, took refuge in Venice. Thither the treachery of the Duke pursued him, and emissaries were employed to procure his assassination. The plot, however, proved abortive, and Carmagnola was elected captain-general of the Venetian armies, during the league formed by that republic against the Duke of Milan. The war was at first carried on with much spirit and success, and the battle of Maclodio, gained by Carmagnola, was one of the most important and decisive actions of those times. The night after the combat, the victorious soldiers gave liberty to almost all their prisoners. The Venetian envoys having made a complaint on this subject to the Count, he enquired what was become of the captives; and upon being informed that all, except four hundred, had been set free, he gave orders that the remaining ones also should be released immediately, according to the custom which prevailed amongst the armies of those days, the object of which was to prevent a speedy termination of the war. This proceeding of Carmagnola's occasioned much distrust and irritation in the minds of the Venetian rulers, and their displeasure was increased when the armada of the republic, commanded by Il Trevisani, was defeated upon the Po, without any attempt in its favor having been made by the Count. The failure of their attempt upon Cremona was also imputed to him as a crime, and the Senate, resolving to free themselves from a powerful chief, now become an object of suspicion, after many deliberations on the best method of carrying their designs into effect, at length determined to invite him to Venice, under pretence of consulting him on their negotiations for peace. He obeyed their summons without hesitation or mistrust, and was every where received with extraordinary honors during the course of his journey. On his arrival at Venice, and before he entered his own house, eight gentlemen were sent to meet him, by whom he was escorted to St. Mark's Place. When he was introduced into the ducal palace, his attendants were dismissed, and informed that he would be in private with the Doge for a considerable time. He was arrested in the palace, then examined by the Secret Council, put to the torture, which a wound he had received in the service of the Republic rendered still more agonizing, and condemned to death. On the 5th May, 1432, he was conducted to execution, with his mouth gagged, and beheaded between the two columns of St. Mark's Place. With regard to the innocence or guilt of this distinguished character, there exists no authentic information. The author of the tragedy, which we are about to analyse, has chosen to represent him as entirely innocent, and probability at least is on this side. It is possible, that the haughtiness of an aspiring warrior, accustomed to command, and impatient of control, might have been the principal cause of offence to the Venetians; or perhaps their jealousy was excited by his increasing power over the minds of an obedient army; and, not considering it expedient to displace him, they resolved upon his destruction.

This tragedy, which is formed upon the model of the English and German drama, comprises the history of Carmagnola's life, from the day on which he was made commander of the Venetian armies to that of his execution, thus embracing a period of about seven years The extracts we are about to present to our readers, will enable them to form their own opinion of a piece which has excited so much attention in Italy. The first act opens in Venice, in the hall of the Senate. The Doge proposes that the Count di Carmagnola should be consulted on the projected league between the Republic and the Florentines, against the Duke of Milan. To this all agree; and the Count is introduced. He begins by justifying his conduct from the imputations to which it might be liable, in consequence of his appearing as the enemy of the Prince whom he had so recently served:—

―――― He cast me down
From the high place my blood had dearly won,
And when I sought his presence, to appeal
For justice there, 'twas vain! my foes had form'd
Around his throne a barrier; e'en my life
Became the mark of hatred, but in this
Their hopes have fail'd—I gave them not the time.
My life!—I stand prepared to yield it up
On the proud field, and in some noble cause
For glory well exchanged; but not a prey,
Not to be caught ignobly in the toils
Of those I scorn. I left him, and obtain'd
With you a place of refuge; yet e'en here
His snares were cast around me. Now all ties
Are broke between us; to an open foe,
An open foe I come.――――

He then gives counsel in favor of war, and retires, leaving the senate engaged in deliberation. War is resolved upon, and he is elected commander. The fourth scene represents the house of Car magnola. His soliloquy is noble; but its character is much more that of English than of Italian poetry, and may be traced without difficulty, to the celebrated monologue of Hamlet.

A leader—or a fugitive!—to drag
Slow years along in idle vacancy,
As a worn veteran living on the fame
Of former deeds; to offer humble prayers
And blessings for protection—owing all
Yet left me of existence to the might
Of other swords, dependent on some arm
Which soon may cast me off—or on the field
To breathe once more, to feel the tide of life
Rush proudly through my veins—to hail again
My lofty star, and at the trumpet's voice
To wake! to rule! to conquer!—Which must be
My fate, this hour decides. And yet, if peace

Should be the choice of Venice, shall I cling
Still poorly to ignoble safety here,
Secluded as a homicide, who cowers
Within a temple's precincts? Shall not he
Who made a kingdom's fate, control his own?
Is there not one among the many lords
Of this divided Italy—not one
With soul enough to envy that bright crown
Encircling Philip's head? And know they not
'Twas won by me from many a tyrant's grasp,
Snatch'd by my hand, and placed upon the brow
Of that ingrate, from whom my spirit burns
Again to wrest it, and bestow the prize
On him who best shall call the prowess forth
Which slumbers in my arm?

 Marco, a senator, and a friend of the Count, now arrives, and announces to him that war is resolved upon, and that he is appointed to the command of the armies, at the same time advising him to act with caution towards his enemies in the Republic.

 Car. Think'st thou I know not whom to deem my foes?
Ay, I could number all.
 Mar. And know'st thou, too,
What fault hath made them such?—'Tis, that thou art
So high above them; 'tis that thy disdain
Doth meet them undisguised. As yet not one
Hath done thee wrong; but who, when so resolved,
Finds not his time to injure?—In thy thoughts,
Save when they cross thy path, no place is theirs;
But they remember *thee.* The high in soul
Scorn and forget; but to the grovelling heart
There is delight in hatred. Rouse it not,
Subdue it, while the power is yet thine own.
I counsel no vile arts, from which my soul
Revolts indignantly—thou know'st it well;
But there is yet a wisdom, not unmeet
For the most lofty nature—there is power
Of winning meaner minds, without descent
From the high spirit's glorious eminence,—
And would'st thou seek that magic, it were thine.

 The first scene of the second act represents part of the Duke of Milan's camp near Maclodio. Malatesti, the commander-in-chief, and Pergola, a Condottiere of great distinction, are deliberating upon the state of the war. Pergola considers it imprudent to give battle, Malatesti is of a contrary opinion. They are joined by Sforza and Fortebraccio, who are impatient for action, and Torello, who endeavors to convince them of its inexpediency.

 Sfo. Torello, didst thou mark the ardent soul
Which fires each soldier's eye?
 Tor. I mark'd it well.

I heard th' impatient shout, th' exulting voice
Of Hope and Courage, and I turned aside,
That on my brow the warrior might not read
Th' involuntary thought, whose sudden gloom
Had cast deep shadows there. It was a thought,
That this vain semblance of delusive joy
Soon like a dream shall fade. It was a thought
On wasted valour doom'd to perish here.
* * * * * * *

For these—what boots it to disguise the truth ?—'
These are no wars in which, for all things loved,
And precious, and revered—for all the ties
Clinging around the heart—for those whose smile
Makes home so lovely—for his native land,
And for its laws, the patriot soldier fights!
These are no wars in which the chieftain's aim
Is but to station his devoted bands,
And theirs, thus fix'd—to die ! It is *our* fate
To lead a hireling train, whose spirits breathe
Fury, not fortitude. With burning hearts
They rush where Victory smiling waves them on;
But if delay'd, if between flight and death,
Pausing they stand—is there no cause to doubt
What choice were theirs? And but too well our hearts
That choice might here foresee. Oh ! evil times,
When for the leader, care augments, the more
Bright glory fades away !—Yet, once again,
This is no field for us.

After various debates, Malatesti resolves to attack the enemy.—The fourth and fifth scenes of the second act represent the tent of the Count in the Venetian camp, and his preparations for battle. And here a magnificent piece of lyric poetry is introduced, in which the battle is described, and its fatal effects lamented, with all the feeling of a patriot and a Christian. It appears to us, however, that this ode, hymn, or chorus as the author has entitled it, striking as its effect may be in a separate recitation, produces a much less powerful impression in the situation it occupies at present. It is even necessary, in order to appreciate its singular beauty, that it should be re-perused, as a thing detached from the tragedy. The transition is too violent, in our opinion, from a tragic action, in which the characters are represented as clothed with existence, and passing before us with all their contending motives and feelings laid open to our inspection, to the comparative coldness of a lyric piece, where the author's imagination expatiates alone. The poet may have been led into this error by a definition of Schlegel's, who, speaking of the Greek choruses, gives it as his opinion, that " the chorus is to be considered as a personification of the moral thoughts inspired by the action—as the organ of the poet who speaks in the name of the whole human race. The chorus, in short, is the *ideal* spectator."

But the fact was not exactly thus : The Greek chorus was composed of *real* characters, and expressed the sentiments of the people before whose eyes the action was imagined to be passing; thus the **true** spectator, after witnessing in representation the triumphs or misfortunes of kings and heroes, heard from the chorus the idea supposed **to be** entertained on the subject by the more enlightened part of the multitude. If the author, availing himself of his talent for lyric poetry, and varying the measure in conformity to the subject, had brought his chorus into action, introducing, for example, a veteran looking down upon the battle from an eminence, and describing its vicissitudes to the persons below, with whom he might interchange a variery of national and moral reflections, it appears to us that the dramatic effect would have been considerably heightened, and the assertion that the Greek chorus is not compatible with the system of the modern drama, possibly disapproved. We shall present our readers with the entire chorus of which we have spoken, as a piece to be read separately, and one to which the following title would be much more appropriate.

The Battle of Maclodio (or Macalo), an Ode.

Hark! from the right bursts forth a trumpet's sound,
A loud shrill trumpet from the left replies!
On every side hoarse echoes from the ground
To the quick tramp of steeds and warriors rise,
Hollow and deep—and banners, all around,
Meet hostile banners waving to the skies;
Here steel-clad bands in marshall'd order shine,
And there a host confronts their glittering line.

Lo! half the field already from the sight
Hath vanish'd, hid by closing groups of foes!
Swords crossing swords, flash lightning o'er the fight,
And the strife deepens, and the life-blood flows!
Oh! who are these? What stranger in his might
Comes bursting on the lovely land's repose?
What patriot hearts have nobly vow'd to save
Their native soil, or make its dust their grave?

One race, alas! these foes—one kindred race,
Were born and rear'd the same fair scenes among!
The stranger calls them brothers—and each face
That brotherhood reveals;—one common tongue
Dwells on their lips—the earth on which we trace
Their heart's blood—is the soil from whence they sprung.
One mother gave them birth—this chosen land,
Circled with Alps and seas, by Nature's guardian hand.

O grief and horror! who the first could dare
Against a brother's breast the sword to wield?
What cause unhallow'd and accursed, declare,
Hath bathed with carnage this ignoble field?
Think'st thou they know?—they but inflict and share
Misery and death, the motive unreveal'd!
—Sold to a leader, sold *himself* to die,
With him they strive,—they fall—and ask not why.

But are there none who love them? Have they none—
No wives, no mothers, who might rush between,

And win with tears the husband and the son
Back to his home, from this polluted scene?
And they, whose hearts, when life's bright day is done,
Unfold to thoughts more solemn and serene,
Thoughts of the tomb; why cannot *they* assuage
The storms of passion with the voice of age?

Ask not!—the peasant at his cabin-door
Sits calmly pointing to the distant cloud
Which skirts th' horizon, menacing to pour
Destruction down o'er fields he hath not plough'd.
Thus, where no echo of the battle's roar
Is heard afar, even thus the reckless crowd,
In tranquil safety number o'er the slain,
Or tell of cities burning on the plain.

There may'st thou mark the boy, with earnest gaze
Fix'd on his mother's lips, intent to know
By names of insult, those, whom future days
Shall see him meet in arms, their deadliest foe.
There proudly many a glittering dame displays
Bracelet and zone, with radiant gems that glow,
By lovers, husbands, home in triumph borne,
From the sad brides of fall'n warriors torn.

Woe to the victors and the vanquish'd woe!
The earth is heap'd, is loaded with the slain;
Loud and more loud the cries of fury grow,
A sea of blood is swelling o'er the plain.
But from th' embattled front, already, lo!
A band recedes—it flies—all hope is vain,
And venal hearts, despairing of the strife,
Wake to the love, the clinging love of life.

As the light grain disperses in the air,
Borne from the winnowing by the gales around,
Thus fly the vanquish'd, in their wild despair,
Chased, sever'd, scatter'd—o'er the ample ground.
But mightier bands, that lay in ambush there,
Burst on their flight—and hark! the deepening sound
Of fierce pursuit!—still nearer and more near,
The rush of war-steeds trampling in the rear.

The day is won!—they fall—disarm'd they yield,
Low at the conqueror's feet all suppliant lying!
'Midst shouts of victory pealing o'er the field,
Ah! who may hear the murmurs of the dying?
Haste! let the tale of triumph be reveal'd!
E'en now the courier to his steed is flying,
He spurs—he speeds—with tidings of the day,
To rouse up cities in his lightning way.

THE CARMAGNOLA OF MANZONI.

Why pour ye forth from your deserted homes,
O eager multitudes! around him pressing?
Each hurrying where his breathless courser foams,
Each tongue, each eye, infatuate hope confessing!
Know ye not *whence* th' ill-omen'd herald comes,
And dare ye dream he comes with words of blessing?
Brothers, by brothers slain, lie low and cold,—
Be ye content! the glorious tale is told.

I hear the voice of joy, th' exulting cry!
They deck the shrine, they swell the choral strains,
E'en now the homicides assail the sky
With pæans, which indignant Heavens disdains!—
But from the soaring Alps the stranger's eye
Looks watchful down on our ensanguin'd plains,
And, with the cruel rapture of a foe,
Numbers the mighty, stretch'd in death below.

Haste! form your lines again, ye brave and true!
Haste, haste! your triumph and your joys suspending;
Th' invader comes, your banners raise anew,
Rush to the strife, your country's call attending!
Victors! why pause ye?—Are ye weak and few?—
Ay! such he deem'd you, and for *this* descending,
He waits you on the field ye know too well,
The same red war-field where your brethren fell.

O thou devoted land! that canst not rear
In peace thine offspring; thou, the lost and won,
The fair and fatal soil, that dost appear
Too narrow still for each contending son;
Receive the stranger, in his fierce career
Parting thy spoils! Thy chastening is begun!
And, wresting from thy kings the guardian sword,
Foes whom thou n'er hadst wrong'd sit proudly at thy board.

Are these infatuate too?—Oh! who hath known
A people e'er by guilt's vain triumph blest?
The wrong'd, the vanquish'd suffer not alone,
Brief is that joy that swells th' oppressor's breast.
What though not yet his day of pride be flown,
Though yet Heaven's vengeance spare his haughty crest,
Well hath it mark'd him—and decreed the hour,
When his last sigh shall own, the terror of its power.

Are we not creatures of one hand divine,
Form'd in one mould, to one redemption born?
Kindred alike where'er our skies may shine,
Where'er our sight first drank the vital morn!
Brothers! one bond around our souls should twine,
And woe to him by whom that bond is torn!

Who mounts by trampling broken hearts to earth,
Who bows down spirits of immortal birth!

The third act, which passes entirely in the tent of the Count, is composed of long discourses between Carmagnola and the Venetian envoys. One of these requires him to pursue the fugitives after his victory, which he haughtily refuses to do, declaring that he will not leave the field until he has gained possession of the surrounding fortresses Another complains that the Condottieri and the soldiers have released their prisoners, to which he replies, that it is an established military custom; and, sending for the remaining four hundred captives, he gives them their liberty also. This act, which terminates with the suspicious observations of the envoys on Carmagnola's conduct, is rather barren of interest, though the episode of the younger Pergola, which we shall lay before our readers, is happily imagined.

As the prisoners are departing, the Count observes the younger Pergola, and stops him.

Car. Thou art not, youth!
One to be number'd with the vulgar crowd.
Thy garb, and more, thy towering mien, would speak
Of nobler parentage. Yet with the rest
Thou minglest, and art silent!
Per. Silence best,
O chief! befits the vanquish'd.
Car. Bearing up
Against thy fate thus proudly, thou art proved
Worthy a better star. Thy name?
Per. 'Tis one
Whose heritage doth impose no common task
On him that bears it. One, which to adorn
With brighter blazonry were hard emprize.
My name is Pergola.
Car. And art thou then
That warrior's son?
Per. I am.
Car. Approach! embrace
Thy father's early friend! What thou art now
I was, when first we met. Oh! thou dost bring
Back on my heart remembrance of the days,
The young, and joyous, and adventurous days
Of hope and ardor. And despond not thou!
My dawn, 'tis true, with brighter omens smiled,
But still fair Fortune's glorious promises
Are for the brave, and though delay'd awhile,
She soon or late fulfils them. Youth! salute
Thy sire for me; and say, though not of *thee*
I ask'd it, yet my heart is well assured
He counsell'd not this battle.
Per. Oh! he gave
Far other counsels, but his fruitless words
Were spoken to the winds.

Car. Lament thou not.
Upon his chieftain's head the shame will rest
Of this defeat; and he who firmly stood
Fix'd at his post of peril, hath begun
A soldier's race full nobly. Follow me,
I will restore thy sword.

The fourth act is occupied by the machinations of the Count's enemies at Venice; and the jealous and complicated policy of that Republic, and the despotic authority of the Council of Ten, are skilfully developed in many of the scenes.

The first scene of the fifth act opens at Venice in the hall of the Council of Ten. Carmagnola is consulted by the Doge on the terms of peace offered by the Duke of Milan. His advice is received with disdain, and after various insults he is accused of treason. His astonishment and indignation at this unexpected charge are expressed with all the warmth and simplicity of innocence.

Car. A traitor! I!—that name of infamy
Reaches not me. Let him the title bear
Who best deserves such meed—it is not mine.
Call me a dupe, and I may well submit,
For such my part is here; yet would I not
Exchange that name, for 'tis the worthiest still.
A traitor!—I retrace in thought the time,
When for your cause I fought; 'tis all one path
Strew'd o'er with flowers. Point out the day on which
A traitor's deeds were mine; the day which pass'd
Unmark'd by thanks, and praise, and promises
Of high reward! What more? Behold me here!
And when I came to seeming honor call'd,
When in my heart most deeply spoke the voice
Of love, and grateful zeal, and trusting faith—
Of trusting faith!—Oh, no! Doth he who comes
Th' invited guest of friendship, dream of faith?
I came to be ensnared! Well! 'it is done,
And be it so! but since deceitful hate
Hath thrown at length her smiling mask aside,
Praise be to Heaven! an open field at least
Is spread before us. Now 'tis yours to speak,
Mine to defend my cause; declare ye then
My treasons!
Doge. By the secret college soon
All shall be told thee.
Car. I appeal not there.
What I have done for you hath all been done
In the bright noonday, and its tale shall not
Be told in darkness. Of a warrior's deeds
Warriors alone should judge; and such I choose
To be mine arbiters; my proud defence
Shall not be made in secret. All shall hear.
Doge. The time for choice is past.
Car. What! Is there force

Employ'd against me?—Guards! (*raising his voice.*
  Doge. They are not nigh.
Soldiers! (*enter armed men.*)
Thy guards are these.
  Car. I am betray'd!
  Doge. 'Twas then a thought of wisdom to disperse
Thy followers. Well and justly was it deem'd
That the bold traitor, in his plots surprised,
Might prove a rebel too.
  Car. E'en as ye list,
Now be it yours to charge me.
  Doge. Bear him hence,
Before the secret college.
  Car. Hear me yet
One moment first. That ye have doom'd my death
I well perceive; but with that death ye doom
Your own eternal shame. Far o'er these towers
Beyond its ancient bounds, majestic floats
The banner of the Lion, in its pride
Of conquering power, and well doth Europe know
I bore it thus to empire. *Here,* 'tis true,
No voice will speak men's thoughts; but far beyond
The limits of your sway, in other scenes,
Where that still, speechless terror hath not reach'd.
Which is your sceptre's attribute, my deeds,
And your reward, will live in chronicles
For ever to endure. Yet, yet, respect
Your annals, and the future! Ye will need
A warrior soon, and who will then be yours?
Forget not, though your captive now I stand,
I was not born your subject. No! my birth
Was 'midst a warlike people, one in soul,
And watchful o'er its rights, and used to deem
The honor of each citizen its own.
Think ye this outrage will be there unheard?
There is some treachery here. Our common foes
Have urged you on to this. Full well ye know
I have been faithful still. There yet is time.
  Doge. The time is past. When thou didst meditate
Thy guilt, and in thy pride of heart defy
Those destined to chastise it, then the hour
Of foresight should have been.
  Car. O mean in soul!
And dost thou dare to think a warrior's breast
For worthless life can tremble? Thou shalt soon!
Learn how to die. Go! When the hour of fate
On thy vile couch o'ertakes thee, thou wilt meet
Its summons with far other mien than such
As I shall bear to ignominious death.

Scene II.—*The House of* Carmagnola.
Antonietta, Matilda.

Mat. The hours fly fast, the morn is risen, and yet
My father comes not!
  Ant. Ah! thou hast not learn'd
By sad experience, with how slow a pace
Joys ever come; expected long, and oft
Deceiving expectation! while the steps
Of grief o'ertake us, ere we dream them nigh.
But night is past, the long and lingering hours
Of hope deferr'd are o'er, and those of bliss
Must soon succeed. A few short moments more,
And he is with us. E'en from this delay
I augur well. A council held so long
Must be to give us peace. He will be ours,
Perhaps for years our own.
  Mat. O mother! thus
My hopes too whisper. Nights enough in tears,
And days in all the sickness of suspense
Our anxious love hath pass'd. It is full time
That each sad moment, at each rumor'd tale,
Each idle murmur of the people's voice,
We should not longer tremble, that no more
This thought should haunt our souls—E'en now, perchance,
He for whom thus our hearts are yearning—dies!
  Ant. Oh! fearful thought! but vain and distant now!
Each joy my daughter must be bought with grief.
Hast thou forgot the day, when proudly led
In triumph 'midst the noble and the brave,
Thy glorious father to the temple bore
The banners won in battle from his foes?
  Mat. A day to be remember'd!
  Ant. By his side
Each seem'd inferior. Every breath of air
Swell'd with his echoing name; and we, the while,
Station'd on high and sever'd from the throng,
Gazed on that one who drew the gaze of all,
While with the tide of rapture half o'erwhelm'd,
Our hearts beat high, and whisper'd—" We are his."
  Mat. Moments of joy!
  Ant. What have we done, my child,
To merit such? Heaven, for so high a fate,
Chose us from thousands, and upon thy brow
Inscribed a lofty name, a name so bright,
That he to whom thou bear'st the gift, whate'er
His race, may boast it proudly. What a mark
For envy is the glory of our lot!
And we should weigh its joys against these hours
Of fear and sorrow.
  Mat. They are past e'en now.
Hark! 'twas the sound of oars!—it swells—'tis hush'd!

The gates unclose—O mother! I behold
A warrior clad in mail—he comes, 'tis he!
  Ant. Whom should it be if not himself?—my husband!
                              (*She comes forward.*

(*Enter* GONZAGA *and others.*)

  Ant. Gonzaga!—Where is he we look'd for? Where?
Thou answerest not!—O heaven! thy looks are fraught
With prophecies of woe!
  Gon. Alas! too true
The omens they reveal!
  Mat. Of woe to whom?
  Gon. Oh! why hath such a task of bitterness
Fallen to my lot?
  Ant. Thou would'st be pitiful,
And thou art cruel. Close this dread suspense;
Speak! I adjure thee in the name of God!
Where is my husband?
  Gon. Heaven sustain your souls
With fortitude to bear the tale!—my chief——
  Mat. Is he return'd unto the field?
  Gon. Alas!
Thither the warrior shall return no more.
The senate's wrath is on him   He is now
A prisoner!
  Ant. He is a prisoner!—and for what!
  Gon. He is accused of treason.
  Mat. Treason! *He*
A traitor!—Oh! my father!
  Ant. Haste! proceed,
And pause no more. Our hearts are nerved for all.
Say, what shall be his sentence?
  Gon. From my lips
It shall not be reveal'd.
  Ant, Oh! he is slain!
  Gon. He lives, but yet his doom is fix'd.
  Ant. He lives!
Weep not, my daughter! 'tis the time to act.
For pity's sake, Gonzaga, be thou not
Wearied of our afflictions. Heaven to thee
Intrusts the care of two forsaken ones.
He was thy friend—Ah! haste, then, be our guide;
Conduct us to his judges. Come, my child.
Poor innocent, come with me. There yet is left
Mercy upon the earth. Yes! they themselves
Are husbands, they are fathers! When they sign'd
The fearful sentence, they remember'd not
He was a father, and a husband too.
But when their eyes behold the agony
One word of theirs hath caused, their hearts will melt
They will, they *must* revoke it. Oh! the sight
Of mortal woe is terrible to man!

Perhaps the warrior's lofty soul disdain'd
To vindicate his deeds, or to recall
His triumphs won for them. It is for us
To wake each high remembrance. Ah! we know
That he implored not, but *our* knees shall bend,
And we will pray.
    Gon. Oh heaven! that I could leave
Your hearts one ray of hope! There is no ear,
No place for prayers. The judges here are deaf,
Implacable, unknown. The thunderbolt
Falls heavy, and the hand by which 'tis launch'd
Is veil'd in clouds. There is one comfort still,
The sole sad comfort of a parting hour,
I come to bear. Ye may behold him yet.
The moments fly. Arouse your strength of heart.
Oh! fearful is the trial, but the God
Of mourners will be with you.
    Mat. Is there not
One hope?
    Ant. Alas! my child!

Scene IV.—*A Prison.*

CARMAGNOLA.

They must have heard it now.—Oh! that at least
I might have died far from them! Though their hearts
Had bled to hear the tidings, yet the hour,
The solemn hour of Nature's parting pangs,
Had then been past. It meets us darkly now,
And we must drain its draught of bitterness
Together, drop by drop. O ye wide fields;
Ye plains of fight, and thrilling sounds of arms!
O proud delights of danger! Battle cries,
And thou, my war-steed! and ye trumpet notes
Kindling the soul! 'Midst your tumultuous joys
Death seem'd all beautiful.—And must I then,
With shrinking cold reluctance, to my fate
Be dragg'd, e'en as a felon, on the winds
Pouring vain prayers and impotent complaints?
And Marco! hath he not betray'd me too?
Vile doubt! That I could cast it from my soul
Before I die!—But no! What boots it now
Thus to look back on life with eye that turns
To linger where my footstep may not tread?
Now, Philip! thou wilt triumph! Be it so!
I too have proved such vain and impious joys,
And know their value now. But oh! again
To see those loved ones, and to hear the last,
Last accents of their voices! By those arms
Once more to be encircled, and from thence
To tear myself for ever!—Hark! they come!—
O God of Mercy, from thy throne look down
In pity on their woes!

Scene V.

Antonietta, Matilda, Gonzaga, *and* Carmagnola.

Ant. My husband!
Mat. Oh! my father!
Ant. Is it thus
That thou returnest? and is this the hour
Desired so long?
  Car. O ye afflicted ones!
Heaven knows I dread its pangs for you alone.
Long have my thoughts been used to look on Death,
And calmly wait his time. For you alone
My soul hath need of firmness; will ye, then,
Deprive me of its aid?—When the Most High
On virtue pours afflictions, he bestows
The courage to sustain them. Oh! let yours
Equal your sorrows! Let us yet find joy
In this embrace, 'tis still a gift of Heaven.
Thou weep'st my child! and thou, beloved wife!
Ah! when I made thee mine, thy days flow'd on
In peace and gladness; I united thee
To my disastrous fate, and now the thought
Embitters death. Oh! that I had not seen
The woes I cause thee!
  Ant. Husband of my youth!
Of my bright days, thou who didst make them bright,
Read thou my heart! the pangs of death are there,
And yet e'en now—I would not but be thine.
  Car. Full well I know how much I lose in thee;
Oh! make me not too deeply feel it now.
  Mat. The homicides!
  Car. No, sweet Matilda, no!
Let no dark thought of rage or vengeance rise
To cloud thy gentle spirit, and disturb
These moments—they are sacred. Yes! my wrongs
Are deep, but thou, forgive them, and confess,
That, e'en 'midst all the fulness of our woe,
High, holy joy remains.—Death! death!—our foes,
Our most relentless foes, can only speed
Th' inevitable hour. Oh! man hath not
Invented death for man; it would be *then*
Madd'ning and insupportable; from Heaven
'Tis sent, and Heaven doth temper all its pangs
With such blest comfort, as no mortal power
Can give or take away. My wife! my child!
Hear my last words—they wring your bosoms now
With agony, but yet, some future day,
'Twill soothe you to recall them. Live, my wife!
Sustain thy grief, and live! this ill-starr'd girl
Must not be reft of all. Fly swiftly hence,
Conduct her to thy kindred, she is theirs,

Of their own blood—and they so loved thee once!
Then, to their foe united, thou becamest
Less dear; for feuds and wrongs made warring sounds
Of Carmagnola's and Visconti's names.
But to their bosoms thou wilt now return
A mourner; and the object of their hate
Will be no more.—Oh! there is joy in death!—
And thou, my flower! that 'midst the din of arms,
Wert born to cheer my soul, thy lovely head
Droops to the earth! Alas! the tempest's rage
Is on thee now. Thou tremblest, and thy heart
Can scarce contain the heavings of its woe.
I feel thy burning tears upon my breast—
I feel, and cannot dry them. Dost thou claim
Pity from me, Matilda? Oh! thy sire
Hath now no power to aid thee, but thou know'st
That the forsaken have a Father still
On high. Confide in him, and live to days
Of peace, if not of joy; for such to thee
He surely destines. Wherefore hath he pour'd
The torrent of affliction on thy youth,
If to thy future years be not reserved
All his benign compassion? Live! and soothe
Thy suffering mother. May she to the arms
Of no ignoble consort lead thee still!—
Gonzaga! take the hand which thou hast pressed
Oft in the morn of battle, when our hearts
Had cause to doubt if we should meet at eve.
Wilt thou yet press it, pledging me thy faith
To guide and guard these mourners, till they join
Their friends and kindred?
   Gon. Rest assured, I will.
   Car. I am content. And if, when this is done,
Thou to the field returnest, there for me
Salute my brethren; tell them that I died
Guiltless; thou hast been witness of my deeds,
Hast read my inmost thoughts—and know'st it well.
Tell them I never, with a traitor's shame,
Stain'd my bright sword.—Oh! never—I myself
Have been ensnared by treachery. Think of me
When trumpet-notes are stirring every heart,
And banners proudly waving in the air,
Think of thine ancient comrade! And the day
Following the combat, when upon the field,
Amidst the deep and solemn harmony
Of dirge and hymn, the priest of funeral rites,
With lifted hands, is offering for the slain
His sacrifice to heaven;—forget me not!
For I, too, hoped upon the battle plain
E'en so to die.
   Ant. Have mercy on us, Heaven!

Car. My wife! Matilda! now the hour is nigh,
And we must part.—Farewell!
Mat. No, father! no!
Car. Come to this breast yet, yet once more, and then
For pity's sake depart!
Ant. No! force alone
Shall tear us hence.
     (*A sound of arms is heard.*)
Mat. Hark! what dread sound!
Ant. Great God!
  (*The door is half opened, and armed men enter, the chief of whom advances to the Count. His wife and daughter fall senseless.*)
Car. O God! I thank thee. O most merciful!
Thus to withdraw their senses from the pangs
Of this dread moment's conflict!
     Thou, my friend,
Assist them, bear them from this scene of woe,
And tell them, when their eyes unclose
To meet the day—that nought is left to fear.

 Notwithstanding the pathetic beauties of the last act, the attention which this tragedy has excited in Italy, must be principally attributed to the boldness of the author in so completely emancipating himself from the fetters of the dramatic unities. The severity with which the tragic poets of that country have, in general, restricted themselves to those rules, has been sufficiently remarkable, to obtain, at least, temporary distinction for the courage of the writer who should attempt to violate them. Although this piece comprises a period of several years, and that, too, in days so troubled and so "full of fate"—days in which the deepest passions and most powerful energies of the human mind were called into action by the strife of conflicting interests; there is nevertheless, as great a deficiency of incident, as if "to be born and die" made all the history of aspiring natures contending for supremacy. The character of the hero is portrayed in words, not in actions; it does not unfold itself in any struggle of opposite feelings and passions, and the interest excited for him only commences at the moment when it ought to have reached its climax. The merits of the piece may be summed up in the occasional energy of the language and dignity of the thoughts; and the truth with which the spirit of the age is characterised, as well in the developement of that suspicious policy distinguishing the system of the Venetian government, as in the pictures of the fiery Condottieri, holding their councils of war,

   "Jealous of honor, sudden and quick in quarrel."

CAIUS GRACCHUS,

A TRAGEDY.—BY MONTI.

 This tragedy, though inferior in power and interest to the *Aristodemo* of the same author, is, nevertheless, distinguished by beauties of a high order, and such as, in our opinion, fully establish its claims to more general attention than it has hitherto received. Although the loftiness and severity of Roman manners, in the days of the Republic, have been sufficiently preserved to give an impressive character to the piece; yet those workings of passion and tenderness, without which dignity soon becomes monotonous, and heroism unnatural, have not been (as in the tragedies of Alfieri upon similar subjects) too rigidly suppressed.

The powerful character of the high-hearted Cornelia, with all the calm collected majesty which our ideas are wont to associate with the name of a Roman matron; and the depth and sublimity of maternal affection more particularly belonging to the mother of the Gracchi, are beautifully contrasted with the softer and more womanish feelings, the intense anxieties, the sensitive and passionate attachment, embodied in the person of Sicinia, the wife of Gracchus. The appeals made by Gracchus to the people are full of majestic eloquence, and the whole piece seems to be animated by that restless and untamable spirit of freedom, whose immortalized struggles for ascendency give so vivid a coloring, so exalted an interest, to the annals of the ancient republics.

The tragedy opens with the soliloquy of Caius Gracchus, who is returned in secret to Rome, after having been employed in rebuilding Carthage, which Scipio had utterly demolished.

Caius, in Rome behold thyself! The night
Hath spread her favoring shadows o'er thy path:
And thou, be strong, my country! for thy son
Gracchus is with thee! All is hush'd around,
And in deep slumber; from the cares of day,
The worn plebeians rest. Oh! good and true,
And only Romans! your repose is sweet,
For toil hath given it zest; 'tis calm and pure,
For no remorse hath troubled it. Meanwhile,
My brother's murderers, the patricians, hold
Inebriate vigils o'er their festal boards,
Or in dark midnight councils sentence me
To death, and Rome to chains. They little deem
Of the unlook'd for and tremendous foe
So near at hand!—It is enough. I tread
In safety my paternal threshold.—Yes!
This is my own! Oh mother! oh my wife!
My child!—I come to dry your tears. I come
Strengthen'd by three dread furies. One is wrath,
Fired by my country's wrongs; and one deep love,
For those, my bosom's inmates; and the third—
Vengeance, fierce vengeance, for a brother's blood!

His soliloquy is interrupted by the entrance of Fulvius, his friend, with whose profligate character, and unprincipled designs, he is represented as unacquainted. From the opening speech made by Fulvius (before he is aware of the presence of Caius) to the slave by whom he is attended, it appears that he is just returned from the perpetration of some crime, the nature of which is not disclosed until the second act.

The suspicions of Caius are, however, awakened, by the obscure allusions to some act of signal, but secret vengeance, which Fulvius throws out in the course of the ensuing discussion.

Ful. This is no time for grief and feeble tears,
But for high deeds.
   Caius. And we will make it such.
But prove we first our strength. Declare, what friends
(If yet misfortune hath her friends) remain
True to our cause?
   Ful. Few, few, but valiant hearts!
      *   *   *   *   *   *
Oh! what a change is here! There was a time,
When, over all supreme, thy word gave law
To nations and their rulers; in thy presence
The senate trembled, and the citizens
Flock'd round thee in deep reverence. Then a word,
A look from Caius—a salute, a smile,
Fill'd them with pride. Each sought to be the friend,
The client, ay, the very slave, of him,
The people's idol; and beholding them
Thus prostrate in thy path, thou, thou thyself,
Didst blush to see their vileness!—But thy fortune
Is waning now, her glorious phantoms melt
Into dim vapor, and the earthly god,
So worshipp'd once, from his forsaken shrines,
Down to the dust is hurl'd.
   Caius. And what of this?
There is no power in Fortune to deprive
Gracchus of Gracchus. Mine is such a heart
As meets the storm exultingly; a heart
Whose stern delight it is to strive with fate,
And conquer. Trust me, fate is terrible
But because man is vile. A coward first
Made her a deity.
      *   *   *   *
                        But say, what thoughts
Are foster'd by the people? Have they lost
The sense of their misfortunes? Is the name
Of Gracchus in their hearts—reveal the truth—
Already number'd with forgotten things?
   Ful. A breeze, a passing breeze, now here, now there,
Borne on light pinion—such the people's love!
Yet have they claims on pardon, for their faults
Are of their miseries; and their feebleness
Is to their woes proportion'd. Haply still
The secret sigh of their full hearts is thine,
But their lips breathe it not. Their grief is mute;
And the deep paleness of their timid mein,
And eyes in fix'd despondence bent on earth,
And sometimes a faint murmur of thy name,
Alone accuse them. They are hush'd, for now
Not one, nor two, their tyrants; but a host
Whose numbers are the numbers of the rich,
And the patrician Romans. Yes; and well
May proud oppression dauntlessly go forth,

For Rome is widow'd ! Distant wars engage
The noblest of her youth, by Fabius led,
And but the weak remain. Hence every heart
Sickens with voiceless terror ; and the people,
Subdued and trembling, turn to thee in thought,
But yet are silent.
  Caius. I will make them heard.
Rome is a slumbering lion, and my voice
Shall wake the mighty. Thou shalt see I came
Prepared for all ; and as I track'd the deep
For Rome, my dangers to my spirit grew
Familiar in its musings. With a voice
Of wrath, the loud winds fiercely swell'd ; the waves
Mutter'd around ; Heaven flash'd in lightning forth,
And the pale steersman trembled : I the while
Stood on the tossing and bewilder'd bark,
Retired and shrouded in my mantle's folds,
With thoughtful eyes cast down, and all absorb'd
In a far deeper storm ! Around my heart,
Gathering in secret, then my spirit's powers
Held council with themselves—and on my thoughts
My country rose,—and I foresaw the snares,
The treacheries of Opimius, and the senate,
And my false friends, awaiting my return.
        *   *   *   *   *

Fulvius ! I wept ! but they were tears of rage !
For I was wrought to frenzy, by the thought
Of my wrong'd country, and of him, that brother
Whose shade through ten long years hath sternly cried
" Vengeance !"—nor found it yet.
  Ful. It is fulfill'd.
  Caius. And how ?
  Ful. Thou shalt be told.
  Caius. Explain thy words.
  Ful. Then know—(incautious that I am !)
  Caius. Why thus
Falters thy voice ? Why speak'st thou not ?
  Ful. Forgive !
E'en friendship sometimes hath its secrets.
  Caius. No !
True friendship, never !

Caius afterwards enquires what part his brother-in law, Scipio Emilianus, is likely to adopt in their enterprises.

                    His high renown—
The glorious deeds, whereby was earn'd his name
Of second Africanus ; and the blind,
Deep reverence paid him by the people's hearts,
Who, knowing him their foe, respect him still ;
All this disturbs me : hardly will be won
Our day of victory, if by him withstood.

Ful. Yet won it *shall* be. If but this thou fear'st,
Then be at peace.
  Caius. I understand thee not.
  Ful. Thou wilt ere long. But here we vainly waste
Our time and words. Soon will the morning break,
Nor know thy friends as yet of thy return;
I fly to cheer them with the tidings.
  Caius. Stay!
  Ful. And wherefore?
  Caius. To reveal thy meaning.
  Ful. Peace!
I hear the sound of steps.

This conversation is interrupted by the entrance of Cornelia, with the wife and child of Caius. They are about to seek an asylum in the house of Emilianus, by whom Cornelia has been warned of the imminent danger which menaces the family of her son from the fury of the patricians, who intend, on the following day, to abrogate the laws enacted by the Gracchi in favor of the plebeians. The joy and emotion of Gracchus, on thus meeting with his family, may appear somewhat inconsistent with his having remained so long engaged in political discussion, on the threshold of their abode, without ever having made an enquiry after their welfare; but it would be somewhat unreasonable to try the conduct of a Roman (particularly in a tragedy) by the laws of *nature*. Before, however, we are disposed to condemn the principles which seem to be laid down for the delineation of Roman character in dramatic poetry, let us recollect that the general habits of the people whose institutions gave birth to the fearful grandeur displayed in the actions of the elder Brutus, and whose towering spirit was fostered to enthusiasm by the contemplation of it, must have been deeply tinctured by the austerity of even their virtues. Shakspeare alone, without compromising the dignity of his Romans, has disencumbered them of the formal scholastic drapery which seems to be their *official* garb, and has stamped their features with the general attributes of human nature, without effacing the impress which distinguished "the men of iron," from the nations who "stood still before them."

The first act concludes with the parting of Caius and Fulvius in wrath and suspicion, Cornelia having accused the latter of an attempt to seduce her daughter, the wife of Scipio, and of concealing the most atrocious designs under the mask of zeal for the cause of liberty.

         Of liberty
What speak'st thou, and to whom? Thou hast no shame—
No virtue—and thy boast is, to be free!
Oh! zeal for liberty! eternal mask
Assumed by every crime!

In the second act, the death of Emilianus is announced to Opimius the consul, in the presence of Gracchus, and the intelligence is accompanied by a rumor of his having perished by assassination. The mysterious expressions of Fulvius, and the accusation of Cornelia, immediately recur to the mind of Caius. The following scene, in which his vehement emotion, and high sense of honor, are well contrasted with the cold-blooded sophistry of Fulvius, is powerfully wrought up.

Caius. Back on my thoughts the words of Fulvius rush,
Like darts of fire. All hell is in my heart! (*Fulvius enters.*
Thou com'st in time. Speak, thou perfidious friend!
Scipio lies murdered on his bed of death!—
Who slew him?
 Ful. Ask'st thou me?
 Caius. Thee! thee, who late
Did'st in such words discourse of him, as now
Assure me thou'rt his murderer. Traitor, speak!
 Ful. If thus his fate doth weigh upon thy heart,
Thou art no longer Gracchus, or thou ravest!
More grateful praise, and warmer thanks might well
Reward the gen'rous courage which hath freed
Rome from a tyrant, Gracchus from a foe!
 Caius. Then he was slain by thee?
 Ful. Ungrateful friend!
Why dost thou tempt me? Danger menaces
Thy honor. Freedom's wavering light is dim;
Rome wears the fetters of a guilty senate;
One Scipio drove thy brother to a death
Of infamy, another seeks *thy* fall;
And when one noble, one determined stroke,
To thee and thine assures the vict'ry, wreaks
The people's vengeance, gives thee life and fame,
And pacifies thy brother's angry shade,
Is it a cause for wailing? Am I call'd
For *this* a murderer? Go!—I say once more,
Thou art no longer Gracchus, or thou ravest!
 Caius. I know thee now, barbarian! Would'st thou serve
My cause with crimes?
 Ful. And those of that proud man
Whom I have slain, and thou dost mourn, are *they*
To be forgotten? Hath oblivion then
Shrouded the stern destroyer's ruthless work,
The famine of Numantia? Such a deed,
As on our name the world's deep curses drew!
Or the four hundred Lusian youths betray'd,
And with their bleeding, mutilated limbs,
Back to their parents sent? Is this forgot?
Go, ask of Carthage!—bid her wasted shores
Of him, this reveller in blood, recount
The terrible achievements!—At the cries,
The groans, th' unutterable pangs of those,
The more than hundred thousand wretches, doom'd
(Of every age and sex) to fire, and sword,
And fetters, I could marvel that the earth
In horror doth not open!—They were foes,
They were barbarians, but unarm'd, subdued,
Weeping, imploring mercy! And the law
Of Roman virtue is, to spare the weak,
To tame the lofty! But in other lands,
Why should I seek for records of his crimes,

If here the suffering people ask in vain
A little earth to lay their bones in peace?
If the decree which yielded to their claims
So brief a heritage, and the which to seal
Thy brother's blood was shed; if this remain
Still fruitless, still delusive, who was he
That mock'd its power?—Who to all Rome declared
Thy brother's death was just, was needful?—Who
But Scipio?—And remember thou the words
Which burst in thunder from thy lips e'en then,
Heard by the people! Caius, in my heart
They have been deeply treasured. He must die,
(Thus did'st thou speak) this tyrant! We have need
That he should perish!—I have done the deed;
And call'st thou *me* his murderer? If the blow
Was guilt, then *thou* art guilty. From thy lips
The sentence came—the crime is thine alone.
I, thy devoted friend, did but obey
Thy mandate.
   Caius. Thou my friend! I am not one,
To call a villain friend. Let thunders fraught
With fate and death, awake, to scatter those,
Who bringing liberty through paths of blood
Bring chains!—degrading Freedom's lofty self
Below e'en Slavery's level!—Say thou not,
Wretch! that the sentence and the guilt were mine!
I wish'd him slain!—'tis so—but by the axe
Of high and public justice; that whose stroke
On thy vile head will fall. Thou hast disgraced
Unutterably my name—I bid thee tremble!
   Ful. Caius, let insult cease, I counsel thee,
Let insult cease! Be the deed just or guilty,
Enjoy its fruits in silence. Force me not
To utter more.
   Caius. And what hast thou to say?
   Ful. That which I now suppress.
   Caius. How! are there yet,
Perchance, more crimes to be reveal'd?
   Ful. I know not.
   Caius. Thou know'st not!—Horror chills my curdling veins,
I dare not ask thee farther.
   Ful. Thou dost well.
   Caius. What saidst thou?
   Ful. Nothing.
   Caius. On my heart the words
Press heavily. Oh! what a fearful light
Bursts o'er my soul!—Hast thou accomplices?
   Ful. Insensate! ask me not.
   Caius. I must be told.
   Ful. Away!—thou wilt repent.
   Caius. No more of this, for I *will* know.
   Ful. Thou wilt?

Ask then thy sister.
 Caius (alone). Ask my sister!—What!
Is she a murderess?—Hath my sister slain
Her lord?—Oh! crime of darkest dye!—Oh! name
Till now unstain'd, name of the Gracchi, thus
Consign'd to infamy!—to infamy?
The very hair doth rise upon my head,
Thrill'd by the thought!—Where shall I find a place
To hide my shame, to lave the branded stains
From this dishonor'd brow?—What should I do?
There is a voice whose deep tremendous tones
Murmurs within my heart, and sternly cry,
" Away!—and pause not—slay thy guilty sister!"
Voice of lost honor of a noble line
Disgraced, I will obey thee!—terribly
Thou call'st for blood, and thou shalt be appeased.

PATRIOTIC EFFUSIONS

OF THE ITALIAN POETS.

WHOEVER has attentively studied the works of the Italian poets, from the days of Dante and Petrarch to those of Foscolo and Pindemonte, must have been struck with those allusions to the glory and the fall, the renown and the degradation, of Italy, which give a melancholy interest to their pages. Amidst all the vicissitudes of that devoted country, the warning voice of her bards has still been heard to prophesy the impending storm, and to call up such deep and spirit-stirring recollections from the glorious past, as have resounded through the land, notwithstanding the loudest tumults of those discords which have made her—

> Long, long, a bloody stage
> For petty kinglings tame,
> Their miserable game
> Of puny war to wage."

There is something very affecting in these vain, though exalted aspirations, after that independence which the Italians, as a nation, seem destined never to regain. The strains in which their high-toned feelings on this subject are recorded, produce on our minds the same effect with the song of the imprisoned bird, whose melody is fraught, in our imagination, with recollections of the green woodland, the free air, and unbounded sky. We soon grow weary of the perpetual *violets and zephyrs,* whose cloying sweetness pervades the sonnets and canzoni of the minor Italian poets, till we are ready to " die in aromatic pain ;" nor is our interest much more excited even by the everlasting *laurel* which inspires the enamored Petrarch with so ingenious a variety of *concetti,* as might reasonably cause it to be doubted whether the beautiful Laura, or the emblematic tree, are the real object of the bard's affection ; but the moment a patriotic chord is struck our feelings are awakened, and we find it easy to sympathize with the emotions of a modern Roman, surrounded by the ruins of the capitol ; a Venetian when contemplating the proud trophies won by his ancestors at Byzantium ; or a Florentine amongst the tombs of the mighty dead, in the church of Santa Croce It is not, perhaps, *now*, the time to plead, with any effect, the cause of Italy; yet cannot we consider that nation as altogether degraded, whose literature' from the dawn of its majestic immortality, has been consecrated to the nurture of every generous principle and ennobling recollection; and whose " choice and master spirits," under the most adverse circumstances, have kept alive a flame, which may well be considered as imperishable, since the "ten thousand tyrants" of the land have failed to quench its brightness. We present our readers with a few of the minor effusions, in which the indignant though unavailing regrets of those, who, to use the words of Alfieri, are "slaves, yet still *indignant* slaves,"* have been feelingly portrayed.

The first of these productions must, in the original, be familiar to every reader who has any acquaintance with Italian literature.

VINCENZO DA FILICAJA.

'Quando giù dai gran monti bruna bruna," &c.

WHEN from the mountain's brow, the gathering shades
  Of twilight fall, on one deep thought I dwell:
Day beams o'er other lands, if here she fades,
  Nor bids the universe at once farewell.

But thou, I cry, my country! what a night
  Spreads o'er thy glories one dark sweeping pall;
Thy thousand triumphs won by valor's might,
  And wisdom's voice—what now remains of all?

And see'st thou not th' ascending flame of war
Burst through thy darkness, redd'ning from afar?
  Is not thy misery's evidence complete?
But if endurance can thy fall delay,
Still, still endure, devoted one! and say,
  If it be victory thus but to retard defeat!

CARLO MARIA MAGGI.

"Io grido, e griderò finche mi senta," &c.

I CRY aloud, and ye shall hear my call,
  Arno, Sessino, Tiber; Adrian deep,
  And blue Tyrrhene! Let him first roused from sleep
Startle the next! one peril broods o'er all.
It nought avails that Italy should plead,
  Forgetting valor, sinking in despair,

---

* "Schiavi siam, ma schiavi ognor frementi."—ALFIERI.

At strangers' feet!—our land is all too fair;
Nor tears, nor prayers, can check ambition's speed.
In vain her faded cheek, her humbled eye,
For pardon sue; 'tis not her agony,
　Her death alone may now appease her foes.
Be theirs to suffer who to combat shun!
But oh! weak pride, thus feeble and undone,
　Nor to wage battle, nor endure repose!

ALESSANDRO MARCHETTI.

"Italia! Italia! ah! non più Italia! appena," &c.

ITALIA! oh! no more Italia now!
　Scarce of her form a vestige dost thou wear;
She was a queen with glory mantled;—Thou,
　A slave, degraded, and compell'd to bear.

Chains gird thy hands and feet; deep clouds of care
　Darken thy brow, once radiant as thy skies;
And shadows, born of terror and despair—
　Shadows of death have dimm'd thy glorious eyes.
Italia! oh! Italia, now no more!
　For thee my tears of shame and anguish flow;
And the glad strains my lyre was wont to pour,
　Are changed to dirge-notes: but my deepest woe
Is, that base herds of thine own sons the while,
　Behold thy miseries with insulting smile.

ALESSANDRO PEGOLOTTI.

"Quella, ch'ambi le mani entro la chioma," &c

SHE that cast down the empires of the world,
　And, in her proud triumphal course through Rome,
Dragg'd them, from freedom and dominion hurl'd,
　Bound by the hair, pale, humbled, and o'ercome.

I see her now, dismantled of her state,
　Spoil'd of her sceptre; crouching to the ground
Beneath a hostile car, and lo! the weight
　Of fetters, her imperial neck around!

Oh! that a stranger's envious hands had wrought
　This desolation! for I then would say,
"Vengeance, Italia!"—in the burning thought
　Losing my grief: but 'tis th' ignoble sway
Of vice hath bow'd thee! Discord, slothful ease,
　Theirs is that victor car; thy tyrant lords are these.

FRANCESCO MARIA DE CONTI.

THE SHORE OF AFRICA.

"O peregrin, chi muovi erranti il passo," &c.

PILGRIM! whose steps those desert sands explore,
  Where verdure never spreads its bright array:
Know, 'twas on this inhospitable shore,
  From Pompey's heart the life-blood ebb'd away.
'Twas here betray'd he fell, neglected lay;
  Nor found *his* relics a sepulchral stone,
Whose life, so long a bright, triumphal day,
  O'er Tiber's wave supreme in glory shone!

Thou, stranger! if from barbarous climes thy birth,
Look round exultingly, and bless the earth,
  Where Rome, with him, saw power and virtue die;
But if 'tis Roman blood that fills thy veins,
Then, son of heroes! think upon thy chains,
  And bathe with tears the grave of liberty.

THE SCEPTIC.

"Leur raison, qu'ils prennent pour guide, ne présente à leur esprit que des conjectures et des embarras ; les absurdités où ils tombent en niant la Religion deviennent plus insoutenables que les verités dont la hauteur les étonne ; et pour ne vouloir pas croire des mystères incompréhensibles, ils suivent l'une après l'autre d'incompréhensibles erreurs." BOSSUET, *Oraisons Funèbres*.

WHEN the young Eagle, with exulting eye,
Has learn'd to dare the splendor of the sky,
And leave the Alps beneath him in his course,
To bathe his crest in morn's empyreal source ;
Will his free wing, from that majestic height,
Descend to follow some wild meteor's light,
Which, far below, with evanescent fire,
Shines to delude, and dazzles to expire?

No! still through clouds he wins his upward way,
And proudly claims his heritage of day!
—And shall the spirit, on whose ardent gaze
The dayspring from on high hath pour'd its blaze,
Turn from that pure effulgence, to the beam
Of earth-born light, that sheds a treacherous gleam,
Luring the wanderer, from the star of faith,
To the deep valley of the shades of death?
What bright exchange, what treasure shall be given,
For the high birthright of its hope in Heaven?
If lost the gem which empires could not buy,
What yet remains?—a dark eternity!

Is earth still Eden?—might a Seraph guest,
Still 'midst its chosen bowers delighted rest?
Is all so cloudless and so calm below,
We seek no fairer scenes than *life* can show?
That the cold Sceptic, in his pride elate,
Rejects the promise of a brighter state,
And leaves the rock, no tempest shall displace,
To rear his dwelling on the quicksand's base?

Votary of doubt! then join the festal throng,
Bask in the sunbeam, listen to the song,
Spread the rich board, and fill the wine-cup high,
And bind the wreath ere yet the roses die!
'Tis well, thine eye is yet undimm'd by time,
And, thy heart bounds, exulting in its prime :

Smile then unmoved at Wisdom's warning voice,
And, in the glory of thy strength, rejoice!

But life hath sterner tasks; e'en youth's brief hours
Survive the beauty of their loveliest flowers;
The founts of joy, where pilgrims rest from toil,
Are few and distant on the desert soil,
The soul's pure flame the breath of storms must fan,
And pain and sorrow claim their nursling—Man!
Earth's noblest sons the bitter cup have shared—
Proud child of reason! how art *thou* prepared?
When years, with silent might, thy frame have bow'd,
And o'er thy spirit cast their wintry cloud,
Will Memory soothe thee on thy bed of pain
With the bright images of pleasure's train?

Yes! as the sight of some far-distant shore,
Whose well-known scenes his foot shall tread no more,
Would cheer the seaman, by the eddying wave
Drawn, vainly struggling, to th' unfathom'd grave!
Shall Hope, the faithful cherub, hear thy call,
She who, like heaven's own sunbeam, smiles for all?
Will *she* speak comfort?—Thou hast shorn her plume,
That might have raised thee far above the tomb,
And hush'd the only voice whose angel tone
Soothes when all melodies of joy are flown!

For she was born beyond the stars to soar,
And kindling at the source of life, adore;
Thou could'st not, mortal! rivet to the earth
Her eye, whose beam is of celestial birth;
She dwells with those who leave her pinion free,
And sheds the dews of heaven on all but thee.

Yet few there are so lonely, so bereft,
But some true heart, that beats to theirs, is left,
And, haply, one whose strong affection's power
Unchanged may triumph through misfortune's hour,
Still with fond care supports thy languid head,
And keeps unwearied vigils by thy bed.

But thou whose thoughts have no blest home above!
Captive of earth! and canst thou dare to *love?*
To nurse such feelings as delight to rest,
Within that hallow'd shrine—a parent's breast,
To fix each hope, concentrate every tie,
On one frail Idol—destined but to die;
Yet mock the faith that points to worlds of light,
Where severed souls, made perfect, re-unite?
Then tremble! cling to every passing joy,
Twined with a life a moment may destroy!

THE SCEPTIC.

If there be sorrow in a parting tear,
Still let "*for ever*" vibrate on thine ear!
If some bright hour on rapture's wing hath flown,
Find more than anguish in the thought—'tis gone!

Go! to a voice such magic influence give,
Thou canst not lose its melody, and live;
And make an eye the lode-star of thy soul,
And let a glance the springs of thought control;
Gaze on a mortal form with fond delight,
Till the fair vision mingles with thy sight;
There seek thy blessings, there repose thy trust,
Lean on the willow, idolize the dust!
Then, when thy treasure best repays thy care,
Think on that dread "*for ever*"—and despair!

And oh! no strange, unwonted storm there needs,
To wreck at once thy fragile ark of reeds.
Watch well its course—explore with anxious eye
Each little cloud that floats along the sky—
Is the blue canopy serenely fair?
Yet may the thunderbolt unseen be there,
And the bark sink, when peace and sunshine sleep
On the smooth bosom of the waveless deep!
Yes! ere a sound, a sign announce thy fate,
May the blow fall which makes thee desolate!
Not always Heaven's destroying angel shrouds
His awful form in tempest and in clouds;
He fills the summer air with latent power,
He hides his venom in the scented flower,
He steals upon thee in the Zephyr's breath,
And festal garlands veil the shafts of death!

Where art thou *then*, who thus didst rashly cast
Thine all upon the mercy of the blast,
And vainly hope the tree of life to find
Rooted in sands that flit before the wind?
Is not that earth thy spirit loved so well
It wish'd not in a brighter sphere to dwell,
Become a desert *now*, a vale of gloom,
O'ershadow'd with the midnight of the tomb?
Where shalt thou turn?—it is not thine to raise
To yon pure heaven thy calm confiding gaze,
No gleam reflected from that realm of rest
Steals on the darkness of thy troubled breast;
Not for thine eye shall Faith divinely shed
Her glory round the image of the dead;
And if, when slumber's lonely couch is prest,
The form departed be thy spirit's guest,
It bears no light from purer worlds to this;
Thy future lends not e'en a dream of bliss

But who shall dare the gate of life to close,
Or say, *thus far* the stream of mercy flows?
That fount unseal'd, whose boundless waves embrace
Each distant isle, and visit every race,
Pours from the throne of God its current free,
Nor yet denies th' immortal draught to thee.
O! while the doom impends, not yet decreed,
While yet th' Atoner hath not ceased to plead,
While still suspended by a single hair,
The sharp bright sword hangs quivering in the air,
Bow down thy heart to Him who will not break
The bruised reed; e'en yet, awake, awake!
Patient, because Eternal,[1] He may hear
Thy prayer of agony with pitying ear,
And send his chastening Spirit from above,
O'er the deep chaos of thy soul to move.

But seek thou mercy through His name alone,
To whose unequall'd sorrows none was shown.
Through Him, who here in mortal garb abode,
As man to suffer, and to heal as God;
And, born the sons of utmost time to bless,
Endured all scorn, and aided all distress.

Call thou on Him—for He, in human form,
Hath walk'd the waves of life, and still'd the storm.
He, when her hour of lingering grace was past,
O'er Salem wept, relenting to the last,
Wept with such tears as Judah's monarch pour'd
O'er his lost child, ungrateful, yet deplored;
And offering guiltless blood that guilt might live,
Taught from his Cross the lesson—to forgive!

Call thou on Him—his prayer e'en then arose,
Breathed in unpitied anguish for his foes.
And haste!—ere bursts the lightning from on high,
Fly to the City of thy Refuge, fly![2]
So shall th' Avenger turn his steps away,
And sheath his falchion, baffled of its prey.

Yet must long days roll on, ere peace shall brood,
As the soft halcyon, o'er thy heart subdued;
Ere yet the dove of Heaven descend, to shed
Inspiring influence o'er thy fallen head.
—He, who hath pined in dungeons, 'midst the shade
Of such deep night as man for man hath made,
Through lingering years; if call'd at length to be,
Once more, by nature's boundless charter, free,
Shrinks feebly back, the blaze of noon to shun,
Fainting at day, and blasted by the sun.

Thus, when the captive soul hath long remain'd
In its own dread abyss of darkness chain'd,

If the Deliverer, in his might, at last,
Its fetters, born of earth, to earth should cast,
The beam of truth o'erpowers its dazzled sight,
Trembling it sinks, and finds no joy in light,
But this will pass away—that spark of mind,
Within thy frame unquenchably enshrined,
Shall live to triumph in its bright'ning ray,
Born to be foster'd with ethereal day.
Then wilt thou bless the hour, when o'er thee pass'd,
On wing of flame, the purifying blast,
And sorrow's voice, through paths before untrod,
Like Sinai's trumpet, call'd thee to thy God!

But hopest thou, in thy panoply of pride,
Heaven's messenger, affliction, to deride?
In thine own strength unaided to defy,
With Stoic smile, the arrows of the sky?
Torn by the vulture, fetter'd to the rock,
Still, demigod! the tempest wilt thou mock?
Alas! the tower that crests the mountain's brow
A thousand years may awe the vale below,
Yet not the less be shatter'd on its height,
By one dread moment of the earthquake's might!
A thousand pangs thy bosom may have borne,
In silent fortitude, or haughty scorn,
Till comes the one, the master-anguish, sent
To break the mighty heart that ne'er was bent.

Oh! what is nature's strength? the vacant eye,
By mind deserted, hath a dread reply!
The wild delirious laughter of despair,
The mirth of frenzy—seek an answer there!
Turn not away, though pity's cheek grow pale,
Close not thine ear against their awful tale.
They tell thee, Reason, wandering from the ray
Of Faith, the blazing pillar of her way,
In the mid-darkness of the stormy wave,
Forsook the struggling soul she could not save!
Weep not, sad moralist! o'er desert plains,
Strew'd with the wrecks of grandeur—mouldering fanes,
Arches of triumph, long with weeds o'ergrown,
And regal cities, now the serpent's own:
Earth has more awful ruins—one lost mind,
Whose star is quench'd, hath lessons for mankind,
Of deeper import than each prostrate dome,
Mingling its marble with the dust of Rome.

But who, with eye unshrinking, shall explore
That waste, illumed by reason's beam no more?
Who pierce the deep, mysterious clouds that roll
Around the shattered temple of the soul,

Curtain'd with midnight?—low its columns lie,
And dark the chambers of its imag'ry,[3]
Sunk are its idols now—and God alone
May rear the fabric, by their fall o'erthrown!
Yet, from its inmost shrine, by storms laid bare,
Is heard an oracle that cries—" Beware!
Child of the dust! but ransomed of the skies!
One breath of Heaven—and thus thy glory dies!
Haste, ere the hour of doom—draw nigh to him
Who dwells above between the cherubim!"

Spirit dethroned! and check'd in mid career,
Son of the morning! exiled from thy sphere,
Tell us thy tale!—Perchance thy race was run
With science, in the chariot of the sun;
Free as the winds the paths of space to sweep,
Traverse the untrodden kingdoms of the deep,
And search the laws that Nature's springs control,
These tracing all—save Him who guides the whole!

Haply thine eye its ardent glance had cast
Through the dim shades, the portals of the past;
By the bright lamp of thought thy care had fed
From the far beacon-lights of ages fled,
The depths of time exploring, to retrace
The glorious march of many a vanish'd race.

Or did thy power pervade the living lyre,
Till its deep chords became instinct with fire,
Silenced all meaner notes, and swell'd on high,
Full and alone, their mighty harmony,
While woke each passion from its cell profound,
And nations started at th' electric sound?

Lord of th' ascendant! what avails it now,
Though bright the laurels waved upon thy brow?
What, though thy name, through distant empires heard,
Bade the heart bound, as doth a battle-word?
Was it for *this* thy still-unwearied eye,
Kept vigil with the watchfires of the sky,
To make the secrets of all ages thine,
And commune with majestic thoughts that shine
O'er Time's long shadowy pathway?—hath thy mind
Sever'd its lone dominions from mankind,
For *this* to woo their homage?—Thou hast sought
All, save the wisdom with salvation fraught,
Won every wreath—but that which will not die,
Nor aught neglected—save eternity!

And did all fail thee, in the hour of wrath,
When burst the o'erwhelming vials on thy path?

Could not the voice of Fame inspire thee then,
O spirit! scepter'd by the sons of men,
With an immortal's courage, to sustain
The transient agonies of earthly pain?
—One, one there was, all-powerful to have saved,
When the loud fury of the billow raved;
But him thou knew'st not—and the light he lent
Hath vanish'd from its ruin'd tenement,
But left thee breathing, moving, lingering yet,
A thing we shrink from—vainly to forget!
—Lift the dread veil no further—hide, oh! hide
The bleeding form, the couch of suicide!
The dagger, grasp'd in death—the brow, the eye,
Lifeless, yet stamp'd with rage and agony;
The soul's dark traces left in many a line
Graved on *his* mein, who died,—" and made no sign!"
Approach not, gaze not—lest thy fever'd brain
Too deep that image of despair retain;
Angels of slumber! o'er the midnight hour,
Let not such visions claim unhallow'd power,
Lest the mind sink with terror, and above
See but th' Avenger's arm, forget th' Atoner's love!

O Thou! th' unseen th' all-seeing!—Thou, whose ways,
Mantled with darkness, mock all finite gaze,
Before whose eyes the creatures of Thy hand,
Seraph and man, alike in weakness stand,
And countless ages, trampling into clay
Earth's empires on their march, are but a day!
Father of worlds unknown, unnumber'd!—Thou,
With whom all time is one eternal *now*,
Who know'st no past, nor future—Thou whose breath
Goes forth, and bears to myriads, life or death!
Look on us, guide us!—wanderers of a sea
Wild and obscure, what are we, reft of Thee?
A thousand rocks, deep-hid, elude our sight,
A star may set—and we are lost in night;
A breeze may waft us to the whirlpool's brink,
A treach'rous song allure us—and we sink!

Oh! by *His* love, who, veiling Godhead's light,
To moments circumscribed the Infinite,
And Heaven and Earth disdain'd not to ally
By that dread union—Man with Deity;
Immortal tears o'er mortal woes who shed,
And, ere he raised them, wept above the dead;
Save, or we perish!—Let Thy word control
The earthquakes of that universe—the soul;
Pervade the depths of passion—speak once more
The mighty mandate, guard of every shore,
" Here shall thy waves be stay'd"—in grief, in pain,
The fearful poise of reason's sphere maintain,

Thou, by whom suns are balanced!—thus secure
In Thee shall Faith and Fortitude endure;
Conscious of Thee, unfaltering, shall the just
Look upward still, in high and holy trust,
And by affliction guided to Thy shrine,
The first, last thought of suffering hearts be Thine.

And oh! be near, when, clothed with conquering power,
The King of Terrors claims his own dread hour;
When, on the edge of that unknown abyss,
Which darkly parts us from the realm of bliss,
Awe-struck alike the timid and the brave,
Alike subdued the monarch and the slave,
Must drink the cup of trembling[4] —when we see
Nought in the universe but Death and Thee,
Forsake us not—if still, when life was young,
Faith to thy bosom, as her home, hath sprung,
If Hope's retreat hath been, through all the past,
The shadow by the Rock of Ages cast,
Father, forsake us not!—when tortures urge
The shrinking soul to that mysterious verge;
When from Thy justice to Thy love we fly,
On Nature's conflict look with pitying eye,
Bid the strong wind, the fire, the earthquake cease,
Come in the still small voice, and whisper—peace![5]

For oh! 'tis awful—He that hath beheld
The parting spirit, by its fears repell'd,
Cling in weak terror to its earthly chain,
And from the dizzy brink recoil, in vain;
He that hath seen the last convulsive throe
Dissolve the union form'd and closed in woe,
Well knows that hour is awful.—In the pride
Of youth and health, by suffering yet untried,
We talk of Death, as something, which 'twere sweet
In Glory's arms exultingly to meet,
A closing triumph, a majestic scene,
Where gazing nations watch the hero's mien,
As, undismay'd amidst the tears of all,
He folds his mantle, regally to fall!

Hush, fond enthusiast!—still, obscure and lone,
Yet not less terrible because unknown,
Is the last hour of thousands—they retire
From life's throng'd path, unnoticed to expire;
As the light leaf, whose fall to ruin bears
Some trembling insect's little world of cares,
Descends in silence—while around waves on
The mighty forest, reckless what is gone!
Such is man's doom—and ere an hour be flown,
— Start not, thou trifler!—such may be thine own.

But, as life's current in its ebb draws near
The shadowy gulf, there wakes a thought of fear,
A thrilling thought, which haply mock'd before,
We fain would stifle—but it sleeps no more!
There are who fly its murmurs 'midst the throng,
That join the masque of revelry and song;
Yet still Death's image, by its power restored,
Frowns 'midst the roses of the festal board,
And when deep shades o'er earth and ocean brood,
And the heart owns the might of solitude,
Is its low whisper heard?—a note profound,
But wild and startling as the trumpet sound,
That bursts, with sudden blast, the dead repose
Of some proud city, storm'd by midnight foes!

Oh! vainly Reason's scornful voice would prove
That life hath nought to claim such lingering love,
And ask if e'er the captive, half unchain'd,
Clung to the links which yet his step restrain'd?
In vain Philosophy, with tranquil pride,
Would mock the feelings she perchance can hide,
Call up the countless armies of the dead,
Point to the pathway beaten by their tread,
And say—" What wouldst thou? Shall the fix'd decree,
Made for creation, be reversed for *thee?*"
—Poor, feeble aid!—proud Stoic! ask not why,
It is enough, that nature shrinks to die!
Enough, *that* horror, which thy words upbraid,
Is her dread penalty, and must be paid!
—Search thy deep wisdom, solve the scarce defined
And mystic questions of the parting mind,
Half check'd, half utter'd—tell her, what shall burst,
In whelming grandeur, on her vision first,
When freed from mortal films?—what viewless world
Shall first receive her wing, but half unfurl'd?
What awful and unbodied beings guide
Her timid flight through regions yet untried?
Say, if at once, her final doom to hear,
Before her God the trembler must appear,
Or wait that day of terror, when the sea
Shall yield its hidden dead, and heaven and earth shall flee?

Hast thou no answer?—Then deride no more
The thoughts that shrink, yet cease not to explore
Th' unknown, th' unseen, the future—through the heart,
As at unearthly sounds, before them start;
Though the frame shudder, and the spirit sigh,
They have their source in immortality!
Whence, then, shall strength, which reason's aid denies,
An equal to the mortal conflict rise?
When, on the swift pale horse, whose lightning pace,
Where'er we fly, still wins the dreadful race,

The mighty rider comes—O whence shall aid
Be drawn, to meet his rushing, undismay'd?
—Whence, but from thee, Messiah!—thou hast drain'd
The bitter cup, till not the dregs remain'd;
To thee the struggle and the pang were known,
The mystic horror—all became thine own!

But did no hand celestial succor bring,
Till scorn and anguish haply lost their sting?
Came not th' Archangel, in the final hour,
To arm thee with invulnerable power?
No, Son of God! upon thy sacred head
The shafts of wrath their tenfold fury shed,
From man averted—and thy path on high
Pass'd through the strait of fiercest agony;
For thus th' Eternal, with propitious eyes,
Received the last, th' almighty sacrifice!

But wake! be glad, ye nations! from the tomb
Is won the vict'ry, and is fled the gloom!
The vale of death in conquest hath been trod,
Break forth in joy, ye ransom'd! saith your God!
Swell ye the raptures of the song afar,
And hail with harps your bright and Morning Star.

He rose! the everlasting gates of day
Received the King of Glory on his way!
The hope, the comforter of those who wept,
And the first-fruits of them, in Him that slept.
He rose, he triumph'd! he will yet sustain
Frail nature sinking in the strife of pain.
Aided by Him, around the martyr's frame
When fiercely blazed a living shroud of flame,
Hath the firm soul exulted, and the voice
Raised the victorious hymn, and cried, Rejoice!
Aided by Him, though none the bed attend,
Where the lone sufferer dies without a friend,
He whom the busy world shall miss no more
Than morn one dewdrop from her countless store,
Earth's most neglected child, with trusting heart,
Call'd to the hope of glory, shall depart!

And say, cold Sophist! if by thee bereft
Of that high hope, to misery what were left?
But for the vision of the days to be,
But for the comforter, despised by thee,
Should we not wither at the Chastener's look,
Should we not sink beneath our God's rebuke,
When o'er our heads the desolating blast,
Fraught with inscrutable decrees, hath pass'd,
And the stern power who seeks the noblest prey,
Hath call'd our fairest and our best away?

Should we not madden when our eyes behold
All that we loved in marble stillness cold,
No more responsive to our smile or sigh,
Fix'd—frozen—silent—all mortality?
But for the promise, all shall yet be well,
Would not the spirit in its pangs rebel,
Beneath such clouds as darken'd, when the hand
Of wrath lay heavy on our prostrate land;
And thou,* just lent thy gladden'd isles to bless,
Then snatch'd from earth with all thy loveliness,
With all a nation's blessings on thy head,
O England's flower! wert gather'd to the dead?
But thou didst teach us. Thou to every heart,
Faith's lofty lesson didst thyself impart!
When fled the hope through all thy pangs which smiled,
When thy young bosom, o'er thy lifeless child,
Yearn'd with vain longing—still thy patient eye,
To its last light, beam'd holy constancy!
Torn from a lot in cloudless sunshine cast,
Amidst those agonies—thy first and last,
Thy pale lip, quivering with convulsive throes,
Breathed not a plaint—and settled in repose;
While bow'd thy royal head to Him, whose power
Spoke in the fiat of that midnight hour,
Who from the brightest vision of a throne,
Love, glory, empire, claim'd thee for his own,
And spread such terror o'er the sea-girt coast,
As blasted Israel, when her Ark was lost!

" It is the will of God!"—yet, yet we hear
The words which closed thy beautiful career;
Yet should we mourn thee in thy blest abode,
But for that thought—" It is the will of God!"
Who shall arraign th' Eternal's dark decree,
If not one murmur then escaped from thee?
Oh!—still, though vanishing without a trace,
Thou hast not left one scion of thy race;
Still may thy memory bloom our vales among,
Hallow'd by freedom, and enshrined in song!
Still may thy pure, majestic spirit dwell,
Bright on the isles which loved thy name so well,
E'en as an angel, with presiding care,
To wake and guard thine own high virtues there.

For lo! the hour when storm-presaging skies
Call on the watchers of the land to rise.
To set the sign of fire on every height,[6]
And o'er the mountains rear, with patriot might,
Prepar'd, if summon'd in its cause to die,
The banner of our faith, the Cross of victory!

---
* The Princess Charlotte.

By this hath England conquer'd—field and flood
Have own'd her sov'reignty—alone she stood,
When chains o'er all the scepter'd earth were thrown,
In high and holy singleness, alone,
But mighty in her God—and shall she now
Forget before th' Omnipotent to bow?
From the bright fountain of her glory turn,
Or bid strange fire upon his altars burn?
No! sever'd land, 'midst rocks and billows rude,
Throned in thy majesty of solitude,
Still in the deep asylum of thy breast
Shall the pure elements of greatness rest,
Virtue and faith, the tutelary powers,
Thy hearths that hallow, and defend thy towers!

Still, where thy hamlet-vales, O chosen isle!
In the soft beauty of their verdure smile,
Where yew and elm o'ershade the lonely fanes,
That guard the peasant's records and remains,
May the blest echoes of the Sabbath-bell
Sweet on the quiet of the woodlands swell,
And from each cottage-dwelling of thy glades,
When starlight glimmers through the deep'ning shades,
Devotion's voice in choral hymns arise,
And bear the land's warm incense to the skies.

There may the mother, as with anxious joy
To Heaven her lessons consecrate her boy,
Teach his young accent still the immortal lays
Of Zion's bards, in inspiration's days,
When angels, whispering through the cedar shade,
Prophetic tones to Judah's harp convey'd
And as, her soul all glistening in her eyes,
She bids the prayer of infancy arise,
Tell of his name, who left his Throne on high,
Earth's lowliest lot to bear and sanctify,
His love divine, by keenest anguish tried,
And fondly say—" My child, for thee He died!"

NOTES.

Note 1, page 250, line 13.
Patient, because Eternal.
'He is patient, because he is eternal."—St. Augustine.

Note 2, page 250, line 34.
Fly to the City of thy Refuge, fly!
"Then ye shall appoint you cities, to be cities of refuge for you; that the slayer may flee thither which killeth any person at unawares.—And they shall be unto you cities of refuge from the avenger."—Numbers, chap. 35.

Note 3, page 252, line 2.
And dark the chambers of its imag'ry,
"Every man in the chambers of his imagery."—Ezekiel, chap. 8.

Note 4, page 254, line 13.
Must drink the cup of trembling.
"Thou hast drunken the dregs of the cup of trembling, and wrung them out."—Isaiah, chap. 51.

Note 5, page 254, line 24.
Come in the still small voice, and whisper peace.
"And behold, the Lord passed by, and a great and strong wind rent the mountains, and brake in pieces the rocks before the Lord; but the Lord was not in the wind: and after the wind an earthquake; but the Lord was not in the earthquake: and after the earthquake a fire; but the Lord was not in the fire: and after the fire a still small voice."—Kings, book i. chap. 19.

Note 6, page 257, line 45.
To set the sign of fire on every height.
"And set up a sign of fire."—Jeremiah, chap. 6

CRITICAL ANNOTATIONS

ON "THE SCEPTIC."

"In 1820 Mrs. Hemans published *The Sceptic*, a poem of great merit for its style and its sentiments, of which we shall give a rapid sketch. She considers the influence of unbelief on the affections and gentler part of our nature, and, after pursuing the picture of the misery consequent on doubt, shows the relief that may be found in the thoughts that have their source in immortality. Glancing at pleasure as the only resort of the sceptic, she turns to the sterner tasks of life.

'E'en youth's brief hours
Survive the beauty of their loveliest flowers; * * *
The soul's pure flame the breath of storms must fan;
And pain and sorrow claim their nursling—Man.

But then the sceptic has no relief in memory, for memory recalls no joys but such as were transitory, and known to be such; and as for hope—

'She, who like heaven's own sunbeam, smiles for all,
Will she speak comfort?—Thou hast shorn her plume,
That might have raised thee far above the tomb,
And hush'd the only voice whose angel-tone
Soothes when all melodies of joy are flown.'

"The poet then asks, if an infidel dare love; and, having no home for his thoughts in a better world, nurse such feelings as delight to enshrine themselves in the breast of a parent. She addresses him on the insecurity of an attachment to a vain idol, from which death may at any time divide him '*for ever.*' . . . For relief the infidel is referred to the Christian religion, in a strain, which unites the fervor of devotion with poetic sensibility. . . . The poem proceeds to depict, in a forcible manner the unfortunate state of a mind which acquires every kind of knowledge but that which gives salvation; and, having gained possession of the secrets of all ages, and communed with the majestic minds that shine along the pathway of time, neglects nothing but eternity. Such a one, in the season of suffering, finds relief in suicide, and escapes to death as to an eternal rest. The thought of death recurs to the mind of the poet, and calls forth a fervent prayer for the divine presence and support in the hour of dissolution; for the hour, when the soul is brought to the mysterious verge of another life, is an 'awful one.' . . . . . This is followed by an allusion to the strong love of life which belongs to human nature, and the instinctive apprehension with which the parting mind muses on its future condition, and asks of itself mystic questions, that it cannot solve But through the influence of religion—

'He whom the busy world shall miss no more
Than morn one dewdrop from her countless store,
Earth's most neglected child, with trusting heart,
Call'd to the hope of glory, shall depart!'

"After some lines expressing the spirit of English patriotism, in a manner with which foreigners can only be pleased, the poem closes with the picture of a mother teaching her child the first lessons of religion, by holding up the divine example of the Saviour.

"We have been led into a longer notice of this poem, for it illustrates the character of Mrs. Hemans's manner. We perceive in it a loftiness of purpose, an earnestness of thought, sometimes made more interesting by a tinge of melancholy, a depth of religious feeling, a mind alive to all the interests, gratifications, and sorrows of social life."—PROFESSOR NORTON (in *North American Review*, April, 1827.)

"We have, on more than one occasion, expressed the very high opinion which we entertain of the talents of this lady; and it is gratifying to find that she gives us no reason to retract or modify in any degree the applause already bestowed, and that every fresh ex nibition of her powers enhances and confirms her claims upon our admiration. Mrs. Hemans is indeed but in the infancy of her poetical career; but it is an infancy of unrivalled beauty, and of very high promise. Not but that she has already performed more than has often been sufficient to win for other candidates no mean place in the roll of fame, but because what she has already done, shrinks, when compared with what we consider to be her own great capacity, to mere incipient excellence—the intimation rather than the fulfilment of the high destiny of her genius.

The verses of Mrs. Hemans appear the spontaneous offspring of intense and noble feeling, governed by a clear understanding, and fashioned into elegance by an exquisite delicacy and precision of taste. With more than the force of many of her masculine competitors, she never ceases to be strictly *feminine* in the whole current of her thought and feeling, nor approaches by any chance the verge of that free and intrepid course of speculation, of which the boldness is more conspicuous than the wisdom, but into which some of the most remarkable among the female literati of our times have freely and fearlessly plunged. She has, in the poem before us, made choice of a subject of which it would have been very difficult to have reconciled the treatment, in the hands of some female authors, to the delicacy which belongs to the sex, and the tenderness and enthusiasm which form its finest characteristics. A coarse and chilling cento of the exploded fancies of modern scepticism, done into rhyme by the hand of a woman, would have been doubly disgusting, by the revival of absurdities long consigned to oblivion, and by the revolting exhibition of a female mind shorn of all its attractions, and wrapt in darkness and defiance. But Mrs. Hemans has chosen the better and the nobler cause, and, while she has left in the poem before us every trace of vigorous intellect of which the subject admitted, and has far transcended in energy of thought the prosing pioneers of unbelief, she has sustained throughout a tone of warm and confiding piety, and has thus proved that the humility of hope and of faith has in it none of the weakness with which it has been charged by the arrogance of impiety, but owns a divine and mysterious vigor residing under the very aspect of gentleness and devotion."—*Edinburgh Monthly Review*, vol. iii.

"Her last two publications are works of a higher stamp; works, indeed, of which no living poet need to be ashamed. The first of them is entitled *The Sceptic*, and is devoted, as our readers will easily anticipate, to advocating the cause of religion. Undoubtedly the poem must have owed its being to the circumstances of the times—to a laudable indignation at the course which literature in many departments seemed lately to be taking in this country, and at the doctrines disseminated with industry, principally (but by no means exclusively, as has been falsely supposed) among the lower orders. Mrs. Hemans, however, does not attempt to reason learnedly or laboriously in verse; few poems, ostensibly philosophical or didactic, have ever been of use, except to display the ingenuity and talent of the writers. People are not often taught a science or an art in poetry, and much less will an infidel be converted by a theological treatise in verse. But the argument of *The Sceptic* is one of irresistible force to confirm a wavering mind; it is simply resting the truth of religion on the necessity of it—on the utter misery and helplessness of man without it. This argument is in itself available for all the purposes of poetry: it appeals to the imagination and passions of man; it is capable of interesting all our affectionate hopes and charities, of acting upon all our natural fears. Mrs. Hemans has gone through this range with great feeling and ability; and, when she comes to the mind which has clothed itself in its own strength, and relying proudly on that alone in the hour of affliction, has sunk into distraction in the contest, she rises into a strain of moral poetry not often surpassed:—

'Oh, what is nature's strength?—the vacant eye,
By mind deserted, hath a dread reply,' &c."

Quarterly Review, vol. xxiv.

A TALE OF THE SECRET TRIBUNAL.

The Secret Tribunal,* which attained such formidable power towards the close of the fourteenth century, is mentioned in history as an institution publicly known so early as in the year 1211. Its members, who were called Free Judges, were unknown to the people, and were bound by a tremendous oath, to deliver up their dearest friends and relatives, without exception, if they had committed any offence cognizable by the tribunal. They were also under an obligation to relate all they knew concerning the affair, to cite the accused, and, in case of his condemnation, to pursue and put him to death, wherever he might be met with. The proceedings of this tribunal were carried on at night, and with the greatest mystery; and though it was usual to summon a culprit three times before sentence was passed, yet persons obnoxious to it were sometimes accused and condemned without any citation. After condemnation, it was almost impossible for any one to escape the vengeance of the Free Judges, for their commands set thousands of assassins in motion, who had sworn not to spare the life of their nearest relation, if required to sacrifice it, but to execute the decrees of the order with the most devoted obedience, even should they consider the object of their pursuit as the most innocent of men. Almost all persons of rank and fortune sought admission into the society; there were Free Judges even amongst the magistrates of the imperial cities, and every prince had some of their order in his council. When a member of this tribunal was not of himself strong enough to seize and put to death a criminal, he was not to lose sight of him until he met with a sufficient number of his comrades for the purpose, and these were obliged, upon his making certain signs, to lend him immediate assistance, without asking any questions. It was usual to hang up the persons condemned, with a willow branch, to the first tree; but if circumstances obliged them to dispatch him with a poinard, they left it in his body, that it might be known he had not been assassinated, but executed by a Free Judge. All the transactions of the *Sages* or *Seers* (as they called themselves,) were enveloped in mystery, and it is even now unknown by what signs they revealed themselves to each other. At length their power became so extensive and redoubtable, that the Princes of the Empire found it necessary to unite their exertions for its suppression, in which they were at length successful.

The following account of this extraordinary association is given by Madame de Staël:—" Des juges mysterieux, inconnus l'un à l'autre, toujours masqués, et se rassemblant pendant la nuit, punissoient dans le silence, et gravoient seulement sur le poignard qu'ils enforçoient dans le sein du coupable ce mot terrible: Tribunal Secret. Ils prévenoient le condamné, en faisant crier trois fois sous les fenêtres de sa maison, Malheur, Malheur, Malheur! Alors l'infortuné savoit que par-tout, dans l'étranger, dans son concitoyen, dans son parent même, il pouvoit trouver son meurtrier. La solitude, la foule, les villes, les campagnes, tout étoit rempli par la presence invisible de cette conscience armée qui poursuivoit les criminels. On conçoit comment cette terrible institution pouvoit être necessaire, dans un

---

* See the works of Baron Bock and Professor Kramer.

A TALE OF THE SECRET TRIBUNAL.

temps où chaque homme étoit fort contre tous, au lieu, que tous doivent être forts contre chacun. Il falloit que la justice surprît le criminel avant qu'il pût s'en defendre; mais cette punition qui planoit dans les airs comme une ombre vengeresse, cette sentence mortelle qui pouvoit receller le sein même d'un ami, frappoit d'une invincible terreur." *L'Allemagne, Vol. II.*

Night veil'd the mountains of the vine,
And storms had roused the foaming Rhine,
And, mingling with the pinewood's roar,
Its billows hoarsely chafed the shore,
While glen and cavern, to their moans,
Gave answer with a thousand tones:
Then, as the voice of storms appall'd
The peasant of the Odenwald,*
Shuddering he deem'd, that, far on high,
'Twas the wild huntsman rushing by,
Riding the blast with phantom speed,
With cry of hound, and tramp of steed,
While his fierce train, as on they flew,
Their horns in savage chorus blew,
Till rock, and tower, and convent round,
Rung to the shrill unearthly sound.

Vain dreams! far other footsteps traced
The forest path, in secret haste;
Far other sounds were on the night,
Though lost amidst the tempest's might,
That fill'd the echoing earth and sky,
With its own awful harmony.
There stood a lone and ruin'd fane,
Far in the Odenwald's domain,
'Midst wood and rock, a deep recess
Of still and shadowy loneliness.
Long grass its pavement had o'ergrown.
The wild-flower waved o'er the altar-stone,
The night-wind rock'd the tottering pile,
As it swept along the roofless aisle,
For the forest-boughs, and the stormy sky,
Were all that minster's canopy.

Many a broken image lay
In the mossy mantle of decay,
And partial light the moonbeams darted
O'er trophies of the long departed;
For there the chiefs of other days,
The mighty, slumber'd, with their praise:

---

* The Odenwald, a forest-district near the Rhine, adjoining the territories of Darmstadt.

'Twas long since aught but the dews of Heaven
A tribute to their bier had given,
Long since a sound but the moaning blast
Above their voiceless home had pass'd.

So slept the proud, and with them all
The records of their fame and fall;
Helmet, and shield, and sculptured crest,
Adorn'd the dwelling of their rest,
And emblems of the Holy Land
Were carved by some forgotten hand;
But the helm was broke, the shield defaced,
And the crest through weeds might scarce be traced;
And the scatter'd leaves of the northern pine
Half hid the palm of Palestine.
So slept the glorious—lowly laid,
As the peasant in his native shade;
Some hermit's tale, some shepherd's rhyme,
All that high deeds could win from time!

What footsteps move, with measured tread,
Amid those chambers of the dead?
What silent, shadowy beings glide
Low tombs and mouldering shrines beside,
Peopling the wild and solemn scene
With forms well suited to its mien?
Wanderer, away! let none intrude
On their mysterious solitude!
Lo! these are they, that awful band,
The secret Watchers of the land,
They that, unknown and uncontroll'd,
Their dark and dread tribunal hold.
They meet not in the monarch's dome,
They meet not in the chieftain's home;
But where, unbounded o'er their heads,
All heaven magnificently spreads,
And from its depths of cloudless blue
The eternal stars their deeds may view!
Where'er the flowers of the mountain sod
By roving foot are seldom trod;
Where'er the pathless forest waves,
Or the ivy clothes forsaken graves;
Where'er wild legends mark a spot,
By mortals shunn'd, but unforgot,
There, circled by the shades of night,
They judge of crimes that shrink from light,
And guilt that deems its secret known
To the One unslumbering eye alone,
Yet hears their name with a sudden start,
As an icy touch had chill'd its heart,
For the shadow of th' avenger's hand
Rests dark and heavy on the land.

There rose a voice from the ruin's gloom
And woke the echoes of the tomb,
As if the noble hearts beneath
Sent forth deep answers to its breath.

"When the midnight stars are burning
And the dead to earth returning;
When the spirits of the blest
Rise upon the good man's rest;
When each whisper of the gale
Bids the cheek of guilt turn pale;
In the shadow of the hour
That o'er the soul hath deepest power,
Why thus meet we, but to call
For judgment on the criminal?
Why, but the doom of guilt to seal,
And point th' avenger's holy steel?
A fearful oath has bound our souls,
A fearful power our arm controls!
There is an ear, awake on high,
E'en to thought's whispers, ere they die;
There is an eye, whose beam pervades
All depths, all deserts, and all shades;
That ear hath heard our awful vow,
That searching eye is on us now!
Let him whose heart is unprofaned,
Whose hand no blameless blood hath stain'd—
Let him, whose thoughts no record keep
Of crimes, in silence buried deep,
Here, in the face of Heaven, accuse
The guilty whom its wrath pursues!"

'Twas hushed—that voice of thrilling sound,
And a dead silence reign'd around.
Then stood forth one, whose dim-seen form,
Tower'd like a phantom in the storm;
Gathering his mantle, as a cloud,
With its dark folds his face to shroud,
Through pillar'd arches on he pass'd,
With stately step, and paused at last,
Where, on the altar's mouldering stone,
The fitful moonbeam brightly shone;
Then on the fearful stillness broke
Low, solemn tones, as thus he spoke :

"Before that eye, whose glance pervades
All depths, all deserts, and all shades;
Heard by that ear awake on high
E'en to thought's whispers ere they die;
With all a mortal's awe I stand,
Yet with pure heart, and stainless hand.

To Heaven I lift that hand and call
For judgment on the criminal;
The earth is dyed with bloodshed's hues,
It cries for vengeance—I accuse!"

" Name thou the guilty! say for whom
Thou claim'st th' inevitable doom!"

" Albert of Lindheim—to the skies
The voice of blood against him cries;
A brother's blood—his hand is dyed
With the deep stain of fratricide.
One hour, one moment, hath reveal'd,
What years in darkness had conceal'd,
But all in vain—the gulf of time
Refused to close upon his crime;
And guilt that slept on flowers, shall know,
The earthquake was but hush'd below!

Here, where amidst the noble dead,
Awed by their fame, he dare not tread;
Where, left by him to dark decay,
Their trophies moulder fast away;
Around us and beneath us lie
The relics of his ancestry;
The chiefs of Lindheim's ancient race,
Each in his last low dwelling-place:
But one is absent—o'er *his* grave
The palmy shades of Syria wave;
Far distant from his native Rhine,
He died unmourn'd, in Palestine;
The Pilgrim sought the Holy Land,
To perish by a brother's hand!
Peace to his soul! though o'er his bed
No dirge be pour'd, no tear be shed,
Though all he loved his name forget,
They live who shall avenge him yet!"

" Accuser! how to thee alone
Became the fearful secret known?"

" There is an hour when vain remorse
First wakes in her eternal force;
When pardon may not be retrieved,
When conscience will not be deceived.
He that beheld the victim bleed,
Beheld, and aided in the deed—
When earthly fears had lost their power
Reveal'd the tale in such an hour,
Unfolding, with his latest breath,
All that gave keene pangs to death."

"By Him, th' All-seeing and Unseen,
Who is for ever, and hath been,
And by th' Atoner's cross adored,
And by th' avenger's holy sword,
By truth eternal and divine,
Accuser! wilt thou swear to thine?"
—"The cross upon my heart is prest,
I hold the dagger to my breast;
If false the tale whose truth I swear,
Be mine the murderer's doom to bear!"

Then sternly rose the dread reply—
"His days are number'd—he must die!
There is no shadow of the night,
So deep as to conceal his flight;
Earth doth not hold so lone a waste,
But there his footstep shall be traced;
Devotion hath no shrine so blest,
That there in safety he may rest.
Where'er he treads, let Vengeance there
Around him spread her secret snare!
In the busy haunts of men,
In the still and shadowy glen,
When the social board is crown'd,
When the wine-cup sparkles round;
When his couch of sleep is prest,
And a dream his spirit's guest;
When his bosom knows no fear,
Let the dagger still be near,
Till, sudden as the lightning's dart,
Silent and swift it reach his heart!
One warning voice, one fearful word,
Ere morn beneath his towers be heard,
Then vainly may the guilty fly,
Unseen, unaided,—he must die!
Let those he loves prepare his tomb,
Let friendship lure him to his doom!
Perish his deeds, his name, his race,
Without a record or a trace!
Away! be watchful, swift, and free,
To wreak th' invisible's decree.
'Tis pass'd—th' avenger claims his prey,
On to the chase of death—away!"

And all was still—the sweeping blast
Caught not a whisper as it pass'd;
The shadowy forms were seen no more
The tombs deserted as before;
And the wide forest waved immense,
In dark and lone magnificence.
In Lindheim's towers the feast had closed;
The song was hush'd, the bard reposed;

Sleep settled on the weary guest,
And the castle's lord retired to rest.
To rest!—the captive doom'd to die
May slumber, when his hour is nigh;
The seaman, when the billows foam,
Rock'd on the mast, may dream of home;
The warrior, on the battle's eve,
May win from care a short reprieve;
But earth and heaven alike deny
Their peace to guilt's o'erwearied eye;
And night, that brings to grief a calm,
To toil a pause, to pain a balm,
Hath spells terrific in her course,
Dread sounds and shadows, for remorse,
Voices that long from earth had fled,
And steps and echoes from the dead;
And many a dream, whose forms arise,
Like a darker world's realities!
Call them not vain illusions—born
But for the wise and brave to scorn!
Heaven, that the penal doom defers,
Hath yet its thousand ministers,
To scourge the heart, unseen, unknown,
In shade, in silence, and alone,
Concentrating in one brief hour
Ages of retribution's power!

If thou wouldst know the lot of those,
Whose souls are dark with guilty woes
Ah! seek them not where pleasure's throng
Are listening to the voice of song;
Seek them not where the banquet glows,
And the red vineyard's nectar flows:
There mirth may flush the hollow cheek,
The eye of feverish joy may speak,
And smiles, the ready mask of pride,
The canker-worm within may hide:
Heed not those signs! they but delude;
Follow, and mark their solitude!

The song is hush'd, the feast is done,
And Lindheim's lord remains alone,
Alone, in silence and unrest,
With the dread secret of his breast:
Alone with anguish and with fear;
—There needs not an avenger here!
Behold him!—Why that sudden start?
Thou hear'st the beating of thy heart!
Thou hear'st the night-wind's hollow sigh,
Thou hear'st the rustling tapestry!
No sound but these may near thee be;
Sleep! all things earthly sleep—but thee.

No! there are murmurs on the air,
And a voice is heard that cries—" Despair!"
And he who trembles fain would deem
'Twas the whisper of a waking dream.
Was it but this?—again 'tis there,
Again is heard—" Despair! Despair!"
'Tis past—its tones have slowly died
In echoes on the mountain side ;
Heard but by him, they rose, they fell,
He knew their fearful meaning well,
And shrinking from the midnight gloom,
As from the shadow of the tomb,
Yet, shuddering, turn'd in pale dismay
When broke the dawn's first kindling ray,
And sought, amidst the forest wild,
Some shade where sunbeam never smiled.

Yes! hide thee, guilt!—the laughing morn
Wakes in a heaven of splendor born!
The storms that shook the mountain crest
Have sought their viewless world of rest.
High from his cliffs, with ardent gaze,
Soars the young eagle in the blaze,
Exulting, as he wings his way,
To revel in the fount of day,
And brightly past his banks of vine,
In glory, flows the monarch Rhine ;
And joyous peals the vintage song
His wild luxuriant shores along,
As peasant bands, from rock and dell,
Their strains of choral transport swell ;
And cliffs of bold fantastic forms,
Aspiring to the realm of storms ;
And woods around, and waves below,
Catch the red Orient's deepening glow,
That lends each tower, and convent-spire,
A tinge of its ethereal fire.
Swell high the song of festal hours!
Deck ye the shrine with living flowers!
Let music o'er the waters breathe!
Let beauty twine the bridal wreath!
While she, whose blue eye laughs in light,
Whose cheek with love's own hue is bright,
The fair-hair'd maid of Lindheim's hall,
Wakes to her nuptial festival.
Oh! who hath seen, in dreams that soar
To worlds the soul would fain explore,
When, for her own blest country pining,
Its beauty o'er her thought is shining,
Some form of heaven, whose cloudless eye
Was all one beam of ecstacy!

Whose glorious brow no traces wore
Of guilt, or sorrow known before!
Whose smile, undimm'd by aught of earth,
A sunbeam of immortal birth,
Spoke of bright realms, far distant lying,
Where love and joy are both undying!
E'en thus—a vision of delight,
A beam to gladden mortal sight,
A flower whose head no storm had bow'd,
Whose leaves ne'er droop'd beneath a cloud,
Thus, by the world unstain'd, untried,
Seem'd that belov'd and lovely bride;
A being all too soft and fair,
One breath of earthly woe to bear!
Yet lives there many a lofty mind,
In light and fragile form enshrined;
And oft smooth cheek, and smiling eye,
Hide strength to suffer and to die!
Judge not of woman's heart in hours
That strew her path with summer flowers,
When joy's full cup is mantling high,
When flattery's blandishments are nigh;
Judge her not then! within her breast
Are energies unseen, that rest!
They wait their call—and grief alone
May make the soul's deep secrets known.
Yes! let her smile, 'midst pleasure's train
Leading the reckless and the vain!
Firm on the scaffold she hath stood,
Besprinkled with the martyr's blood;
Her voice the patriot's heart hath steel'd,
Her spirit glow'd on battle-field;
Her courage freed from dungeon's gloom
The captive brooding o'er his doom;
Her faith the fallen monarch saved,
Her love the tyrant's fury braved;
No scene of danger or despair,
But she hath won her triumph there!

Away! nor cloud the festal morn
With thoughts of boding sadness borne!
Far other, lovelier dreams are thine,
Fair daughter of a noble line!
Young Ella! from thy tower, whose height
Hath caught the flush of Eastern light,
Watching, while soft the morning air
Parts on thy brow the sunny hair,
Yon bark, that o'er the calm blue tide
Bears thy loved warrior to his bride—
He, whose high deeds romantic praise
Hath hallow'd with a thousand lays.

He came—that youthful chief—he came
That favor'd lord of love and fame!
His step was hurried—as if one
Who seeks a voice within to shun;
His cheek was varying, and express'd
The conflict of a troubled breast:
His eye was anxious—doubt, and dread,
And a stern grief might there be read;
Yet all that mark'd his alter'd mien
Seem'd struggling to be still unseen.

With shrinking heart, with nameless fear,
Young Ella met the brow austere,
And the wild look, which seem'd to fly
The timid welcome of her eye.
Was that a lover's gaze, which chill'd
The soul, its awful sadness thrill'd?
A lover's brow, so darkly fraught
With all the heaviest gloom of thought?
She trembled—ne'er to grief inured,
By its dread lessons ne'er matured:
Unused to meet a glance of less
Than all a parent's tenderness,
Shuddering she felt, through every sense
The death-like faintness of suspense.

High o'er the windings of the flood,
On Lindheim's terraced rocks they stood,
Whence the free sight afar might stray
O'er that imperial river's way,
Which, rushing from its Alpine source,
Makes one long triumph of its course,
Rolling in tranquil grandeur by,
'Midst Nature's noblest pageantry.
But they, o'er that majestic scene,
With clouded brow and anxious mien,
In silence gazed:—for Ella's heart
Fear'd its own terrors to impart;
And he, who vainly strove to hide
His pangs, with all a warrior's pride,
Seem'd gathering courage to unfold
Some fearful tale that must be told.

At length his mien, his voice, obtain'd
A calm, that seem'd by conflicts gain'd,
As thus he spoke—" Yes! gaze a while
On the bright scenes that round thee smile
For, if thy love be firm and true,
Soon must thou bid their charms adieu!
A fate hangs o'er us, whose decree
Must bear me far from them or thee;

Our path is one of snares and fear,
I lose thee if I linger here!
Droop not, beloved! thy home shall rise
As fair, beneath far distant skies;
As fondly tenderness and truth
Shall cherish there thy rose of youth.
But speak! and when yon hallow'd shrine
Hath heard the vows which make thee mine
Say, wilt thou fly with me, no more
To tread thine own loved mountain-shore,
But share and soothe, repining not
The bitterness of exile's lot?"

"Ulric! thou know'st how dearly loved
The scenes where first my childhood roved;
The woods, the rocks, that tower supreme
Above our own majestic stream,
The halls where first my heart beat high
To the proud songs of chivalry.
All, all are dear—yet *these* are ties
Affection well may sacrifice;
Loved though they be, where'er thou art,
There is the country of my heart!
Yet, is there one, who, reft of me,
Were lonely as a blasted tree;
One, who still hoped my hand should close
His eyes, in Nature's last repose;
Eve gathers round him—on his brow
Already rests the wintry snow;
His form is bent, his features wear
The deepening lines of age and care,
His faded eye hath lost its fire;
Thou wouldst not tear me from my sire?
Yet tell me all –thy woes impart,
My Ulric! to a faithful heart,
Which sooner far—oh, doubt not this—
Would share *thy* pangs, than others' bliss!"

"Ella, what would'st thou?—'tis a tale
Will make that cheek as marble pale!
Yet what avails it to conceal
All thou too soon must know and feel?
It must, it must be told—prepare,
And nerve that gentle heart to bear—
But I—oh, was it then for *me*
The herald of thy woes to be!
Thy soul's bright calmness to destroy,
And wake thee first from dreams of joy?
Forgive!—I would not ruder tone
Should make the fearful tidings known,
I would not that unpitying eyes
Should coldly watch thine agonies!

Better 'twere mine—that task severe,
To cloud thy breast with grief and fear.

" Hast thou not heard, in legends old,
Wild tales that turn the life-blood cold,
Of those who meet in cave or glen,
Far from the busy walks of men;
Those who mysterious vigils keep,
When earth is wrapt in shades and sleep,
To judge of crimes, like Him on high,
In stillness and in secresy?
Th' unknown avengers, whose decree
'Tis fruitless to resist or flee?
Whose name hath cast a spell of power,
O'er peasant's cot and chieftain's tower?
Thy sire—oh, Ella! hope is fled!
Think of him, mourn him, as the dead!
Their sentence, theirs, hath seal'd his doom,
And thou may'st weep as o'er his tomb!
Yes, weep!—relieve thy heart oppress'd,
Pour forth thy sorrows on my breast!
Thy cheek is cold—thy tearless eye
Seems fix'd in frozen vacancy;
Oh, gaze not thus!—thy silence break,
Speak! if 'tis but in anguish, speak!"

She spoke at length, in accents low,
Of wild and half-indignant woe:
—" *He* doom'd to perish! *he* decreed
By their avenging arm to bleed!
He, the renown'd in holy fight,
The Paynim's scourge, the Christian's might!
Ulric! what mean'st thou?—not a thought
Of that high mind with guilt is fraught!
Say, for which glorious trophy won,
Which deed of martial prowess done;
Which battle-field, in days gone by,
Gain'd by his valor, must he die?
Away! 'tis not *his* lofty name
Their sentence hath consign'd to shame,
'Tis not his life they seek—recall
Thy words, or say he shall not fall!"

Then sprung forth tears, whose blest relief
Gave pleading softness to her grief:
" And wilt thou not, by all the ties
Of our affianced love," she cries,
" By all my soul hath fix'd on thee,
Of cherish'd hope for years to be,
Wilt *thou* not aid him? wilt not thou
Shield his grey head from danger now?

And didst thou not, in childhood's morn,
That saw our young affection born,
Hang round his neck, and climb his knee,
Sharing his parent-smile with me?
Kind, gentle Ulric! best beloved!
Now be thy faith in danger proved!
Though snares and terrors round him wait,
Thou wilt not leave him to his fate!
Turn not away in cold disdain!
—Shall thine own Ella plead in vain?
How art thou changed! and must I bear
That frown, that stern, averted air?
What mean they?"

"Maiden, need'st thou ask?
These features wear no specious mask!
Doth sorrow mark this brow and eye
With characters of mystery?
This—*this* is anguish!—can it be?
And plead'st thou for thy sire to *me*?
Know though thy prayers a death-pang give,
He must not meet my sight—and live!
Well may'st thou shudder!—of the band
Who watch in secret o'er the land,
Whose thousand swords 'tis vain to shun,
Th' unknown, th' unslumbering—I am one!
My arm defend him!—what were *then*
Each vow that binds the souls of men,
Sworn on the cross, and deeply seal'd
By rites that may not be reveal'd?
—A breeze's breath, an echo's tone,
A passing sound, forgot when gone!
Nay, shrink not from me—I would fly,
That he by other hands may die!
What! think'st thou I would live to trace
Abhorrence in that angel-face?
Beside thee should the lover stand,
The father's life-blood on his brand?
No! I have bade my home adieu,
For other scenes mine eyes must view;
Look on me, love! now all is known,
O Ella! must I fly alone?"

But she was changed; scarce heaved her breath
She stood like one prepared for death,
And wept no more; then, casting down
From her fair brows the nuptial crown,
As joy's last vision from her heart,
Cried, with sad firmness, "We must part!
'Tis past—these bridal flowers, so frail
They may not brook one stormy gale,

Survive—too dear as still thou art,
Each hope they imaged—we must part!
One struggle yet—and all is o'er—
We love—and may we meet no more!
Oh! little know'st thou of the power
Affection lends in danger's hour,
To deem that fate should thus divide
My footsteps from a father's side!
Speed thou to other shores—I go
To share his wanderings and his woe;
Where'er his path of thorns may lead,
Whate'er his doom, by Heaven decreed,
If there be guardian powers above,
To nerve the heart of filial love;
If courage may be won by prayer,
Or strength by duty—I can bear!
Farewell!—though in that sound be years
Of blighted hopes and fruitless tears,
Though the soul vibrate to its knell
Of joys departed—yet, farewell!"

Was *this* the maid who seem'd, erewhile,
Born but to meet life's vernal smile?
A being, almost on the wing,
As an embodied breeze of spring?
A child of beauty and of bliss,
Sent from some purer sphere to this,
Not, in her exile, to sustain
The trial of one earthly pain;
But, as a sunbeam, on to move,
Wak'ning all hearts to joy and love?
That airy form, with footsteps free,
And radiant glance—could this be she?
From her fair cheek the rose was gone,
Her eye's blue sparkle thence had flown,
Of all its vivid glow bereft,
Each playful charm her lip had left;
But what were these? on that young face,
Far nobler beauty fill'd their place!
'Twas not the pride that scorns to bend,
Though all the bolts of Heaven descend;
Not the fierce grandeur of despair,
That half exults its fate to dare;
Nor that wild energy which leads
Th' enthusiast to fanatic deeds;
Her mien, by sorrow unsubdued,
Was fix'd in silent fortitude;
Not in its haughty strength elate,
But calmly, mournfully sedate.
'Twas strange, yet lovely to behold
That spirit in so fair a mould,

As if a rose-tree's tender form,
Uubent, unbroke, should meet the storm.

One look she cast, where firmness strove
With the deep pangs of parting love;
One tear a moment in her eye
Dimm'd the pure light of constancy;
And pressing, as to still her heart,
She turn'd in silence to depart.
But Ulric, as to frenzy wrought,
Then started from his trance of thought:
" Stay thee, oh, stay!—it must not be—
All, all were well resigned for thee!
Stay! till my soul each vow disown,
But those which make me thine alone;
If there be guilt—there is no shrine
More holy than that heart of thine;
There be my crime absolved—I take
The cup of shame for thy dear sake.
Of *shame!* oh no! to virtue true,
Where *thou* art, there is glory too!
Go now! and to thy sire impart,
He hath a shield in Ulric's heart,
And thou a home!—remain, or flee,
In life, in death—I follow thee!"

" There shall not rest one cloud of shame,
O Ulric! on thy lofty name;
There shall not one accusing word
Against thy spotless faith be heard!
Thy path is where the brave rush on,
Thy course must be where palms are won;
Where banners wave, and falchions glare,
Son of the mighty! be thou there!
Think on the glorious names that shine
Along thy sire's majestic line;
Oh, last of that illustrious race!
Thou wert not born to meet disgrace!
Well, well I know each grief, each pain,
Thy spirit nobly could sustain;
E'en I unshrinking see them near,
And what hast thou to do with fear?
But when hath warriors calmly borne
The cold and bitter smile of scorn?
'Tis not for thee—thy soul hath force
To cope with all things—but remorse;
And this my brightest thought shall be,
Thou hast not braved its pangs for me.
Go! break thou not one solemn vow;
Closed be the fearful conflict now;
Go! but forget not how my heart
Still at thy name will proudly start,

When chieftains hear and minstrels tell
Thy deeds of glory—fare thee well!"

And thus they parted—why recall
The scene of anguish known to all?
The burst of tears, the blush of pride,
That fain those fruitless tears would hide
The lingering look, the last embrace,
Oh! what avails it to retrace?
They parted—in that bitter word
A thousand tones of grief are heard,
Whose deeply-seated echoes rest
In the far cells of every breast;
Who hath not known, who shall not know
That keen, yet most familiar woe?
Where'er affection's home is found,
It meets her on the holy ground;
The cloud of every summer hour,
The canker-worm of every flower;
Who but hath proved, or yet shall prove,
That mortal agony of love?

The autumn moon slept bright and still
On fading wood and purple hill;
The vintager had hush'd his lay,
The fisher shunn'd the blaze of day,
And silence, o'er each green recess,
Brooded in misty sultriness.
But soon a low and measured sound
Broke on the deep repose around;
From Lindheim's towers, a glancing oar
Bade the stream ripple to the shore.
Sweet was that sound of waves which parted
The fond, the true, the noble-hearted;
And smoothly seem'd the bark to glide,
And brightly flow'd the reckless tide,
'Though, mingling with its current, fell
The last warm tears of love's farewell.

Part II.

Sweet is the gloom of forest shades,
Their pillar'd walks and dim arcades,
With all the thousand flowers that blow,
A waste of loveliness, below.
To him whose soul the world would fly,
For Nature's lonely majesty:
To bard when wrapt in mighty themes,
To lover, lost in fairy dreams,

To hermit, whose prophetic thought
By fits a gleam of heaven hath caught,
And, in the visions of his rest,
Held bright communion with the blest;
'Tis sweet, but solemn—there alike
Silence and sound with awe can strike.
The deep Eolian murmur made
By sighing breeze and rustling shade,
And cavern'd fountain gushing nigh,
And wild-bee's plaintive lullaby,
Or the dead stillness of the bowers,
When dark the summer tempest lowers;
When silent Nature seems to wait
The gathering Thunder's voice of fate,
When the aspin scarcely waves in air,
And the clouds collect for the lightning's glare,
Each, each alike is awful there,
And thrills the soul with feelings high,
As some majestic harmony.

But she, the maid, whose footsteps traced
Each green retreat, in breathless haste,
Young Ella linger'd not, to hear
The wood-notes, lost on mourner's ear;
The shivering leaf, the breeze's play,
The fountain's gush, the wild-bird's lay;
These charm not now—her sire she sought,
With trembling frame, with anxious thought,
And, starting, if a forest deer,
But moved the rustling branches near,
First felt that innocence may fear.

She reach'd a lone and shadowy dell,
Where the free sunbeam never fell;
'Twas twilight there at summer-noon,
Deep night beneath the harvest-moon,
And scarce might one bright star be seen
Gleaming the tangled boughs between;
For many a giant rock around,
Dark, in terrific grandeur, frown'd,
And the ancient oaks, that waved on high,
Shut out each glimpse of the blessed sky.
There the cold spring, in its shadowy cave,
Ne'er to Heaven's beam one sparkle gave,
And the wild flower on its brink that grew,
Caught not from day one glowing hue.

'Twas said, some fearful deed untold,
Had stain'd that scene in days of old;
Tradition o'er the haunt had thrown
A shade yet deeper than its own

And still, amidst th' umbrageous gloom,
Perchance above some victim's tomb,
O'ergrown with ivy and with moss,
There stood a rudely-sculptured Cross,
Which haply silent record bore,
Of guilt and penitence of yore.

Who by that holy sign was kneeling,
With brow unutter'd pangs revealing,
Hands clasp'd convulsively in prayer,
And lifted eyes and streaming hair,
And cheek, all pale as marble mould,
Seen by the moonbeam's radiance cold?
Was it some image of despair,
Still fix'd that stamp of woe to bear?
—Oh! ne'er could Art her forms have wrought,
To speak such agonies of thought!
Those death-like features gave to view
A mortal's pangs, too deep and true!
Starting he rose, with frenzied eye,
As Ella's hurried step drew nigh;
He turn'd, with aspect darkly wild,
Trembling he stood—before his child!
On, with a burst of tears, she sprung,
And to her father's bosom clung.

"Away! what seek'st thou here?" he cried,
"Art thou not now thine Ulric's bride?
Hence, leave me, leave me to await,
In solitude, the storm of Fate;
Thou know'st not what my doom may be
Ere evening comes in peace to thee."

"My father! shall the joyous throng
Swell high for me the bridal song?
Shall the gay nuptial board be spread,
The festal garland bind my head,
And thou in grief in peril roam,
And make the wilderness thy home?
No! I am here with thee to share
All suffering mortal strength may bear;
And, oh! whate'er thy foes decree,
In life, in death, in chains, or free;
Well, well I feel, in thee secure,
Thy heart and hand alike are pure!"

Then was there meaning in his look.
Which deep that trusting spirit shook;
So wildly did each glance express
The strife of shame and bitterness,
As thus he spoke: "Fond dreams, oh hence!
Is this the mien of Innocence?

This furrow'd brow, this restless eye,
Read thou this fearful tale—and fly!
Is it enough? or must I seek
For *words*, the tale of guilt to speak?
Then be it so—I will not doom
Thy youth to wither in its bloom;
I will not see thy tender frame
Bow'd to the earth with fear and shame.
No! though I teach thee to abhor
The sire, so fondly loved before;
Though the dread effort rend my breast,
Yet shalt thou leave me and be blest!
Oh! bitter penance! thou wilt turn
Away in horror and in scorn;
Thy looks, that still through all the past
Affection's gentlest beams have cast,
As lightning on my heart will fall,
And I must mark and bear it all!
Yet though of life's best ties bereaved,
Thou shalt not, must not be deceived!
I linger—let me speed the tale,
Ere voice, and thought, and memory fail,
Why should I falter thus, to tell
What Heaven so long hath known too well?
Yes! though from mortal sight conceal'd,
There hath a brother's blood appeal'd.
He died—'twas not where banners wave,
And war-steeds trample on the brave,
He died—it was in Holy Land;
Yet fell he not by Paynim hand;
He sleeps not with his sires at rest,
With trophied shield and knightly crest;
Unknown his grave to kindred eyes,
—But I can tell thee where he lies!
It was a wild and savage spot,
But once beheld—and ne'er forgot!
I see it now—that haunted scene
My spirit's dwelling still hath been;
And he is there—I see him laid
Beneath that palm-tree's lonely shade.
The fountain-wave that sparkles nigh,
Bears witness with its crimson dye!
I see th' accusing glance he raised,
Ere that dim eye by death was glazed;
—Ne'er will that parting look forgive!
I still behold it—and I live!
I live! from hope, from mercy driven,
A mark for all the shafts of Heaven!

 "Yet had I wrongs: by fraud he won
My birth-right—and my child, my son,

Heir to high name, high fortune born,
Was doom'd to penury and scorn,
An alien 'midst his fathers' halls,
An exile from his native walls.
Could I bear this?—the rankling thought,
Deep, dark, within my bosom wrought;
Some serpent, kindling hate and guile,
Lurk'd in my infant's rosy smile,
And when his accents lisp'd my name,
They woke my inmost heart to flame!
I struggled—are there evil powers
That claim their own ascendant hours?
—Oh! what should thine unspotted soul
Or know or fear of *their* control?
Why on the fearful conflict dwell?
Vainly I struggled—and I fell:
Cast down from every hope of bliss,
Too well thou know'st to what abyss!

" 'Twas done—that moment hurried by
To darken all eternity!
Years roll'd away, long, evil years,
Of woes, of fetters, and of fears;
Nor aught but vain remorse I gain'd,
By the deep guilt my soul which stain'd;
For, long a captive in the lands
Where Arabs tread their burning sands,
The haunted midnight of the mind
Was round me while in chains I pined.
By all forgotten save by one
Dread presence—which I could not shun.

" How oft, when o'er the silent waste
Nor path nor landmark might be traced,
When slumbering by the watch-fire's ray,
The Wanderers of the Desert lay,
And stars, as o'er an ocean shone,
Vigil I kept—but not alone!
That form, that image from the dead,
Still walk'd the wild with soundless tread!
I've seen it in the fiery blast,
I've seen it where the sand-storms pass'd;
Beside the desert's fount it stood,
Tinging the clear cold wave with blood;
And e'en when viewless, by the fear
Curdling my veins, I knew 'twas near!
—*Was* near!—I feel th' unearthly thrill,
Its power is on my spirit still!
A mystic influence, undefined,
The spell, the shadow of my mind!

"Wilt thou yet linger?—time speeds on
One last farewell, and then begone!
Unclasp the hands that shade thy brow,
And let me read thine aspect *now!*
No stay thee yet, and learn the meed
Heaven's justice to my crime decreed.
Slow came the day that broke my chain,
But I at length was free again;
And freedom brings a burst of joy,
E'en guilt itself can scarce destroy;
I thought upon my own fair towers,
My native Rhine's gay vineyard bowers,
And, in a father's visions, press'd
Thee and thy brother to my breast.

"'Twas but in visions—canst thou yet
Recall the moment when we meet?
Thy step to greet me lightly sprung,
Thy arms around me fondly clung;
Scarce aught than infant-seraph less,
Seem'd thy pure childhood's loveliness;
But he was gone—that son, for whom
I rush'd on guilt's eternal doom,
He for whose sake alone were given
My peace on earth, my hope in Heaven,
He met me not.—A ruthless band,
Whose name with terror fill'd the land,
Fierce outlaws of the wood and wild
Had reft the father of his child.
Foes to my race, the hate they nursed,
Full on that cherish'd scion burst.
Unknown his fate.—No parent nigh,
My boy! my first-born! didst thou die?
Or did they spare thee for a life
Of shame, of rapine, and of strife?
Livest thou, unfriended, unallied,
A wanderer, lost without a guide?
Oh! to thy fate's mysterious gloom
Blest were the darkness of the tomb!

"Ella! 'tis done—my guilty heart
Before thee all unveil'd—depart!
Few pangs 'twill cost thee now to fly
From one so stained, so lost as I;
Yet peace to thine untainted breast,
E'en though it hate me—be thou blest!
Farewell! thou shalt not linger here;
E'en now th' avenger may be near:
Where'er I turn, the foe, the snare,
The dagger, may be ambush'd there;
One hour—and haply all is o'er,
And we must meet on earth no more;

No, nor beyond!—to those pure skies
Where thou shalt be, I may not rise;
Heaven's will forever parts our lot,
Yet, oh! my child! abhor me not!
Speak once! to soothe this broken heart,
Speak to me once! and then depart!"

But still—as if each pulse were dead,
Mute—as the power of speech were fled,
Pale—as if life-blood ceas'd to warm
The marble beauty of her form;
On the dark rock she lean'd her head,
That seem'd as there 'twere riveted,
And dropt the hands, till then which press'd
Her burning brow, or throbbing breast.
There beam'd no tear-drop in her eye,
And from her lips there breathed no sigh,
And on her brow no trace their dwelt,
That told she suffer'd or she felt.
All that once glow'd, or smil'd, or beam'd,
Now fix'd, and quench'd, and frozen seem'd
And long her sire, in wild dismay,
Deem'd her pure spirit pass'd away.

But life return'd. O'er that cold frame
One deep convulsive shudder came,
And a faint light her eye relumed,
And sad resolve her mien assumed;
But there was horror in the gaze,
Which yet to his she dared not raise,
And her sad accents, wild and low,
As rising from a depth of woe,
At first with hurried trembling broke,
But gather'd firmness as she spoke.

"I leave thee not—whate'er betide,
My footsteps shall not quit thy side;
Pangs, keen as death my soul may thrill,
But yet thou art my father still!
And, oh! if stain'd by guilty deed,
For some kind spirit, tenfold need,
To speak of Heaven's absolving love,
And waft desponding thought above.
Is there not power in mercy's wave,
The blood-stain from thy soul to lave?
Is there not balm to heal despair,
In tears, in penitence, in prayer?
My father! kneel at His pure shrine
Who died to expiate guilt like thine,
Weep—and my tears with thine shall blend
Pray—while my prayers with thine ascend,

And, as our mingling sorrows rise,
Heaven will relent, though earth despise!"

"My child, my child! these bursting tears,
The first mine eyes have shed for years,
Though deepest conflicts they express,
Yet flow not all in bitterness!
Oh! thou hast bid a wither'd heart
From desolation's slumber start,
Thy voice of pity and of love
Seems o'er its icy depths to move
E'en as a breeze of health, which brings
Life, hope, and healing, on its wings.
And there is mercy yet! I feel
Its influence o'er my spirit steal,
How welcome were each pang below,
If guilt might be atoned by woe!
Think'st thou I yet may be forgiven?
Shall prayers unclose the gate of Heaven?
Oh! if it yet avail to plead,
If judgment be not yet decreed,
Our hearts shall blend their suppliant cry,
Till pardon shall be seal'd on high!
Yet, yet I shrink!—will Mercy shed
Her dews upon this fallen head?
—Kneel, Ella, kneel! till full and free
Descend forgiveness, won by thee!"

They knelt:—before the Cross, that sign
Of love eternal and divine;
That symbol, which so long hath stood
A rock of strength on time's dark flood,
Clasp'd by despairing hands and laved
By the warm tears of nations saved;
In one deep prayer their spirits blent,
The guilty and the innocent!
Youth, pure as if from Heaven its birth,
Age, soil'd with every stain of earth,
Knelt, offering up one heart, one cry,
One sacrifice of agony.

Oh! blest, though bitter be their source,
Though dark the fountain of remorse,
Blest are the tears which pour from thence,
Th' atoning stream of penitence!
And let not pity check the tide,
By which the heart is purified;
Let not vain comfort turn its course
Or timid love repress its force!
Go! bind the flood, whose waves expand,
To bear luxuriance o'er the land;

Forbid the life-restoring rains
To fall on Afric's burning plains;
Close up the fount that gush'd to cheer
    The pilgrim o'er the waste who trode;
But check thou not one holy tear,
    Which Penitence devotes to God!

Through scenes so lone the wild-deer ne'er
Was roused by huntsman's bugle there;
So rude, that scarce might human eye
Sustain their dread sublimity;
So awful, that the timid swain,
Nurtured amidst their dark domain,
Had peopled, with unearthly forms,
Their mists, their forests, and their storms;
She, whose blue eye, of laughing light,
Once made each festal scene more bright;
Whose voice in song of joy was sweetest,
Whose step in dance of mirth was fleetest.
By torrent-wave, and mountain-brow,
Is wandering as an out-cast now,
To share with Lindheim's fallen chief,
His shame, his terror, and his grief.

Hast thou not mark'd the ruin's flower,
    That blooms in solitary grace,
And, faithful to its mouldering tower,
    Waves in the banner's place?
From those grey haunts renown hath pass'd
Time wins his heritage at last;
This day of glory hath gone by,
With all its pomp and minstrelsy;
Yet still the flower of golden hues
There loves its fragrance to diffuse,
To fallen and forsaken things
With constancy unalter'd clings,
And, smiling o'er the wreck of state,
With beauty clothes the desolate.

E'en such was she, the fair-hair'd maid,
In all her light of youth array'd,
Forsaking every joy below,
To soothe a guilty parent's woe,
And clinging thus, in beauty's prime,
To the dark ruin made by crime.
Oh! ne'er did Heaven's propitious eyes
Smile on a purer sacrifice;
Ne'er did young love, at duty's shrine,
More nobly brighter hopes resign!
O'er her own pangs she brooded not,
Nor sunk beneath her bitter lot;

No! that pure spirit's lofty worth
Still rose more buoyantly from earth,
And drew from an eternal source
Its gentle, yet triumphant force;
Roused by affliction's chastening might
To energies more calmly bright,
Like the wild harp of airy sigh,
Woke by the storm to harmony!
He that in mountain holds hath sought
A refuge for unconquer'd thought,
A charter'd home, where Freedom's child
Might rear her altars in the wild,
And fix her quenchless torch on high,
A beacon for Eternity;
Or they, whose martyr-spirits wage
Proud war with Persecution's rage,
And to the deserts bear the faith
That bids them smile on chains and death
Well may *they* draw, from all around,
Of grandeur clothed in form and sound,
From the deep power of earth and sky,
Wild nature's might of majesty,
Strong energies, immortal fires,
High hopes, magnificent desires!

But dark, terrific, and austere,
To *him* doth Nature's mien appear,
Who, 'midst her wilds, would seek repose
From guilty pangs and vengeful foes!
For him the winds hath music dread,
A dirge-like voice that mourns the dead;
The forest's whisper breathes a tone,
Appalling, as from world's unknown;
The mystic gloom of wood and cave
Is fill'd with shadows of the grave;
In noon's deep calm the sunbeams dart
A blaze that seems to search his heart;
The pure, eternal stars of night,
Upbraid him with their silent light,
And the dread spirit, which pervades,
And hallows earth's most lonely shades,
In every scene, in every hour,
Surrounds him with chastising power
With nameless fear his soul to thrill,
Heard, felt, acknowledged, present still!

'Twas the chilly close of an Autumn day,
And the leaves fell thick o'er the wanderer's way,
The rustling pines, with a hollow sound,
Foretold the tempest gathering round,
And the skirts of the western clouds were spread
With a tinge of wild and stormy red,

That seem'd, through the twilight forest bowers
Like the glare of a city's blazing towers;
But they, who far from cities fled,
And shrunk from the print of human tread,
Had reach'd a desert-scene unknown,
So strangely wild, so deeply lone,
That a nameless feeling, unconfess'd
And undefined, their souls oppress'd.
Rocks piled on rocks, around them hurl'd,
Lay like the ruins of a world,
Left by an earthquake's final throes
In deep and desolate repose;
Things of eternity whose forms
Bore record of ten thousand storms!
While, rearing its colossal crest
In sullen grandeur o'er the rest,
One, like a pillar, vast and rude,
Stood monarch of the solitude.
Perchance by Roman conqueror's hand
Th' enduring monument was plann'd;
Or Odin's sons, in days gone by,
Had shaped its rough immensity,
To rear, 'midst mountain, rock, and wood,
A temple meet for rites of blood.
But they were gone, who might have told
That secret of the times of old,
And there, in silent scorn it frown'd,
O'er all its vast coevals round.
Darkly those giant masses lower'd,
Countless and motionless they tower'd;
No wild-flower o'er their summits hung,
No fountain from their caverns sprung;
Yet ever on the wanderers' ear
Murmur'd a sound of waters near,
With music deep of lulling falls,
And louder gush at intervals.
Unknown its source—nor spring nor stream
Caught the red sunset's lingering gleam,
But ceaseless, from its hidden caves,
Arose that mystic voice of waves.[1]
Yet bosom'd 'midst that savage scene,
One chosen spot of gentler mien
Gave promise to the pilgrim's eye
Of shelter from the tempest nigh.
Glad sight! the ivied cross it bore,
The sculptured saint that crown'd its door;
Less welcome now were monarch's dome,
Than that low cell, some hermit's home.
Thither the outcasts bent their way,
By the last lingering gleam of day,
When from a cavern'd rock, which cast
Deep shadows o'er them as they pass'd,

A form, a warrior-form of might,
As from earth's bosom sprung to sight.
His port was lofty—yet the heart
Shrunk from him with recoiling start;
His mien was youthful—yet his face
Had nought of youth's ingenious grace;
Nor chivalrous, nor tender thought,
Its traces on his brow had wrought;
Yet dwelt no fierceness in his eye,
But calm and cold severity,
A spirit haughtily austere,
Stranger to pity as to fear.
It seem'd as pride had thrown a veil
O'er that dark brow and visage pale,
Leaving the searcher nought to guess,
All was so fix'd and passionless.

He spoke—and they who heard the tone
Felt, deeply felt, all hope was flown.
"I've sought thee far in forest bowers,
I've sought thee long in peopled towers,
I've borne the dagger of th' UNKNOWN
Trough scenes explored by me alone;
My search is closed—nor toils, nor fears,
Repel the servant of the Seers;
We meet—'tis vain to strive or fly
Albert of Lindheim—thou must die!"

Then with clasp'd hands the fair-hair'd maid
Sunk at his feet and wildly pray'd:—
"Stay, stay thee! sheath that lifted steel!
Oh! thou art human, and canst feel!
Hear me! if e'er 'twas thine to prove
The blessing of a parent's love;
By thine own father's hoary hair,
By her who gave thee being, spare!
Did they not o'er thy infant years,
Keep watch, in sleepless hopes and fears!
Young warrior! thou wilt heed my prayers,
As thou would'st hope for grace to theirs!"

But cold th' Avenger's look remain'd,
His brow its rigid calm maintain'd:
"Maiden! 'tis vain—my bosom ne'er
Was conscious of a parent's care;
The nurture of my infant years
Froze in my soul the source of tears;
'Tis not for me to pause or melt,
Or feel as happier hearts have felt.
Away! the hour of fate goes by,
Thy prayers are fruitless—he must die!"

"Rise, Ella! rise," with steadfast brow
The father spoke; unshrinking now,
As if from heaven a martyr's strength
Had settled on his soul at length;
"Kneel thou no more, my noble child,
Thou by no taint of guilt defiled;
Kneel not to man!—for mortal prayer,
Oh! when did mortal vengeance spare?
Since hope of earthly aid is flown,
Lift thy pure hands to Heaven alone,
And know, to calm thy suffering heart,
My spirit is resign'd to part,
Trusting in Him, who reads and knows
This guilty breast with all its woes
Rise! I would bless thee once again,
Be still, be firm—for all is vain!"

And she *was* still—she heard him not,
Her prayers were hush'd—her pangs forgot;
All thought, all memory pass'd away,
Silent and motionless she lay,
In a brief death, a blest suspense,
Alike of agony and sense.
She saw not when the dagger gleam'd
In the last red light from the west that stream'd;
She mark'd not when the life-blood's flow
Came rushing to the mortal blow;
While, unresisting, sunk her sire,
Yet gather'd firmness to expire,
Mingling a warrior's courage high,
With a penitent's humility.
And o'er him there th' Avenger stood,
And watch'd the victim's ebbing blood,
Still calm, as if his faithful hand
Had but obey'd some just command,
Some power, whose stern, yet righteous will,
He deem'd it virtue to fulfil,
And triumph'd, when the palm was won,
For duty's task austerely done.

But a feeling dread, and undefin'd
A mystic presage of the mind,
With strange and sudden impulse ran
Chill through the heart of the dying man
And his thoughts found voice, and his bosom breath,
And it seem'd as fear suspended death,
And Nature from her terrors drew
Fresh energy, and vigor new.

"Thou said'st thy lonely bosom ne'er
Was conscious of a parent's care·

Thou said'st, thy lot, in childhood's years,
Froze in thy soul the source of tears:
The time will come, when thou, with me,
The judgment-throne of God wilt see.
Oh! by thy hopes of mercy then,
By His blest love who died for men,
By each dread rite, and shrine, and vow
Avenger! I adjure thee now!
To him who bleeds beneath thy steel,
Thy lineage and thy name reveal,
And haste thee! for his closing ear
Hath little more on earth to hear—
Haste! for the spirit almost flown,
Is lingering for thy words alone."

Then first a shade, resembling fear,
Pass'd o'er th'Avenger's mien austere;
A nameless awe his features cross'd,
Soon in their haughty coldness lost.

"What wouldst thou? Ask the rock and wild,
And bid them tell thee of their child!
Ask the rude winds, and angry skies,
Whose tempests were his lullabies!
His chambers were the cave and wood,
His fosterers men of wrath and blood;
Outcasts alike of earth and heaven,
By wrongs to desperation driven!
Who, in their pupil, now could trace
The features of a nobler race?
Yet such was mine! if one who cast
A look of anguish o'er the past,
Bore faithful record on the day,
When penitent in death he lay.
But still deep shades my prospects veil,
He died—and told but half the tale;
With him it sleeps—I only know
Enough for stern and silent woe,
For vain ambition's deep regret,
For hopes deceived, deceiving yet,
For dreams of pride that vainly tell
How high a lot had suited well
The heir of some illustrious line,
Heroes and chieftains of the Rhine!

Then swift through Albert's bosom pass'd,
One pang, the keenest and the last,
Ere with his spirit fled the fears,
The sorrows, and the pangs of years;
And, while his grey hairs swept the dust,
Faltering he murmur'd, "Heaven is just!

For thee that deed of guilt was done,
By thee avenged, my Son! my Son!"

The day was closed—the moonbeam shed
Light on the living and the dead,
And as through rolling clouds it broke,
Young Ella from her trance awoke—
Awoke to bear, to feel, to know
E'en more than all an orphan's woe.
Oh! ne'er did moonbeam's light serene
With beauty clothe a sadder scene!
There, cold in death, the father slept,
There, pale in woe, the daughter wept!
Yes! *she* might weep—but one stood nigh
With horror in his tearless eye,
That eye which ne'er again shall close
In the deep quiet of repose;
No more on earth beholding aught,
Save one dread vision, stamp'd on thought.
But, lost in grief, the Orphan Maid
His deeper woe had scarce survey'd,
Till his wild voice reveal'd a tale,
Which seem'd to bid the Heavens turn pale!
He call'd her, "Sister!" and the word
In anguish breathed, in terror heard,
Reveal'd enough—all else were weak,
That sound a thousand pangs could speak.
He knelt beside that breathless clay,
Which, fix'd in utter stillness, lay—
Knelt till his soul imbibed each trace,
Each line of that unconscious face;
Knelt, till his eye could bear no more,
Those marble features to explore;
Then, starting, turning, as to shun
The image thus by Memory won,
A wild farewell to her he bade,
Who by the dead in silence pray'd,
And, frenzied by his bitter doom,
Fled thence—to find all earth a tomb!

Days pass'd away—and Rhine's fair shore
In the light of summer smiled once more;
The vines were purpling on the hill,
And corn-fields waved in the sunshine still:
There came a bark up the noble stream,
With pennons that shed a golden gleam,
With the flash of arms, and the voice of song,
Gliding triumphantly along;
For warrior-forms were glittering there,
Whose plumes waved light in the whispering air;
And as the tones of oar and wave
Their measured cadence mingling gave,

'Twas thus th' exulting chorus rose,
While many an echo swell'd the close:

From the fields where dead and dying,
On their battle-bier are lying,
Where the blood unstanch'd is gushing,
Where the steed uncheck'd is rushing,
Trampling o'er the noble-hearted,
Ere the spirit yet be parted;
Where each breath of Heaven is swaying
Knightly plumes and banners playing,
And the clarion's music swelling
Calls the vulture from his dwelling;
He comes, with trophies worthy of his line,
The son of heroes, Ulric of the Rhine!
To his own fair woods, enclosing
Vales in sunny peace reposing,
Where his native stream is laving
Banks, with golden harvests waving,
And the summer light is sleeping
On the grape, through tendrils peeping;
To the halls where harps are ringing,
Bards the praise of warriors singing,
Graceful footsteps bounding fleetly,
Joyous voices mingling sweetly;
Where the cheek of mirth is glowing,
And the wine-cup brightly flowing,
He comes with trophies worthy of his line,
The son of heroes, Ulric of the Rhine.

He came—he sought his Ella's bowers,
He traversed Lindheim's lonely towers;
But voice and footstep thence had fled,
As from the dwellings of the dead,
And the sounds of human joy and woe
Gave place to the moan of the wave below.
The banner still the rampart crown'd,
But the tall rank grass waved thick around;
Still hung the arms of a race gone by,
In the blazon'd halls of their ancestry
But they caught no more, at fall of night,
The wavering flash of the torch's light;
And they sent their echoes forth no more,
To the Minnesinger's[2] tuneful lore,
For the hands that touch'd the harp were gone,
And the hearts were cold that loved its tone;
And the soul of the chord lay mute and still,
Save when the wild wind bade it thrill,
And woke from its depths a dream-like moan,
For life, and power and beauty gone.

The warrior turn'd from that silent scene,
Where a voice of woe had welcome been,

And his heart was heavy with boding thought,
As the forest-path alone he sought.
He reach'd a convent's fane, that stood
Deep bosom'd in luxuriant wood;
Still, solemn, fair—it seem'd a spot
Where earthly care might be all forgot,
And sounds and dreams of Heaven alone,
To musing spirit might be known.

And sweet e'en then were the sounds that rose
On the holy and profound repose.
Oh! they came o'er the warrior's breast,
Like a glorious anthem of the blest;
And fear and sorrow died away,
Before the full, majestic lay.
He enter'd the secluded fane,
Which sent forth that inspiring strain;
He gazed—the hallow'd pile's array
Was that of some high festal day;
Wreath's of all hues its pillars bound,
Flowers of all scents were strew'd around;
The rose exhaled its fragrant sigh,
Blest on the altar to smile and die;
And a fragrant cloud from the censer's breath
Half hid the sacred pomp beneath;
And still the peal of choral song
Swell'd the resounding aisles along;
Wakening, in its triumphant flow,
Deep echoes from the graves below.

Why, from its woodland birth place **torn**,
Doth summer's rose that scene adorn?
Why breathes the incense to the sky?
Why swells th' exulting harmony?
—And see'st thou not yon form, so light,
It seems half floating on the sight,
As if the whisper of a gale,
That did but wave its snowy veil,
Might bear it from the earth afar,
A lovely, but receding star?
Know that devotion's shrine e'en now,
Receives that youthful vestal's vow,
For this, high hymns, sweet odours rise,
A jubilee of sacrifice!
Mark yet a moment! from her brow
Yon priest shall lift the veil of snow,
Ere yet a darker mantle hide
The charms to Heaven thus sanctified;
Stay thee! and catch their parting gleam,
That ne'er shall fade from memory's dream
A moment! oh! to Ulric's soul,
Poised between hope and fear's control,

What slow, unmeasured hours went by,
Ere yet suspense grew certainty ;
It came at length—once more that face
Reveal'd to man its mournful grace ;
A sunbeam on its features fell,
As if to bear the world's farewell ;
And doubt was o'er—his heart grew chill—
'Twas she—though changed—'twas Ella still !
Though now her once-rejoicing mien,
Was deeply, mournfully serene ;
Though clouds her eye's blue lustre shaded,
And the young cheek beneath had faded,
Well, well he knew the form, which cast
Light on his soul through all the past !
'Twas with him on the battle plain,
'Twas with him on the stormy main,
'Twas in his visions, when the shield
Pillow'd his head on tented field ;
'Twas a bright dream that led him on
Where'er a triumph might be won,
In danger as in glory nigh,
An angel-guide to victory !

She caught his pale bewilder'd gaze
Of grief half lost in fix'd amaze—
Was it some vain illusion, wrought
By frenzy of impassion'd thought ?
Some phantom, such as Grief hath power
To summon, in her wandering hour ?
No ! it was he ! the lost, the mourn'd,
Too deeply loved, too late return'd !

A fever'd blush, a sudden start,
Spoke the last weakness of her heart,
'Twas vanquish'd soon—the hectic red
A moment flush'd her cheek, and fled.
Once more serene—her steadfast eye
Look'd up as to Eternity ;
Then gaz'd on Ulric with an air,
That said—the home of Love is *there !*

Yes ! *there* alone it smiled for him,
Whose eye before that look grew dim ;
Not long 'twas his e'en *thus* to view
The beauty of its calm adieu ;
Soon o'er those features, brightly pale,
Was cast th' impenetrable veil ;
And, if one human sigh were given
By the pure bosom vow'd to Heaven,
'Twas lost, as many a murmur'd sound
Of grief, " not loud, but deep," is drown'd,

In hymns of joy, which proudly rise,
To tell the calm untroubled skies,
That earth hath banish'd care and woe,
And man holds festivals below!

NOTES

Note 1, page 287, line 40.

THE original of the scene here described is presented by the mountain called the Feldberg, in the Bergstrasse:—"Des masses énormes de rochers, entassées l'une sur l'autre depuis le sommet de la montagne jusqu'à son pied, viennent y présenter un aspect superbe qu' aucune description ne saurait rendre. Ce furent, dit-on, des géans, qui en se livrant un combat du haut des montagnes, lancèrent les uns sur les autres ces énormes masses de rochers. On arrive, avec beaucoup de peine, jusqu'au sommet du Feldberg, en suivant un sentier qui passe à côté de cette chaine de rochers. On entend continuellement un bruit sourd, qui parait venir d'un ruisseau au dessous des rochers; mais on a beau decendre, en se glissant à travers les ouvertures qui s'y trouvent, on ne decouvrira jamais le ruisseau. La colonne, dite Riesensäule, se trouve un peu plus haut qu'à la moitie de la montagne; c'est un bloc de granit taillé, d'une longueur de 30 pieds et d'un diamètre de 4 pieds. Il y a plus de probabilité de croire que les anciens Germains voulaient faire de ce bloc une colonne pour l'ériger en l'honneur de leur dieu Odin, quede prétendre, comme le fort plusieurs auteurs, que les Romains aient eu le dessein de la transporter dans leur capitale. On voit un peu plus haut un autre bloc d'une forme presque carrée, qu'on appelle Riesenaltar (autel du géant) qui, à en juger par sa grosseur et sa forme, était destiné à servir de piédestal à la colonne susdite."—*Manuel pour les Voyageurs sur le Rhin*.

Note 2, page 292, line 42

Minnesingers (bards of love), the appellation of the German minstrels in the Middle Ages.

SUPERSTITION AND REVELATION.

AN UNFINISHED POEM.

I.

BEINGS of brighter worlds! that rise at times
As phantoms, with ideal beauty fraught,
In those brief visions of celestial climes,
Which pass, like sunbeams, o'er the realms of thought,
Dwell ye around us?—are ye hovering nigh,
Throned on the cloud, or buoyant in the air?
And in deep solitudes, where human eye
Can trace no step, Immortals! are ye there?
Oh! who can tell?—what power, but Death alone
Can lift the mystic veil that shades the world unknown?

II.

But Earth hath seen the days, ere yet the flowers
Of Eden wither'd, when reveal'd ye shone,
In all your brightness, 'midst those holy bowers—
Holy, but not unfading, as your own!
While He, the child of that primeval soil,
With you its paths in high communion trode,
His glory yet undimm'd by guilt or toil,
And beaming in the image of his God.
And his pure spirit glowing from the sky
Exulting in its light, a spark of Deity.

III.

Then, haply mortal and celestial lays
Mingling their tones, from Nature's temple rose,
When nought but that majestic song of praise
Broke on the sanctity of night's repose,
With music since unheard: and man might trace,
By stream and vale, in deep embow'ring shade,
Devotion's first and loveliest dwelling-place,
The footsteps of th' Omnipotent, who made
That spot a shrine, where youthful nature cast
Her consecrated wealth, rejoicing as He pass'd.

IV.

Short were those days, and soon, O sons of Heaven!
Your aspect changed from man; in that dread hour,
When from his paradise the alien driven,
Beheld your forms in angry splendor tower,

Guarding the clime where he no more might dwell,
With meteor-swords: he saw the living flame,
And his first cry of misery was—"Farewell!"
His heart's first anguish, exile: he became
A pilgrim on the earth, whose children's lot
Is still for happier lands to pine—and reach them not.

v.

Where now the chosen bowers that once beheld
Delight and Love their first bright Sabbath keep?
From all its founts the world of waters swell'd,
And wrapt them in the mantle of the deep!
For He, to whom the elements are slaves,
In wrath unchain'd the oceans of the cloud,
And heaved the abyss beneath; till waves on waves
Folded creation in their mighty shroud,
Then left the earth a solitude, o'erspread
With its own awful wreck—a desert of the dead.

vi.

But onward flow'd life's busy course again,
And rolling ages with them bore away—
As to be lost amidst the boundless main,
Rich orient streams their golden sands convey—
The hallow'd lore of old—the guiding light
Left by tradition to the sons of earth,
And the blest memory of each sacred rite,
Known in the region of their father's birth,
When in each breeze around his fair abode
Whisper'd a seraph's voice, or lived the breath of **God.**

vii.

Who hath not seen, what time the orb of day,
Cinctured with glory, seeks the ocean's breast,
A thousand clouds, all glowing in his ray,
Catching brief splendor from the purple west?
So round thy parting steps, fair Truth! awhile
With borrow'd hues unnumber'd phantoms shone;
And Superstition, from thy lingering smile,
Caught a faint glow of beauty not her own,
Blending her rites with thine—while yet afar
Thine eye's last radiance beam'd, a slow-receding star.

viii.

Yet still one stream was pure—one sever'd shrine
Was fed with holier fire, by chosen hands,
And sounds, and dreams, and impulses divine,
Where in the dwellings of the patriarch bands.
There still the father to his child bequeathed
The sacred torch of never-dying flame;
There still Devotion's suppliant accents breathed
The One adored and everlasting Name;

And angel guests would linger and repose
Where those primeval tents amid their palm-trees rose

IX.

But far o'er earth the apostate wanderers bore
Their alien rites:—for them, by fount or shade.
Nor voice, nor vision, holy as of yore,
In thrilling whispers to the soul convey'd
High inspiration: yet in every clime,
Those sons of doubt and error fondly sought
With beings, in their essence more sublime,
To hold communion of mysterious thought;
On some dread power in trembling hope to lean,
And hear in every wind the accents of th' Unseen

X.

Yes! we have need to bid our hopes repose
On some protecting influence; here confined,
Life hath no healing balm for mortal woes,
Earth is too narrow for th' immortal mind.
Our spirits burn to mingle with the day,
As exiles panting for their native coast,
Yet lured by every wild-flower from their way,
And shrinking from the gulf that must be cross'd;
Death hovers round us—in the zephyr's sigh,
As in the storm, he comes—and lo! Eternity!

XI.

As one left lonely on the desert sands
Of burning Afric, where, without a guide,
He gazes as the pathless waste expands—
Around, beyond, interminably wide;
While the red haze, presaging the Simoom,
Obscures the fierce resplendence of the sky,
Or suns of blasting light perchance illume
The glistening Serab* which illudes his eye;
Such was the wanderer Man, in ages flown,
Kneeling in doubt and fear before the dread Unknown.

XII.

His thoughts explored the past—and where were they,
The chiefs of men, the mighty ones gone by?
He turn'd—a boundless void before him lay,
Wrapp'd in the shadows of futurity.
How knew the child of Nature that the flame
He felt within him, struggling to ascend,
Should perish not with that terrestrial frame
Doom'd with the earth on which it moved, to blend?
How, when affliction bade his spirit bleed,
If 'twere a Father's love or Tyrant's wrath decreed?

Serab, mirage.

XIII.

Oh! marvel not, it then he sought to trace,
In all sublimities of sight and sound,
In rushing winds that wander through all space,
Or 'midst deep woods, with holy gloom embrown'd,
The oracles of Fate! or if the train
Of floating forms, that throng the world of sleep,
And sounds that vibrate on the slumberer's brain.
When mortal voices rest in stillness deep,
Were deem'd mysterious revelations, sent
From viewless powers, the lords of each dread element.

XIV.

Was not wild Nature, in that elder time,
Clothed with a deeper power?—earth's wandering race,
Exploring realms of solitude sublime,
Not as *we* see, beheld her awful face!
Art had not tamed the mighty scenes which met
Their searching eyes: unpeopled kingdoms lay
In savage pomp before them—all was yet
Silent and vast, but not as in decay,
And the bright daystar, from his burning throne,
Look'd o'er a thousand shores, untrodden, voiceless, lone.

XV.

The forests in their dark luxuriance waved,
With all their swell of strange Æolian sound;
The fearful deep, sole region, ne'er enslaved,
Heaved, in its pomp of terror darkly round;
Then brooding o'er the images, imprest
By forms of grandeur thronging on his eye,
And faint traditions, guarded in his breast,
'Midst dim remembrances of infancy,
Man shaped unearthly presences, in dreams,
Peopling each wilder haunt of mountains, groves, and streams.

XVI.

Then bled the victim—then in every shade
Of rock or turf arose the votive shrine;
Fear bow'd before the phantoms she portray'd,
And nature teem'd with many a mystic sign.
Meteors, and storms, and thunders! ye whose course
E'en yet is awful to th' enlighten'd eye,
As wildly rushing from your secret source,
Your sounding chariot sweeps the realms on high,
Then o'er the earth prophetic gloom ye cast
And the wide nations gazed and trembled as ye pass'd.

XVII.

But you, ye stars! in distant glory burning,
Nurtured with flame, bright altars of the sky!

To whose far climes the spirit, vainly turning,
Would pierce the secrets of infinity—
To you the heart, bereft of other light,
Its first deep homage paid, on Eastern plains,
Where Day hath terrors, but majestic Night,
Calm in her pomp, magnificently reigns,
Cloudless and silent, circled with the race
Of some unnumber'd orbs, that light the depths of space.

XVIII.
Shine on! and brightly plead for erring thought,
Whose wing, unaided in its course, explored
The wide creation, and beholding nought
Like your eternal beauty, then adored
Its living splendors; deeming them inform'd
By natures temper'd with a holier fire—
Pure beings, with ethereal effluence warm'd,
Who to the source of spirit might aspire,
And mortal prayers benignantly convey
To some presiding Power, more awful far than they.

XIX.
Guides o'er the desert and the deep! to you
The seaman turn'd, rejoicing at the helm,
When from the regions of empyreal blue
Ye pour'd soft radiance o'er the ocean-realm;
To you the dweller of the plains address'd
Vain prayers, that called the clouds and dews your own;
To you the shepherd, on the mountain's crest,
Kindled the fires that far through midnight shone,
As earth would light up all her hills, to vie
With your immortal host, and image back the sky.

XX.
Hail to the queen of heaven! her silvery crown
Serenely wearing, o'er her high domain
She walks in brightness, looking cloudless down,
As if to smile on her terrestrial reign.
Earth should be hush'd in slumber—but the night
Calls forth her worshippers; the feast is spread,
On hoary Lebanon's umbrageous height
The shrine is raised, the rich libation shed
To her, whose beams illume those cedar shades
Faintly as Nature's light the 'wildered soul pervades.

XXI.
But when *thine* orb, all earth's rich hues restoring,
Came forth, O sun! in majesty supreme,
Still, from thy pure exhaustless fountain, pouring
Beauty and life in each triumphant beam,
Through thine own east what joyous rites prevail'd!
What choral songs re-echo'd! while thy fire

Shone o'er its thousand altars, and exhaled
The precious incense of each odorous pyre,
Heap'd with the richest balms of spicy vales,
And aromatic woods that scent the Arabian gales.

XXII.
Yet not with Saba's fragrant wealth alone,
Balsam and myrrh, the votive pile was strewed ;
For the dark children of the burning zone
Drew frenzy from thy fervors, and bedew'd
With their own blood thy shrine ; while that wild scene,
Haply with pitying eye, thine angel view'd,
And, though with glory mantled, and serene
In his own fulness of beatitude,
Yet mourn'd for those whose spirits from thy ray
Caught not one transient spark of intellectual day.

XXIII.
But earth had deeper stains: ethereal powers!
Benignant seraphs! wont to leave the skies,
And hold high converse, 'midst his native bowers,
With the once-glorious son of Paradise,
Looked ye from heaven in sadness ? were your strains
Of choral praise suspended in dismay,
When the polluted shrine of Syria's plains,
With clouds of incense dimm'd the blaze of day ?
Or did ye veil indignantly your eyes,
While demons hail'd the pomp of human sacrifice ?

XXIV.
And well the powers of evil might rejoice,
When rose from Tophet's vale the exulting cry,
And, deaf to Nature's supplicating voice,
The frantic mother bore her child to die !
Around her vainly clung his feeble hands
With sacred instinct: love hath lost its sway,
While ruthless zeal the sacrifice demands,
And the fires blaze, impatient for their prey.
Let not his shrieks reveal the dreadful tale!
Well may the drum's loud peal o'erpower an infant's wail !

XXV.
A voice of sorrow! not from thence it rose ;
'Twas not the childless mother—Syrian maids,
Where with red wave the mountain streamlet flows,
Keep tearful vigil in their native shades.
With dirge and plaint the cedar-groves resound,
Each rock's deep echo for Adonis mourns :
Weep for the dead !—away! the lost is found,
To life and love the buried god returns!
Then wakes the timbrel—then the forests ring,
And shouts of frenzied joy are on each breeze's wing!

XXVI.

But fill'd with holier joy the Persian stood,
In silent reverence on the mountain's brow
At early dayspring, while the expanding flood
Of radiance burst around above, below—
Bright, boundless as eternity : he gazed
Till his full soul, imbibing heaven, o'erflow'd
In worship of th' Invisible, and praised
In thee, O Sun ! the symbol and abode
Of life, and power, and excellence ; the throne
Where dwelt the Unapproach'd, resplendently alone.*

XXVII.

What if his thoughts, with erring fondness, gave
Mysterious sanctity to things which wear
Th' Eternal's impress ?—if the living wave,
The circling heavens, the free and boundless air—
If the pure founts of everlasting flame,
Deep in his country's hallow'd vales enshrined,
And the bright stars maintain'd a silent claim
To love and homage from his awestruck mind?
Still with his spirit dwelt a lofty dream
Of uncreated Power, far, far o'er these supreme.

XXVIII.

And with that faith was conquest. He whose name
To Judah's harp of prophecy had rung ;
He, of whose yet unborn and distant fame
The mighty voice of Inspiration sung,
He came, the victor Cyrus !—as he pass'd,
Thrones to his footstep rock'd, and monarch's lay
Suppliant and clothed with dust ; while nations cast
Their ancient idols down before *his* way,
Who, in majestic march, from shore to shore,
The quenchless flame revered by Persia's children bore

* * * * * *

---

* At an earlier stage in the composition of this poem, the following stanza was here inserted :—

> ' Nor rose the Magian's hymn, sublimely swelling
> In full-toned homage to the source of flame,
> From fabric rear'd by man—the gorgeous dwelling
> Of such bright idol-forms as art could frame ;
> He rear'd no temple, bade no walls contain
> The breath of incense, or the voice of prayer ·
> But made the boundless universe his fane,
> The rocks his altar-stone, adoring there
> The Being whose Omnipotence pervades
> All deserts and all depths, and hallows loneliest shades.

THE CARAVAN IN THE DESERT.

Call it not loneliness, to dwell
In woodland shade or hermit dell,
Or the deep forest to explore,
Or wander Alpine regions o'er ;
For Nature there all joyous reigns,
And fills with life her wild domains:
A bird's light wing may break the air,
A wave, a leaf, may murmur there ;
A bee the mountain flowers may seek,
A chamois bound from peak to peak ;
An eagle, rushing to the sky,
Wake the deep echoes with his cry ;
And still some sound, thy heart to cheer,
Some voice, though not of man is near.
But he, whose weary step hath traced
Mysterious Afric's awful waste—
Whose eye Arabia's wilds hath view'd,
Can tell thee what is solitude !
It is, to traverse lifeless plains,
Where everlasting stillness reigns,
And billowy sands and dazzling sky,
Seem boundless as infinity !
It is to sink, with speechless dread,
In scenes unmeet for mortal tread,
Sever'd from earthly being's trace,
Alone, amidst eternal space !
'Tis noon—and fearfully profound,
Silence is on the desert round ;
Alone she reigns, above, beneath
With all the attributes of death !
No bird the blazing heaven may dare,
No insect bide the scorching air :
The ostrich, though of sun-born race,
Seeks a more shelter'd dwelling-place
The lion slumbers in his lair,
The serpent shuns the noontide glare ;
But slowly wind the patient train
Of camels o'er the blasted plain,
Where they and man may brave alone
The terrors of the burning zone.

Faint not, O pilgrims! though on high,
As a volcano, flame the sky;
Shrink not, though as a furnace glow
The dark-red seas of sand below;
Though not a shadow save your own,
Across the dread expanse is thrown;
Mark! where your feverish lips to lave,
Wide spreads the fresh transparent wave,
Urge your tired camels on, and take
Your rest beside yon glistening lake:
Thence, haply, cooler gales may spring,
And fan your brows with lighter wing.
Lo! nearer now, its glassy tide,
Reflects the date-tree on its side—
Speed on! pure draughts and genial air,
And verdant shade, await you there.
Oh glimpse of Heaven! to him unknown,
That hath not trod the burning zone!
Forward they press—they gaze dismay'd—
The waters of the desert fade!
Melting to vapors that elude
The eye, the lip, they vainly woo'd.*
What meteor comes?—a purple haze
Hath half obscured the noontide rays: †
Onward it moves in swift career,
A blush upon the atmosphere;
Haste, haste! avert th' impending doom,
Fall prostrate! 'tis the dread Simoom!
Bow down your faces—till the blast
On its red wing of flame hath pass'd,
Far bearing o'er the sandy wave,
The viewless Angel of the Grave.

It came—'tis vanish'd—but hath left
The wanderers e'en of hope bereft;
The ardent heart, the vigorous frame,
Pride, courage, strength, its power could tame
Faint with despondence, worn with toil,
They sink upon the burning soil,
Resign'd, amist those realms of gloom,
To find their death-bed and their tomb.‡

But onward still!—yon distant spot
Of verdure can deceive you not;
Yon palms, which tremulously seem'd
Reflected as the waters gleam'd,

---

* The mirage, or vapor assuming the appearance of water.
† See the description of the Simoom in Bruce's Travels.
‡ The extreme languor and despondence produced by the Simoom, even when its effects are not fatal, have been described by many travellers

Along the horizon's verge display'd,
Still rear their slender colonnade—
A landmark, guiding o'er the plain
The Caravan's exhausted train.
Fair is that little Isle of Bliss
The desert's emerald oasis!
A rainbow on the torrent's wave,
A gem embosom'd in the grave,
A sunbeam on a stormy day
Its beauty's image might convey!
' Beauty, in horror's lap that sleeps,
While silence round her vigil keeps.'
—Rest, weary pilgrims! calmly laid
To slumber in the acacia shade :
Rest, where the shrubs your camels bruise,
Their aromatic breath diffuse ;
Where softer light the sunbeams pour
Through the tall palm and sycamore ;
And the rich date luxuriant spreads
Its pendant clusters o'er your heads.
Nature once more, to seal your eyes,
Murmurs her sweetest lullabies ;
Again each heart the music hails
Of rustling leaves and sighing gales,
And oh! to Afric's child how dear
The voice of fountains gushing near!
Sweet be your slumbers! and your dreams
Of waving groves and rippling streams!
Far be the serpent's venom'd coil
From the brief respite won by toil;
Far be the awful shades of those
Who deep beneath the sands repose—
The hosts, to whom the desert's breath
Bore swift and stern the call of death.
Sleep! nor may scorching blast invade
The freshness of the acacia shade,
But gales of heaven your spirits bless,
With life's best balm—Forgetfulness!
Till night from many an urn diffuse
The treasures of her world of dews.

The day hath closed—the moon on high
Walks in her cloudless majesty.
A thousand stars to Afric's heaven
Serene magnificence have given ;
Sure beacon's of the sky, whose flame
Phines forth eternally the same.
Blest be their beams, whose holy light
Shall guide the camel's footsteps right,
And lead, as with a track divine,
The pilgrim to his prophet's shrine!

THE CARAVAN IN THE DESERTS.

Rise! bid your Isle of Palms adieu!
Again your lonely march pursue,
While airs of night are freshly blowing,
And heavens with softer beauty glowing.
—'Tis silence all: the solemn scene
Wears, at each step, a ruder mien;
For giant-rocks, at distance piled,
Cast their deep shadows o'er the wild.
Darkly they rise—what eye hath view'd
The caverns of their solitude?
Away! within those awful cells
The savage lord of Afric dwells!
Heard ye his voice?—the lion's roar
Swells as when billows break on shore.
Well may the camel shake with fear,
And the steed pant—his foe is near;
Haste! light the torch, bid watchfires throw,
Far o'er the waste a ruddy glow;
Keep vigil—guard the bright array,
Of flames that scare him from his prey;
Within their magic circle press,
O wanderers of the wilderness!
Heap high the pile, and by its blaze
Tell the wild tales of elder days.
Arabia's wond'rous lore—that dwells
On warrior deeds, and wizard spells;
Enchanted domes, 'mid scenes like these,
Rising to vanish with the breeze;
Gardens, whose fruits are gems, that shed
Their light where mortal may not tread,
And spirits, o'er whose pearly halls
Th' eternal billow heaves and falls.
—With charms like these, of mystic power,
Watchers! beguile the midnight hour.
—Slowly that hour hath roll'd away,
And star by star withdraws its ray.
Dark children of the sun! again
Your own rich orient hails his reign.
He comes, but veil'd—with sanguine glare
Tinging the mists that load the air;
Sounds of dismay, and signs of flame,
Th' approaching hurricane proclaim.
'Tis death's red banner streams on high—
Fly to the rocks for shelter!—fly!
Lo! dark'ning o'er the fiery skies,
The pillars of the desert rise!
On, in terrific grandeur wheeling,
A giant-host, the heavens concealing,
They move, like mighty genii forms,
Towering immense 'midst clouds and storms.
Who shall escape?—with awful force
The whirlwind bears them on their course;

They join, they rush resistless on,
The landmarks of the plain are gone ;
The steps, the forms, from earth effaced,
Of those who trod the burning waste !
All whelm'd, all hush'd !—none left to bear
Sad record how they perish'd there !
No stone their tale of death shall tell—
The desert guards its mysteries well ;
And o'er th' unfathom'd sandy deep,
Where low their nameless relics sleep,
Oft shall the future pilgrim tread,
Nor know his steps are on the dead.

MARIUS AMONGST THE RUINS OF CARTHAGE.

[" Marius, during the time of his exile, seeking refuge in Africa, had landed at Carthage, when an officer, sent by the Roman governor of Africa, came and thus addressed him :—" Marius, I come from the Prætor Sextilius, to tell you that he forbids you to set foot in Africa. If you obey not, he will support the Senate's decree, and treat you as a public enemy." Marius, upon hearing this, was struck dumb with grief and indignation. He uttered not a word for some time, but regarded the officer with a menacing aspect. At length the officer enquired what answer he should carry to the governor. " Go and tell him," said the unfortunate man, with a sigh, " that thou hast seen the exiled Marius sitting on the ruins of Carthage."—See PLUTARCH.

'TWAS noon, and Afric's dazzling sun on high,
With fierce resplendence fill'd th' unclouded sky ;
No zephyr waved the palm's majestic head,
And smooth alike the seas and deserts spread ;
While desolate, beneath a blaze of light,
Silent and lonely as at dead of night,
The wreck of Carthage lay. Her prostrate fanes
Had strew'd their precious marble o'er the plains ;
Dark weeds and grass the column had o'ergrown,
The lizard bask'd upon the altar-stone ;
Whelm'd by the ruins of their own abodes,
Had sunk the forms of heroes and of gods ;
While near, dread offspring of the burning day !
Coil'd 'midst forsaken halls, the serpent lay.

There came an exile, long by fate pursued,
To shelter in that awful solitude.
Well did that wanderer's high yet faded mien,
Suit the sad grandeur of the desert-scene ;
Shadow'd, not veil'd, by locks of wintry snow
Pride sat, still mighty, on his furrow'd brow
Time had not quench'd the terrors of his eye,
Nor tamed his glance of fierce ascendency ;
While the deep meaning of his features told,
Ages of thought had o'er his spirit roll'd,
Nor dimm'd the fire that might not be controll'd ;
And still did power invest his stately form,
Shatter'd, but yet unconquer'd, by the storm.

But slow his step—and where, not yet o'erthrown
Still tower'd a pillar 'midst the waste alone,
Faint, with long toil, his weary limbs he laid,
To slumber in its solitary shade.
He slept—and darkly, on his brief repose,
Th' indignant genius of the scene arose.
Clouds robed his dim unearthly form, and spread
Mysterious gloom around his crownless head,
Crownless, but regal still. With stern disdain,
The kingly shadow seem'd to lift his chain,
Gazed on the palm, his ancient sceptre torn,
And his eye kindled with immortal scorn !

" And sleep'st thou, Roman ?" cry'd his voice austere
" Shall son of Latium find a refuge *here* ?
Awake ! arise ! to speed the hour of Fate,
When Rome shall fall, as Carthage desolate !
Go ! with her children's flower, the free, the brave,
People the silent chambers of the grave ;
So shall the course of ages yet to be,
More swiftly waft the day, avenging me !

" Yes, from the awful gulf of years to come,
I hear a voice that prophesies her doom ;
I see the trophies of her pride decay,
And her long line of triumphs pass away,
Lost in the depths of time—while sinks the star
That led her march of heroes from afar !
Lo ! from the frozen forests of the north,
The sons of slaughter pour in myriads forth .
Who shall awake the mighty ?—will thy woe,
City of thrones ! disturb the realms below ?
Call on the dead to hear thee ! let thy cries
Summon their shadowy legions to arise,
Array the ghosts of conquerors on thy walls !
—Barbarians revel in their ancient halls,
And their lost children bend the subject knee,
'Midst the proud tombs and trophies of the free.

RUINS OF CARTHAGE.

Bird of the sun! dread eagle! borne on high,
A creature of the empyreal—Thou, whose eye
Was lightning to the earth—whose pinion waved
In haughty triumph o'er a world enslaved;
Sink from thy Heavens! for glory's noon is o'er,
And rushing storms shall bear thee on no more!
Closed is thy regal course—thy crest is torn,
And thy plume banish'd from the realms of morn.
The shaft hath reach'd thee?—rest with chiefs and kings,
Who conquer'd in the shadow of thy wings;
Sleep! while thy foes exult around their prey,
And share thy glorious heritage of day!
" But darker years shall mingle with the past,
And deeper vengeance shall be mine at last.
O'er the seven hills I see destruction spread,
And Empire's widow veils with dust her head!
Her gods forsake each desolated shrine,
Her temples moulder to the earth, like mine:
'Midst fallen palaces she sits alone,
Calling heroic shades from ages gone,
Or bids the nations 'midst her deserts wait
To learn the fearful oracles of Fate!

" Still sleep'st thou, Roman? Son of Victory, rise!
Wake to obey th' avenging Destinies!
Shed by thy mandate, soon thy country's blood
Shall swell and darken Tiber's yellow flood!
My children's manès call—awake! prepare
The feast they claim!—exult in Rome's despair!
Be thine ear closed against her suppliant cries,
Bid thy soul triumph in her agonies;
Let carnage revel, e'en her shrines among,
Spare not the valiant, pity not the young!
Haste! o'er her hills the sword's libation shed,
And wreak the curse of Carthage on her head!'"

The vision flies—a mortal step is near,
Whose echoes vibrate on the slumberer's ear;
He starts, he wakes to woe—before him stands
Th' unwelcome messenger of harsh commands,
Whose falt'ring accents tell the exiled chief,
To seek on other shores a home for grief.
—Silent the wanderer sat—but on his cheek
The burning glow far more than words might speak;
And, from the kindling of his eye, there broke
Language, where all th' indignant soul awoke,
Till his deep thought found voice—then, calmly stern,
And sovereign in despair, he cried, " Return!
Tell him who sent thee hither, thou hast seen
Marius, the exile, rest where Carthage once hath been!"

SONG.

FOUNDED ON AN ARABIAN ANECDOTE.

Away ! though still thy sword is red
   With life-blood from my sire,
No drop of thine may now be shed
   To quench my bosom's fire ;
Though on my heart 'twould fall more blest,
Than dews upon the desert's breast.

I've sought thee 'midst the sons of men,
   Through the wide city's fanes ;
I've sought thee by the lion's den,
   O'er pathless, boundless plains ;
No step that mark'd the burning waste,
But mine its lonely course hath traced.

Thy name hath been a baleful spell,
   O'er my dark spirit cast ;
No thought may dream, no words may tell
   What there unseen hath pass'd :
This wither'd cheek, this faded eye,
Are seals of thee—behold ! and fly !

Hath not my cup for thee been pour'd
   Beneath the palm-tree's shade ?
Hath not soft sleep thy frame restored
   Within my dwelling laid ?
What though unknown—yet who shall rest
Secure—if not the Arab's guest ?

Haste thee ; and leave my threshold-floor,
   Inviolate and pure !
Let not thy presence tempt me more,
   —Man may not thus endure !
Away ! I bear a fetter'd arm,
A heart that burns—but must not harm.

Begone ! outstrip the swift gazelle !
   The wind in speed subdue !
Fear cannot fly so swift, so well,
   As vengeance shall pursue ;
And hate, like love, in parting pain,
Smiles o'er *one* hope—we meet again !

To-morrow—and th' avenger's hand,
    The warrior's dart is free!
E'en now, no spot in all thy land,
    Save *this*, had shelter'd thee,
Let blood the monarch's hall profane,—
The Arab's tent must bear no stain!

Fly! may the desert's fiery blast
    Avoid thy secret way!
And sternly, till thy steps be past,
    Its whirlwinds sleep to-day!
I would not that thy doom should be
Assign'd by Heaven to aught but me.

ALP-HORN SONG.

TRANSLATED FROM THE GERMAN OF TIECK.

WHAT dost thou here, brave Swiss?
Forget'st thou thus thy native clime—
The lovely land of thy bright spring-time?
The land of thy home, with its free delights,
And fresh green valleys and mountain heights?
    Can the stranger's yield the bliss?

What welcome cheers thee now?
Dar'st thou lift thine eye to gaze around?
Where are the peaks, with their snow-wreaths crown'd?
Where is the song, on the wild winds borne,
Or the ringing peal of the joyous horn,
    Or the peasant's fearless brow?

But thy spirit is far away!
Where a greeting waits thee in kindred eyes,
Where the white Alps look through the sunny skies,
With the low senn-cabins, and pastures free,
And the sparkling blue of the glacier-sea,
    And the summits, clothed with day!

Back, noble child of Tell!
Back to the wild and the silent glen,
And the frugal board of peasant-men!
Dost thou seek the friend, the loved one, here?—
Away! not a true Swiss heart is near,
    Against thine own to swell!

TRANSLATIONS FROM HORACE.

TO VENUS.

BOOK 1st, ODE 30th.

"O Venus, Regina Cnidi Paphique," &c.

OH! leave thine own loved isle,
Bright Queen of Cyprus and the Paphian shores!
And here in Glycera's fair temple smile,
Where vows and incense lavishly she pours.

Waft here thy glowing son;
Bring Hermes; let the Nymphs thy path surround,
And youth unlovely till thy gifts be won,
And the light Graces with the zone unbound.

TO HIS ATTENDANT.

BOOK 1st, ODE 38th.

"Persicos odi, puer, apparatus," &c.

I HATE the Persian's costly pride—
The wreaths with bands of linden tied—
    These, boy, delight me not;
Nor where the lingering roses bide,
    Seek thou for me the spot.

For me be nought but myrtle twined—
The modest myrtle, sweet to bind
    Alike thy brows and mine;
While thus I quaff the bowl, reclined
    Beneath th' o'erarching vine.

TO DELIUS

BOOK 2d, ODE 3d.

"Æquam memento rebus in arduis,' &c.

FIRM be thy soul!—serene in power,
    When adverse fortune clouds the sky;

Undazzled by the triumph's hour,
   Since, Delius, thou must die!

Alike, if still to grief resign'd,
   Or if, through festal days, 'tis thine
To quaff in grassy haunts reclined,
   The old Falernian wine:

Haunts where the silvery poplar boughs
   Love with the pine's to blend on high,
And some clear fountain brightly flows
   In graceful windings by.

There be the rose with beauty fraught,
   So soon to fade, so brilliant now,
There be the wine, the odors brought,
   While time and fate allow!

For thou, resigning to thine heir
   Thy halls, thy bowers, thy treasured store,
Must leave that home, those woodlands fair,
   On yellow Tiber's shore.

What then avails it if thou trace
   From Inachus thy glorious line?
Or, sprung from some ignoble race,
   If not a roof be thine?

Since the dread lot for all must leap
   Forth from the dark revolving urn,
And we must tempt the gloomy deep,
   Whence exiles ne'er return.

TO THE FOUNTAIN OF BANDUSIA.

BOOK 3d, ODE 13th.

"Oh! Fons Bandusiæ, splendidior vitro," &c.

OH! worthy fragrant gifts of flowers and wine,
   Bandusian fount, than christal far more bright!
To-morrow shall a sportive kid be thine,
   Whose forehead swells with horns of infant might:
Ev'n now of love and war he dreams in vain,
Doom'd with his blood thy gelid wave to stain.

Let the red dog-star burn!—his scorching beam,
   Fierce in resplendence shall molest not thee!
Still shelter'd from his rays, thy banks, fair stream,
   To the wild flock around thee wandering free,

And the tired oxen from the furrow'd field
The genial freshness of their breath shall yield.

And thou, bright fount! ennobled and renown'd
　Shalt by thy poet's votive song be made ;
Thou and the oak with deathless verdure crown'd
　Whose boughs, a pendant canopy, o'ershade
Those hollow rocks, whence, murmuring many a tale
Thy chiming waters pour upon the vale.

TO FAUNUS.

BOOK 3d, ODE 18th.

"Faune, Nympharum fugentium amator," &c

Faunus, who lov'st the flying nymphs to chase
　O let thy steps with genial influence tread
My sunny fields, and be thy fostering grace,
　Soft on my nursling groves and borders, shed.

If at the mellow closing of the year
　A tender kid in sacrifice be thine ;
Nor fail the liberal bowls to Venus dear ;
　Nor clouds of incense to thine antique shrine.

Joyous each flock in meadow herbage plays,
　When the December feast returns to thee ;
Calmly the ox along the pasture strays,
　With festal villages from toil set free.

Then from the wolf no more the lambs retreat,
　Then shower the woods to thee their foliage round ;
And the glad laborer triumphs that his feet
　In triple dance have struck the hated ground.

THE CROSS OF THE SOUTH.

The beautiful constellation of the Cross is seen only in the southern hemisphere. The following lines are supposed to be addressed to it by a Spanish traveller in South America.]

In the silence and grandeur of midnight I tread,
Where savannahs, in boundless magnificence, spread,
And bearing sublimely their snow-wreaths on high,
The far Cordilleras unite with the sky.

'The fir-tree waves o'er me, the fire-flies' red light
With its quick-glancing splendor illumines the night;
And I read in each tint of the skies and the earth,
How distant my steps from the land of my birth.

But to thee, as thy lode-stars resplendently burn
In their clear depths of blue, with devotion I turn,
Bright Cross of the South! and beholding thee shine,
Scarce regret the loved land of the olive and vine.

Thou recallest the ages when first o'er the main
My fathers unfolded the ensign of Spain,
And planted their faith in the regions that see
Its unperishing symbol emblazon'd in thee.

How oft in their course o'er the oceans unknown,
Where all was mysterious, and awful and lone,
Hath their spirit been cheer'd by thy light, when the deep
Reflected its brilliance in tremulous sleep?

As the vision that rose to the Lord of the world,*
When first his bright banner of faith was unfurl'd;
Even such, to the heroes of Spain, when their prow
Made the billows the path of their glory, wert thou.

And to me as I traversed the world of the west,
Through deserts of beauty in stillness that rest;
By forests and rivers untamed in their pride,
Thy hues have a language, thy course is a guide.

Shine on—my own land is a far distant spot,
And the stars of thy sphere can enlighten it not;
And the eyes that I love, though e'en now they may be
O'er the firmament wandering, can gaze not on thee!

But thou to my thoughts art a pure-blazing shrine,
A fount of bright hopes, and of visions divine;
And my soul as an eagle exulting and free,
Soars high o'er the Andes to mingle with thee.

THE SLEEPER OF MARATHON.

I LAY upon the solemn plain,
   And by the funeral mound,
Where those who died not there in vain,
   Their place of sleep had found.

---

* Constantine

TO MISS F. A. L. ON HER BIRTHDAY.

'Twas silent where the free blood gush'd
    When Persia came array'd—
So many a voice had there been hush'd,
    So many a foot-step stay'd.

I slumber'd on the lonely spot
    So sanctified by death :
I slumber'd—but my rest was not
    As theirs who lay beneath.

For on my dreams, that shadowy hour,
    They rose—the chainless dead—
All arm'd they sprang, in joy, in power,
    Up from their grassy bed.

I saw their spears on that red field,
    Flash as in time gone by—
Chased to the seas without his shield
    I saw the Persian fly.

I woke—the sudden trumpet's blast
    Call'd to another fight—
From visions of our glorious past,
    Who doth not wake in might ?

TO MISS F. A. L. ON HER BIRTHDAY

WHAT wish can Friendship form for thee
    What brighter star invoke to shine ?
Thy path from every thorn is free,
    And every rose is thine !

Life hath no purer joy in store,
    Time hath no sorrow to efface ;
Hope cannot paint one blessing more
    Than memory can retrace !

Some hearts a boding fear might own,
    Had fate to *them* thy portion given,
Since many an eye by tears alone,
    Is taught to gaze on Heaven !

And there are virtues oft conceal'd,
    Till roused by anguish from repose,
As odorous trees no balm will yield,
    Till from their wounds it flows.

But fear not *thou* the lesson fraught
    With Sorrow's chast'ning power to know ;
Thou need'st not thus be sternly taught,
    " To melt at others' woe."

TO THE SAME.

Then still, with heart as blest, as warm,
  Rejoice thou in thy lot on earth :
Ah ! why should virtue dread the *storm*.
  If *Sunbeams* prove her worth?

WRITTEN IN THE FIRST LEAF OF THE ALBUM OF THE SAME.

WHAT first should consecrate as thine,
  The volume, destined to be fraught
With many a sweet and playful line,
  With many a pure and pious thought?

It should be, what a loftier strain
  Perchance less meetly would impart ;
What never yet was pour'd in vain,—
  The blessing of a grateful heart—

For kindness, which hath soothed the hour
  Of anxious grief, of weary pain,
And oft, with its beguiling power,
  Taught languid Hope to smile again ;

Long shall that fervent blessing rest
  On thee and thine, and heavenwards borne,
Call down such peace to soothe *thy* breast.
  As *thou* would'st bear to all that mourn.

TO THE SAME—ON THE DEATH OF HER MOTHER.

SAY not 'tis fruitless, nature's holy tear.
Shed by affection o'er a parent's bier !
More blest than dew on Hermon's brow that falls,
Each drop to life some latent virtue calls ;
Awakes some purer hope, ordain'd to rise,
By earthly sorrow strengthen'd for the skies,
Till the sad heart, whose pangs exalt its love,
With its lost treasure, seeks a home—above.

But grief will claim her hour,—and He, whose eye
Looks pitying down on nature's agony,
He, in whose love the righteous calmly sleep,
Who bids us hope, forbids not to weep !
He too, hath wept—and sacred be the woes
Once borne by him, their inmost source who knows,
Searches each wound, and bids His Spirit bring
Celestial healing on its dove-like wing !

FROM THE ITALIAN OF LA VEGA.

And who but he shall soothe, when one dread stroke,
Ties, that were fibres of the soul, hath broke?
Oh! well may those, yet lingering here, deplore
The vanish'd light, that cheers their path no more!
Th' Almighty hand, which many a blessing dealt,
Sends its keen arrows not to be unfelt!
By fire and storm, Heaven tries the Christian's worth,
And joy departs to wean us from the earth,
Where still too long, with beings born to die,
Time hath dominion o'er Eternity.

Yet not the less, o'er all the heart hath lost,
Shall Faith rejoice, when Nature grieves the most;
Then comes her triumph! through the shadowy gloom,
Her star in glory rises from the tomb,
Mounts to the day-spring, leaves the cloud below,
And gilds the tears that cease not yet to flow!
Yes, all is o'er! fear, doubt, suspense are fled,
Let brighter thoughts be with the virtuous dead!
The final ordeal of the soul is past,
And the pale brow is seal'd to Heaven at last!*

And thou, loved spirit! for the skies mature,
Steadfast in faith, in meek devotion pure;
Thou that didst make the home thy presence blest,
Bright with the sunshine of thy gentle breast,
Where peace a holy dwelling-place had found,
Whence beam'd her smile benignantly around;
Thou, that to bosoms widow'd and bereft
Dear, precious records of thy worth hast left,
The treasured gem of sorrowing hearts to be
Till Heaven recall surviving love to thee!—
O cherish'd and revered! fond memory well
On thee, with sacred, sad delight, may dwell'.
So pure, so blest thy life, that death alone
Could make more perfect happiness thine own;
He came—thy cup of joy, serenely bright,
Full to the last, still flow'd in cloudless light;
He came—an angel, bearing from on high
The all it wanted—immortality!

FROM THE ITALIAN OF GARCILASSO DE LA VEGA.

Divine Eliza!—since the sapphire sky
Thou measur'st now on angel wings, and feet
Sandall'd with immortality—oh why
Of me forgetful!—Wherefore not entreat

---

* "Till we have sealed the servants of God in their foreheads."—*Revelations*.

FROM THE ITALIAN OF SANNAZARO.

To hurry on the time when I shall see
The veil of mortal being rent in twain,
  And smile that I am free?

In the third circle of that happy land
Shall we not seek together, hand in hand,
Another lovelier lanscape, a new plain,
Other romantic streams and mountains blue,
And other vales, and a new shady shore,
When I may rest, and ever in my view
Keep thee, without the terror and surprise
  Of being sunder'd more!

FROM THE ITALIAN OF SANNAZARO.

  Oh! pure and blessed soul
  That, from thy clay's control
Escaped, hast sought and found thy native sphere,
  And from thy crystal throne
  Look'st down, with smiles alone,
On this vain scene of mortal hope and fear;

  Thy happy feet have trod
  The starry spangled road,
Celestial flocks by field and fountain guiding,
  And from their erring track
  Thou charm'st thy shepherds back
With the soft music of thy gentle chiding,

  Oh! who shall Death withstand—
  Death, whose impartial hand
Levels the lowest plant and loftiest pine!
  When shall our ears again
  Drink in so sweet a strain.
Our eyes behold so fair a form as thine.

APPEARANCE OF THE SPIRIT OF THE CAPE TO VASCO DE GAMA.

(TRANSLATED FROM THE FIFTH BOOK OF THE LUSIAD OF CAMOENS.)

Propitious winds our daring bark impell'd,
O'er seas which mortal n'er till then beheld,
When as one eve, devoid of care, we stood
Watching the prow glide swiftly through the flood,

High o'er our heads arose a cloud so vast,
O'er sea and heaven a fearful shade it cast:
Awful, immense, it came! so thick, so drear,
Its gloomy grandeur chill'd our hearts with fear,
And the dark billow heaved with distant roar,
Hoarse, as if bursting on some rocky shore.

Thrill'd with amaze, I cried, "Supernal Power!
What mean the omens of this threatening hour?
What the dread mystery of this ocean-clime,
So darkly grand, so fearfully sublime?"
Scarce had I spoke, when lo! a mighty form,
Tower'd through the gathering shadows of the storm;
Of rude proportions and gigantic size,
Dark features, rugged beard, and deep-sunk eyes;
Fierce was his gesture, and his tresses flew,
Sable his lips, and earthly pale his hue.
Well may I tell thee, that his limbs and height,
In vast dimensions and stupendous might,
Surpass'd that wonder, once the sculptor's boast,
The proud Colossus of the Rhodian coast.
Deep was his voice, in hollow tones he spoke,
As if from ocean's inmost caves they broke;
And but that form to view, that voice to hear,
Spread o'er our flesh and hair cold deadly thrills of fear.

"Oh! daring band," he cried, "far, far more bold
Than all whose deeds recording fame has told;
Adventurous spirits! whom no bounds of fear
Can teach one pause in rapine's fierce career;
Since, bursting thus the barriers of the main,
Ye dare to violate my lonely reign,
Where, till this moment, from the birth of time,
No sail e'er broke the solitude sublime:
Since thus ye pierce the veil by Nature thrown
O'er the dark secrets of the deep Unknown,
Ne'er yet revealed to aught of mortal birth,
Howe'er supreme in power, unmatch'd in worth;
Hear from my lips what chastisements of fate,
Rash, bold intruders! on your course await!
What countless perils, woes of darkest hue,
Haunt the vast main and shores your arms must yet subdue!

"Know that o'er every bark, whose fearless helm
Invades, like yours, this wide mysterious realm,
Unmeasured ills my arm in wrath shall pour,
And guard with storms my own terrific shore!
And on the fleet which first presumes to brave
The dangers throned on this tempestuous wave,
Shall vengeance burst, ere yet a warning fear
Have time to prophesy destruction near!

"Yes, desperate band! if right my hopes divine,
Revenge, fierce, full, unequall'd shall be mine!
Urge your bold prow, pursue your venturous way,
Pain, Havoc, Ruin, wait their destined prey!
And your proud vessels, year by year, shall find,
(If no false dreams delude my prescient mind,)
My wrath so dread in many a fatal storm,
Death shall be deem'd misfortune's mildest form.

* * * * * *

"Lo! where my victim comes!—of noble birth,
Of cultured genius, and exalted worth,
With her,* his best beloved, in all her charms,
Pride of his heart, and treasure of his arms!
From foaming waves, from raging winds they fly,
Spared for revenge, reserved for agony!
Oh dark the fate that calls them from their home,
On this rude shore, my savage reign to roam,
And sternly save them from a billowy tomb,
For woes more exquisite, more dreadful doom!
—Yes! he shall see the offspring, loved in vain,
Pierced with keen famine, die in lingering pain;
Shall see fierce Caffres every garment tear
From her, the soft, the idolized, the fair;
Shall see those limbs of Nature's finest mould,
Bare to the sultry sun, or midnight-cold,
And, in long wanderings o'er a desert land
Those tender feet imprint the scorching sand.

"Yet more, yet deeper woe, shall those behold,
Who live through toils unequall'd and untold!
On the wild shore, beneath the burning sky,
The hapless pair, exhausted, sink to die!
Bedew the rock with tears of pain intense,
Of bitterest anguish, thrilling every sense,
Till in one last embrace, with mortal throes,
Their struggling spirits mount from anguish to repose!"

As the dark phantom sternly thus portray'd
Our future ills, in Horror's deepest shade,—
"Who then art *thou?*" I cried, "dread being, tell
Each sense thus bending in amazement's spell?"
—With fearful shriek, far echoing o'er the tide,
Writhing his lips and eyes, he thus replied—
"Behold the genius of that secret shore,
Where the wind rages, and the billows roar;
That stormy Cape, for ages mine alone,
To Pompey, Strabo, Pliny, all unknown!
Far to the southern pole my throne extends,
That hidden rock, which Afric's region ends.

* Don Emanuel de Sonza, and his wife, Leonora de Sà.

Behold that spirit, whose avenging might,
Whose fiercest wrath your daring deeds excite."

* * * * * *

Thus having said, with strange, terrific cries,
The giant-spectre vanish'd from our eyes;
In sable clouds dissolved—while far around,
Dark ocean's heaving realms his parting yells resound!

A DIRGE.

Weep for the early lost!—
How many flowers were mingled in the crown
Thus, with the lovely, to the grave gone down,
 E'en when life promised most,
How many hopes have wither'd—they that bow
To Heaven's dread will, feel all its mysteries now

 Did the young mother's eye,
Behold her child, and close upon the day,
Ere from its glance th' awakening spirit's ray
 In sunshine could reply?
—Then look for clouds to dim the fairest morn!
Oh! strong is faith, if woe like this be borne.

 For there is hush'd on earth
A voice of gladness—there is veil'd a face,
Whose parting leaves a dark and silent place,
 By the once-joyous hearth.
A smile hath pass'd, which fill'd its home with light
A soul, whose beauty made that smile so bright!

 But there *is* power with faith!
Power, e'en though nature, o'er the untimely grave
Must weep, when God resumes the gem He gave;
 For sorrow comes of Death,
And with a yearning heart we linger on,
When they, whose glance unlock'd its founts, are gone!

 But glory from the dust,
And praise to Him, the merciful, for those
On whose bright memory love may still repose,
 With an immortal trust!
Praise for the dead, who leave us, when they part,
Such hope as she hath left—" the pure in heart."

THE MAREMMA.

["NELLO DELLA PIETRA had espoused a lady of noble family at Sienna, named Madonna Pia. Her beauty was the admiration of Tuscany, and excited in the heart of her husband a jealousy, which, exasperated by false reports and groundless suspicions, at length drove him to the desperate resolution of Othello. It is difficult to decide whether the lady was quite innocent, but so Dante represents her. Her husband brought her into the Maremma, which, then as now, was a district destructive of health. He never told his unfortunate wife the reason of her banishment to so dangerous a country. He did not deign to utter complaint or accusation. He lived with her alone, in cold silence, without answering her questions, or listening to her remonstrances. He patiently waited till the pestilential air should destroy the health of this young lady. In a few months she died. Some chronicles, indeed, tell us that Nello used the dagger to hasten her death. It is certain that he survived her, plunged in sadness and perpetual silence. Dante had in this incident, all the materials of an ample and very poetical narrative. But he bestows on it only four verses. He meets in Purgatory three spirits. One was a captain who fell fighting on the same side with him in the battle of Campaldino; the second, a gentleman assassinated by the treachery of the House of Este; the third, was a woman unknown to the poet, and who, after the others had spoken, turned towards him with these words:—

'Recorditi di me ; che son la Pia,
Sienna, mi fe, disfecemi Maremma,
Salsi colui che inanellata pria
Disposando m' avea con la sua gemma.'"
Purgatorio, cant. **5**.

—*Edinburgh Review*, No. lviii.]

" Mais elle etait du monde, ou les plus belles choses,
　　Ont le pire destin ;
Et Rose elle a vécu ce que vivent les roses,
　　L'espace d'un Matin." 　　MALHERBE.

THERE are bright scenes beneath Italian skies,
Where glowing suns their purest light diffuse,
Uncultured flowers in wild profusion rise,
And nature lavishes her warmest hues ;
But trust thou not her smile, her balmy breath,
Away ! her charms are but the pomp of Death !

He, in the vine-clad bowers, unseen is dwelling,
Where the cool shade its freshness round thee throws,
His voice, in every perfumed zephyr swelling,
With gentlest whisper lures thee to repose :

And the soft sounds that through the foliage sigh,
But woo thee still to slumber and to die,

Mysterious danger lurks, a syren, there,
Not robed in terrors, or announced in gloom,
But stealing o'er thee in the scented air,
And veil'd in flowers, that smile to deck thy tomb;
How may we deem, amidst their deep array,
That heaven and earth but flatter to betray?

Sunshine, and bloom, and verdure? Can it be,
That these but charm us with destructive wiles?
Where shall we turn, O Nature, if in *thee*
Danger is mask'd in beauty—death in smiles?
Oh! still the Circe of that fatal shore,
Where she, the sun's bright daughter, dwelt of yore!

There, year by year, that secret peril spreads,
Disguised in loveliness, its baleful reign,
And viewless blights o'er many a landscape sheds,
Gay with the riches of the south, in vain,
O'er fairy bowers and palaces of state,
Passing unseen to leave them desolate.

And pillar'd halls, whose airy colonades
Were formed to echo music's choral tone,
Are silent now, amidst deserted shades,*
Peopled by sculpture's graceful forms alone;
And fountains dash unheard, by lone alcoves,
Neglected temples, and forsaken groves.

And there were marble nymphs, in beauty gleaming,
'Midst the deep shades of plane and cypress rise,
By wave or grot might fancy linger, dreaming
Of old Arcadia's woodland deities,—
Wild visions!—there no sylvan powers convene,
Death reigns the genius of the Elysian scene.

Ye, too illustrious hills of Rome! that bear
Traces of Mightier beings on your brow,
O'er you that subtle spirit of the air
Extends the desert of his empire now;
Broods o'er the wreck of altar, fane, and dome,
And makes the Cæsars' ruin'd halls his home.

Youth, valor, beauty, oft have felt his power,
His crown'd and chosen victims: o'er their lot
Hath fond affection wept each blighted flower
In turn was loved and mourn'd, and is forgot.

---

* See Madame de Staël's fine description, in her *Corinne*, of the Villa Borghese, deserted on account of malaria.

THE MAREMMA.

But one who perish'd, left a tale ot woe,
Meet for as deep a sigh as pity can bestow.

A voice of music, from Sienna's walls,
Is floating joyous on the summer air,
And there are banquets in her stately halls,
And graceful revels of the gay and fair,
And brilliant wreaths the altar have array'd,
Where meet her noblest youth, and loveliest maid.

To that young bride each grace hath Nature given,
Which glows on Art's divinest dream,—her eye
Hath a pure sunbeam of her native heaven—
Her cheek a tinge of morning's richest dye;
Fair as that daughter of the south, whose form
Still breathes and charms, in Vinci's colors warm.*

But is she blest ?—for sometimes o'er her smile
A soft sweet shade of pensiveness is cast;
And in her liquid glance there seems a-while
To dwell some thought whose soul is with the past;
Yet soon it flies—a cloud that leaves no trace,
On the sky's azure, of its dwelling-place.

Perchance, at times, within her heart may rise
Remembrance of some early love or woe,
Faded, yet scarce forgotten—in her eyes
Wakening the half-form'd tear that may not flow;
Yet radiant seems her lot as aught on earth,
Where still some pining thought comes darkly o'er our mirth

The world before her smiles—its changeful gaze
She hath not proved as yet; her path seems gay
With flowers and sunshine, and the voice of praise
Is still the joyous herald of her way;
And beauty's light around her dwells, to throw
O'er every scene is own resplendent glow.

Such is the young Bianca—graced with all
That nature, fortune, youth, at once can give;
Pure in their loveliness—her looks recall
Such dreams, as ne'er life's early bloom survive;
And, when she speaks, each thrilling tone is fraught
With sweetness, born of high and heavenly thought.

And he, to whom are breathed her vows of faith
Is brave and noble—child of high descent,
He hath stood fearless in the ranks of death,
'Mid slaughter'd heaps, the warrior's monument:

---

* An allusion to Leonardo da Vinci's picture of his wife Mona Lisa, supposed to be the most perfect imitation of Nature ever exhibited in painting.—See Vasari in his *Lives of the Painters*.

And proudly marshall'd his Carroccio's* way
Amidst the wildest wreck of war's array.

And his the chivalrous, commanding mien,
Where high-born grandeur blends with courtly grace;
Yet may a lightning glance at times be seen,
Of fiery passions, darting o'er his face,
And fierce the spirit kindling in his eye—
But e'en while yet we gaze, its quick, wild flashes die.

And calmly can Pietra smile, concealing,
As if forgotten, vengeance, hate, remorse;
And veil the workings of each darker feeling,
Deep in his soul concentrating its force:
But yet, he loves—O! who hath loved nor known
Affection's power exalt the bosom all its own?

The days roll on—and still Bianca's lot
Seems as a path of Eden—thou might's deem
That grief, the mighty chastener, had forgot
To wake her soul from life's enchanted dream;
And, if her brow a moment's sadness wear,
It sheds but grace more intellectual there.

A few short years, and all is changed—her fate
Seems with some deep mysterious cloud o'ercast.
Have jealous doubts transform'd to wrath and hate,
The love whose glow expression's power surpass'd?
Lo! on Pietra's brow a sullen gloom
Is gathering day by day, prophetic of her doom.

O! can he meet that eye, of light serene,
Whence the pure spirit looks in radiance forth,
And view that bright intelligence of mien
Form'd to express but thoughts of loftiest worth,
Yet deem that vice within that heart can reign?
—How shall he e'er confide in aught on earth again?

In silence oft, with strange vindictive gaze,
Transient, yet fill'd with meaning, stern and wild,
Her features, calm in beauty he surveys,
Then turns away, and fixes on her child
So dark a glance as thrills a mother's mind
With some vague fear, scarce own'd and undefined.

There stands a lonely dwelling, by the wave
Of the blue deep which bathes Italia's shore,
Far from all sounds, but rippling seas that lave
Grey rocks with foliage richly shadow'd o'er;

---

* See the description of this sort of consecrated war-chariot in
Sismondi's *Histoire des Republiques Italiennes*, &c.,—vol. i. p 394.

And sighing winds, that murmur through the wood,
Fringing the beach of that Hesperian flood.

Fair is that house of solitude—and fair
The green Maremma, far around it spread,
A sun-bright waste of beauty—yet an air
Of brooding sadness o'er the scene is shed,
No human footstep tracks the lone domain,
The desert of luxuriance glows in vain.

And silent are the marble halls that rise
'Mid founts, and cypress walks, and olive groves
All sleeps in sunshine, 'neath cerulean skies,
And still around the sea-breeze lightly roves;
Yet every trace of man reveals alone,
That there life once hath flourish'd—and is gone.

There, till around them slowly, softly stealing,
The summer air, deceit in every sigh,
Came fraught with death, its power no sign revealing
Thy sires, Pietra, dwelt, in days gone by;
And strains of mirth and melody have flow'd
Where stands, all voiceless now, the still abode.

And thither doth her lord, remorseless, bear
Bianca with her child—his alter'd eye
And brow a stern and fearful calmness wear,
While his dark spirit seals their doom—to die;
And the deep bodings of his victim's heart
Tell her, from fruitless hope at once to part.

It is the summer's glorious prime—and blending
Its blue transparence with the skies, the deep,
Each tint of Heaven upon his breast descending,
Scarce murmurs as it heaves, in glassy sleep,
And on its wave reflects, more softly bright,
That lovely shore of solitude and light.

Fragrance in each warm southern gale is breathing,
Deck'd with young flowers the rich Maremma glows,
Neglected vines the trees are wildly wreathing,
And the fresh myrtle in exuberance blows,
And far around, a deep and sunny bloom
Mantles the scene, as garlands robe the tomb.

Yes! 'tis *thy* tomb Bianca! fairest flower!
The voice that calls thee speaks in every gale,
Which o'er thee breathing with insidious power,
Bids the young roses of thy cheek turn pale,
And, fatal in its softness, day by day,
Steals from that eye some trembling spark away.

But sink not yet ; for there are darker woes,
Daughter of Beauty ! in thy spring-morn fading,
Sufferings more keen for thee reserved than those
Of lingering death, which thus thine eye are shading !
Nerve then thy heart to meet that bitter lot ;
'Tis agony—but soon to be forgot !

What deeper pangs maternal hearts can wring,
Than hourly to behold the spoiler's breath
Shedding, as mildews on the bloom of spring,
O'er Infancy's fair cheek the blight of death ?
To gaze and shrink, as gathering shades o'ercast
The pale smooth brow, yet watch it to the last !

Such pangs were thine, young mother !—Thou did'st bend
O'er thy fair boy, and raise his drooping head ;
And faint and hopeless, far from every friend,
Keep thy sad midnight-vigils near his bed,
And watch his patient, supplicating eye,
Fix'd upon thee—on thee !—who could'st no aid supply !

There was no voice to cheer thy lonely woe
Through those dark hours—to thee the wind's low sigh,
And the faint murmur of the ocean's flow,
Came like some spirit whispering—" He must die !"
And thou didst vainly clasp him to the breast
His young and sunny smile so oft with hope had blest.

'Tis past—that fearful trial—he is gone ;
But thou, sad mourner ! hast not long to weep ;
The hour of nature's charter'd peace comes on,
And thou shalt share thine infant's holy sleep,
A few short sufferings yet—and death shall be
As a bright messenger from Heaven to thee.

But ask not—hope not—one relenting thought
From him who doom'd thee thus to waste away,
Whose heart with sullen, speechless vengeance fraught,
Broods in dark triumph o'er thy slow decay ;
And coldly, sternly, silently can trace
The gradual withering of each youthful grace.

And yet the day of vain remorse shall come,
When thou, bright victim ! on his dreams shall rise
As an accusing angel—and thy tomb,
A martyr's shrine be hallow'd in his eyes !
Then shall thine innocence his bosom wring,
More than thy fancied guilt with jealous pangs could sting.

Lift thy meek eyes to Heaven—for all on earth,
Young sufferer fades before thee—'Thou art lone—
Hope, Fortune, Love, smiled brightly on thy birth,

'Thine hour of death is all Affliction's own!
It is our task to suffer—and our fate
To learn that mighty lesson, soon or late.

The season's glory fades—the vintage-lay
Through joyous Italy resounds no more;
But mortal loveliness hath pass'd away,
Fairer than aught in summer's glowing store.
Beauty and youth are gone—behold them such
As Death hath made them with his blighting touch!

The summer's breath came o'er them—and they died!
Softly it came to give luxuriance birth,
Call'd forth young nature in her festal pride,
But bore to them their summons from the earth!
Again shall blow that mild, delicious breeze,
And wake to life and light all flowers—but these.

No sculptured urn, nor verse thy virtues telling,
O lost and loveliest one! adorns thy grave;
But o'er that humble cypress-shaded dwelling
The dew-drops glisten, and the wild-flowers wave—
Emblems more meet, in transient light and bloom,
For thee, who thus didst pass in brightness to the tomb!

STANZAS TO THE MEMORY OF GEORGE THE THIRD.

"Among many nations was there no King like him."—NEHEMIAH.
"Know ye not that there is a prince and a great man fallen this day in Israel!"—SAMUEL.

ANOTHER warning sound! the funeral bell,
   Startling the cities of the isle once more
With measured tones of melancholy swell,
   Strikes on th' awaken'd heart from shore to shore.
he, at whose coming monarchs sink to dust,
   The chambers of our palaces hath trod,
And the long-suffering spirit of the just,
   Pure from its ruins, hath return'd to God!
Yet may not England o'er her Father weep;
   Thoughts to her bosom crowd, too many, and too deep.

Vain voice of Reason, hush!—they yet must flow,
   The unrestrain'd, involuntary tears;
A thousand feelings sanctify the woe,
   Roused by the glorious shades of vanish'd years.

Tell us no more 'tis not the time for grief,
　Now that the exile of the soul is past,
And Death, blest messenger of Heaven's relief,
　Hath borne the wanderer to his rest at last ;
For him, eternity hath tenfold day,
We feel, we know, 'tis thus—yet nature will have way.

What though amidst us, like a blasted oak,
　Sadd'ning the scene where once it nobly reign'd,
A dread memorial of the lightning stroke,
　Stamp'd with its fiery record, he remain'd ;
Around that shatter'd tree still fondly clung
　Th' undying tendrils of our love, which drew
Fresh nurture from its deep decay, and sprung
　Luxuriant thence, to Glory's ruin true ;
While England hung her trophies on the stem,
That desolately stood, unconscious e'en of THEM.

Of *them* unconscious ! Oh mysterious doom !
　Who shall unfold the counsels of the skies ?
His was the voice which roused, as from the tomb,
　The realm's high soul to loftiest energies !
His was the spirit o'er the isles which threw
　The mantle of its fortitude ; and wrought
In every bosom, powerful to renew
　Each dying spark of pure and generous thought ;
The star of tempests ! beaming on the mast,*
The seaman's torch of Hope, 'midst perils deepening fast.

Then from th' unslumbering influence of his worth,
　Strength, as of inspiration, fill'd the land ;
A young, but quenchless flame went brightly forth,
　Kindled by him—who saw it not expand !
Such was the will of heaven—the gifted seer,
　Who with his God had communed, face to face,
And from the house of bondage, and of fear,
　In faith victorious, led the chosen race ;
He through the desert and the waste their guide,
Saw dimly from afar, the promised land—and died.

O full of days and virtues ! on thy head
　Centred the woes of many a bitter lot ;
Fathers have sorrow'd o'er their beauteous dead,
　Eyes, quench'd in night, the sunbeam have forgot ;
Minds have striven buoyantly with evil years,
　And sunk beneath their gathering weight at length ;
But Pain for thee had fill'd a cup of tears,
　Where every anguish mingled all its strength ;

---

* The glittering meteor, like a star, which often appears about a ship during tempests ; if seen upon the main-mast, is considered by the sailors as an omen of good weather.—See DAMPIER'S *Voyages*.

By thy lost child we saw thee weeping stand,
And shadows deep around fell from th' Eternal's hand.

Then came the noon of glory, which thy dreams
   Perchance of yore had faintly prophesied ;
But what to *thee* the splendor of its beams ?
   The ice-rock glows not 'midst the summer's pride !
Nations leap'd up to joy—as streams that burst,
   At the warm touch of spring, their frozen chain,
And o'er the plains, whose verdure once they nursed,
   Roll in exulting melody again ;
And bright o'er earth the long majestic line
Of England's triumphs swept, to rouse all hearts—but thine.

Oh ! what a dazzling vision, by the veil
   That o'er thy spirit hung, was shut from thee,
When sceptred chieftains throng'd with palms to hail
   The crowning isle, th' anointed of the sea !
Within thy palaces the lords of earth
   Met to rejoice—rich pageants glitter'd by,
And stately revels imaged, in their mirth,
   The old magnificence of chivalry.
They reach'd not thee—amidst them, yet alone,
Stillness and gloom begirt one dim and shadowy throne,

Yet there was mercy still—if joy no more
   Within that blasted circle might intrude,
Earth had no grief whose footstep might pass o'er
   The silent limits of its solitude !
If all unheard the bridal song awoke
   Our hearts' full echoes, as it swell'd on high ;
Alike unheard the sudden dirge, that broke
   On the glad strain, with dread solemnity !
If the land's rose unheeded wore its bloom,
Alike unfelt the storm that swept it to the tomb.

And she, who, tried through all the stormy past,
   Severely, deeply proved, in many an hour,
Watch'd o'er thee, firm and faithful to the last,
   Sustain'd, inspired, by strong affection's power ;
If to thy soul her voice no music bore—
   If thy closed eye and wandering spirit caught
No light from looks, that fondly would explore
   Thy mien, for traces of responsive thought ;
Oh ! thou wert spared the pang that would have thrill'd
Thine inmost heart, when death that anxious bosom still'd.

Thy loved ones fell around thee. Manhood's prime,
   Youth, with its glory, in its fulness, age,
All, at the gates of their eternal clime
   Lay down, and closed their mortal pilgrimage ;
The land wore ashes for its perish'd flowers,

The grave's imperial harvest. Thou, meanwhile,
Didst walk unconscious through thy royal towers,
 The one that wept not in the tearful isle!
As a tired warrior, on his battle-plain,
Breathes deep in dreams amidst the mourners and the slain.

And who can tell what visions might be thine?
 The stream of thought, though broken, still was pure!
Still o'er that wave the stars of heaven might shine,
 Where earthly image would no more endure!
Though many a step, of once-familiar sound,
 Came as a stranger's o'er thy closing ear,
And voices breathed forgotten tones around,
 Which that paternal heart once thrill'd to hear;
The mind hath senses of its own, and powers
To people boundless worlds, in its most wandering hours.

Nor might the phantoms to thy spirit known
 Be dark or wild, creations of remorse;
Unstained by thee, the blameless past had thrown
 No fearful shadows o'er the future's course:
For thee no cloud from memory's dread abyss,
 Might shape such forms as haunt the tyrant's eye;
And, closing up each avenue of bliss,
 Murmur their summons, to " despair and die!"
No! e'en though joy depart, though reason cease,
Still virtue's ruin'd home is redolent of peace.

They might be with thee still—the loved, the tried,
 The fair, the lost—they might be with thee still!
More softly seen, in radiance purified
 From each dim vapour of terrestrial ill;
Long after earth received them, and the note
 Of the last requiem o'er their dust was pour'd,
As passing sunbeams o'er thy soul might float
 Those forms, from us withdrawn—to thee restored!
Spirits of holiness, in light reveal'd,
To commune with a mind whose source of tears was seal'd

Came they with tidings from the worlds above.
 Those viewless regions where the weary rest?
Sever'd from earth, estranged from mortal love,
 Was thy mysterious converse with the blest?
Or shone their visionary presence bright
 With human beauty?—did their smiles renew
Those days of sacred and serene delight,
 When fairest beings in thy pathway grew?
Oh! Heaven hath balm for every wound it makes,
Healing the broken heart; it smites, but ne'er forsakes.

These may be fantasies—and this alone,
 Of all we picture in our dreams, is sure;

That rest, made perfect, is at length thine own,
   Rest, in thy God immortally secure!
Enough for tranquil faith; released from all
   The woes that graved Heaven's lessons on thy brow,
No cloud to dim, no fetter to enthral,
   Haply thine eye is on thy people now;
Whose love around thee still its offerings shed,
Though vainly sweet, as flowers, grief's tribute to the dead.

But if th' ascending, disembodied mind,
   Borne, on the wings of morning, to the skies,
May cast one glance of tenderness behind
   On scenes once hallow'd by its mortal ties,
How much hast thou to gaze on! all that lay
   By the dark mantle of thy soul conceal'd,
The might, the majesty, the proud array
   Of England's march o'er many a noble field,
All spread beneath thee, in a blaze of light,
Shine like some glorious land, view'd from an Alpine height.

Away, presumptuous thought!—departed saint!
   To thy freed vision what can earth display
Of pomp, of royalty, that is not faint,
   Seen from the birth-place of celestial day?
Oh! pale and weak the sun's reflected rays,
   E'en in their fervor of meridian heat,
To him, who in the sanctuary may gaze
   On the bright cloud that fills the mercy-seat!
And thou may'st view, from thy divine abode,
The dust of empires flit before a breath of God.

And yet we mourn thee! Yes! thy place is void
   Within our hearts—there veil'd thine image dwelt,
But cherish'd still; and o'er that tie destroy'd,
   Though faith rejoice, fond nature still must melt.
Beneath the long-loved sceptre of thy sway,
   Thousands were born, who now in dust repose,
And many a head, with years and sorrows grey,
   Wore youth's bright tresses, when thy star arose;
And many a glorious mind, since that fair dawn,
Hath fill'd our sphere with light, now to its source withdrawn

Earthquakes have rock'd the nations:—things revered,
   Th' ancestral fabrics of the world went down
In ruins, from whose stones Ambition rear'd
   His lonely pyramid of dread renown.
But when the fires that long had slumber'd, pent
   Deep in men's bosoms, with volcanic force,
Bursting their prison-house, each bulwark rent,
   And swept each holy barrier from their course,
Firm and unmoved, amidst that lava-flood,
Still, by thine arm upheld, our ancient landmarks stood.

Be they eternal!—Be thy children found
  Still to their country's altars true like thee!
And, while "the name of Briton" is a sound
  Of rallying music to the brave and free,
With the high feelings, at the word which swell,
  To make the breast a shrine for Freedom's flame,
Be mingled thoughts of him, who loved so well,
  Who left so pure, its heritage of fame!
Let earth with trophies guard the conqueror's dust,
Heaven in our souls embalms the memory of the just.

All else shall pass away—the thrones of kings,
  The very traces of their *tombs* depart;
But number not with perishable things
  The holy records Virtue leaves the heart,
Heir-looms from race to race!—and oh! in days,
  When, by the yet unborn, thy deeds are blest,
When our sons learn, " as household words," thy praise,
  Still on thine offspring, may thy spirit rest!
And many a name of that imperial line,
Father and patriot! blend, in England's songs, with thine!

CRITICAL ANNOTATION.

"The last poem is to the memory of his late Majesty: unlike courtly themes in general, this is one of the deepest and most lasting interest. Buried as the King had long been in mental and visual darkness, and dead to the common joys of the world, his death, perhaps, did not occasion the shock, or the piercing sorrow which we have felt on some other public losses; but the heart must be cold indeed, that could, on reflection, regard the whole fortune and fate of that venerable, gallant, tender-hearted, and pious man, without a more than common sympathy. There was something in his character so truly national; his very errors were of so amiable a kind, his excellencies bore so high a stamp, his nature was so genuine and unsophisticated, he stood in his splendid court, amidst his large and fine family, so true a husband, so good a father, so safe an example; he so thoroughly understood the feelings, and so duly appreciated the virtues, even the uncourtly virtues of his subjects; and, with all this, the sorrows from heaven rained down upon his head in so 'pitiless and pelting a storm,'—all these—his high qualities and unparalleled sufferings, form such a subject for poetry, as nothing, we should imagine, but its difficulty and the expectation attending it, would prevent from being seized upon by the greatest poets of the day. We will not say that Mrs. Hemans has filled the whole canvass as it might have been filled, but unquestionably her poem is beyond all comparison with any which we have seen on the subject; it is full of fine and pathetic passages, and it leads us up through all the dismal colorings of the foreground to that bright and consoling prospect which should close every Christian's reflections on such a matter. An analysis of so short a poem is wholly unnecessary, and we have already transgressed our limits; we will, therefore, give but one extract of that soothing nature alluded to, and release our readers:—

'Yet was there mercy still—*if joy no more,*' &c.

"It is time to close this article.* Our readers will have seen, and we do not deny, that we have been much interested by our subject: who or what Mrs. Hemans is we know not: we have been told that, like a poet of antiquity:

——'Tristia vitæ
Solatur cantu.'——

If it be so (and the most sensible hearts are not uncommonly nor unnaturally the most bitterly wounded,) she seems, from the tenor of her writings, to bear about her a higher and a surer balsam than the praises of men, or even the 'sacred muse' herself can impart. Still there is a pleasure, an innocent and an honest pleasure, even to a wounded spirit, in fame fairly earned; and such fame as may wait upon our decision, we freely and conscientiously bestow; in our opinion, all her poems are elegant and pure in thought and language; her later poems are of higher promise, they are vigorous, picturesque, and pathetic." *Quarterly Review*, vol. xxiv.

A TALE OF THE FOURTEENTH CENTURY.

A FRAGMENT.

The moonbeam, quivering o'er the wave,
   Sleeps in pale gold on wood and hill,
The wild wind slumbers in its cave,
   And heaven is cloudless—earth is still!
The pile, that crowns yon savage height
With battlements of Gothic might,
   Rises in softer pomp array'd,
   Its massy towers half lost in shade,
Half touch'd with mellowing light!
The rays of night, the tints of time,
   Soft-mingling on its dark-grey stone,
O'er its rude strength and mien sublime,
   A placid smile have thrown;
And far beyond, where wild and high,
Bounding the pale blue summer sky,
A mountain-vista meets the eye,
Its dark, luxuriant woods assume
A pencil'd shade, a softer gloom;
Its jutting cliffs have caught the light,
Its torrents glitter through the night,
While every cave and deep recess
Frowns in more shadowy awfulness.
Scarce moving on the glassy deep
Yon gallant vessel seems to sleep,

---

* This critique, from the pen of the venerable and distinguished Editor, Wm. Gifford, Esq., comprehended strictures on "The Restoration of the Works of Art to Italy,"—"Tales and Historic Scenes in Verse,"—"Translations from Camoens," &c.,—"The Sceptic," and "Stanzas to the Memory of the late King"

But darting from its side,
How swiftly does its boat design
A slender, silvery, waving line
　Of radiance o'er the tide!
No sound is on the summer seas,
　But the low dashing of the oar,
And faintly sighs the midnight breeze
　Through woods that fringe the rocky shore.
—That boat has reached the silent bay,
The dashing oar has ceased to play,
The breeze has murmur'd and has died
In forest-shades, on ocean's tide.
No step, no tone, no breath of sound,
Disturbs the loneliness profound;
And midnight spreads o'er earth and main
　A calm so holy and so deep,
That voice of mortal were profane,
　To break on nature's sleep!
It is the hour for thought to soar,
　High o'er the cloud of earthly woes;
For rapt devotion to adore,
　For passion to repose;
And virtue to forget her tears,
In visions of sublimer spheres!
For oh! those transient gleams of heaven,
To calmer, purer spirits given,
Children of hallow'd peace, are known
In solitude and shade alone!
Like flowers that shun the blaze of noon,
To blow beneath the midnight moon,
The garish world they will not bless,
But only live in loneliness!

Hark! did some note of plaintive swell
　Melt on the stillness of the air?
Or was it fancy's powerful spell
　That woke such sweetness there?
For wild and distant it arose,
Like sounds that bless the bard's repose,
When in lone wood, or mossy cave
He dreams beside some fountain-wave,
And fairy worlds delight the eyes,
Wearied with life's realities.
—Was it illusion?—yet again
Rises and falls th' enchanted strain
　Mellow, and sweet, and faint,
As if some spirit's touch had given
The soul of sound to harp of heaven
　To soothe a dying saint!
Is it the mermaid's distant shell,
　Warbling beneath the moonlit wave?
—Such witching tones might lure full well

The seaman to his grave!
Sure from no mortal touch ye rise,
Wild, soft, aerial melodies!
—Is it the song of woodland-fay
   From fairy grot, or haunted bower?
Hark! borne on, the magic lay
    near yon ivied tower!
Nearer still, the listening ear
May catch sweet harp notes, faint, yet clear;
And accents low, as if in fear,
   Thus murmur, half suppress'd :—
" Awake! the moon is bright on high,
The sea is calm, the bark is nigh,
   The world is hush'd to rest!"
Then sinks the voice—the strain is o'er,
Its last low cadence dies along the shore.

Fair Bertha hears th' expected song,
Swift from her tower she glides along ;
No echo to her tread awakes,
Her fairy step no slumber breaks,
And, in that hour of silence deep,
While all around the dews of sleep
O'erpower each sense, each eyelid steep,
Quick throbs her heart with hope and fear,
Her dark eye glistens with a tear.
Half-wavering now, the varying cheek
And sudden pause, her doubts bespeak,
The lip now flush'd, now pale as death,
The trembling frame, the fluttering breath!
Oh! in that moment, o'er her soul,
What struggling passions claim control!
Fear, duty, love, in conflict high,
By turns have won th' ascendency ;
And as, all tremulously bright,
Streams o'er her face the beam of night,
What thousand mix'd emotions play
O'er that fair face, and melt away :
Like forms whose quick succession gleams
O'er fancy's rainbow-tinted dreams ;
Like the swift glancing lights that rise
'Midst the wild cloud of stormy skies,
   And traverse ocean o'er;
So in that full, impassion'd eye
The changeful meanings rise and die,
   Just seen—and then no more!
But oh! too short that pause—again
Thrills to her heart that witching strain :—
" Awake! the midnight moon is bright,
Awake! the moments wing their flight,
   Haste! or they speed in vain!"

O, call of love! thy potent spell,
O'er that weak heart prevails too well;
The "still small voice" is heard no more
That pleaded duty's cause before,
And fear is hush'd, and doubt is gone,
And pride forgot, and reason flown!
Her cheek, whose color came and fled,
Resumes its warmest, brightest red,
Her step its quick elastic tread,
   Her eye its beaming smile!
Through lonely court and silent hall,
Flits her light shadow o'er the wall,
And still that low, harmonious call
   Melts on her ear the while!
Though love's quick ear alone could tell
The words its accents faintly swell:—
"Awake, while yet the lingering night
And stars and seas befriend our flight,
   O! haste, while all is well!"

The halls, the courts, the gates, are past,
She gains the moonlit beach at last.
Who waits to guide her trembling feet?
Who flies the fugitive to greet?
He, to her youthful heart endear'd
By all it e'er had hoped and feared,
Twined with each wish, with every thought,
Each day-dream fancy e'er had wrought,
Whose tints portray, with flattering skill,
What brighter worlds alone fulfil!
—Alas! that aught so fair should fly,
Thy blighting wand, Reality!

A chieftain's mien her Osbert bore,
A pilgrim's lowly robes he wore,
Disguise that vainly strove to hide
Bearing and glance of martial pride;
For he in many a battle scene,
On many a rampart-breach had been,
Had sternly smiled at danger nigh,
Had seen the valiant bleed and die,
And proudly rear'd on hostile tower,
'Midst falchion-clash, and arrowy shower,
   Britannia's banner high!
And though some ancient feud had taught
   His Bertha's sire to loathe his name,
More noble warrior never fought,
   For glory's prize, or England's fame.
And well his dark, commanding eye,
   And form and step of stately grace,
Accorded with achievements high,
Soul of emprize and chivalry,

Bright name, and generous race!
His cheek, embrown'd by many a sun,
Tells a proud tale of glory won,
Of vigil, march, and combat rude,
Valor, and toil, and fortitude!
E'en while youth's earliest blushes threw
Warm o'er that cheek, their vivid hue,
His gallant soul, his stripling-form,
Had braved the battle's rudest storm;
When England's conquering archers stood,
And dyed thy plain, Poitiers, with blood,
When shiver'd axe, and cloven shield,
And shatter'd helmet, strew'd the field,
And France around her King in vain,
Had marshal'd valor's noblest train;
In that dread strife, his lightning eye,
Had flash'd with transport keen and high,
And 'midst the battle's wildest tide,
Throbb'd his young heart with hope and pride.
Alike that fearless heart could brave,
Death on the war-field or the wave;
Alike in tournament or fight,
That ardent spirit found delight!
Yet oft, 'midst hostile scenes afar,
 Bright o'er his soul a vision came,
Rising, like some benignant star,
On stormy seas, or plains of war,
 To soothe, with hopes more dear than fame,
 The heart that throbb'd to Bertha's name!
And 'midst the wildest rage of fight,
And in the deepest calm of night,
To her his thoughts would wing their flight,
 With fond devotion warm;
Oft would those glowing thoughts portray
Some home, from tumults far away,
 Graced with that angel form!
And now his spirit fondly deems
Fulfill'd its loveliest, dearest dreams!

Who, with pale cheek, and locks of snow,
 In minstrel garb, attends the chief?
The moonbeam on his thoughtful brow
 Reveals a shade of grief.
Sorrow and time have touch'd his face,
With mournful yet majestic grace,
Soft as the melancholy smile
Of sunset on some ruin'd pile!
—It is the bard, whose song had power,
To lure the maiden from her tower;
The bard whose wild, inspiring lays,
E'en in gay childhood's earliest days,

First woke, in Osbert's kindling breast.
The flame that will not be represt,
The pulse that throbs for praise!
Those lays had banish'd from his eye,
The bright, soft tears of infancy,
Had soothed the boy to calm repose,
Had hush'd his bosom's earliest woes;
And when the light of thought awoke,
When first young reason's day-spring broke,
More powerful still, they bade arise
His spirit's burning energies!
Then the bright dream of glory warm'd,
Then the loud pealing war-song charm'd,
The legends of each martial line,
The battle-tales of Palestine;
And oft, since then, *his* deeds had proved,
Themes of the lofty lays he loved!
Now, at triumphant love's command,
Since Osbert leaves his native land,
Forsaking glory's high career,
For her, than glory far more dear;
Since hope's gay dream, and meteor ray,
To distant regions points his way,
That there Affection's hands may dress,
A fairy bower for happiness;
That fond, devoted bard, though now
Time's wint'ry garland wreathes his brow,
Though quench'd the sunbeam of his eye,
And fled his spirit's buoyancy;
And strength and enterprise are past,
Still follows constant to the last!

Though his sole wish was but to die
Midst the calm scenes of days gone by;
And all that hallows and endears
The memory of departed years—
Sorrow, and joy, and time, have twined
To those loved scenes, his pensive mind;
Ah! what can tear the links apart,
That bind his chieftain to his heart!
What smile but *his* with joy can light
The eye obscured by age's night?
Last of a loved and honor'd line,
Last tie to earth in life's decline,
Till death its lingering spark shall dim,
That faithful eye must gaze on him!
Silent and swift, with footstep light,
Haste on those fugitives of night,
They reach the boat—the rapid oar
Soon wafts them from the wooded shore
The bark is gain'd—a gallant few,
Vassals of Osbert, form its crew;

The pennant, in the moonlight beam,
  With soft suffusion glows;
From the white sail a silvery gleam,
  Falls on the wave's repose;
Long shadows undulating play,
From mast and streamer, o'er the bay;
But still so hush'd the summer-air,
They tremble, 'midst that scene so fair,
Lest morn's first beam behold them there
—Wake, viewless wanderer! breeze of night,
From river-wave, or mountain-height,
Or dew-bright couch of moss and flowers,
By haunted spring, in forest bowers;
Or dost thou lurk in pearly cell,
In amber grot, where mermaids dwell,
And cavern'd gems their lustre throw,
O'er the red sea-flowers' vivid glow?
Where treasures, not for mortal gaze,
In solitary splendor blaze;
And sounds, ne'er heard by mortal ear,
Swell through the deep's unfathom'd sphere?
What grove of that mysterious world,
Holds thy light wing in slumber furl'd?
Awake! o'er glittering seas to rove,
Awake! to guide the bark of love!
Swift fly the midnight hours, and soon
Shall fade the bright propitious moon;
Soon shall the waning stars grow pale,
E'en now—but lo! the rustling sail
Swells to the new-sprung ocean gale!
The bark glides on—their fears are o'er,
Recedes the bold romantic shore,
  Its features mingling fast;
Gaze, Bertha, gaze, thy lingering eye
May still each lovely scene descry
  Of years forever past!
There wave the woods, beneath whose shade,
With bounding step, thy childhood play'd;
'Midst ferny glades, and mossy lawns,
Free as their native birds and fawns;
Listening the sylvan sounds that float
On each low breeze, 'midst dells remote;
The ringdove's deep, melodious moan,
The rustling deer in thickets lone;
The wild-bee's hum, the aspen's sigh,
The wood-stream's plaintive harmony.
Dear scenes of many a sportive hour,
There thy own mountains darkly tower!
'Midst their grey rocks no glen so rude,
But thou hast loved its solitude!
No path so wild but thou hast known,
And traced its rugged course alone!

'The earliest wreath that bound thy hair,
Was twined of glowing heath-flowers there.
There, in the day-spring of thy years,
Undimm'd by passions or by tears,
Oft, while thy bright, enraptured eye
Wandered o'er ocean, earth, or sky,
While the wild breeze that round thee blew,
Tinged thy warm cheek with richer hue;
Pure as the skies that o'er thy head
Their clear and cloudless azure spread;
Pure as that gale, whose light wing drew
Its freshness from the mountain dew;
Glow'd thy young heart with feelings high,
A heaven of hallow'd ecstacy!
Such days were thine! ere love had drawn
A cloud o'er that celestial dawn!
As the clear dews in morning's beam,
With soft reflected coloring stream,
Catch every tint of eastern gem,
To form the rose's diadem;
But vanish when the noon-tide hour
Glows fiercely on the shrinking flower;
Thus in thy soul each calm delight,
Like morn's first dew-drops, pure and bright,
Fled swift from passion's blighting fire,
Or linger'd only to expire!

Spring, on thy native hills again,
  Shall bid neglected wild-flowers rise,
And call forth, in each grassy glen,
  Her brightest emerald dyes!
There shall the lonely mountain-rose,
Wreath of the cliffs, again disclose;
'Midst rocky dells, each well-known stream,
Shall sparkle in the summer beam;
The birch, o'er precipice and cave,
Its feathery foliage still shall wave;
The ash 'midst rugged clefts unveil
Its coral clusters to the gale,
And autumn shed a warmer bloom,
O'er the rich heath and glowing broom.
But thy light footstep there no more,
Each path, each dingle shall explore;
In vain may smile each green recess,
—Who now shall pierce its loneliness?
The stream through shadowy glens may stray,
—Who now shall trace its glistening way?
In solitude, in silence deep,
Shrined 'midst her rocks, shall echo sleep,
No lute's wild swell again shall rise,
To wake her mystic melodies.

All soft may blow the mountain air,
—It will not wave thy graceful hair!
The mountain-rose may bloom and die,
—It will not meet thy smiling eye!
But like those scenes of vanish'd days,
 Shall others ne'er delight;
Far lovelier lands shall meet thy gaze,
 Yet seem not half so bright!
O'er the dim woodlands' fading hue,
 Still gleams yon Gothic pile on high;
Gaze on, while yet 'tis thine to view
 That home of infancy!
Heed not the night-dew's chilling power,
Heed not the sea-wind's coldest hour,
But pause, and linger on the deck,
Till of those towers no trace, no speck,
 Is gleaming o'er the main;
For when the mist of morn shall rise,
Blending the sea, the shore, the skies,
That home, once vanish'd from thine eyes,
 Shall bless them ne'er again!
There the dark tales and songs of yore,
 First with strange transport thrill'd thy soul,
E'en while their fearful, mystic lore,
 From thy warm cheek the life-bloom stole;
There, while thy father's raptured ear,
Dwelt fondly on a strain so dear,
And in his eye the trembling tear,
 Reveal'd his spirit's trance;
How oft, those echoing halls along,
Thy thrilling voice hath swell'd the song,
Tradition wild of other days,
Or troubadour's heroic lays,
 Or legend of romance!
Oh! many an hour hath there been thine,
 That memory's pencil oft shall dress
In softer shades, and tints that shine
 In mellow'd loveliness!
While thy sick heart, and fruitless tears,
 Shall mourn, with fond and deep regret,
The sunshine of thine early years,
 Scarce deem'd so radiant—till it set!
The cloudless peace, unprized till gone,
The bliss, till vanish'd, hardly known!

On rock and turret, wood and hill,
The fading moonbeams linger still;
Still, Bertha, gaze on yon grey tower,
At evening's last and sweetest hour,
While varying still, the western skies
Flush'd the clear seas with rainbow-dyes,

Whose warm suffusions glow'd and pass'd,
Each richer, lovelier, than the last;
How oft, while gazing on the deep,
That seem'd a heaven of peace to sleep,
As if its wave, so still, so fair,
More frowning mien might never wear,
The twilight calm of mental rest,
Would steal in silence o'er thy breast,
And wake that dear and balmy sigh,
That softly breathes the spirit's harmony!
—Ah! ne'er again shall hours to thee be given,
Of joy on earth—so near allied to Heaven!

Why starts the tear to Bertha's eye?
Is not her long-loved Osbert nigh?
Is there a grief his voice, his smile,
His words, are fruitless to beguile?
—Oh! bitter to the youthful heart,
  That scarce a pang, a care has known,
The hour when first from scenes we part,
  Where life's bright spring has flown!
Forsaking, o'er the world to roam,
That little shrine of peace—our home!
E'en if delighted fancy throw
O'er that cold world, her brightest glow,
Painting its untried paths with flowers,
That will not live in earthly bowers;
(Too frail, too exquisite, to bear
One breath of life's ungenial air;)
E'en if such dreams of hope arise,
As Heaven alone can realize;
Cold were the breast that would not heave
One sigh, the home of youth to leave;
Stern were the heart that would not swell
To breathe life's saddest word—farewell!
Though earth has many a deeper woe,
Though tears, more bitter far, must flow,
That hour, whate'er our future lot,
That first fond grief, is ne'er forgot!

Such was the pang of Bertha's heart,
The thought, that bade the tear-drop start
  And Osbert by her side
Heard the deep sigh, whose bursting swell
Nature's fond struggle told too well;
And days of future bliss portray'd,
And love's own eloquence essay'd,
  To soothe his plighted bride!
Of bright Arcadian scenes he tells,
  In that sweet land to which they fly;
The vine-clad rocks, the fragrant dells
  Of blooming Italy.

For he had roved a pilgrim there,
And gazed on many a spot so fair,
It seem'd like some enchanted grove,
Where only peace, and joy, and love,
Those exiles of the world, might rove,
  And breathe its heavenly air;
And, all unmix'd with ruder tone,
Their " wood-notes wild " be heard alone!

Far from the frown of stern control,
That vainly would subdue the soul,
There shall their long-affianced hands,
Be join'd in consecrated bands,
And in some rich, romantic vale ,
  Circled with heights of Alpine snow,
Where citron-woods enrich the gale,
And scented shrubs their balm exhale,
  And flowering myrtles blow ;
And 'midst the mulberry boughs on high,
Weaves the wild vine her tapestry :
On some bright streamlet's emerald side,
Where cedars wave, in graceful pride,
Bosom'd in groves, their home shall rise,
A shelter'd bower of Paradise !

Thus would the lover soothe to rest
With tales of hope her anxious breast ;
Nor vain that dear enchanting lore,
Her soul's bright visions to restore,
And bid gay phantoms of delight
Float in soft coloring, o'er her sight.
—Oh ! youth, sweet May-morn, fled so soon,
Far brighter than life's loveliest noon,
How oft thy spirit's buoyant power
Will triumph e'en in sorrow's hour
  Prevailing o'er regret !
As rears its head th' elastic flower
Though the dark tempest's recent shower
Hang on its petals yet !

Ah ! not so soon can hope's gay smile
 The aged bard to joy beguile :
Those silent years that steal away
The cheek's warm rose, the eye's bright ray,
Win from the mind a nobler prize,
E'en all its buoyant energies !
For him the April days are past,
  When grief was but a fleeting cloud ;
No transient shade will sorrow cast,
  When age the spirit's might has bow'd !
And as he sees the land grow dim,
That native land, now lost to him,

Fix'd are his eyes, and clasp'd his hands,
And long in speechless grief he stands.
  So desolately calm his air,
He seems an image, wrought to bear
The stamp of deep, though hush'd despair;
Motion and life no sign bespeaks
Save that the night-breeze, o'er his cheeks,
  Just waves his silvery hair!
Nought else could teach the eye to know
He was no sculptured form of woe!

Long gazing o'er the dark'ning flood,
Pale in that silent grief he stood;
Till the cold moon was waning fast,
  And many a lovely star had died,
And the grey heavens deep shadows cast
  Far o'er the slumbering tide;
And robed in one dark solemn hue,
Arose the distant shore to view.
Then, starting from his trance of woe,
Tears, long suppress'd, in freedom flow,
While thus his wild and plaintive strain,
Blends with the murmur of the main,

THE BARD'S FAREWELL.

Thou setting moon! when next thy rays
  Are trembling on the shadowy deep,
The land, now fading from my gaze,
  These eyes in vain shall weep;
And wander o'er the lonely sea,
And fix their tearful glance on thee.
On thee! whose light so softly gleams,
Through the green oaks that fringe my native streams

But, 'midst those ancient groves, no more
  Shall I thy quivering lustre hail,
Its plaintive strain my harp must pour.
  To swell a foreign gale;
The rocks, the woods, whose echoes woke,
When its full tones their stillness broke,
Deserted now, shall hear alone,
The brook's wild voice, the wind's mysterious moan.

And oh! ye fair, forsaken halls,
  Left by your lord to slow decay,
Soon shall the trophies on your walls
  Be mouldering fast away!
There shall no choral songs resound,
There shall no festal board be crown'd;
But ivy wreath the silent gate,
And all be hush'd, and cold, and desolate.

No banner from the stately tower,
  Shall spread its blazon'd folds on high,
There the wild brier and summer flower,
  Unmark'd, shall wave and die.
Home of the mighty! thou art lone,
The noonday of thy pride is gone,
And, 'midst thy solitude profound,
A step shall echo like unearthly sound!

From thy cold hearths no festal blaze
  Shall fill the hall with ruddy light,
Nor welcome, with convivial rays,
  Some pilgrim of the night;
But there shall grass luxuriant spread,
As o'er the dwellings of the dead;
And the deep swell of every blast,
Seem a wild dirge for years of grandeur past.

And I—my joy of life is fled,
  My spirit's power, my bosom's glow,
The raven locks that graced my head,
  Wave in a wreath of snow!
And where the star of youth arose,
I deem'd life's lingering ray should close,
And those loved trees my tomb o'ershade,
Beneath whose arching bowers my childhood play'd.

Vain dream! that tomb in distant earth
  Shall rise, forsaken and forgot;
And thou, sweet land, that gav'st me birth,
  A grave must yield me not!
Yet, haply he for whom I leave
Thy shores, in life's dark winter-eve,
When cold the hand, and closed the lays,
And mute the voice he loved to praise,
O'er the hush'd harp one tear may shed,
And one frail garland o'er the minstrel's bed!

BELSHAZZAR'S FEAST.

'Twas night in Babylon: yet many a beam,
Of lamps far glittering from her domes on high,
Shone, brightly mingling in Euphrates' stream
With the clear stars of that Chaldean sky,
Whose azure knows no cloud: each whisper'd sigh
Of the soft night-breeze through her terrace bowers,
Bore deepening tones of joy and melody,

O'er an illumined wilderness of flowers;
And the glad city's voice went up from all her towers.

But prouder mirth was in the kingly hall,
Where, 'midst adoring slaves, a gorgeous band,
High at the stately midnight festival,
Belshazzar sat enthroned. There luxury's hand
Had shower'd around all treasures that expand
Beneath the burning East; all gems that pour
The sunbeams back; all sweets of many a land,
Whose gales waft incense from their spicy shore!
—But mortal pride look'd on, and still demanded more.

With richer zest the banquet may be fraught,
A loftier theme may swell the exulting strain!
The Lord of nations spoke,—and forth were brought
The spoils of Salem's devastated fane.
Thrice holy vessels!—pure from earthly stain,
And set apart, and sanctified to Him,
Who deign'd within the oracle to reign,
Reveal'd, yet shadow'd; making noonday dim,
To that most glorious cloud between the cherubim.

They came, and louder peal'd the voice of song,
And pride flash'd brighter from the kindling eye,
And He who sleeps not heard the elated throng,
In mirth that plays with thunderbolts, defy
The Rock of Zion!—Fill the nectar high,
High in the cups of consecrated gold!
And crown the bowl with garlands, ere they die,
And bid the censers of the temple hold
Offerings to Babel's gods, the mighty ones of old!

Peace!—is it but a phantom of the brain,
Thus shadow'd forth, the senses to appal,
Yon fearful vision?—Who shall gaze again
To search its cause?—Along the illumined wall,
Startling, yet riveting the eyes of all.
Darkly it moves,—a hand, a human hand,
O'er the bright lamps of that resplendent hall,
In silence tracing, as a mystic wand,
Words all unknown, the tongue of some far distant land!

There are pale cheeks around the regal board,
And quivering limbs, and whispers deep and low,
And fitful starts!—the wine, in triumph pour'd,
Untasted foams, the song hath ceased to flow,
The waving censer drops to earth—and lo!
The king of men, the ruler, girt with mirth,
Trembles before a shadow!—Say not so!
—The child of dust, with guilt's foreboding sight,
Shrinks from the dread Unknown, the avenging Infinite!

"But haste ye!—bring Chaldea's gifted seers,
The men of prescience!—haply to *their* eyes,
Which track the future through the rolling spheres,
Yon mystic sign may speak in prophecies."
They come—the readers of the midnight skies,
They that gave voice to visions—but in vain!
Still wrapt in clouds the awful secret lies,
It hath no language 'midst the starry train,
Earth has no gifted tongue Heaven's mysteries to explain.

Then stood forth one, a child of other sires,
And other inspiration!—one of those
Who on the willows hung their captive lyres,
And sat, and wept, where Babel's river flows.
His eye was bright, and yet the pale repose
Of his pure features half o'erawed the mind,
Telling of inward mysteries—joys and woes
In lone recesses of the soul enshrined;
Depths of a being seal'd and sever'd from mankind.

Yes!—what was earth to him, whose spirit pass'd
Time's utmost bounds?—on whose unshrinking sight
Ten thousand shapes of burning glory cast
Their full resplendence?—Majesty and might
Were in his dreams;—for him the veil of light
Shrouding Heaven's inmost sanctuary and throne,
The curtain of th' unutterably bright
Was raised!—to him, in fearful splendor shown,
Ancient of Days! e'en Thou mad'st thy dread presence known.

He spoke:—the shadows of the things to come
Pass'd o'er his soul:—" O King, elate in pride!
God hath sent forth the writing of thy doom—
The one, the living, God by thee defied!
He, in whose balance earthly lords are tried,
Hath weigh'd, and found thee wanting. 'Tis decreed
The conqueror's hands thy kingdom shall divide,
The stranger to thy throne of power succeed!
Thy days are full—they come,—the Persian and the Mede!"

There fell a moment's thrilling silence round—
A breathless pause!—the hush of hearts that beat,
And limbs that quiver:—Is there not a sound,
A gathering cry, a tread of hurrying feet?
—'Twas but some echo in the crowded street,
Of far-heard revelry; the shout, the song,
The measured dance to music wildly sweet,
That speeds the stars their joyous course along—
Away; nor let a dream disturb the festal throng!

Peace yet again! Hark! steps in tumult flying,
Steeds rushing on, as o'er a battle-field!

The shouts of hosts exulting or defying,
The press of multitudes that strive or yield!
And the loud startling clash of spear and shield,
Sudden as earthquake's burst; and blent, with these,
The last wild shriek of those whose doom is seal'd
In their full mirth;—all deepening on the breeze,
As the long stormy roll of far-advancing seas!

And nearer yet the trumpet's blast is swelling,
Loud, shrill, and savage, drowning every cry;
And, lo! the spoiler in the regal dwelling,
Death—bursting on the halls of revelry!
Ere on their brows one fragile rose-leaf die,
The sword hath raged through joy's devoted train:
Ere one bright star be faded from the sky,
Red flames, like banners, wave from dome and fane;
Empire is lost and won—Belshazzar with the slain.*

---

* As originally written, the following additional stanzas (afterwards omitted) concluded this poem:

<pre>
Fallen is the golden city!—in the dust,
Spoil'd of her crown, dismantled of her state,
She that hath made the strength of towers her trust,
Weeps by her dead, supremely desolate!
She that beheld the nations at her gate,
Thronging in homage, shall be call'd no more
Lady of kingdoms! Who shall mourn her fate?
Her guilt is full, her march of triumph o'er—
What widow'd land shall now her widowhood deplore?

Sit thou in silence! Thou that wert enthroned
On many waters!—thou, whose augurs read
The language of the planets, and disown'd
The Mighty Name it blazons:—veil thy head,
Daughter of Babylon!—the sword is red
From thy destroyer's harvest, and the yoke
Is on thee, O most proud!—for thou hast said,
"I am, and none beside!" Th' Eternal spoke,
Thy glory was a spoil, thine idol-gods were broke!

But go thou forth, O Israel?—wake! rejoice!
Be clothed with strength, as in thine ancient day!
Renew the sound of harps, th' exulting voice,
The mirth of timbrels!—loose the chain, and say
God hath redeem'd his people!—from decay
The silent and the trampled shall arise!
—Awake!—put on thy beautiful array,
O long-forsaken Zion!—to the skies
Send up on every wind thy choral melodies!

And lift thy head!—Behold thy sons returning,
Redeem'd from exile, ransom'd from the chain,
Light hath revisited the house of mourning,
She that on Judah's mountains wept in vain,
Because her children were not—dwells again,
Girt with the lovely!—through thy streets, once more,
City of God! shall pass the bridal train,
And the bright lamps their festive radiance pour,
And the triumphal hymns thy joy of youth restore.
</pre>

THE LAST CONSTANTINE.

> .... "Thou strivest nobly,
> When hearts of sterner stuff perhaps had sunk;
> And o'er thy fall, if it be so decreed,
> Good men will mourn, and brave men will shed tears,
> . . . .
> .... Fame I look not for,
> But to sustain, in Heaven's all-seeing eye,
> Before my fellow men, in mine own sight,
> With graceful virtue and becoming pride,
> The dignity and honor of a man,
> Thus station'd as I am, I will do all
> That man may do."
>   Miss Baillie's *Constantine Palæologus.*

I.

The fires grew pale on Rome's deserted shrines,
In the dim grot the Pythia's voice had died ;
- Shout, for the City of the Constantines,
The rising city of the billow-side,
The City of the Cross !—great ocean's bride,
Crown'd with her birth she sprung !—long ages past,
And still she look'd in glory o'er the tide,
Which at her feet barbaric riches cast,
Pour'd by the burning East, all joyously and fast.

II.

Long ages past !—they left her porphyry halls
Still trod by kingly footsteps. Gems and gold
Broider'd her mantle, and her castled walls
Frown'd in their strength ; yet there were signs which told
The days were full. The pure high faith of old
Was changed ; and on her silken couch of sleep
She lay, and murmur'd if a rose-leaf's fold
Disturb'd her dreams ; and call'd her slaves to keep
Their watch, that no rude sound might reach her o'er the deep

III.

But there are sounds that from the regal dwelling
Free hearts and fearless only may exclude ;
'Tis not alone the wind, at midnight swelling,
Breaks on the soft repose by luxury woo'd !
There are unbidden footsteps, which intrude
Where the lamps glitter, and the wine-cup flows,
And darker hues have stain'd the marble, strew'd
With the fresh myrtle, and the short-lived rose,
And Parian walls have rung to the dread march of foes.

IV.

A voice of multitudes is on the breeze,
Remote yet solemn as the night-storm's roar
Through Ida's giant-pines! Across the seas
A murmur comes, like that the deep winds bore
From Tempé's haunted river to the shore
Of the reed-crown'd Eurotas; when, of old,
Dark Asia sent her battle-myriads o'er
Th' indignant wave, which would not be controll'd,
But past the Persian's chain in boundless freedom roll'd.

V.

And it is thus again?—Swift oars are dashing
The parted waters, and a light is cast
On their white foam-wreaths, from the sudden flashing
Of Tartar spears, whose ranks are thickening fast
There swells a savage trumpet on the blast,
A music of the deserts, wild and deep,
Wakening strange echoes, as the shores are pass'd
Where low 'midst Ilion's dust her conquerors sleep;
O'ershadowing with high names each rude sepulchral heap.

VI.

War from the West!—the snows on Thracian hills
Are loosed by Spring's warm breath; yet o'er the lands
Which Hæmus girds, the chainless mountain rills
Pour down less swiftly than the Moslem bands.
War from the East!—'midst Araby's lone sands,
More lonely now the few bright founts may be,
While Ismael's bow is bent in warrior-hands
Against the Golden City of the sea : [1]
—Oh! for a soul to fire thy dust, Thermopylæ!

VII.

Hear yet again ye mighty!—Where are they,
Who, with their green Olympic garlands crown'd,
Leap'd up, in proudly beautiful array,
As to the banquet gathering, at the sound
Of Persia's clarion?—Far and joyous round,
From the pine-forests, and the mountain-snows,
And the low sylvan valleys, to the bound
Of the bright waves, at freedom's voice they rose!
—Hath it no thrilling tone to break the tomb's repose?

VIII.

They slumber with their swords!—The olive-shades
In vain are whispering their immortal tale!
In vain the spirit of the past pervades
The soft winds, breathing through each Grecian vale.
—Yet must *Thou* wake, though all unarm'd and pale,
Devoted City!—Lo! the Moslem's spear,
Red from its vintage, at thy gates; his sail

Upon thy waves, his trumpet in thine ear!
—Awake! and summon those, who yet, perchance, may hear!

IX.
Be hush'd, thou faint and feeble voice of weeping!
Lift ye the banner of the Cross on high,
And call on chiefs, whose noble sires are sleeping
In their proud graves of sainted chivalry,
Beneath the palms and cedars, where they sigh
To Syrian gales!—The sons of each brave line,
From their baronial halls shall hear your cry,
And seize the arms which flash'd round Salem's shrine,
And wield for you the swords once waved for Palestine!

X.
All still, all voiceless!—and the billow's roar
Alone replies!—Alike *their* soul is gone
Who shared the funeral-feast on Œta's shore,
And *theirs* that o'er the field of Ascalon
Swell'd the crusader's hymn!—Then gird thou on
Thine armor, Eastern Queen! and meet the hour
Which waits thee ere the day's fierce work is done
With a strong heart; so may thy helmet tower
Unshiver'd through the storm, for generous hope is power!

XI.
But linger not,—array thy men of might!
The shores, the seas, are peopled with thy foes.
Arms through thy cypress groves are gleaming bright,
And the dark huntsmen of the wild, repose
Beneath the shadowy marble porticoes
Of thy proud villas. Nearer and more near,
Around thy walls the sons of battle close;
Each hour, each moment, hath its sound of fear,
Which the deep grave alone is charter'd not to hear!

XII.
Away! bring wine, bring odors, to the shade,[2]
Where the tall pine and poplar blend on high!
Bring roses, exquisite, but soon to fade!
Snatch every brief delight,—since we must die!—
Yet is the hour, degenerate Greeks! gone by,
For feast in vine-wreath'd bower, or pillar'd hall;
Dim gleams the torch beneath yon fiery sky,
And deep and hollow is the tambour's call,
And from the startled hand th' untasted cup will fall.

XIII.
The night—the glorious oriental night,
Hath lost the silence of her purple heaven,
With its clear stars! The red artillery's light
Athwart her worlds of tranquil splendor driven,

To the still firmament's expanse hath given
Its own fierce glare, wherein each cliff and tower
Starts wildly forth; and now the air is riven
With thunder-bursts, and now dull smoke-clouds lower
Veiling the gentle moon, in her most hallow'd hour.

XIV.
Sounds from the waters, sounds upon the earth,
Sounds in the air, of battle! Yet with these
A voice is mingling, whose deep tones give birth
To Faith and Courage! From luxurious ease
A gallant few have started! O'er the seas,
From the Seven Towers,[3] their banner waves its sign,
And Hope is whispering in the joyous breeze,
  Which plays amidst its folds. That voice was *thine;*
Thy soul was on that band devoted Constantine!

XV.
Was Rome thy parent? Didst thou catch from *her*
The fire that lives in thine undaunted eye?
—That city of the throne and sepulchre
Hath given proud lessons how to reign and die!
Heir of the Cæsars! did that lineage high,
Which, as a triumph to the grave, hath pass'd
With its long march of sceptered imag'ry,[4]
Th' heroic mantle o'er thy spirit cast?
—Thou! of an eagle-race the noblest and the last!

XVI.
Vain dreams! upon that spirit hath descended
Light from the living Fountain, whence each thought
Springs pure and holy! In that eye is blended
A spark, with Earth's triumphal memories fraught,
And, far within, a deeper meaning, caught
From worlds unseen. A hope, a lofty trust,
Whose resting-place on buoyant wing is sought
(Though through its veil, seen darkly from the dust,)
In realms where Time no more hath power upon the just.

XVII.
Those were proud days, when on the battle plain,
And in the sun's bright face, and 'midst the array
Of awe-struck hosts, and circled by the slain,
The Roman cast his glittering mail away,[5]
And while a silence, as of midnight, lay
O'er breathless thousands at his voice who started,
Call'd on the unseen, terrific powers that sway
  The heights, the depths, the shades; then, fearless-hearted,
Girt on his robe of death, and for the grave departed!

XVIII.
But then, around him as the javelins rush'd,
From earth to heaven swell'd up the loud acclaim;

And, ere his heart's last free libation gush'd,
With a bright smile the warrior caught his name
Far-floating on the winds! And Vict'ry came,
And made the hour of that immortal deed
A life, in fiery feeling! Valor's aim
Had sought no loftier guerdon. Thus to bleed,
Was to be Rome's high star!—He died—and had his meed.

XIX.

But praise—and dearer, holier praise, be theirs,
Who, in the stillness and the solitude
Of hearts press'd earthwards by a weight of cares,
Uncheer'd by Fame's proud hope, th' ethereal food
Of restless energies, and only view'd
By Him whose eye, from his eternal throne,
Is on the soul's dark palaces; have subdued
And vow'd themselves with strength till then unknown,
To some high martyr-task, in secret and alone.

XX.

Theirs be the bright and sacred names, enshrined
Far in the bosom! for their deeds belong,
Not to the gorgeous faith which charm'd mankind
With its rich pomp of festival and song,
Garland, and shrine, and incense-bearing throng;
But to that Spirit, hallowing, as it tries
Man's hidden soul in whispers, yet more strong
Than storm or earthquake's voice; for *thence* arise
All that mysterious world's unseen sublimities.

XXI.

Well might *thy* name, brave Constantine! awake
Such thought, such feeling!—But the scene again
Bursts on my vision, as the day-beams break
Through the red sulphurous mists: the camp, the plain,
The terraced palaces, the dome-capt fane,
With its bright cross fix'd high in crowning grace;
Spears on the ramparts, galleys on the main,
And, circling all with arms, that turban'd race,
The sun, the desert, stamp'd in each dark haughty face.

XXII.

Shout, ye seven hills! Lo! Christian pennons streaming
Red o'er the waters![6] Hail, deliverers, hail!
Along your billowy wake the radiance gleaming,
Is Hope's own smile! They crowd the swelling sail,
On, with the foam, the sunbeam and the gale,
Borne, as a victor's car! The batteries pour
Their clouds and thunders; but the rolling veil
Of smoke floats up the exulting winds before!
—And oh! the glorious burst of that bright sea and shore!

XXIII.

The rocks, waves, ramparts, Europe's, Asia's coast,
All throng'd! one theatre for kingly war!
A monarch girt with his barbaric host,
Points o'er the beach his flashing scymitar!
Dark tribes are tossing javelins from afar,
Hands waving banners o'er each battlement,
Decks, with their serried guns, array'd to bar
The promised aid: but hark! a shout is sent
Up from the noble barks!—the Moslem line is rent!

XXIV.

On, on through rushing flame, and arrowy shower,
The welcome prows have cleft their rapid way;
And, with the shadows of the vesper hour,
Furl'd their white sails, and anchor'd in the bay.
Then were the streets with song and torch-fire gay,
Then the Greek wines flow'd mantling in the light
Of festal halls—and there was joy!—the ray
Of dying eyes, a moment wildly bright,
The sunset of the soul, ere lost to mortal sight!

XXV.

For vain that feeble succour! Day by day
Th' imperial towers are crumbling, and the sweep
Of the vast engines, in their ceaseless play,
Comes powerful, as when Heaven unbinds the deep!
—Man's heart is mightier than the castled steep,
Yet will it sink when earthly hope is fled;
Man's thoughts work darkly in such hours, and sleep
Flies far; and in *their* mien, the walls who tread,
Things by the brave untold, may fearfully be read!

XXVI.

It was a sad and solemn task, to hold
Their midnight-watch on that beleaguer'd wall!
As the sea-wave beneath the bastions roll'd,
A sound of fate was in its rise and fall;
The heavy clouds were as an empire's pall,
The giant-shadows of each tower and fane
Lay like the grave's; a low mysterious call
Breathed in the wind, and, from the tented plain,
A voice of omens rose with each wild martial strain.

XXVII.

For they might catch the Arab chargers neighing,
The Thracian drum, the Tartar's drowsy song;
Might almost hear the soldan's banner swaying,
The watch-word mutter'd in some eastern tongue.
Then flash'd the gun's terrific light along
The marble streets, all stillness—not repose;
And boding thoughts came o'er them, dark and strong;

For heaven, earth, air, speak auguries to those
Who see their number'd hours fast pressing to the close.

XXVIII.
But strength is from the mightiest! There is one
Still in the breach, and on the rampart seen,
Whose cheek shows paler with each morning sun,
And tells in silence, how the night hath been,
In kingly halls, a vigil : yet serene
The ray set deep within his thoughtful eye ;
And there is that in his collected mien,
To which the hearts of noble men reply,
With fires, partaking not this frame's mortality !

XXIX.
Yes ! call it not of lofty minds the fate
To pass o'er earth in brightness, but alone ;
High power was made their birthright, to create
A thousand thoughts responsive to their own !
A thousand echoes of their spirit's tone
Start into life, where'er their path may be,
Still following fast ; as when the wind hath blown
O'er Indian groves,[7] a wanderer wild and free,
Kindling and bearing flames afar from tree to tree !

XXX.
And it is thus with thee ! thy lot is cast
On evil days, thou Cæsar ! yet the few
That set their generous bosom'to the blast
Which rocks thy throne—the fearless and the true,
Bear hearts wherein thy glance can still renew
The free devotion of the years gone by,
When from bright dreams th' ascendant Roman drew
Enduring strength ! States vanish—ages fly—
But leave one task unchanged—to suffer and to die !

XXXI.
These are our nature's heritage. But thou,
The crown'd with empire ! thou wert call'd to share
A cup more bitter. On thy fever'd brow
The semblance of that buoyant hope to wear,
Which long had pass'd away ; alone to bear
The rush and pressure of dark thoughts, that came
As a strong billow in their weight of care ;
And, with all this, to smile ! for earth-born fame
These are stern conflicts, yet they pass, unknown to fav.

XXXII.
Her glance is on the triumph, on the field,
On the red scaffold ; and where'er, in sight
Of human eyes, the human soul is steel'd
To deeds that seem as of immortal might,

    Yet are proud nature's! But her meteor-light
Can pierce no depths, no clouds; it falls not where
In silence, and in secret, and in night,
The noble heart doth wrestle with despair,
And rise more strong than death from its unwitness'd prayer.

XXXIII.
Men have been firm in battle: they have stood
With a prevailing hope on ravaged plains,
And won the birthright of their hearths with blood,
And died rejoicing, 'midst their ancient fanes,
That so their children, undefiled with chains,
Might worship there in peace. But they that stand
When not a beacon o'er the wave remains,
Link'd but to perish with a ruin'd land,
Where Freedom dies with them—call *these* a martyr-band!

XXXIV.
But the world heeds them not. Or if, perchance,
Upon their strife it bend a careless eye,
It is but as the Roman's stoic glance
Fell on that stage where man's last agony
Was made *his* sport, who, knowing *one* must die,
Reck'd not *which* champion; but prepared the strain,
And bound the bloody wreath of victory,
To greet the conquerer; while, with calm disdain,
The vanquish'd proudly met the doom he met in vain.

XXXV.
The hour of Fate comes on! and it is fraught
With *this* of Liberty, that now the need
Is past to veil the brow of anxious thought,
And clothe the heart, which still beneath must bleed,
With Hope's fair-seeming drapery. We are freed
From tasks like these by misery; one alone
Is left the brave, and rest shall be thy meed,
Prince, watcher, wearied-one! when thou hast shown
How brief the cloudy space which parts the grave and throne.

XXXVI.
The signs are full. They are not in the sky,
Nor in the many voices of the air,
Nor the swift clouds. No fiery hosts on high
Toss their wild spears: no meteor-banners glare,
No comet fiercely shakes its blazing hair;
And yet the signs are full: too truely seen
In the thinn'd ramparts, in the pale despair
Which lends one language to a people's mien,
And in the ruin'd heaps where walls and towers have been!

XXXVII.
It is a night of beauty: such a night
As, from the sparry grot or laurel shade,

Or wave in marble cavern rippling bright,
Might woo the nymphs of Grecian fount and glade
To sport beneath its moonbeams, which pervade
Their forest-haunts ; a night to rove alone
Where the young leaves by vernal winds are sway'd,
And the reeds whisper, with a dreamy tone
Of melody, that seems to breathe from worlds unknown.

XXXVIII.
A night, to call from green Elysium's bowers
The shades of elder bards ; a night, to hold
Unseen communion with th' inspiring powers
That made deep groves their dwelling-place of old ;
A night, for mourners o'er the hallow'd mould,
To strew sweet flowers ; for revellers to fill
And wreath the cup ; for sorrows to be told
Which love ha' 'herish'd long—vain thoughts! be still!
It is a night of fa   amp'd with Almighty Will!

XXXIX.
It *should* come sweeping in the storm, and rending
The ancient summits in its dread career!
And with vast billows wrathfully contending,
And with dark clouds o'ershadowing every sphere!
But He, whose footstep shakes the earth with fear,
Passing to lay the sovereign cities low
Alike in His omnipotence is near,
When the soft winds o'er spring's green pathway blow,
And when His thunders cleave the monarch-mountain's brow.

XL.
The heavens in still magnificence look down
On the hush'd Bosphorus, whose ocean stream
Sleeps, with its paler stars : the snowy crown
Of far Olympus,[8] in the moonlight-gleam
Towers radiantly, as when the Pagan's dream
Throng'd it with gods, and bent th' adoring knee !
—But that is past—and now the One Supreme
Fills not alone *those* haunts ; but ear'h, air, sea,
And Time, which presses on, to finish his decree.

XLI.
Olympus, Ida, Delphi ! ye, the thrones
And temples of a visionary might,
Brooding in clouds above your forest-zones,
And mantling thence the realms beneath with night.
Ye have look'd down on battles ! Fear, and Flight,
And arm'd Revenge, all hurrying past below !
But there is yet a more appalling sight
For earth prepared, than e'er, with tranquil brow,
Ye gazed or from your world of solitude and snow !

XLII.

Last night a sound was in the Moslem camp,
And Asia's hills re-echoed to a cry
Of savage mirth!—Wild horn, and war-steeds' tramp,
Blent with the shout of barbarous revelry,
The clash of desert-spears! Last night the sky
A hue of menace and of wrath put on,
Caught from red watch-fires, blazing far and high,
And countless, as the flames, in ages gone,
Streaming to heaven's bright queen from shadowy Lebanon!

XLIII.

But all is stillness now. May this be sleep
Which wraps those eastern thousands? Yes perchance
Along yon moonlit shore and dark-blue deep,
Bright are their visions with the Houri's glance,
And they behold the sparkling fountains, once
Beneath the bowers of paradise, that shed
Rich odors o'er the faithful; but the lance,
The bow, the spear, now round the slumberers spread,
Ere Fate fulfil such dreams, must rest beside the dead.

XLIV.

May this be sleep, this hush?—A sleepless eye
Doth hold its vigil 'midst that dusky race!
One that would scan th' abyss of destiny,
E'en now is gazing on the skies, to trace,
In those bright worlds, the burning isles of space,
Fate's mystic pathway: they the while, serene,
Walk in their beauty; but Mohammed's face
Kindles beneath their aspect,[9] and his mien,
All fired with stormy joy, by that soft light is seen.

XLV.

Oh! wild presumption of a conqueror's dream,
To gaze on those pure altar-fires, enshrined
In depths of blue infinitude, and deem
They shine to guide the spoiler of mankind
O'er fields of blood!—But with the restless mind
It hath been ever thus! and they that weep
For worlds to conquer, o'er the bounds assign'd
To human search, in daring pride would sweep,
As o'er the trampled dust wherein they soon must sleep.

XLVI.

But ye! that beam'd on Fate's tremendous night,
When the storm burst o'er golden Babylon,
And ye, that sparkled with your wonted light
O'er burning Salem, by the Roman won;
And ye, that calmly view'd the slaughter done
In Rome's own streets, when Alaric's trumpet-blast
Rung through the Capitol; bright spheres! roll on!

Still bright, though empires fall; and bid man cast
His humbled eyes to earth, and commune with the past

XLVII.
For it hath mighty lessons! from the tomb,
And from the ruins of the tomb, and where,
'Midst the wreck'd cities in the desert's gloom,
All tameless creatures make their savage lair,
Thence comes its voice, that shakes the midnight air,
And calls up clouds to dim the laughing day,
And thrills the soul;—yet bids us not despair,
But make one rock our shelter and our stay,
Beneath whose shade all else is passing to decay!

XLVIII.
The hours move on. I see a wavering gleam
O'er the hush'd waters tremulously fall,
Pour'd from the Cæsar's palace: now the beam
Of many lamps is brightening in the hall,
And from its long arcades and pillars tall
Soft graceful shadows undulating lie
On the wave's heaving bosom, and recall
A thought of Venice, with her moonlight sky,
And festal seas and domes, and fairy pageantry.

XLIX.
But from that dwelling floats no mirthful sound!
The swell of flute and Grecian lyre no more,
Wafting an atmosphere of music round,
Tells the hush'd seaman, gliding past the shore,
How monarchs revel there!—Its feasts are o'er—
Why gleam the lights along its colonnade?
—I see a train of guests in silence pour
Through its long avenues of terraced shade,
Whose stately founts and bowers for joy alone were made!

L.
In silence, and in arms!—With helm—with sword—
These are no marriage-garments!—Yet e'en now
Thy nuptial feast should grace the regal board,
Thy Georgian bride should wreath her lovely brow
With an imperial diadem![10]—but thou,
O fated prince! art call'd, and these with thee,
To darker scenes; and thou hast learn'd to bow
Thine Eastern sceptre to the dread decree,
And count it joy enough to perish—being free!

LI.
On through long vestibules, with solemn tread,
As men, that in some time of fear and wo,
Bear darkly to their rest the noble dead,
O'er whom by day their sorrows may not flow,
The warriors pass: their measured steps are slow,

And hollow echoes fill the marble halls,
Whose long-drawn vistas open as they go
In desolate pomp; and from the pictured walls,
Sad seems the light itself which on their armour falls!

LII.
And they have reach'd a gorgeous chamber, bright
With all we dream of splendor; yet a gloom
Seems gather'd o'er it to the boding sight,
A shadow that anticipates the tomb!
Still from its fretted roof the lamps illume
A purple canopy, a golden throne;
But it is empty!—Hath the stroke of doom
Fallen there already?—Where is He, the One,
Born that high seat to fill, supremely and alone?

LIII.
Oh! there are times whose pressure doth efface
Earth's vain distinctions!—when the storm beats loud,
When the strong towers are tottering to their base,
And the streets rock,—who mingle in the crowd?
—Peasant and chief, the lowly and the proud,
Are in that throng!—Yes, life hath many an hour
Which makes us kindred, by one chast'ning bow'd,
And feeling but, as from the storm we cower,
What shrinking weakness feels before unbounded power!

LIV.
Yet then that power, whose dwelling is on high,
Its loftiest marvels doth reveal, and speak,
In the deep human heart more gloriously,
Than in the bursting thunder!—Thence the weak,
They that seem'd form'd, as flower-stems, but to break
With the first wind, have risen to deeds, whose name
Still calls up thoughts that mantle to the cheek,
And thrill the pulse!—Ay, strength no pangs could tame
Hath look'd from woman's eye upon the sword and flame!

LV.
And this is of such hours!—That throne is void,
And its lord comes uncrown'd. Behold him stand,
With a calm brow, where woes have not destroy'd
The Greek's heroic beauty, 'midst his band,
The gather'd virtue of a sinking land.
Alas! how scanty!—Now is cast aside
All form of princely state; each noble hand
Is press'd by turns in his: for earthly pride
There is no room in hearts where earthly hope hath died!

LVI.
A moment's hush—and then he speaks—he speaks!
But not of hope! *that* dream hath long ago gone by:

His words are full of memory—as he seeks,
By the strong names of Rome and Liberty,
Which yet are living powers that fire the eye,
And rouse the heart of manhood ; and by all
The sad yet grand remembrances that lie
 Deep with earth's buried heroes ; to recall
The soul of other years, if but to grace their fall!

LVII.

His words are full of faith !—And thoughts, more high
Than Rome e'er knew, now fill his glance with light ;
Thoughts which give nobler lessons how to die
Than e'er were drawn from Nature's haughty might!
And to that eye, with all the spirit bright,
Have theirs replied in tears, which may not shame
The bravest in such moments !—'Tis a sight
To make all earthly splendors cold and tame,
—That generous burst of soul, with its electric flame!

LVIII.

They weep—those champions of the Cross—they weep,
Yet vow themselves to death !—Ay, 'midst that train
Are martyrs, privileged in tears to steep
Their lofty sacrifice !—The pang is vain,
And yet its gush of sorrow shall not stain
A warrior's sword.—Those men are strangers here—[11]
The homes they never may behold again,
Lie far away, with all things blest and dear,
On laughing shores, to which their barks no more shall steer !

LIX.

Know'st thou the land where bloom the orange bowers? [12]
Where, through dark foliage, gleam the citron's dyes?
—It is their own. They see their fathers' towers,
'Midst its Hesperian groves in sunlight rise :
They meet in soul, the bright Italian eyes,
Which long and vainly shall explore the main
For their white sails' return : the melodies
Of that sweet land are floating o'er their brain—
Oh ! what a crowded world one moment may contain !

LX.

Such moments come to thousands !—few may die
Amidst their native shades. The young, the brave,
The beautiful, whose gladdening voice and eye
Made summer in a parent's heart, and gave
Light to their peopled homes ; o'er land and wave
Are scatter'd fast and far, as rose-leaves fall
From the deserted stem. They find a grave
Far from the shadow of th' ancestral hall,
A lonely bed is theirs, whose smiles were hope to all!

LXI.

But life flows on, and bears us with its tide,
Nor may we, lingering, by the slumberers dwell,
Though they were those once blooming at our side
In youth's gay home!—Away! what sound's deep swell
Comes on the wind?—It is an empire's knell,
Slow, soft, majestic, pealing through the night!
For the last time speaks forth the solemn bell,
Which calls the Christians to their holiest rite,
With a funereal voice of solitary might.

LXII.

Again, and yet again!—A startling power
In sounds like these lives ever; for they beat
Full on remembrance, each eventful hour,
Chequering life's crowded path. They fill the air
When conquerors pass, and fearful cities wear
A mien like joy's; and when young brides are led
From their paternal homes; and when the glare
Of burning streets on midnight's cloud waves red,
And when the silent house receives its guest—the dead.[13]

LXIII.

But to those tones what thrilling soul was given,
On that last night of empire!—As a spell
Whereby the life-blood to its source is driven,
On the chill'd heart of multitudes they fell.
Each cadence seem'd a prophecy, to tell
Of sceptres passing from their line away,
An angel-watcher's long and sad farewell,
The requiem of a faith's departing sway,
A throne's, a nation's dirge, a wail for earth's decay.

LXIV.

Again, and yet again!—from yon high dome
Still the slow peal comes awfully; and they
Who never more, to rest in mortal home,
Shall throw the breastplate off at fall of day,
Th' imperial band, in close and arm'd array,
As men that from the sword must part no more,
Take through the midnight streets their silent way,
Within their ancient temple to adore,
Ere yet its thousand years of Christian pomp are o'er.

LXV.

It is the hour of sleep: yet few the eyes
O'er which forgetfulness her balm hath shed
In the beleaguer'd city. Stillness lies
With moonlight, o'er the hills and waters spread,
But not the less, with signs and sounds of dread,
The time speeds on. No voice is raised to greet
The last brave Constantine; and yet the tread

Of many steps is in the echoing street,
And pressure of pale crowds, scarce conscious why they meet

LXVI.
Their homes are luxury's yet: why pour they thence
With a dim terror in each restless eye?
Hath the dread car which bears the pestilence,
In darkness, with its heavy wheels roll'd by,
And rock'd their palaces, as if on high
The whirlwind pass'd?—From couch and joyous board
Hath the fierce phantom beckon'd them to die?[14]
—No!—what are these?—for them a cup is pour'd [sword.
More dark with wrath;—*Man* comes—the spoiler and the

LXVII.
Still, as the monarch and his chieftains pass
Through those pale throngs, the streaming torchlight throws
On some wild form, amidst the living mass,
Hues, deeply red like lava's, which disclose
What countless shapes are worn by mortal woes!
Lips bloodless, quivering limbs, hands clasp'd in prayer,
Starts, tremblings, hurryings, tears; all outward shows
Betokening inward agonies, were there:
—Greeks! Romans! all but such as image brave despair'

LXVIII.
But high above that scene, in bright repose,
And beauty borrowing from the torches' gleams
A mien of life, yet where no life-blood flows,
But all instinct with loftier being seems
Pale, grand, colossal; lo! th' embodied dreams
Of yore!—Gods, heroes, bards, in marble wrought,
Look down, as powers, upon the wild extremes
Of mortal passion!—Yet 'twas man that caught,
And in each glorious form enshrined immortal thought!

LXIX.
Stood ye not thus amidst the streets of Rome?
That Rome which witness'd, in her sceptred days,
So much of noble death?—When shrine and dome,
'Midst clouds of incense, rung with choral lays,
As the long triumph pass'd, with all its blaze
Of regal spoil, were yet not proudly borne,
O sovereign forms! cencent'ring all the rays
Of the soul's lightnings?—did ye not adorn
The pomp which earth stood still to gaze on, and to mourn?

LXX.
Hath it been thus?—Or did ye grace the halls,
Once peopled by the mighty?—Haply there,
In your still grandeur, from the pillar'd walls,
Serene ye smiled on banquets of despair,[15]
Where hopeless courage wrought itself to dare

The stroke of its deliverance, 'midst the glow
Of living wreaths, the sighs of perfumed air,
The sound of lyres, the flower-crown'd goblet's flow:
—Behold again!—high hearts make nobler offerings now!

LXXI.

The stately fane is reach'd—and at its gate
The warriors pause ; on life's tumultuous tide
A stillness falls, while he whom regal state
Hath mark'd from all, to be more sternly tried
By suffering, speaks:—each ruder voice hath died,
While his implores forgiveness!—" If there be
One 'midst your throngs, my people! whom, in pride
Or passion, I have wrong'd ; such pardon, free
As mortals hope from Heaven, accord that man to me!"

LXXII.

By all is silence ; and a gush of tears
Alone replies!—He hath not been of those
Who, fear'd by many, pine in secret fears
Of all ; th' environ'd but by slaves and foes,
To whom day brings not safety, night repose,
For they have *heard the voice cry*, " *Sleep no more!*"
Of them he hath not been, nor such as close
Their hearts to misery, till the time is o'er,
When it speaks low and kneels th' oppressor's throne before!

LXXIII.

He hath been loved—but who may trust the love
Of a degenerate race?—in other mould
Are cast the free and lofty hearts, that prove
Their faith through fiery trials.— Yet behold,
And call him not forsaken!—Thoughts untold
Have lent his aspect calmness, and his tread
Moves firmly to the shrine. What pomps unfold
Within its precincts!—Isles and seas have shed
'Their gorgeous treasures there, around the imperial dead.

LXXIV.

'Tis a proud vision—that most regal pile
Of ancient days!—The lamps are streaming bright
From its rich altar, down each pillar'd aisle,
Whose vista fades in dimness ; but the sight
Is lost in splendors, as the wavering light
Developes, on those walls, the thousand dyes
Of the vein'd marbles, which array their height,
And from yon dome, the lode-star of all eyes,[16]
Pour such an iris-glow as emulates the skies.

LXXV.

But gaze thou not on these ; though heaven's own **hues,**
In their soft clouds and radiant tracery vie ;

Though tints, of sun-born glory, may suffuse
Arch, column, rich mosaic: pass thou by
The stately tombs, where eastern Cæsars lie,
Beneath their trophies; pause not here; for know,
A deeper source of all sublimity
Lives in man's bosom, than the world can show,
In nature or in art—above, around, below.

LXXVI.
Turn thou to mark (though tears may dim thy gaze)
The steel-clad group before yon altar-stone:
Heed not though gems and gold around it blaze;
Those heads unhelm'd, those kneeling forms alone,
Thus bow'd, look glorious here. The light is thrown
Full from the shrine on one, a nation's lord,
A sufferer!—but his task shall soon be done—
E'en now, as Faith's mysterious cup is pour'd,
See to that noble brow, peace, not of earth, restored!

LXXVII.
The rite is o'er. The band of brethren part,
Once—and *but* once—to meet on earth again!
Each, in the strength of a collected heart,
To dare what man may dare—and know 'tis vain!
The rite is o'er: and thou, majestic fane!—
The glory is departed from thy brow!—
Be clothed with dust!—the Christian's farewell strain
Hath died within thy walls; thy cross must bow;
Thy kingly tombs be spoil'd; thy golden shrines laid low!

LXXVIII.
The streets grow still and lonely—and the star,
The last bright lingerer in the path of morn,
Gleams faint; and in the very lap of war,
As if young Hope with twilight's ray were born,
Awhile the city sleeps:—her throngs, o'erworn
With fears and watchings, to their homes retire;
Nor is the balmy air of dayspring torn
With battle-sounds;[17] the winds in sighs expire,
And quiet broods in mists that veil the sunbeam's fire.

LXXIX.
The city sleeps!—ay! on the combat's eve,
And by the scaffold's brink, and 'midst the swell
Of angry seas, hath nature won repreive
Thus from her cares. The brave have slumber'd well,
And e'en the fearful, in their dungeon-cell,
Chain'd between life and death! Such rest be thine,
For conflicts wait thee still!—Yet who can tell
In that brief hour, how much of heaven may shire
Full on thy spirit's dream?—Sleep, weary Constantine!

LXXX.

Doth the blast rise?—the clouded east is red,
As if a storm were gathering; and I hear
What seems like heavy rain-drops, or the tread,
The soft and smother'd step of those that fear
Surprise from ambush'd foes. Hark! yet more near
It comes, a many-toned and mingled sound;
A rustling, as of winds, where boughs are sear,
A rolling, as of wheels that shake the ground
From far; a heavy rush, like seas that burst their bound!

LXXXI.

Wake, wake! They come from sea and shore, ascending
In hosts your ramparts! Arm ye for the day!
Who now may sleep amidst the thunders rending,
Through tower and wall, a path for their array?
Hark how the trumpet cheers them to the prey,
With its wild voice, to which the seas reply,
And the earth rocks beneath their engines' sway,
And the far hills repeat their battle-cry,
Till that fierce tumult seems to shake the vaulted sky!

LXXXII.

They fail not now, the generous band, that long
Have ranged their swords around a falling throne;
Still in those fearless men the walls are strong,
Hearts, such as rescue empires, are their own!
—Shall those high energies be vainly shown?
No! from their towers th' invading tide is driven
Back, like the Red-sea waves, when God had blown
With his strong winds! the dark-brow'd ranks are riven—[18]
Shout, warriors of the cross!—for victory is of Heaven!

LXXXIII

Stand firm!—Again the crescent host is rushing,
And the waves foam, as on the galleys sweep,
With all their fires and darts, though blood is gushing
Fast o'er their sides, as rivers to the deep.
Stand firm!—there yet is hope, th' ascent is steep,
And from on high no shaft descends in vain;
—But those that fall swell up the mangled heap,
In the red moat, the dying and the slain,
And o'er that fearful bridge th' assailants mount again!

LXXXIV.

Oh! the dread mingling, in that awful hour,
Of all terrific sounds!—the savage tone
Of the wild horn, the cannon's peal, the shower
Of hissing darts, the crash of walls o'erthrown,
The deep dull tambour's beat—man's voice alone
Is there unheard! Ye may not catch the cry
Of trampled thousands—prayer, and shriek, and moan,

All drown'd, as that fierce hurricane sweeps by,
But swell the unheeded sum earth pays for victory!

LXXXV.
War-clouds have wrapt the city!—through their dun,
O'erloaded canopy, at times a blaze,
As of an angry storm-presaging sun,
From the Greek fire shoots up;[19] and lightning rays
Flash, from the shock of sabres, through the haze,
And glancing arrows cleave the dusky air!
—Ay! *this* is in the compass of our gaze,—
But fearful things, unknown, untold, are there,
Workings of wrath and death, and anguish, and despair!

LXXXVI.
Woe, shame and woe!—A chief, a warrior flies,
A red-cross champion, bleeding, wild, and pale!
—O God! that nature's passing agonies,
Thus, o'er the spark which dies not, should prevail!
Yes! rend the arrow from thy shatter'd mail,
And stanch the blood-drops, Genoa's fallen son![20]
Fly swifter yet! the javelins pour as hail!
—But there are tortures which thou canst not shun,
The spirit is *their* prey—thy pangs are but begun!

LXXXVII.
Oh, happy in their homes, the noble dead!
The seal is set on their majestic fame;
Earth has drunk deep the generous blood they shed,
Fate has no power to dim their stainless name!
They may not, in one bitter moment, shame
Long glorious years; from many a lofty stem
Fall graceful flowers, and eagle-hearts grow tame,
And stars drop, fading, from the diadem;
But the bright *past* is theirs—there is no change for *them!*

LXXXVIII.
Where art thou, Constantine?—where death is reaping
His sevenfold harvest!—where the stormy light,
Fast as th' artillery's thunderbolts are sweeping,
Throws meteor-bursts o'er battle's noonday-night!
Where the towers rock and crumble from their height,
As to the earthquake, and the engines ply,
Like red Vesuvio: and where human might
Confronts all this, and still brave hearts beat high,
While scymitars ring loud on shivering panoply.

LXXXIX.
Where art thou, Constantine?—where Christian blood
Hath bathed the walls in torrents, and in vain!
Where faith and valor perish in the flood,
Whose billows, rising o'er their bosoms, gain

Dark strength each moment: where the gallant slain
Around the banner of the cross lie strew'd,
Thick as the vine-leaves on the autumnal plain;
Where all, save one high spirit is subdued,
And through the breach press on th' o'erwhelming multitude.

XC.

Now is he battling 'midst a host alone,
As the last cedar stems awhile the sway
Of mountain-storms, whose fury hath o'erthrown
Its forest-brethren in their green array!
And he hath cast his purple robe away,
With its imperial bearings; that his sword
An iron ransom from the chain may pay,
And win, what haply fate may yet accord,
A soldier's death—the all now left an empire's lord!

XCI.

Search for him now where bloodiest lie the files
Which once were men, the faithful and the brave!
Search for him now where loftiest rise the piles
Of shatter'd helms and shields which could not save;
And crests and banners, never more to wave
In the free winds of heaven! He is of those
O'er whom the host may rush, the tempest rave,
And the steeds trample, and the spearmen close,
Yet wake them not!—so deep their long and last repose!

XCII.

Woe to the vanquish'd!—thus it hath been still
Since Time's first march!—Hark, hark, a people's cry!
Ay, now the conquerors in the streets fulfil
Their task of wrath! In vain the victims fly;
Hark! now each piercing tone af agony
Blends in the city's shriek! The lot is cast.
Slaves, 'twas your *choice* thus, rather thus, to die,
Than where the warrior's blood flows warm and fast,
And roused and mighty hearts beat proudly to the last!

XCIII.

Oh! well doth freedom battle! Men have made,
E'en 'midst their blazing roofs, a noble stand,
And on the floors, where once their children play'd,
And by the hearths, round which their household band
At evening met; ay, struggling hand to hand,
Within the very chambers of their sleep,
There have they taught the spoilers of the land,
In chainless hearts what fiery strength lies deep,
To guard free homes!—but ye!—kneel, tremblers! kneel, and
weep!

XCIV.

'Tis eve—the storm hath died, the valiant rest
Low on their shields; the day's fierce work is done,

And blood-stain'd seas, and burning towers attest
Its fearful deeds. An empire's race is run!
Sad, 'midst his glory, looks the parting sun
Upon the captive city. Hark! a swell
(Meet to proclaim barbaric war-fields won)
Of fierce triumphal sounds, that wildly tell
The Soldan comes within the Cæsars' halls to dwell

XCV.

Yes! with the peal of cymbal and of gong,
He comes,—the Moslem treads those ancient halls!
But all is stillness there, as death had long
Been lord alone within those gorgeous walls.
And half that silence of the grave appals
The conqueror's heart. Ay, thus with triumph's hour,
Still comes the boding whisper, which recalls
A thought of those impervious clouds that lower
O'er grandeur's path, a sense of some far mightier Power!

XCVI.

" The owl upon Afrasiab's towers hath sung
Her watch-song,[21] and around th' imperial throne
The spider weaves his web!" So darkly hung
That verse of omen, as a prophet's tone,
O'er his flush'd spirit. Years on years have flown
To prove its truth: kings pile their domes in air,
That the coil'd snake may bask on sculptured stone,
And nations clear the forest, to prepare
For the wild fox and wolf more stately dwellings there!

XCVII.

But thou! that on thy ramparts proudly dying,
As a crown'd leader in such hour should die,
Upon thy pyre of shiver'd spears art lying,
With the heavens o'er thee for a canopy,
And banners for thy shroud! No tear, no sigh,
Shall mingle with thy dirge; for thou art now
Beyond vicissitude! Lo! rear'd on high,
The Crescent blazes, while the Cross must bow;
But where no change can reach, there, Constantine, art thou

XCVIII.

" After life's fitful fever thou sleep'st well!
We may not mourn thee! Sceptred chiefs, from whom!
The earth received her destiny, and fell
Before them trembling—to a sterner doom
Have oft been call'd. For them the dungeon's gloom,
With its cold starless midnight, hath been made
More fearful darkness, where, as in a tomb,
Without a tomb's repose, the chain hath weigh'd
Their very soul to dust, with each high power decay'd.

XCIX.
Or in the eye of thousands they have stood,
To meet the stroke of death; but not like thee!
From bonds and scaffolds hath appeal'd *their* blood,
But thou didst fall unfetter'd, arm'd, and free,
And kingly to the last!—And if it be,
That, from the viewless world, whose marvels none
Return to tell, a spirit's eye can see
The things of earth; still may'st thou hail the sun,
Which o'er thy land shall dawn, when freedom's fight is won!

C.
And the hour comes, in storm! A light is glancing
Far through the forest-god's Arcadian shades!
—'Tis not the moonbeam, tremulously dancing,
Where lone Alpheus bathes his haunted glades;
A murmur, gathering power, the air pervades,
Round dark Cithæron, and by Delphi's steep;
—'Tis not the song and lyre of Grecian maids,
Nor pastoral reed that lulls the vales to sleep,
Nor yet the rustling pines, nor yet the sounding deep!

CI.
Arms glitter on the mountains, which, of old,
Awoke to freedom's first heroic strain,
And by the streams, once crimson, as they roll'd
The Persian helm and standard to the main;
And the blue waves of Salamis again
Thrill to the trumpet; and the tombs reply,
With their ten thousand echoes, from each plain,
Far as Platæa's, where the mighty lie,
Who crown'd so proudly there the bowl of liberty!"[22]

CII.
Bright land, with glory mantled o'er by song!
Land of the vision-peopled hills, and streams,
And fountains, whose deserted banks along,
Still the soft air with inspiration teems;
Land of the graves, whose dwellers shall be themes
To verse for ever; and of ruin'd shrines,
That scarce look desolate beneath such beams,
As bathe in gold thine ancient rocks and pines?
—When shall thy sons repose in peace beneath their vines?

CIII.
Thou wert not made for bonds, nor shame, nor fear!
—Do the hoar oaks and dark-green laurels wave
O'er Mantinea's earth?—doth Pindus rear
His snows, the sunbeam, and the storm to brave?
And is there yet on Marathon a grave?
And doth Eurotas lead his silvery line
By Sparta's ruins?—And shall man, a slave,

Bow'd to the dust, amid such scenes repine?
—If e'er a soil was mark'd for freedom's step—'tis thine!

CIV.

Wash from that soil the stains, with battle-showers!
—Beneath Sophia's dome the Moslem prays,
The crescent gleams amidst the olive-bowers,
In the Comneni's halls the Tartar sways:[23]
But not for long!—the spirit of those days,
When the three hundred made their funeral pile
Of Asia's dead, is kindling, like the rays
Of thy rejoicing sun, when first his smile
Warms the Parnassian rock, and gilds the Delian isle.

CV.

If then 'tis given thee to arise in might,
Trampling the scourge, and dashing down the chain,
Pure be thy triumphs, as thy name is bright!
The cross of victory should not know a stain!
So may that faith once more supremely reign,
Through which we lift our spirits from the dust!
And deem not, e'en when virtue dies in vain,
She dies forsaken; but repose our trust
On Him whose ways are dark, unsearchable—but just.

NOTES.

Note 1, page 352, line 26.
While Ismael's bow, &c.

The army of Mohammed the Second, at the siege of Constantinople, was thronged with fanatics of all sects and nations, who were not enrolled amongst the regular troops. The Sultan himself marched upon the city from Adrianople; but his army must have been principally collected in the Asiatic provinces, which he had previously visited.

Note 2, page 353, line 30.
Away! bring wine, bring odors, &c.

"Huc vina, et unguenta, et nimium breves
Flores amœnæ ferre jube rosæ."
Hor. lib. ii. od. 3.

Note 3, page 354, line 11.
From the Seven Towers, &c.

The castle of the Seven Towers is mentioned in the Byzantine history, as early as the sixth century of the Christian era, as an edifice which contributed materially to the defence of Constantinople; and it was the principal bulwark of the town on the coast of the Propontis, in the later periods of the empire. For a description of this building, see POUQUEVILLE'S *Travels*.

Note 4, page 354, line 21.
With its long march of sceptred imag'ry.
An allusion to the Roman custom of carrying in procession, at the unerals of their great men, the images of their ancestors.

Note 5, page 354, line 36.
The Roman cast his glittering mail away.
The following was the ceremony of consecration with which Decius devoted himself in battle:—He was ordered by Valerius, the Pontifex Maximus, to quit his military habit, and put on the robe he wore in the senate. Valerius then covered his head with a veil, commanded him to put forth his hand under his robe to his chin, and, standing with both feet upon a javelin, to repeat these words: —" O Janus, Jupiter, Mars, Romulus, Bellona! and ye, Lares and Novensiles! All ye heroes who dwell in heaven! and all ye gods who rule over us and our enemies—especially ye gods of hell!—I honor you, invoke you, and humbly entreat you to prosper the arms of the Romans, and to transfer all fear and terror from them to their enemies; and I do for the safety of the Roman people, and their legions, devote myself, and with myself the army and auxiliaries of the enemy, to the infernal gods, and the goddess of the earth." Decius then, girding his robe around him, mounted his horse, and rode full speed into the thickest of the enemy's battalions. The Latins were, for a while, thunderstruck at this spectacle; but at length recovering themselves, they discharged a shower of darts, under which the Consul fell.

Note 6, page 355, line 36.
Shout, ye seven hills! Lo! Christian pennons streaming
Red o'er the waters.
See Gibbon's animated description of the arrival of five Christian ships, with men and provisions, for the succor of the besieged, not many days before the fall of Constantinople.—*Decline and Fall of the Roman Empire*, vol. xii. p. 215.

Note 7, page 357, line 19.
As when the wind hath blown
O'er Indian groves, &c.
The summits of the lofty rocks in the Carnatic, particularly about the Ghauts, are sometimes covered with the bamboo tree, which grows in thick clumps, and is of such uncommon aridity, that in the sultry season of the year the friction occasioned by a strong dry wind will literally produce sparks of fire, which frequently setting the woods in a blaze, exhibit to the spectator stationed in a valley surrounded by rocks, a magnificent though imperfect circle of fire.—*Notes to* KINDERSLEY'S *Specimens of Hindoo Literature.*

Note 8, page 359, line 29.
—— *The snowy crown*
Of far Olympus, &c.
Those who steer their westward course through the middle of the Propontis, may at once descry the high lands of Thrace and Bithynia, and never lose sight of the lofty summit of Mount Olympus, covered with eternal snows.—*Decline and Fall, &c.*, vol. iii. p. 8.

Note 9, page 360, line 26.
——— *Mohammed's face*
Kindles beneath their aspect, &c.

Mohammed II. was greatly addicted to the study of astrology. His calculations in this science led him to fix upon the morning of the 29th of May as the fortunate hour for a general attack upon the city.

Note 10, page 361, line 34.
Thy Georgian bride, &c

Constantine Palæologus was betrothed to a Georgian princess ; and the very spring which witnessed the fall of Constantinople had been fixed upon as the time for conveying the imperial bride to that city.

Note 11, page 363, line 22.
Those men are strangers here.

Many of the adherents of Constantine, in his last noble stand for the liberties, or rather the honor, of a falling empire, were foreigners, and chiefly Italians.

Note 12, page 363, line 26.
Know'st thou the land, &c.

This and the next line are an almost literal translation from a beautiful song of Goethe's :—

"Kennst du das land, wo die zitronen blühn,
Mit dunkeln laub die gold orangen glühn ?" &c.

Note 13, page 364, line 18.

The idea expressed in this stanzas is beautifully amplified in Schiller's poem, " Das Lied der Glocke."

Note 14, page 365, line 9.
Hath the fierce phantom, &c.

It is said to be a Greek superstition that the plague is announced by the heavy rolling of an invisible chariot, heard in the streets at midnight ; and also by the appearance of a gigantic spectre, who summons the devoted person by name.

Note 15, page 365, line 42.
Ye smiled on banquets of despair.

Many instances of such banquets, given and shared by persons resolved upon death, might be adduced from ancient history. That of Vibius Virius, at Capua, is amongst the most memorable.

Note 16, page 366, line 39.
Yon dome, the lode-star of all eyes.

For a minute description of the marbles, jaspers, and porphyries employed in the construction of St. Sophia, see *The Decline and Fall,* &c., vol. vii. page 120.

Note 17, page 367, line 33.
Nor is the balmy air of dayspring torn
With battle-sounds, &c.

The assault of the city took place at daybreak, and the Turks were strictly enjoined to advance in silence, which had also been commanded, on pain of death, during the preceding night. This circumstance is finely alluded to by Miss Baillie, in her tragedy of *Constantine Palæologus*:

"Silent shall be the march ; nor drum, nor trump,
Nor clash of arms, shall to the watchful foe

Our near approach betray: silent and soft,
As the pard's velvet foot on Lybia's sands,
Slow stealing with crouch'd shoulders on her prey."
Constantine Palæologus, act. iv.

"The march and labor of thousands" must, however, as Gibbon observes, "have inevitably produced a strange confusion of discordant clamors, which reached the ears of the watchmen on the towers."

Note 18, page, 368 line 26,
The dark-brow'd ranks are riven.

"After a conflict of two hours, the Greeks still maintained and preserved their advantage," says Gibbon. The strenuous exertions of the janizaries first turned the fortune of the day.

Note 19, page 369, line 6.
From the Greek fire shoots up, &c.

"A circumstance that distinguishes the siege of Constantinople is the union of the ancient and modern artillery. The bullet and the battering-ram were directed against the same wall; nor had the discovery of gun-powder superseded the use of the liquid and inextinguishable fire."—*Decline and Fall, &c.*, vol. xii. page 213.

Note 20, page 369, line 17.
And stanch the blood-drops, Genoa's fallen son!

"The immediate loss of Constantinople may be ascribed to the bullet, or arrow, which pierced the gauntlet of John Justiniani (a Genoese chief.) The sight of his blood, and exquisite pain, appalled the courage of the chief, whose arms and counsels were the firmest rampart of the city."—*Decline and Fall, &c.*, vol. xii. page 229.

Note 21, page 371, line 18.
"*The owl upon Afrasiab's towers hath sung*
Her watch-song," *&c.*

Mohammed II., on entering, after his victory, the palace of the Byzantine emperors, was strongly impressed with the silence and desolation which reigned within its precincts. "A melancholy reflection on the vicissitudes of human greatness forced itself on his mind, and he repeated an elegant distich of Persian poetry; 'The spider has wove his web in the imperial palace, and the owl bath sung her watch-song on the towers of Afrasiab.'"—*Decline and Fall &c.*, vol. xii. page 240.

Note 22, page 372, line 27.
The bowl of liberty.

One of the ceremonies by which the battle of Platæa was annually commemorated was, to crown with wine a cup called the *Bowl of Liberty*, which was afterwards poured forth in libation.

Note 23, page 373, line 6.
In the Comneni's halls the Tartar sways.

The Comneni were amongst the most distinguished of the families who filled the Byzantine throne in the declining years of the eastern empire.

GREEK SONGS.

I.—THE STORM OF DELPHI.*

Far through the Delphian shades
　　An Eastern trumpet rung!
And the startled eagle rush'd on high,
With a sounding flight through the fiery sky;
　　And banners, o'er the shadowy glades,
　　　To the sweeping winds were flung.

Banners, with deep-red gold
　　All waving as a flame,
And a fitful glance from the bright spear-head
On the dim wood-paths of the mountain shed,
　　And a peal of Asia's war-notes told
　　　That in arms the Persian came.

He came with starry gems
　　On his quiver and his crest;
With starry gems, at whose heart the day
Of the cloudless orient burning lay,
　　And they cast a gleam on the laurel-stems.
　　　As onward his thousands press'd.

But a gloom fell o'er their way,
　　And a heavy moan went by!
A moan, yet not like the wind's low swell,
When its voice grows wild amidst cave and dell,
　　But a mortal murmur of dismay,
　　　Or a warrior's dying sigh!

A gloom fell o'er their way!
　　'Twas not the shadow cast
By the dark pine boughs, as they cross'd the blue
Of the Grecian heavens with their solemn hue;—
　　The air was fill'd with a mightier sway—
　　　But on the spearmen pass'd!

And hollow to their tread,
　　Came the echoes of the ground,

---

* See the account cited from Herodotus, in Mitford's *Greece.*

And banners droop'd, as with dews o'erborne,
And the wailing blast of the battle horn
  Had an alter'd cadence, dull and dead,
    Of strange foreboding sound.

But they blew a louder strain,
  When the steep defiles were pass'd!
And afar the crown'd Parnassus rose,
To shine through heaven with his radiant snows,
  And in golden light the Delphian fane
    Before them stood at last!

In golden light it stood,
  'Midst the laurels gleaming lone,
For the Sun-god yet, with a lovely smile,
O'er its graceful pillars look'd awhile.
  Through the stormy shade on cliff and wood
    Grew deep round its mountain-throne.

And the Persians gave a shout!
  But the marble-walls replied,
With a clash of steel and a sullen roar
Like heavy wheels on the ocean-shore,
  And a savage trumpet's note peal'd out,
    Till their hearts for terror died!

On the armor of the god,
  Then a viewless hand was laid;
There were helm and spear, with a clanging din,
And corslet brought from the shrine within,
  From the inmost shrine of the dread abode,
    And before its front array'd.

And a sudden silence fell
  Through the dim and loaded air!
On the wild-bird's wing, and the myrtle spray,
And the very founts, in their silvery way,
  With a weight of sleep came down the spell,
    Till man grew breathless there.

But the pause was broken soon!
  'Twas not by song or lyre;
For the Delphian maids had left their bowers,
And the hearths were lone in the city's towers,
  But there burst a sound through the misty noon—
    That battle-noon of fire!

It burst forth from earth and heaven!
  It roll'd from crag and cloud!
For a moment of the mountain-blast,
With a thousand stormy voices pass'd,
  And the purple gloom of the sky was riven,
    When the thunder peal'd aloud.

And the lightnings in their play
　　Flash'd forth, like javelins thrown;
Like sun-darts wing'd from the silver bow,
They smote the spear and the turban'd brow,
　　And the bright gems flew from the crests like spray,
　　And the banners were struck down!

And the massy oak-boughs crash'd
　　To the fire-bolts from on high,
And the forest lent its billowy roar,
While the glorious tempest onward bore,
　　And lit the streams, as they foam'd and dash'd,
　　With the fierce rain sweeping by.

Then rush'd the Delphian men
　　On the pale and scatter'd host;
Like the joyous burst of a flashing wave,
They rush'd from the dim Corycian cave,
　　And the singing blast o'er wood and glen
　　Roll'd on, with the spears they toss'd.

There were cries of wild dismay,
　　There were shouts of warrior glee,
There were savage sounds of the tempest's mirth,
That shook the realm of their eagle-birth;
　　But the mount of song, when they died away,
　　Still rose, with its temple, free!

And the Pæan swell'd erelong,
　　Io Pæan! from the fane;
Io Pæan! for the war-array,
On the crown'd Parnassus riven that day!
　　—Thou shalt rise *as* free, thou mount of song!
　　With thy bounding streams again.

II.—THE BOWL OF LIBERTY.*

BEFORE the fiery sun,
The sun that looks on Greece with cloudless eye,
In the free air, and on the war-field won,
Our fathers crown'd the Bowl of Liberty.

　　Amidst the tombs they stood,
The tombs of heroes! with the solemn skies,
And the wide plain around, where patriot-blood
Had steep'd the soil in hues of sacrifice.

* This and the following piece appeared originally in the *New Monthly Magazine.*

They call'd the glorious dead,
In the strong faith which brings the viewless nigh,
And pour'd rich odors o'er their battle-bed,
And bade them to their rite of Liberty.

They call'd them from the shades,
The golden-fruited shades, where minstrels tell
How softer light th' immortal clime pervades,
And music floats o'er meads of Asphodel.

Then fast the bright-red wine*
Flow'd to *their* names who taught the world to die
And made the land's green turf a living shrine,
Meet for the wreath and Bowl of Liberty.

So the rejoicing earth
Took from her vines again the blood she gave,
And richer flowers to deck the tomb drew birth
From the free soil thus hallow'd to the brave.

We have the battle-fields,
The tombs, the names, the blue majestic sky,
We have the founts the purple vintage yields;
When shall *we* crown the Bowl of Liberty?

III.—THE VOICE OF SCIO.

A voice from Scio's isle—
A voice of song, a voice of old
Swept far as cloud or billow roll'd,
And earth was hush'd the while—

The souls of nations woke!
Where lies the land whose hills among,
That voice of Victory hath not rung,
As if a trumpet spoke?

To sky, and sea, and shore,
Of those whose blood, on Ilion's plain,
Swept from the rivers to the main,
A glorious tale it bore.

Still, by our sun-bright deep,
With all the fame that fiery lay
Threw round them, in its rushing way,
The sons of battle sleep.

---

* For an account of this ceremony, anciently performed in commemoration of the battle of Platæa, see POTTER'S *Antiquities of Greece*, vol. i., p. 389.

And kings their turf have crown'd!
And pilgrims o'er the foaming wave
Brought garlands there: so rest the brave,
    Who thus their bard have found!

A voice from Scio's isle,
A voice as deep hath risen again
As far shall peal its thrilling strain,
    Where'er our sun may smile!

Let not its tones expire!
Such power to waken earth and heaven,
And might and vengeance, ne'er was given
    To mortal song or lyre!

Know ye not whence it comes?
—From ruin'd hearths, from burning fanes,
From kindred blood on yon red plains,
    From desolated homes!

'Tis with us through the night!
'Tis on our hills, 'tis in our sky—
Hear it, ye heavens! when swords flash high,
    O'er the mid-waves of fight!

IV.—THE SPARTANS' MARCH.*

"The Spartans used not the trumpet in their march into battle," says Thucydides, "because they wished not to excite the rage of their warriors. Their charging-step was made to the 'Dorian, mood of flutes and soft recorders.' The valor of a Spartan was too highly tempered to require a stunning or a rousing impulse. His spirit was like a steed too proud for the spur."
    CAMPBELL *on the Elegiac Poetry of the Greeks.*

'Twas morn upon the Grecian hills,
    Where peasants dress'd the vines;
Sunlight was on Cithæron's rills,
    Arcadia's rocks and pines.

And brightly, through his reeds and flowers,
    Eurotas wander'd by,
When a sound arose from Sparta's towers
    Of solemn harmony.

Was it the hunters' choral strain
    To the woodland-goddess pour'd?
Did virgin hands in Pallas' fane
    Strike the full sounding chord?

---

* Originally published in the *Edinburgh Magazine*

But helms were glancing on the stream,
  Spears ranged in close array,
And shields flung back a glorious beam
  To the morn of a fearful day!

And the mountain-echoes of the land
  Swell'd through the deep-blue sky;
While to soft strains moved forth a band
  Of men that moved to die.

They march'd not with the trumpet's blast,
  Nor bade the horn peal out,
And the laurel groves, as on they pass'd,
  Rung with no battle shout!

They ask'd no clarion's voice to fire
  Their souls with an impulse high;
But the Dorian reed and the Spartan lyre
  For the sons of liberty!

And still sweet flutes, their path around
  Sent forth Æolian breath;
They needed not a sterner sound
  To marshal them for death!

So moved they calmly to their field,
  Thence never to return,
Save bearing back the Spartan shield,
  Or on it proudly borne!

V.—THE URN AND SWORD.

THEY sought for treasures in the tomb,
Where gentler hands were wont to spread
Fresh boughs and flowers of purple bloom,
And sunny ringlets, for the dead.*

They scatter'd far the greensward heap,
Where once those hands the bright wine pour'd;
—What found they in the home of sleep?—
A mouldering urn, a shiver'd sword!

An urn, which held the dust of one
Who died when hearths and shrines were free;
A sword, whose work was proudly done
Between our mountains and the sea.

---

* See Potter's *Grecian Antiquities*, vol. ii. p. 234.

And these are treasures ?—undismay'd,
Still for the suffering land we trust,
Wherein the past its fame hath laid,
With freedom's sword, and valor's dust.

VI.—THE MYRTLE BOUGH.

STILL green, along our sunny shore,
 The flowering myrtle waves,
As when its fragrant boughs of yore
 Were offer'd on the graves—
The graves, wherein our mighty men
Had rest, unviolated then.

Still green it waves! as when the hearth
 Was sacred through the land;
And fearless was the banquet's mirth,
 And free the minstrel's hand;
And guests, with shining myrtle crown'd,
Sent the wreath'd lyre and wine-cup round.

Still green! as when on holy ground
 The tyrant's blood was pour'd:
Forget ye.not what garlands bound
 The young deliverer's sword!
Though earth may shroud Harmodius now,
We still have sword and myrtle bough!

ELYSIUM.

"In the Elysium of the ancients, we find none but heroes and persons who had either been fortunate or distinguished on earth; the children, and apparently the slaves and lower classes, that is to say, Poverty, Misfortune, and Innocence, were banished to the infernal Regions."   CHATEAUBRIAND, *Génie du Christianisme.*

FAIR wert thou in the dreams
Of elder time, thou land of glorious flowers
And summer winds and low-toned silvery streams,
Dim with the shadows of thy laurel bowers,
 Where, as they pass'd, bright hours
Left no faint sense of parting, such as clings
To earthly love, and joy in loveliest things!

Fair wert thou, with the light
On thy blue hills and sleepy waters cast,
From purple skies ne'er deep'ning into night,
Yet soft, as if each moment were their last
　　Of glory, fading fast
Along the mountains!—but *thy* golden day
Was not as those that warn us of decay.

And ever, through thy shades,
A swell of deep Æolian sound went by,
From fountain-voices in their secret glades,
And low reed-whispers, making sweet reply
　　To summer's breezy sigh,
And young leaves trembling to the wind's light breath,
Which ne'er had touch'd them with a hue of death!

And the transparent sky
Rung as a dome, all thrilling to the strain
Of harps that, 'midst the woods, made harmony
Solemn and sweet; yet troubling not the brain
　　With dreams and yearnings vain,
And dim remembrances, that still draw birth
From the bewild'ring music of the earth.

And who, with silent tread,
Moved o'er the plains of waving asphodel?
Call'd from the dim procession of the dead,
Who, 'midst the shadowy amaranth-bowers might dwell,
　　And listen to the swell
Of those majestic hymn-notes, and inhale
The spirit wand'ring in the immortal gale?

They of the sword, whose praise,
With the bright wine at nations' feasts, went round!
They of the lyre, whose unforgotten lays
Forth on the winds had sent their mighty sound,
　　And in all regions found
Their echoes 'midst the mountains!—and become
In man's deep heart as voices of his home!

They of the daring thought!
Daring and powerful, yet to dust allied—
Whose flight through stars, and seas, and depths, had sough.
The soul's far birthplace—but without a guide!
　　Sages and seers, who died,
And left the world their high mysterious dreams,
Born 'midst the olive woods, by Grecian streams.

But the most *loved* are they
Of whom fame speaks not with her clarion voice,
In regal halls!—the shades o'erhang their way,

The vale, with its deep fountains, is their choice,
  And gentle hearts rejoice
Around their steps ; till silently they die,
As a stream shrinks from summer's burning eye.

  And these—of whose abode,
'Midst her green valleys, earth retain'd no trace,
Save a flower springing from their burial-sod,
A shade of sadness on some kindred face,
  A dim and vacant place
In some sweet home ;—thou hadst no wreaths for *these*,
Thou sunny land ! with all thy deathless trees !

  The peasant at his door
Might sink to die when vintage feasts were spread,
And songs on every wind ! From *thy* bright shore
No lovelier vision floated round his head—
  Thou wert for nobler dead !
He heard the bounding steps which round him fell,
And sigh'd to bid the festal sun farewell !

  The slave, whose very tears
Were a forbidden luxury, and whose breast
Kept the mute woes and burning thoughts of years,
As embers in a burial-urn compress'd ;
  He might not be thy guest !
No gentle breathings from thy distant sky
Came o'er *his* path, and whisper'd " Liberty !"

  Calm, on its leaf-strewn bier,
Unlike a gift of Nature to Decay,
Too rose-like still, too beautiful, too dear,
The child at rest before the mother lay,
  E'en so to pass away,
With its bright smile !—Elysium ! what wert *thou*
To her, who wept o'er that young slumb'rer's brow ?

  Thou hadst no home, green land !
For the fair creature from her bosom gone,
With life's fresh flowers just opening in its hand,
And all the lovely thoughts and dreams unknown
  Which, in its clear eye, shone
Like spring's first wakening ! but that light was past—
Where went the dewdrop swept before the blast ?

  Not where thy soft winds play'd,
Not where thy waters lay in glassy sleep !
Fade with thy bowers, thou Land of Visions, fade !
From thee no voice came o'er the gloomy deep,
  And bade man cease to weep !

Fade, with the amaranth plain, the myrtle grove,
Which could not yield one hope to sorrowing love!*

THE FUNERAL GENIUS.

AN ANCIENT STATUE.

"Debout, couronné de fleurs, les bras élevés et posés sur sa tête, et le dos appuyé contre un pin, ce génie semble exprimer par son attitude le repos des morts. Les bas-reliefs des tombeaux offrent souvent des figures semblables."—VISCONTI, *Description des Antiques du Musée Royal.*

THOU shouldst be look'd on when the starlight falls
Through the blue stillness of the summer-air,
Not by the torch-fire wavering on the walls—
It hath too fitful and too wild a glare!
And thou!—thy rest, the soft, the lovely, seems
To ask light steps, that will not break its dreams.

Flowers are upon thy brow; for so the dead
Were crown'd of old, with pale spring flowers like these
Sleep on thine eye hath sunk; yet softly shed,
As from the wing of some faint southern breeze:
And the pine-boughs o'ershadow thee with gloom
Which of the grove seems breathing—not the tomb.

They fear'd not death, whose calm and gracious thought
Of the last hour, hath settled thus in thee!
They who thy wreath of pallid roses wrought,
And laid thy head against the forest tree,
As that of one by music's dreamy close,
On the wood-violets lull'd to deep repose.

* The form of this poem was a good deal altered by Mrs. Hemans some years after its first publication, and, though done so perhaps to advantage, one verse was omitted. As originally written, the two following stanzas concluded the piece:—

> For the most loved are they
> Of whom Fame speaks not with her clarion voice,
> In regal halls! the shades o'erhang their way.
> The vale, with its deep fountains, is their choice,
> And gentle hearts rejoice
> Around their steps; till silently they die,
> As a streams shrinks from summer's burning eye.
>
> And the world knows not then,
> Not then, nor ever, what pure thoughts are fled!
> Yet these are they, who on the souls of men
> Come back, when night her folding veil hath spread,
> The long-remember'd dead!
> But not with *thee* might aught save glory dwell—
> Fade, fade away, thou shore of asphodel!

They fear'd not death!—yet who shall say his touch
Thus lighty falls on gentle things and fair?
Doth he bestow, or will he leave so much
Of tender beauty as thy features wear?
Thou sleeper of the bower! on whose young eyes
So still a night, a night of summer, lies!

Had they seen aught like thee?—Did some fair boy
Thus, with his graceful hair, before them rest?
—His graceful hair, no more to wave in joy,
But drooping, as with heavy dews oppress'd:
And his eye veil'd so softly by its fringe,
And his lip faded to the white-rose tinge!

Oh! happy, if to them the one dread hour
Made known its lessons from a brow like thine!
If all their knowledge of the spoiler's power
Came by a look so tranquilly divine!
—Let him, who *thus* hath seen the lovely part,
Hold well that image to his thoughtful heart!

But thou, fair slumberer! was there less of woe,
Or love, or terror, in the days of old,
That men pour'd out their gladdening spirit's flow,
Like sunshine, on the desolate and cold,
And gave thy semblance to the shadowy king,
Who for deep souls had then a deeeper sting?

In the dark bosom of the earth they laid
Far more than we—for loftier faith is ours!
Their gems were lost in ashes—yet they made
The grave a place of beauty and of flowers,
With fragrant wreaths, and summer boughs array'd,
And lovely sculpture gleaming through the shade.

Is it for *us* a darker gloom to shed
O'er its dim precincts?—do we not intrust
But for a time, its chambers with our dead,
And strew immortal seed upon the dust?
—Why should *we* dwell on that which lies beneath,
When living light hath touch'd the brow of death?

THE TOMBS OF PLATÆA.

FROM A PAINTING BY WILLIAMS.

AND there they sleep!—the men who stood
In arms before th' exulting sun,
And bathed their spears in Persian blood.
And taught the earth how freedom might be won.

THE TOMBS OF PLATÆA.

They sleep!—th' Olympic wreaths are dead,
Th' Athenian lyres are hush'd and gone;
The Dorian voice of song is fled—
Slumber, ye mighty! slumber deeply on.

They sleep, and seems not all around
As hallow'd unto glory's tomb?
Silence is on the battle ground,
The heavens are loaded with a breathless gloom.

And stars are watching on their height,
But dimly seen through mist and cloud,
And still and solemn is the light
Which folds the plain, as with a glimmering shroud.

And thou, pale night-queen! here thy beams
Are not as those the shepherd loves,
Nor look they down on shining streams,
By Naiads haunted in their laurel groves:

Thou seest no pastoral hamlet sleep,
In shadowy quiet, 'midst its vines
No temple gleaming from the steep,
'Midst the grey olives, or the mountain pines:

But o'er a dim and boundless waste,
Thy rays, e'en like a tomb-lamp's, brood,
Where man's departed steps are traced
But by his dust, amidst the solitude.

And be it thus!—What slave shall tread
O'er freedom's ancient battle-plains?
Let deserts wrap the glorious dead,
When their bright Land sits weeping o'er her chains.

Here, where the Persian clarion rung,
And where the Spartan sword flash'd high,
And where the pæan strains were sung,
From year to year swell'd on by liberty!

Here should no voice, no sound, be heard,
Until the bonds of Greece be riven,
Save of the leader's charging word,
Or the shrill trumpet pealing up through heaven!

Rest in your silent homes, ye brave!
No vines festoon your lonely tree!*
No harvest o'er your war-field wave,
Till rushing winds proclaim—the land is free!

---

* A single tree appears in Mr. Williams' impressive picture.

THE VIEW FROM CASTRI.

FROM A PAINTING BY WILLIAMS

There have been bright and glorious pageants here,
Where now grey stones and moss-grown columns lie ;
There have been words, which earth grew pale to hear,
Breath'd from the cavern's misty chambers nigh :
There have been voices, through the sunny sky,
And the pine-woods, their choral hymn-notes sending,
And reeds and lyres, their Dorian melody,
With incense-clouds around the temple blending,
And throngs with laurel-boughs, before the altar bending.

There have been treasures of the seas and isles
Brought to the day-god's now-forsaken throne ;
Thunders have peal'd along the rock-defiles,
When the far-echoing battle-horn made known
That foes were on their way !—the deep-wind's moan
Hath chill'd th' invader's heart with secret fear,
And from the Sybil-grottos, wild and lone,
Storms have gone forth, which, in their fierce career,
From his bold hand have struck the banner and the spear.

The shrine hath sunk !—but thou unchanged art there !
Mount of the voice and vision, robed with dreams !
Unchanged, and rushing through the radiant air,
With thy dark waving pines, and flashing streams,
And all thy founts of song ! their bright course teems
With inspiration yet ; and each dim haze,
Or golden cloud which floats around thee, seems
As with its mantle veiling from our gaze
The mysteries of the past, the gods of elder days !

Away, vain phantasies !—doth less of power
Dwell round thy summit, or thy cliffs invest,
Though in deep stillness now, the ruin's flower
Wave o'er the pillars mouldering on thy breast ?
—Lift through the free blue heavens thine arrowy crest !
Let the great rocks their solitude regain !
No Delphian lyres now break thy noontide rest
With their full chords :—but silent be the strain !
Thou hast a mightier voice to speak th' Eternal's reign !*

---

* This, with the preceding, and several of the following pieces first appeared in the *Edinburgh Magazine*.

THE FESTAL HOUR.

When are the lessons given
That shakes the startled earth? When wakes the foe
While the friend sleeps! When falls the traitor's blow?
　When are proud sceptres riven,
High hope o'erthrown?—It is when lands rejoice,
When cities blaze and lift the' exulting voice,
And wave their banners to the kindling heaven!

　Fear ye the festal hour!
When mirth o'erflows, then tremble!—'Twas a night
Of gorgeous revel, wreaths, and dance, and light,
　When through the regal bower
The trumpet peal'd, ere yet the song was done,
And there were shrieks in golden Babylon,
And trampling armies, ruthless in their power.

　The marble shrines were crown'd:
Young voices, through the blue Athenian sky,
And Dorian reeds, made summer-melody,
　And censers waved around;
And lyres were strung and bright libations pour'd!
When, through the streets, flash'd out th' avenging sword
Fearless and free, the sword with myrtles bound!*

Through Rome a triumph pass'd.
Rich in her sun-god's mantling beams went by
That long array of glorious pageantry,
　With shout and trumpet-blast.
An empire's gems their starry splendor shed
O'er the proud march; a king in chains was led;
A stately victor, crown'd and robed, came last.†

　And many a Dryad's bower
Had lent the laurels which, in waving play,
Stirr'd the warm air, and glisten'd round his way,
　As a quick-flashing shower.
—O'er his own porch, meantime, the cypress hung,
Through his fair halls a cry of anguish rung—
Woe for the dead!—the father's broken flower!

　A sound of lyre and song,
In the still night, went floating o'er the Nile,
Whose waves, by many an old mysterious pile,
　Swept with that voice along;

---

* The sword of Harmodius.
† Paulus Æmilius, one of whose sons died a few days before, and another shortly after, his triumph on the conquest of Macedon, when Perseus, king of that country, was led in chains.

And lamps were shining o'er the red wine's foam
Where a chief revell'd in a monarch's dome,
And fresh rose-garlands deck'd a glittering throng.

    'Twas Antony that bade
The joyous chords ring out!—but strains arose
Of wilder omen at the banquet's close!
    Sounds, by no mortal made,*
Shook Alexandria through her streets that night,
And pass'd—and with another sunset's light,
The kingly Roman on his bier was laid,

    Bright 'midst its vineyards lay
The fair Campanian city,† with its towers
And temples gleaming through dark olive-bowers,
    Clear in the golden day;
Joy was around it as the glowing sky,
And crowds had fill'd its halls of revelry,
And all the sunny air was music's way.

    A cloud came o'er the face
Of Italy's rich heaven!—its crystal blue
Was changed, and deepen'd to a wrathful hue
    Of night, o'ershadowing space,
As with the wings of death!—in all his power
Vesuvius woke, and hurl'd the burning shower,
And who could tell the buried city's place?

    Such things have been of yore,
In the gay regions where the citrons blow,
And purple summers all their sleepy glow
    On the grape-clusters pour;
And where the palms to spicy winds are waving,
Along clear seas of melting sapphire, laving,
As with a flow of light, their southern shore.

    Turn we to other climes!—
Far in the Druid-Isle a feast was spread,
'Midst the rock-altars of the warrior dead:‡
    And ancient battle-rhymes
Were chanted to the harp; and yellow mead
Went flowing round, and tales of martial deed,
And lofty songs of Britain's elder time;

---

* See the description given by Plutarch, in his life of Antony, of the supernatural sounds heard in the streets of Alexandria, the night before Antony's death.

† Herculaneum, of which it is related, that all the inhabitants were assembled in the theatres, when the shower of ashes which covered the city descended.

‡ Stonehenge, said by some traditions to have been erected to the memory of Ambrosius, an early British king; and by others mentioned as a monumental record of the massacre of British chiefs here alluded to.

But ere the giant-fane
Cast its broad shadows on the robe of even,
Hush'd were the bards, and in the face of heaven,
    O'er that old burial-plain
Flashed the keen Saxon dagger!—Blood was streaming
Where late the mead-cup to the sun was gleaming,
And Britain's hearths were heap'd that night in vain—

    For they return'd no more!
They that went forth at morn, with reckless heart,
In that fierce banquet's mirth to bear their part;
    And, on the rushy floor,
And the bright spears and bucklers of the walls,
The high wood-fires were blazing in their halls;
But not for them—they slept—their feast was o'er!

    Fear ye the festal hour!
Ay, tremble when the cup of joy o'erflows!
Tame down the swelling heart!—the bridal rose,
    And the rich myrtle's flower
Have veil'd the sword!—Red wines have sparkled fast
From venom'd goblets, and soft breezes pass'd,
With fatal perfume, through the revel's bower.

    Twine the young glowing wreath!
But pour not all your spirit in the song,
Which through the sky's deep azure floats along,
    Like summer's quickening breath!
The ground is hollow in the path of mirth:
Oh! far too daring seems the joy of earth,
So darkly press'd and girdled in by death!

SONG OF THE BATTLE OF MORGARTEN

["In the year 1315, Switzerland was invaded by Duke Leopold of Austria, with a formidable army. It is well attested that this prince repeatedly declared he 'would trample the audacious rustics under his feet;' and that he had procured a large stock of cordage, for the purpose of binding their chiefs, and putting them to death.

"The 15th of October, 1315, dawned. The sun darted its first rays on the shields and armor of the advancing host; and this being the first army ever known to have attempted the frontiers of the cantons, the Swiss viewed its long line with various emotions. Montfort de Tettnang led the cavalry into the narrow pass, and soon filled the whole space between the mountain (Mount Sattel) and the lake. The fifty men on the eminence (above Morgarten)

BATTLE OF MORGARTEN.

raised a sudden shout, and rolled down heaps of rocks and stones among the crowded ranks. The confederates on the mountain, perceiving the impression made by this attack, rushed down in close array, and fell upon the flank of the disordered column. With massy clubs they dashed in pieces the armor of the enemy, and dealt their blows and thursts with long pikes. The narrowness of the defile admitted of no evolutions, and a slight frost having injured the road, the horses were impeded in all their motions; many leaped into the lake; all were startled; and at last the whole column gave way, and fell suddenly back on the infantry; and these last, as the nature of the country did not allow them to open their files, were run over by the fugitives, and many of them trampled to death. A general route ensued, and Duke Leopold was, with much difficulty, rescued by a peasant, who led him to Winterthur, where the historian of the times saw him arrive in the evening, pale, sullen, and dismayed."—PLANTA'S *History of the Helvetic Confederacy.*]

THE wine-month* shone in its golden prime,
   And the red grapes clustering hung,
But a deeper sound, through the Switzer's clime,
   Than the vintage music, rung.
      A sound, through vaulted cave,
      A sound, through echoing glen,
   Like the hollow swell of a rushing wave;
      —'Twas the tread of steel-girt men.

And a trumpet, pealing wild and far,
   'Midst the ancient rocks was blown,
Till the Alps replied to that voice of war
   With a thousand of their own.
      And through the forest-glooms
      Flash'd helmets to the day,
   And the winds were tossing knightly plumes,
      Like the larch-boughs in their play.

In Hasli's † wilds there was gleaming steel,
   As the host of the Austrian pass'd;
And the Schreckhorn's‡ rocks, with a savage peal,
   Made mirth of his clarion's blast.
      Up 'midst the Righi's§ snows,
      The stormy march was heard;
   With the charger's tramp, whence fire-sparks rose,
      And the leader's gathering word.

But a band, the noblest band of all,
   Through the rude Morgarten strait,
With blazon'd streamers, and lances tall,
   Moved onwards in princely state,

---

* *Wine-month*, the German name for October.
† Hasli, a wild district in the canton of Berne.
‡ Schreckhorn, the *peak of terror*, a mountain in the canton of Berne.
§ Righi, a mountain in the canton of Schwytz.

They came with heavy chains,
    For the race despised so long—
But amidst his Alp-domains,
    The herdsman's arm is strong!

The sun was reddening the clouds of morn
    When they enter'd the rock-defile,
And shrill as a joyous hunter's horn
    Their bugles rung the while.
        But on the misty height,
        Where the mountain-people stood,
    There was stillness, as of night,
        When storms at distance brood.

There was stillness, as of deep dead night,
    And a pause—but not of fear,
While the Switzers gazed on the gathering might
    Of the hostile shield and spear.
        On wound those columns bright
        Between the lake and wood,
    But they look'd not to the misty height
        Where the mountain-people stood.

The pass was fill'd with their serried power,
    All helm'd and mail-array'd,
And their steps had sounds like a thunder-shower
    In the rustling forest-shade.
        There were prince and crested knight,
        Hemm'd in by cliff and flood,
    When a shout arose from the misty height
        Where the mountain-people stood.

And the mighty rocks came bounding down,
    Their startled foes among,
With a joyous whirl from the summit thrown—
    —Oh! the herdsman's arm is strong!
        They came like lauwine* hurl'd
        From Alp to Alp in play,
    When the echoes shout through the snowy world
        And the pines are borne away.

The fir-woods crash'd on the mountain-side,
    And the Switzers rush'd from high,
With a sudden charge, on the flower and pride
    Of the Austrian chivalry:
        Like hunters of the deer,
        They storm'd the narrow dell,
    And first in the shock, with Uri's spear,
        Was the arm of William Tell.†

---

* *Lauwine*, the Swiss name for the avalanche.
† William Tell's name is particularly mentioned amongst the confederates at Morgarten.

There was tumult in the crowded strait,
  And a cry of wild dismay,
And many a warrior met his fate
  From a peasant's hand that day!
    And the empire's banner then
    From its place of waving free,
  Went down before the shepherd-men,
    The men of the Forest-sea.*

With their pikes and massy clubs they brake
  The cuirass and the shield,
And the war-horse dash'd to the reddening lake
  From the reapers of the field!
    The field—but not of sheaves—
    Proud crests and pennons lay,
  Strewn o'er it thick as the birch-wood leaves,
    In the autumn tempest's way.

Oh! the sun in heaven fierce havoc view'd,
  When the Austrian turn'd to fly,
And the brave, in the trampling multitude,
  Had a fearful death to die!
    And the leader of the war
    At eve unhelm'd was seen,
  With a hurrying step on the wilds afar,
    And a pale and troubled mien.

But the sons of the land which the freeman tills,
  Went back from the battle-toil,
To their cabin homes 'midst the deep green hills,
  All burden'd with royal spoil.
    There were songs and festal fires
    On the soaring Alps that night,
  When children sprung to meet their sires
    From the wild Morgarten fight.

---

* *Forest-sea*, the lake of the four cantons is also so called.

SEBASTIAN OF PORTUGAL.

A DRAMATIC FRAGMENT.

Dram. Pers.

SEBASTIAN.   ZAMOR, *A young Arab.*
GONZALEZ *his friend.*   SYLVEIRA.

SCENE I.

The sea-shore near Lisbon.

SEBASTIAN—GONZALEZ—ZAMOR.

Seb. With what young life and fragrance in its breath
My native air salutes me! from the groves
Of citron, and the mountains of the vine,
And thy majestic tide thus foaming on
In power and freedom o'er its golden sands,
Fair stream, my Tajo! youth, with all its glow
And pride of feeling, through my soul and frame
Again seems rushing, as these noble waves
Past their bright shores flow joyously. Sweet land,
My own, my Fathers' land, of sunny skies
And orange-bowers!—Oh! is it not a dream
That thus I tread thy soil? Or do I wake
From a dark dream but now! Gonzalez, say,
Doth it not bring the flush of early life
Back on th' awakening spirit thus to gaze
On the far-sweeping river, and the shades
Which in their undulating motion speak
Of gentle winds amidst bright waters born,
After the fiery skies and dark-red sands
Of the lone desert? Time and toil must needs
Have changed *our* mien; but this, our blessed land,
Hath gained but richer beauty since we bade
Her glowing shores farewell. Seems it not thus?
Thy brow is clouded.—
   Gon.   To mine eye the scene
Wears, amidst all its quiet loveliness,
A hue of desolation, and the calm,
The solitude and silence which pervade
Earth, air, and ocean, seem belonging less
To peace than sadness! We have proudly stood
Even on this shore, beside the Atlantic wave,
When it hath look'd not thus

SEBASTIAN OF PORTUGAL.

Seb.   Ay, now thy soul
Is in the past! Oh no, it look'd not thus
When the morn smiled upon our thousand sails,
And the winds blew for Afric! How that hour
With all its hues of glory, seems to burst
Again upon my vision! I behold
The stately barks, the arming, the array,
The crests, the banners of my chivalry
Swayed by the sea-breeze till their motion show'd
Like joyous life! How the proud billows foam'd!
And the oars flash'd, like lightnings of the deep,
And the tall spears went glancing to the sun,
And scattering round quick rays, as if to guide
The valiant unto fame! Ay, the blue heaven
Seemed for that noble scene a canopy
Scarce too majestic, while it rung afar
To peals of warlike sound! My gallant bands!
Where are you now?
  Gon.   Bid the wide desert tell
Where sleep its dead! To mightier hosts than them
Hath it lent graves ere now; and on its breast
Is room for nations yet!
  Seb.   It cannot be
That all have perished! Many a noble man,
Made captive on that war-field, may have burst
His bonds like ours. Cloud not this fleeting hour,
Which to my soul is as the fountain's draught
To the parched lip of fever, with a thought
So darkly sad!
  Gon.   Oh never, never cast
That deep remembrance from you! When once more
Your place is 'midst earth's rulers, let it dwell
Around you, as the shadow of your throne,
Wherein the land may rest. My king, this hour
(Solemn as that which to the voyager's eye,
In far and dim perspective, doth unfold
A new and boundless world) may haply be
The last in which the courage and the power
Of truth's high voice may reach you. Who may stand
As man to man, as friend to friend, before
The ancestral throne of monarchs? Or, perchance,
Toils, such as tame the loftiest to endurance,
Henceforth may wait us here! But howsoe'er
This be, the lessons now from sufferings past
Befit all time, all change. Oh! by the blood,
The free, the generous blood of Portugal,
Shed on the sands of Afric,—by the names
Which, with their centuries of high renown,
There died, extinct for ever,—let not those
Who stood in hope and glory at our side
Here, on this very sea-beach, whence they pass'd
To fall, and leave no trophy,—let them not

Be soon, be e'er forgotten! for their fate
Bears a deep warning in its awfulness,
Whence power might well learn wisdom!
   Seb.   Think'st thou, then,
That years of sufferance and captivity,
Such as have bow'd down eagle hearts ere now,
And made high energies their spoil, have pass'd
So lightly o'er my spirit? It is not thus!
The things thou wouldst recall are not of those
To be forgotten! But my heart hath still
A sense, a bounding pulse for hope and joy,
And it is joy which whispers in the breeze
Sent from my own free mountains. Brave Gonzalez!
Thou art one to make thy fearles heart a shield
Unto thy friend, in the dark stormy hour
When knightly crests are trampled, and proud helms
Cleft, and strong breastplates shiver'd. Thou art one
To infuse the soul of gallant fortitude
Into the captive's bosom, and beguile
The long slow march beneath the burning noon
With lofty patience; but for those quick bursts
Those buoyant efforts of the soul to cast
Her weight of care to earth, those brief delights
Whose source is in a sunbeam, or a sound
Which stirs the blood, or a young breeze, whose wing
Wanders in chainless joy; for things like these
Thou hast no sympathies!—And thou, my Zamor,
Art wrapt in thought! I welcome thee to this,
The kingdom of my fathers. Is it not
A goodly heritage?
   Zam.   The land is fair:
But he, the archer of the wilderness,
Beholdeth not the palms beneath whose shade
His tents are scatter'd, and his camels rest;
And therefore is he sad!
   Seb.   Thou must not pine
With that sick yearning of the impatient heart,
Which makes the exile's life one fever'd dream
Of skies, and hills, and voices far away,
And faces wearing the familiar hues
Lent by his native sunbeams. I have known
Too much of this, and would not see another
Thus daily die. If it be so with thee,
My gentle Zamor, speak. Behold, our bark
Yet, with her white sails catching sunset's glow,
Lies within signal reach. If it be thus,
Then fare thee well—farewell, thou brave, and true,
And generous friend! How often is our path
Cross'd by some being whose bright spirit sheds
A passing gladness o'er it, but whose course
Leads down another current, never more
To blend with ours! Yet far within our souls,

Amidst the rushing of the busy world,
Dwells many a secret thought which lingers yet
Around that image. And e'en so, kind Zamor,
Shalt thou be long remembered!
   Zam.   By the fame
Of my brave sire, whose deeds the warrior tribes
Tell round the desert's watchfire, at the hour
Of silence, and of coolness, and of stars,
I will not leave thee! 'Twas in such an hour
The dreams of rest were on me, and I lay
Shrouded in slumber's mantle, as within
The chambers of the dead. Who saved me then,
When the pard, soundless as the midnight, stole
Soft on the sleeper? Whose keen dart transfix'd
The monarch of the solitudes? I woke,
And saw *thy* javelin crimson'd with his blood,
Thou, my deliverer! and my heart e'en then
Call'd thee its brother.
   Seb.   For that gift of life
With one of tenfold price, even freedom's self,
Thou hast repaid me well.
   Zam.   Then bid me not
Forsake thee! Though my father's tents may rise
At times upon my spirit, yet my home
Shall be amidst thy mountains, Prince, and thou
Shalt be my chief, until I see thee robed
With all thy power. When thou canst need no more
Thine Arab's faithful heart and vigorous arm,
From the green regions of the setting sun
Then shall the wanderer turn his steps, and seek
His orient wild's again.
   Seb.   Be near me still,
And ever, O my warrior! I shall stand
Again amidst my hosts a mail-clad king,
Begirt with spears and banners, and the pomp
And the proud sounds of battle. Be thy place
Then at my side. When doth a monarch cease
To need true hearts, bold hands? Not in the field
Of arms, nor on the throne of power, nor yet
The couch of sleep. Be our friend, we will not part.
   Gon. Be all thy friends then faithful, for e'en yet
They may be fiercely tried.
   Seb.   I doubt them not.
Even now my heart beats high to meet their welcome.
Let us away!
   Gon.   Yet hear once more my liege:
The humblest pilgrim from his distant shrine
Returning, finds not e'en his peasant home
Unchanged amidst its vineyards. Some loved face,
Which made the sun-light of his lowly board,
Is touch'd by sickness; some familiar voice
Greets him no more; and shall not fate and time

Have done their work, since last we parted hence,
Upon an empire? Ay, within those years,
Hearts from their ancient worship have fall'n off
And bow'd before new stars: high names have sunk
From their supremacy of place, and others
Gone forth, and made themselves the mighty sounds
At which thrones tremble. Oh! be slow to trust
E'en those to whom your smiles were wont to seem
As light is unto flowers. Search well the depths
Of bosoms in whose keeping you would shrine
The secret of your state. Storms pass not by
Leaving earth's face unchanged.
   Seb. Whence didst thou learn
The cold distrust which casts so deep a shadow
O'er a most noble nature?
   Gon. Life hath been
My stern and only teacher. I have known
Vicissitudes in all things, but the most
In human hearts. Oh! yet awhile tame down
That royal spirit, till the hour be come
When it may burst its bondage! On thy brow
The suns of burning climes have set their seal,
And toil, and years, and perils, have not pass'd
O'er the bright aspect, and the ardent eye,
As doth a breeze of summer. Be that change
The mask beneath whose shelter thou may'st read
Men's thoughts, and veil thine own.
   Seb. Am I thus changed
From all I was? And yet it needs must be,
Since e'en my soul hath caught another hue
From its long sufferings. Did I not array
The gallant flower of Lusian chivalry,
And lead the mighty of the land, to pour
Destruction on the Moslem? I return,
And as a fearless and a trusted friend,
Bring, from the realms of my captivity,
An Arab of the desert!—But the sun
Hath sunk below th' Atlantic. Let us hence—
Gonzalez, fear me not.   [*Exeunt.*

Scene II.

A Street in Lisbon illuminated.

Many Citizens.

   1st Cit. In sooth our city wears a goodly mien
With her far-blazing fanes, and festive lamps
Shining from all her marble palaces,
Countless as heaven's fair stars. The humblest lattice
Sends forth its radiance. How the sparkling waves
Fling back the light!
   2d Cit.   Ay, 'tis a gallant show;
And one which serves, like others, to conceal

Things which must not be told.
3d Cit.   What wouldst thou say?
2d Cit. That which may scarce, in perilous times like these,
Be said with safety. Hast thou look'd within
Those stately palaces? Were they but peopled
With the high race of warlike nobles, once
Their princely lords, think'st thou, good friend, that now
They would be glittering with this hollow pomp,
To greet a conqueror's entrance?
3d Cit.   Thou say'st well.
None but a land forsaken of its chiefs
Had been so lost and won.
4th Cit.   The lot is cast;
We have but to yield. Hush! for some strangers come:
Now friends, beware.
1st Cit.   Did the king pass this way
At morning, with his train?
2d Cit.   Ay: saw you not
The long and rich procession?
            [SEBAST. *enters with* GONZAL. *and* ZAMOR.
Seb. to Gon   This should be
The night of some high festival. E'en thus
My royal city to the skies sent up
From her illumined fanes and towers a voice
Of gladness, welcoming our first return
From Afric's coast. Speak thou, Gonzalez, ask
The cause of this rejoicing. To my heart
Deep feelings rush, so mingled and so fast,
My voice perchance might tremble.
Gon.   Citizen,
What festal night is this, that all your streets
Are throng'd and glittering thus?
1st Cit.   Hast thou not heard
Of the king's entry, in triumphal pomp,
This very morn?
Gon.   The king! triumphal pomp!
Thy words are dark.
Seb.   Speak yet again: mine ears
Ring with strange sounds. Again!
1st Cit.   I said, the king,
Philip of Spain, and now of Portugal,
This morning enter'd with a conqueror's train
Our city's royal palace: and for this
We hold our festival.
Seb. (*in a low voice.*) Thou said'st—the king!
His name?—I heard it not.
1st Cit.   Philip of Spain.
Seb. Philip of Spain! We slumber, till aroused
By th' earthquake's bursting shock. Hath there not fall'n
A sudden darkness? All things seem to float
Obscurely round me. Now 'tis past. The streets
Are blazing with strange fire. Go, quench those lamps;

They glare upon me till my very brain
Grows dizzy, and doth whirl. How dare ye thus
Light up your shrines for *him*?
   Gon.   Away, away!
This is no time, no scene—
   Seb.   Philip of Spain!
How name ye this fair land? Why—is it not
The free, the chivalrous Portugal? the land
By the proud ransom of heroic blood
Won from the Moor of old? Did that red stream
Sink to the earth, and leave no fiery current
In the veins of noble men, that so its tide,
Full swelling at the sound of hostile steps,
Might be a kingdom's barrier?
   2d Cit.   That high blood
Which should have been our strength, profusely shed
By the rash King Sebastian, bathed the plains
Of fatal Alcazar. Our monarch's guilt
Hath brought this ruin down.
   Seb.   Must this be heard,
And borne, and unchastised. Man, darest thou stand
Before me face to face, and thus arraign
Thy sovereign?
   Zam. (*aside to Seb.*) Shall I lift the sword, my Prince,
Against thy foes?
   Gon.   Be still—or all is lost.
   2d Cit. I dare speak that which all men think and know.
'Tis to Sebastian, and his waste of life,
And power, and treasure, that we owe these bonds.
   3d Cit. Talk not of bonds. May our new monarch rule
The weary land in peace! But who art thou?
Whence com'st thou, haughty stranger, that these things,
Known to all nations, should be new to thee?
   Seb. (*wildly.*) I come from regions where the cities lie
In ruins, not in chains.
                [*Exit with* GONZAL. *and* ZAMOR.
   2d Cit.   He wears the mien
Of one that hath commanded; yet his looks
And words were strangely wild.
   1st Cit.   Mark'd you his fierce
And haughty gestures, and the flash that broke
From his dark eye, when King Sebastian's name
Became our theme?
   2d Cit.   Trust me, there's more in this
Than may be lightly said. These are no times
To breathe men's thoughts i' th' open face of heaven
And ear of multitudes. They that would speak
Of monarchs and their deeds, should keep within
Their quiet homes. Come, let us hence, and then
We'll commune of this stranger.

The Portico of a Palace.
SEBASTIAN.—GONZALEZ.—ZAMOR.

Seb. Withstand me not! I tell thee that my soul,
With all its passionate energies, is roused
Unto that fearful strength which *must* have way
E'en like the elements, in their hour of might
And mastery o'er creation.
   Gon.   But they *wait*
That hour in silence. O! be calm awhile,
Thine is not come. My king—
   Seb.   I am no king,
While in the very palace of my sires,
Ay, where mine eyes first drank the glorious light,
Where my soul's thrilling echoes first awoke
To the high sound of earth's immortal names,
Th' usurper lives and reigns. I am no king
Until I cast him thence.
   Zam.   Shall not thy voice
Be as a trumpet to the awak'ning land?
Will not the bright swords flash like sun-bursts forth,
When the brave hear their chief?
   Gon.   Peace, Zamor, peace!
Child of the desert, what hast thou to do
With the calm hour of counsel?
                     —Monarch, pause,
A kingdom's destiny should not be th' sport
Of passion's reckless winds. There is a time
When men, in very weariness of heart
And careless desolation, tamed to yield
By misery, strong as death, will lay their souls
E'en at the conqueror's feet, as nature sinks,
After long torture, into cold and dull,
And heavy sleep. But comes there not an hour
Of fierce atonement? Ay, the slumberer wakes
With gather'd strength and vengeance; and the sense
And the remembrance of his agonies
Are in themselves a power, whose fearful path
Is like the path of ocean, when the heavens
Take off its interdict. Wait then the hour
Of that high impulse.
   Seb.   Is it not the sun
Whose radiant bursting through the embattled clouds
Doth make it morn? The hour of which thou speak'st,
Itself, with all its glory, is the work
Of some commanding nature, which doth bid
The sullen shades disperse. Away!—e'en now
The land's high hearts, the fearless and the true,
Shall know they have a leader. Is not this
The mansion of mine own, mine earliest, friend
Sylveira?
   Gon. Ay, its glittering lamps too well

Illume the stately vestibule to leave
Our sight a moment's doubt. He ever loved
Such pageantries.
   Seb.   *His* dwelling thus adorn'd
On such a night! Yet will I seek him here.
He must be faithful, and to him the first
My tale shall be reveal'd. A sudden chill
Falls on my heart; and yet I will not wrong
My friend with dull suspicion. He hath been
Link'd all too closely with mine inmost soul.
And what have I to lose?
   Gon.   Is their blood nought
Who without hope will follow where thou lead'st,
E'en unto death?
   Seb.   Was that a brave man's voice?
Warrior, and friend! how long then hast thou learn'd
To hold thy blood thus dear?
   Gon. Of *mine,* mine own
Think'st thou I spoke? When all is shed for thee
Thou'lt know me better.
   Seb. (*entering the palace.*) For a while farewell.   [*Exit*
   Gon. Thus princes lead men's hearts. Come, follow me,
And if a home is left me still, brave Zamor,
There will I bid thee welcome.   [*Exeunt.*

Scene IV.

A Hall within the palace.

Sebastian.—Sylveira.

   Sylv. Whence art thou, stranger?—what would'st thou with
       me?
There is a fiery wildness in thy mien,
Startling and almost fearful.
   Seb.   From the stern,
And vast, and desolate wilderness, whose lord
Is the fierce lion, and whose gentlest wind
Breathes of the tomb, and whose dark children make
The bow and spear their law, men bear not back
That smilingness of aspect, wont to mask
The secrets of their spirits 'midst the stir
Of courts and cities. I have look'd on scenes
Boundless, and strange, and terrible; I have known
Sufferings which are not in the shadowy scope
Of wild imagination; and these things
Have stamp'd me with their impress. Man of peace,
Thou look'st on one familiar with the extremes
Of grandeur and of misery.
   Sylv.   Stranger, speak
Thy name and purpose briefly, for the time
Ill suits these mysteries. I must hence; to-night
I feast the lords of Spain.

Seb.   Is that a task
For King Sebastian's friend?
   Sylv.   Sebastian's friend!
That name hath lost its meaning. Will the dead
Rise from their silent dwellings, to upbraid
The living for their mirth. The grave sets bounds
Unto all human friendship.
   Seb.   On the plain
Of Alcazar full many a stately flower,
The pride and crown of some high house, was laid
Low in the dust of Afric; but of these
Sebastian was not one.
   Sylv.   I am not skill'd
To deal with men of mystery. Take, then, off
The strange dark scrutiny of thine eye from mine.
What mean'st thou?—Speak!
   Seb.   Sebastian died not **there**.
I read no joy in that cold doubting mien,
Is not thy name Sylveira?
   Sylv.   Ay.
   Seb.   Why, then,
Be glad! I tell thee that Sebastian lives!
Think thou on this—he lives! Should he return
—For he may yet return—and find the friend
In whom he trusted with such perfect trust
As should be heaven's alone—mark'st thou my words?
—Should he then find this man, not girt and arm'd,
And watching o'er the heritage of his lord,
But, reckless of high fame and loyal faith,
Holding luxurious revels with his foes,
How wouldst thou meet his glance?
   Sylv.   As I do thine,
Keen though it be, and proud.
   Seb.   Why, thou dost quail
Before it, even as if the burning eye
Of the broad sun pursued thy shrinking soul
Through all its depths.
   Sylv.   Away! he died not there!
He *should* have died there, with the chivalry
And strength and honor of his kingdom, lost
By his impetuous rashness.
   Seb.   This from *thee?*
Who hath given power to falsehood, that one gaze
At its unmask'd and withering mien, should blight
High souls at once? I wake. And this from thee?
There are, whose eyes discern the secret springs
Which lie beneath the desert, and the gold
And gems within earth's caverns, far below
The everlasting hills: but who hath dared
To dream that heaven's most awful attribute
Invested his mortality, and to boast
That through its inmost folds his glance could **read**

One heart, one human heart? Why, then, to love
And trust is but to lend a traitor arms
Of keenest temper and unerring aim,
Wherewith to pierce our souls. But thou, beware!
Sebastian lives!
  Sylv.   If it be so, and thou
Art of his followers still, then bid him seek
Far in the wilds, which gave one sepulchre
To his proud hosts, a kingdom and a home,
For none is left him here.
  Seb.   This is to live
An age of wisdom in an hour! The man
Whose empire, as in scorn, o'erpass'd the bounds
E'en of the infinite deep; whose orient realms
Lay bright beneath the morning, while the clouds
Were brooding in their sunset mantle still,
O'er his majestic regions of the west;
This heir of far dominion shall return,
And, in the very city of his birth,
Shall find no home! Ay, I *will* tell him this,
And he will answer that the tale is false,
False as a traitor's hollow words of love;
And that the stately dwelling, in whose halls
We commune now—a friend's, a monarch's gift,
Unto the chosen of his heart, Sylveira,
Should yield him still a welcome.
  Sylv.   Fare thee well!
I may not pause to hear thee, for thy words
Are full of danger, and of snares, perchance
Laid by some treacherous foe. But all in vain.
I mock thy wiles to scorn.
  Seb.   Ha! ha! The snake
Doth pride himself in his distorted cunning,
Deeming it wisdom. Nay, thou go'st not thus.
My heart is bursting, and I *will* be heard.
What! know'st thou not my spirit was born to hold
Dominion over thine? Thou shalt not cast
Those bonds thus lightly from thee. Stand thou there,
And tremble in the presence of thy lord!
  Sylv. This is all madness.
  Seb.   Madness! no—I say
'Tis Reason starting from her sleep, to feel,
And see, and know, in all their cold distinctness,
Things which come o'er her, as a sense of pain
O' th' sudden wakes the dreamer. Stay thee yet:
Be still. Thou'rt used to smile and to obey;
Ay, and to weep. I have seen thy tears flow fast,
As from the fulness of a heart o'ercharged
With loyal love. Oh! never, never more
Let tears or smiles be trusted! When thy king
Went forth on his disastrous enterprise
Upon thy bed of sickness thou wast laid,

And he stood o'er thee with the look of one
Who leaves a dying brother, and his eyes
Were fill'd with tears like thine. No! *not* like thine:
His bosom knew no falsehood, and he deem'd
Thine clear and stainless as a warrior's shield,
Wherein high deeds and noble forms alone
Are brightly imaged forth.
 Sylv.   What now avail
These recollections?
 Seb.   What? I have seen thee shrink,
As the murd'rer from the eye of light, before me :
I have earn'd (how dearly and how bitterly
It matters not, but I *have* earn'd at last)
Deep knowledge, fearful wisdom. Now, begone!
Hence to thy guests, and fear not, though arraign'd
E'en of Sebastian's friendship. Make his scorn
(For he *will* scorn thee, as a crouching slave
By all high hearts is scorn'd) thy right, thy charter
Unto vile safety. Let the secret voice,
Whose low upbraidings will not sleep within thee,
Be as a sign, a token of thy claim
To all such guerdons as are shower'd on traitors,
When noble men are crush'd. And fear thou not:—
'Tis but the kingly cedar which the storm
Hurls from his mountain throne :—th' ignoble shrub,
Groveling beneath, may live.
 Sylv.   It is *thy* part
To tremble for thy life.
 Seb.   They that have look'd
Upon a heart like thine, should know too well
The worth of life to tremble. Such things make
Brave men, and reckless. Ay, and they whom fate
Would trample should be thus. It is enough—
Thou may'st depart.
 Sylv.   And thou, if thou dost prize
Thy safety, speed thee hence. [*Exit* SILVEIRA.
 Seb. (*alone.*) And this is he
Who was as mine own soul : whose image rose,
Shadowing my dreams of glory with the thought
That on the sick man's weary couch he lay,
Pining to share my battles!

CHORUS.

Ye winds that sweep
The conquer'd billows of the western deep,
Or wander where the morn
'Midst the resplendent Indian heavens is born,
Waft o'er bright isles, and glorious worlds the fame
Of the crown'd Spaniard's name :
Till in each glowing zone
Its might the nations own,

And bow to him the vassal knee
Whose sceptre shadows realms from sea to sea.

Seb. Away—away! this is no place for him
Whose name hath thus resounded, but is now
A word of desolation.   [*Exit.*

ODE ON THE DEFEAT OF KING SEBASTIAN OF PORTUGAL AND HIS ARMY, IN AFRICA.

TRANSLATED FROM THE SPANISH OF HERRERA

FERDINAND DE HERRERA, surnamed the Divine, was a Spanish poet, who lived in the reign of Charles V., and is still considered by the Castilians as one of their classic writers. He aimed at the introduction of a new style into Spanish poetry, and his lyrics are distinguished by the sustained majesty of their language, the frequent recurrence of expressions and images, derived apparently from a fervent study of the prophetic books of Scripture, and the lofty tone of national pride maintained throughout, and justified indeed by the nature of the subjects to which some of these productions are devoted. This last characteristic is blended with a deep and enthusiastic feeling of religion, which rather exalts than tempers the haughty confidence of the poet in the high destinies of his country. Spain is to him what Judea was to the bards who sung beneath the shadow of her palm-trees—the chosen and favored land, whose people, severed from all others by the purity and devotedness of their faith, are peculiarly called to wreak the vengeance of Heaven upon the infidel. This triumphant conviction is powerfully expressed in his magnificent Ode on the Battle of Lepanto.

The impression of deep solemnity left upon the mind of the Spanish reader, by another of Herrera's lyric compositions, will, it is feared, be very inadequately conveyed through the medium of the following translation.

"Voz de dolor, y canto de gemido," &c.

A VOICE of woe, a murmur of lament,
A spirit of deep fear and mingled ire;
Let such record the day, the day of wail
For Lusitania's bitter chastening sent!
She who hath seen her power, her fame expire,
And mourns them in the dust, discrown'd and pale!
    And let the awful tale
With grief and horror every realm o'ershade,
    From Afric's burning main
To the far sea, in other hues array'd,
And the red limits of the Orient's reign,
Whose nations, haughty though subdued, behold
Christ's glorious banner to the winds unfold.

Alas! for those that in embattled power,
And vain array of chariots and of horse,
O desert Libya! sought thy fatal coast!
And trusting not in Him, the eternal source
Of might and glory, but in earthly force,
Making the strength of multitudes their boast,
    A flush'd and crested host,
Elate in lofty dreams of victory, trode
Their path of pride, as o'er a conquer'd land
Given for the spoil; nor raised their eyes to God:
And Israel's Holy One withdrew his hand,
Their sole support;—and heavily and prone
They fell—the car, the steed, the rider, all o'erthrown!

It came, the hour of wrath, the hour of woe,
Which to deep solitude and tears consign'd
The peopled realm, the realm of joy and mirth;
A gloom was on the heavens, no mantling glow
Announced the morn—it seem'd as nature pined,
And boding clouds obscured the sunbeam's birth;
    While, startling the pale earth,
Bursting upon the mighty and the proud
    With visitation dread,
Their crests the Eternal, in his anger, bow'd,
And raised barbarian nations o'er their head,
The inflexible, the fierce, who seek not gold,
But vengeance on their foes, relentless, uncontroll'd.

Then was the sword let loose, the flaming sword
Of the strong infidel's ignoble hand,
Amidst that host, the pride, the flower, the crown
Of thy fair knighthood; and the insatiate horde,
Not with thy life content, O ruin'd land!
Sad Lusitania! even thy bright renown
    Defaced and trampled down;
And scatter'd, rushing as a torrent flood,
Thy pomp of arms and banners;—till the sands
Became a lake of blood—thy noblest blood!—
The plain a mountain of thy slaughter'd bands.
Strength on thy foes, resistless might was shed;
On thy devoted sons—amaze, and shame, and dread.

Are *these* the conquerors, *these* the lords of fight,
The warrior men, the invincible, the famed,
Who shook the earth with terror and dismay,
Whose spoils were empires?—They that in their might
The haughty strength of savage nations tamed,
And gave the spacious orient realms of day
    To desolation's sway,
Making the cities of imperial name
    E'en as the desert place?

Where now the fearless heart, the soul of flame?
Thus has their glory closed its dazzling race
In one brief hour? Is this their valor's doom,
On distant shores to fall, and find not even a tomb?

Once were they in their splendor and their pride,
As an imperial cedar on the brow
Of the Great Lebanon! It rose, array'd
In its rich pomp of foliage, and of wide
Majestic branches, leaving far below
All children of the forest. To its shade
    The waters tribute paid,
Fostering its beauty. Birds found shelter there
Whose flight is of the loftiest through the sky,
And the wild mountain-creatures made their lair
Beneath; and nations by its canopy
Were shadow'd o'er. Supreme it stood, and ne'er
Had earth beheld a tree so excellently fair.

By all elated, on its verdant stem,
Confiding solely in its regal height,
It soar'd presumptuous, as for empire born;
And God for this removed its diadem,
And cast it from its regions of delight,
Forth to the spoiler, as a prey and scorn,
    By the deep roots uptorn!
And lo! encumb'ring the lone hills it lay,
Shorn of its leaves, dismantled of its state,
While, pale with fear, men hurried far away,
Who in its ample shade had found so late
Their bower of rest; and nature's savage race
'Midst the great ruin sought their dwelling-place.

But thou, base Libya, thou whose arid sand
Hath been a kingdom's death-bed, where one fate
Closed her bright life, and her majestic fame,—
Though to thy feeble and barbarian hand
Hath fall'n the victory, be not thou elate!
Boast not thyself, though thine that day of shame,
    Unworthy of a name!
Know, if the Spaniard in his wrath advance,
Aroused to vengeance by a nation's cry,
    Pierced by his searching lance,
Soon shalt thou expiate crime with agony,
And thine affrighted streams to ocean's flood
An ample tribute bear of Afric's Paynim blood.

THE SIEGE OF VALENCIA.

A DRAMATIC POEM.

Judicio ha dado esta no vista hazanna,
Del valor que en los siglos venideros
Tendran los Hijos de la fuerte Espanna,
Hijos de tal padres herederos.

Hallo sola en Numancia todo quanto
Debe con justo titulo cantarse,
Y lo que puede dar materia al canto.
Numancia de Cervantes.

ADVERTISEMENT.

The history of Spain records two instances of the severe and self-devoting heroism, which forms the subject of the following dramatic poem. The first of these occurred at the siege of Tarifa, which was defended, in 1294, for Sancho, King of Castile, during the rebellion of his brother, Don Juan, by Guzman, surnamed the Good.* The second is related of Alonzo Lopez de Texeda, who, until his garrison had been utterly disabled by pestilence, maintained the city of Zamora for the children of Don Pedro the Cruel, against the forces of Henrique of Trastamara.†

Impressive as were the circumstances which distinguished both these memorable sieges, it appeared to the author of the following pages that a deeper interest, as well as a stronger color of nationality, might be imparted to the scenes in which she has feebly attempted "to describe high passions and high actions," by connecting a religious feeling with the patriotism and high-minded loyalty which had thus been proved "faithful unto death," and by surrounding her ideal *dramatis personæ* with recollections derived from the heroic legends of Spanish chivalry. She has, for this reason, employed the agency of imaginary characters, and fixed upon Valencia del Cid as the scene to give them

"A local habitation and a name."

Dram. Pers,

ALVAR GONZALEZ,   *Governor of Valencia.*
ALPHONSO, CARLOS,   *His Sons.*
HERNANDEZ,   *A Priest.*
ABDULLAH,   *A Moorish Prince, Chief of the Army besieging Valencia.*
GARCIAS,   *A Spanish Knight.*

ELMINA   *Wife to Gonzalez.*
XIMENA,   *Her Daughter.*
THERESA,   *An Attendant.*
Citizens, Soldiers, Attendants, &c.

* See Quintana's *Vidas de Espanoles Célèbres*, p. 53.
† See the Preface to Southey's *Chronicle of the Cid.*

THE SIEGE OF VALENCIA.

Scene I.

Room in a Palace of Valencia.—Ximena *Singing to a Lute*

BALLAD.

"Thou hast not been with a festal throng
   At the pouring of the wine;
Men bear not from the hall of song
   A mien so dark as thine!
    There's blood upon thy shield,
    There's dust upon thy plume,
Thou hast brought from some disastrous field
    That brow of wrath and gloom!"

"And is there blood upon my shield?
   Maiden, it well may be!
We have sent the streams, from our battle-field,
   All darken'd to the sea!
    We have given the founts a stain,
    'Midst their woods of ancient pine;
And the ground is wet—but not with rain,
    Deep dyed—but not with wine!

"The ground it wet—but not with rain—
   We have been in war array,
And the noblest blood of Christian Spain
   Hath bathed her soil to-day.
    I have seen the strong man die,
    And the stripling meet his fate,
Where the mountain-winds go sounding by,
    In the Roncesvalles' Strait.

"In the gloomy Roncesvalles' Strait
   There are helms and lances left;
And they that moved at morn elate
   On a bed of heath are left!
    There's many a fair young face
    Which the war-steed hath gone o'er;
At many a board there is kept a place
    For those that come no more!"

"Alas! for love, for woman's breast,
   If woe like this must be!
Hath thou seen a youth with an eagle crest,
   And a white plume waving free?
    With his proud quick-flashing eye,
    And his mien of knightly state?
Doth he come from where the swords flash'd high
    In the Roncesvalles' Strait?"

"In the gloomy Roncesvalles' Strait
   I saw, and mark'd him well;
For nobly on his steed he sate,
   When the pride of manhood fell!

But it is not *youth* which turns
From the field of spears again;
For the boy's high heart too wildly burns,
Till it rests admidst the slain!"

" Thou canst not say that *he* lies low,
The lovely and the brave?
Oh! none could look on his joyous brow,
And think upon the grave!
Dark, dark perchance the day,
Hath been with valor's fate;
But *he* is on his homeward way,
From the Roncesvalles' Strait!"

"There is dust upon his joyous brow,
And o'er his graceful head;
And the war-horse will not wake him now
Though it browse his greensward bed!
I have seen the stripling die,
And the strong man meet his fate,
Where the mountain-winds go sounding by,
In the Roncesvalles' Strait!"

[ELMINA *enters.*
Elm. Your songs are not as those of other days,
Mine own Ximena! Where is now the young
And buoyant spirit of the morn, which once
Breathed in your spring-like melodies, and woke
Joy's echo from all hearts?
Xim. My mother, this
Is not the free air of our mountain-wilds;
And these are not the halls wherein my voice
First pour'd those gladd'ning strains.
Elm. Alas! thy heart
(I see it well) doth sicken for the pure
Free-wand'ring breezes of the joyous hills,
Where thy young brothers, o'er the rock and heath,
Bound in glad boyhood, e'en as torrent streams
Leap brightly from the heights. Had we not been
Within these walls, thus suddenly begirt,
Thou shouldst have track'd ere now, with step as light
Their wild-wood paths.
Xim. I would not but have shared
These hours of woe and peril, though the deep
And solemn feelings wak'ning at their voice,
Claim all the wrought-up spirit to themselves,
And will not blend with mirth. The storm doth hush
All floating whispery sounds, all bird-notes wild
O' th' summer-forest, filling earth and heaven
With its own awful music. And 'tis well!
Should not a hero's child be train'd to hear
The trumpet's blast unstartled, and to look

34

In the fix'd face of death without dismay?
  Elm. Woe! woe! that aught so gentle and so young
Should thus be call'd to stand i' the tempest's path,
And bear the token and the hue of death
On a bright soul so soon! I had not shrunk
From mine own lot; but thou, my child, shouldst move,
As a light breeze of heaven, through summer-bowers,
And not o'er foaming billows. We are fall'n
On dark and evil days!
  Xim.   Ay, days, that wake
All to their tasks!—Youth may not loiter now
In the green walks of spring; and womanhood
Is summon'd unto conflicts, heretofore
The lot of warrior-souls. Strength is born
In the deep silence of long-suffering hearts:
Not amidst joy.
  Elm.   Hast thou some secret woe
That thus thou speak'st?
  Xim.   What sorrow should be mine,
Unknown to thee?
  Elm.   Alas! the baleful air
Wherewith the pestilence in darkness walks
Through the devoted city, like a blight
Amidst the rose-tints of thy cheek hath fall'n,
And wrought an early withering!—Thou hast cross'd
The paths of death, and minister'd to those
O'er whom his shadow rested, till thine eye
Hath changed its glancing sunbeam for a still,
Deep, solemn radiance, and thy brow hath caught
A wild and high expression, which at times
Fades into desolate calmness, most unlike
What youth's bright mien should wear. My gentle child!
I look on thee in fear!
  Xim.   Thou hast no cause
To fear for me. When the wild clash of steel,
And the deep tambour, and the heavy step
Of armed men, break on our morning dreams!
When, hour by hour, the noble and the brave
Are falling round us, and we deem it much
To give them funeral-rites, and call them blest
If the good sword, in its own stormy hour,
Hath done its work upon them, ere disease
Had chill'd their fiery blood;—it is no time
For the light mien wherewith, in happier hours,
We trode the woodland mazes, when young leaves
Were whisp'ring in the gale.—My father comes—
Oh! speak of me no more. I would not shade
His princely aspect with a thought less high
Than his proud duties claim.
         [G<small>ONZALEZ</small> ***enters.***
  Elm.   My noble lord!
Welcome from this day's toil!—It is the hour

Whose shadows, as they deepen, bring repose
Unto all weary men! and wilt not thou
Free thy mail'd bosom from the corslet's weight,
To rest at fall of eve?
    Gon.   There may be rest
For the tired peasant, when the vesper-bell
Doth send him to his cabin, and beneath
His vine and olive he may sit at eve,
Watching his children's sport: but unto *him*
Who keeps the watch-place on the mountain-height,
When Heaven lets loose the storms that chasten realms
—Who speaks of rest?
    Xim.   My father, shall I fill
The wine-cup for thy lips, or bring the lute
Whose sounds thou lovest?
    Gon.   If there be strains of **power**
To rouse a spirit, which in triumphant scorn
May cast off nature's feebleness, and hold
Its proud career unshackled, dashing down
Tears and fond thoughts to earth; give voice to those!
I have need of such, Ximena!—we must hear
No melting music now!
    Xim.   I know all high
Heroic ditties of the elder-time,
Sung by the mountain-Christians,[1] in the holds
Of th' everlasting hills, whose snows yet bear
The print of Freedom's step; and all wild strains
Wherein the dark serranos* teach the rocks,
And the pine forests, deeply to resound
The praise of later champions. Wouldst thou hear
The war-song of thine ancestor, the Cid?
    Gon. Ay, speak of him; for in that name is power,
Such as might rescue kingdoms! Speak of him!
We are his children! They that can look back
I' th' annals of their house on such a name,
How should *they* take dishonor by the hand,
And o'er the threshold of their father's halls
First lead her as a guest?
    Elm.   Oh, why is this?
How my heart sinks!
    Gon.   It must not fail thee *yet*,
Daughter of heroes!—thine inheritance
Is strength to meet all conflicts. Thou canst number
In thy long line of glorious ancestry
Men, the bright offering of whose blood hath made
The ground it bathed e'en as an altar, whence
High thoughts shall rise for ever. Bore they not,
'Midst flame and sword, their witness of the Cross,
With its victorious inspiration girt
As with a conqueror's robe, till th' infidel

Serranos, mountaineers.

O'erawed, shrank back before them?—Ay, the earth
Doth call them martyrs, but *their* agonies
Were of a moment, tortures whose brief aim
Was to destroy, within whose powers and scope
Lay nought but dust.—And earth doth call them *martyrs!*
Why, Heaven but claim'd their blood, their lives, and not
The things which grow as tendrils round their hearts;
No, not their children!
   Elm.   Mean'st thou?—know'st thou augnt?—
I cannot utter it—My sons! my sons!
Is it of them?—Oh! wouldst thou speak of them?
   Gon. A mother's heart divineth but too well!
   Elm. Speak, I adjure thee!—I can bear it all.—
Where are my children?
   Gon.   In the Moorish camp
Whose lines have girt the city.
   Xim.   But they live?
—All is not lost, my mother!
   Elm.   Say, they live.
   Gon. Elmina, still they live.
   Elm. But captives!—They
Whom my fond heart had imaged to itself
Bounding from cliff to cliff amidst the wilds
Where the rock-eagle seem'd not more secure
In its rejoicing freedom!—and my boys
Are captives with the Moor!—Oh! how was this?
   Gon. Alas! our brave Alphonso, in the pride
Of boyish daring, left our mountain-halls,
With his young brother, eager to behold
The face of noble war. Thence on their way
Were the rash wanderers captured.
   Elm.   'Tis enough.
— And when shall they be ransom'd?
   Gon.   There is ask'd
A ransom far too high.
   Elm   What! have we wealth
Which might redeem a monarch, and our sons
The while wear fetters?—Take thou all for them,
And we will cast our worthless grandeur from us,
As 'twere a cumbrous robe!—Why *thou* art one.
To whose high nature pomp hath ever been
But as the plumage to a warrior's helm,
Worn or thrown off as lightly. And for me,
Thou know'st not how serenely I could take
The peasant's lot upon me, so my heart,
Amidst its deep affections undisturb'd,
May dwell in silence.
   Xim.   Father! doubt thou not
But we will bind ourselves to poverty,
With glad devotedness, if this, but this,
May win them back.—Distrust us not, my father!
We can bear all things.

Gon.   Can ye bear disgrace?
Xim. We were not born for this.
Gon.   No, thou say'st well!
Hold to that lofty faith.—My wife, my child!
Hath earth no treasures richer than the gems
Torn from her secret caverns?—If by them
Chains may be riven, then let the captive spring
Rejoicing to the light!—But he, for whom
Freedom and life may but be worn with shame,
Hath nought to do, save fearlessly to fix
His stedfast look on the majestic heavens,
And proudly die!
  Elm.   Gonzalez, *who* must die?
  Gon. (*hurridly.*) They on whose lives a fearful price is set,
But to be paid by treason!—Is't enough!
Or must I yet seek words?
  Elm.   That look saith more!—
Thou canst not mean——
  Gon. I do!—why dwells there not
Power in a glance to speak it?—They must die!
They—must their names be told—*Our sons* must die
Unless I yield the city!
  Xim.   Oh! look up!
My mother, sink not thus!—Until the grave
Shut from our sight its victims, there is hope.
  Elm. (*in a low voice.*) Whose knell was in the breeze?—No,
      no, not *theirs?*
Whose was the blessed voice that spoke of hope?
—And there is hope!—I will not be subdued—
I will not hear a whisper of despair!
For nature is all-powerful, and her breath
Moves like a quickening spirit o'er the depths
Within a father's heart.—Thou too, Gonzalez,
Wilt tell me there is hope!
  Gon. (*solemnly.*)   Hope but in Him
Who bade the patriarch lay his fair young son
Bound on the shrine of sacrifice, and when
The bright steel quiver'd in the father's hand
Just raised to strike, sent forth his awful voice
Through the still clouds, and on the breathless air
Commanding to withhold!—Earth has no hope:
It rests with Him,
  Elm.   *Thou* canst not tell me this!
Thou father of my sons, within whose hands
Doth lie thy children's fate.
  Gon.   If there have been
Men in whose bosoms nature's voice hath made
Its accents as the solitary sound
Of an o'erpowering torrent, silencing
Th' austere and yet divine remonstrances
Whisper'd by faith and honor, lift thy hands;
And, to that heaven which arms the brave with strength,

Pray, that the father of thy sons may ne'er
Be thus found wanting!
    Elm.   Then their doom is seal'd!—
Thou wilt not save thy children?
    Gon.   Hast thou cause,
Wife of my youth! to deem it lies within
The bounds of possible things, that I should link
My name to that word—*traitor?*—They that sleep
On their proud battle-fields, thy sires and mine,
Died not for this!
    Elm.   Oh, cold and hard of heart!
Thou shouldst be born for empire, since thy soul
Thus lightly from all human bonds can free
Its haughty flight!—Men! men! too much is yours
Of vantage; ye that with a sound, a breath,
A shadow, thus can fill the desolate space
Of rooted up affections, o'er whose void
Our yearning hearts must wither!—So it is,
Dominion must be won!—Nay, leave me not—
My heart is bursting, and I *must* be heard!
Heaven hath given power to mortal agony,
As to the elements in their hour of might
And mastery o'er creation!—Who shall dare
To mock that fearful strength!—I *must* be heard!
Give me my sons!
    Gon.   That they may live to hide
With covering hands th' indignant flush of shame
On their young brows, when men shall speak of him
They call'd their father!—Was the oath, whereby,
On th' altar of my faith, I bound myself,
With an unswerving spirit to maintain
This free and Christian city for my God,
And for my king, a writing traced on sand?
That passionate tears should wash it from the earth,
Or e'en the life-drops of a bleeding heart
Efface it, as a billow sweeps away
The last light vessel's wake?—Then never more
Let man's deep vows be trusted!—though enforced
By all th' appeals of high remembrances,
And silent claims o' th' sepulchres, wherein
His fathers with their stainless glory sleep,
On their good swords! Think'st thou *I* feel no pangs?
He that hath given me sons doth know the heart
Whose treasure he recalls.—Of this no more.
'Tis vain. I tell thee that the inviolate cross
Still from our ancient temples, must look up
Through the blue heavens of Spain, thought at its foot
I perish, with my race. Thou *darest* not ask
That I, the son of warriors—men who died
To fix it on that proud supremacy—
Should tear the sign of our victorious faith,

From its high place of sunbeams, for the Moor
In impious joy to trample!
    Elm.   Scorn me not
In mine extreme of misery!—Thou art strong—
Thy heart is not as mine.—My brain grows wild;
I know not what I ask!—And yet 'twere but
Anticipating fate—since it must fall,
That cross *must* fall at last! There is no power,
No hope within this city of the grave,
To keep its place on high. Her sultry air
Breathes heavily of death, her warriors sink
Beneath their ancient banners, ere the Moor
Hath bent his bow against them; for the shaft
Of pestilence flies more swiftly to its mark,
Than the arrow of the desert. Even the skies
O'erhang the desolate splendor of·her domes
With an ill omen's aspect, shaping forth,
From the dull clouds, wild menacing forms and signs
Foreboding ruin. *Man* might be withstood,
But who shall cope with famine and disease
When leagued with armed foes?—Where now the aid
Where the long-promised lances, of Castile?
—We are forsaken in our utmost need—
By Heaven and earth forsaken!
    Gon.   If this be
(And yet I will not deem it,) we must fall
As men that in severe devotedness
Have chosen their part, and bound themselves to death,
Through high conviction that their suffering land,
By the free blood of martyrdom alone,
Shall call deliverance down.
    Elm   Oh! I have stood
Beside thee through the beating storms of life,
With the true heart of unrepining love,
As the poor peasant's mate doth cheerily,
In the parch'd vineyard, or the harvest-field,
Bearing her part, sustain with him the heat
And burden of the day;—But now the hour,
The heavy hour is come, when human strength
Sinks down, a toil-worn pilgrim, in the dust,
Owning that woe is mightier!—Spare me yet
This bitter cup, my husband!—Let not her,
The mother of the lovely, sit and mourn
In her unpeopled home, a broken stem,
O'er its fallen roses dying!
    Gon.   Urge me not,
Thou that through all sharp conflicts has been found
Worthy a brave man's love!—oh, urge me not
To guilt, which through the midst of blinding tears,
In its own hues thou seest not!—Death may scarce
Bring aught like this!

Elm. All, all thy gentle race,
The beautiful beings that around thee grew,
Creatures of sunshine! Wilt thou doom them all?
—She too, thy daughter—doth her smile unmark'd
Pass from thee, with its radiance, day by day?
Shadows are gathering round her—seest thou not
The misty dimness of the spoiler's breath
Hangs o'er her beauty, and the face which made
The summer of our hearts, now doth but send,
With every glance, deep bodings through the soul,
Telling of early fate.
   Gon. I see a change
Far nobler on her brow!—She is as one,
Who, at the trumpet's sudden call, hath risen
From the gay banquet, and in scorn cast down
The wine-cup, and the garland, and the lute
Of festal hours, for the good spear and helm,
Beseeming sterner tasks.—Her eye hath lost
The beam which laugh'd upon th' awakening heart,
E'en as morn breaks o'er earth. But far within
Its full dark orb, a light hath sprung, whose source
Lies deeper in the soul.—And let the torch
Which but illumed the glittering pageant, fade!
The altar-flame, i' th' sanctuary's recess,
Burns quenchless, being of heaven!—She hath put on
Courage, and faith, and generous constancy,
Even as a breastplate.—Ay, men look on her,
As she goes forth, serenely to her tasks,
Binding the warrior's wounds, and bearing fresh
Cool draughts to fever'd lips; they look on her,
Thus moving in her beautiful array
Of gentle fortitude, and bless the fair
Majestic vision, and unmurmuring turn
Unto their heavy toils.
   Elm. And seest thou not
In that high faith and strong collectedness,
A fearful inspiration?—*They* have cause
To tremble, who behold th' unearthly light
Of high, and, it may be prophetic thought,
Investing youth with grandeur!—From the grave
It rises, on whose shadowy brink thy child
Waits but a father's hand to snatch her back
Into the laughing sunshine.—Kneel with me;
Ximena, kneel beside me, and implore
That which a deeper, more prevailing voice
Than ours doth ask, and will not be denied;
—His children's lives!
   Xim. Alas! this may not be,
Mother!—I cannot. [*Exit* XIMENA.
   Gon. My heroic child!
—A terrible sacrifice thou claim'st, O God!

From creatures in whose agonizing hearts
Nature is strong as death!
  Elm.   Is't thus in thine?
Away!—what time is given thee to resolve
On—what I cannot utter?—Speak! thou know'st
Too well what I would say.
  Gon.   Until—ask not!
The time is brief.
  Elm.   Thou said'st—I heard not right—
  Gon. The time is brief.
  Elm. What! must we burst all ties
Wherewith the thrilling chords of life are twined;
And, for this task's fulfilment, can it be
That man in his cold heartlessness, hath dared,
To number and to mete us forth the sands
Of hours, nay, moments?—Why, the sentenced **wretch,**
He on whose soul there rests a brother's blood
Pour'd forth in slumber, is allow'd more time
To wean his turbulent passions from the world
His presence doth pollute!—It is not thus!
We must have time to school us.
  Gon.   We have but
To bow the head in silence, when Heaven's voice
Calls back the things we love.
  Elm. Love! love!—there are soft smiles and gentle **words**
And there are faces, skilful to put on
The look we trust in—and 'tis mockery all!
—A faithless mist, a desert-vapor, wearing
The brightness of clear waters, thus to cheat
The thirst that semblance kindled!—There is none,
In all this cold and hollow world, no fount
Of deep, strong, deathless love, save that within
A mother's heart.—It is but pride, wherewith
To his fair son the father's eye doth turn,
Watching his growth. Ay, on the boy he looks,
The bright glad creature springing in his path,
But as the heir of his great name, the young
And stately tree, whose rising strength erelong
Shall bear his trophies well.—And this is love!
This is *man's* love!—What marvel?—*you* ne'er made
Your breast the pillow of his infancy,
While to the fulness of your heart's glad heavings
His fair cheek rose and fell! and his bright hair
Waved softly to your breath!—*You* ne'er kept watch
Beside him, till the last pale star had set,
And morn, all dazzling, as in triumph, broke
On your dim weary eye; yet *yours* the face
Which, early faded through fond care for him,
Hung o'er his sleep, and, duly as heaven's light,
Was there to greet his wak'ning! *You* ne'er smooth'd
His couch, ne'er sung him to his rosy rest,
Caught his least whisper, when his voice from your,

Had learn'd soft utterance ; press'd your lip to his,
When fever parch'd it ; hush'd his wayward cries,
With patient, vigilant, never-wearied love !
No ! these are *woman's* tasks !—In these her youth,
And bloom of cheek, and buoyancy of heart,
Steal from her all unmark'd !—My boys ! my boys !
Hath vain affection borne with all for this ?
—Why were ye given me ?
  Gon.   Is there strength in man
Thus to endure ? That thou couldst read, through all
Its depths of silent agony, the heart
Thy voice of woe doth rend !
  Elm. Thy heart—*thy* heart !—Away ! it feels not *now*
But an hour comes to tame the mighty man
Unto the infant's weakness ; nor shall heaven
Spare you that bitter chastening !—May you live
To be alone, when loneliness doth seem
Most heavy to sustain !—For me, my voice
Of prayer and fruitless weeping shall be soon
With all forgotten sounds ; my quiet place
Low with my lovely ones, and we shall sleep,
Though kings lead armies o'er us, we shall sleep,
Wrapt in earth's covering mantle !—you the while
Shall sit within your vast, forsaken halls,
And hear the wild and melancholy winds
Moan through their drooping banners, never more
To wave above your race. Ay, then call up
Shadows—dim phantom's from ancestral tombs,
But all, all—*glorious*—conquerors, chieftains, kings,
To people that cold void !—And when the strength
From your right arm hath melted, when the blast
Of the shrill clarion gives your heart no more
A fiery wakening ; if at last you pine
For the glad voices and the bounding steps,
Once through your home re-echoing, and the clasp
Of twining arms, and all the joyous light
Of eyes that laughed with youth, and made your board
A place of sunshine ; when those days are come.
Then in your utter desolation, turn
To the cold world, the smiling, faithless world,
Which hath swept past you long, and bid it quench
Your soul's deep thirst with *fame !* immortal *fame !*
Fame to the sick of heart !—a gorgeous robe.
A crown of victory, unto him that dies
I' th' burning waste, for water !
  Gon.   This from *thee* !
Now the last drop of bitterness is pour'd.
Elmina—I forgive thee !   [*Exit* ELMINA.
                Aid me, Heaven !
From whom alone is power !—Oh ! thou hast set
Duties so stern of aspect in my path,
They almost, to my startled gaze, assume

The hue of things less hallow'd! Men have sunk
Unblamed beneath such trials! Doth not He
Who made us know the limits of our strength?
My wife! my sons!—Away! I must not pause
To give my heart one moment's mastery thus!
          [*Exit* GONZALEZ.

SCENE II.—*The Aisle of a Gothic Church.*

HERNANDEZ, GARCIAS, *and others.*

 Her. The rites are closed. Now, valiant men depart,
Each to his place—I may not say, of rest—
Your faithful vigils for your sons may win
What must not be your own. Ye are as those
Who sow, in peril and in care, the seed
Of the fair tree, beneath whose stately shade
They may not sit. But bless'd be those who toil
For after-days!—All high and holy thoughts
Be with you, warriors, through the lingering hours
Of the night-watch!
 Gar.   Ay, father! we have need
Of high and holy thoughts, wherewith to fence
Our hearts against despair. Yet have I been
From youth a son of war. The stars have look'd
A thousand times upon my couch of heath,
Spread 'midst the wild sierras, by some stream
Whose dark-red waves look'd e'en as though their source
Lay not in rocky caverns, but the veins
Of noble hearts; while many a knightly crest
Roll'd with them to the deep. And, in the years
Of my long exile and captivity,
With the fierce Arab I have watch'd beneath
The still, pale shadow of some lonely palm,
At midnight in the desert; while the wind
Swell'd with the lion's roar, and heavily
The fearfulness and might of solitude
Press'd on my weary heart.
 Her. (*thoughtfully.*) Thou little know'st
Of what is solitude!—I tell thee, those
For whom—in earth's remotest nook, howe'er
Divided from their path by chain on chain
Of mighty mountains, and the amplitude
Of rolling seas—there beats one human heart,
Their breathes one being, unto whom their name
Comes with a thrilling and a gladd'ning sound
Heard o'er the din of life, are not alone!
Not on the deep, nor in the wild, alone;
For there is that on earth with which they hold
A brotherhood of soul!—Call *him* alone,
Who stands shut out from this!—and let not those
Whose homes are bright with sunshine and with love,

Put on the insolence of happiness,
Glorying in that proud lot!—A lonely hour
Is on its way to each, to all; for Death
Knows no companionship.
 Gar.   I have look'd on Death
In field, and storm, and flood. But never yet
Hath aught weigh'd down my spirit to a mood
Of sadness, dreaming o'er dark auguries,
Like this, our watch by midnight. Fearful things,
Are gathering round us. Death upon the earth,
Omens in heaven!—The summer skies put forth
No clear bright stars above us, but at times,
Catching some comet's fiery hue of wrath,
Marshal their clouds to armies, traversing
Heaven with the rush of meteor-steeds, th' array
Of spears and banners, tossing like the pines
Of Pyrenean forests, when the storm
Doth sweep the mountains.
 Her.   Ay, last night I too
Kept vigil, gazing on the angry heavens;
And I beheld the meeting and the shock
Of those wild hosts i' th' air, when, as they closed,
A red and sultry mist, like that which mantles
The thunder's path, fell o'er them. Then were flung
Through the dull glare, broad cloudy banners forth,
And chariots seem'd to whirl, and steeds to sink,
Bearing down crested warriors. But all this
Was dim and shadowy;—then swift darkness rush'd
Down on the unearthly battle, as the deep
Swept o'er the Egyptian's armament.—I look'd—
And all that fiery field of plumes and spears
Was blotted from heaven's face!—I look'd again—
And from the brooding mass of cloud leap'd forth
One meteor-sword, which o'er the reddening sea
Shook with strange motion, such as earthquakes give
Unto a rocking citadel!—I beheld,
And yet my spirit sunk not.
 Gar.   Neither deem
That mine hath blench'd. But these are sights and sounds
To awe the firmest.—Know'st thou what we hear
At midnight from the walls?—Were 't but the deep
Barbaric horn, or Moorish tambour's peal,
Thence might the warrior's heart catch impulses
Quickening its fiery currents. But our ears
Are pierced by other tones. We hear the knell
For brave men in their noon of strength cut down,
And the shrill wail of woman, and the dirge
Faint swelling through the streets. Then e'en the air
Hath strange and fitful murmurs of lament,
As if the viewless watchers of the land
Sigh'd on its hollow breezes!—To my soul,
The torrent rush of battle, with its din

Of trampling steeds and ringing panoply,
Were, after these faint sounds of drooping woe,
As the free sky's glad music unto him
Who leaves a couch of sickness.
 Her. (*with solemnity.*)   If to plunge
In the mid-waves of combat, as they bear
Chargers and spearmen onwards; and to make
A reckless bosom's front the buoyant mark,
On that wild current, for ten thousand arrows;
If *thus* to dare were valor's noblest aim,
Lightly might fame be won! But there are things
Which ask a spirit of more exalted pitch,
And courage temper'd with a holier fire!
Well may'st thou say that these are fearful times,
Therefore be firm, be patient!—There is strength,
And a fierce instinct, e'en in common souls,
To bear up manhood with a stormy joy,
When red swords meet in lightning!—But our task
Is more and nobler!—We have to endure,
And to keep watch, and to arouse a land,
And to defend an altar!—If we fall,
So that our blood make but the millionth part
Of Spain's great ransom, we may count it joy
To die upon her bosom, and beneath
The banner of her faith!—Think but on this,
And gird your hearts with silent fortitude,
Suffering, yet hoping all things—Fare ye well.
 Gar. Father, farewell.
       [*Exeunt* GARCIAS *and his followers.*
 Her.   These men have earthly ties
And bondage on their natures! To the cause
Of God, and Spain's revenge, they bring but half
Their energies and hopes. But he whom Heaven
Hath call'd to be th' awakener of a land,
Should have his soul's affections all absorb'd
In that majestic purpose, and press on
To its fulfilment, as a mountain-born
And mighty stream, with all its vassal-rills,
Sweeps proudly to the ocean, pausing not
To dally with the flowers. Hark! What quick step
Comes hurrying through the gloom at this dead hour?
            [ELMINA *enters*
 Elm. Are not all hours as one to misery? Why
Should *she* take note of time, for whom the day
And night have lost their blessed attributes
Of sunshine and repose?
 Her.   I know thy griefs;
But there are trials for the noble heart,
Wherein its own deep fountains must supply
All it can hope of comfort. Pity's voice
Comes with vain sweetness to th' unheeding ear
Of anguish e'en as music heard afar

On the green shore, by him who perishes
'Midst rocks and eddying waters.
 Elm.   Think thou not
I sought thee but for pity. I am come
For that which grief is priv'leged to demand
With an imperious claim, from all whose form,
Whose human form, doth seal them unto suffering!
Father! I ask thine *aid*.
 Her.   There is no aid
For thee or for thy children, but with Him
Whose presence is around us in the cloud,
As in the shining and the glorious light.
 Elm. There is no aid!—art thou a man of God
Art thou a man of sorrow?—for the world
Doth call thee such—and hast thou not been taught
By God and sorrow?—mighty as they are,
To own the claims of misery?
 Her.   Is there power
With me to save thy sons?—implore of Heaven!
 Elm. Doth not Heaven work its purposes by man?
I tell thee *thou* canst save them! Art thou not
Gonzalez' counsellor? Unto him thy words
Are e'en as oracles——
 Her,   And therefore?—Speak!
The noble daughter of Pelayo's line
Hath nought to ask, unworthy of the name
Which is a nation's heritage. Dost thou shrink?
 Elm. Have pity on me, father! I must speak
That, from the thought of which but yesterday
I had recoiled in scorn!—But this is past.
Oh! we grow humble in our agonies,
And to the dust—their birthplace—bow the heads
That wore the crown of glory!—I am weak—
My chastening is far more than I can bear.
 Her. These are no times for weakness. On our hills
The ancient cedars, in their gather'd might,
Are battling with the tempest; and the flower
Which cannot meet its driving blast must die,
—But thou hast drawn thy nurture from a stem
Unwont to bend or break.—Lift thy proud head,
Daughter of Spain!—What would'st thou with thy lord?
 Elm. Look not upon me thus!—I have no power
To tell thee. Take thy keen disdainful eye
Off from my soul!—What! am I sunk to this?
I, whose blood sprung from heroes!—How my sons
Will scorn the mother that would bring disgrace
On their majestic line!—My sons! my sons!
—Now is all else forgotten!—I had once
A babe that in the early spring-time lay
Sickening upon my bosom, till at last,
When earth's young flowers were opening to the sun,
Death sunk on his meek eyelid, and I deem'd

All sorrow light to mine!—But now the fate
Of all my children seems to brood above me
In the dark thunder-clouds!—Oh! I have power
And voice unfaltering now to speak my prayer
And my last lingering hope, that thou should'st win
The father to relent, to save his sons!
 Her. By yielding up the city?
 Elm.   Rather say
By meeting that which gathers close upon us
Perchance one day the sooner!—Is 't not so?
Must we not yield at last?--How long shall man
Array his single breast against disease,
And famine, and the sword?
 Her.   How long?—While he
Who shadows forth his power more gloriously
In the high deeds and sufferings of the soul,
Than in the circling heavens, with all their stars,
Or the far-sounding deep, doth send abroad
A spirit, which takes affliction for its mate,
In the good cause, with solemn joy!—How long?
—And who art *thou*, that, in the littleness
Of thine own selfish purpose, would'st set bounds
To the free current of all noble thought
And generous action, bidding its bright waves
Be stay'd, and flow no further?—But the Power
Whose interdict is laid on seas and orbs,
To chain them in from wandering, hath assign'd
No limits unto that which man's high strength
Shall, through its aid achieve!
 Elm.   Oh! there are times,
When *all* that hopeless courage can achieve
But sheds a mournful beauty o'er the fate
Of those who die in vain.
 Her   *Who* dies in vain
Upon his country's war-fields, and within
The shadow of her altars?—Feeble heart!
I tell thee that the voice of noble blood,
Thus pour'd for faith and freedom, hath a tone
Which, from the night of ages, from the gulf
Of death, shall burst, and make its high appeal
Sound unto earth and heaven! Ay, let the land,
Whose sons, through centuries of woe hath striven,
And perish'd by her temples, sink awhile,
Borne down in conflict!—But immortal seed
Deep, by heroic suffering, hath been sown
On all her ancient hills; and generous hope
Knows that the soil, in its good time, shall yet
Bring forth a glorious harvest!—Earth receives
Not one red drop from faithful hearts in vain.
 Elm. Then it must be!—And ye will make those lives,
Those young bright lives, an offering—to retard
Our doom one day!

Her.   The mantle of that day
May wrap the fate of Spain!
   Elm.   What led me here?
Why did I turn to *thee* in my despair?
Love hath no ties upon thee; what had I
To hope from *thee*, thou lone and childless man!
Go to thy silent home!—there no young voice
Shall bid thee welcome, no light footstep spring
Forth at the sound of thine!—What knows thy heart?
   Her. Woman! how darest thou taunt me with my woes?
Thy children too shall perish, and I say
It shall be well!—Why takest thou thought for them!
Wearing thy heart, and wasting down thy life
Unto its dregs, and making night thy time
Of care yet more intense, and casting health,
Unprized, to melt away, i' th' bitter cup
Thou minglest for thyself?—Why, what hath earth
To pay thee back for this? Shall they not live
(If the sword spare them now) to prove how soon
All love may be forgotten?—Years of thought,
Long faithful watchings, looks of tenderness,
That changed not, though to change be this world's law—
Shall they not flush thy cheek with shame, whose blood
Marks, e'en like branding iron?—to thy sick heart
Make death a want, as sleep to weariness?
Doth not all hope end thus?—or e'en at best,
Will they not leave thee?—far from thee seek room
For the o'erflowings of their fiery souls,
On life's wide ocean?—give the bounding steed,
Or the wing'd bark to youth, that his free course
May be o'er hills and seas; and weep thou not
In thy forsaken home, for the bright world
Lies all before him, and be sure he wastes
No thought on thee!
   Elm.   Not so! it is not so!
Thou dost but torture me!—*My* sons are kind,
And brave, and gentle.
   Her.   Others too have worn
The semblance of all good. Nay, stay thee yet;
I will be calm, and thou shalt learn how earth,
The fruitful in all agonies, hath woes
Which far outweigh thine own.
   Elm.   It may not be!
Whose grief is like a mother's for her sons?
   Her. *My* son lay stretch'd upon his battle-bier,
And there were hands wrung o'er him which had caught
Their hue from his young blood!
   Elm.   What tale is this?
   Her. Read you no records in this mien, of things
Whose traces on man's aspect are not such
As the breeze leaves on water?—Lofty birth,
War, peril, power?—Affliction's hand is strong,

If it erase the haughty characters
They grave so deep!—I have not always been
That which I am. The name I bore is not
Of those which perish!—I was once a chief—
A warrior—nor as now, a lonely man!
I was a father!
    Elm.   Then thy heart can *feel!*
Thou wilt have pity!
    Her.   Should I pity *thee?*
Thy sons will perish gloriously—their blood——
    Elm. Their blood! my children's blood!—Thou speak'st as 'twere
Of casting down a wine-cup, in the mirth
And wantonness of feasting!—My fair boys!
—Man! hast *thou* been a father?
    Her.   Let them die!
Let them die *now*, thy children! so thy heart
Shall wear their beautiful image all undimm'd
Within it, to the last! Nor shalt thou learn
The bitter lesson, of what worthless dust
Are framed the idols, whose false glory binds
Earth's fetter on our souls?—Thou think'st it much
To mourn the early dead; but there are tears
Heavy with deeper anguish! We endow
Those whom we love, in our fond passionate blindness,
With power upon our souls, too absolute
To be a mortal's trust! Within their hands
We lay the flaming sword, whose stroke alone
Can reach our hearts, and *they* are merciful,
As they are strong, that wield it not to pierce us!
—Ay, fear them, fear the loved!—Had I but wept
O'er my son's grave, or o'er a babe's, where tears
Are as spring dew-drops, glittering in the sun,
And brightening the young verdure, *I* might still
Have loved and trusted!
    Elm. (disdainfully.) But he fell in war!
And hath not glory medicine in her cup,
For the brief pangs of nature?
    Her.   Glory!—Peace,
And listen!—By my side the stripling grew,
Last of my line. I rear'd him to take joy
I' th' blaze of arms, as eagles train their young
To look upon the day-king!—His quick blood
Even to his boyish cheek would mantle up,
When the heavens rang with trumpets, and his eye
Flash with the spirit of a race whose deeds—
—But this availeth not!—Yet he *was* brave.
I've seen him clear himself a path in fight
As lightning through a forest, and his plume
Waved like a torch, above the battle-storm,
The soldier's guide, when princely crests had sunk,
And banners were struck down.—Around my steps

Floated his fame, like music, and I lived
But in the lofty sound. But when my heart
In one frail ark had ventured all, when most
He seem'd to stand between my soul and heaven,
—Then came the thunder-stroke!
   Elm.   'Tis ever thus!
And the unquiet and foreboding sense
That thus 'twill ever be, doth link itself
Darkly with all deep love!—He died?
   Her.   Not so!
—Death! Death!—Why, earth should be a paradise,
To make that name so fearful!—Had he died,
With his young fame about him for a shroud,
I had not learn'd the might of agony,
To bring proud natures low!—No! he fell off—
—Why do I tell thee this;—What right hast *thou*
To learn how pass'd the glory from my house?
Yet listen!—He forsook me!—He, that was
As mine own soul, forsook me! trampled o'er
The ashes of his sires!—ay, leagued himself
E'en with the infidel, the curse of Spain;
And for the dark eye of a Moorish maid,
Abjured his faith, his God!—Now, talk of death!
   Elm. Oh! I can pity thee——
   Her.   There's more to hear.
I braced the corslet o'er my heart's deep wound,
And cast my troubled spirit on the tide
Of war and high events, whose stormy waves
Might bear it up from sinking;——
   Elm.   And ye met
No more?
   Her. Be still!—We did!—we met *once* more.
God had his own high purpose to fulfil,
Or think'st thou that the sun in his bright heaven
Had look'd upon such things?—We met *once more.*
That was an hour to leave its lightning-mark
Sear'd upon brain and bosom! There had been
Combat on Ebro's banks, and when the day
Sank in red clouds, it faded from a field
Still held by Moorish lances. Night closed round—
A night of sultry darkness, in the shadow
Of whose broad wing, e'en unto death, I strove
Long with a turban'd champion; but my sword
Was heavy with God's vengeance—and prevail'd.
He fell—my heart exulted—and I stood
In gloomy triumph o'er him. Nature gave
No sign of horror, for 'twas Heaven's decree!
He strove to speak—but I had done the work
Of wrath too well;—yet in his last deep moan
A dreadful something of familiar sound
Came o'er my shuddering sense. The moon look'd forth,
And I beheld—speak not!—'twas he—my son!

My boy lay dying there! He raised one glance,
And knew me—for he sought with feeble hand
To cover his glazed eyes. A darker veil
Sank o'er them soon.—I will not have thy look
Fix'd on me thus!—Away?
  Elm.   Thou hast seen this,
Thou hast *done* this—and yet thou liv'st?
  Her.   I live!
And know'st thou wherefore?—On my soul there fell
A horror of great darkness, which shut out
All earth, and heaven, and hope. I cast away
The spear and helm, and made the cloister's shade
The home of my despair. But a deep voice
Came to me through the gloom, and sent its tones
Far through my bosom's depths. And I awoke,
Ay, as the mountain-cedar doth shake off
Its weight of wintry snow, e'en so I shook
Despondence from my soul, and knew myself
Seal'd by that blood wherewith my hands were dyed,
And set apart, and fearfully mark'd out
Unto a mighty task!—To rouse the soul
Of Spain as from the dead; and to lift up
The cross, her sign of victory, on the hills,
Gathering her sons to battle!—And my voice
Must be as freedom's trumpet on the winds,
From Roncesvalles to the blue sea-waves
Where Calpe looks on Afric; till the land
Have fill'd her cup of vengeance!—Ask me *now*
To yield the Christian city, that its fanes
May rear the minaret in the face of Heaven!—
But death shall have a bloodier vintage-feast
Ere that day come!
  Elm.   I ask thee this no more,
For I am hopeless now.—But yet one boon—
Hear me, by all thy woes!—Thy voice hath power
Through the wide city—here I cannot rest:—
Aid me to pass the gates!
  Her.   And wherefore?
  Elm.   Thou,
That *wert* a father, and art now—alone!
Canst *thou* ask "wherefore?"—Ask the wretch whose sands
Have not an hour to run, whose failing limbs
Have but one earthly journey to perform,
Why, on his pathway to the place of death,
Ay, when the very axe is glistening cold
Upon his dizzy sight, his pale, parch'd lip
Implores a cup of water?—Why, the stroke
Which trembles o'er him in itself shall bring
Oblivion of all wants, yet who denies
Nature's last prayer?—I tell thee that the thirst
Which burns my spirit up is agony
To be endured no more!—And I *must* look

Upon my children's faces, I must hear
Their voices, ere they perish!—But hath Heaven
Decreed that they *must* perish?—Who shall say
If in yon Moslem camp there beats no heart
Which prayers and tears may melt?
 Her.   There! with the Moor
Let him fill up the measure of his guilt!
—'Tis madness all?—How would'st thou pass th' array
Of armed foes?
 Elm.   Oh! free doth sorrow pass,
Free and unquestioned, through a suffering world!
 Her. This must not be. Enough of woe is laid
E'n now upon thy lord's heroic soul,
For man to bear, unsinking. Press thou not
Too heavily th' o'erburthen'd heart.—Away!
Bow down the knee, and send thy prayers for strength
Up to Heaven's gate.—Farewell!
             [*Exit* HERNANDEZ.
 Elm.   Are all men thus?
—Why, were 't not better they should fall e'n now
Than live to shut their hearts, in haughty scorn,
Against the sufferer's pleading?—But no, no!
Who can be like *this* man that slew his son,
Yet wears his life still proudly, and a soul
Untamed upon his brow?   [*After a pause.*
      There's one, whose arms
Have borne my children in their infancy,
And on whose knees they sported, and whose hand
Hath led them oft—a vassal of there sire's;
And I will seek him: he may lend me aid,
When all beside pass on.

    DIRGE, HEARD WITHOUT.

  Thou to thy rest art gone,
   High heart! and what are we,
While o'er our heads the storm sweeps on,
   That we should mourn for thee?

  Free grave and peaceful bier
   To the buried son of Spain!
To those that live, the lance and spear,
   And well if not the chain!

  Be *theirs* to weep the dead,
   As they sit beneath their vines,
Whose flowery land hath borne no tread
   Of spoilers o'er its shrines!

  Thou hast thrown off the load
   Which we must yet sustain,
And pour our blood where *thine* hath flow'd
   Too blest if not in vain!

THE SIEGE OF VALENCIA.

  We give thee holy rite,
   Slow knell, and chaunted strain.
 —For those that fall to-morrow night,
   May be left no funeral-train.

  Again, when trumpets wake,
   We must brace our armor on?
 But a deeper note *thy* sleep must break—
   Thou to thy rest art gone!

  Happier in *this* than all,
   That, now thy race is run,
 Upon thy name no stain may fall,
   Thy work hath well been done!

Elm. " Thy work hath well been done!"—so thou may'st rest!
—There is a solemn lesson in those words—
But now I may not pause.   [*Exit* ELMINA.

  SCENE III.—*A Street in the City.*
   HERNANDEZ—GONZALEZ.

Her. Would they not hear?
Gon.   .   They heard, as one that stands
By the cold grave which hath but newly closed
O'er his last friend doth hear some passer-by
Bid him be comforted!—Their hearts have died
Within them!—We must perish, not as those
That fall when battle's voice doth shake the hills,
And peal through heaven's great arch, but silently,
And with a wasting of the spirit down,
A quenching, day by day, of some bright spark,
Which lit us on our toils!—Reproach me not;
My soul is darken'd with a heavy cloud—
—Yet fear not I shall yield!
Her.   Breathe not the word,
Save in proud scorn!—Each bitter day o'erpass'd
By slow endurance, is a triumph won
For Spain's red cross. And be of trusting heart!
A few brief hours, and those that turn'd away
In cold despondence, shrinking from your voice,
May crowd around their leader, and demand
To be array'd for battle. We must watch
For the swift impulse, and await its time,
As the bark waits the ocean's. You have chosen
To kindle up their souls, an hour, perchance,
When they were weary; they had cast aside
Their arms to slumber; or a knell, just then,
With its deep hollow tone, had made the blood
Creep shuddering through their veins; or they had caught
A glimpse of some new meteor, and shaped forth

Strange omens from its blaze.
  Gon.   Alas! the cause
Lies deeper in their misery!—I have seen,
In my night's course through this beleaguer'd city,
Things whose remembrance doth not pass away
As vapors from the mountains.—There were some,
That sat beside their dead, with eyes wherein
Grief had ta'en place of sight, and shut out all
But its own ghastly object. To my voice
Some answer'd with a fierce and bitter laugh,
As men whose agonies were made to pass
The bounds of sufferance, by some reckless word
Dropt from the light of spirit.—Others lay—
—Why should I tell thee, father! how despair
Can bring the lofty brow of manhood down
Unto the very dust?—And yet for this,
Fear not that I embrace my doom—Oh God!
That 'twere *my* doom alone!—with less of fix'd
And solemn fortitude.—Lead on, prepare
The holiest rites of faith, that I by them
Once more may consecrate my sword, my life;
—But what are these?—Who hath not dearer lives
Twined with his own?—I shall be lonely soon—
Childless!—Heaven wills it so. Let us begone.
Perchance before the shrine my heart may beat
With a less troubled motion.
      [*Exeunt* Gonzalez *and* Hernandez.

  Scene IV.—*A Tent in the Moorish Camp.*
    Abdullah—Alphonso—Carlos.

 Abd. These are bold words: but hast thou look'd on death,
Fair stripling?—On thy cheek and sunny brow
Scarce fifteen summers of their laughing course
Have left light traces. If thy shaft hath pierced
The ibex of the mountains, if thy step
Hath climb'd some eagle's nest, and thou hast made
His nest thy spoil, 'tis much!—And fear'st thou not
The leader of the mighty?
 Alph.   I have been
Rear'd amongst fearless men, and 'midst the rocks
And the wild hills, whereon my fathers fought
And won their battles. There are glorious tales
Told of their deeds, and I have learn'd them all.
How should I fear thee, Moor?
 Abd.   So, thou hast seen
Fields, where the combat's roar hath died away
Into the whispering breeze, and where wild flowers
Bloom o'er forgotten graves!—But know'st thou aught
Of those, where sword from crossing sword strikes fire,
And leaders are borne down, and rushing steeds
Trample the life from out the mighty hearts

THE SIEGE OF VALENCIA.

That ruled the storm so late?—Speak not of death
Till thou hast look'd on such.
   Alph.   I was not born
A shepherd's son, to dwell with pipe and crook,
And peasant men, amidst the lowly vales;
Instead of ringing clarions, and bright spears,
And crested knights!—I am of princely race;
And, if my father would have heard my suit,
I tell thee, infidel, that long ere now,
I should have seen how lances meet, and swords
Do the field's work.
   Abd.   Boy!—know'st thou there are sights
A thousand times more fearful?—Men may die
Full proudly, when the skies and mountains ring
To battle-horn and tecbir.* But not all
So pass away in glory. There are those,
'Midst the dead silence of pale multitudes,
Led forth in fetters—dost thou mark me, boy?
To take their last look of th' all gladdening sun,
And bow, perchance, the stately head of youth.
Unto the death of shame!—Hadst thou seen this——   [not!
   Alph. (*to Carlos.*) Sweet brother, God is with us, fear thou
We have had heroes for our sires:—this man
Should not behold us tremble.
   Abd.   There are means
To tame the loftiest natures. Yet, again
I ask thee, wilt thou, from beneath the walls
Sue to thy sire for life?—or would'st thou die
With this thy brother?
   Alph.   Moslem!—on the hills,
Around my father's castle, I have heard
The mountain-peasants, as they dress'd the vines,
Or drove the goats, by rock and torrent, home,
Singing their ancient songs; and these were all
Of the Cid Campeador; and how his sword
Tizona,³ clear'd its way through turban'd hosts,
And captured Afric's kings, and how he won
Valencia from the Moor⁴—I will not shame
The blood we draw from him!   [*A Moorish soldier enters.*
   Sol.   Valencia's lord
Sends messengers, my chief.
   Abd.   Conduct them hither.
     [*The soldier goes out and re-enters with*
       Elmina, *disguised, and an attendant.*
   Car. (*springing forward to the attendant.*) Oh! take me
      hence, Diego! take me hence
With thee, that I may see my mother's face
At morning when I wake. Here, dark-brow'd men
Frown strangely, with their cruel eyes, upon us.
Take me with thee, for thou art good and kind,
And well I know thou lov'st me, my Diego!

      * *Tecbir*, the war-cry of the Moors and Arabs.

Abd. Peace, boy!—What tidings, Christian, from thy lord?
Is he grown humbler?—doth he set the lives
Of these fair nurslings at a city's worth?
    Alph. (*rushing forward impatiently.*) Say not he doth!—
Yet wherefore art thou here?
If it be so, I could weep burning tears
For very shame! If this *can* be, return!
Tell him, of all his wealth, his battle-spoils,
I will but ask a war-horse and a sword,
And that beside him in the mountain-chase,
And in his halls, and at his stately feasts,
My place shall be no more!—but, no!—I wrong,
I wrong my father! Moor, believe it not,
He is a champion of the cross and Spain,
Sprung from the Cid!—and I, too, I can die
As a warrior's high-born child!
    Elm.   Alas, alas!
And would'st thou die, thus early die, fair boy?
What hath life done to thee that thou should'st cast
Its flower away, in very scorn of heart,
Ere yet the blight be come?
    Alph.   That voice doth sound——
    Abd. Stranger, who art thou?—this is mockery! speak.
    Elm. (*throwing off a mantle and helmet, and embracing her
sons.*) My boys! whom I have rear'd through many hours
Of silent joys and sorrows, and deep thoughts
Untold and unimagined; let me die
With you, now I have held you to my heart,
And seen once more the faces, in whose light
My soul hath lived for years!
    Car.   Sweet mother! now
Thou shalt not leave us more.
    Abd.   Enough of this!
Woman! what seek'st thou here? How hast thou dared
To front the mighty thus amidst his hosts?
    Elm. Think'st thou there dwells no courage but in breasts
That set their mail against the ringing spears,
When helmets are struck down? Thou little know'st
Of nature's marvels. Chief, my heart is nerved
To make its way through things which warrior men,
Ay, they that master death by field or flood,
Would look on, ere they braved!—I have no thought,
No sense of fear! Thou'rt mighty! but a soul
Wound up like mine is mightier, in the power
Of that one feeling pour'd through all its depths,
Than monarchs with their hosts! Am I not come
To die with these my children?
    Abd.   Doth thy faith
Bid thee do this, fond Christian? Hast thou not
The means to save them?
    Elm.   I have prayers, and tears,
And agonies!—and he, my God, the God

Whose hand, or soon or late, doth find its hour
To bow the crested head—hath made these things
Most powerful in a world where all must learn
That one deep language, by the storm call'd forth
From the bruis'd reeds of earth! For thee, perchance,
Affliction's chastening lesson hath not yet
Been laid upon thy heart, and thou may'st love
To see the creatures, by its might brought low,
Humbled before thee.   [*She throws herself at his feet.*
                                   Conqueror, I can kneel!
I, that drew birth from princes, bow myself
E'en to thy feet! Call in thy chiefs, thy slaves
If this will swell thy triumph, to behold
The blood of kings, of heroes, thus abased!
Do this, but spare my sons!
    Alph. (*attempting to raise her.*) Thou should'st not kneel
Unto this infidel! Rise, rise, my mother!
This sight doth shame our house!
    Abd.   Thou daring boy!
They that in arms have taught thy father's land
How chains are worn, shall school that haughty mien
Unto another language.
    Elm.   Peace, my son!
Have pity on my heart!—Oh, pardon, chief!
He is of noble blood. Hear, hear me yet!
Are there no lives through which the shafts of Heaven
May reach your soul? He that loves aught on earth,
Dares far too much, if he be merciless!
Is it for those, whose frail mortality
Must one day strive alone with God and death,
To shut their souls against th' appealing voice
Of nature, in her anguish?—warrior, man,
To you, too, ay, and haply with your hosts,
By thousands and ten thousands marshall'd round,
And your strong armor on, shall come that stroke
Which the lance wards not!—where shall your high heart
Find refuge then, if in the day of might
Woe hath lain prostrate, bleeding at your feet,
And you have pitied not?
    Abd.   These are vain words.
    Elm. Have you no children?—fear you not to bring
The lightning on their heads.—In your own land
Doth no fond mother, from the tents beneath
Your native palms, look o'er the deserts out,
To greet your homeward step?—You have not yet
Forgot so utterly her patient love;—
For is not woman's in all climes the same?
That you should scorn *my* prayer!—O Heaven! his eye
Doth wear no mercy!
    Abd.   Then it mocks you not.
I have swept o'er mountains of your land,
Leaving my traces, as the visitings

Of storms upon them! Shall I now be stay'd?
Know, unto me it were as light a thing
In this my course, to quench your children's lives,
As journeying through a forest, to break off
The young wild branches that obstruct the way
With their green sprays and leaves.
  Elm.   Are there such hearts
Amongst thy works, O God!
  Abd.   Kneel not to me.
Kneel to your lord! on his resolves doth hang
His children's doom. He may be lightly won
By a few bursts of passionate tears and words. [bears a sou*
  Elm. (rising indignantly.) Speak not of noble men!—He
Stronger than love or death.
  Alph. (with exultation.) I knew 'twas thus!
He could not fail!
  Elm.   There is no mercy, none,
On this cold earth!—To strive with such a world,
Hearts should be void of love!—We will go hence,
My children! we are summon'd. Lay your heads,
In their young radiant beauty, once again
To rest upon this bosom. He that dwells
Beyond the clouds which press us darkly round,
Will yet have pity, and before his face
We three will stand together! Moslem! now
Let the stroke fall at once!
  Abd.   'Tis thine own will.
These might e'en yet be spared.
  Elm.   *Thou* wilt not spare!
And he beneath whose eye their childhood grew,
And in whose paths they sported, and whose ear
From their first lisping accents caught the sound
Of that word—*Father*—once a name of love—
Is——Men shall call him *steadfast.*
  Abd.   Hath the blast
Of sudden trumpets ne'er at dead of night,
When the land's watchers fear'd no hostile step,
Startled the slumberers from their dreamy world,
In cities, whose heroic lords have been
Stedfast as thine?
  Elm.   There's meaning in thine eye,
More than thy words.
  Abd. (pointing to the city.) Look to yon towers and walls
Think you no hearts within their limits pine,
Weary of hopeless warfare, and prepared
To burst the feeble links which bind them still
Unto endurance?
  Elm.   Thou hast said too well.
But what of this?
  Abd.   Then there are those, to whom
The prophet's armies not as foes would pass
Yon gates, but as deliverers. Might they not

In some still hour, when weariness takes rest,
Be won to welcome us?—Your children's steps
May yet bound lightly through their father's halls!
   Alph. (*indignantly.*) Thou treacherous Moor!
   Elm.   Let me not thus be tried
Beyond all strength, oh, Heaven!
   Abd.   Now, 'tis for *thee,*
Thou Christian mother! on thy sons to pass
The sentence—life or death!—the price it set
On their young blood, and rests within thy hands.
   Alph. Mother! thou tremblest!
   Abd.   Hath thy heart resolved?
   Elm. (*covering her face with her hands.*) My boy's proud
    eye is on me, and the things
Which rush in stormy darkness through my soul,
Shrink from his glance. I cannot answer *here.*
   Abd. Come forth. We'll commune elsewhere.
   Car. (*to his mother.*)   Wilt thou go?
Oh! let me follow thee!
   Elm.   Mine own fair child!
Now that thine eyes have pour'd once more on mine
The light of their young smile, and thy sweet voice
Hath sent its gentle music through my soul,
And I have felt the twining of thine arms—
How shall I leave thee?
   Abd.   Leave him, as 'twere but
For a brief slumber, to behold his face
At morning, with the sun's.
   Alph.   Thou hast no look
For me, my mother!
   Elm.   Oh! that I should live
To say, I *dare* not look on thee!—Farewell.
My first born, fare thee well!
   Alph.   Yet, yet beware!
It were a grief more heavy on thy soul,
That I should blush for thee, than o'er my grave
That thou should'st proudly weep!
   Abd. Away! we trifle here. The night wanes fast.
Come forth!
   Elm. Once more embrace! My sons, farewell!
   [*Exeunt* ABDULLAH *with* ELMINA *and her attendant.*
   Alph. Hear me yet once, my mother!—Art thou gone?
But one word more! [*He rushes out, followed by* CARLOS.

       SCENE V.—*The Garden of a Palace in Valencia.*
               XIMENA, THERESA.

   Ther. Stay yet awhile. A purer air doth rove
Here through the myrtles whispering, and the limes,
And shaking sweetness from the orange boughs,
Than waits you in the city.
   Xim.   There are those

In their last need, and on their bed of death,
At which no hand doth minister but mine
That wait me in the city. Let us hence.
    Ther. You have been wont to love the music made
By founts, and rustling foliage, and soft winds,
Breathing of citron-groves. And will you turn
From these to scenes of death?
    Xim.   To me the voice
Of summer, whispering through young flowers and leaves,
Now speaks too deep a language! and of all
Its dreamy and mysterious melodies,
The breathing soul is sadness!—I have felt
That summons through my spirit, after which
The hues of earth are changed, and all her sounds
Seem fraught with secret warnings.—There is cause
That I should bend my footsteps to the scenes
Where Death is busy, taming warrior-hearts,
And pouring winter through the fiery blood,
And lett'ring the strong arm!—For now no sigh
In the dull air, nor floating cloud in heaven,
No, not the lightest murmur of a leaf,
But of his angel's silent coming bears
Some token to my soul.—But nought of this
Unto my mother!—These are awful hours!
And on their heavy steps afflictions crowd
With such dark pressure, there is left no room
For one grief more.
    Ther.   Sweet lady, talk not thus!
Your eye this morn doth wear a calmer light,
There's more of life in its clear trem'lous ray
Than I have mark'd of late. Nay, go not yet;
Rest by this fountain, where the laurels dip
Their glossy leaves. A fresher gale doth spring
From the transparent waters, dashing round
Their silvery spray, with a sweet voice of coolness,
O'er the pale glistening marble. 'Twill call up
Faint bloom, if but a moment's, to your cheek.
Rest here, ere you go forth, and I will sing
The melody you love.
                THERESA *sings.*

    Why is the Spanish maiden's grave
        So far from her own bright land?
    The sunny flowers that o'er it wave
        Were sown by no kindred hand.

    'Tis not the orange-bough that sends
        Its breath on the sultry air,
    'Tis not the myrtle-stem that bends
        To the breeze of evening there!

    But the rose of Sharon's eastern bloom
        By the silent dwelling fades,

And none but strangers pass the tomb
    Which the palm of Judah shades.

The lowly Cross, with flowers o'ergrown,
    Marks well that place of rest;
But who hath graved, on its mossy stone,
    A sword, a helm, a crest?

These are the trophies of a chief,
    A lord of the axe and spear!
—Some blossom pluck'd, some faded leaf,
    Should grace a maiden's bier!

Scorn not her tomb—deny not her
    The honors of the brave!
O'er that forsaken sepulchre,
    Banner and plume might wave.

She bound the steel, in battle tried,
    Her fearless heart above,
And stood with brave men, side by side,
    In the strength and faith of love!

That strength prevail'd—that faith was bless'd!
    True was the javelin thrown,
Yet pierced it not her warrior's breast:
    She met it with her own!

And nobly won, where heroes fell
    In arms for the holy shrine,
A death which saved what she loved so well,
    And a grave in Palestine.

Then let the rose of Sharon spread
    Its breast to the glowing air,
And the palm of Judah lift its head,
    Green and immortal there!

And let yon grey stone, undefaced,
    With its trophy mark the scene,
Telling the pilgrim of the waste,
    Where Love and Death have been.

Xim. Those notes were wont to make my heart beat quick,
As at a voice of victory; but to-day
The spirit of the song is changed, and seems
All mournful. Oh! that, ere my early grave
Shuts out the sunbeam, I might hear one peal
Of the Castilian trumpet, ringing forth
Beneath my father's banner!—In that sound
Were life to you, sweet brothers!—But for me—
Come on—our tasks await us. They who know
Their hours are number'd out, have little time
To give the vague and slumberous languor way,

Which doth steal o'er them in the breath of flowers,
And whisper of soft winds.
                    [ELMINA *enters hurriedly*.
    Elm. The air will calm my spirit, ere yet I meet
His eye, which must be met.—Thou here, Ximena!
                    [*She starts back on seeing* XIMENA.
    Xim. Alas! my mother! In that hurrying step
And troubled glance I read——
    Elm. (*wildly*.)   Thou read'st it not!
Why, who would live, if unto mortal eye
The things lay glaring, which within our hearts
We treasure up for God's?—Thou read'st it not!
I say, thou canst not!—There's not one on earth
Shall know the thoughts, which for themselves have made
And kept dark places in the very breast
Whereon he hath laid his slumber, till the hour
When the graves open!
    Xim.   Mother! what is this?
Alas! your eye is wandering, and your cheek
Flush'd, as with fever! To your woes the night
Hath brought no rest.
    Elm.   Rest!—who should rest?—not he
That holds one earthly blessing to his heart
Nearer than life!—No! if this world have aught
Of bright or precious, let not him who calls
Such things his own, take rest!—Dark spirits keep watch,
And they to whom fair honor, chivalrous fame,
Were as heaven's air, the vital element
Wherein they breathed, may wake, and find their souls
Made marks for human scorn!—Will they bear on
With life struck down, and thus disrobed of all
Its glorious drapery?—Who shall tell us this?
—Will *he* so bear it?
    Xim.   Mother! let us kneel
And blend our hearts in prayer!—What else is left
To mortals when the dark hour's might is on them?
—Leave us, Theresa.—Grief like this doth find
Its balm in solitude.   [*Exit* THERESA.
            My mother! peace
Is heaven's benignant answer to the cry
Of wounded spirits. Wilt thou kneel with me?
    Elm. Away! 'tis but for souls unstain'd, to wear
Heaven's tranquil image on their depths. The stream
Of my dark thoughts, all broken by the storm,
Reflects but clouds and lightnings! Didst thou speak
Of peace? 'tis fled from earth! but there is joy!
Wild, troubled joy! And who shall know, my child!
It is not happiness? Why, our own hearts
Will keep the secret close! Joy, joy! if but
To leave this desolate city, with its dull
Slow knells and dirges, and to breathe again
Th' untainted mountain-air! But hush! the trees,

The flowers, the waters, must hear nought of this!
They are full of voices, and will whisper things——
—We'll speak of it no more.
    Xim.   Oh! pitying Heaven!
This grief doth shake her reason!
    Elm. (starting.)   Hark! a step!
'Tis—'tis thy father's!—come away—not now—
He must not see us now!
    Xim.   Why should this be?
        [GONZALEZ *enters and detains* ELMINA.
    Gon. Elmina, dost thou shun me?—Have we not,
E'en from the hopeful and the sunny time
When youth was as a glory round our brows,
Held on through life together?—And is this,
When eve is gathering round us, with the gloom
Of stormy clouds, a time to part our steps
Upon the darkening wild?
    Elm. (coldly.)   There needs not this.
Why should'st thou think I shunn'd thee?
    Gon.   Should the love
That shone o'er many years, th' unfading love,
Whose only change hath been from gladd'ning smiles
To mingling sorrows and sustaining strength,
Thus lightly be forgotten?
    Elm.   Speak'st *thou* thus?
—I have knelt before thee with that very plea,
When it avail'd me not!—But there are things
Whose very breathings from the soul erase
All record of past love, save the chill sense,
Th' unquiet memory of its wasted faith,
And vain devotedness!—Ay! they that fix
Affection's perfect trust on aught of earth,
Have many a dream to start from!
    Gon.   This is but
The wildness and the bitterness of grief,
Ere yet the unsettled heart hath closed its long
Impatient conflicts with a mightier power,
Which makes all conflict vain.
            ——Hark! was there not
A sound of distant trumpets, far beyond
The Moorish tents, and of another tone
Than th' Afric horn, Ximena?
    Xim.   Oh, my father!
I know that horn too well.—'Tis but the wind,
Which, with a sudden rising, bears its deep
And savage war-note from us, wafting it
O'er the far hills.
    Gon.   Alas! this woe must be!
I do not shake my spirit from its height,
So startling it with hope!—But the dread hour
Shall be met bravely still. I can keep down
Yet for a little while—and Heaven will ask

No more—the passionate workings of my heart
—And thine—Elmina?
 Elm.   'Tis—I am prepared.
I *have* prepared for all.
 Gon.   Oh, well I knew
Thou would'st not fail me!—Not in vain my soul,
Upon thy faith and courage, hath built up
Unshaken trust.
 Elm. (*wildly.*) Away!—thou know'st me not.
Man dares too far, his rashness would invest
This our mortality with an attribute
Too high and awful, boasting that he knows
One human heart!
 Gon.   These are wild words, but yet
I will not doubt thee!—Hast thou not been found
Noble in all things, pouring thy soul's light
Undimm'd o'er every trial?—And, as our fates,
So must our names be, undivided!—Thine,
I' th' record of a warrior's life, shall find
Its place of stainless honor.—By his side—
 Elm. May this be borne?—How much of agony
Hath the heart room for?—Speak to me in wrath
—I can endure it!—But no gentle words!
No words of love! no praise!—Thy sword might slay,
And be more merciful!
 Gon,   Wherefore art thou thus?
Elmina, my beloved!
 Elm.   No more of love!
—Have I not said there's that within my heart,
Whereon it falls as living fire would fall
Upon an unclosed wound?
 Gon.   Nay, lift thine eyes,
That I may read *their* meaning!
 Elm.   Never more
With a free soul—What have I said?—'twas nought!
Take thou no heed! The words of wretchedness
Admit not scrutiny. Would'st thou mark the speech
Of troubled dreams?
 Gon.   I have seen thee in the hour
Of thy deep spirit's joy, and when the breath
Of grief hung chilling round thee; in all change,
Bright health and drooping sickness; hope and fear;
Youth and decline; but never yet, Elmina,
Ne'er hath thine eye till now shrunk back perturb'd
With shame or dread, from mine!
 Elm.   Thy glance doth search
A wounded heart too deeply.
 Gon.   Hast thou there
Aught to conceal?
 Elm. Who hath not?
 Gon.   Till this hour
Thou never hadst!—Yet hear me!—by the free

And unattainted fame which wraps the dust
Of thine heroic fathers—
    Elm.   This to me!
—Bring your inspiring war-notes, and your sounds
Of festal music round a dying man!
Will his heart echo them?—But if thy words
Were spells, to call up, with each lofty tone,
The grave's most awful spirits, they would stand
Powerless, before my anguish!
    Gon.   Then, by her,
Who there looks on thee in the purity
Of her devoted youth, and o'er whose name
No blight must fall, and whose pale cheek must ne'er
Burn with that deeper tinge, caught painfully
From the quick feeling of dishonor.—Speak!
Unfold this mystery?—By thy sons—
    Elm.   My sons!
And canst *thou* name them?
    Gon.   Proudly!—Better far
They died with all the promise of their youth,
And the fair honor of their house upon them,
Than that, with manhood's high and passionate soul,
To fearful strength unfolded, they should live,
Barr'd from the lists of crested chivalry,
And pining, in the silence of a woe,
Which from the heart shuts daylight—o'er the shame
Of those who gave them birth!—But *thou* could'st ne'er
Forget their lofty claims!
    Elm. (*wildly.*)   'Twas but for them!
'Twas for them only!—Who shall dare arraign
Madness of crime?—And He who made us knows
There are dark moments of all hearts and lives,
Which bear down reason!
    Gon.   Thou, whom I have loved
With such high trust as o'er our nature threw
A glory scarce allow'd;—what hast thou done?
—Ximena, go thou hence!
    Elm.   No, no! my child!
There's pity in thy look!—All other eyes
Are full of wrath and scorn!—Oh! leave me not!
    Gon. That I should live to see thee thus abased!
—Yet speak?—What hast thou done?
    Elm.   Look to the gate!
Thou art worn with toil—but take no rest to-night!
The western gate!—Its watchers have been won—
The Christian city hath been bought and sold!—
They will admit the Moor!
    Gon.   They have been won!
Brave men and tried so long!—Whose work was this?
    Elm. Think'st thou all hearts like thine?—Can mothers
        stand
To see their children perish?

Gon.   Then the guilt
Was thine?
Elm.   Shall mortal dare to call it guilt?
I tell thee, Heaven, which made all holy things,
Made nought more holy than the boundless love
Which fills a mother's heart!—I say, 'tis woe
Enough, with such an aching tenderness,
To love aught earthly!—and in vain! in vain!
—We are press'd down too sorely!
  Gon. (*In a low desponding voice.*) Now my life
Is struck to worthless ashes!—In my soul
Suspicion hath ta'en root. The nobleness
Henceforth is blotted from all human brows;
And fearful power, a dark and troublous gift,
Almost like prophecy, is pour'd upon me,
To read the guilty secrets in each eye
That once look'd bright with truth!
                        —Why, then, I have gain'd
What men call wisdom!—A new sense, to which
All tales that speak of high fidelity,
And holy courage, and proud honor, tried,
Search'd, and found steadfast, even to martyrdom,
Are food for mockery!—Why should I not cast
From my thinn'd locks the wearing helm at once,
And in the heavy sickness of my soul
Throw the sword down for ever?—Is there aught
In all this world of gilded hollowness,
Now the bright hues drop off its loveliest things,
Worth striving for again?
  Xim   Father! look up!
Turn unto me, thy child!
  Gon.   Thy face is fair;
And hath been unto me, in other days,
As morning to the journeyer of the deep;
But now—'tis too like hers!
  Elm. (*falling at his feet.*) Woe, shame and woe,
Are on me in their might!—forgive, forgive!
  Gon. (*starting up.*) Doth the Moor deem that *I* have part,
         or share,
Or counsel in this vileness?—Stay me not!
Let go thy hold—'tis powerless on me now—
I linger here, while treason is at work!   [*Exit* GONZALEZ.
  Elm. Ximena, dost *thou* scorn me?
  Xim.   I have found
In mine own heart too much of feebleness,
Hid, beneath many foldings, from all eyes
But His whom nought can blind, to dare do aught
But pity thee, dear mother!
  Elm.   Blessings light
On thy fair head, my gentle child, for this!—
Thou kind and merciful!—My soul is faint—
Worn with long strife!—Is there aught else to do,

THE SIEGE OF VALENCIA.

Or suffer, ere we die?—Oh God! my sons!
—I have betrayed them!—All their innocent blood
Is on my soul!
   Xim.   How shall I comfort thee?
—Oh! hark! what sounds come deepening on the wind,
So full of solemn hope!

*(A procession of Nuns passes across the Scene, bearing
relics, and chanting.)*

CHANT.

        A sword is on the land!
He that bears down young tree and glorious flower,
Death is gone forth, he walks the wind in power!
      Where is the warrior's hand?
Our steps are in the shadows of the grave,
Hear us, we perish! Father, hear and save.

      If, in the days of song,
The days of gladness, we have call'd on thee,
When mirthful voices rang from sea to sea,
      And joyous hearts were strong;
Now that alike the feeble and the brave
Must cry, " We perish!"—Father, hear and save!

      The days of song are fled!
The winds come loaded, wafting dirge-notes by,
But they that linger soon unmourn'd must die;—
      The dead weep not the dead!—
Wilt thou forsake us 'midst the stormy wave?
We sink, we perish!—Father, hear and save!

      Helmet and lance are dust!
Is not the strong man wither'd from our eye?
The arm struck down that held our banners high?—
      Thine is our spirits' trust!
Look through the gath'ring shadows of the grave!
Do we not perish?—Father, hear and save!

                          [HERNANDEZ *enters.*
   Elm. Why com'st thou, man of vengeance?—What have I
To do with thee?—Am I not bow'd enough?—
Thou art no mourner's comforter!
   Her.   Thy lord
Hath sent me unto thee. Till this day's task
Be closed, thou daughter of the feeble heart!
He bids thee seek him not, but lay thy ways
Before Heaven's altar, and in penitence
Make thy soul's peace with God.
   Elm.   Till this day's task
Be closed!—there is strange triumph in thine eyes—
Is it that I have fall'n from that high place

Whereon I stood in fame?—But I can feel
A wild and bitter pride in thus being past
The power of thy dark glance!—My spirit now
Is wound about by one sole mighty grief;
Thy scorn hath lost its sting. Thou may'st reproach—
  Her. I come not to reproach thee. Heaven doth work
By many agencies; and in its hour
There is no insect which the summer breeze
From the green leaf shakes trembling, but may serve
Its deep unsearchable purposes, as well
As the great ocean, or th' eternal fires
Pent in earth's caves!—Thou hast but speeded that,
Which, in th' infatuate blindness of thy heart,
Thou would'st have trampled o'er all holy ties
But to avert one day!
  Elm.   My senses fail—
Thou said'st—speak yet again—I could not catch
The meaning of thy words.
  Her.   E'en now thy lord
Hath sent our foes defiance. On the walls
He stands in conference with the boastful Moor,
And awful strength is with him. Through the blood
Which this day must be pour'd in sacrifice
Shall Spain be free. On all her olive-hills
Shall men set up the battle-sign of fire,
And round its blaze, at midnight, keep the sense
Of vengeance wakeful in each other's hearts
E'en with thy children's tale!
  Xim.   Peace, father! peace!
Behold she sinks!—the storm hath done its work
Upon the broken reed. Oh! lend thine aid
To bear her hence.   [*They lead her away.*

SCENE VI.—*A Street in Valencia. Several Groups of Citizens and Soldiers, many of them lying on the steps of a church. Arms scattered on the ground around them.*

  An Old Cit. The air is sultry, as with thunder-clouds.
I left my desolate home, that I might breathe
More freely in heaven's face, but my heart feels
With this hot gloom o'erburden'd. I have now
No sons to tend me. Which of you, kind friends,
Will bring the old man water from the fount,
To moisten his parch'd lip?   [*A citizen goes out*
  2d Cit. This wasting siege,
Good Father Lopez, hath gone hard with you!
'Tis sad to hear no voices through the house.
Once peopled with fair sons!
  3d Cit.   Why, better thus,
Than to be haunted with their famish'd cries,
E'en in your very dreams!
  Old Cit.   Heaven's will be done!
These are dark times! I have not been alone

In my affliction.
 3d Cit. (with bitterness.) Why we have but this thought
Left for our gloomy comfort !—And 'tis well !
Ay, let the balance be awhile struck even
Between the noble's palace and the hut,
Where the worn peasant sickens !—They that bear
The humble dead unhonor'd to their homes,
Pass now i' th' streets no lordly bridal train
With its exulting music ; and the wretch
Who on the marble steps of some proud hall
Flings himself down to die, in his last need
And agony of famine, doth behold
No scornful guests, with their long purple robes,
To the banquet sweeping by. Why, this is just !
These are the days when pomp is made to feel
Its human mould !
 4th Cit.   Heard ye last night the sound
Of Saint Iago's bell ?—How sullenly
From the great tower it peal'd !
 5th Cit.   Ay, and 'tis said
No mortal hand was near when so it seem'd
To shake the midnight streets.
 Old Cit.   Too well I know
The sound of coming fate !—'Tis ever thus
When Death is on his way to make it night
In the Cid's ancient house.⁵—Oh ! there are things
In this strange world of which we've all to learn
When its dark bounds are pass'd.—Yon bell, untouch'd
(Save by the hands we see not,) still doth speak—
When of that line some stately head is mark'd—
With a wild hollow peal, at dead of night,
Rocking Valencia's towers. I've heard it oft,
Nor known its warning false.
 4th Cit.   And will our chief
Buy with the price of his fair children's blood
A few more days of pining wretchedness
For this forsaken city ?
 Old Cit.   Doubt it not !
—But with that ransom he may purchase still
Deliverance for the land !—And yet 'tis sad
To think that such a race, with all its fame,
Should pass away !—For she, his daughter too,
Moves upon earth as some bright thing whose time
To sojourn there is short.
 5th Cit.   Then woe for us
When she is gone !—Her voice—the very sound
Of her soft step was comfort, as she moved
Through the still house of mourning !—Who like her
Shall give us hope again ?
 Old Cit.   Be still !—she comes,
And with a mien how changed !—A hurrying step,
And a flush'd cheek !—What may this bode !—Be still !

XIMENA *enters, with Attendants carrying a Banner*

Xim. Men of Valencia! in an hour like this,
What do ye here?
 A Cit. We die!
 Xim.   Brave men die *now*
Girt for the toil, as travellers suddenly
By the dark night o'ertaken on their way!
These days require such death!—It is too much
Of luxury for our wild and angry times,
To fold the mantle round us, and to sink
From life, as flowers that shut up silently,
When the sun's heat doth scorch them! Hear ye not?
 A Cit. Lady! what would'st thou with us?
 Xim.   Rise and arm!
E'en now the children of your chief are led
Forth by the Moor to perish!—Shall this be,
Shall the high sound of such a name be hush'd,
I' th' land to which for ages it hath been
A battle-word, as 'twere some passing note
Of shepherd-music?—Must this work be done,
And ye lie pining here, as men in whom
·The pulse which God hath made for noble thought
Can so be thrill'd no longer?
 Cit.   'Tis e'en so!
Sickness and toil, and grief, have breathed upon us,
Our hearts beat faint and low.
 Xim.   Are ye so poor
Of soul, my countrymen! that ye can draw
Strength from no deeper source than that which sends
The red blood mantling through the joyous veins,
And gives the fleet step wings?—Why, how have age
And sens'tive womanhood ere now endured,
Through pangs of searching fire, in some proud cause,
Blessing that agony? Think ye the Power
Which bore them nobly up, as if to teach
The torturer where eternal Heaven had set
Bounds to his sway, was earthy, of this earth—
This dull mortality?—Nay, then look on me!
Death's touch hath mark'd me, and I stand amongst **you**,
As one whose place, i' th' sunshine of your world,
Shall soon be left to fill!—I say, the breath
Of th' incense, floating through yon fane, shall scarce
Pass from your path before me! But even now,
I've that within me, kindling through the dust,
Which from all time hath made high deeds its voice
And token to the nations;—Look on me!
Why hath Heaven pour'd forth courage, as a flame
Wasting the womanish heart, which must be still'd
Yet sooner for its swift consuming brightness,
If not to shame your doubt and your despair,
And your soul's torpor?—Yet, arise and arm
It may not be too late.

A Cit.   Why, what are we,
To cope with hosts?—Thus faint, and worn and few,
O'ernumber'd and forsaken, is't for us
To stand against the mighty?
    Xim.   And for whom
Hath He, who shakes the mighty with a breath
From their high places, made the fearfulness,
And ever-wakeful presence of his power,
To the pale startled earth most manifest,
But for the weak?—Was't for the helm'd and crown'd
That suns were stay'd at noonday?—Stormy seas
As a rill parted?—Mail'd archangels sent
To wither up the strength of kings with death?
—I tell you, if these marvels have been done,
'Twas for the wearied and th' oppress'd of men.
They needed such!—And generous faith hath power
By her prevailing spirit, e'en to work
Deliverances, whose tale shall live with those
Of the great elder-time!—Be of good of heart!
Who is forsaken?—He that gives the thought
A place within his breast!—'Tis not for you.
—Know ye this banner?
    Cits. (*murmuring to each other.*) Is she not inspired?
Doth not Heaven call us by her fervent voice?
    Xim. Know ye this banner?
    Cit.   'Tis the Cid's.
    Xim.   The Cid's!
Who breathes that name but in th' exulting tone
Which the heart rings to?—Why, the very wind,
As it swells out the noble standard's fold,
Hath a triumphant sound!—The Cid's!—it moved
Even as a sign of victory through the land,
From the free skies ne'er stooping to a foe!
    Old Cit. Can ye still pause, my brethren? Oh! that youth
Through this worn frame were kindling once again!
    Xim. Ye linger still? Upon this very air,
He that was born in happy hour for Spain,[6]
Pour'd forth his conquering spirit! 'Twas the breeze
From your own mountains which came down to wave
This banner of his battles, as it droop'd
Above the champion's deathbed. Nor even then
Its tale of glory closed. They made no moan
O'er the dead hero, and no dirge was sung,[7]
But the deep tambor and shrill horn of war
Told when the mighty pass'd! They wrapt him not
With the pale shroud, but braced the warrior's form
In war array, and on his barbed steed,
As for a triumph, rear'd him; marching forth
In the hush'd midnight from Valencia's walls,
Beleagur'd then as now. All silently
The stately funeral moved. But who was he
That follow'd charging on the tall white horse,

And with the solemn standard, broad and pale,
Waving in sheets of snowlight? And the cross,
The bloody cross, far-blazing from his shield,
And the fierce meteor-sword? They fled, they fled,
The kings of Afric, with their countless hosts,
Were dust in his red path. The scimitar
Was shiver'd as a reed ;—for in that hour
The warrior-saint that keeps the watch for Spain,
Was arm'd betimes. And o'er that fiery field
The Cid's high banner stream'd all joyously,
For still its lord was there.
    Cits. (*rising tumultuously.*) Even unto death
Again it shall be follow'd!
    Xim.   Will he see
The noble stem hewn down, the beacon-light
Which from his house for ages o'er the land
Hath shone through cloud and storm, thus quench'd at once?
Will he not aid his children in the hour
Of this their utmost peril?—Awful power
Is with the holy dead, and there are times
When the tomb hath no chain they cannot burst!
Is it a thing forgotten how he woke
From its deep rest of old ; remembering Spain
In her great danger? At the night's mid-watch
How Leon started, when the sound was heard
That shook her dark and hollow-echoing streets,
As with the heavy tramp of steel-clad men,
By thousands marching through. For he had risen!
The Campeador was on his march again,
And in his arms, and follow'd by his hosts
Of shadowy spearmen. He had left the world
From which we are dimly parted, and gone forth,
And call'd his buried warriors from their sleep,
Gathering them round him to deliver Spain ;
For Afric was upon her. Morning broke,
Day rush'd through clouds of battle ; but at eve
Our God had triumph'd, and the rescued land
Sent up a shout of victory from the field,
That rock'd her ancient mountains.
    The Cits.   Arm! to arms!
On to our chief! We have strength within us yet
To die with our blood roused! Now, be the word
For the Cid's house!   [*They begin to arm themselves.*
    Xim.   Ye know his battle song?
The old rude strain wherewith his bands went forth
To strike down Paynim swords!   [*She sings.*

THE CID'S BATTLE SONG.

    The Moor is on his way,
With the tambour peal and the tecbir-shout,
And the horn o'er the blue seas ringing out,
    He hath marshall'd his dark array!

Shout through the vine-clad land!
That her sons on all their hills may hear,
And sharpen the point of the red wolf-spear,
    And the sword for the brave man's hand!

[*The* Citizens *join in the song, while they continue arming themselves.*

Banners are in the field!
The chief must rise from his joyous board,
And turn from the feast ere the wine be pour'd,
    And take up his father's shield!

The Moor is on his way!
Let the peasant leave his olive-ground,
And the goats roam wild through the pine-woods round!
    There is nobler work to-day!

Send forth the trumpet's call!
Till the bridegroom cast the goblet down,
And the marriage-robe, and the flowery crown;
    And arm in the banquet-hall!

And stay the funeral train:
Bid the chanted mass be hush'd awhile,
And the bier laid down in the holy aisle,
    And the mourners girt for Spain.

[*They take up the banner and follow* Ximena *out. Their voices are heard gradually dying away at a distance.*

Ere night must swords be red!
It is not an hour for knells and tears,
But for helmets braced, and serried spears!
    To-morrow for the dead!

The Cid is in array!
His steed is barded,* his plume waves high,
His banner is up in the sunny sky,
    Now joy for the Cross to-day!

Scene VII.—*The Walls of the City. The Plains beneath with the Moorish Camp and Army*

Gonzalez—Garcias—Hernandez.

(*A wild sound of Moorish Music heard from below.*)

Her. What notes are these in their deep mournfulness
So strangely wild?
Gar.   'Tis the shrill melody
Of the Moor's ancient death-song. Well I know
The rude barbaric sound; but, till this hour,
It seem'd not fearful.—Now, a shuddering chill

---

* *Barded,* caparisoned for battle.

Comes o'er me with its tones.—Lo! from yon tent
They lead the noble boys!
 Her.   The young, and pure,
And beautiful victims!—'Tis on things like these
We cast our hearts in wild idolatry,
Sowing the winds with hope!—Yet this is well,
Thus brightly crown'd with life's most gorgeous flowers,
And all unblemish'd, earth should offer up
Her treasures unto Heaven!
 Gar. (*to* GONZALEZ.) My chief, the Moor
Hath led your children forth.
 Gon. (*starting.*)   Are my sons there?
I knew they could not perish; for yon Heaven
Would ne'er behold it!---Where is he that said
I was no more a father?---They look changed---
Pallid and worn, as from a prison-house!
Or is't mine eye sees dimly?---But their steps
Seem heavy, as with pain.—I hear the clank—
Oh God! their limbs are fetter'd!
 Abd. (*coming forward beneath the walls.*) Christian ook
Once more upon thy children. There is yet
One moment for the trembling of the sword;
Their doom is still with thee.
 Gon.   Why should this man
So mock us with the semblance of our kind?
---Moor! Moor! thou dost too daringly provoke,
In thy bold cruelty, th' all-judging One,
Who visits for such things!---Hast thou no sense
Of thy frail nature?---'Twill be taught thee yet,
And darkly shall the anguish of my soul,
Darkly and heavily, pour itself on thine,
When thou shalt cry for mercy from the dust,
And be denied!
 Abd.   Nay, is it not thyself,
That hast no mercy and no love within thee?
These are thy sons, the nurslings of thy house;
Speak! must they live or die?
 Gon. (*in violent emotion.*) Is it Heaven's will
To try the dust it kindles for a day,
With infinite agony!---How have I drawn
This chastening on my head!---They bloom'd around me,
And my heart grew too fearless in its joy,
Glorying in their bright promise!---If we fall,
Is there no pardon for our feebleness?
 [HERNANDEZ, *without speaking, holds up a cross before him.*
 Abd. Speak!
 Gon. (*snatching the cross, and lifting it up.*) Let the earth
  be shaken through its depths,
But *this* must triumph!
 Abd. (*coldly.*) Be it as thou wilt.
---Unsheath the scimitar!   [*To his guards.*
 Gar. (*to* GONZALEZ.) Away, my chief!

This is your place no longer. There are things
No human heart, though battle-proof as yours,
Unmadden'd may sustain.
 Gon.   Be still! I have now
No place on earth but this!
Alph. (from beneath.) Men! give me way,
That I may speak forth once before I die!
 Gar. The princely boy!---how gallantly his brow
Wears its high nature in the face of death!
 Alph. Father!
 Gon. My son! my son!---Mine eldest-born!
 Alph. Stay but upon the ramparts! Fear thou not
---There is good courage in me: oh! my father!
I will not shame thee!---only let me fall
Knowing thine eye looks proudly on thy child,
So shall my heart have strength.
 Gon.   Would, would to **God,**
That I might die for thee, my noble boy!
Alphonso, my fair son!
 Alph.   Could I have lived,
I might have been a warrior!---Now, farewell!
But look upon me still!---I will not blench
When the keen sabre flashes---Mark me well!
Mine eyelids shall not quiver as it falls,
So thou wilt look upon me!
 Gar. (to Gonzalez.) Nay, my lord!
We must begone!---Thou *canst* not bear it!
 Gon.   Peace!
---Who hath told *thee* how much man's heart can bear?
---Lend me thine arm---my brain whirls fearfully---
How thick the shades close round!---my boy! my boy!
Where art thou in this gloom?
 Gar.   Let us go hence!
This is a dreadful moment!
 Gon.   Hush!---what saidst thou!
Now let me look on him!---Dost *thou* see aught
Through the dull mist which wraps us?
 Gar.   I behold---
O! for a thousand Spaniards! to rush down---
 Gon. Thou seest---My heart stands still to hear thee **speak!**
---There seems a fearful hush upon the air,
As 'twere the dead of night!
 Gar.   The hosts have closed
Around the spot in stillness. Through the spears,
Ranged thick and motionless, I see him not;
---But now---
 Gon. He bade me keep mine eye upon him,
And all is darkness round me!---Now?
 Gar.   A sword,
A sword, springs upward, like a lightning burst,
Through the dark serried mass!---Its cold blue glare
Is wavering to and fro---'tis vanish'd---hark!

Gon. I heard it, yes!—I heard the dull dead sound
That heavily broke the silence!—Didst thou speak?
—I lost thy words—come nearer!
Gar. 'Twas—'tis past!—
The sword fell *then!*
Her. (*with exultation.*) Flow forth, thou noble blood!
Fount of Spain's ransom and deliverance, flow
Uncheck'd and brighty forth!—Thou kingly stream!
Blood of our heroes! blood of martyrdom!
Which through so many warrior-hearts hast pour'd
Thy fiery currents, and hast made our hills
Free, by thine own free offering!—Bathe the land,
But there thou shalt not sink!—Our very air
Shall take thy coloring, and our loaded skies
O'er th' infidel hang dark and ominous,
With battle-hues of thee!—And thy deep voice
Rising above them to the judgment-seat
Shall call a burst of gather'd vengeance down,
To sweep th' oppressor from us!—for thy wave
Hath made his guilt run o'er!
Gon. (*endeavoring to rouse himself.*) 'Tis all a dream!
There is not one—no hand on earth could harm
That fair boy's graceful head!—Why look you thus?
Abd. (*pointing to* Carlos.) Christian? e'en yet thou hast a son!
Gon. E'en yet!
Car. My father! take me from these fearful men!
Wilt thou not save me, father?
Gon. (*attempting to unsheath his sword.*) Is the strength
From mine arm shiver'd?—Garcias, follow me!
Gar. Whither, my chief?
Gon. Why, we can die as well
On yonder plain,—ay, a spear's thrust will do
The little that our misery doth require,
Sooner than e'en this anguish! Life is best
Thrown from us in such moments.
 [*Voices heard at a distance.*
Her. Hush! what strain
Floats on the wind?
Gar. 'Tis the Cid's battle-song!
What marvel hath been wrought?
 [*Voices approaching heard in chorus.*
 The Moor is on his way!
With the tambour peal and the tecbir-shout,
And the horn o'er the blue seas ringing out;
 He hath marshall'd his dark array!
[Ximena *enters, followed by* Citizens, *with the banner.*
Xim. Is it too late?—My father, these are men
Through life and death prepared to follow thee
Beneath this banner!—Is their zeal too late?
—Oh! There's a fearful history on thy brow!
What hast thou seen?

Gar. It is not *all* too late.
Xim. My brothers!
Her. All is well. (*To* GARCIAS.) Hush would'st
    thou chill
That which has sprung within them, as a flame
From th' altar-embers mounts in sudden brightness?
I say, 'tis not too late, ye men of Spain!
On to the rescue!
    Xim. Bless me, O my father!
And I will hence, to aid thee with my prayers,
Sending my spirit with thee through the storm
Lit up by flashing swords!
    Gon. (*falling upon her neck.*) Hath aught been spared?
Am I not bereft?—Thou 'rt left me still!
Mine own, my loveliest one, thou 'rt left me still!
Farewell!—thy father's blessing and thy God's,
Be with thee, my Ximena!
    Xim. Fare thee well!
If e'er thy steps turn homeward from the field,
The voice is hush'd that still hath welcomed thee,
Think of me in thy victory!
    Her. Peace! no more!
This is no time to melt our nature down
To a soft stream of tears!—Be of strong heart!
Give me the banner! Swell the song again!
    The Cits. Ere night must swords be red!
    It is not an hour for knells and tears,
    But for helmets braced and serried spears!
    —To-morrow for the dead! [*Exeunt omnes.*

SCENE VIII.—*Before the Altar of a Church.*

ELMINA *rises from the steps of the Altar.*

Elm. The clouds are fearful that o'erhang thy ways,
Oh, thou mysterious Heaven!—It cannot be
That I have drawn the vials of thy wrath,
To burst upon me through the lifting up
Of a proud heart, elate in happiness!
No! in my day's full noon, for me life's flowers
But wreath'd a cup of trembling; and the love,
The boundless love, my spirit was form'd to bear,
Hath ever, in its place of silence, been
A trouble and a shadow, tinging thought
With hues too deep for joy!—I never look'd
On my fair children, in their buoyant mirth
Or sunny sleep, when all the gentle air
Seem'd glowing with their quiet blessedness,
But o'er my soul there came a shudd'ring sense
Of earth, and its pale changes; ev'n like that
Which vaguely mingles with our glorious dreams
A restless and disturbing consciousness
That the bright things must fade!—How have I shrunk

From the dull murmur of th' unquiet voice,
With its low tokens of mortality,
Till my heart fainted 'midst their smiles!—their smiles!
—Where are those glad looks now?—Could they go down,
With all their joyous light, that seem'd not earth's,
To the cold grave!—My children!—righteous Heaven!
There floats a dark remembrance o'er my brain
Of one who told me, with relentless eye,
That *this* should be the hour! [XIMENA *enters.*
   Xim. They are gone forth
Unto the rescue!—strong in heart and hope,
Faithful, though few!—My mother, let thy prayers
Call on the land's good saints to lift once more
The sword and cross that sweep the field for Spain,
As in old battle, so thine arms e'en yet
May clasp thy son!—For me, my part is done!
The flame which dimly might have linger'd yet
A little while, hath gather'd all its rays
Brightly to sink at once; and it is well!
The shadows are around me; to thy heart
Fold me, that I may die.
   Elm. My child!—What dream
Is on thy soul?—Even now thine aspect wears
Life's brightest inspiration!
   Xim. Death's!
   Elm. Away!
Thine eye hath starry clearness; and thy cheek
Doth glow beneath it with a richer hue
Than tinged its earliest flower!
   Xim. It well may be!
There are far deeper and far warmer hues
Than those which draw their coloring from the founts
Of youth, or health, or hope.
   Elm. Nay, speak not thus!
There's that about thee shining which would send
E'en through *my* heart a sunny glow of joy,
Were 't not for these sad words. The dim cold air
And solemn light, which wrap these tombs and shrines
As a pale gleaming shroud, seem kindled up
With a young spirit of etherial hope
Caught from thy mien!—Oh no! this is not death!
   Xim. Why should not He, whose touch dissolves our chain,
Put on his robes of beauty when he comes
As a deliverer?—He hath many forms,
They should not all be fearful!—If his call
Be but our gathering to that distant land
For whose sweet waters we have pined with thirst,
Why should not its prophetic sense be borne
Into the heart's deep stillness, with a breath
Of summer-winds, a voice of melody,
Solemn, yet lovely?—Mother, I depart!—
Be it thy comfort, in the after-days,

That thou hast seen me thus!
  Elm.   Distract me not
With such wild fears! Can I bear on with life
When thou art gone?—Thy voice, thy step, thy smile,
Pass'd from my path?—Alas! even now thine eye
Is changed—thy cheek is fading!
  Xim.   Ay, the clouds
Of the dim hour are gathering o'er my sight,
And yet I fear not, for the God of Help
Comes in that quiet darkness!—It may soothe
Thy woes, my mother! if I tell thee now
With what glad calmness I behold the veil
Falling between me and the world, wherein
My heart so ill hath rested.
  Elm.   Thine!
  Xim.   Rejoice
For her, that, when the garland of her life
Was blighted, and the springs of hope were dried,
Received her summons hence; and had no time,
Bearing the canker at th' impatient heart,
To wither, sorrowing for that gift of Heaven,
Which lent one moment of existence light,
That dimm'd the rest for ever!
  Elm.   How is this?
My child, what mean'st thou?
  Xim.   Mother! I have loved,
And been beloved!—the sunbeam of an hour,
Which gave life's hidden treasures to mine eye,
As they lay shining in their secret founts,
Went out and left them colorless.—'Tis past—
And what remains on earth?—the rainbow mist,
Through which I gazed, hath melted, and my sight
Is clear'd to look on all things as they are!—
But this is far too mournful!—Life's dark gift
Hath fall'n too early and too cold upon me!—
Therefore I would go hence!
  Elm.   And thou hast loved
Unknown——
  Xim.   Oh! pardon, pardon that 1 veil'd
My thoughts from thee!—But thou hadst woes enough,
And mine came o'er me when thy soul had need
Of more than mortal strength!—For I had scarce
Given the deep consciousness that I was loved
A treasure's place within my secret heart,
When earth's brief joy went from me!
            'Twas at morn
I saw the warriors to their field go forth,
And he—my chosen—was there amongst the rest,
With his young, glorious brow!—I look'd again--
The strife grew dark beneath me—but his plume
Waved free above the lances. Yet again—
It had gone down! and steeds were trampling o'er

The spot to which mine eyes were riveted,
Till blinded by th' intenseness of their gaze!—
And then—at last—I hurried to the gate,
And met him there!—I met him!—on his shield,
And with his cloven helm, and shiver'd sword,
And dark hair steep'd in blood!—They bore him past—
Mother!—I saw his face!—Oh! such a death
Works fearful changes on the fair of earth,
The pride of woman's eye!
   Elm.   Sweet daughter, peace!
Wake not the dark remembrance; for thy frame——
   Xim. There will be peace ere long. I shut my heart,
Even as a tomb, o'er that lone silent grief,
That I might spare it thee!—But now the hour
Is come when that which would have pierced thy soul
Shall be its healing balm. Oh! weep thou not,
Save with a gentle sorrow!
   Elm.   Must it be?
Art thou indeed to leave me?
   Xim. (exultingly.)   Be thou glad!
I say, rejoice above thy favor'd child!
Joy, for the soldier when his field is fought,
Joy, for the peasant when his vintage-task
Is closed at eve!—But most of all for her,
Who, when her life had changed its glittering robes
For the dull garb of sorrow, which doth cling
So heavily around the journeyers on,
Cast down its weight—and slept!
   Elm,
                      Alas! thine eye
Is wandering—yet how brightly!—Is this death,
Or some high wondrous vision?—Speak, my child!
How is it with thee now?
   Xim. (wildly.)   I see it still!
'Tis floating, like a glorious cloud on high,
My father's banner!—Hear'st thou not a sound?
The trumpet of Castile?—Praise, praise to Heaven!
—Now may the weary rest!—Be still!—Who calls
The night so fearful?—   *[She dies.*
   Elm.   No! she is not dead!—
Ximena!—speak to me!—Oh yet a tone
From that sweet voice, that I may gather in
One more remembrance of its lovely sound,
Ere the deep silence fall!—What, is all hush'd?—
No, no!—it cannot be!—How should we bear
The dark misgivings of our souls, if Heaven
Left not such beings with us?—But is this
Her wonted look?—too sad a quiet lies
On its dim fearful beauty?—Speak, Ximena!
Speak!—my heart dies within me!—She is gone,
With all her blessed smiles!—my child! my child!
Where art thou?—Where is that which answer'd me,
From thy soft-shining eyes?—Hush! doth she move?

—One light lock seem'd to tremble on her brow,
As a pulse throbb'd beneath ;—'twas but the voice
Of my despair that stirr'd it!—She is gone!
    [*She throws herself on the body.* GONZALEZ *enters,
    alone, and wounded.*
  Elm. (*rising as he approaches.*) I must not *now* be scorn'd
       No, not a look,
A whisper of reproach!—Behold my woe!—
Thou canst not scorn me now!
      Gon.   Hast thou heard *all?*
  Elm. Thy daughter on my bosom laid her head,
And pass'd away to rest.—Behold her there,
Even such as death hath made her!⁸
  Gon. (*bending over* XIMENA's *body.*) Thou art gone
A little while before me, oh, my child!
Why should the traveller weep to part with those
That scarce an hour will reach their promised land
Ere he too cast his pilgrim staff away,
And spread his couch beside them?
      Elm.   Must it be
Henceforth enough that *once* a thing so fair
Had its bright place amongst us?—Is this all
Left for the years to come?—We will not stay!
Earth's chain each hour grows weaker.
       Gon. (*still gazing upon* XIMENA.) And thou'rt laid
To slumber in the shadow, blessed child!
Of a yet stainless altar, and beside
A sainted warrior's tomb!—Oh, fitting place
For thee to yield thy pure heroic soul
Back unto him that gave it!—And thy cheek
Yet smiles in its bright paleness!
      Elm.   Hadst thou seen
The look with which she pass'd!
      Gon. (*still bending over her.*) Why, 'tis almost
Like joy to view thy beautiful repose!
The faded image of that perfect calm
Floats, e'en as long-forgotten music, back
Into my weary heart!—No dark wild spot
On *thy* clear brow doth tell of bloody hands
That quench'd young life by violence!—We 've seen
Too much of horror, in one crowded hour,
To weep for aught so gently gather'd hence!
—Oh! *man* leaves other traces!
  Elm. (*suddenly starting.*)   It returns
On my bewilder'd soul?—Went ye not forth
Unto the rescue?—And thou'rt here alone!
—Where are my sons?
  Gon. (*solemnly.*)   We were too late!
  Elm.   'Too late!
Hast thou nought else to tell me?
  Gon.   I brought back
From that last field the banner of my sires,

38

And my own death-wound.
Elm.   Thine!
Gon.   Another hour
Shall hush its throb for ever. I go hence,
And with me——
    Elm.   No!—Man *could* not lift his hands—
Where hast thou left thy sons?
    Gon.   I *have* no sons.
    Elm. What hast thou said?
    Gon.   That now there lives not one
To wear the glory of mine ancient house,
When I am gone to rest.
    Elm. (*throwing herself on the ground, and speaking in a
low hurried voice.*) In one brief hour, all gone!—and *such* a
        death!
—I see their blood gush forth!—their graceful heads—
Take the dark vision from me, oh, my God!
And such a death for *them!*—I was not there!
They were but mine in beauty and in joy,
Not in that mortal anguish—All, all gone!
—Why should I struggle more?—What *is* this Power,
Against whose might, on all sides pressing us,
We strive with fierce impatience, which but lays
Our own frail spirits prostrate?   [*After a long pause.*
                    Now I know
Thy hand, my God!—and they are soonest crush'd
That most withstand it!—I resist no more.
                                        [*She rises.*
A light, a light springs up from grief and death,
Which with its solemn radiance doth reveal
Why we have thus been tried!
    Gon.   Then I may still
Fix my last look on thee, in holy love,
Parting, but yet with hope!
    Elm. (*falling at his feet.*) Canst thou forgive?
—Oh, I have driven the arrow to thy heart,
That should have buried it within mine own,
And borne the pang in silence!—I have cast
Thy life's fair honor, in my wild despair,
As an unvalued gem upon the waves,
Whence thou hast snatch'd it back, to bear from earth,
All stainless on thy breast.—Well hast thou done—
But I—canst thou forgive?
    Gon.   Within this hour
I've stood upon that verge whence mortals fall,
And learn'd how 'tis with one whose sight grows dim,
And whose foot trembles on the gulf's dark side,
—Death purifies all feeling—We will part
In pity and in love.
    Elm.   Death!—And thou too
Art on thy way!—Oh, joy for thee, high heart!
Glory and joy for thee!—The day is closed,

And well and nobly hast thou borne thyself
Through its long battle-toils, though many swords
Have enter'd thine own soul!—But on my head
Recoil the fierce invokings of despair,
And I am left far distanced in the race.
The lonely one of earth!—Ay, this is just.
I am not worthy that upon my breast
In this, thine hour of vict'ry, thou should'st yield
Thy spirit unto God!
  Gon.   Thou art! thou art!
Oh! a life's love, a heart's long faithfulness,
Even in the presence of eternal things,
Wearing their chasten'd beauty all undimm'd,
Assert their lofty claims; and these are not
For one dark hour to cancel!—We are here,
Before that altar which received the vows
Of our unbroken youth, and meet it is
For such a witness, in the sight of Heaven,
And in the face of death, whose shadowy arm
Comes dim between us, to record th' exchange
Of our tried hearts' forgiveness.—Who are they,
That in one path have journey'd, needing not
Forgiveness at its close? [A CITIZEN *enters hastily.*
  Cit.   The Moors! the Moors!
  Gon. How! is the city storm'd?
O righteous Heaven! for this I look'd not yet!
Hath all been done in vain? Why, then, 'tis time
For prayer, and then to rest!
  Cit.   The sun shall set,
And not a Christian voice be left for prayer,
To-night, within Valencia. Round our walls
The Paynim host is gathering for th' assault,
And we have none to guard them.
  Gon.   Then my place
Is here no longer. I had hoped to die
E'en by the altar and the sepulchre
Of my brave sires; but this was not to be!
Give me my sword again, and lead me hence
Back to the ramparts. I have yet an hour,
And it hath still high duties. Now, my wife!
Thou mother of my children—of the dead—
Whom I name unto thee in steadfast hope—
  Elm. No, *not* farewell! My soul hath risen
To mate itself with thine; and by thy side,
Amidst the hurling lances, I will stand,
As one on whom a brave man's love hath been
Wasted not utterly.
  Gon.   I thank thee, Heaven!
That I have tasted of the awful joy
Which thou hast given, to temper hours like this
With a deep sense of thee, and of thine ends
In these dread visitings!

 (*To* ELMINA.)   We will not part,
But with the spirit's parting.
 Elm.   One farewell
To her, that, mantled with sad loveliness,
Doth slumber at our feet! My blessed child!
Oh! in thy heart's affliction thou wert strong,
And holy courage did pervade thy woe,
As light the troubled waters! Be at peace!
Thou whose bright spirit made itself the soul
Of all that were around thee! And thy life
E'en then was struck and withering at the core!
Farewell! thy parting look hath on me fallen,
E'en as a gleam of heaven, and I am now
More like what thou hast been. My soul is hush'd
For a still sense of purer worlds hath sunk
And settled on its depths with that last smile
Which from thine eye shone forth. Thou hast not lived
In vain—my child, farewell!
 Gon.   Surely for thee
Death had no sting, Ximena! We are blest,
To learn one secret of the shadowy pass,
From such an aspect's calmness. Yet once more
I kiss thy pale young cheek, my broken flower!
In token of th' undying love and hope
Whose land is far away.   [*Exeunt*

    SCENE IX.—*The Walls of the City.*

 HERNANDEZ.—*A few Citizens gathered round him.*

 Her. Why, men have cast the treasures, which their lives
Had been worn down in gathering, on the pyre,
Ay, at their household hearths have lit the brand,
Even from that shrine of quiet love to bear
The flame which gave their temples and their homes,
In ashes, to the winds! They have done this,
Making a blasted void where once the sun
Look'd upon lovely dwellings; and from earth
Razing all record that on such a spot
Childhood hath sprung, age faded, misery wept,
And frail humanity knelt before her God;
They have done *this*, in their free nobleness,
Rather than see the spoiler's tread pollute
Their holy places. Praise, high praise be theirs,
Who have left man such lessons! And these things,
Made your own hills their witnesses! The sky,
Whose arch bends o'er you, and the seas, wherein
Your rivers pour their gold, rejoicing saw
The altar, and the birthplace, and the tomb,
And all memorials of man's heart and faith,
Thus proudly honor'd! Be ye not outdone
By the departed! Though the godless foe
Be close upon us, we have power to snatch

The spoils of victory from him. Be but strong!
A few bright torches and brief moments yet
Shall baffle his flush'd hope, and we may die,
Laughing him unto scorn. Rise, follow me,
And thou, Valencia! triumph in thy fate,
The ruin, not the yoke, and make thy towers
A beacon unto Spain!
  Cits.   We'll follow thee!
Alas! for our fair city, and the homes
Wherein we rear'd our children! But away!
The Moor shall plant no crescent o'er our fanes! [Castile!
 Voice. (*from a Tower on the Walls.*) Succors!—Castile!
 Cits. (*rushing to the spot.*) It is even so!
Now blessing be to Heaven, for we are saved!—
Castile! Castile!
 Voice. (*from the Tower.*) Line after line of spears,
Lance after lance, upon the horizon's verge,
Like festal lights from cities bursting up,
Doth skirt the plain. In faith, a noble host! [to front
 Another Voice. The Moor hath turn'd him from our walls,
Th' advancing might of Spain!
  Cits. (*shouting.*)   Castile! Castile!
  [GONZALEZ *enters, supported by* ELMINA *and a Citizen.*
 Gon. What shouts of joy are these?
 Her.   Hail! chieftain, hail!
Thus, even in death, 'tis given thee to receive
The conqueror's crown! Behold our God hath heard,
And arm'd himself with vengeance! Lo! they come!
The lances of Castile!
 Gon.   I knew, I knew
Thou would'st not utterly, my God, forsake
Thy servant in his need! My blood and tears
Have not sunk vainly to th' attesting earth!
Praise to thee, thanks and praise, that I have lived
To see this hour!
 Elm.   And I, too, bless thy name,
Though thou hast proved me unto agony!
O God!—thou God of chastening!
 Voice. (*from the Tower.*) They move on!
I see the royal banner in the air,
With its emblazon'd towers!
 Gon.   Go, bring ye forth
The banner of the Cid, and plant it here,
To stream above me, for an answering sign
That the good cross doth hold its lofty place
Within Valencia still! What see ye now?
 Her. I see a kingdom's might upon its path,
Moving, in terrible magnificence,
Unto revenge and victory! With the flash
Of knightly swords, up-springing from the ranks,
As meteors from a still and gloomy deep,
And with the waving of ten thousand plumes,

Like a land's harvest in the autumn-wind,
And with fierce light, which is not of the sun,
But flung from sheets of steel—it comes, it comes,
The vengeance of our God!
 Gon.   I hear it now,
The heavy tread of mail-clad multitudes,
Like thunder showers upon the forest paths.
 Her. Ay, earth knows well the omen of that sound,
And she hath echoes, like a sepulchre's,
Pent in her secret hollows to respond
Unto the step of death!
 Gon.   Hark! how the wind
Swells proudly with the battle-march of Spain!
Now the heart feels its power!—A little while
Grant me to live, my God! What pause is this?
 Her. A deep and dreadful one!—the serried files
Level their spears for combat; now the hosts
Look on each other in their brooding wrath,
Silent and face to face.

    Voices heard Without, Chanting.

  Calm on the bosom of thy God,
   Fair spirit! rest thee now!
  E'en while with ours thy footsteps trode
   His seal was on thy brow.

  Dust to its narrow house beneath!
   Soul, to its place on high!
  They that have seen thy look in death,
   No more may fear to die.

 Elm. (*to* GONZALEZ.) It is the death-hymn o'er thy daughter's
  bier!
But I am calm; and e'en like gentle winds,
That music, through the stillness of my heart,
Sends mournful peace.
 Gon.   Oh! well those solemn tones
Accord with such an hour, for all her life
Breath'd of a hero's soul!
 [*A sound of trumpets and shouting from the plain.*
 Her. Now, now they close! Hark! what a dull dead sound
Is in the Moorish war-shout!—I have known
Such tones prophetic oft.—The shock is given—
Lo! they have placed their shields before their hearts,
And lower'd their lances with the streamers on,
And on their steeds bent forward!—God for Spain!
The first bright sparks of battle have been struck
From spear to spear, across the gleaming field!—
There is no sight on which the blue sky looks
To match with this!—'Tis not the gallant crests,
Nor banners with their glorious blazonry;

The very nature and high soul of man
Doth now reveal itself?
 Gon.   Oh, raise me up,
That I may look upon the noble scene!—
It will not be!—That this dull mist would pass
A moment from my sight!—Whence rose that shout,
As in fierce triumph?
 Her. (*clasping his hands.*) Must I look on this?
The banner sinks—'tis taken!
 Gon.   Whose?
 Her.   Castile's!
 Gon. Oh, God of Battles!
 Elm.   Calm thy noble heart!
Thou wilt not pass away without thy meed.
Nay, rest thee on my bosom.
 Her.   Cheer thee yet!
Our knights have spurr'd to rescue.—There is now
A whirl, a mingling of all terrible things,
Yet more appalling than the fierce distinctness
Wherewith they moved before!—I see tall plumes
All wildly tossing o'er the battle's tide,
Sway'd by the wrathful motion, and the press
Of desperate men, as cedar-boughs by storms.
Many a white streamer there is dyed with blood,
Many a false corslet broken, many a shield
Pierced through!—Now, shout for Santiago, shout!
Lo! javelins with a moment's brightness cleave
The thickening dust, and barbed steeds go down
With their helm'd riders!—Who, but One, can tell
How spirits part amidst that fearful rush
And trampling on of furious multitudes?
 Gon. Thou'rt silent!—See'st thou more?—My soul grows
  dark.
 Her. And dark and troubled, as an angry sea,
Dashing some gallant armament in scorn
Against its rocks, is all on which I gaze!—
I can but tell thee how tall spears are cross'd,
And lances seem to shiver, and proud helms
To lighten with the stroke!—But round the spot,
Where, like a storm-fell'd mast, our standard sank.
The heart of battle burns.
 Gon.   Where is that spot?
 Her. It is beneath the lonely tuft of palms,
That lift their green heads o'er the tumult still
In calm and stately grace.
 Gon.   *There* didst thou say?
Then God is with us, and we *must* prevail!
For on that spot they died!—My children's blood
Calls on th' avenger thence!
 Elm.   They perish'd there!
—And the bright locks that waved so joyously
To the free winds, lay trampled and defiled

Even on that place of death!—Oh, Merciful!
Hush the dark thought within me!
   Her. (*with sudden exultation.*) Who is he,
On the white steed, and with the castled helm,
And the gold-broider'd mantle, which doth float
E'en like a sunny cloud above the fight;
And the pale cross, which from his breast-plate gleams
With star-like radiance?
   Gon. (*eagerly.*)   Didst thou say the cross?
   Her. On his mail'd bosom shines a broad white cross,
And his long plumage through the dark'ning air
Streams like a snow-wreath.
   Gon.   That should be—
   Her.   The king!
—Was it not told us how he sent, of late,
To the Cid's tomb, e'en for the silver cross
Which he who slumbers there was wont to bind
O'er his brave heart in fight?⁹
   Gon. (*springing up joyfully.*) My king: my king!
Now all good saints for Spain!—My noble king!
And thou art there!—That I might look once more
Upon thy face!—But yet I thank thee, Heaven!
That thou hast sent him, from my dying hands
Thus to receive his city!
                         [*He sinks back into* ELMINA'S *arms.*
   Her.   He hath clear'd
A pathway 'midst the combat, and the light
Follows his charge through yon close living mass,
E'en as a gleam on some proud vessel's wake
Along the stormy waters!—'Tis redeem'd—
The castled banner!—It is flung once more
In joy and glory to the sweeping winds!
—There seems a wavering through the paynim hosts—
Castile doth press them sore—Now, now rejoice!
   Gon. What hast thou seen?
   Her.   Abdullah falls! He falls!
The man of blood!—the spoiler!—he hath sunk
In our king's path!—Well hath that royal sword
Avenged thy cause, Gonzalez!
                          They give way,
The Crescent's van is broken!—On the hills
And the dark pine-woods may the infidel
Call vainly in his agony of fear,
To cover him from vengeance!—Lo! they fly!
They of the forest and the wilderness
Are scatter'd, e'en as leaves upon the wind!
Woe to the sons of Afric!—Let the plains,
And the vine-mountains, and Hesperian seas,
Take their dead unto them!—that blood shall wash
Our soil from stains of bondage.
   Gon. (*attempting to raise himself.*) Set me free!

THE SIEGE OF VALENCIA. 469

Come with me forth, for I must greet my king,
After his battle-field!
 Her.   Oh, blest in death!
Chosen of Heaven, farewell!—Look on the Cross,
And part from earth in peace!
 Gon.   Now, charge once more!
God is with Spain, and Santiago's sword
Is reddening all the air!—Shout forth " Castile !"
The day is ours!—I go ; but fear ye not!
For Afric's lance is broken, and my sons
Have won their first good field!   [*He dies.*
 Elm.   Look on me yet!
Speak one farewell, my husband!—must thy voice
Enter my soul no more!—Thine eye is fix'd—
Now is my life uprooted,—And 'tis well.
 [*A sound of triumphant music is heard, and many Castilian Knights and Soldiers enter.*
 A Cit. Hush your triumphant sounds, although ye come
E'en as deliverers!—But the noble dead,
And those that mourn them, claim from human hearts
Deep silent reverence.
 Elm. (*rising proudly.*) No, swell forth, Castile!
Thy trumpet-music, till the seas and heavens,
And the deep hills, give every stormy note
Echoes to ring through Spain!—How, know ye not
That all array'd for triumph, crown'd and robed
With the strong spirit which hath saved the land,
E'en now a conqueror to his rest is gone?
—Fear not to break that sleep, but let the wind
Swell on with victory's shout!—*He* will not hear—
Hath earth a sound more sad?
 Her.   Lift ye the dead,
And bear him with the banner of his race
Waving above him proudly, as it waved
O'er the Cid's battles, to the tomb wherein
His warrior-sires are gather'd. [*They raise the body.*
 Elm.   Ay, 'tis thus
Thou should'st be honor'd!—And I follow thee
With an unfaltering and a lofty step,
To that last home of glory. She that wears
In her deep heart the memory of thy love,
Shall thence draw strength for all things, till the God
Whose hand around her hath unpeopled earth,
Looking upon her still and chasten'd soul,
Call it once more to thine!
 (*To the Castilians.*) Awake, I say,
Tambour and trumpet, awake!—And let the land
Through all her mountains hear your funeral peal
 So should a hero pass to his repose. [*Exeunt omnes.*

NOTES.

Note 1, page, 415, line 25,

MOUNTAIN CHRISTIANS, those natives of Spain, who under their prince, Pelayo, took refuge amongst the mountains of the northern provinces, where they maintained their religion and liberty, whilst the rest of their country was overrun by the Moors.

Note 2, page 432, line 11.
Oh, free doth sorrow pass, &c.
"Frey geht das Unglück durch die ganze Erde."
SCHILLER's *Death of Wallenstein*, act iv. sc. 2.

Note 3, page 435, line 37.

Tizona, the fire-brand. The name of the Cid's favorite sword, taken in battle from the Moorish king Bucar.

Note 4, page 435, line 39.
How he won Valencia from the Moor, &c.

Valencia, which has been repeatedly besieged and taken by the armies of different nations, remained in the possession of the Moors for a hundred and seventy years after the Cid's death. It was regained from them by King Don Jayme of Aragon, surnamed the Conqueror; after whose success I have ventured to suppose it governed by a descendant of the Campeador.

Note 5, page 449, line 26.

It was a Spanish tradition, that the great bell of the cathedral of Saragossa always tolled spontaneously before a king of Spain died.

Note 6, page 451, line 37.

"El que en buen hora nasco," he that was born in happy hour An appellation given to the Cid in the ancient chronicles.

Note 7, page 451, line 43.

For this, and the subsequent allusion to Spanish legends, see *The Romances, and Chronicle of the Cid.*

Note 8, page 461, line 13.

"La voilà, telle que la mort nous l'a faite!"—BOSSUET, *Oraisons Funèbres.*

Note 9, page 468, line 18.

This circumstance is recorded of King Don Alfonso, the last of that name. He sent to the Cid's tomb for the cross which that warrior was accustomed to wear upon his breast when he went to battle, and had it made into one for himself; "Because of the faith which he had, that through it he should obtain the victory."—*Southey's Chronicle of the Cid.*

CRITICAL ANNOTATIONS

ON

"THE SIEGE OF VALENCIA," "THE LAST CONSTANTINE," &c.

"THE present publication appears to us, in every respect superior to any thing Mrs. Hemans has yet written—more powerful in particular passages—more interesting in the narrative part—as pathetic and delicate in the reflective—as elaborately faultless in its versification—as copious in imagery. Of the longer poems, *The Last Constantine* is our favorite. The dramatic poem which follows it, entitled *The Siege of Valencia*, exhibits too evidently the weak points of Mrs. Hemans's poetry—a want of dramatic invention, a penury of incident, and the substitution of lyrical for passionate dialogue. The leading features of Constantine's character seem to be taken from the unequal, but, on the whole, admirable play of *Constantine Palæologus*, by the gifted rival of our authoress, Joanna Baillie; and the picture of that enduring and Christian courage, which, in the midst of 'a ruined city and a fallen state,' sustained the last of the Cæsars, when all earthly hope and help had failed him, is eminently touching and poetical. The following stanzas appears to us particularly beautiful.

 'Sounds from the waters, sounds upon the earth,
  Sounds in the air, of battle,' &c.

The following stanzas, too, in which the leading idea of Constantine's character is still more fully brought out, are likewise excellent.

 'It was a sad and solemn task to hold
  Their midnight watch on that beleaguer'd wall,' &c,

"These are splendid passages, justly conceived, admirably expressed, full of eloquence and melody; and the poem contains many others equally beautiful. As we have already hinted, the story might have been better told; or rather, there is scarcely any story at all, but the reader is borne down the stream of pensive reflection, so gently and so easily, that he scarcely perceives the want of it.

"Of the *Siege of Valencia* we say little, for we by no means consider it as the happiest of Mrs. Hemans's efforts. Not that it does not contain, nay, abound with fine passages; but the whole wants vigor, coherence, and compression. The story is meagre, and the dialogue too diffuse.

" *The Festal Hour* certainly appears to us to be one of the noblest regular and classical odes in the English language—happy in the general idea, and rich in imagery and illustration."—The Rev. Dr. MOREHEAD, in *Constable's Magazine* for September, 1823.

" *The Siege of Valencia* is a dramatic poem, but not intended for representation. The story is extremely simple. The Moors, who besiege Valencia, take the two sons of the Governor, Gonzalez, captive, as they come to visit their father, and now the ransom demanded for them is the surrender of the city: they are to die if the place is not yielded up. Elmina, the mother of the boys, and Ximena, their sister, are the remaining members of a family to which so dreadful an option is submitted. The poem is one of the highest merit. The subject is of great dignity, being connected with the defence of Spain against the Moors, and at the same time it is of the greatest tenderness, offering a succession of the most moving scenes that can be imagined to occur in the bosom of a family. The father is firm, the daughter is heroic; the mother falters. She finds her way to the Moorish camp, sees her children, forms her plan for betraying the town, and then is not able to conceal her grief and her design from her husband. He immediately sends a defiance to the Moors, his children are brought out and beheaded, a *sortie* is made from the besieged city: finally, the king of Spain arrives to the rescue; the wrongs of Gonzalez are avenged, he himself dies in victory; and the poem closes with a picture of his wife, moved by the strongest grief, of which she is yet able to restrain the expression. The great excellence of the poem lies in the description of the struggle between the consciousness of duty and maternal fondness. We believe none but a mother could have written it."—PROFESSOR NORTON, in *North American Review* for April 1827.

THE FOREST SANCTUARY.

> Ihr Plätze aller meiner stillen freuden,
> Euch lass' ich hinter mir auf immerdar!
> * * * * * * * *
> So ist des geistes ruf an mich ergangen,
> Mich treibt nicht eitles, irdisches verlangen.
> *Die Jungfrau von Orleans*

> Long time against oppression have I fought,
> And for the native liberty of faith
> Have bled and suffer'd bonds.
> *Remorse, a Tragedy.*

The following Poem is intended to describe the mental conflicts, as well as outward sufferings, of a Spaniard, who, flying from the religious persecutions of his own country, in the sixteenth century, takes refuge with his child, in a North American forest. The story is supposed to be related by himself, amidst the wilderness which has afforded him an asylum.

I.

The voices of my home!—I hear them still!
They have been with me through the dreamy night—
The blessed household voices, wont to fill
My heart's clear depths with unalloy'd delight!
I hear them still, unchanged:—though some from earth
Are music parted, and the tones of mirth—
Wild, silvery tones, that rang through days more bright!
Have died in others,—yet to me they come,
Singing of boyhood back—the voices of my home!

II.

They call me through this hush of woods reposing,
In the grey stillness of the summer morn;
They wander by when heavy flowers are closing,
And thoughts grow deep, and winds and stars are born;
Even as a fount's remember'd gushings burst
On the parch'd traveller in his hour of thirst,
E'en thus they haunt me with sweet sounds, till worn
By quenchless longings, to my soul I say—
Oh! for the dove's swift wings, that I might flee away,—

III.

And find mine ark!—yet whither?—I must bear
A yearning heart within me to the grave.
I am of those o'er whom a breath of air—
Just darkening in its course the lake's bright wave,
And sighing through the feathery canes¹—hath power
To call up shadows, in the silent hour,
From the dim past, as from a wizard's cave!—

So must it be!—These skies above me spread,
Are they my own soft skies?—Ye rest not here, my dead!

IV.
Ye far amidst the southern flowers lie sleeping,
Your graves all smiling in the sunshine clear,
Save one! a blue, lone, distant main is sweeping
High o'er *one* gentle head—ye rest not here!—
'Tis not the olive, with a whisper swaying,
Not thy low ripplings, glassy water, playing
Through my own chestnut groves, which fill mine ear;
But the faint echoes in my breast that dwell,
And for their birthplace moan, as moans the ocean-shell.²

V.
Peace!—I will dash these fond regrets to earth,
Even as an eagle shakes the cumbering rain
From his strong pinion. Thou that gavest me birth,
And lineage, and once home,—my native Spain!
My own bright land—my father's land—my child's!
What hath thy son brought from thee to the wilds?
He hath brought marks of torture and the chain,
Traces of things which pass not as a breeze; [these.
A blighted name, dark thoughts, wrath, woe,—thy gifts are

VI.
A blighted name!—I hear the winds of morn—
Their sounds are not of this!—I hear the shiver
Of the green reeds, and all the rustlings, borne
From the high forest, when the light leaves quiver.
Their sounds are not of this!—the cedars, waving,
Lend it no tone: His wide savannahs laving,
It is not murmur'd by the joyous river!
What part hath mortal name, where God alone
Speaks to the mighty waste, and through its heart is known?

VII.
Is it not much that I may worship Him,
With nought my spirit's breathings to control,
And feel His presence in the vast, and dim,
And whispery woods, where dying thunders roll
From the far cat'racts?—Shall I not rejoice
That I have learn'd at last to know *His* voice
From man's?—I will rejoice!—my soaring soul
Now hath redeem'd her birthright of the day,
And won, through clouds, to Him, her own unfetter'd way!

VIII.
And thou, my boy! that silent at my knee
Dost lift to mine thy soft, dark, earnest eyes,
Fill'd with the love of childhood, which I see
Pure through its depths, a thing without disguise;
Thou that hast breathed in slumber on my breast,
When I have check'd its throbs to give thee rest,
Mine own! whose young thoughts fresh before me rise!

Is it not much that I may guide thy prayer,
And circle thy glad soul with free and healthful air?

IX.

Why should I weep on thy bright head, my boy?
Within thy fathers' halls thou wilt not dwell,
Nor lift their banner, with a warrior's joy,
Amidst the sons of mountain chiefs, who fell
For Spain of old.—Yet what if rolling waves
Have borne us far from our ancestral graves?
Thou shalt not feel thy bursting heart rebel,
As mine hath done; nor bear what I have borne,
Casting in falsehood's mould th' indignant brow of scorn.

X.

This shall not be thy lot, my blessed child!
I have not sorrow'd, struggled, lived in vain—
Hear me! magnificent and ancient wild;
And mighty rivers, ye that meet the main,
As deep meets deep; and forests, whose dim shade
The flood's voice, and the wind's, by swells pervade;
Hear me!—'tis well to die, and not complain,
Yet there are hours when the charged heart must speak,
E'en in the desert's ear to pour itself, or break!

XI.

I see an oak before me:[3] it hath been
The crown'd one of the woods; and might have flung
Its hundred arms to heaven, still freshly green,
But a wild vine around the stem hath clung,
From branch to branch close wreaths of bondage throwing,
Till the proud tree, before no tempest bowing,
Hath shrunk and died those serpent folds among,
Alas! alas! what is it that I see?
An image of man's mind, land of my sires, with thee!

XII.

Yet art thou lovely!—Song is on thy hills—
Oh, sweet and mournful melodies of Spain,
That lull'd my boyhood, how your memory thrills
The exile's heart with sudden-wakening pain!
Your sounds are on the rocks:—That I might hear
Once more the music of the mountaineer!
And from the sunny vales the shepherd's strain
Floats out, and fills the solitary place
With the old tuneful names of Spain's heroic race.

XIII.

But there was silence one bright, golden day,
Through my own pine-hung mountains. Clear, yet lone,
In the rich autumn light the vineyards lay,
And from the fields the peasant's voice was gone;
And the red grapes untrodden strew'd the ground,
And the free flocks, untended, roam'd around:
Where was the pastor?—where the pipe's wild tone?

Music and mirth were hush'd the hills among,
While to the city's gates each hamlet pour'd its throng.

XIV.
Silence upon the mountains! But within
The city's gate a rush, a press, a swell
Of multitudes, their torrent way to win;
And heavy boomings of a dull deep bell,
A dead pause following each—like that which parts
The dash of billows, holding breathless hearts
Fast in the hush of fear—knell after knell;
And sounds of thickening steps, like thunder-rain
That plashes on the roof of some vast echoing fane!

XV.
What pageant's hour approach'd? The sullen gate
Of a strong ancient prison-house was thrown
Back to the day. And who, in mournful state,
Came forth, led slowly o'er its threshold-stone?
They that had learn'd, in cells of secret gloom,
How sunshine is forgotten! They, to whom
The very features of mankind were grown
Things that bewilder'd! O'er their dazzled sight
They lifted their wan hands, and cower'd before the light!

XVI.
To this, man brings his brother! Some were there,
Who, with their desolation, had entwined
Fierce strength, and girt the sternness of despair
Fast round their bosoms, even as warriors bind
The breastplate on for fight; but brow and cheek
Seem'd *theirs* a torturing panoply to speak!
And there was some, from whom the very mind
Had been wrung out:—they smiled—oh! startling smile,
Whence man's high soul is fled! Where doth it sleep the while?

XVII.
But onward moved the melancholy train,
For their false creeds in fiery pangs to die.
This was the solemn sacrifice of Spain—
Heaven's offering from the land of chivalry!
Through thousands, thousands of their race they moved—
Oh! how unlike all others!—the beloved,
The free, the proud, the beautiful! whose eye
Grew fix'd before them, while a people's breath
Was hush'd, and its one soul bound in the thought of death!

XVIII.
It might be that amidst the countless throng,
There swell'd some heart with pity's weight oppress'd
For the wide stream of human love is strong;
And woman, on whose fond and faithful breast
Childhood is rear'd, and at whose knee the sigh
Of its first prayer is breathed, she, too, was nigh.
But life is dear, and the free footstep bless'd,

And home a sunny place, where each may fill
Some eye with glistening smiles,—and therefore all were still.

XIX.

All still,—youth, courage, strength!—a winter laid,
A chain of palsy cast, on might and mind!
Still, as at noon a southern forest's shade
They stood, those breathless masses of mankind;
Still, as a frozen torrent!—but the wave
Soon leaps to foaming freedom—they, the brave,
Endured—they saw the martyr's place assign'd
In the red flames—whence is the withering spell
That numbs each human pulse?—they saw, and thought it well.

XX.

And I, too, thought it well! That very morn
From a far land I came, yet round me clung
The spirit of my own. No hand had torn
With a strong grasp away the veil which hung
Between my eyes and truth. I gazed, I saw
Dimly, as through a glass. In silent awe
I watch'd the fearful rites; and if there sprung
One rebel feeling from its deep founts up,
Shuddering, I flung it back, as guilt's own poison-cup.

XXI.

But I was waken'd as the dreamers waken
Whom the shrill trumpet and the shriek of dread
Rouse up at midnight, when their walls are taken,
And they must battle till their blood is shed
On their own threshold-floor. A path for light
Through my torn breast was shatter'd by the might
Of the swift thunder-stroke—and freedom's tread
Came in through ruins, late, yet not in vain,
Making the blighted place all green with life again.

XXII.

Still darkly, slowly, as a sullen mass
Of cloud, o'ersweeping, without wind, the sky,
Dream-like I saw the sad procession pass,
And mark'd its victims with a tearless eye.
They moved before me but as pictures, wrought
Each to reveal some secret of man's thought,
On the sharp edge of sad mortality,
Till in his place came one—oh! could it be?
My friend, my heart's first friend!—and did I gaze on thee?

XXIII.

On thee! with whom in boyhood I had play'd,
At the grape-gatherings, by my native streams!
And to whose eye my youthful soul had laid
Bare, as to Heaven's, its glowing world of dreams;
And by whose side 'midst warriors I had stood,
And in whose helm was brought—oh! earn'd with blood!
The fresh wave to my lips, when tropic beams

Smote on my fever'd brow!—Ay, years had pass'd,
Severing our paths, brave friend!—and *thus* we met at ast!

XXIV.

I see it still—the lofty mien thou borest—
On thy pale forehead sat a sense of power!
The very look that once thou brightly worest,
Cheering me onward through a fearful hour,
When we were girt by Indian bow and spear,
'Midst the white Andes—even as mountain deer,
Hemm'd in our camp—but through the javelin shower
We rent our way, a tempest of despair!
And thou—hadst thou but died with thy true brethren there!

XXV.

I call the fond wish back—for thou hast perish'd
More nobly far, my Alvar!—making known
The might of truth;[4] and be thy memory cherish'd
With theirs, the thousands that around her throne
Have pour'd their lives out smiling, in that doom
Finding a triumph, if denied a tomb!—
Ay, with their ashes hath the wine been sown,
And with the wind their spirit shall be spread,
Filling man's heart and home with records of the dead.

XXVI.

Thou Searcher of the soul! in whose dread sight
Not the bold guilt alone that mocks the skies,
But the scarce-owned, unwhisper'd thought of night,
As a thing written with the sunbeam lies;
Thou know'st—whose eye through shade and depth can see,
That this man's crime was but to worship thee,
Like those that made their hearts thy sacrifice,
The call'd of yore—wont by the Saviour's side
On the dim Olive-Mount to pray at eventide.

XXVII.

For the strong spirit will at times awake,
Piercing the mists that wrap her clay abode;
And, born of thee, she may not always take
Earth's accents for the oracles of God;
And even for this—O dust, whose mask is power!
Reed, that would'st be a scourge thy little hour!
Spark, whereon yet the mighty hath not trod,
And therefore thou destroyest!—where were flown
Our hopes, if man were left to man's decree alone?

XXVIII.

But this I felt not yet. I could but gaze
On him, my friend; while that swift moment threw
A sudden freshness back on vanish'd days,
Like water-drops on some dim picture's hue;
Calling the proud time up, when first I stood
Where banners floated, and my heart's quick blood
Sprang to a torrent as the clarion blew,

And he—his sword was like a brother's worn,
That watches through the field his mother's youngest born.

XXIX.
But a lance met me in that day's career,
Senseless I lay amidst th' o'ersweeping fight,
Wak'ning at last—how full, how strangely clear,
That scene on memory flash'd!—the shivery light,
Moonlight, on broken shields—the plain of slaughter.
The fountain-side—the low sweet sound of water—
And Alvar bending o'er me—from the night
Covering me with his mantle!—all the past
Flow'd back—my soul's far chords all answer'd to the blast.

XXX.
Till, in that rush of visions, I became
As one that, by the bands of slumber wound,
Lies with a powerless but all-thrilling frame,
Intense in consciousness of sight and sound,
Yet buried in a wildering dream which brings
Loved faces round him, girt with fearful things!
Troubled even thus I stood, but chain'd and bound
On that familiar form mine eye to keep:—
Alas! I might not fall upon his neck and weep!

XXXI.
He pass'd me—and what next?—I look'd on two,
Following his footsteps to the same dread place,
For the same guilt—his sisters![5]—Well I knew
The beauty on those brows, though each young face
Was changed—so deeply changed!—a dungeon's air
Is hard for loved and lovely things to bear;
And ye, O daughters of a lofty race,
Queen-like Theresa! radiant Inez!—flowers
So cherish'd! were ye then but rear'd for those dark hours?

XXXII.
A mournful home, young sisters! had ye left,
With your lutes hanging hush'd upon the wall,
And silence round the aged man, bereft
Of each glad voice, once answering to his call.
Alas, that lonely father! doom'd to pine
For sounds departed in his life's decline,
And, 'midst the shadowing banners of his hall,
With his white hair to sit, and deem the name
A hundred chiefs had borne, cast down by you to shame![6]

XXXIII.
And woe for you, 'midst looks and words of love,
And gentle hearts and faces, nursed so long!
How had I seen you in your beauty move,
Wearing the wreath, and listening to the song!
—Yet sat, even then, what seem'd the crowd to shun,
Half-veil'd upon the clear pale brow of one,
And deeper thoughts than oft to youth belong,

Thoughts, such as wake to evening's whispery sway,
Within the drooping shade of her sweet eyelids lay.

XXXIV.

And if she mingled with the festive train,
It was but as some melancholy star
Beholds the dance of shepherds on the plain,
In its bright stillness present, though afar.
Yet would she smile—and that, too, hath its smile—
Circled with joy which reach'd her not the while,
And bearing a lone spirit, not at war
With earthly things, but o'er their form and hue
Shedding too clear a light, too sorrowfully true.

XXXV.

But the dark hours wring forth the hidden might
Which hath lain bedded in the silent soul,
A treasure all undreamt of ;—as the night
Calls out the harmonies of streams that roll
Unheard by day. It seem'd as if her breast
Had hoarded energies, till then suppress'd
Almost with pain, and bursting from control,
And finding first that hour their pathway free :—
Could a rose brave the storm, such might her emblem be !

XXXVI.

For the soft gloom whose shadow still had hung
On her fair brow, beneath its garlands worn,
Was fled ; and fire, like prophecy's, had sprung
Clear to her kindled eye. It might be scorn—
Pride—sense of wrong—ay, the frail heart is bound
By these at times, even as with adamant round,
Kept so from breaking !—yet not *thus* upborne
She moved, though some sustaining passion's wave
Lifted her fervent soul—a sister for the brave !

XXXVII.

And yet, alas ! to see the strength which clings
Round women in such hours !—a mournful sight,
Though lovely !—an o'erflowing of the springs,
The full springs of affection, deep as bright !
And she, because her life is ever twined
With other lives, and by no stormy wind
May thence be shaken, and because the light
Of tenderness is round her, and her eye
Doth weep such passionate tears—therefore she thus can die.

XXXVIII.

Therefore didst *thou*, through that heart-shaking scene,
As through a triumph move ; and cast aside
Thine own sweet thoughtfulness for victory's mien,
O faithful sister ! cheering thus the guide,
And friend, and brother of thy sainted youth,
Whose hand had led thee to the source of truth,
Where thy glad soul from earth was purified ;

Nor wouldst thou, following him through all the past,
That he should see thy step grow tremulous at last.

XXXIX.

For thou hadst made no deeper love a guest
'Midst thy young spirit's dreams, than that which grows
Between the nurtured of the same fond breast,
The shelter'd of one roof; and thus it rose
Twined in with life.—How is it that the hours
Of the same sport, the gathering early flowers
Round the same tree, the sharing one repose,
And mingling one first prayer in murmurs soft,
From the heart's memory fade, in this world's breath so oft?

XL.

But thee that breath had touch'd not; thee, nor him,
The true in all things found!—and thou wert blest
Even then, that no remember'd change could dim
The perfect image of affection, press'd
Like armor to thy bosom!—thou hadst kept
Watch by thy brother's couch of pain, and wept,
Thy sweet face covering with thy robe, when rest
Fled from the sufferer; thou hadst bound his faith
Unto thy soul;—one light, one hope ye chose—one death.

XLI.

So didst thou pass on brightly!—but for her,
Next in that path, how may *her* doom be spoken!
All merciful! to think that such things were,
And *are*, and seen by men with hearts unbroken!
To think of that fair girl, whose path had been
So strew'd with rose-leaves, all one fairy scene!
And whose quick glance came ever as a token
Of hope to drooping thought, and her glad voice
As a free bird's in spring, that makes the woods rejoice!

XLII.

And she to die!—she loved the laughing earth
With such deep joy in its fresh leaves and flowers!
Was not her smile even as the sudden birth
Of a young rainbow, coloring vernal showers?
Yes! but to meet her fawn-like step, to hear
The gushes of wild song, so silvery clear,
Which oft, unconsciously, in happier hours
Flow'd from her lips, was to forget the sway
Of Time and Death below, blight, shadow, dull decay!

XLIII.

Could this change be?—the hour, the scene, where last
I saw that form, came floating o'er my mind:—
A golden vintage-eve; the heats were pass'd,
And, in the freshness of the fanning wind,
Her father sat where gleam'd the first faint star
Through the lime-boughs; and with her light guitar,
She, on the greensward at his feet reclined,

In his calm face laugh'd up; some shepherd lay
Singing, as childhood sings on the lone hills at play.

XLIV.

And now—oh God!—the bitter fear of death,
The sore amaze, the faint o'ershadowing dread,
Had grasp'd her!—panting in her quick-drawn breath,
And in her white lips quivering;—onward led,
She look'd up with her dim bewilder'd eyes,
And there smiled out her own soft brilliant skies,
Far in their sultry southern azure spread,
Glowing with joy, but silent!—still they smiled,
Yet sent down no reprieve for earth's poor trembling child.

XLV.

Alas! that earth had all too strong a hold,
Too fast, sweet Inez! on thy heart, whose bloom
Was given to early love, nor knew how cold
The hours which follow. There was one, with whom,
Young as thou wert, and gentle, and untried,
Thou might'st, perchance, unshrinkingly have died:
But he was far away;—and with thy doom
Thus gathering, life grew so intensely dear,
That all thy slight frame shook with its cold mortal fear!

XLVI.

No aid! thou too didst pass!—and all had pass'd,
The fearful—and the desperate—and the strong!
Some like the bark that rushes with the blast,
Some like the leaf swept shiveringly along,
And some as men, that have but one more field
To fight, and then may slumber on their shield,—
Therefore they arm in hope. But now the throng
Roll'd on, and bore me with their living tide,
Even as a bark wherein is left no power to guide.

XLVII.

Wave swept on wave. We reach'd a stately square,
Deck'd for the rites. An altar stood on high,
And gorgeous, in the midst: a place for prayer,
And praise, and offering. Could the earth supply
No fruits, no flowers for sacrifice, of all
Which on her sunny lap unheeded fall?
No fair young firstling of the flock to die,
As when before their God the patriarchs stood?— [blood!
Look down! man brings thee, Heaven! his brother's guiltless

XLVIII.

Hear its voice, hear!—a cry goes up to thee,
From the stain'd sod; make thou thy judgment known
On him the shedder!—let his portion be
The fear that walks at midnight—give the moan
In the wind haunting him, a power to say,
"Where is thy brother?"—and the stars a ray
To search and shake his spirit, when alone,

XLIX.

Sounds of triumphant praise!—the mass was sung -
Voices that die not might have pour'd such strains!
Through Salem's towers might that proud chant have rung
When the Most High, on Syria's palmy plains,
Had quell'd her foes!—so full it swept, a sea
Of loud waves jubilant, and rolling free!
—Oft when the wind, as through resounding fanes,
Hath fill'd the choral forests with its power,
Some deep tone brings me back the music of that hour

L.

It died away;—the incense-cloud was driven
Before the breeze—the words of doom were said;
And the sun faded mournfully from heaven:
—He faded mournfully! and dimly red,
Parting in clouds from those that look'd their last,
And sigh'd—" Farewell, thou sun!"—Eve glow'd and pass'd
Night—midnight and the moon—came forth and shed
Sleep, even as dew, on glen, wood, peopled spot—
Save one—a place of death—and there men slumber'd not.

LI.

'Twas not within the city—⁷ but in sight
Of the snow-crown'd sierras, freely sweeping,
With many an eagle's eyrie on the height,
And hunter's cabin, by the torrent peeping
Far off: and vales between, and vineyards lay,
With sound and gleam of waters on their way,
And chestnut woods, that girt the happy sleeping
In many a peasant-home!—the midnight sky
Brought softly that rich world round those who came to die.

LII.

The darkly-glorious midnight sky of Spain,
Burning with stars!—What had the torches' glare
To do beneath that temple, and profane
Its holy radiance?—By their wavering flare,
I saw beside the pyres—I see thee *now*,
O bright Theresa! with thy lifted brow,
And thy clasp'd hands, and dark eyes fill'd with prayers!
And thee, sad Inez! bowing thy fair head,
And mantling up thy face, all colorless with dread!

LIII.

And Alvar, Alvar!—I beheld thee too,
Pale, steadfast, kingly; till thy clear glance fell
On that young sister; then perturb'd it grew
And all thy laboring bosom seem'd to swell
With painful tenderness. Why came I there,
That troubled image of my friend to bear
Thence, for my after-years?—a thing to dwell

In my heart's core, and on the darkness rise,
Disquieting my dreams with its bright mournful eyes?

LIV.
Why came I? oh! the heart's deep mystery!--Why
In man's last hour doth vain affection's gaze
Fix itself down on struggling agony,
To the dimm'd eyeballs freezing as they gaze?
It might be--yet the power to will seem'd o'er--
That my soul yearn'd to hear his voice once more!
But mine was fetter'd!--mute in strong amaze,
I watch'd his features as the night-wind blew,
And torch-light or the moon's pass'd o'er their marble hue.

LV.
The trampling of a steed!--a tall white steed,
Rending his fiery way the crowds among--
A storm's way through a forest--came at speed,
And a wild voice cried " Inez!" Swift she flung
The mantle from her face, and gazed around,
With a faint shriek at that familiar sound;
And from his seat a breathless rider sprung,
And dash'd off fiercely those who came to part,
And rush'd to that pale girl, and clasp'd her to his heart.

LVI.
And for a moment all around gave way
To that full burst of passion!--on his breast,
Like a bird panting yet from fear she lay,
But blest--in misery's very lap--yet blest!--
Oh love, love strong as death!--from such an hour
Pressing out joy by thine immortal power;
Holy and fervent love! had earth but rest
For thee and thine, this world were all too fair!
How could we thence be wean'd to die without despair?

LVII.
But she--as falls a willow from the storm,
O'er its own river streaming--thus reclined
On the youth's bosom hung her fragile form,
And clasping arms, so passionately twined
Around his neck--with such a trusting fold,
A full deep sense of safety in their hold,
As if nought earthly might th' embrace unbind!
Alas! a child's fond faith, believing still
Its mother's breast beyond the lightning's reach to kill!

LVIII.
Brief rest! upon the turning billow's height,
A strange, sweet moment of some heavenly strain,
Floating between the savage gusts of night,
That sweep the seas to foam! Soon dark again
The hour--the scene--th' intensely present, rush'd
Back on her spirit, and her large tears gush'd
Like blood-drops from a victim; with swift rain

Bathing the bosom where she lean'd that hour,
As if her life would melt into th' o'erswelling shower.

LIX.

But he whose arm sustain'd her!--oh! I knew
'Twas vain,--and yet he hop'd!--he fondly strove
Back from her faith her sinking soul to woo,
As life might yet be hers!--A dream of love
Which could not look upon so fair a thing,
Remembering how like hope, like joy, like spring,
Her smile was wont to glance, her step to move,
And deem that men indeed, in very truth,
Could mean the sting of death for her soft flowering youth!

LX.

He woo'd her back to life.--"Sweet Inez, live!
My blessed Inez!--visions have beguiled
Thy heart; abjure them! thou wert form'd to give,
And to find, joy; and hath not sunshine smiled
Around thee ever? Leave me not, mine own!
Or earth will grow too dark!--for thee alone,
Thee have I loved, thou gentlest! from a child,
And borne thine image with me o'er the sea,
Thy soft voice in my soul--speak!--Oh! yet live for me!"

LXI.

She look'd up wildly; there were anxious eyes
Waiting that look--sad eyes of troubled thought,
Alvar's--Theresa's!--Did her childhood rise,
With all its pure and home-affections fraught,
In the brief glance?—She clasp'd her hands—the strife
Of love, faith, fear, and that vain dream of life,
Within her woman's breast so deeply wrought,
It seem'd as if a reed so slight and weak
Must, in the rending storm not quiver only—break!

LXII.

And thus it was—the young cheek flush'd and faded,
As the swift blood in currents came and went,
And hues of death the marble brow o'ershaded,
And the sunk eye a wat'ry lustre sent
Through its white fluttering lids. Then tremblings pass'd
O'er the frail form that shook it, as the blast
Shakes the sere leaf, until the spirit rent
Its way to peace—the fearful way unknown—
Pale in love's arms she lay—*she!*—what had loved was gone

LXIII.

Joy for thee, trembler!—thou redeem'd one, joy!
Young dove set free!—earth, ashes, soulless clay,
Remain'd for baffled vengeance to destroy;
—*Thy* chain was riven!—nor hadst thou cast away
Thy hope in thy last hour!—though love was there
Striving to wring thy troubled soul from prayer,
And life seem'd robed in beautiful array,

Too fair to leave!—but this might be forgiven,
Thou wert so richly crown'd with precious gifts of Heaven!

LXIV.

But woe for him who felt the heart grow still,
Which, with its weight of agony, had lain
Breaking on his!—scarce could the mortal chill
Of the hush'd bosom, ne'er to heave again,
And all the silence curdling round the eye,
Bring home the stern belief that she could die—
That she indeed could die!—for wild and vain
As hope might be—his soul *had* hoped—'twas o'er—
Slowly his failing arms dropp'd from the form they bore.

LXV.

They forced him from that spot. It might be well,
That the fierce, reckless words by anguish wrung
From his torn breast, all aimless as they fell,
Like spray-drops from the strife of torrents flung,
Were mark'd as guilt.—There are, who note these things
Against the smitten heart; its breaking strings
—On whose low thrills once gentle music hung—
With a rude hand of touch unholy trying,   [ing.
And numbering then as crimes, the deep, strange tones reply-

LXVI.

But ye in solemn joy, O faithful pair!
Stood gazing on your parted sister's dust;
I saw your features by the torch's glare,
And they were brightning with a heavenward trust!
I saw the doubt, the anguish, the dismay,
Melt from my Alvar's glorious mien away;
And peace was there—the calmness of the just!
And, bending down the slumb'rer's brow to kiss,
"Thy rest is won," he said; "sweet sister! praise for this!"

LXVII.

I started as from sleep;—yes! he had spoken—
A breeze had troubled memory's hidden source!
At once the torpor of my soul was broken—
Thought, feeling, passion, woke in tenfold force.
—There are soft breathings in the southern wind,
That so your ice-chains, O ye streams! unbind,
And free the foaming swiftness of your course!
—I burst from those that held me back, and fell   [well!"
Even on his neck, and cried—" Friend! brother! fare thee

LXVIII.

Did *he* not say, " Farewell?"—Alas! no breath
Came to mine ear. Hoarse murmurs from the throng
Told that the mysteries in the face of death
Had from their eager sight been veil'd too long.
And we were parted as the surge might part
Those that would die together, true of heart.—
His hour was come—but in mine anguish strong,

Like a fierce swimmer through the midnight sea,
Blindly I rush'd away from that which was to be.

LXIX.

Away—away I rush'd—but swift and high
The arrowy pillars of the firelight grew,
Till the transparent darkness of the sky
Flush'd to a blood-red mantle in their hue;
And, phantom-like, the kindling city seem'd
To spread, float, wave, as on the wind they stream'd,
With their wild splendor chasing me!—I knew
The death-work was begun—I veil'd mine eyes,
Yet stopp'd in spell-bound fear to catch the victims' cries

LXX.

What heard I then?—a ringing shriek of pain,
Such as forever haunts the tortured ear?—
I heard a sweet and solemn-breathing strain
Piercing the flames, untremulous and clear!—
The rich, triumphal tones!—I knew them well,
As they came floating with a breezy swell!
Man's voice was there—a clarion voice to cheer
In the mid-battle—ay, to turn the flying—
Woman's—that might have sung of heaven beside the **dying**

LXXI.

It was a fearful, yet a glorious thing,
To hear that hymn of martyrdom, and know
That its glad stream of melody could spring
Up from the unsounded gulfs of human woe!
Alvar! Theresa!—what is deep? what strong?
—God's breath within the soul!—It fill'd that song
From your victorious voices!—but the glow
On the hot air and lurid skies increased—   [ceased
Faint grew the sounds—more faint—I listen'd—they had

LXXII.

And thou indeed had'st perish'd, my soul's friend!
I might form other ties—but thou alone
Could'st with a glance the veil of dimness rend,
By other years o'er boyhood's memory thrown!
Others might aid me ownward:—thou and I
Had mingled the fresh thoughts that early die,
Once flowering—never more!—And thou wert gone!
Who could give back my youth, my spirit free,
Or be in aught again what thou hadst been to me?

LXXIII.

And yet I wept thee not, thou true and brave!
I could not weep!—there gather'd round thy name
Too deep a passion!—*thou* denied a grave!
Thou, with the light flung on thy soldier's fame!
Had I not known thy heart from childhood's time?
Thy heart of hearts?—and could'st thou die for **crime?**—
No! had all earth decreed that death of shame,

I would have set, against all earth's decree,
Th' inalienable trust of my firm soul in thee!
LXXIV.
There are swift hours in life—strong, rushing hours,
That do the work of tempests in their might!
They shake down things that stood as rocks and towers
Unto th' undoubting mind;—they pour in light
Where it but startles—like a burst of day
For which the uprooting of an oak makes way;—
They sweep the coloring mists from off our sight,
They touch with fire thought's graven page, the roll
Stamp'd with past years—and lo! it shrivels as a scroll!
LXXV.
And this was of such hours!—the sudden flow
Of my soul's tide seem'd whelming me; the glare
Of the red flames, yet rocking to and fro,
Scorch'd up my heart with breathless thirst for air,
And solitude, and freedom. It had been
Well with me then, in some vast desert scene,
To pour my voice out, for the winds to bear
On with them, wildly questioning the sky,
Fiercely the untroubled stars, of man's dim destiny.
LXXVI.
I would have call'd, adjuring the dark cloud;
To the most ancient heavens I would have said—
"Speak to me! show me truth!" 8—through night aloud
I would have cried to him, the newly dead,
"Come back! and show me truth!" My spirit seem'd
Gasping for some free burst, its darkness teem'd
With such pent storms of thought!—again I fled.
I fled, a refuge from man's face to gain.
Scarce conscious when I paused, entering a lonely fane
LXXVII.
A mighty minster, dim, and proud, and vast!
Silence was round the sleepers whom its floor
Shut in the grave; a shadow of the past,
A memory of the sainted steps that wore,
Erewhile, its gorgeous pavement, seem'd to brood
Like mist upon the stately solitude;
A halo of sad fame, to mantle o'er
Its white sepulcral forms of mail-clad men,
And all was hush'd as night in some deep Alpine glen.
LXXVIII.
More hush'd, far more!—for there the wind sweeps by
Or the woods tremble to the streams' loud play;
Here a strange echo made my very sigh
Seem for the place too much a sound of day!
To much my footsteps broke the moonlight, fading,
Yet arch through arch in one soft flow pervading!
And I stood still:—prayer, chant, had died away;

Yet past me floated a funereal breath
Of incense. I stood still—as before God and death.

LXXIX.

For thick ye girt me round, ye long departed![9]
Dust—imaged forms—with cross, and shield, and crest;
It seem'd as if your ashes would have started,
Had a wild voice burst forth above your rest!
Yet ne'er, perchance, did worshipper of yore
Bear to your thrilling presence what *I* bore
Of wrath, doubt, anguish, battling in the breast!
I could have pour'd out words, on that pale air,
To make your proud tombs ring—no, no! I could not *there*!

LXXX.

Not 'midst those aisles, through which a thousand years,
Mutely as clouds and reverently, had swept;
Not by those shrines, which yet the trace of tears
And kneeling votaries on their marble kept!
Ye were too mighty in your pomp of gloom
And trophied age, O temple, altar, tomb!
And you, ye dead!—for in that faith ye slept,
Whose weight had grown a mountain's on my heart,
Which could not *there* be loosed. I turn'd me to depart.

LXXXI.

I turn'd—what glimmer'd faintly on my sight,
Faintly, yet bright'ning as a wreath of snow
Seen through dissolving haze?—The moon, the night,
Had waned, and dawn pour'd in—grey, shadowy, slow,
Yet dayspring still!—a solemn hue it caught,
Piercing the storied windows, darkly fraught
With stoles and draperies of imperial glow;
And soft, and sad, that coloring gleam was thrown,
Where, pale, a pictured form above the altar shone.

LXXXII.

Thy form, thou Son of God!—a wrathful deep,
With foam and cloud, and tempest round Thee spread,
And such a weight, of night!—a night, when sleep
From the fierce rocking of the billows fled.
A bark show'd dim beyond Thee, with its mast
Bow'd, and its rent sail shivering to the blast;
But, like a spirit in thy gliding tread,
Thou, as o'er glass, didst walk that stormy sea
Through rushing winds, which left a silent path for Thee

LXXXIII.

So still thy white robes fell!—no breath of air
Within their long and slumb'rous folds had sway.
So still the waves of parted, shadowy hair
From thy clear brow flow'd droopingly away!
Dark were the heavens above thee Saviour!—dark
The gulfs, Deliverer! round the straining bark!
But Thou!—o'er all thine aspect and array

Was pour'd one stream of pale, broad silvery light—
Thou wert the single star of that all-shrouding night!

LXXXIV.
Aid for one sinking!—Thy lone brightness gleam'd
On his wild face, just lifted o'er the wave,
With its worn, fearful, *human* look, that seem'd
To cry, through surge and blast—" I perish—save!"
Not to the winds—not vainly!—Thou wert nigh,
Thy hand was stretch'd to fainting agony,
Even in the portals of th' unquiet grave!
O Thou that art the life! and yet didst bear
Too much of mortal woe to turn from mortal prayer!

LXXXV.
But was it not a thing to rise on death,
With its remember'd light, that face of thine,
Redeemer! dimm'd by this world's misty breath,
Yet mournfully, mysteriously divine?
O! that calm, sorrowful, prophetic eye,
With its dark depths of grief, love, majesty!
And the pale glory of the brow!—a shrine
Where power sat veil'd, yet shedding softly round
What told that *Thou* could'st be but for a time uncrown'd.

LXXXVI.
And, more than all, the Heaven of that sad smile!
The lip of mercy, our immortal trust!
Did not that look, that very look, erewhile
Pour its o'ershadow'd beauty on the dust? [Thee?—
Wert thou not such when earth's dark cloud hung o'er
Surely thou wert!—my heart grew hush'd before Thee,
Sinking, with all its passions, as the gust
Sank at thy voice, along its billowy way—
What had I there to do but kneel, and weep, and pray?

LXXXVII.
Amidst the stillness rose my spirit's cry,
Amidst the dead—" By that full cup of woe,
Press'd from the fruitage of mortality,
Saviour! for Thee—give light! that I may know
If by *thy* will, in thine all-healing name,
Men cast down human hearts to blighting shame,
And early death—and say, if this be so,
Where then is mercy? Whither shall we flee,
So unallied to hope, save by our hold on Thee?

LXXXVIII.
"But didst Thou not, the deep sea brightly treading,
Lift from despair that struggler with the wave;
And wert Thou not, sad tears, yet awful, shedding,
Beheld a weeper at a mortal's grave?
And is this weight of anguish, which they bind
On life, this searing to the quick of mind,
That but to God its own free path would crave,

This crushing out of hope, and love, and youth,
Thy will, indeed? Give light! that I may know the truth!
LXXXIX.
" For my sick soul is darken'd unto death,
With shadows from the suffering it hath seen;
The strong foundations of mine ancient faith
Sink from beneath me—whereon shall I lean?
Oh! if from thy pure lips was wrung the sigh
Of the dust's anguish! if like man to die,
And earth round *him* shuts heavily—hath been
Even to *Thee* bitter, aid me!—guide me!—turn [bourne!"
My wild and wandering thoughts back from their starless
XC.
And calm'd I rose :—but how the while had risen
Morn's sun, dissolving mist and shade!
Could there indeed be wrong, or chain, or prison,
In the bright world such radiance might pervade!
It fill'd the fane, it mantled the pale form
Which rose before me through the pictured storm,
Even the grey tombs it kindled, and array'd
With life!—how hard to see thy race begun,
And think man wakes to grief, wakening to *thee*, O Sun!
XCI.
I sought my home again :—and thou, my child,
There at thy play beneath yon ancient pine,
With eyes, whose lightning laughter[10] hath beguiled
A thousand pangs thence flashing joy to mine;
Thou in thy mother's arms, a babe didst meet
My coming with young smiles, which yet, though sweet,
Seem'd on my soul all mournfully to shine,
And ask a happier heritage for thee,
Than but in turn the blight of human hope too see.
XCII.
Now sport, for thou art free, the bright birds chasing
Whose wings waft star-like gleams from tree to tree;
Or with the fawn, thy swift wood-playmate, racing,
Sport on, my joyous child! for thou art free!
Yes, on that day I took thee to my heart,
And inly vow'd for thee a better part
To choose; that so thy sunny bursts of glee
Should wake no more dim thoughts of far-seen woe,
But, gladdening fearless eyes, flow on—as now they flow.
XCIII.
Thou hast a rich world round thee :—Mighty shades
Weaving their gorgeous tracery o'er thy head,
With the light melting through their high arcades,
As through a pillar'd cloister's[11] but the dead
Sleep not beneath; nor doth the sunbeam pass
To marble shrines through rainbow-tinted glass;
Yet thou, by fount and forest-murmur led
To worship, thou art blest!—to thee is shown
Earth in her holy pomp, deck'd for her God alone.

PART SECOND.

> Wie diese treue liebe seele
> Von ihrem Glauben Voll,
>   Der ganz allein
>   Ihr selig marchend ist, sich heilig quale,
> Das sie den liebsten Mann verloren halten soll!
> *Faust.*
>
> I never shall smile more—but all my days
> Walk with still footsteps and with humble eyes,
> An everlasting hymn within my soul.
> *Wilson.*

I.
BRING me the sounding of the torrent-water,
With yet a nearer swell—fresh breeze, awake![12]
And river, dark'ning ne'er with hues of slaughter
Thy wave's pure silvery green,—and shining lake,
Spread far before my cabin, with thy zone
Of ancient woods, ye chainless things and lone!
Send voices through the forest aisles, and make
Glad music round me, that my soul may dare,
Cheer'd by such tones, to look back on a dungeon's air!

II.
Oh, Indian hunter of the desert's race!
That with the spear at times, or bended bow,
Dost cross my footsteps in thy fiery chase
Of the swift elk or blue hill's flying roe ;
Thou that beside the red night-fire thou heapest,
Beneath the cedars and the star-light sleepest,
Thou know'st not, wanderer—never may'st thou know!
Of the dark holds wherewith man cumbers earth,
To shut from human eyes the dancing seasons' mirth.

III.
There, fetter'd down from day, to think the while
How bright in heaven the festal sun is glowing,
Making earth's loneliest places, with his smile,
Flush like the rose ; and how the streams are flowing
With sudden sparkles through the shadowy grass,
And water-flowers, all trembling as they pass ;
And how the rich, dark summer-trees are bowing
With their full foliage ;—this to know, and pine
Bound unto midnight's heart, seems a stern lot—'twas mine.

IV.
Wherefore was this !—Because my soul had drawn
Light from the book whose words are graved in light !
There, at its well-head, had I found the dawn,
And day, and noon of freedom : but too bright
It shines on that which man to man hath given,
And call'd the truth—the very truth, from heaven !
And therefore seeks he, in his brother's sight,
To cast the mote ; and therefore strives to bind
With his strong chains to earth, what is not earth's—the mind

THE FOREST SANCTUARY.

V.

It is a weary and a bitter task
Back from the lip the burning word to keep,
And to shut out heaven's air with falsehood's mask,
And in the dark urn of the soul to heap
Indignant feelings—making e'en of thought
A buried treasure, which may but be sought
When shadows are abroad—and night—and sleep.
I might not brook it long—and thus was thrown
Into that grave-like cell, to wither there alone.

VI.

And I, a child of danger, whose delights
Were on dark hills and many-sounding seas—
I, that amidst the Cordillera heights
Had given Castilian banners to the breeze,
And the full circle of the rainbow seen
There, on the snows;[13] and in my country been
A mountain wanderer, from the Pyrenees
To the Morena crags—how left I not
Life, or the soul's life, quench'd, on that sepulchral spot?

VII.

Because *Thou* didst not leave me, O my God!
Thou wert with those that bore the truth of old
Into the deserts from the oppressor's rod,
And made the caverns of the rock their fold;
And in the hidden chambers of the dead,
Our guiding lamp with fire immortal fed;
And met when stars met, by their beams to hold
The free heart's communing with Thee,—and Thou
Wert in the midst, felt, own'd—the Strengthener then as now

VIII.

Yet once I sank. Alas! man's wavering mind?
Wherefore and whence the gusts that o'er it blow?
How they bear with them, floating uncombined,
The shadows of the past, that come and go,
As o'er the deep the old long-buried things,
Which a storm's working to the surface brings!
Is the reed shaken,—and must *we* be so,
With every wind?—So, Father! must we be,
Till we can fix undimm'd our steadfast eyes on Thee.

IX.

Once my soul died within me. What had thrown
That sickness o'er it?—Even a passing thought
Of a clear spring, whose side, with flowers o'ergrown,
Fondly and oft my boyish steps had sought
Perchance the damp roof's water-drops, that fell
Just then low tinkling through my vaulted cell,
Intensely heard amidst the stillness, caught
Some tone from memory, of the music, welling
Ever with that fresh rill, from its deep rocky dwelling.

X.

But so my spirit's fever'd longings wrought,
Wakening, it might be, to the faint, sad sound,
That from the darkness of the walls they brought
A loved scene round me, visibly around.[14]
Yes, kindling, spreading, bright'ning, hue by hue,
Like stars from midnight, through the gloom it grew,
That haunt of youth, hope, manhood!—till the bound
Of my shut cavern seem'd dissolved, and I
Girt with the solemn hills and burning pomp of sky.

XI.

I look'd—and lo! the clear, broad river flowing,
Past the old Moorish ruin on the steep,
The lone tower dark against a heaven all glowing,
Like seas of glass and fire!—I saw the sweep
Of glorious woods far down the mountain side,
And their still shadows in the gleaming tide,
And the red evening on its waves asleep;
And 'midst the scene—oh! more than all—there smiled
My child's fair face, and hers, the mother of my child!

XII.

With their soft eyes of love and gladness raised
Up to the flushing sky, as when we stood
Last by that river, and in silence gazed
On the rich world of sunset:—but a flood
Of sudden tenderness my soul oppress'd,
And I rush'd forward, with a yearning breast,
To clasp—alas!—a vision!—Wave and wood,
And gentle faces, lifted in the light
Of day's last hectic blush, all melted from my sight.

XIII.

Then darkness!—oh! th' unutterable gloom
That seem'd as narrowing round me, making less
And less my dungeon, when, with all its bloom,
That bright dream vanish'd from my loneliness!
It floated off, the beautiful! yet left
Such deep thirst in my soul, that thus bereft,
I lay down, sick with passion's vain excess,
And pray'd to die.—How oft would sorrow weep
Her weariness to death, if he might come like sleep!

XIV.

But I was roused—and how?—It is no tale
Even 'midst *thy* shades, thou wilderness, to tell!
I would not have my boy's young cheek made pale,
Nor haunt his sunny rest with what befell
In that drear prison-house. His eye must grow
More dark with thought, more earnest his fair brow,
More high his heart in youthful strength must swell;
So shall it fitly burn when all is told:—
Let childhood's radiant mist the free child yet enfold.

XV.

It is enough that through such heavy hours,
As wring us by our fellowship of clay,
I lived, and undegraded. We have powers
To snatch th' oppressor's bitter joy away!
Shall the wild Indian, for his savage fame,
Laugh and expire, and shall not Truth's high name
Bear up her martyrs with all-conquering sway?
It is enough that torture may be vain—
I had seen Alvar die—the strife was won from Pain.

XVI.

And faint not, heart of man! though years wane slow!
There have been those that from the deepest caves,
And cells of night, and fastnesses below
The stormy dashing of the ocean-waves,
Down, farther down than gold lies hid, have nursed
A quenchless hope, and watch'd their time, and burst
On the bright day, like wakeners from the graves!
I was of such at last!—unchain'd I trode
This green earth, taking back my freedom from my God!

XVII.

That was an hour to send its fadeless trace
Down life's far-sweeping tide!—A dim, wild night,
Like sorrow, hung upon the soft moon's face,
Yet how my heart leap'd in her blessed light!
The shepherd's light—the sailor's on the sea—
The hunter's homeward from the mountains free,
Where its lone smile makes tremulously bright
The thousand streams!—I could but gaze through tears—
Oh! what a sight is heaven, thus first beheld for years!

XVIII.

The rolling clouds!—they have the whole blue space
Above to sail in—all the dome of sky!
My soul shot with them in their breezy race
O'er star and gloom!—but I had yet to fly,
As flies the hunted wolf. A secret spot
And strange, I knew—the sunbeam knew it not;—
Wildest of all the savage glens that lie
In far sierras, hiding their deep springs,
And traversed but by storms, or sounding eagles' wings.

XIX.

Ay, and I met the storm there!—I had gain'd
The covert's heart with swift and stealthy tread:
A moan went past me, and the dark trees rain'd
Their autum foliage rustling on my head;
A moan—a hollow gust—and there I stood
Girt with majestic night, and ancient wood,
And foaming water.—Thither might have fled
The mountain Christian with his faith of yore,
When Afric's tambour shook the ringing western shore!

XX.

But through the black ravine the storm came swelling,
—Mighty thou art amidst the hills, thou blast!
In thy lone course the kingly cedars felling,
Like plumes upon the path of battle cast!—
A rent oak thunder'd down beside my cave,
Booming it rush'd, as booms a deep sea-wave;
A falcon soar'd; a startled wild-deer pass'd;
A far-off bell tol'd faintly through the roar:—
How my glad spirit swept forth with the winds once more!

XXI.

And with the arrowy lightnings!—for they flash'd.
Smiting the branches in their fitful play,
And brightly shivering where the torrents dash'd
Up, even to crag and eagle's nest, their spray!
And there to stand amidst the pealing strife,
The strong pines groaning with tempestuous life,
And all the mountain-voices on their way,—
Was it not joy?—'twas joy in rushing might,
After those years that wove but one long dead of night!

XXII.

There came a softer hour, a lovelier moon,
And lit me to my home of youth again,
Through the dim chestnut shade, where oft at noon,
By the fount's flashing burst, my head had lain
In gentle sleep: but now I pass'd as one
That may not pause where wood-streams whispering run,
Or light sprays tremble to a bird's wild strain,
Because th' avenger's voice is in the wind,
The foe's quick, rustling step close on the leaves behind.

XXIII.

My home of youth!—oh! if indeed to part
With the soul's loved ones be a mournful thing,
When we go forth in buoyancy of heart,
And bearing all the glories of our spring
For life to breathe on,—is it less to meet,
When these are faded?—who shall call it sweet?
—Even though love's mingling tears may haply bring
Balm as they fall, too well their heavy showers
Teach us how much is lost of all that once was ours!

XXIV.

Not by the sunshine, with its golden glow,
Nor the green earth, nor yet the laughing sky,
Nor the fair flower scents, [15] as they come and go
In the soft air, like music wandering by;
—Oh! not by these, th' unfailing, are we taught
How time and sorrow on our frames have wrought;
But by the sadden'd eye, the darken'd brow
Of kindred aspect, and the long dim gaze,
Which tells us *we* are changed—how changed from other days

XXV.

Before my father—in my place of birth,
I stood an alien. On the very floor
Which oft had trembled to my boyish mirth,
The love that rear'd me, knew my face no more!
There hung the antique armor, helm and crest,
Whose every stain woke childhood in my breast;
There droop'd the banner, with the marks it bore
Of Paynim spears; and I, the worn in frame
And heart, what there was I?—another and the same!

XXVI.

Then bounded in a boy, with clear, dark eye—
How should *he* know his father?—when we parted,
From the soft cloud which mantles infancy,
His soul, just wakening into wonder, darted
Its first looks around. Him follow'd one, the bride
Of my young days, the wife how loved and tried!
Her glance met mine—I could not speak—she started
With a bewilder'd gaze;—until there came
Tears to my burning eyes, and from my lips her name.

XXVII.

She knew me then!—I murmur'd "*Leonor!*"
And her heart answer'd!—oh! the voice is known
First from all else, and swiftest to restore
Love's buried images, with one low tone
That strikes like lightning, when the cheek is faded,
And the brow heavily with thought o'ershaded,
And all the brightness from the aspect gone!
—Upon my breast she sunk, when doubt was fled,
Weeping as those may weep, that meet in woe and dread.

XXVIII.

For there we might not rest. Alas! to leave
Those native towers, and know that they must fall
By slow decay, and none remain to grieve
When the weeds cluster'd on the lonely wall!
We were the last—my boy and I—the last
Of a long line which brightly thence had pass'd!
My father bless'd me as I left his hall—
With his deep tones and sweet, though full of years, [tears.
He bless'd me there, and bathed my child's young head with

XXIX.

I had brought sorrow on his grey hairs down,
And cast the darkness of my branded name
(For so *he* deem'd it) on the clear renown,
My own ancestral heritage of fame.
And yet he bless'd me!—Father! if the dust
Lie on those lips benign, my spirit's trust
Is to behold thee yet, where grief and shame
Dim the bright day no more; and thou will know
That not through guilt thy son thus bow'd thine age with woe!

XXX.

And thou, my Leonor! that unrepining,
If sad in soul, didst quit all else for me,
When stars—the stars that earliest rise—are shining,
How their soft glance unseals each thought of thee!
For on our flight they smiled; their dewy rays,
Through the last olives, lit thy tearful gaze
Back to the home we never more might see;
So pass'd we on, like earth's first exiles, turning
Fond looks where hung the sword above their Eden burning.

XXXI.

It was a woe to say, "Farewell, my Spain!
The sunny and the vintage land, farewell!"
—I could have died upon the battle-plain
For thee, my country! but I might not dwell
In thy sweet vales, at peace.—The voice of song
Breathes, with the myrtle scent, thy hills along;
The citron's glow is caught from shade and dell;
But what are these?—upon thy flowery sod
I might not kneel, and pour my free thoughts out to God!

XXXII.

O'er the blue deep I fled, the chainless deep!—
Strange heart of man! that e'en 'midst woe swells high,
When through the foam he sees his proud bark sweep,
Flinging out joyous gleams to wave and sky!
Yes! it swells high, whate'er he leaves behind,
His spirit rises with the rising wind;
For, wedded to the far futurity,
On, on, it bears him ever, and the main
Seems rushing, like his hope, some happier shore to gain.

XXXIII.

Not thus is woman. Closely *her* still heart
Doth twine itself with even each lifeless thing,
Which, long remember'd, seem'd to bear its part
In her calm joys. For ever would she cling,
A brooding dove, to that sole spot of earth
Where she hath loved, and given her children birth,
And heard their first sweet voices. There may Spring
Array no path, renew no flower, no leaf,
But hath its breath of home, its claim to farewell grief.

XXXIV.

I look'd on Leonor,—and if there seem'd
A cloud of more than pensiveness to rise
In the faint smiles that o'er her features gleam'd,
And the soft darkness of her serious eyes,
Misty with tender gloom, I call'd it nought
But the fond exile's pang, a lingering thought
Of her own vale, with all its melodies
And living light of streams. Her soul would rest
Beneath your shades, I said, bowers of the gorgeous west!

XXXV.

Oh! could we live in visions! could we hold
Delusion faster, longer, to our breast,
When it shuts from us, with its mantle's fold,
That which we see not, and are therefore blest!
But they, our loved and loving—they to whom
We have spread out our souls in joy and gloom,
Their looks and accents, unto ours address'd,
Have been a language of familiar tone
Too long to breathe, at last, dark sayings and unknown.

XXXVI.

I told my heart, 'twas but the exile's woe
Which press'd on that sweet bosom ;—I deceived
My heart but half:—a whisper, faint and low,
Haunting it ever, and at times believed,
Spoke of some deeper cause. How oft we seem
Like those that dream, and *know* the while they dream,
'Midst the soft falls of airy voices grieved,
And troubled, while bright phantoms round them play,
By a dim sense that all will float and fade away!

XXXVII.

Yet, as if chasing joy, I woo'd the breeze
To speed me onward with the wings of morn.
—Oh! far amidst the solitary seas,
Which were not made for man, what man hath borne,
Answering their moan with his!—what *thou* didst bear,
My lost and loveliest! while that secret care
Grew terror, and thy gentle spirit, worn
By its dull brooding weight, gave way at last,
Beholding me as one from hope for ever cast!

XXXVIII.

For unto thee, as through all change, reveal'd
Mine inward being lay. In other eyes
I had to bow me yet, and make a shield,
To fence my burning bosom, of disguise ;
By the still hope sustain'd, erelong to win
Some sanctuary, whose green retreats within,
My thoughts unfetter'd to their source might rise,
Like songs and scents of morn.—But thou didst look
Through all my soul, and thine even unto fainting shook.

XXXIX.

Fallen, fallen, I seem'd--yet, oh! not less beloved,
Though from thy love was pluck'd the early pride,
And harshly, by a gloomy faith reproved, [died,
And sear'd with shame!—though each young flower had
There was the root,—strong, living, not the less
That all it yielded now was bitterness ;
Yet still such love as quits not misery's side,
Nor drops from guilt its ivy-like embrace,
Nor turns away from death's its pale heroic face.

XL.

Yes! thou hadst follow'd me through fear and flight!
Thou would'st have follow'd had my pathway led
Even to the scaffold; had the flashing light
Of the raised axe made strong men shrink with dread,
Thou, 'midst the hush of thousands, would'st have been
With thy clasp'd hands beside me kneeling seen,
And meekly bowing to the shame thy head—
  The shame!—oh! making beautiful to view
The might of human love—fair thing! so bravely true!

XLI.

There was thine agony—to love so well
Where fear made love life's chastener.—Heretofore
Whate'er of earth's disquiet round thee fell,
Thy soul, o'erpassing its dim bounds, could soar
Away to sunshine, and thy clear eye speak
Most of the skies when grief most touch'd thy cheek
Now, that far brightness faded, never more
  Could thou lift heavenwards for its hope thy heart,
Since at heaven's gate it seem'd that thou and I must part

XLII.

Alas! and life hath moments when a glance—
(If thought to sudden watchfulness be stirr'd)—
A flush—a fading of the cheek, perchance—
A word—less, less—the *cadence* of a word,
Lets in our gaze the mind's dim veil beneath,
Thence to bring haply knowledge fraught with death.
—Even thus, what never from thy lip was heard
  Broke on my soul.—I knew that in thy sight
I stood—howe'er beloved—a recreant from the light!

XLIII.

Thy sad, sweet hymn, at eve, the seas along,—
Oh! the deep soul it breathed!—the love, the woe,
The fervor, pour'd in that full gush of song,
As it went floating through the fiery glow
Of the rich sunset!—bringing thoughts of Spain,
With all her vesper-voices, o'er the main,
Which seem'd responsive in its murmuring flow.
  —" *Ave sanctissima!*"—how oft that lay
Hath melted from my heart the martyr-strength away.

  Ave, sanctissima!
    'Tis nightfall on the sea;
  Ora pro nobis!
    Our souls rise to thee!

  Watch us, while shadows lie
    O'er the dim waters spread;
  Hear the heart's lonely sigh—
    Thine too hath bled!

  Thou that hast look'd on death,
    Aid us when death is near!

Whisper of heaven to faith;
  Sweet Mother, hear!
  Ora pro nobis!
  The wave must rock our sleep,
  Ora, Mater, ora!
  Thou star of the deep!

XLIV.

"*Ora pro nobis Mater!*"—What a spell
Was in those notes, with day's last glory dying
On the flush'd waters—seem'd they not to swell
From the far dust, wherein my sires were lying
With crucifix and sword?—Oh! yet how clear
Comes their reproachful sweetness to mine ear!
"*Ora,*"—with all the purple waves replying,
  All my youth's visions rising in the strain—
And I had thought it much to bear the rack and chain!

XLV.

Torture! the sorrow of affection's eye,
Fixing its meekness on the spirit's core,
Deeper, and teaching more of agony,
May pierce than many swords!—and this I bore
With a mute pang. Since I had vainly striven
From its free springs to pour the truth of Heaven
Into thy trembling soul, my Leonor!
Silence rose up where hearts no hope could share!
Alas! for those that love, and may not blend in prayer!

XLVI.

We could not pray together 'midst the deep,
Which, like a floor of sapphire, round us lay,
Through days of splendor, nights too bright for sleep,
Soft, solemn, holy!—We were on our way
Unto the mighty Cordillera-land,
With men whom tales of that world's golden strand
Had lured to leave their vines.—Oh! who shall say
What thoughts rose in us, when the tropic sky
Touched all its molten seas with sunset's alchemy!

XLVII.

Thoughts no more mingled!—Then came night—th' intense
Dark blue—the burning stars!—I saw *thee* shine
Once more, in thy serene magnificence,
O Southern Cross![16] as when thy radiant sign
First drew my gaze of youth.—No, not as then;
I had been stricken by the darts of men
Since those fresh days; and now thy light divine
Look'd on mine anguish, while within me strove
The still small voice against the might of suffering love.

XLVIII.

But thou, the clear, the glorious! thou wert pouring
Brilliance and joy upon the chrystal wave,

While she that met thy ray with eyes adoring,
Stood in the lengthening shadow of the grave!
—Alas! I watch'd her dark religious glance,
As it still sought thee through the heaven's expanse,
Bright Cross! and knew not that I watch'd what gave
But passing lustre—shrouded soon to be—
A soft light found no more—no more on earth or sea!

XLIX.

I knew not all—yet something of unrest
Sat on my heart. Wake, ocean-wind! I said;
Waft us to land in leafy freshness drest,
Where, through rich clouds of foliage o'er her head,
Sweet day may steal, and rills unseen go by,
Like singing voices, and the green earth lie
Starry with flowers, beneath her graceful tread!
—But the calm bound us 'midst the glassy main;
Ne'er was her step to bend earth's living flowers again.

L.

Yes! as if Heaven upon the waves were sleeping,
Vexing my soul with quiet, there they lay,
All moveless, through their blue transparence keeping
The shadows of our sails, from day to day;
While she—oh! strongest is the strong heart's woe—
And yet I live! I feel the sunshine's glow—
And I am he that look'd, and saw decay
Steal o'er the fair of earth, th' adored too much!—
It is a fearful thing to love what death may touch.

LI.

A fearful thing that love and death may dwell
In the same world!—She faded on—and I,
Blind to the last, there needed death to tell
My trusting soul that she *could* fade to die!
Yet, ere she parted, I had mark'd a change,
But it breathed hope—'twas beautiful though strange:
Something of gladness in the melody
Of her low voice, and in her words a flight
Of airy thought—alas! too perilously bright!

LII.

And a clear sparkle in her glance, yet wild,
And quick, and eager, like the flashing gaze
Of some all-wondering and awakening child,
That first the glories of the earth surveys.
How could it thus deceive me?—she had worn
Around her, like the dewy mists of morn,
A pensive tenderness through happiest days;
And a soft world of dreams had seemed to lie
Still in her dark, and deep, and spiritual eye.

LIII.

And I could hope in that strange fire!—she died,
She died, with all its lustre on her mien!

The day was melting from the waters wide,
And through its long bright hours her thoughts had been,
It seem'd, with restless and unwonted yearning,
To Spain's blue skies and dark sierras turning;
For her fond words were all of vintage-scene,
And flowering myrtle, and sweet citron's breath:
Oh! with what vivid hues life comes back oft on death!

LIV.

And from her lips the mountain-songs of old,
In wild, faint snatches fitfully had sprung;
Songs of the orange bower, the Moorish hold,
The "*Rio verde*,"[17] on her soul that hung,
And thence flow'd forth.—But now the sun was low;
And watching by my side its last red glow,
That ever stills the heart, one more she sung
Her own soft "*Ora Mater!*"—and the sound
Was even like love's farewell—so mournfully profound.

LV.

The boy had dropp'd to slumber at our feet;
" And I have lull'd him to his smiling rest
Once more !" she said:—I raised him—it was sweet,
Yet sad, to see the perfect calm which bless'd
His look that hour;—for now her voice grew weak;
And on the flowery crimson of his cheek,
With her white lips, a long, long kiss she press'd,
Yet light, to wake him not.—Then sank her head
Against my bursting heart:—What did I clasp?—the dead!

LVI.

I call'd—to call what answers not our cries,
By what we loved to stand unseen, unheard,
With the loud passion of our tears and sighs,
To see but some cold glittering ringlet stirr'd
And in the quench'd eye's fixedness to gaze,
All vainly searching for the parted rays;
This is what waits us!—Dead!—with that chill word
To link our bosom-names!—For this we pour
Our souls upon the dust—nor tremble to adore!

LVII.

But the true parting came!—I look'd my last
On the sad beauty of that slumbering face;
How could I think the lovely spirit pass'd,
Which there had left so tenderly its trace!
Yet a dim awfulness was on the brow—
No! not like sleep to look upon art Thou,
Death, Death!—She lay, a thing for earth's embrace,
To cover with spring-wreaths. For earth's?—the wave
That gives the bier no flowers—makes moan above her grave!

LVIII.

On the mid-seas a knell!—for man was there,
Anguish and love—the mourner with his dead!

A long, low-rolling knell—a voice of prayer—
Dark glassy waters, like a desert spread,—
And the pale-shining Southern Cross on high,
Its faint stars fading from a solemn sky,
Where mighty clouds before the dawn grew red:
Were these things round me? Such o'er memory sweep
Wildly, when aught brings back that burial of the deep.

LIX.
Then the broad, lonely sunrise!—and the plash
Into the sounding waves![18]—around her head
They parted, with a glancing moment's flash,
Then shut—and all was still. And now thy bed
Is of their secrets, gentlest Leonor!
Once fairest of young brides!—and never more,
Loved as thou wert, may human tear be shed
Above thy rest!—No mark the proud seas keep,
To show where he that wept may pause again to weep!

LX.
So the depths took thee!—Oh! the sullen sense
Of desolation in that hour compress'd!
Dust going down, a speck amidst th' immense
And gloomy waters, leaving on their breast
The trace a weed might leave there!—Dust!—the thing
Which to the heart was as a living spring
Of joy, with fearfulness of love possess'd,
Thus sinking!—Love, joy, fear, all crush'd to this—
And the wide heaven so far—so fathomless th' abyss!

LXI.
Where the line sounds not, where the wrecks lie low,
What shall wake thence the dead?—Blest, blest are they
That earth to earth intrust; for they may know
And tend the dwelling whence the slumberer's clay
Shall rise at last; and bid the young flowers bloom,
That waft a breath of hope around the tomb;
And kneel upon the dewy turf to pray!
But thou, what cave hath dimly chamber'd *thee!*
Vain dreams!—oh! art thou not where there is no more sea?[19]

LXII.
The wind rose free and singing:—when for ever,
O'er that sole spot of all the watery plain,
I could have bent my sight with fond endeavor
Down, where its treasure was, its glance to strain;
Then rose the reckless wind! Before our prow
The white foam flash'd—ay, joyously, and thou
Wert left with all the solitary main
Around thee—and thy beauty in my heart,
And thy meek, sorrowing love—oh, where could *that* depart?

LXIII.
I will not speak of woe; I may not tell—
Friend tells not such to friends—the thoughts which rent

My fainting spirit, when its wild farewell
Across the billows to thy grave was sent,
Thou, there most lonely!—He that sits above,
In his calm glory, will forgive the love
His creatures bear each other, even if blent
With a vain worship; for its close is dim
Ever with grief which leads the wrung soul back to Him

LXIV.

And with a milder pang if now I bear
To think of thee in thy forsaken rest,
If from my heart be lifted the despair,
The sharp remorse with healing influence press'd,
If the soft eyes that visit me in sleep
Look not reproach, though still they seem to weep;
It is that He my sacrifice hath bless'd,
And fill'd my bosom, through its inmost cell,
With a deep chastening sense that all at last is well.

LXV.

Yes! thou art now—Oh! wherefore doth the thought
Of the wave dashing o'er thy long bright hair,
The sea-weed into its dark tresses wrought,
The sand thy pillow—thou that wert so fair!
Come o'er me still!—Earth, earth!—it is the hold
Earth ever keeps on that of earthly mould!
But *thou* art breathing now in purer air,
I well believe, and freed from all of error,
Which blighted here the root of thy sweet life with terror.

LXVI.

And if the love, which here was passing light,
Went with what died not—Oh! that *this* we knew,
But this!—that through the silence of the night,
Some voice, of all the lost ones and the true,
Would speak, and say, if in their far repose,
We are yet aught of what we were to those
We call the dead!—their passionate adieu,
Was it but breath, to perish?—Holier trust
Be mine!—thy love *is* there, but purified from dust!

LXVII.

A thing all heavenly!—clear'd from that which hung
As a dim cloud between us, heart and mind!
Loosed from the fear, the grief, whose tendrils flung
A chain, so darkly with its growth entwined.
This is my hope!—though when the sunset fades,
When forests rock the midnight on their shades,
When tones of wail are in the rising wind,
Across my spirit some faint doubt may sigh;
For the strong hours *will* sway this frail mortality!

LXVIII.

We have been wand'rers since those days of woe,
Thy boy and I!—As wild birds tend their young,

So have I tended him—my bounding roe!
The high Peruvian solitudes among;
And o'er the Andes' torrents borne his form,
Where our frail bridge hath quiver'd 'midst the storm.[20]
But there the war-notes of my country rung,
And, smitten deep of Heaven and man, I fled
To hide in shades unpierced a mark'd and weary head.

LXIX.
But he went on in gladness—that fair child!
Save when at times his bright eye seem'd to dream,
And his young lips, which then no longer smiled.
Ask'd of his mother!—that was but a gleam
Of memory, fleeting fast;[21] and then his play
Through the wide Llanos cheer'd again our way,
And by the mighty Oronoco stream,[22]
On whose lone margin we have heard at morn,
From the mysterious rocks, the sunrise-music borne.

LXX.
So like a spirit's voice! a harping tone,
Lovely, yet ominous to mortal ear,
Such as might reach us from a world unknown,
Troubling man's heart with thrills of joy and fear!
'Twas sweet!—[23] yet those deep southern shades oppress'd
My soul with stillness, like the calms that rest
On melancholy waves: I sigh'd to hear
Once more earth's breezy sounds, her foliage fann'd,
And turn'd to seek the wilds of the red hunter's land.

LXXI.
And we have won a bower of refuge now,
In this fresh waste, the breath of whose repose
Hath cool'd, like dew, the fever of my brow,
And whose green oaks and cedars round me close
As temple-walls and pillars, that exclude
Earth's haunted dreams from their free solitude;
All, save the image and the thought of those
Before us gone; our loved of early years,
Gone where affection's cup hath lost the taste of tears.

LXXII.
I see a star—eve's first-born!—in whose train
Past scenes, words, looks, come back. The arrowy spire
Of the lone cypress, as of wood-girt fane,
Rests dark and still amidst a heaven of fire;
The pine gives forth its odors, and the lake
Gleams like one ruby, and the soft winds wake,
Till every string of nature's solemn lyre
Is touch'd to answer; its most secret tone
Drawn from each tree, for each hath whispers all its own.

LXXIII.
And hark! another murmur on the air,
Not of the hidden rills, or quivering shades!—

That is the cataract's, which the breezes bear,
Filling the leafy twilight of the glades
With hollow surge-like sounds, as from the bed
Of the blue, mournful seas, that keep the dead:
But *they* are far!—the low sun here pervades
Dim forest-arches, bathing with red gold
Their stems, till each is made a marvel to behold,—

LXXIV.

Gorgeous, yet full of gloom!- -In such an hour,
The vesper-melody of dying bells
Wanders through Spain, from each grey convent's tower
O'er shining rivers pour'd, and olive-dells,
By every peasant heard, and muleteer,
And hamlet, round my home:—and I am here,
Living again through all my life's farewells,
In these vast woods, where farewell ne'er was spoken,
And sole I lift to Heaven a sad heart—yet unbroken!

LXXV.

In such an hour are told the hermit's beads;
With the white sail the seaman's hymn floats by:
Peace be with all! whate'er their varying creeds,
With all that send up holy thoughts on high!
Come to me, boy!—by Guadalquiver's vines,
By every stream of Spain, as day declines,
Man's prayers are mingled in the rosy sky.
—We, too, will pray; not yet unheard, my child!
Of Him whose voice *we* hear at eve amidst the wild.

LXXVI.

At eve?—O through all hours!—From dark dreams oft
Awakening, I look forth, and learn the might
Of solitude, while thou art breathing soft,
And low, my loved one! on the breast of night:
I look forth on the stars—the shadowy sleep
Of forests—and the lake whose gloomy deep
Sends up red sparkles to the fire-flies' light.
A lonely world!—even fearful to man's thought
But for His presence felt, whom here my soul hath sought.

NOTES.

Note 1, page 472, line 23.
And sighing through the feathery canes, &c.

The canes, in some parts of the American forests, form a thick undergrowth for many hundred miles. — *See* HODGSON's *Letters from North America,* vol. i. p. 242.

NOTES.

Note 2, page 473, line 11.

And for their birthplace moan, as moans the ocean-shell.

Such a shell as Wordsworth has beautifully described.

"I have seen
A curious child who dwelt upon a tract
Of inland ground, applying to his ear
The convolutions of a smooth-lipp'd shell;
To which, in silence hush'd, his very soul
Listen'd intently, and his countenance soon
Brighten'd with joy; for murmurings from within
Were heard—sonorous cadences! whereby
To his belief, the monitor express'd
Mysterious union with its native sea.
—Even such a shell the universe itself
Is to the ear of Faith." *The Excursion.*

Note 3, page 474, line 21.

I see an oak before me: &c.

"I recollect hearing a traveller, of poetical temperament, expressing the kind of horror which he felt on beholding, on the banks of the Missouri, an oak of prodigious size, which had been in a manner overpowered by an enormous wild-grape vine. The vine had clasped its huge folds round the trunk, and from thence had wound about every branch and twig, until the mighty tree had withered in its embrace. It seemed like Laocoon struggling ineffectually in the hideous coils of the monster Python."—*Bracebridge Hall.* Chapter on Forest-Trees.

Note 4, page 477, line 14.

The might of truth.

For a most interesting account of the Spanish Protestants, and the heroic devotion with which they met the spirit of persecution in the sixteenth century, see the *Quarterly Review*, No. 57, Art. 'Quin's Visit to Spain.'

Note 5, page 478, line 23.

For the same guilt—his sisters!

"A priest, named Gonzalez, had, among other proselytes, gained over two young females, his sisters, to the Protestant faith. All three were confined in the dungeons of the Inquisition. The torture, repeatedly applied, could not draw from them the least evidence against their religious associates. Every artifice was employed to obtain a recantation from the two sisters, since the constancy and learning of Gonzalez precluded all hopes of a theological victory. Their answer, if not exactly logical, is wonderfully simple and affecting. 'We will die in the faith of our brother: he is too wise to be wrong, and too good to deceive us'—The three stakes on which they died were near each other. The priest had been gagged till the moment of lighting up the wood. The few minutes that he was allowed to speak he employed in comforting his sisters, with whom he sung the 109th Psalm, till the flames smothered their voices."—*Ibid.*

Note 6, page 478, line 38.

A hundred chiefs had borne, cast down by you to shame.

The names, not only of the immediate victims of the Inquisition were devoted to infamy, but those of all their relations were branded with the same indelible stain, which was likewise to descend as an inheritance to their latest posterity.

THE FOREST SANCTUARY.

Note 7, page 482, line 21
*T'was not within the city—but in sight
Of the snow-crown'd sierras.*
The piles erected for these executions were without the towns, and the final scene of an Auto da Fe was sometimes, from the length of the preceding ceremonies, delayed till midnight.

Note 8, page 487, line 23.
" *Speak to me! show me truth!*"
For one of the most powerful and impressive pictures perhaps ever drawn, of a young mind struggling against habit and superstition in its first aspirations after truth, see the admirable *Letters from Spain* by Don Leucadio Doblado.

Note 9, page 488, line 3.
*For thick ye girt me round, ye long departed!
Dust—imaged forms—with cross, and shield, and crest.*
" You walk from end to end over a floor of tombstones, inlaid in brass with the forms of the departed, mitres, and crosiers, and spears, and shields, and helmets, all mingled together—all worn into glass-like smoothness by the feet and the knees of long-departed worshippers. Around, on every side, each in their separate chapel, sleep undisturbed from age to age the venerable ashes of the holiest or the loftiest that of old came thither to worship—their images and their dying prayers sculptured among the resting-places of their remains.'' From a beautiful description of ancient Spanish Cathedrals, in *Peter's Letters to his Kinsfclk.*

Note 10, page 490, line 23.
*With eyes, whose lightning laughter hath beguiled
A thousand pangs.*
" El' *lampeggiar* de l'angelico riso."—PETRARCH

Note 11, page 490, line 42.
As through a pillar'd cloister's.
" Sometimes their discourse was held in the deep shades of moss-grown forests, whose gloom and interlaced boughs first suggested that Gothic architecture beneath whose pointed arches, where they had studied and prayed, party colored windows shed a tinged light; scenes which the gleams of sunshine, penetrating the deep foliage, and flickering on the variegated turf below, might have recalled to their memory."—Webster's Oration on the Landing of the Pilgrim Fathers in New England.—See HODGSON's *Letters from North America*, vol. ii. p. 305.

Note 12, page 490, line 2.
With yet a nearer swell—fresh breeze, awake.
The varying sounds of waterfalls are thus alluded to in an interesting work of Mrs. Grant's. " On the opposite side the view was bounded by steep hills, covered with lofty pines, from which a waterfall descended, which not only gave animation to the sylvan scene, but was the best barometer imaginable; foretelling by its varied and intelligible sounds every approaching change, not only of the weather but of the wind."—*Memoirs of an American Lady*, vol. i. p. 143.

Note 13, page 492, line 15.
There, on the snows.
The circular rainbows, occasionally seen amongst the Andes, are described by Ulloa.

Note 14, page 493, line 4.
A loved scene round me, visibly around.

Many striking instances of the vividness with which the mind, when strongly excited, has been known to renovate past impressions, and embody them into visible imagery, are noticed and accounted for in Dr. Hibbert's *Philosophy of Apparitions.* The following illustrative passage is quoted in the same work, from the writings of the late Dr. Ferriar:—"I remember that, about the age of fourteen, it was a source of great amusement to myself, if I had been viewing any interesting object in the course of the day, such as a romantic ruin, a fine seat, or a review of a body of troops, as soon as evening came on, if I had occasion to go into a dark room, the whole scene was brought before my eyes with a brilliancy equal to what it had possessed in daylight, and remained visible for several minutes. I have no doubt that dismal and frightful images have been thus presented to young persons after scenes of domestic affliction or public horror."

The following passage from the *Alcazar of Seville* a tale or historical sketch, by the author of Doblado's *Letters*, affords a further illustration of this subject. "When, descending fast into the vale of years, I strongly fix my mind's eye on those narrow, shady, silent streets, where I breathed the scented air which came rustling through the surrounding groves; where the footsteps re-echoed from the clean watered porches of the houses, and where every object spoke of quiet and contentment;   *   *   *   *   the objects around me begin to fade into a mere delusion, and not only the thoughts, but the external sensations, which I then experienced, revive with a reality that almost makes me shudder—it has so much the character of a trance or vision."

Note 15, page 495, line 39.
Nor the faint flower-scents as they come
In the soft air, like music wandering by.

"For because the breath of flowers is farre sweeter in the aire (where it comes and goes like the warbling of music) than in the hand, therefore nothing is more fit for that delight than to know what be the flowers and plants which doe best perfume the aire."—LORD BACON'S *Essay on Gardens.*

Note 16, page 500, line 37.
O Southern Cross!

. "The pleasure we felt on discovering the Southern Cross was warmly shared by such of the crew as had lived in the colonies. In the solitude of the seas, we hail a star as a friend from whom we have long been separated. Among the Portuguese and the Spaniards, peculiar motives seem to increase this feeling; a religious sentiment attaches them to a constellation, the form of which recalls the sign of the faith planted by their ancestors in the deserts of the New World. . . . . . . It has been observed at what hour of the night, in different seasons, the Cross of the South is erect or inclined. It is a time-piece that advances very regularly near four minutes a day, and no other group of stars exhibits to the naked eye an observation of Time so easily made. How often have we heard our guides exclaim, in the savannahs of Venezuela, or in the desert extending from Lima to Truxillo, 'Midnight is past, the Cross begins to bend!' How often these words reminded us of that affecting scene where Paul and Virginia, seated near the source of the river of Lataniers, conversed together for the last time; and where the old man, at the sight of the Southern Cross, warns them that it is time to separate!"—DE HUMBOLDT'S *Travels.*

Note 17, page 502, line 11.
The "Rio verde."
"Rio verde, rio verde," the popular Spanish romance, known to the English reader in Percy's translation.

> "Gentle river, gentle river,
> Lo, thy streams are stain'd with gore!
> Many a brave and noble captain
> Floats along thy willow'd shore," &c. &c.

Note 18, page 503, line 9.
Into the sounding waves!
De Humboldt, in describing the burial of a young Asturian at sea, mentions the entreaty of the officiating priest, that the body, which had been brought upon deck during the night, might not be committed to the waves until after sunrise, in order to pay it the last rites according to the usage of the Romish Church.

Note 19, page 503, line 34.
Oh! art thou not where there is no more sea?
And there was no more sea.—*Rev.* chap. xxi. v. 1.

Note 20, page 505, line 4.
Where our frail bridge hath quiver'd 'midst the storm.
The bridges over many deep chasms amongst the Andes are pendulous, and formed only of the fibres of equinoctial plants. Their tremulous motion has afforded a striking image to one of the stanzas in *Gertrude of Wyoming*.

> "Anon some wilder portraiture he draws,
> Of nature's savage glories he would speak;
> The loneliness of earth, that overawes,
> Where, resting by the tomb of old Cacique,
> The lama-driver, on Peruvia's peak,
> Nor voice nor living motion marks around
> But storks that to the boundless forest shriek,
> Or wild-cane arch, high flung o'er gulf profound,
> That fluctuates when the storms of El Dorado sound."

Note 21, page 505, line 12.
And then his play
Through the wide Llanos cheer'd again our way.
Llanos, or savannahs, the great plains in South America.

Note 22, page 505, line 14.
And by the mighty Oronoco stream.
On whose lone margin we have heard at morn,
From the mysterious rocks the sunrise-music borne
De Humboldt speaks of these rocks on the shores of the Oronoco. Travellers have heard from time to time subterraneous sounds proceed from them at sunrise, resembling those of an organ. He believes in the existence of this mysterious music, although not fortunate enough to have heard it himself; and thinks that it may be produced by currents of air issuing through the crevices.

Note 23, page 505, line 21.
Yet those deep southern shades oppress'd
My soul with stillness, like the calms that rest
On melancholy waves.
The same distinguished traveller frequently alludes to the extreme stillness of the air in the equatorial regions of the new continent, and particularly on the thickly wooded shores of the Oronoco. "In this neighborhood," he says," no breath of wind ever agitates the foliage."

CRITICAL ANNOTATIONS.

ON

"THE FOREST SANCTUARY.'

"Mrs. Hemans may be considered as the representative of a new school of poetry, or to speak more precisely, her poetry discovers characteristics of the highest kind, which belong almost exclusively to that of latter times, and have been the result of the gradual advancement, and especially the moral progress of mankind. It is only when man, under the influence of true religion, feels himself connected with whatever is infinite, that his affections and powers are fully developed. The poetry of an immortal being must be of a different character from that of an earthly being. But, in recurring to the classic poets of antiquity, we find that in their conceptions the element of religious faith was wanting. Their mythology was to them no object of sober belief; and, had it been so, was adapted not to produce but to annihilate devotion. They had no thought of regarding the universe as created, animated, and ruled, by God's all-powerful and omniscient goodness."—PROFESSOR NORTON, in *Christian Examiner.*

"We will now say a few words of *The Forest Sanctuary*; but it so abounds with beauty, is so highly finished, and animated by so generous a spirit of moral heroism, that we can do no justice to our views of it in the narrow space which our limits allow us. A Spanish Protestant flies from persecution at home to religious liberty in America. He has imbibed the spirit of our own fathers, and his mental struggles are described in verses, with which the descendants of the pilgrims must know how to sympathize. We dare not enter on an analysis. From one scene at sea, in the second part, we will make a few extracts. The exile is attended by his wife and child; but his wife remains true to the faith of her fathers.

"'*Ora pro nobis, Mater*! what a spell
Was in those notes,'' &c.

"But we must cease making extracts, for we could not transfer all that is beautiful in the poem without transferring the whole."—*North American Review* for April 1827.

"If taste and elegance be titles to enduring fame, we might venture securely to promise that rich boon to the author before us; who adds to those great merits a tenderness and loftiness of feeling, and an ethereal purity of sentiment, which could only emanate from the soul of a woman. She must beware of becoming too voluminous; and must not venture again on any thing so long as *The Forest Sanctuary.* But if the next generation inherits our taste for short poems, we are persuaded it will not readily allow her to be forgotten. For we do not hesitate to say, that she is, beyond all comparison, the most touching and accomplished writer of occasional verses that our literature has yet to boast of."—LORD JEFFREY, in *Edinburgh Review,* October 1829.

LAYS OF MANY LANDS.

The following pieces may so far be considered a series, as each is intended to be commemorative of some national recollection, popular custom, or tradition. The idea was suggested by Herder's "*Stimmen der Volker in Liedern ;*" the execution is, however, different, as the poems in his collection are chiefly translations.

MOORISH BRIDAL SONG.

["It is a custom among the Moors, that a female who dies unmarried is clothed for interment in wedding apparel, and the bridal-song is sung over her remains before they are borne from her home."—See *the Narrative of a Ten Years' Residence in Tripoli, by the Sister-in-law of Mr. Tully.*]

THE citron-groves their fruit and flowers were strewing
Around a Moorish palace, while the sigh
Of low sweet summer-winds, the branches wooing
With music through their shadowy bowers went by ;
  Music and voices, from the marble halls,
Through the leaves gleaming, and the fountain-falls.

A song of joy, a bridal-song came swelling,
To blend with fragrance in those southern shades,
And told of feasts within the stately dwelling,
Bright lamps, and dancing steps, and gem-crown'd maids
  And thus it flow'd ; yet something in the lay
Belong'd to sadness, as it died away.

" The bride comes forth ! her tears no more are falling
To leave the chamber of her infant years ;
Kind voices from a distant home are calling ;
She comes like day-spring—she hath done with tears ;
  Now must her dark eye shine on other flowers,
Her soft smile gladden other hearts than ours !—
              Pour the rich odours round !

" We haste ! the chosen and the lovely bringing ;
Love still goes with her from her place of birth ;
Deep, silent joy within her soul is springing,
Though in her glance the light no more is mirth !
  Her beauty leaves us in its rosy years ;
Her sisters weep—but she hath done with tears !—
              Now may the timbrel sound !"

Know'st thou for *whom* they sang the bridal numbers ?—
One, whose rich tresses were to wave no more !
One, whose pale cheek soft winds, nor gentle slumbers,
Nor Love's own sigh, to rose-tints might restore !

Her graceful ringlets o'er a bier were spread.—
Weep for the young, the beautiful,—the dead!

THE BIRD'S RELEASE.

[The Indians of Bengal and of the coast of Malabar bring cages filled with birds to the graves of their friends, over which they set the birds at liberty. This custom is alluded to in the description of Virginia's funeral.—See *Paul and Virginia*.]

Go forth, for she is gone!
With the golden light of her wavy hair,
She is gone to the fields of the viewless air;
   She hath left her dwelling lone!

Her voice hath pass'd away!
It hath pass'd away like a summer breeze,
When it leaves the hills for the far blue seas,
   Where we may not trace its way.

Go forth, and like her be free!
With thy radiant wing, and thy glancing eye,
Thou hast all the range of the sunny sky,
   And what is our grief to thee?

Is it aught even to her we mourn?
Doth she look on the tears by her kindred shed?
Doth she rest with the flowers o'er her gentle head,
   Or float, on the light wind borne?

We know not—but she is gone!
Her step from the dance, her voice from the song,
And the smile of her eye from the festal throng;
   She hath left her dwelling lone!

When the waves at sunset shine,
We may hear thy voice amidst thousands more,
In the scented woods of our glowing shore;
   But we shall not know 'tis thine!

Even so with the loved one flown!
Her smile in the starlight may wander by,
Her breath may be near in the wind's low sigh,
   Around us—but all unknown.

Go forth, we have loosed thy chain!
We may deck thy cage with the richest flowers
Which the bright day rears in our eastern bowers;
   But thou will not be lured again.

Even thus may the summer pour
All fragrant things on the land's green breast,
And the glorious earth like a bride be dress'd,
   But it wins *her* back no more!

THE SWORD OF THE TOMB.

A NORTHERN LEGEND.

[The idea of this ballad is taken from a scene in *Starkother*, a tragedy by the Danish poet Ochlenschlager. The sepulchral fire here alluded to, and supposed to guard the ashes of deceased heroes, is frequently mentioned in the Northern Sagas. Severe sufferings to the departed spirit, were supposed by the Scandinavian mythologists to be the consequence of any profanation of the sepulchre.—See OCHLENSCHLAGER'S *Plays*.]

' VOICE of the gifted elder time!
Voice of the charm and the Runic rhyme!
Speak! from the shades and the depths disclose
How Sigurd may vanquish his mortal foes;
 Voice of the buried past!

" Voice of the grave! 'tis the mighty hour,
When night with her stars and dreams hath power.
And my step hath been soundless on the snows,
And the spell I have sung hath laid repose
 On the billow and the blast."

  Then the torrents of the North,
  And the forest pines were still,
  While a hollow chant came forth
  From the dark sepulchral hill.

" There shines no sun 'midst the hidden dead;
But where the day looks not the brave may tread:
There is heard no song, and no mead is pour'd;
But the warrior may come to the silent board,
 In the shadow of the night.

" There is laid a sword in thy father's tomb,
And its edge is fraught with thy foeman's doom
But soft be thy step through the silence deep,
And move not the urn in the house of sleep,
 For the viewless have fearful might!"——

  Then died the solemn lay,
  As a trumpet's music dies,
  By the night-wind borne away
  Through the wild and stormy skies.

The fir-trees rock'd to the wailing blast,
As on through the forest the warrior pass'd—
Through the forest of Odin, the dim and old—
The dark place of visions and legends, told
 By the fires of Northern pine.

The fir-trees rock'd, and the frozen ground
Gave back to his footstep a hollow sound;
And it seem'd that the depths of those awful shades,
From the dreary gloom of their long arcades,
 Gave warning, with voice and sign.

THE SWORD OF THE TOMB.

    But the wind strange magic knows,
    To call wild shape and tone
    From the grey wood's tossing boughs,
    When Night is on her throne.

The pines closed o'er him with deeper gloom,
As he took the path to the monarch's tomb:
The Pole-star shone, and the heavens were bright
With the arrowy streams of the Northern light;
    But his road through dimness lay!

He pass'd, in the heart of that ancient wood,
The dark shrine stain'd with the victim's blood;
Nor paused till the rock, where a vaulted bed
Had been hewn of old for the kingly dead,
    Arose on his midnight way.

    Then first a moment's chill
    Went shuddering through his breast,
    And the steel-clad man stood still
    Before that place of rest.

But he cross'd at length, with a deep-drawn breath,
The threshold-floor of the hall of Death,
And look'd on the pale mysterious fire
Which gleam'd from the urn of his warrior-sire
    With a strange and solemn light.
Then darkly the words of the boding strain
Like an omen rose on his soul again,
—" Soft be thy step through the silence deep,
And move not the urn in the house of sleep,
    For the viewless have fearful might!"

    But the gleaming sword and shield
    Of many a battle-day
    Hung o'er that urn, reveal'd
    By the tomb-fire's waveless ray;

With a faded leaf of oak-leaves bound,
They hung o'er the dust of the far-renown'd,
Whom the bright Valkyriur's warning voice
Had call'd to the banquet where gods rejoice,
    And the rich mead flows in light.

With a beating heart his son drew near,
And still rang the verse in his thrilling ear,
—" Soft be thy step through the silence deep,
And move not the urn in the house of sleep,
    For the viewless have fearful might!"

    And many a Saga's rhyme,
    And legend of the grave,
    That shadowy scene and time
    Call'd back, to daunt the brave.

But he raised his arm—and the flame grew dim,
And the sword in its light seem'd to wave and swim,

And his faltering hand could not grasp it well—
From the pale oak-wreath, with a clash it fell
   Through the chamber of the dead!

The deep tomb rang with the heavy sound,
And the urn lay shiver'd in fragments round;
And a rush, as of tempests, quench'd the fire,
And the scatter'd dust of his warlike sire
     Was strewn on the Champion's head.

     One moment—and all was still
     In the slumberer's ancient hall,
     When the rock had ceas'd to thrill
     With the mighty weapon's fall.

The stars were just fading, one by one,
The clouds were just tinged by the early sun,
When there stream'd through the cavern a torch's flame,
And the brother of Sigurd the valiant came
     To seek him in the tomb.

Stretch'd on his shield, like the steel-girt slain,
By moonlight seen on the battle-plain,
In a speechless trance lay the warrior there;
But he wildly woke when the torch's glare
     Burst on him through the gloom.

     "The morning wind blows free,
     And the hour of chace is near:
     Come forth, come forth with me!
     What do'st thou, Sigurd, here?"

"I have put out the holy sepulchral fire,
I have scatter'd the dust of my warrior-sire!
It burns on my head, and it weighs down my heart;
But the winds shall not wander without their part
     To strew o'er the restless deep!

"In the mantle of death he was here with me now—
There was wrath in his eye, there was gloom on his brow;
And his cold still glance on my spirit fell
With an icy ray and a withering spell—
     Oh! chill is the house of sleep!"

     "The morning wind blows free,
     And the reddening sun shines clear;
     Come forth, come forth with me!
     It is dark and fearful here!"

"He is there, he is there, with his shadowy frown!
But gone from his head is the kingly crown—
The crown from his head, and the spear from his hand—
They have chased him far from the glorious land
     Where the feast of the gods is spread!

'He must go forth alone on his phantom steed,
He must ride o'er the grave-hills with stormy speed·

His place is no longer at Odin's board,
He is driven from Valhalla without his sword;
But the slayer shall avenge the dead!"

    That sword its fame had won
    By the fall of many a crest;
    But it fiercest work was done
    In the tomb, on Sigurd's breast!

VALKYRIUR SONG.

[The Valkyriur, or Fatal Sisters of Northern mythology, were supposed to single out the warriors who were to die in battle, and be received into the halls of Odin.

When a northern chief fell gloriously in war, his obsequies were honored with all possible magnificence. His arms, gold and silver, war-horse, domestic attendants, and whatever else he held most dear, were placed with him on the pile. His dependants and friends frequently made it a point of honor to die with their leader, in order to attend on his shade in Valhalla, or the palace of Odin And, lastly, his wife was generally consumed with him on the same pile.—See MALLET's *Northern Antiquities*, HERBERT's *Helga, &c.*

    "Tremblingly flash'd th' inconstant meteor light,
    Showing thin forms like virgins of this earth;
    Save that all signs of human joy or grief,
    The flush of passion, smile, or tear, had seem'd
    On the fix'd brightness of each dazzling cheek
    Strange and unnatural." *Milman.*

THE sea-king woke from the troubled sleep
    Of a vision-haunted night,
And he look'd from his bark o'er the gloomy deep,
    And counted the streaks of light;
        For the red sun's earliest ray
        Was to rouse his bands that day
    To the stormy joy of fight!

But the dreams of rest were still on earth,
    And the silent stars on high,
And there waved not the smoke of one cabin hearth
    'Midst the quiet of the sky;
        And along the twilight bay,
        In their sleep the hamlets lay,
For they knew not the Norse were nigh!

The Sea-king look'd o'er the brooding wave:
    He turn'd to the dusky shore,
And there seem'd, through the arch of a tide-worn cave,
    A gleam, as of snow, to pour;
        And forth, in watery light,
        Moved phantoms, dimly white,
    Which the garb of woman bore.

Slowly they moved to the billow side;
  And the forms, as they grew more clear,
Seem'd each on a tall pale steed to ride,
  And a shadowy crest to rear,
    And to beckon with faint hand
    From the dark and rocky strand,
  And to point a gleaming spear.

Then a stillness on his spirit fell,
  Before th' unearthly train.
For he knew Valhalla's daughters well,
  The Choosers of the slain!
    And a sudden rising breeze
    Bore, across the moaning seas,
  To his ear their thrilling strain.

    "There are songs in Odin's Hall
    For the brave ere night to fall!
    Doth the great sun hide his ray?—
    He must bring a wrathful day!
    Sleeps the falchion in its sheath?
    Swords must do the work of death!
    Regner!—Sea-king!—*thee* we call!—
    There is joy in Odin's Hall.

    "At the feast and in the song,
    Thou shalt be remember'd long!
    By the green isles of the flood,
    Thou hast left thy track in blood!
    On the earth and on the sea,
    There are those will speak of thee!
    'Tis enough,—the war-gods call,—
    There is mead in Odin's Hall!

    "Regner! tell thy fair-hair'd bride
    She must slumber at thy side!
    Tell the brother of thy breast
    Even for him thy grave hath rest!
    Tell the raven steed which bore thee,
    When the wild wolf fled before thee,
    He too with his lord must fall,—
    There is room in Odin's Hall!

    "Lo! the mighty sun looks forth—
    Arm! thou leader of the north!
    Lo! the mists of twilight fly,—
    We must vanish, thou must die!
    By the sword and by the spear,
    By the hand that knows not fear,
    Sea-king! nobly shalt thou fall!—
    There is joy in Odin's Hall!"

There was arming heard on land and wave,
  When afar the sunlight spread,
And the phantom forms of the tide-worn cave

With the mists of morning fled;
But at eve, the kingly hand
Of the battle-axe and brand
Lay cold on a pile of dead!

THE CAVERN OF THE THREE TELLS.

A SWISS TRADITION.

"The three founders of the Helvetic Confederacy are thought to sleep in a cavern near the Lake of Lucerne. The herdsmen call them the Three Tells; and say that they lie there in their antique garb, in quiet slumber; and when Switzerland is in her utmost need, they will awaken and regain the liberties of the land.—*See Quarterly Review*, No. 44.

The Grütli, where the confederates held their nightly meetings, is a meadow on the shore of the Lake of Lucerne, or Lake of the Forest-cantons, here called the Forest-sea.

OH! enter not yon shadowy cave,
 Seek not the bright spars there,
Though the whispering pines that o'er it wave
 With freshness fill the air:
  For there the Patriot Three
  In the garb of old array'd
  By their native Forest-sea,
   On a rocky couch are laid.

The Patriot Three that met of yore
 Beneath the midnight sky,
And leagued their hearts on the Grütli shore
 In the name of liberty!
  Now silently they sleep
   Amidst the hills they freed!
  But their rest is only deep
   Till their country's hour of need.

They start not at the hunter's call,
 Nor the Lammer-geyer's cry,
Nor the rush of a sudden torrent's fall,
 Nor the Lauwine thundering by!
  And the Alpine herdsman's lay,
   To a Switzer's heart so dear!
  On the wild wind floats away,
   No more for them to hear.

But when the battle-horn is blown
 Till the Schreckhorn's peaks reply,
When the Jungfrau's cliffs send back the tone
 Through their eagles' lonely sky;
  When the spear-heads light the lakes,
   When trumpets loose the snows,
  When the rushing war-steed shakes
   The glacier's mute repose;

When Uri's beechen woods wave red
  In the burning hamlet's light;—
Then from the cavern of the dead
  Shall the sleepers wake in might!
    With a leap, like Tell's proud leap
      When away the helm he flung,
    And boldly up the steep
      From the flashing billow sprung*

They shall wake beside their Forest-sea,
  In the ancient garb they wore
When they link'd the hands that made us free,
  On the Grütli's moonlight shore:
    And their voices shall be heard,
      And be answered with a shout,
    Till the echoing Alps are stirr'd,
      And the signal-fires blaze out.

And the land shall see such deeds again
  As those of that proud day,
When Winkelried, on Sempach's plain,
  Through the serried spears made way;
    And when the rocks came down
      On the dark Morgarten dell,
    And the crown'd casques,† o'erthrown,
      Before our fathers fell!

For the Kühreihen's‡ notes must never sound
  In the land that wears the chain,
And the vines on freedom's holy ground
  Untrampled must remain!
    And the yellow harvests wave
      For no stranger's hand to reap,
    While within their silent cave
      The men of Grütli sleep.

SWISS SONG,

ON THE ANNIVERSARY OF AN ANCIENT BATTLE.

[The Swiss, even to our days, have continued to celebrate the anniversaries of their ancient battles with much solemnity; assembling in the open air on the fields where their ancestors fought, to hear thanksgivings offered up by the priests, and the names of all who shared in the glory of the day enumerated. They afterwards walk in procession to chapels, always erected in the vicinity of such scenes, where masses are sung for the souls of the departed.—See PLANTA's *History of the Helvetic Confederacy*.]

  Look on the white Alps round!
    If yet they gird a land

---

* The point of rock on which Tell leaped from the boat of Gessler is marked by a chapel, and called the *Tellensprung*.

† *Crowned Helmets*, as a distinction of rank, are mentioned in Simond's *Switzerland*.

‡ The Kühreihen, the celebrated *Ranz des Vaches*.

SWISS SONG.

Where Freedom's voice and step are found,
    Forget ye not the band,—
The faithful band, our sires, who fell
Here in the narrow battle dell!

If yet, the wilds among,
    Our silent hearts may burn,
When the deep mountain-horn hath rung,
    And home our steps may turn,—
Home!—home!—if still that name be dear,
Praise to the men who perish'd here!

Look on the white alps round!
    Up to their shining snows
That day the stormy rolling sound,
    The sound of battle, rose!
Their caves prolong'd the trumpet's blast,
Their dark pines trembled as it pass'd!

They saw the princely crest,
    They saw the knightly spear,
The banner and the mail-clad breast,
    Borne down, and trampled here!
They saw—and glorying there they stand,
Eternal records to the land!

Praise to the mountain-born,
    The brethren of the glen!
By them no steel array was worn,
    They stood as peasant-men!
They left the vineyard and the field,
To break an empire's lance and shield!

Look on the white Alps round!
    If yet, along their steeps,
Our children's fearless feet may bound,
    Free as the chamois leaps:
Teach them in song to blesss the band
Amidst whose mossy graves we stand!

If, by the wood-fire's blaze,
    When winter stars gleam cold,
The glorious tales of elder days
    May proudly yet be told,
Forget not then the shepherd race,
Who made the hearth a holy place!

Look on the white Alps round!
    If yet the Sabbath-bell
Comes o'er them with a gladdening sound,
    Think on the battle dell!
For blood first bathed its flowery sod.
That chainless hearts might worship God!

THE MESSENGER BIRD.

[Some of the native Brazilians pay great veneration to a certain bird that sings mournfully in the night-time. They say it is a messenger which their deceased friends and relations have sent, and that it brings them news from the other world.—See PICART'S *Ceremonies and Religious Customs.*]

Thou art come from the spirits' land, thou bird!
    Thou art come from the spirit's land:
Through the dark pine grove let thy voice be heard,
    And tell of the shadowy band!

We know that the bowers are green and fair
    In the light of that summer shore,
And we know that the friends we have lost are there,
    They are there—and they weep no more!

And we know they have quenched their fever's thirst
    From the Fountain of youth ere now,*
For *there* must the stream in its freshness burst
    Which none may find below!

And we know that they will not be lured to earth
    From the land of deathless flowers,
By the feast, or the dance, or the song of mirth,
    Though their hearts were once with ours:

Though they sat with us by the night-fire's blaze,
    And bent with us the bow,
And heard the tales of our fathers' days,
    Which are told to others now!

But tell us, thou bird of the solemn strain!
    Can those who have loved forget!
We call—and they answer not again—
    Do they love—do they love us yet?

Doth the warrior think of his brother *there*,
    And the father of his child?
And the chief, of those that were wont to share
    His wandering through the wild?

We call them far through the silent night,
    And they speak not from cave or hill;

---

* An expedition was actually undertaken by Juan Ponce de Leon, in the 16th century, with a view of discovering a wonderful fountain, believed by the natives of Puerto Rico to spring in one of the Lucayo Isles, and to possess the virtue of restoring youth to all who bathed in its waters.—See ROBERTSON'S *History of America.*

We know, thou bird! that their land is bright,
But say, do they love there still?*

THE STRANGER IN LOUISIANA.

An early traveller mentions people on the banks of the Mississippi who burst into tears at the sight of a stranger. The reason of this is, that they fancy their deceased friends and relations to be only gone on a journey, and being in constant expectation of their return, look for them vainly amongst these foreign travellers.—PICART's *Ceremonies and Religious Customs.*]

" J'ai passé-moi-même," says Chateaubriand in his Souvenirs d'Amerique, " chez une peuplade Indienne qui se prenait à pleurer à la vue d'un voyageur, parce qu'il lui rappelait des amis partis pour la Contrée des Ames, et depuis long-tems *en voyage.*"]

WE saw thee, O stranger, and wept!
We look'd for the youth of the sunny glance
Whose step was the fleetest in chase or dance!
The light of his eye was a joy to see,
The path of his arrows a storm to flee!
But there came a voice from a distant shore:
He was call'd—he is found 'midst his tribe no more!

* ANSWER TO THE MESSENGER BIRD.

BY AN AMERICAN QUAKER LADY.

YES, I came from the spirits' land,
  From the land that is bright and fair;
I came with a voice from the shadowy band,
  To tell that they love you there.

To say, if a wish or a vain regret
  Could live in Elysian bowers,
'Twould be for the friends they can ne'er forget,
  The beloved of their youthful hours.

To whisper the dear deserted band,
  Who smiled on their tarriance here,
That a faithful guard in the dreamless land,
  Are the friends they have loved so dear

'Tis true, in the silent night you call,
  And they answer you not again;
But the spirits of bliss are voiceless all—
  Sound only was made for pain.

That their land is bright and they weep no more,
  I have warbled from hill to hill;
But my plaintive strain should have told before,
  That they love, oh! they love you still.

They bid me say that unfading flowers
  You'll find in the path they trode;
And a welcome true to their deathless bowers,
  Pronounced by the voice of God.

He is not in his place when the night-fires burn,
But we look for him still—he will yet return!
His brother sat with a drooping brow
In the gloom of the shadowing cypress bough:
We roused him—we bade him no longer pine,
For we heard a step—but the step was thine.

We saw thee, O stranger, and wept!
We look'd for the maid of the mournful song—
Mournful, though sweet—she hath left us long!
We told her the youth of her love was gone,
And she went forth to seek him—she pass'd alone;
We hear not her voice when the woods are still,
From the bower where it sang, like a silvery rill.
The joy of her sire with her smile is fled.
The winter is white on his lonely head,
He hath none by his side when the wilds we track,
He hath none when we rest—yet she comes not back!
We look'd for her eye on the feast to shine,
For her breezy step—but the step was thine!

We saw thee, O stranger, and wept!
We look'd for the chief who hath left the spear
And the bow of his battles forgotten here!
We look'd for the hunter, whose bride's lament
On the wind of the forest at eve is sent:
We look'd for the first-born, whose mother's cry
Sounds wild and shrill through the midnight sky!—
Where are they?—thou'rt seeking some distant coast
O ask of them, stranger!—send back the lost!
Tell them we mourn by the dark blue streams,
Tell them our lives but of them are dreams!
Tell, how we sat in the gloom to pine,
And to watch for a step—but the step was thine!

THE ISLE OF FOUNTS.

AN INDIAN TRADITION.

" The river St. Mary has its source from a vast lake or marsh, which lies between Flint and Oakmulge rivers, and occupies a space of near three hundred miles in circuit. This vast accumulation of waters, in the wet season, appears as a lake, and contains some large islands or knolls of rich high land; one of which the present generation of the Creek Indians represent to be a most blissful spot of earth: they say it is inhabited by a peculiar race of Indians, whose women are incomparably beautiful. They also tell you that this terrestial paradise has been seen by some of their enterprising hunters, when in pusuit of game; but that in their endeavors to approach it, they were involved in perpetual labyrinths, and, like enchanted land, still as they imagined they had just gained it, it seemed to fly before them, alternately appearing and disappearing. They resolved, at length, to leave the delusive

pursuit, and to return; which, after a number of difficulties, they effected. When they reported their adventures to their countrymen, the young warriors were inflamed with an irresistible desire to invade, and make a conquest of so charming a country; but all their attempts have hitherto proved abortive, never having been able again to find that enchanting spot."—BERTRAM'S *Travels through North and South Carolina, &c.*

The additional circumstances in the "Isle of Founts" are merely imaginary.]

 SON of the stranger! wouldst thou take
  O'er yon blue hills thy lonely way,
 To reach the still and shinning lake
  Along whose banks the west winds play?—
Let no vain dreams thy heart beguile,
Oh! seek thou not the Fountain Isle!

 Lull but the mighty serpent king,*
  'Midst the grey rocks, his old domain;
 Ward but the cougar's deadly spring,—
  Thy step that lake's green shore may gain,
And the bright Isle, when all is pass'd,
Shall vainly meet thine eye at last!

 Yes! there, with all its rainbow streams,
  Clear as within thine arrow's flight,
 The Isle of Founts, the Isle of dreams,
  Floats on the wave in golden light;
And lovely will the shadows be
Of groves whose fruit is not for thee!

 And breathings from their sunny flowers,
  Which are not of the things that die,
 And singing voices from their bowers,
  Shall greet the in the purple sky;
Soft voices, e'en like those that dwell
Far in the green reed's hollow cell.

 Or hast thou heard the sounds that rise
  From the deep chambers of the earth?
 The wild and wondrous melodies
  To which the ancient rocks gave birth?†
Like that sweet song of hidden caves
Shall swell those wood-notes o'er the waves.

---

* The Cherokees believe that the recesses of their mountains, overgrown with lofty pines and cedars, and covered with old mossy rocks, are inhabited by the kings or chiefs of rattlesnakes, whom they denominate the "bright old inhabitants." They represent them as snakes of an enormous size, and which possess the power of drawing to them every living creature that comes within the reach of their eyes. Their heads are said to be crowned with a carbuncle of dazzling brightness.—See *Notes to* LEYDEN'S *Scenes of Infancy.*

† The stones on the banks of the Oronoco, called by the South American missionaries *Laxas de Musica*, and alluded to in a former note.

The emerald waves!—they take their hue
　　And image from that sunbright shore;
　But wouldst thou launch thy light canoe,
　　And wouldst thou ply thy rapid oar,—
Before thee, hadst thou morning's speed,
The dreamy land should still recede!

　Yet on the breeze thou still wouldst hear
　　The music of its flowering shades,
　And ever should the sound be near
　　Of founts that ripple through its glades;
The sound, and sight, and flashing ray
Of joyous waters in their play!

　But woe for him who sees them burst
　　With their bright spray-showers to the lake.
　Earth has no spring to quench the thirst
　　That semblance in his soul shall wake,
For ever pouring through his dreams,
The gush of those untasted streams!

　Bright, bright in many a rocky urn,
　　The waters of our deserts lie,
　Yet at their source his lip shall burn,
　　Parch'd with the fever's agony!
From the blue mountains to the main,
Our thousand floods may roll in vain.

　E'en thus our hunters came of yore
　　Back from their long and weary quest;—
　Had they not seen th' untrodden shore,
　　And could they 'midst our wilds find rest?
The lightning of their glance was fled,
They dwelt amongst us as the dead!

　They lay beside our glittering rills,
　　With visions in their darken'd eye,
　Their joy was not amidst the hills
　　Where elk and deer before us fly;
Their spears upon the cedar hung,
Their javelins to the wind were flung.

　They bent no more the forest-bow,
　　They arm'd not with the warrior-band,
　The moons waned o'er them dim and slow—
　　They left us for the spirits' land!
Beneath our pines yon greensward heap
Shows where the restless found their sleep.

　Son of the stranger! If at eve
　　Silence be 'midst us in thy place,
　Yet go not where the mighty leave
　　The strength of battle and of chase!
Let no vain dreams thy heart beguile,
Oh! seek thou not the Fountain Isle!

THE BENDED BOW.

[It is supposed that war was anciently proclaimed in Britain by sending messengers in different directions through the land, each bearing a *bended bow* ; and that peace was in a like manner announced by a bow unstrung, and therefore straight.—See the *Cambrian Antiquities*.]

THERE was heard the sound of a coming foe,
There was sent through Britain a bended bow ;
And a voice was pour'd on the free winds far,
As the land rose up at the sign of war.

" Heard you not the battle horn ?—
Reaper ! leave thy golden corn !
Leave it for the birds of heaven,
Swords must flash, and spears be riven !
Leave it for the winds to shed—
Arm ! ere Britain's turf grow red !"

And the reaper arm'd, like a freeman's son ;
And the bended bow and the voice pass'd on.

" Hunter ! leave the mountain-chase !
Take the falchion from its place !
Let the wolf go free to-day,
Leave him for a nobler prey !
Let the deer ungall'd sweep by,—
Arm thee ! Britain's foes are nigh !"

And the hunter arm'd ere the chase was done ;
And the bended bow and the voice pass'd on

" Chieftain ! quit the joyous feast !
Stay not till the song hath ceased :
Though the mead be foaming bright,
Though the fires give ruddy light,
Leave the hearth, and leave the hall—
Arm thee ! Britain's foes must fall."

And the chieftain arm'd, and the horn was blown ;
And the bended bow and the voice pass'd on.

" Prince ! thy father's deeds are told,
In the bower and in the hold !
Where the goatherd's lay is sung,
Where the minstrel's harp is strung !
Foes are on thy native sea—
Give our bards a tale of thee !"

And the prince came arm'd, like a leader's son ;
And the bended bow and the voice pass'd on.

" Mother ! stay thou not thy boy !
He must learn the battle's joy.

Sister! bring the sword and spear,
Give thy brother words of cheer!
Maiden! bid thy lover part,
Britain calls the strong in heart!"

And the bended bow and the voice pass'd on;
And the bards made song for a battle won

HE NEVER SMILED AGAIN.

It is recorded of Henry the First, that after the death of his son, Prince William, who perished in a shipwreck off the coast of Normandy, he was never seen to smile.]

THE bark that held a prince went down,
  The sweeping waves roll'd on;
And what was England's glorious crown
  To him that wept a son?
He lived—for life may long be borne
  Ere sorrow break its chain;
Why comes not death to those who mourn?—
  He never smiled again!

There stood proud forms around his throne,
  The stately and the brave;
But which could fill the place of one,
  That one beneath the wave?
Before him pass'd the young and fair,
  In pleasure's reckless train;
But seas dash'd o'er his son's bright hair—
  He never smiled again!

He sat where festal bowls went round,
  He heard the minstrel sing,
He saw the tourney's victor crown'd,
  Amidst the knightly ring:
A murmur of the restless deep
  Was blent with every strain,
A voice of winds that would not sleep—
  He never smiled again!

Hearts, in that time, closed o'er the trace
  Of vows once fondly pour'd,
And strangers took the kinsman's place
  At many a joyous board;
Graves, which true love had bathed with tears,
  Were left to heaven's bright rain,
Fresh hopes were born for other years—
  He never smiled again!

CŒUR DE LION AT THE BIER OF HIS FATHER.

[The body of Henry the Second lay in state in the abbey-church of Fontevraud, where it was visited by Richard Cœur de Lion who, on beholding it, was struck with horror and remorse, and bitterly reproached himself for that rebellious conduct which had been the means of bringing his father to an untimely grave.]

Torches were blazing clear,
  Hymns pealing deep and slow,
Where a king lay stately on his bier
  In the church of Fontevraud.
Banners of battle o'er him hung,
  And warriors slept beneath,
And light, as noon's broad light was flung
  On the settled face of death.

On the settled face of death
  A strong and ruddy glare,
Though dimm'd at times by the censer's breath,
  Yet it fell still brightest there:
As if each deeply furrow'd trace
  Of earthly years to show,—
Alas! that sceptred mortal's race
  Had surely closed in woe!

The marble floor was swept
  By many a long dark stole,
As the kneeling priests, round him that slept,
  Sang mass for the parted soul:
And solemn were the strains they pour'd
  Through the stillness of the night,
With the cross above, and the crown and sword,
  And the silent king in sight.

There was heard a heavy clang,
  As of steel-girt men the tread,
And the tombs and the hollow pavement rang
  With a sounding thrill of dread;
And the holy chant was hush'd awhile,
  As, by the torch's flame,
A gleam of arms up the sweeping aisle,
  With a mail-clad leader came.

He came with haughty look,
  An eagle-glance and clear;
But his proud heart through its breastplate shook,
  When he stood beside the bier!
He stood there still with a drooping brow,
  And clasp'd hands o'er it raised;—
For his father lay before him low,
  It was Cœur de Lion gazed!

And silently he strove
  With the workings of his breast;
But there's more in late repentant love
  Than steel may keep suppress'd!
And his tears brake forth, at last, like rain,—
  Men held their breath in awe,
For his face was seen by his warrior-train,
  And he reck'd not that they saw.

He look'd upon the dead,
  And sorrow seem'd to lie,
A weight of sorrow, even like lead,
  Pale on the fast-shut eye.
He stoop'd—and kiss'd the frozen cheek,
  And the heavy hand of clay,
Till bursting words—yet all too weak—
  Gave his soul's passion way.

"Oh, father! is it vain,
  This late remorse and deep?
Speak to me, father! once again,
  I weep—behold, I weep!
Alas! my guilty pride and ire!
  Were but this work undone,
I would give England's crown, my sire!
  To hear thee bless thy son.

"Speak to me! mighty grief
  Ere now the dust hath stirr'd!
Hear me, but hear me!—father, chief,
  My king! I *must* be heard!—
Hush'd, hush'd—how is it that I call,
  And that thou answerest not?
When was it thus, woe, woe for all
  The love my soul forgot!

"Thy silver hairs I see,
  So still, so sadly bright!
And father, father! but for me,
  They had not been so white!
I bore thee down, high heart! at last,
  No longer could'st thou strive;—
Oh! for one moment of the past,
  To kneel and say—'forgive!'

"Thou wert the noblest king,
  On royal throne ere seen;
And thou didst wear in knightly ring,
  Of all, the stateliest mien;
And thou didst prove, where spears are proved,
  In war, the bravest heart—
Oh! ever the renown'd and loved
  Thou wert—and *there* thou art!

"Thou that my boyhood's guide
  Didst take fond joy to be!—
The times I've sported at thy side,
  And climb'd thy parent knee!
And there before the blessed shrine,
  My sire! I see thee lie,—
How will that sad still face of thine
  Look on me till I die!"

THE VASSAL'S LAMENT FOR THE FALLEN TREE.

["Here (at Bereton in Cheshire) is one thing incredibly strange, but attested, as I myself have heard, by many persons, and commonly believed. Before any heir of this family dies, there are seen, in a lake adjoining, the bodies of trees swimming on the water for several days."—CAMDEN's *Britannia*.]

YES! I have seen the ancient oak
  On the dark deep water cast,
And it was not fell'd by the woodman's stroke,
  Or the rush of the sweeping blast;
For the axe might never touch that tree,
And the air was still as a summer sea.

I saw it fall, as falls a chief
  By an arrow in the fight,
And the old woods shook, to their loftiest leaf,
  At the crashing of its might!
And the startled deer to their coverts drew,
And the spray of the lake as a fountain's flew!

'Tis fallen! but think thou not I weep
  For the forest's pride o'erthrown;
An old man's tears lie far too deep
  To be pour'd for this alone!
But by that sign too well I know,
That a youthful head must soon be low!

A youthful head, with its shining hair,
  And its bright quick-flashing eye—
Well may I weep! for the boy is fair,
  Too fair a thing to die!
But on his brow the mark is set—
Oh! could *my* life redeem him yet!

He bounded by me as I gazed
  Alone on the fatal sign,
And it seem'd like sunshine when he raised
  His joyous glance to mine!
With a stag's fleet step he bounded by,
So full of life—but he must die!

He must, he must! in that deep dell,
  By that dark water's side,
'Tis known that ne'er a proud tree fell
  But an heir of his fathers died.
And he—there's laughter in his eye,
Joy in his voice—yet he must die!

I've borne him in these arms, that now
  Are nerveless and unstrung;
And must I see, on that fair brow,
  The dust untimely flung?
I must!—yon green oak, branch and crest,
Lies floating on the dark lake's breast!

The noble boy!—how proudly sprung
  The falcon from his hand!
It seem'd like youth to see *him* young,
  A flower in his father's land!
But the hour of the knell and the dirge is nigh,
For the tree hath fall'n, and the flower must die

Say not 'tis vain!—I tell thee, some
  Are warn'd by a meteor's light,
Or a pale bird, flitting, calls them home,
  Or a voice on the winds by night;
And they must go!—and he too, he—
Woe for the fall of the glorious Tree!

THE WILD HUNTSMAN.

[It is a popular belief in the Odenwald, that the passing of the Wild Huntsman announces the approach of war. He is supposed to issue with his train from the ruined castle of Rodenstein, and traverse the air to the opposite castle of Schnellerts. It is confidently asserted, that the sound of his phantom horses and hounds was heard by the Duke of Baden before the commencement of the last war in Germany.]

T<small>HY</small> rest was deep at the slumberer's hour,
  If thou didst not hear the blast
Of the savage horn from the mountain tower,
  As the Wild Night-Huntsman pass'd,
And the roar of the stormy chase went by,
  Through the dark unquiet sky!

The stag sprung up from his mossy bed
  When he caught the piercing sounds,
And the oak-boughs crash'd to his antler'd head
  As he flew from the viewless hounds;
And the falcon soar'd from her craggy height,
  Away through the rushing night!

The banner shook on its ancient hold,
  And the pine in its desert place,
As the cloud and tempest onward roll'd

With the din of the trampling race;
And the glens were fill'd with the laugh and shout,
　And the bugle ringing out!

From the chieftain's hand the wine-cup fell,
　At the castle's festive board;
And a sudden pause came o'er the swell
　Of the harp's triumphal chord;
And the Minnesinger's* thrilling lay
　　In the hall died fast away.

The convent's chanted rite was stay'd
　And the hermit dropp'd his beads,
And a trembling ran through the forest-shade,
　At the neigh of the phantom steeds,
And the church-bells peal'd to the rocking blast
　As the Wild Night-Huntsman pass'd.

The storm hath swept with the chase away.
　There is stillness in the sky;
But the mother looks on her son to-day,
　With a troubled heart and eye,
And the maiden's brow hath a shade of care
　'Midst the gleam of her golden hair!

The Rhine flows bright; but its waves erelong
　Must hear a voice of war,
And a clash of spears our hills among,
　And a trumpet from afar;
And the brave on a bloody turf must lie.
　For the Huntsman hath gone by!

BRANDENBURG HARVEST-SONG.†

FROM THE GERMAN OF LA MOTTE FOUQUE.

The corn, in golden light
　Waves o'er the plain;
The sickle's gleam is bright;
　Full swells the grain.

Now send we far around
　Our harvest lay!—
Alas! a heavier sound
　Comes o'er the day!

Earth shrouds with burial sod
　Her soft eye's blue,—
How o'er the gifts of God
　Fall tears like dew!

---

* Minnesinger, *love-singer*,—the wandering minstrels of Germany were so called in the middle ages.
† For the year of the Queen of Prussia's death

On every breeze a knell
    The hamlets pour,—
We know its cause too well,
    She is no more!

THE SHADE OF THESEUS.

AN ANCIENT GREEK TRADITION.

Know ye not when our dead
    From sleep to battle sprung?—
When the Persian charger's tread
    On their covering greensward rung.
When the trampling march of foes
    Had crush'd our vines and flowers,
When jewel'd crests arose
    Through the holy laurel bowers;

    When banners caught the breeze,
        When helms in sunlight shone,
    When masts were on the seas,
        And spears on Marathon.

There was one, a leader crown'd,
    And arm'd for Greece that day;
But the falchions made no sound
    On his gleaming war-array.
In the battle's front he stood,
    With his tall and shadowy crest;
But the arrows drew no blood,
    Though their path was through his breast

    When banners caught the breeze,
        When helms in sunlight shone,
    When masts were on the seas,
        And spears on Marathon.

His sword was seen to flash
    Where the boldest deeds were done;
But it smote without a clash:
    The stroke was heard by none!
His voice was not of those
    That swell'd the rolling blast,
And his steps fell hush'd like snows—
    'Twas the Shade of Theseus pass'd!

    When banners caught the breeze,
        When helms in sunlight shone,
    When masts were on the seas,
        And spears on Marathon.

Far sweeping through the foe,
    With a fiery charge he bore;

And the Mede left many a bow
  On the sounding ocean-shore
And the foaming waves grew red,
  And the sails were crowded fast,
When the sons of Asia fled,
  As the Shade of Theseus pass'd!

When banners caught the breeze,
  When helms in sunlight shone,
When masts were on the seas,
  And spears on Marathon.

ANCIENT GREEK SONG OF EXILE.

WHERE is the summer with her golden sun?—
  That festal glory hath not pass'd from earth:
For me alone the laughing day is done!
  Where is the summer with her voice of mirth?
    —Far in my own bright land?

Where are the Fauns whose flute notes breathe and die
  On the green hills?—the founts, from sparry caves
Through the wild places bearing melody?
  The reeds, low whispering o'er the river waves?
    —Far in my own bright land!

Where are the temples, through the dim wood shining
  The virgin-dances and the choral strains?
Where the sweet sisters of my youth, entwining
  The Spring's first roses for their sylvan fanes?
    —Far in my own bright land!

Where are the vineyards, with their joyous throngs,
  The red grapes pressing when the foliage fades?
The lyres, the wreaths, the lovely Dorian songs,
  And the pine forests, and the olive shades?
    —Far in my own bright land!

Where the deep haunted grots, the laurel bowers,
  The Dryad's footsteps, and the minstrel's dreams?—
Oh! that my life were as a southern flower's!
  I might not languish then by these chill streams,
    Far from my own bright land!

GREEK FUNERAL CHANT, OR MYRIOLOGUE.

" Les Chants Funèbres par lesquels on déplore en Grèce la mort de ses proches, prennent le nom particulier de Myriologia, comme qui dirait, Discours de lamentation; complaintes. Un malade vient-il de rendre le dernier soupir, sa femme, sa mère, ses filles, ses sœurs, celles, en un mot, de ses plus proches parentes qui sont là, lui ferment les yeux et la bouche, en épanchant librement, chacune selon son naturel et sa mesure de tendresse pour le défunt, la douleur qu'elle ressent de sa perte. Ce premier devoir rempli, elles se retirent toutes chez une de leurs parentes ou de leurs amies. Là elles changent de vêtemens, s'habillent de blanc, comme pour la cérémonie nuptiale, avec cette différence, qu'elles gardent la tête nue, les cheveux épars et pendants. Ces apprêts terminés, les parentes reviennent dans leur parure de deuil ; toutes se rangent en circle autour du mort, et leur douleur s'exhale de nouveau, et, comme la première, fois, sans règle et sans constrainte. A ces plaintes spontanées succèdent bientôt des lamentations d'une autre espèce : ce sont les *Myriologues*. Ordinairement c'est la plus proche parente qui prononce le sien la première ; apres elle les autres parentes, les amies, les simples voisines. Les Myriologues sont toujours composés et chantés par les femmes. Ils sont toujours improvisés, toujours en vers, et toujours chantés sur un air qui diffère d'un lieu à un autre, mais qui, dans un lieu donné, reste invariablement consacré à ce genre de poësie." *Chants Populaires de la Grèce Moderne, par C. Fauriel.*]

A WAIL was heard around the bed, the deathbed of the young,
Amidst her tears the Funeral Chant a mournful mother sung.—
"Ianthis! dost thou sleep?—Thou sleep'st!—but this is not the rest,
The breathing and the rosy calm, I have pillow'd on my breast!
I lull'd thee not to *this* repose, Ianthis! my sweet son!
As in thy glowing childhood's time by twilight I have done!
How is it that I bear to stand and look upon thee now?
And that I die not, seeking death on thy pale glorious brow?

" I look upon thee, thou that wert of all most fair and brave!
I see thee wearing still too much of beauty for the grave!
Though mournfully thy smile is fix'd, and heavily thine eye
Hath shut above the falcon-glance that in it loved to lie ;
And fast is bound the springing step, that seem'd on breezes borne, ['tis morn!'
When to thy couch I came and said,—' Wake, hunter, wake!
Yet art thou lovely still, my flower! untouch'd by slow decay,—
And I, the wither'd stem, remain—I would that grief might slay!

" Oh! ever when I met thy look, I knew that *this* would be!
I knew too well that length of days was not a gift for thee!
I saw it in thy kindling cheek, and in thy bearing high!—
A voice came whispering to my soul, and told me thou must die! [ing red.—
That thou must die, my fearless one! where swords were flash-
Why doth a mother live to say—My first-born and my dead?
They tell me of thy youthful fame, they talk of victory won—
Speak *thou*, and I will hear! my child, Ianthis! my sweet son!"

A wail was heard around the bed, the deathbed of the young,
A fair-hair'd bride the Funeral Chant amidst her weeping sung.

"Ianthis! look'st thou not on *me*?—Can love indeed be fled?
When was it woe before to gaze upon thy stately head?
I would that I had follow'd thee, Ianthis, my beloved! [proved!
And stood as woman oft hath stood where faithful hearts are
That I had bound a breastplate on, and battled at thy side—
It would have been a blessed thing together had we died!

"But where was I when thou didst fall beneath the fatal sword?
Was I beside the sparkling fount, or at the peaceful board?
Or singing some sweet song of old, in the shadow of the vine,
Or praying to the saints for thee, before the holy shrine?
And thou wert lying low the while, the life-drops from thy heart
Fast gushing like a mountain-spring!—and couldst thou thus
    depart? [breath?—
Couldst thou depart, nor on my lips pour out thy fleeting
Oh! I was with thee but in joy, that should have been in death!

"Yes I was with thee when the dance through mazy rings was
    led, [was spread!
And when the lyre and voice were tuned, and when the feast
But not where noble blood flow'd forth, where sounding javelins
    flew—
Why did I hear love's first sweet words, and not its last adieu?
What now can breathe of gladness more,—what scene, what
    hour, what tone?
The blue skies fade with all their lights; they fade, since thou
    art gone! [moved—
Even *that* must leave me, that still face, by all my tears un-
Take me from this dark world with thee, Ianthis! my beloved!"

A wail was heard around the bed, the deathbed of the young,
Amidst her tears the Funeral Chant a mournful sister sung.
"Ianthis! brother of my soul!—oh where are now the days
That laugh'd among the deep green hills, on all our infant plays?
When we two sported by the streams, or track'd them to their
    source,
And like a stag's, the rocks along, was thy fleet, fearless course,
I see the pines there waving yet, I see the rills descend,
I see thy bounding step no more—my brother and my friend!

"I come with flowers—for spring is come! Ianthis! art thou
    here?
I bring the garlands she hath brought, I cast them on thy bier!
Thou shouldst be crown'd with victory's crown—but oh! more
    meet *they* seem,
The first faint violets of the wood, and lilies of the stream!
More meet for one os fondly loved, and laid thus early low—
Alas! how sadly sleeps thy face amidst the sunshine's glow:
The golden glow that through thy heart was wont such joy to
    send,— [friend!"
Woe! that it smiles, and not for thee!—my brother and my

THE PARTING SONG.

[This piece is founded on a tale related by Fauriel, in his "Chanson's Populaires de la Grèce Moderne," and accompanied by some very interesting particulars respecting the extempore parting songs, or songs of expatriation, as he informs us they are called, in which the modern Greeks are accustomed to pour forth their feelings on bidding farewell to their country and friends.]

A YOUTH went forth to exile, from a home
Such as to early thought gives images,
The longest treasured, and most oft recall'd,
And brightest kept, of love ;—a mountain home,
That with the murmur of its rocking pines
And sounding waters, first in childhood's heart
Wakes the deep sense of nature unto joy,
And half unconscious prayer ;—a Grecian home,
With the transparence of blue skies o'erhung,
And, through the dimness of its olive shades,
Catching the flash of fountains, and the gleam
Of shining pillars from the fanes of old.
And this was what he left!—Yet many leave
Far more !—the glistening eye, that first from theirs
Call'd out the soul's bright smile ; the gentle hand,
Which through the sunshine led forth infant steps
To where the violets lay ; the tender voice
That earliest taught them what deep melody
Lives in affection's tones.—*He* left not these.
Happy the weeper, that but weeps to part
With all a mother's love !—a bitterer grief
Was his—to part *unloved !*—of her unloved
That should have breath'd upon his heart, like spring
Fostering its young faint flowers !

                       Yet had he friends,
And they went forth to cheer him on his way
Unto the parting spot ;—and she too went,
That mother, tearless for her youngest-born,
The parting spot was reach'd :—a lone deep glen,
Holy, perchance, of yore, for cave and fount
Were there, and sweet-voiced echoes ; and above,
The silence of the blue still upper heaven
Hung round the crags of Pindus, where they wore
Their crowning snows.—Upon a rock he sprung,
The unbeloved one, for his home to gaze
Through the wild laurels back ; but then a light
Broke on the stern proud sadness of his eye,
A sudden quivering light, and from his lips
A burst of passionate song.

                    " Farewell, farewell !
I hear thee, O thou rushing stream !—thou 'rt from my native dell,
Thou 'rt bearing thence a mournful sound—a murmur of fare-[well!

THE PARTING SONG.

And fare *thee* well—flow on, my stream!—flow on thou bright
 and free!
I do but dream that in thy voice one tone laments for me;
But I have been a thing unloved, from childhood's loving year's,
And therefore turns my soul to thee, for thou hast known my
 tears! [known:
The mountains, and the caves, and thou, my secret tears have
The woods can tell where *he* hath wept, that ever wept alone!

" I see thee once again, my home! thou'rt there amidst thy
 vines,
And clear upon thy gleaming roof the light of summer shines.
It is a joyous hour when eve comes whispering through thy
 groves, [loves!—
The hour that brings the son from toil, the hour the mother
The hour *the mother* loves!—for *me* beloved it hath not been;
Yet ever in its purple smile, *thou* smilest, a blessed scene!
Whose quiet beauty o'er my soul through distant years will
 come—
Yet what but as the dead, to thee, shall I be then, my home?

" Not as the dead!—no, not the dead!—We speak of *them*—
 we keep [deep!
Their names, like light that must not fade, within our bosoms
We hallow even the lyre they touch'd, we love the lay they
 sung,
We pass with softer step the place *they* fill'd our band among!
But I depart like sound, like dew, like aught that leaves on
 earth
No trace of sorrow or delight, no memory of its birth!
I go!—the echo of the rock a thousand songs may swell
When mine is a forgotten voice.—Woods, mountains, home,
 farewell!

" And farewell, mother!—I have borne in lonely silence long,
But now the current of my soul grows passionate and strong!
And I will speak! though but the wind that wanders through
 the sky,
And but the dark, deep-rustling pines and rolling streams reply.
Yes! I will speak!—within my breast whate'er hath seem'd
 to be, [thee!
There lay a hidden fount of love, that would have gush'd for
Brightly it would have gush'd, but thou, my mother! thou hast
 thrown [own!
Back on the forests and the wilds what should have been thine

" Then fare thee well! I leave thee not in loneliness to pine,
Since thou hast sons of statelier mien and fairer brow than
 mine!
Forgive me that thou couldst not love!—it may be, that a tone
Yet from my burning heart may pierce through thine, when I
 am gone! [hast smil'd,
And thou, perchance, may'st weep for him on whom thou ne'er

And the grave give his birthright back to thy neglect'd child!
Might but my spirit *then* return, and 'midst its kindred dwell,
And quench its thirst with love's free tears!—'Tis all a dream
    —farewell!"

"Farewell!"—the echo died with that deep word;
Yet died not so the late repentant pang
By the strain quicken'd in the mother's breast!
There had pass'd many changes o'er her brow,
And cheek, and eye; but into one bright flood
Of tears at last all melted; and she fell
On the glad bosom of her child, and cried,
"Return, return, my son!"—The echo caught
A lovelier sound than song, and woke again,
Murmuring—"Return, my son!"——

THE SULIOTE MOTHER.

[It is related, in a French life of Ali Pacha, that several of the Suliote women, on the advance of the Turkish troops into the mountain fastnesses, assembled on a lofty summit, and, after chanting a wild song, precipitated themselves, with their children, into the chasm below, to avoid becoming the slaves of the enemy.]

She stood upon the loftiest peak.
    Amidst the clear blue sky;
A bitter smile was on her cheek,
    And a dark flash in her eye.

"Dost thou see them, boy?—through the dusky pines
Dost thou see where the foeman's armor shines?
Hast thou caught the gleam of the conqueror's crest?
My babe, that I cradled on my breast!
Wouldst thou spring from thy mother's arms with joy?
—That sight hath cost thee a father, boy!"

For in the rocky strait beneath,
    Lay Suliote sire and son:
They had heap'd high the piles of death
    Before the pass was won.

"They have cross'd the torrent, and on they come,
Woe for the mountain hearth and home!
There, where the hunter laid by his spear,
There, where the lyre hath been sweet to hear,
There, where I sang thee, fair babe! to sleep,
Nought but the blood-stain our trace shall keep!"

And now the horn's loud blast was heard,
    And now the cymbal's clang,

  Till even the upper air was stirr'd,
   As cliff and hollow rang.
"Hark! they bring music, my joyous child!
What saith the trumpet to Suli's wild!
Doth it light thine eye with so quick a fire,
As if at a glance of thine armed sire?—
Still!—be thou still!—there are brave men low—
Thou wouldst not smile couldst thou see him now!"

  But nearer came the clash of steel,
   And louder swell'd the horn,
  And farther yet the tambour's peal
   Through the dark pass was borne.

"Hear'st thou the sound of their savage mirth?—
Boy! thou wert free when I gave thee birth,—
Free, and how cherish'd, my warrior's son!
He too hath bless'd thee, as I have done!
Ay, and unchain'd must his loved ones be—
Freedom, young Suliote! for thee and me!"

  And from the arrowy peak she sprung,
   And fast the fair child bore:—
  A veil upon the wind was flung,
   A cry—and all was o'er!

THE FAREWELL TO THE DEAD.

The following piece is founded on a beautiful part of the Greek funeral service, in which relatives and friends are invited to embrace the deceased (whose face is uncovered) and to bid their final adieu.—See *Christian Researches in the Mediterranean*.]

   "'Tis hard to lay into the earth
   A countenance so benign! a form that walk'd
   But yesterday so stately o'er the earth!"
         Wilson.

  Come near!—ere yet the dust
Soil the bright paleness of the settled brow,
Look on your brother; and embrace him now,
   In still and solemn trust!
Come near!—once more let kindred lips be press'd
On his cold cheek; then bear him to his rest!

  Look yet on this young face!
What shall the beauty, from amongst us gone,
Leave of its image, even where most it shone,
   Gladdening its hearth and race?
Dim grows the semblance on man's heart impress'd—
Come near, and bear the beautiful to rest!

  Ye weep, and it is well!
For tears befit earth's partings!—Yesterday,
Song was upon the lips of this pale clay,

   And sunshine seem'd to dwell
Where'er he moved—the welcome and the bless'd!—
Now gaze! and bear the silent unto rest!

   Look yet on him whose eye
Meets yours no more, in sadness or in mirth!
Was he not fair amidst the sons of earth,
   The beings born to die?—
But not where death has power may love be bless'd—
Come near! and bear ye the beloved to rest!

   How may the mother's heart
Dwell on her son, and dare to hope again?
The Spring's rich promise hath been given in vain,
   The lovely must depart!
Is *he* not gone, our brightest and our best?
Come near! and bear the early call'd to rest!

   Look on him! is he laid
To slumber from the harvest or the chase?—
Too still and sad the smile upon his face;
   Yet that, even that must fade!
Death holds not long unchanged his fairest guest!—
Come near! and bear the mortal to his rest!

   His voice of mirth hath ceased
Amidst the vineyards! there is left no place
For him whose dust receives your vain embrace,
   At the gay bridal feast!
Earth must take earth to moulder on her breast;
Come near! weep o'er him! bear him to his rest!

   Yet mourn ye not as they
Whose spirit's light is quench'd!—for him the past
Is seal'd. He may not fall, he may not cast
   His birth-right's hope away!
All is not *here* of our beloved and bless'd—
Leave ye the sleeper with his God to rest!

MISCELLANEOUS PIECES.

THE TREASURES OF THE DEEP.*

What hidest thou in thy treasure-caves and cells?
 Thou hollow-sounding and mysterious main!—
Pale glistening pearls, and rainbow-color'd shells,
 Bright things which gleam unreck'd of and in vain!—
Keep, keep thy riches, melancholy sea!
  We ask not such from thee.

* Originally introduced in the "Forest Sanctuary."

Yet more, the depths have more!—what wealth untold,
   Far down, and shining through their stillness lies!
Thou hast the starry gems, the burning gold,
   Won from ten thousand royal Argosies!—
Sweep o'er thy spoils, thou wild and wrathful main!
       Earth claims not *these* again.

Yet more, the depths have more!—thy waves have roll'd
   Above the cities of a world gone by!
Sand hath fill'd up the palaces of old,
   Sea-weed o'ergrown the halls of revelry.—
Dash o'er them, ocean! in thy scornful play!
       Man yields them to decay.

Yet more! the billows and the depths have more!
   High hearts and brave are gather'd to thy breast!
They hear not now the booming waters roar,
   The battle-thunders will not break their rest.—
Keep thy red gold and gems, thou stormy grave!
       Give back the true and brave!

Give back the lost and lovely!—those for whom
   The place was kept at board and hearth so long!
The prayer went up through midnight's breathless gloom,
   And the vain yearning woke 'midst festal song!
Hold fast thy buried isles, thy towers o'erthrown—
       But all is not thine own.

To thee the love of woman hath gone down,
   Dark flow thy tides o'er manhood's noble head,
O'er youth's bright locks, and beauty's flowery crown;
   Yet must thou hear a voice—Restore the dead!
Earth shall reclaim her precious things from thee!—
       Restore the dead, thou sea!

BRING FLOWERS.

Bring flowers, young flowers, for the festal board,
To wreath the cup ere the wine is pour'd;
Bring flowers! they are springing in wood and vale:
Their breath floats out on the southern gale;
And the touch of the sunbeam hath waked the rose,
To deck the hall where the bright wine flows.

Bring flowers to strew in the conqueror's path—
He hath shaken thrones with his stormy wrath!
He comes with the spoils of nations back,
The vines lie crush'd in his chariot's track,
The turf looks red where he won the day—
Bring flowers to die in the conqueror's way!

Bring flowers to the captive's lonely cell,
They have tales of the joyous woods to tell;
Of the free blue streams, and the glowing sky,
And the bright world shut from his languid eye:
They will bear him a thought of the sunny hours,
And the dream of his youth—bring him flowers, wild flowers!

Bring flowers, fresh flowers, for the bride to wear!
They were born to blush in her shining hair.
She is leaving the home of her childhood's mirth,
She hath bid farewell to her father's hearth,
Her place is now by another's side—
Bring flowers for the locks of the fair young bride!

Bring flowers, pale flowers, o'er the bier to shed,
A crown for the brow of the early dead!
For this through its leaves hath the white rose burst,
For this in the woods was the violet nursed!
Though they smile in vain for what once was ours.
They are love's last gift—bring ye flowers, pale flowers!

Bring flowers to the shrine where we kneel in prayer,
They are nature's offering, their place is *there!*
They speak of hope to the fainting heart,
With a voice of promise they come and part,
They sleep in dust through the wintry hours,
They break forth in glory—bring flowers, bright flowers!

THE CRUSADER'S RETURN.

> "Alas! the mother that him bare,
> If she had been in presence there,
> In his wan cheeks and sunburnt hair
> She had not known her child."
> *Marmion.*

REST, pilgrim, rest!—thou'rt from the Syrian land,
  Thou'rt from the wild and wondrous east, I know
By the long-wither'd palm-branch in thy hand,
  And by the darkness of thy sunburnt brow.
Alas! the bright, the beautiful, who part
  So full of hope, for that far country's bourne!
Alas! the weary and the changed in heart,
  And dimm'd in aspect, who like thee return!

Thou'rt faint—stay, rest thee from thy toils at last:
  Through the high chestnuts lightly plays the breeze,
The stars gleam out, the *Ave* hour is past,
  The sailor's hymn hath died along the seas.
Thou'rt faint and worn—hear'st thou the fountain welling
  By the grey pillars of yon ruin'd shrine?
Seest thou the dewy grapes before thee swelling?
  —He that hath left me train'd that loaded vine!

THE CRUSADER'S RETURN.

He was a child when thus the bower he wove,
  (Oh! hath a day fled since his childhood's time?)
That I might sit and hear the sound I love,
  Beneath its shade—the convent's vesper-chime.
And sit *thou* there!—for he was gentle ever,
  With his glad voice he would have welcomed thee,
And brought fresh fruits to cool thy parch'd lips' fever—
  There in his place thou'rt resting—where is he?

If I could hear that laughing voice again,
  But once again!—how oft it wanders by,
In the still hours, like some remember'd strain,
  Troubling the heart with its wild melody!—
Thou hast seen much, tired pilgrim! hast thou seen
  In that far land, the chosen land of yore,
A youth—my Guido—with the fiery mien
  And the dark eye of this Italian shore?

The dark, clear, lightning eye!—on heaven and earth
  It smiled—as if man were not dust it smiled!
The very air seem'd kindling with his mirth,
  And I—my heart grew young before my child!
My blessed child!—I had but him—yet he
  Fill'd all my home even with o'erflowing joy,
Sweet laughter, and wild song, and footstep free—
  Where is he now?—my pride, my flower, my boy!

His sunny childhood melted from my sight,
  Like a spring dew-drop—then his forehead wore
A prouder look—his eye a keener light—
  I knew these woods might be his world no more!
He loved me—but he left me!—thus they go
  Whom we have rear'd, watch'd, bless'd, too much adored!
He heard the trumpet of the Red-Cross blow,
  And bounded from me with his father's sword!

Thou weep'st—I tremble—thou hast seen the slain
  Pressing a bloody turf; the young and fair,
With their pale beauty strewing o'er the plain
  Where hosts have met—speak! answer!—was *he* there?
Oh! hath his smile departed?—Could the grave
  Shut o'er those bursts of bright and tameless glee?—
No! I shall yet behold his dark locks wave—
  That look gives hope—I knew it could not be!

Still weep'st thou, wand'rer?—some fond mother's glance
  O'er thee, too, brooded in thine early years—
Think'st thou of her, whose gentle eye, perchance,
  Bathed all thy faded hair with parting tears?
Speak, for thy tears disturb me!—what art thou?
  Why dost thou hide thy face, yet weeping on?
Look up!—oh! is it—that wan cheek and brow!—
  Is it—alas! yet joy!—my son, my son!

THEKLA'S SONG; OR, THE VOICE OF A SPIRIT

FROM THE GERMAN OF SCHILLER.

[This song is said to have been composed by Schiller in answer to the enquiries of his friends respecting the fate of *Thekla*, whose beautiful character is withdrawn from the tragedy of *Wallenstein's Death*, after her resolution to visit the grave of her lover is made known.]

> " 'Tis not merely
> The human being's *pride* that peoples space
> With life and mistical predominance;
> Since likewise for the stricken heart of *love*
> This visible nature, and this common world,
> Are all too narrow."
> *Coleridge's Translation of Wallenstein.*

Ask'st thou my home?—my pathway would'st thou know,
  When from thine eye my floating shadow pass'd?
Was not my work fulfill'd and closed below?
  Had I not lived and loved?—my lot was cast.

Would'st thou ask where the nightingale is gone,
  That, melting into song her soul away,
Gave the spring-breeze what witch'd thee in its tone?—
  But while she loved, she lived, in that deep lay!

Think'st thou my heart its lost one hath not found?—
  Yes! we are one: oh! trust me, we have met,
Where nought again may part what love hath bound,
  Where falls no tear, and whispers no regret.

There shalt *thou* find us, there with us be blest,
  If, as *our* love, *thy* love is pure and true!
There dwells my father,* sinless and at rest,
  Where the fierce murd'rer may no more pursue.

And well he feels, no error of the dust
  Drew to the stars of heaven his mortal ken,
There it is with us, even as is our trust,
  He that believes, is near the holy *then*.

There shall each feeling, beautiful and high,
  Keep the sweet promise of its earthly day;—
Oh! fear thou not to dream with waking eye!
  There lies deep meaning oft in childish play.

THE REVELLERS.

Ring, joyous chords!—ring out again!
A swifter still, and a wilder strain!

---
* Wallenstein.

THE REVELLERS.

They are here—the fair face and the careless heart,
And stars shall wane ere the mirthful part.—
But I met a dimly mournful glance,
In a sudden turn of the flying dance ;
I heard the tone of a heavy sigh
In a pause of the thrilling melody!
And it is not well that woe should breathe
On the bright spring-flowers of the festal wreath !—
Ye that to thought or to grief belong,
        Leave, leave the hall of song !

Ring, joyous chords !—but who art *thou*
With the shadowy locks o'er thy pale young brow
And the world of dreamy gloom that lies
In the misty depths of thy soft dark eyes?
Thou hast loved, fair girl ! thou hast loved too well !
Thou art mourning now o'er a broken spell ;
Thou hast pour'd thy heart's rich treasures forth,
And art unrepaid for their priceless worth !
Mourn on !—yet come thou not *here* the while,
It is but a pain to see thee smile !
There is not a tone in our song for thee—
        Home with thy sorrows flee !

Ring, joyous chords !—ring out again !—
But what dost thou with the revel's train ?
A silvery voice through the soft air floats,
But thou hast no part in the gladd'ning notes ;
There are bright young faces that pass thee by,
But they fix no glance of thy wandering eye !
Away, there's a void in thy yearning breast,
Thou weary man ! wilt thou *here* find rest ?
Away ! for thy thoughts from the scene hath fled,
And the love of *thy* spirit is with the dead !
Thou art but more lone 'midst the sounds of mirth,
        Back to thy silent hearth !

Ring, joyous chords !—ring forth again !
A swifter still, and a wilder strain !—
But *thou*, though a reckless mien be thine,
And thy cup be crown'd with the foaming wine,
By the fitful bursts of thy laughter loud,
By thine eye's quick flash through its troubled cloud,
I know thee ! it is but the wakeful fear
Of a haunted bosom that brings thee here !
I know thee !—thou fearest the solemn night,
With her piercing stars and her deep wind's might !
There's a tone in her voice which thou fain would'st shun,
For it asks what the secret soul hath done !
And thou—there's a dark weight on thine—away !—
        Back to thy home, and pray !

Ring joyous chords ! ring out again !
A swifter still, and a wilder strain !

And bring fresh wreaths!—we will banish all
Save the free in heart from our festive hall.
On! through the maze of the fleet dance, on!—
But where are the young and the lovely?—gone!
Where are the brows with the Red Cross crown'd,
And the floating forms with the bright zone bound?
And the waving locks and the flying feet,
That still should be where the mirthful meet?—
They are gone—they are fled—they are parted all—
    Alas! the forsaken hall!

THE CONQUEROR'S SLEEP.

    Sleep 'midst thy banners furl'd!
Yes! thou art there, upon thy buckler lying,
With the soft wind unfelt around thee sighing,
Thou chief of hosts, whose trumpet shakes the world!
Sleep while the babe sleeps on its mother's breast—
Oh! strong is night—for thou too art at rest!

    Stillness hath smooth'd thy brow,
And now might love keep timid vigils by thee,
Now might the foe with stealthy foot draw nigh thee,
Alike unconscious and defenceless thou!
Tread lightly, watchers!—now the field is won,
Break not the rest of Nature's weary son!

    Perchance some lovely dream
Back from the stormy fight thy soul is bearing,
To the green places of thy boyish daring,
And all the windings of thy native stream;—
Why, this were joy!—upon the tented plain,
Dream on, thou Conqueror!—be a child again!

    But thou wilt wake at morn,
With thy strong passions to the conflict leaping,
And thy dark troubled thoughts all earth o'ersweeping;
So wilt thou rise, oh! thou of woman born!
And put thy terrors on, till none may dare
Look upon thee—the tired one, slumbering there!

    Why, so the peasant sleeps
Beneath his vine!—and man must kneel before thee,
And for his birthright vainly still implore thee!
Shalt thou be stay'd because thy brother weeps?—
Wake! and forget that 'midst a dreaming world,
Thou hast lain thus, with all thy banners furl'd!

    Forget that thou, even thou,
Hast feebly shiver'd when the wind pass'd o'er thee
And sunk to rest upon the earth which bore thee,
And felt the night-dew chill thy fever'd brow!
Wake with the trumpet, with the spear press on!—
Yet shall the dust take home its mortal son.

OUR LADY'S WELL.*

Fount of the woods! thou art hid no more,
From heaven's clear eye, as in time of yore.
For the roof hath sunk from thy mossy walls,
And the sun's free glance on thy slumber falls;
And the dim tree-shadows across thee pass,
As the boughs are sway'd o'er thy silvery glass;
And the reddening leaves to thy breast are blown,
When the autumn wind hath a stormy tone:
And thy bubbles rise to the flashing rain—
Bright Fount! thou art nature's own again!

Fount of the vale! thou art sought no more
By the pilgrim's foot, as in time of yore,
When he came from afar, his beads to tell,
And to chant his hymn at Our Lady's Well.
There is heard no *Ave* through thy bowers,
Thou art gleaming lone 'midst thy water-flowers!
But the herd may drink from thy gushing wave,
And there may the reaper his forehead lave,
And the woodman seeks thee not in vain—
Bright Fount! thou art nature's own again!

Fount of the Virgin's ruin'd shrine!
A voice that speaks of the past is thine!
It mingles the tone of a thoughtful sigh,
With the notes that ring through the laughing sky;
'Midst the mirthful song of the summer bird,
And the sound of the breeze, it will yet be heard!
Why is it that thus we may gaze on thee,
To the brilliant sunshine sparkling free?—
'Tis that all on earth is of *Time's* domain—
He hath made thee nature's own again!

Fount of the chapel with ages grey!
Thou art springing freshly amidst decay;
Thy rites are closed, and thy cross lies low,
And the changeful hours breathe o'er thee now:
Yet if at thine altar one holy thought
In man's deep spirit of old hath wrought;
If peace to the mourner hath here been given,
Or prayer, from a chastened heart, to Heaven—
Be the spot still hallow'd while Time shall reign,
Who hath made thee nature's own again!

---

* A beautiful spring in the woods near St. Asaph, formerly covered in with a chapel, now in ruins. It was dedicated to the Virgin and, according to Pennant, much the resort of pilgrims.

MISCELLANEOUS PIECES.

THE PARTING OF SUMMER.

Thou'rt bearing hence thy roses,
  Glad summer, fare thee well!
Thou'rt singing thy last melodies
  In every wood and dell.

But ere the golden sunset.
  Of thy latest lingering day,
Oh! tell me, o'er this chequered earth,
  How hast thou pass'd away?

Brightly, sweet Summer! brightly
  Thine hours have floated by,
To the joyous birds of the woodland boughs,
  The rangers of the sky.

And brightly in the forests,
  To the wild deer wandering free;
And brightly 'midst the garden flowers,
  Is the happy murmuring bee:

But how to human bosoms,
  With all their hopes and fears,
And thoughts that make them eagle-wings,
  To pierce the unborn years?

Sweet Summer! to the captive
  Thou hast flown in burning dreams
Of the woods, with all their whispering leaves
  And the blue rejoicing streams;—

To the wasted and the weary
  On the bed of sickness bound,
In swift delirious fantasies,
  That changed with every sound;—

To the sailor on the billows,
  In longings wild and vain,
For the gushing founts and breezy hills,
  And the homes of earth again!

And unto me, glad Summer!
  How hast thou flown to me?
My chainless footstep nought hath kept
  From thy haunts of song and glee.

Thou hast flown in wayward visions,
  In memories of the dead—
In shadows from a troubled heart,
  O'er thy sunny pathway shed:

In brief and sudden strivings
  To fling a weight aside—
Midst these thy melodies have ceased,
  And all thy roses died.

But oh! thou gentle Summer!
  If I greet thy flowers once more,
Bring me again the buoyancy
  Wherewith my soul should soar!

Give me to hail thy sunshine,
  With song and spirit free;
Or in a purer air than this
  May that next meeting be!

THE SONGS OF OUR FATHERS.

> ———" Sing aloud
> Old Songs, the precious music of the heart.'
> *Wordsworth.*

Sing them upon the sunny hills
  When days are long and bright,
And the blue gleam of shining rills
  Is loveliest to the sight!
Sing them along the misty moor,
  Where ancient hunters roved,
And swell them through the torrent's roar,
  The songs our fathers loved!

The songs their souls rejoiced to hear
  When harps were in the hall,
And each proud note made lance and spear
  Thrill on the banner'd wall:
The songs that through our valleys green,
  Sent on from age to age,
Like his own river's voice, have been
  The peasant's heritage.

The reaper sings them when the vale
  Is fill'd with plumy sheaves;
The woodman, by the starlight pale,
  Cheer'd homeward through the leaves:
And unto them the glancing oars
  A joyous measure keep,
Where the dark rocks that crest our shores
  Dash back the foaming deep.

So let it be!—a light they shed
  O'er each old fount and grove;
A memory of the gentle dead,
  A lingering spell of love.
Murmuring the names of mighty men,
  They bid our streams roll on,
And link high thoughts to every glen
  Where valiant deeds were done.

'Teach them your children round the hearth,
    When evening fires burn clear,
And in the fields of harvest mirth,
    And on the hills of deer:
So shall each unforgotten word,
    When far those loved ones roam,
Call back the hearts which once it stirr'd
    To childhood's holy home.

The green woods of their native land
    Shall whisper in the strain,
The voices of their household band
    Shall breathe their names again;
The heathery heights in vision rise
    Where, like the stag, they roved-
Sing to your sons those melodies,
    The songs your fathers loved!'

THE WORLD IN THE OPEN AIR.

Come, while in freshness and dew it lies,
To the world that is under the free, blue skies!
Leave ye man's home, and forget his care—
There breathes no sigh on the dayspring's air.

Come to the woods, in whose mossy dells
A light all made for the poet dwells;
A light, color'd softly by tender leaves,
Whence the primrose a mellower glow receives.

The stock-dove is there in the beechen tree,
And the lulling tone of the honey-bee;
And the voice of cool waters 'midst feathery fern,
Shedding sweet sounds from some hidden urn.

There is life, there is youth, there is tameless mirth,
Where the streams, with the lilies they wear, have birth;
There is peace where the alders are whispering low:
Come from man's dwellings with all their woe!

Yes! we will come—we will leave behind
The homes and the sorrows of human kind:
It is well to rove where the river leads
Its bright blue vein along sunny meads:

It is well through the rich wild woods to go,
And to pierce the haunts of the fawn and doe;
And to hear the gushing of gentle springs,
Where the heart has been fretted by worldly stings;

And to watch the colors that flit and pass,
With insect-wings, through the wavy grass;
And the silvery gleams o'er the ash-tree's bark,
Borne in with a breeze through the foliage dark.

Joyous and far shall our wanderings be,
As the flight of birds o'er the glittering sea;
To the woods, to the dingles where violets blow,
We will bear no memory of earthly woe.

But if by the forest brook we meet
A line like the pathway of former feet;—
If, 'midst the hills, in some lonely spot,
We reach the grey ruins of tower or cot;—

If the cell, where a hermit of old hath pray'd,
Lift up its cross through the solemn shade;—
Or if some nook where the wild flowers wave,
Bear token sad of a mortal grave,—

Doubt not but *there* will our steps be stay'd,
There our quick spirits awhile delay'd;
There will thought fix our impatient eyes,
And win back our hearts to their sympathies.

For what, though the mountains and skies be fair,
Steep'd in soft hues of the Summer-air,—
'Tis the soul of man, by its hopes and dreams,
That lights up all nature with living gleams.

Where it hath suffer'd and nobly striven,
Where it hath pour'd forth its vows to heaven;
Where to repose it hath brightly pass'd,
O'er this green earth there is glory cast.

And by that soul, 'midst groves and rills,
And flocks that feed on a thousand hills,
Birds of the forest, and flowers of the sod,
We, only we, may be linked to God!

KINDRED HEARTS.

Oh! ask not, hope thou not too much
    Of sympathy below;
Few are the hearts whence one same touch
    Bids the sweet fountains flow:
Few—and by still conflicting powers
    Forbidden here to meet—
Such ties would make this life of ours
    Too fair for aught so fleet.

It may be, that thy brother's eye
    Sees not as thine, which turns
In such deep reverence to the sky,
    Where the rich sunset burns:
It may be, that the breath of spring,
    Born amidst violets lone,
A rapture o'er thy soul can bring—
    A dream, to his unknown.

The tune that speaks of other times—
  A sorrowful delight!
The melody of distant chimes,
  The sound of waves by night,
The wind that, with so many a tone,
  Some chord within can thrill,—
These may have language all thine own
  To *him* a mystery still.

Yet scorn thou not, for this, the true
  And steadfast love of years;
The kindly, that from childhood grew,
  The faithful to thy tears!
If there be one that o'er the dead
  Hath in thy grief borne part,
And watch'd through sickness by thy bed,
  Call *his* a kindred heart!

But for those bonds all perfect made,
  Wherein bright spirit's blend,
Like sister flowers of one sweet shade
  With the same breeze that bend,
For that full bliss of thought allied,
  Never to mortals given,—
Oh! lay thy lovely dreams aside,
  Or lift them unto Heaven.

THE TRAVELLER AT THE SOURCE OF THE NILE.

In sunset's light, o'er Afric thrown,
  A wanderer proudly stood
Beside the well-spring, deep and lone
  Of Egypt's awful flood?
The cradle of that mighty birth,
So long a hidden thing to earth!

He heard its life's first murmuring sound
  A low mysterious tone;
A music sought, but never found
  By kings and warriors gone;
He listen'd—and his heart beat high—
That was the song of victory!

The rapture of a conqueror's mood
  Rush'd burning through his frame,—
The depths of that green solitude
  Its torrents could not tame;
Though stillness lay, with eve's last smile—
Round those far fountains of the Nile,

Night came with stars:—across his soul
  There swept a sudden change;

E'en at the pilgrim's glorious goal
   A shadow dark and strange
Breathed from the thought, so swift to fall
O'er triumph's hour—*and is this all?**

No more than this!—what seem'd it *now*
   First by that spring to stand?
A thousand streams of lovelier flow
   Bathed his own mountain land!
Whence, far o'er waste and ocean track,
Their wild, sweet voices call'd him back.

They call'd him back to many a glade,
   His childhood's haunt of play,
Where brightly through the beechen shade
   Their waters glanced away
They call'd him, with their sounding waves,
Back to his father's hills and graves.

But, darkly mingling with the thought
   Of each familiar scene,
Rose up a fearful vision, fraught
   With all that lay between;
The Arab's lance, the desert's gloom,
The whirling sands, the red simoom!

Where was the glow of power and pride?
   The spirit born to roam?
His alter'd heart within him died
   With yearnings for his home!
All vainly struggling to repress
That gush of painful tenderness.

He wept—the stars of Afric's heaven
   Behold his bursting tears,
E'en on that spot where fate had given
   The meed of toiling years!—
Oh, happiness! how far we flee
Thine own sweet paths in search of thee!

---

* A remarkable description of feelings thus fluctuating from triumph to despondency, is given in Bruce's Abyssinian Travels. The buoyant exultation of his spirits on arriving at the source of the Nile, was almost immediately succeeded by a gloom, which he thus portrays:—" I was, at that very moment, in possession of what had for many years been the principal object of my ambition and wishes; indifference, which, from the usual infirmity of human nature, follows, at least for a time, complete enjoyment, had taken place of it. The marsh and the fountains of the Nile, upon comparison with the rise of many of our rivers, became now a trifling object in my sight. I remembered that magnificent scene in my own native country, where the Tweed, Clyde, and Annan, rise in one hill. I began, in my sorrow, to treat the enquiry about the source of the Nile as a violent effort of a distempered fancy."

CASABIANCA.*

The boy stood on the burning deck
  Whence all but he had fled ;
The flame that lit the battle's wreck,
  Shone round him o'er the dead.

Yet beautiful and bright he stood,
  As born to rule the storm ;
A creature of heroic blood,
  A proud, though child-like form.

The flames roll'd on—he would not go
  Without his Father's word ;
That Father, faint in death below,
  His voice no longer heard.

He call'd aloud :—" Say, Father say,
  If yet my task is done ?"
He knew not that the chieftain lay
  Unconscious of his son.

"Speak, Father!" once again he cried,
  " If I may yet be gone!"
And but the booming shots replied.
  And fast the flames roll'd on.

Upon his brow he felt their breath.
  And in his waving hair,
And look'd from that lone post of death,
  In still, yet brave despair.

And shouted but once more aloud,
  " My Father! must I stay ?"
While o'er him fast, through sail and shroud,
  The wreathing fires made way.

They wrapt the ship in splendor wild,
  They caught the flag on high,
And stream'd above the gallant child,
  Like banners in the sky.

There came a burst of thunder sound—
  The boy—oh ! where was he ?
Ask of the winds that far around
  With fragments strew'd the sea !—

With mast, and helm, and pennon fair,
  That well had borne their part—
But the noblest thing which perish'd there
  Was that young faithful heart !

---

* Young Casabianca, a boy about thirteen years old, son to the Admiral of the Orient, remained at his post, (in the Battle of the Nile,) after the ship had taken fire and all the guns had been abandoned; and perished in the explosion of the vessel, when the flames had reached the powder.

THE DIAL OF FLOWERS.*

'Twas a lovely thought to mark the hours,
    As they floated in light away,
By the opening and the folding flowers,
    That laugh to the summer's day.

Thus had each moment its own rich hue,
    And its graceful cup and bell,
In whose color'd vase might sleep the dew,
    Like a pearl in an ocean-shell.

To such sweet signs might the time have flow'd
    In a golden current on,
Ere from the garden, man's first abode,
    The glorious guests were gone.

So might the days have been brightly told—
    Those days of song and dreams—
When shepherds gather'd their flocks of old
    By the blue Arcadian streams.

So in those isles of delight, that rest
    Far off in a breezeless main,
Which many a bark with a weary quest,
    Has sought, but still in vain.

Yet is not life, in its real flight,
    Mark'd thus—even thus—on earth,
By the closing of one hope's delight,
    And another's gentle birth?

Oh! let us live, so that flower by flower,
    Shutting in turn may leave
A lingerer still for the sunset hour,
    A charm for the shaded eve.

OUR DAILY PATHS.†

> "Nought shall prevail against us, or disturb
> Our cheerful faith that all which we behold
> Is full of blessings."   *Wordsworth*

There's beauty all around our paths, if but our watchful eyes,
Can trace it 'midst familiar things, and through their lowly guise;

---

* This dial was, I believe, formed by Linnæus, and marked the hours by the opening and closing, at regular intervals, of the flowers arranged in it.

† This little poem derives an additional interest, from being affectingly associated with a name no less distinguished than that of the late Mr. Dugald Stewart. The admiration he always expressed for

We may find it where a hedge-row showers its blossoms o'er
    our way,
Or a cottage window sparkles forth in the last red light of day.

We may find it where a spring shines clear beneath an aged
    tree,   [by the bee;
With the foxglove o'er the water's glass, borne downwards
Or where a swift and sunny gleam on the birchen stem is thrown,
As a soft wind playing parts the leaves, in copses green and lone.

We may find it in the winter boughs, as they cross the cold,
    blue sky,
While soft on icy pool and stream their pencil'd shadows lie,
When we look upon their tracery, by the fairy frostwork bound,
Whence the flitting redbreast shakes a shower of crystals to
    the ground.

Yes! beauty dwells in all our paths—but sorrow too is there;
How oft some cloud within us dims the bright, still summer air!
When we carry our sick hearts abroad amidst the joyous things,
That through the leafy places glance on many-color'd wings,

With shadows from the past we fill the happy woodland shades,
And a mournful memory of the dead is with us in the glades:
And our dream-like fancies lend the wind an echo's plaintive
Of voices, and of melodies, and of silvery laughter gone. [tone

But are we free to do even thus—to wander as we will—
Bearing sad visions through the grove, and o'er the breezy hill?

Mrs. Hemans's poetry, was mingled with regret that she so generally made choice of melancholy subjects; and on one occasion, he sent her, through a mutual friend, a message suggestive of his wish that she would employ her fine talents in giving more consolatory views of the ways of Providence, thus infusing comfort and cheer into the bosoms of her readers, in a spirit of Christian philosophy, which, he thought, would be more consonant with the pious mind and loving heart displayed in every line she wrote, than dwelling on what was painful and depressing, however beautifully and touchingly such subjects might be treated of. This message was faithfully transmitted, and almost by return of post, Mrs. Hemans (who was then residing in Wales,) sent to the kind friend to whom it had been forwarded, the poem of "Our Daily Paths," requesting it might be given to Mr. Stewart, with an assurance of her gratitude for the interest he took in her writings, and alleging as the reason of the mournful strain which pervaded them, "that a cloud hung over her life which she could not always rise above."

The letter reached Mr. Stewart just as he was stepping into the carriage, to leave his country residence (Kinneil House, the property of the Duke of Hamilton) for Edinburgh—the last time, alas! his presence was ever to gladden that happy home, as his valuable life was closed very shortly afterward. The poem was read to him by his daughter on his way to Edinburgh, and he expressed himself in the highest degree charmed and gratified with the result of his suggestions; and some of the lines which pleased him more particularly were often repeated to him during the few remaining weeks of his life.

No! in our daily paths lie cares, that ofttimes bind us fast,
While from their narrow round we see the golden day fleet past.
They hold us from the woodlark's haunts, and violet dingles,
    back, [track;
And from all the lovely sounds and gleams in the shining river's
They bar us from our heritage of spring-time, hope, and mirth,
And weigh our burden'd spirits down with the cumbering dust
    of earth.

Yet should this be ?—Too much, too soon despondingly we
A better lesson we are taught by the lilies of the field ! [yield !
A sweeter by the birds of heaven—which tell us in their flight,
Of One that through the desert air for ever guides them right.

Shall not this knowledge calm our hearts, and bid vain con-
    flicts cease? [peace ;
Ay, when they commune with themselves in holy hours of
And feel that by the lights and clouds through which our path-
    way lies,
By the beauty and the grief alike we are training for the skies;

THE CROSS IN THE WILDERNESS.

SILENT and mournful sat an Indian chief,
    In the red sunset, by a grassy tomb :
His eyes, that might not weep, were dark with grief,
    And his arms folded in majestic gloom ;
And his bow lay unstrung, beneath the mound
Which sanctified the gorgeous waste around.

For a pale cross above its greensward rose,
    Telling the cedars and the pines that there
Man's heart and hope had struggled with his woes,
    And lifted from the dust a voice of prayer.
Now all was hush'd—and eve's last splendor shone
With a rich sadness on th' attesting stone.

There came a lonely traveller o'er the wild,
    And he, too, paused in reverence by that grave,
Asking the tale of its memorial, piled
    Between the forest and the lake's bright wave ;
Till, as a wind might stir a wither'd oak,
On the deep dream of age his accents broke.

And the grey chieftain, slowly rising, said—
    " I listen'd for the words, which, years ago,
Pass'd o'er these waters : though the voice is fled
    Which made them as a singing fountain's flow,
Yet, when I sit in their long-faded track,
Sometimes the forest's murmur gives them back.

" Ask'st thou of him whose house is lone beneath?
    I was an eagle in my youthful pride,

When o'er the seas he came with summer's breath,
  To dwell amidst us, on the lake's green side.
Many the times of flowers have been since then—
  Many, but bringing nought like *him* again!

" Not with the hunter's bow and spear he came,
  O'er the blue hills to chase the flying roe ;
Not the dark glory of the woods to tame,
  Laying their cedars, like the corn-stalks, low ;
But to spread tidings of all holy things,
Gladd'ning our souls, as with the morning's wings.

" Doth not yon cypress whisper how we met,
  I and my brethren that from earth are gone,
Under its boughs to hear his voice, which yet
  Seems through their gloom to send a silvery tone ?
He told of one, the grave's dark bands who broke,
And our hearts burn'd within us as he spoke.

" He told of far and sunny lands, which lie
  Beyond the dust wherein our fathers dwell :
Bright must they be !—for *there* are none that die,
  And none that weep, and none that say ' Farewell .
He came to guide us thither ; but away
The Happy call'd him, and he might not stay.

" We saw him slowly fade—athirst, perchance,
  For the fresh waters of that lovely clime ;
Yet was there still a sunbeam in his glance,
  And on his gleaming hair no touch of time—
Therefore we hoped :—but now the lake looks dim,
For the green summer comes—and finds not him !

" We gather'd round him in the dewy hour
  Of one still morn, beneath his chosen tree ;
From his clear voice, at first the words of power
  Came low, like moanings of a distant sea ;
But swell'd and shook the wilderness ere long,
As if the spirit of the breeze grew strong.

" And then once more they trembled on his tongue,
  And his white eyelids flutter'd, and his head
Fell back, and mist upon his forehead hung—
  Know'st thou not how we pass to join the dead ?
It is enough !—he sank upon my breast—
Our friend that loved us, he was gone to rest !

" We buried him where he was wont to pray,
  By the calm lake, e'en here, at eventide ;
We rear'd this Cross in token where he lay,
  For on the Cross, he said, his Lord had died !
Now hath he surely reach'd, o'er mount and wave,
That flowery land whose green turf hides no grave.

" But I am sad !—I mourn the clear light taken
  Back from my people, o'er whose place it shone,

The pathway to the better shore forsaken,
  And the true words forgotten, save by one,
Who hears them faintly sounding from the past,
Mingled with death-songs in each fitful blast."

Then spoke the wand'rer forth with kindling eye:
  "Son of the wilderness! despair thou not,
Though the bright hour may seem to thee gone by,
  And the cloud settled o'er thy nation's lot!
Heaven darkly works—yet, where the seed hath been
There shall the fruitage, glowing yet, be seen.

" Hope on, hope ever!—by the sudden springing
  Of green leaves which the winter hid so long;
And by the bursts of free, triumphant singing,
  After cold silent months, the woods among;
And by the rending of the frozen chains,
Which bound the glorious rivers on their plains!

" Deem not the words of light that here were spoken,
  But as a lovely song, to leave no trace:
Yet shall the gloom which wraps thy hills be broken,
  And the full dayspring rise upon thy race!
And fading mists the better path disclose,
And the wide desert blossom as the rose."

So by the Cross they parted, in the wild,
  Each fraught with musings for life's after-day,
Memories to visit *one*, the forest's child,
  By many a blue stream in its lonely way;
And upon *one*, 'midst busy throngs to press
Deep thoughts and sad, yet full of holiness.

LAST RITES.

By the mighty minster's bell,
Tolling with a sudden swell;
By the colors half-mast high,
O'er the sea hung mounfully;
  Know, a prince hath died!

By the drum's dull muffled sound,
By the arms that sweep the ground,
By the volleying muskets' tone,
Speak ye of a soldier gone
  In his manhood's pride.

By the chanted psalm that fills
Reverently the ancient hills,*

*A custom still retained at rural funerals in some parts of England and Wales

Learn, that from his harvests done,
Peasants bear a brother on
    To his last repose.

By the pall of snowy white
Through the yew-trees gleaming bright;
By the garland on the bier,
Weep! a maiden claims thy tear—
    Broken is the rose!

Which is the tenderest rite of all?—
Buried virgin's coronal,
Requiem o'er the monarch's head,
Farewell gun for warrior dead,
    Herdsman's funeral hymn?

Tells not each of human woe!
Each of hope and strength brought low?
    Number each with holy things,
If one chastening thought it brings
    Ere life's day grow dim!

THE HEBREW MOTHER.

The rose was in rich bloom on Sharon's plain,
When a young mother, with her first-born, thence
Went up to Zion; for the boy was vow'd
Unto the Temple service:—by the hand
She led him, and her silent soul, the while,
Oft as the dewy laughter of his eye
Met her sweet serious glance, rejoiced to think
That aught so pure, so beautiful, was hers,
To bring before her God. So pass'd they on
O'er Judah's hills; and wheresoe'er the leaves
Of the broad sycamore made sounds at noon,
Like lulling rain-drops, or the olive boughs,
With their cool dimness, cross'd the sultry blue
Of Syria's heaven, she paused, that he might rest:
Yet from her own meek eyelids chased the sleep
That weigh'd their dark fringe down, to sit and watch
The crimson deepening o'er his cheek's repose,
As at a red flower's heart. And where a fount
Lay, like a twilight star, 'midst palmy shades,
Making its bank green gems along the wild,
There, too, she linger'd, from the diamond wave
Drawing bright water for his rosy lips,
And softly parting clusters of jet curls
To bathe his brow. At last the fane was reach'd,
The earth's one sanctuary—and rapture hush'd
Her bosom, as before her, through the day,
It rose, a mountain of white marble, steep'd

THE HEBREW MOTHER.

In light like floating gold. But when that hour
Waned to the farewell moment, when the boy
Lifted, through rainbow-gleaming tears, his eye
Beseechingly to hers, and half in fear
Turn'd from the white-robed priest, and round her arm
Clung even as joy clings—the deep spring-tide
Of nature then swell'd high, and o'er her child
Bending, her soul broke forth, in mingled sounds
Of weeping and sad song.—" Alas!" she cried,—

" Alas! my boy, thy gentle grasp is on me;
The bright tears quiver in thy pleading eyes;
    And now fond thoughts arise,
And silver cords again to earth have won me;
And like a vine thou claspest my full heart—
    How shall I hence depart?

" How the lone paths retrace where thou wert playing
So late, along the mountains, at my side?
    And I, in joyous pride,
By every place of flowers my course delaying,
Wove, e'en as pearls, the lilies round thy hair,
    Beholding thee so fair!

" And, oh! the home whence thy bright smile hath parted,
Will it not seem as if the sunny day
    Turn'd from its door away?
While through its chambers wandering, weary-hearted,
I languish for thy voice, which past me still
    Went like a singing rill?

" Under the palm-trees thou no more shalt meet me,
When from the fount at evening I return,
    With the full water-urn;
Nor will thy sleep's low dove-like breathing greet me,
As 'midst the silence of the stars I wake,
    And watch for thy dear sake.

" And thou, will slumber's dewy cloud fall round thee,
Without thy mother's hand to smooth thy bed?
    Wilt thou not vainly spread
Thine arms, when darkness as a veil hath wound thee,
To fold my neck, and lift up, in thy fear,
    A cry which none shall hear?

" What have I said, my child!—Will *He* not hear thee,
Who the young ravens heareth from their nest?
    Shall He not guard thy rest,
And, in the hush of holy midnight hear thee,
Breathe o'er thy soul, and fill its dreams with joy?
    Thou shalt sleep soft, my boy.

" I give thee to thy God—the God that gave thee,
A well-spring of deep gladness to my heart!
    And, precious as thou art,
And pure as dew of Hermon, He shall have thee,

My own, my beautiful, my undefiled!
    And thou shalt be His child.
" Therefore, farewell!—I go, my soul may fail me,
As the heart panteth for the water brooks,
    Yearning for thy sweet looks.
But thou, my first-born, droop not, nor bewail me;
Thou in the Shadow of the Rock shalt dwell,
    The Rock of Strength.—Farewell!"

THE WRECK.

ALL night the booming minute-gun
    Had peal'd along the deep,
And mournfully the rising sun
    Look'd o'er the tide-worn steep.
A barque from India's coral strand,
    Before the raging blast,
Had veil'd her topsails to the sand,
    And bow'd her noble mast.

The queenly ship!—brave hearts had striven
    And true ones died with her!—
We saw her mighty cable riven,
    Like floating gossamer.
We saw her proud flag struck that morn,
    A star once o'er the seas—
Her anchor gone, her deck uptorn—
    And sadder things than these!

We saw her treasures cast away,—
    The rocks with pearls were sown,
And strangely sad, the ruby's ray
    Flash'd out o'er fretted stone.
And gold was strewn the wet sands o'er,
    Like ashes by a breeze;
And gorgeous robes—but oh! that shore
    Had sadder things than these!

We saw the strong man still and low,
    A crush'd reed thrown aside;
Yet, by that rigid lip and brow,
    Not without strife he died.
And near him on the sea-weed lay—
    Till then we had not wept—
But well our gushing hearts might say,
    That there a *mother* slept!

For her pale arms a babe had press'd
    With such a wreathing grasp,
Billows had dash'd o'er that fond breast,
    Yet not undone the clasp.

Her very tresses had been flung
  To wrap the fair child's form,
Where still their wet long streamers hung
  All tangled by the storm.

And beautiful, 'midst that wild scene,
  Gleam'd up the boy's dead face,
Like slumber's, trustingly serene,
  In melancholy grace.
Deep in her bosom lay his head,
  With half-shut violet-eye—
He had known little of her dread,
  Nought of her agony!

Oh! human love, whose yearning heart
  Through all things vainly true,
So stamps upon thy mortal part
  Its passionate adieu—
Surely thou hast another lot;
  There is some home for thee,
Where thou shalt rest, rememb'ring not
  The moaning of the sea!

THE TRUMPET.

THE trumpet's voice hath roused the land—
  Light up the beacon-pyre!—
A hundred hills have seen the brand,
  And waved the sign of fire.
A hundred banners to the breeze,
  Their gorgeous folds have cast—
And, hark! was that the sound of seas?
  A king to war went past.

The chief is arming in his hall,
  The peasant by his hearth;
The mourner hears the thrilling call,
  And rises from the earth.
The mother on her first-born son,
  Looks with a boding eye—
They come not back, though all be won,
  Whose young hearts leap so high.

The bard hath ceased his song, and bound
  The falchion to his side;
E'en for the marriage altar crown'd,
  The lover quits his bride.
And all this haste, and change, and fear,
  By *earthly* clarion spread!—
How will it be when kingdoms hear
  The blast that wakes the dead?

EVENING PRAYER,

AT A GIRLS' SCHOOL.

> "Now in thy youth, beseech of Him
> Who giveth, upbraiding not;
> That his light in thy heart become not dim,
> And his love be unforgot;
> And thy God, in the darkest of days, will be,
> Greenness, and beauty, and strength to thee."—*Bernard Barton*

Hush! 'tis a holy hour—the quiet room
  Seems like a temple, while yon soft lamp sheds
A faint and starry radiance, through the gloom
  And the sweet stillness, down on fair young heads,
With all their clust'ring locks, untouch'd by care,
And bow'd, as flowers are bow'd with night, in prayer.

Gaze on—'tis lovely!—Childhood's lip and cheek,
  Mantling beneath its earnest brow of thought—
Gaze—yet what seest thou in those fair, and meek,
  And fragile things, as but for sunshine wrought?—
Thou seest what grief must nurture for the sky,
What death must fashion for eternity!

O! joyous creatures! that will sink to rest,
  Lightly, when those pure orisons are done,
As birds with slumber's honey-dew opprest,
  'Midst the dim folded leaves, at set of sun—
Lift up your hearts! though yet no sorrow lies
Dark in the summer-heaven of those clear eyes.

Though fresh within your breasts th' untroubled springs
  Of hope make melody where'er ye tread,
And o'er your sleep bright shadows, from the wings
  Of spirits visiting but youth, be spread;
Yet in those flute-like voices, mingling low,
Is woman's tenderness—how soon her woe!

Her lot is on you—silent tears to weep,
  And patient smiles to wear through suffering's hour,
And sumless riches, from affection's deep,
  To pour on broken reeds—a wasted shower!
And to make idols, and to find them clay,
And to bewail that worship—therefore pray!

Her lot is on you—to be found untired,
  Watching the stars out by the bed of pain,
With a pale cheek, and yet a brow inspired,
  And a true heart of hope, though hope be vain;
Meekly to bear with wrong, to cheer decay,
And, oh! to love through all things—therefore pray!

And take the thought of this calm vesper time,
  With its low murmuring sounds and silvery light,

On through the dark days fading from their prime,
　As a sweet dew to keep your souls from blight!
Earth will forsake—O! happy to have given
Th' unbroken heart's first fragrance unto Heaven.

THE HOUR OF DEATH.

"Il est dans la Nature d'aimer à se livrer à l'idée même qu'on redoute." *Corinne*

　　Leaves have their time to fall,
And flowers to wither at the north-wind's breath,
　　And stars to set—but all,
Thou hast *all* seasons for thine own, O Death!

　　Day is for mortal care,
Eve, for glad meetings round the joyous hearth,
　　Night, for the dreams of sleep, the voice of prayer—
But all for thee, thou mightiest of the earth.

　　The banquet hath its hour,
Its feverish hour, of mirth, and song, and wine;
　　There comes a day for grief's o'erwhelming power,
A time for softer tears—but all are thine.

　　Youth and the opening rose
May look like things too glorious for decay,
　　And smile at thee—but thou art not of those
That wait the ripen'd bloom to seize their prey.

　　Leaves have their time to fall,
And flowers to wither at the north-wind's breath,
　　And stars to set—but all,
Thou hast *all* seasons for thine own, O Death!

　　We know when moons shall wane,
When Summer-birds from far shall cross the sea,
　　When autumn's hue shall tinge the golden grain—
But who shall teach us when to look for thee!

　　Is it when Spring's first gale
Comes forth to whisper where the violets lie?
　　Is it when roses in our paths grow pale?—
They have *one* season—*all* are ours to die!

　　Thou art where billows foam,
Thou art where music melts upon the air;
　　Thou art around us in our peaceful home,
And the world calls us forth—and thou art there.

　　Thou art where friend meets friend,
Beneath the shadow of the elm to rest—
　　Thou art where foe meets foe, and trumpets rend
The skies, and swords beat down the princely crest.

Leaves have their time to fall,
And flowers to wither at the north-wind's breath,
And stars to set—but all,
Thou hast all seasons for thine own, O Death!

THE LOST PLEIAD.

"Like the lost Pleiad seen no more below."—*Byron.*

AND is there glory from the heavens departed?—
O void unmark'd!—thy sisters of the sky
Still hold their place on high
Though from its rank thine orb so long hath started,
Thou, that no more art seen of mortal eye;

Hath the night lost a gem, the regal night?
She wears her crown of old magnificence,
Though thou art exiled thence—
No desert seems to part those urns of light,
'Midst the far depths of purple gloom intense.

They rise in joy, the starry myriads burning—
The shepherd greets them on his mountains free;
And from the silvery sea
To them the sailor's wakeful eye is turning—
Unchanged they rise, they have not mourn'd for thee.

Couldst thou be shaken from thy radiant place,
Even as a dew-drop from the myrtle spray,
Swept by the wind away?
Wert thou not peopled by some glorious race,
And was there power to smite them with decay?

Why, who shall talk of thrones, of sceptres riven?—
Bow'd be our hearts to think on what *we* are,
When from its height afar
A world sinks thus—and yon majestic heaven
Shines not the less for that one vanish'd star!

THE CLIFFS OF DOVER.

"The inviolate Island of the sage and free."—*Byron*

ROCKS of my country! let the cloud
Your crested heights array,
And rise ye like a fortress proud,
Above the surge and spray!

My spirit greets you as ye stand,
Breasting the billow's foam:
O! thus forever guard the land,
The sever'd land of home!

I have left rich blue skies behind,
  Lighting up classic shrines ;
And music in the southern wind ;
  And sunshine on the vines.

The breathings of the myrtle flowers
  Have floated o'er my way ;
The pilgrim's voice, at vesper-hours,
  Hath soothed me with its lay.

The isles of Greece, the hills of Spain,
  The purple heavens of Rome,—
Yes, all are glorious ;—yet again
  I bless thee, land of home!

For thine the Sabbath peace, my land!
  And thine the guarded hearth ;
And thine the dead, the noble band,
  That make thee holy earth.

Their voices meet me in thy breeze ;
  Their steps are on thy plains ;
Their names, by old majestic trees,
  Are whisper'd round thy fanes.

Their blood hath mingled with the tide
  Of thine exulting sea :
O be it still a joy, a pride,
  To live and die for thee!

THE GRAVES OF MARTYRS.

The kings of old have shrine and tomb
In many a minster's haughty gloom ;
And green, along the ocean side,
The mounds arise where heroes died ;
But show me, on thy flowery breast,
Earth! where thy *nameless* martyrs rest!

The thousands that, uncheer'd by praise,
Have made one offering of their days ;
For Truth, for Heaven, for Freedom's sake,
Resign'd the bitter cup to take ;
And silently, in fearless faith,
Bowing their noble souls to death.

Where sleep they, Earth?—by no proud stone
Their narrow couch of rest is known ;
The still sad glory of their name
Hallows no mountain unto Fame ;
No—not a tree the record bears
Of their deep thoughts and lonely prayers.

Yet happy all around lie strew'd
The ashes of that multitude ;

It may be that each day we tread,
Where thus devoted hearts have bled ;
And the young flowers our children sow,
Take root in holy dust below.

O that the many-rustling leaves,
Which round our homes the summer weaves,
Or that the streams, in whose glad voice
Our own familiar paths rejoice,
Might whisper through the starry sky,
To tell where those blest slumberers lie !

Would not our inmost hearts be still'd,
With knowledge of their presence fill'd,
And by its breathings taught to prize
The meekness of self-sacrifice ?
—But the old woods and sounding waves
Are silent of those hidden graves.

Yet what if no light footstep there
In pilgrim-love and awe repair,
So let it be be !—like him whose clay
Deep buried by his Maker lay,
They sleep in secret, but their sod,
Unknown to man, is mark'd of God !

THE HOUR OF PRAYER.

" Pregar, pregar, pregar,
Ch' altro ponno i mortali al pianger nati ?"
Alfieri

CHILD, amidst the flowers at play,
While the red light fades away ;
Mother with thine earnest eye,
Ever following silently ;
Father, by the breeze of eve
Call'd thy harvest work to leave
Pray : ere yet the dark hours be,
Lift the heart and bend the knee !

Traveller, in the stranger's land,
Far from thine own household band ;
Mourner, haunted by the tone
Of a voice from this world gone ;
Captive, in whose narrow cell
Sunshine hath not leave to dwell ;
Sailor on the darkening sea—
Lift the heart and bend the knee !

Warrior, that from battle won
Breathest now at set of sun ;
Woman, o'er the lowly slain
Weeping on his burial-plain ;

Ye that triumph, ye that sigh,
Kindred by one holy tie,
Heaven's first star alike ye see—
Lift the heart and bend the knee!

THE VOICE OF HOME TO THE PRODIGAL.

" Von Baumen, aus Wellen, aus Mauern,
Wie ruft es dir freundlich und lind ;
Was hast du zu wandern, zu trauern ?
Komm' spielen, du freundliches Kind !"
La Motte Fouqué.

O! WHEN wilt thou return
 To thy spirit's early loves?
To the freshness of the morn,
 To the stillness of the groves?

The Summer-birds are calling
 Thy household porch around,
And the merry waters falling
 With sweet laughter in their sound.

And a thousand bright-vein'd flowers,
 From their banks of moss and fern,
Breathe of the sunny hours—
 But when wilt thou return ?

Oh! thou hast wander'd long
 From thy home without a guide ;
And thy native woodland song,
 In thine alter'd heart hath died.

Thou hast flung the wealth away,
 And the glory of thy Spring ;
And to thee the leaves' light play
 Is a long-forgotten thing.

But when wilt thou return ?—
 Sweet dews may freshen soon
The flower, within whose urn
 Too fiercely gazed the noon.

O'er the image of the sky,
 Which the lake's clear bosom wore,
Darkly may shadows lie—
 But not for evermore.

Give back thy heart again
 To the freedom of the woods,
To the birds' triumphant strain,
 To the mountain solitudes !

But when wilt thou return ?
 Along thine own pure air,

There are young sweet voices borne—
  Oh! should not thine be there?

Still at thy father's board
  There is kept a place for thee;
And, by thy smile restored,
  Joy round the hearth shall be.

Still hath thy mother's eye,
  Thy coming step to greet,
A look of days gone by,
  Tender and gravely sweet.

Still, when the prayer is said,
  For thee kind bosoms yearn,
For thee kind tears are shed—
  Oh! when wilt thou return!

THE WAKENING.

How many thousands are wakening now!
Some to the songs from the forest bough,
To the rustling of leaves at the lattice-pane,
To the chiming fall of the early rain.

And some far out on the deep mid-sea,
To the dash of the waves in their foaming glee,
As they break into spray on the ship's tall side,
That holds through the tumult her path of pride.

And some—O! well may *their* hearts rejoice—
To the gentle sound of a mother's voice!
Long shall they yearn for that kindly tone,
When from the board and the hearth 'tis gone.

And some in the camp, to the bugle's breath,
And the tramp of the steed on the echoing heath,
And the sudden roar of the hostile gun,
Which tells that a field must ere night be won.

And some, in the gloomy convict-cell,
To the dull deep note of the warning-bell,
As it heavily calls them forth to die,
When the bright sun mounts in the laughing sky.

And some to the peal of the hunter's horn,
And some to the din from the city borne,
And some to the rolling of torrent-floods,
Far 'midst old mountains and solemn woods.

So are we roused on this chequered earth:
Each unto light hath a daily birth;
Though fearful or joyous, though sad or sweet,
Are the voices which first our unspringing meet.

But *one* must the sound be, and *one* the call,
Which from the dust shall awaken us all:
One!—but to sever'd and distant dooms.
How shall the sleepers arise from the tombs?

THE BREEZE FROM SHORE.

["Poetry reveals to us the loveliness of nature, brings back the freshness of youthful feeling, revives the relish of simple pleasures, keeps unqenched the enthusiasm which warmed the spring-time of our being, refines youthful love, strengthens our interest in human nature, by vivid delineations of its tenderest and loftiest feelings; and through the brightness of its prophetic visions, helps faith to lay hold on the future life."] *Channing.*

Joy is upon the lonely seas,
 When Indian forests pour
Forth, to the billow and the breeze,
 Their odors from the shore;
Joy, when the soft air's fanning sigh
Bears on the breath of Araby.

Oh! welcome are the winds that tell
 A wand'rer of the deep,
Where, far away, the jasmines dwell,
 And where the myrrh-trees weep!
Blest, on the sounding surge and foam,
Are tidings of the citron's home!

The sailor at the helm they meet,
 And hope his bosom stirs,
Upspringing, 'midst the waves, to greet
 The fair earth's messengers.
That woo him, from the moaning main,
Back to her glorious bowers again.

They woo him, whispering lovely tales
 Of many a flowering glade,
And fount's bright gleam, in island vales
 Of golden-fruited shade:
Across his lone ship's wake they bring
A vision and a glow of Spring.

And O! ye masters of the lay,
 Come not even thus your songs
That meet us on life's weary way,
 Amidst her toiling throngs?
Yes! o'er the spirit thus they bear
A current of celestial air.

Their power is from the brighter clime
 Than in our birth hath part;

Their tones are of the world, which time
    Sears not within the heart:
They tell us of the living light
    In its green places ever bright.

They call us, with a voice divine,
    Back to our early love,—
Our vows of youth at many a shrine,
    Whence far and fast we rove.
Welcome high thought and holy strain
That makes us Truth's and Heaven's again!

THE DYING IMPROVISATORE.*

"My heart shall be pour'd over thee—and break."
Prophecy of Dante

    The spirit of my land,
It visits me once more!—though I must die
Far from the myrtles which thy breeze hath fann'd,
    My own bright Italy!

    It is, it is thy breath,
Which stirs my soul e'en yet, as wavering flame
Is shaken by the wind;—in life and death
    Still trembling, yet the same!

    Oh! that love's quenchless power
Might waft my voice to fill thy summer sky,
And through thy groves its dying music shower
    Italy! Italy!

    The nightingale is there,
The sunbeam's glow, the citron-flower's perfume,
The south-wind's whisper in the scented air—
    It will not pierce the tomb!

    Never, oh! never more,
On my Rome's purple heaven mine eye shall dwell,
Or watch the bright waves melt along thy shore—
    My Italy! farewell!

    Alas!—thy hills among,
Had I but left a memory of my name,
Of love and grief one deep, true, fervent song,
    Unto immortal fame!

    But like a lute's brief tone,
Like a rose-odor on the breezes cast,
Like a swift flush of dayspring, seen and gone,
    So hath my spirit pass'd—

---

* Sestini, the Roman Improvisatore, when on his death-bed at Paris, is said to have poured forth a Farewell to Italy, in his most impassioned poetry

  Pouring itself away
As a wild bird amidst the foliage turns
That which within him triumphs, beats, or burns
  Into a fleeting lay;

  That swells, and floats, and dies,
Leaving no echo to the summer woods
Of the rich breathings and impassion'd sighs,
  Which thrill'd their solitudes.

  Yet, yet remember me!
Friends! that upon its murmurs oft have hung,
When from my bosom, joyously and free,
  The fiery fountain sprung.

  Under the dark rich blue
Of midnight heavens, and on the star-lit sea,
And when woods kindle into Spring's first hue,
  Sweet friends! remember me!

  And in the marble halls,
Where life's full glow the dreams of beauty wear,
And poet-thoughts embodied light the walls,
  Let me be with you there!

  Fain would I bind, for you,
My memory with all glorious things to dwell;
Fain bid all lovely sounds my name renew—
  Sweet friends! bright land! farewell!

MUSIC OF YESTERDAY.

"O! mein Geist, ich fühle es in mir, strebt nach etwas Ueberir
dischem, das keinem Menschen gegonnt ist."—*Tieck.*

The chord, the harp's full chord is hush'd
  The voice hath died away,
Whence music, like sweet waters, gush'd,
  But yesterday.

Th' awakening note, the breeze-like swell,
  The full o'ersweeping tone,
The sounds that sigh'd "Farewell, farewell!"
  Are gone—all gone!

The love, whose fervent spirit pass'd
  With the rich measure's flow;
The grief, to which it sank at last—
  Where are they now?

They are with the scents, by Summer's breath
  Borne from a rose now shed:
With the words from lips long seal'd in death—
  For ever fled.

The sea-shell, of its native deep
    A moaning thrill retains;
But earth and air no record keep
    Of parted strains.

And all the memories, all the dreams,
    They woke in floating by;
The tender thoughts, th' Elysian gleams—
    Could these too die?

They died—as on the water's breast
    The ripple melts away,
When the breeze that stirr'd it sinks to rest—
    So perish'd they!

Mysterious in their sudden birth,
    And mournful in their close,
Passing, and finding not on earth
    Aim or repose.

Whence were they?—like the breath of flowers
    Why thus to come and go?
A long, long journey must be ours
    Ere this we know!

THE FORSAKEN HEARTH.

" Was mir fehlt?—Mir fehlt ja alles,
Bin so ganz verlassen hier!"   *Tyrolese Melody.*

The Hearth, the Hearth is desolate, the fire is quench'd and
    gone
That into happy children's eyes once brightly laughing shone;
The place where mirth and music met is hush'd through day
    and night.
Oh! for one kind, one sunny face, of all that there made light

But scatter'd are those pleasant smiles afar by mount and shore,
Like gleaming waters from one spring dispersed to meet no
    more.
Those kindred eyes reflect not now each other's joy or mirth,
Unbound is that sweet wreath of home—alas! the lonely
    Hearth!

The voices that have mingled here now speak another tongue,
Or breathe, perchance, to alien ears the songs their mother
    sung.   [hold tone,—
Sad, strangely sad, in stranger lands, must sound each house-
The Hearth, the Hearth, is desolate, the bright fire quench'd
    and gone.

But *are* they speaking, singing yet, as in their days of glee?
Those voices, are they lovely still, still sweet on earth or sea?—
Oh! some are hush'd, and some are changed, and never shall
　　one strain
Blend their fraternal cadences triumphantly again!

And of the hearts that here were link'd by long-remember'd
　　years,
Alas! the brother knows not now when fall the sister's tears!
One haply revels at the feast, while one may droop alone,
For broken is the household chain, the bright fire quench'd
　　and gone!

Not so—'tis *not* a broken chain—thy memory binds them still,
Thou holy Hearth of other days, though silent now and chill!
The smiles, the tears, the rites beheld by thine attesting stone,
Have yet a living power to mark thy children for thine own.

The father's voice, the mother's prayer, though called from
　　earth away,
With music rising from the dead, their spirits yet shall sway;
And by the past, and by the grave, the parted yet are one,
Though the loved hearth be desolate, the bright fire quench'd
　　and gone!

THE DREAMER.

"There is no such thing as *forgetting* possible to the mind; a thousand accidents may, and will, interpose a veil between our present consciousness and the secret inscription on the mind; but alike, whether veiled or unveiled, the inscription remains forever."
　　　　　　　　　　　　　　　　English Opium-Eater.

"Thou hast been call'd, O Sleep! the friend of woe,
But 'tis the *happy* who have call'd thee so." *Southey.*

PEACE to thy dreams!—thou art slumbering now,
The moonlight's calm is upon thy brow;
All the deep love that o'erflows thy breast
Lies 'midst the hush of thy heart at rest,
Like the scent of a flower in its folded bell,
When eve through the woodlands hath sigh'd farewell.

Peace!—the sad memories that through the day
With a weight on thy lonely bosom lay,
The sudden thoughts of the changed and dead,
That bow'd thee as winds bow the willow's head,
The yearnings for faces and voices gone—
All are forgotten!—sleep on, sleep on!

Are they forgotten?—It is not so!
Slumber divides not the heart from its woe.
E'en now o'er thine aspect swift changes pass,
Like lights and shades over wavy grass.

Tremblest thou, Dreamer?—O love and grief!
Ye have storms that shake e'en the closed-up leaf.

On thy parted lips there's a quivering thrill,
As on a lyre ere its chords are still;
On the long silk lashes that fringe thine eye,
There's a large tear gathering heavily;
A rain from the clouds of thy spirit press'd—
Sorrowful dreamer! this is not rest!

It is Thought at work amidst buried hours—
It is Love keeping vigil o'er perish'd flowers.
Oh! we bear within us mysterious things;
Of Memory and Anguish, unfathom'd springs;
And Passion—those gulfs of the heart to fill
With bitter waves, which it ne'er may still.

Well might we pause ere we gave them sway,
Flinging the peace of our couch away!
Well might we look on our souls in fear,
They find no fount of oblivion here!
They forget not, the mantle of sleep beneath—
How know we if under the wings of death?

THE WINGS OF THE DOVE.

"Oh! that I had wings like a dove, for then would I fly away, and be at rest."—*Psalm* lv.

Oh! for thy wings, thou dove!
Now sailing by with sunshine on thy breast;
That, borne like thee above,
I too might flee away, and be at rest!

Where wilt thou fold those plumes,
Bird of the forest shadows, holiest bird?
In what rich leafy glooms,
By the sweet voice of hidden waters stirr'd?

Over what blessed home,
What roof with dark, deep summer foliage crown'd,
O! fair as ocean's foam!
Shall thy bright bosom shed a gleam around?

Or seek'st thou some old shrine,
Of nymph or saint, no more by votary woo'd,
Though still, as if divine,
Breathing a spirit o'er the solitude?

Yet wherefore ask thy way?
Blest, ever blest, whate'er its aim, thou art!
Unto the greenwood spray,
Bearing no dark remembrance at thy heart!

PSYCHE'S DEPARTURE.

  No echoes that will blend
A sadness with the whispers of the grove;
  No memory of a friend
Far off, or dead, or changed to thee, thou dove!

  Oh! to some cool recess
Take, take me with thee on the summer wind,
  Leaving the weariness
And all the fever of this life behind:

  The aching and the void
Within the heart, whereunto none reply,
  The young bright hopes destroy'd—
Bird! bear me with thee through the sunny sky;

  Wild wish, and longing vain,
And brief upspringing to be glad and free!
  Go to thy woodland reign:
My soul is bound and held—I may not flee:

  For even by all the fears
And thoughts that haunt my dreams—untold, unknown
  And burning woman's tears,
Pour'd from mine eyes in silence and alone;

  Had I thy wings, thou dove!
High 'midst the gorgeous isles of cloud to soar,
  Soon the strong cords of love
Would draw me earthwards—homewards—yet once more.

PSYCHE BORNE BY ZEPHYRS TO THE ISLAND OF PLEASURE.*

"Souvent l'ame, fortifiée par la contemplation des choses divines, voudroit déployer ses ailes vers le ciel. Elle croit qu'au terme de sa carrière un rideau va se lever pour lui découvrir des scènes de lumière: mais quand la mort touche son corps périssable, elle jette un regard en arrière vers les plaisirs terrestres et vers ses compagnes mortelles."—SCHLEGEL, *translated by* MADAME DE STAEL.

  FEARFULLY and mournfully
   Thou bidst the earth farewell,
  And yet thou'rt passing, loveliest one!
   In a brighter land to dwell.

  Ascend, ascend rejoicing!
   The sunshine of that shore
  Around thee, as a glorious robe,
   Shall stream for evermore.

  The breezy music wandering
   There through th' Elysian sky,

---

* Written for a picture in which Psyche, on her flight upwards, is represented looking back sadly and anxiously to the earth.

Hath no deep tone that seems to float
  From a happier time gone by.
And there the day's last crimson
  Gives no sad memories birth,
No thought of dead or distant friends,
  Or partings—as on earth.

Yet fearfully and mournfully
  Thou bidd'st that earth farewell,
Although thou'rt passing, loveliest one!
  In a brighter land to dwell.

A land where all is deathless—
  The sunny wave's repose,
The wood with its rich melodies,
  The summer and its rose.

A land that sees no parting,
  That hears no sound of sighs,
That waits thee with immortal air—
  Lift, lift those anxious eyes!

Oh! how like *thee*, thou trembler!
  Man's spirit fondly clings
With timid love, to this, its world
  Of old familiar things!

We pant, we thirst for fountains
  That gush not here below!
On, on we toil, allured by dreams
  Of the living water's flow:

We pine for kindred natures
  To mingle with our own;
For communings more full and high
  Than aught by mortal known:

We strive with brief aspirings
  Against our bonds in vain;
Yet summon'd to be free at last,
  We shrink—and clasp our chain;

And fearfully and mournfully
  We bid the earth farewell,
Though passing from its mists, like thee,
  In a brighter world to dwell.

THE BOON OF MEMORY.

    "Many things answered me."—*Manfred.*

I go, I go!—and must mine image fade
From the green spots wherein my childhood play'd,
  By my own streams?

THE BOON OF MEMORY.

Must my life part from each familiar place,
As a bird's song, that leaves the woods no trace
    Of its lone themes?
Will the friend pass my dwelling, and forget
The welcomes there, the hours when we have met
    In grief or glee?
All the sweet counsel, the communion high,
The kindly words of trust, in days gone by,
    Pour'd full and free?

A boon, a talisman, O Memory! give,
To shrine my name in hearts where I would live
    For evermore?
Bid the wind speak of me where I have dwelt,
Bid the stream's voice, of all my soul hath felt,
    A thought restore!
In the rich rose, whose bloom I loved so well,
In the dim brooding violet of the dell,
    Set deep that though!
And let the sunset's melancholy glow,
And let the Spring's first whisper, faint and low,
    With me be fraught!

And Memory answer'd me:—" Wild wish and vain!
I have no hues the loveliest to detain
    In the heart's core.
The place they held in bosoms all their own,
Soon with new shadows fill'd, new flowers o'ergrown,
    Is theirs no more."

Hast *thou* such power, O Love?—And Love replied,
" It is not mine! Pour out thy soul's full tide
    Of hope and trust,
Prayer, tear, devotedness, that boon to gain—
'Tis but to write with the heart's fiery rain,
    Wild words on dust!"

Song, is the gift with thee?—I ask a lay,
Soft, fervent, deep, that will not pass away
    From the still breast;
Fill'd with a tone—oh! not for deathless fame,
But a sweet haunting murmur of my name,
    Where it would rest.

And Song made answer—" It is not in me,
Though call'd immortal; though my gifts may be
    All but divine.
A place of lonely brightness I can give:
A changeless one, where thou with Love wouldst live—
    This is not mine!"

Death, Death! wilt *thou* the restless wish fulfill?
And Death the Strong One, spoke:—" I can but still
    Each vain regret.

What if forgotten?—All thy soul would crave,
Thou too, within the mantle of the grave,
　　　Wilt soon forget."

Then did my heart in lone faint sadness die,
As from all nature's voices one reply,
　　　But one—was given.
" Earth has *no* heart, fond dreamer! with a tone
To send thee back the spirit of thine own—
　　　Seek it in Heaven."

DARTMOOR.

A PRIZE POEM.

> Come, bright Improvement! on the car of Time,
> And rule the spacious world from clime to clime.
> Thy handmaid, Art, shall every wild explore,
> Trace every wave, and culture every shore.　*Campbell*

> 　　　　　　　　　　　　May ne'er
> That true succession fail of English hearts,
> That can perceive, not less than heretofore
> Our ancestors did feelingly perceive,
> ——————————— the charm
> Of pious sentiment, diffused afar,
> And human charity, and social love.　*Wordsworth.*

AMIDST the peopled and the regal Isle,
Whose vales, rejoicing in their beauty, smile;
Whose cities, fearless of the spoiler, tower,
And send on every breeze a voice of power;
Hath Desolation rear'd herself a throne,
And mark'd a pathless region for her own?
Yes! though thy turf no stain of carnage wore,
When bled the noble hearts of many a shore,
Though not a hostile step thy heath-flowers bent,
When empires totter'd, and the earth was rent;
Yet lone, as if some trampler of mankind
Had still'd life's busy murmurs on the wind,
And, flush'd with power in daring pride's excess,
Stamp'd on thy soil the curse of barrenness;
For thee in vain descend the dews of heaven,
In vain the sunbeam and the shower are given;
Wild Dartmoor! thou that, 'midst thy mountains rude,
Hast robed thyself with haughty solitude,
As a dark cloud on summer's clear blue sky,
A mourner, circled with festivity!
For all beyond is life!—the rolling sea,
The rush, the swell, whose echoes reach not thee.
Yet who shall find a scene so wild and bare,
But man has left his lingering traces there?
E'en on mysterious Afric's boundless plains,

Where noon with attributes of midnight reigns.
In gloom and silence, fearfully profound,
As of a world unwaked to soul or sound,
Though the sad wand'rer of the burning zone
Feels, as amidst infinity, alone,
And nought of life be near; his camel's tread
Is o'er the prostrate cities of the dead!
Some column, rear'd by long-forgotten hands,
Just lifts its head above the billowy sands—
Some mouldering shrine still consecrates the scene
And tells that glory's footstep there hath been.
There hath the spirit of the mighty pass'd,
Not without record; though the desert blast,
Borne on the wings of Time, hath swept away
The proud creations rear'd to brave decay.
But *thou*, lone region! whose unnoticed name
No lofty deeds have mingled with their fame,
Who shall unfold thine annals?—who shall tell
If on thy soil the sons of heroes fell,
In those far ages, which have left no trace,
No sunbeam, on the pathway of their race?
Though, haply, in the unrecorded days
Of kings and chiefs, who pass'd without their praise,
Thou might'st have rear'd the valiant and the free;
In history's page there is no tale of thee.

Yet hast thou thy memorials. On the wild
Still rise the cairns of yore, all rudely piled,[1]
But hallow'd by that instinct which reveres
Things fraught with characters of elder years.
And such are these. Long centuries are flown,
Bow'd many a crest, and shatter'd many a throne,
Mingling the urn, the trophy, and the bust,
With what they hide—their shrined and treasured dust;
Men traverse Alps and oceans, to behold
Earth's glorious works fast mingling with her mould;
But still these nameless chronicles of death,
'Midst the deep silence of the unpeopled heath,
Stand in primeval artlessness, and wear
The same sepulchral mien, and almost share
Th' eternity of nature, with the forms
Of the crown d hills beyond, the dwellings of the storms.

Yet, what avails it, if each moss-grown heap
Still on the waste its lonely vigils keep,
Guarding the dust which slumbers well beneath
(Nor needs such care) from each cold season's breath?
Where is the voice to tell *their* tale who rest,
Thus rudely pillow'd on the desert's breast?
Doth the sword sleep beside them? Hath there been
A sound of battle 'midst the silent scene
Where now the flocks repose?—did the scythed car
Here reap its harvest in the ranks of war?

And raise these piles in memory of the slain,
And the red combat of the mountain-plain?

It may be thus:—the vestiges of strife,
Around yet lingering, mark the steps of life,
And the rude arrow's barb remains to tell [2]
How by its stroke, perchance, the mighty fell
To be forgotten. Vain the warrior's pride,
The chieftain's power—they had no bard, and died.[3]
But other scenes, from their untroubled sphere,
The eternal stars of night have witness'd here.
There stands an altar of unsculptured stone,[4]
Far on the moor, a thing of ages gone,
Propp'd on its granite pillars, whence the rains,
And pure bright dews, have laved the crimson stains
Left by dark rites of blood; for here, of yore,
When the bleak waste a robe of forest wore,
And many a crested oak, which now lies low,
Waved its wild wreath of sacred mistletoe;
Here, at dead midnight, through the haunted shade,
On Druid-harps the quivering moonbeam play'd,
And spells were breath'd, that fill'd the deepening gloom
With the pale, shadowy people of the tomb.
Or, haply, torches waving through the night,
Bade the red cairn-fires blaze from every height,[5]
Like battle signals, whose unearthly gleams
Threw o'er the desert's hundred hills and streams,
A savage grandeur; while the starry skies
Rung with the peal of mystic harmonies,
As the loud harp its deep-toned hymns sent forth
To the storm-ruling powers, the war-gods of the North.

But wilder sounds were there; th' imploring cry
That woke the forest's echo in reply,
But not the heart's!- Unmoved, the wizard train
Stood round their human victim, and in vain
His prayer for mercy rose; in vain his glance
Look'd up, appealing to the blue expanse,
Where, in their calm, immortal beauty, shone
Heaven's cloudless orbs. With faint and fainter moan,
Bound on the shrine of sacrifice he lay,
Till, drop by drop, life's current ebb'd away;
Till rock and turf grew deeply, darkly red,
And the pale moon gleam'd paler on the dead.
Have such things been, and here?—where stillness dwells
'Midst the rude barrows and the moorland swells,
Thus undisturb'd?—Oh! long the gulf of time
Hath closed in darkness o'er those days of crime,
And earth no vestige of their path retains,
Save such as these, which strew her loneliest plains
With records of man's conflicts and his doom,
His spirit and his dust—the altar and the tomb.

But ages roll'd away ; and England stood,
With her proud banner streaming o'er the flood ;
And with a lofty calmness in her eye,
And regal in collected majesty,
To breast the storm of battle.   Every breeze
Bore sounds of triumph o'er her own blue seas ;
And other lands, redeem'd and joyous, drank
The life-blood of her heroes, as they sank
On the red fields they won ; whose wild flowers wave
Now in luxuriant beauty, o'er their grave.

'Twas then the captives of Britannia's war,[6]
Here for their lovely southern climes afar
In bondage pined : the spell-deluded throng
Dragg'd at ambition's chariot-wheels so long
To die—because a despot could not clasp
A sceptre, fitted to his boundless grasp !

Yes ! they whose march had rock'd the ancient thrones
And temples of the world ; the deepening tones
Of whose advancing trumpet, from repose
Had startled nations, wakening to their woes ;
Were prisoners here.—And there were some whose dreams
Were of sweet homes, by chainless mountain-streams,
And of the vine-clad hills, and many a strain,
And festal melody of Loire or Seine,
And of those mothers who had watch'd and wept,
When on the field the unshelter'd conscript slept,
Bathed with the midnight dews.   And some were
Of sterner spirits, harden'd by despair ;
Who, in their dark imaginings, again
Fired the rich palace and the stately fane,
Drank in the victim's shriek, as music's breath,
And lived o'er scenes, the festivals of death !

And there was mirth, too !—strange and savage mirth,
More fearful far than all the woes of earth !
The laughter of cold hearts, and scoffs that spring
From minds for which there is no sacred thing,
And transient bursts of fierce, exulting glee—
The lightning's flash upon its blasted tree !

But still, howe'er the soul's disguise was worn,
If, from wild revelry, or haughty scorn,
Or buoyant hope, it won an outward show,
Slight was the mask, and all beneath it—woe.

Yet, was this all ?—amidst the dungeon-gloom,
The void, the stillness, of the captive's doom,
Were there no deeper thoughts ?—and that dark power,
To whom guilt owes one late but dreadful hour,
The mighty debt through years of crime delay'd,
But, as the grave's, inevitably paid ;
Came he not thither, in his burning force,
The lord, the tamer of dark souls—remorse ?

Yes! as the night calls forth from sea and sky,
From breeze and wood, a solemn harmony,
Lost, when the swift, triumphant wheels of day,
In light and sound, are hurrying on their way:
Thus, from the deep recesses of the heart,
The voice which sleeps, but never dies, might start,
Call'd up by solitude, each nerve to thrill
With accents heard not, save when all is still!

The voice, inaudible when havoc's train
Crush'd the red vintage of devoted Spain;
Mute, when sierras to the war-whoop rung,
And the broad light of conflagration sprung
From the south's marble cities;—hush'd 'midst cries
That told the heavens of mortal agonies;
But gathering silent strength, to wake at last
In concentrated thunders of the past!

And there, perchance, some long-bewilder'd mind,
Torn from its lowly sphere, its path confined
Of village duties, in the Alpine glen,
Where nature cast its lot, 'midst peasant-men;
Drawn to that vortex, whose fierce ruler blent
The earthquake power of each wild element,
To lend the tide, which bore his throne on high,
One impulse more of desperate energy;
Might—when the billow's awful rush was o'er,
Which toss'd its wreck upon the storm-beat shore,
Won from its wand'rings past, by suffering tried,
Search'd by remorse, by anguish purified—
Have fix'd, at length, its troubled hopes and fears,
On the far world, seen brightest through our tears,
And, in that hour of triumph or despair,
Whose secrets all must learn but none declare,
When of the things to come, a deeper sense
Fills the dim eye of trembling penitence,
Have turn'd to Him whose bow is in the cloud,
Around life's limits gathering, as a shroud;—
The fearful mysteries of the heart who knows,
And, by the tempest, calls it to repose!

Who visited that deathbed?—Who can tell
Its brief sad tale, on which the soul might dwell,
And learn immortal lessons?—who beheld
The struggling hope, by shame, by doubt repell'd—
The agony of prayer—the bursting tears—
The dark remembrances of guilty years,
Crowding upon the spirit in their might?
He, through the storm who look'd, and there was light.

That scene is closed!—that wild, tumultuous breast,
With all its pangs and passions, is at rest!
He too, is fallen, the master-power of strife,
Who woke those passions to delirious life;

And days, prepared a brighter course to run,
Unfold their buoyant pinions to the sun!

It is a glorious hour when Spring goes forth
O'er the bleak mountains of the shadowy north,
And with one radiant glance, one magic breath,
Wakes all things lovely from the sleep of death;
While the glad voices of a thousand streams,
Bursting their bondage, triumph in her beams!

But *Peace* hath nobler changes! O'er the mind,
The warm and living spirit of mankind,
Her influence breathes, and bids the blighted heart,
To life and hope from desolation start!
She, with a look, dissolves the captive's chain,
Peopling with beauty widow'd homes again;
Around the mother, in her closing years,
Gathering her sons once more, and from the tears
Of the dim past, but winning purer light,
To make the present more serenely bright.

Nor rests that influence here. From clime to clime,
In silence gliding with the stream of time,
Still doth it spread, borne onwards, as a breeze
With healing on its wings, o'er isles and seas:
And, as Heaven's breath call'd forth, with genial power,
From the dry wand, the almond's living flower;
So doth its deep-felt charm in secret move
The coldest heart to gentle deeds of love;
While round its pathway nature softly glows,
And the wide desert blossoms as the rose.

Yes! let the waste lift up the exulting voice!
Let the far-echoing solitude rejoice!
And thou, lone moor! where no blithe reaper's song
E'er lightly sped the summer hours along,
Bid thy wild rivers, from each mountain-source,
Rushing in joy, make music on their course!
Thou, whose sole records of existence mark
The scene of barbarous rites, in ages dark,
And of some nameless combat: hope's bright eye
Beams o'er thee in the light of prophecy!
Yet shalt thou smile, by busy culture drest,
And the rich harvest wave upon thy breast!
Yet shall thy cottage smoke, at dewy morn,
Rise, in blue wreaths, above the flowering thorn,
And, 'midst thy hamlet shades, the embosom'd spire
Catch from deep-kindling heavens their earliest fire.

Thee too that hour shall bless, the balmy close
Of labor's day, the herald of repose,
Which gathers hearts in peace; while social mirth
Basks in the blaze of each free village hearth;
While peasant-songs are on the joyous gales,
And merry England's voice floats up from all her vales.

Yet are there sweeter sounds ; and thou shalt hear
Such as to Heaven's immortal host are dear.
Oh! if there still be melody on earth,
Worthy the sacred bowers where man drew birth
When angel-steps their paths rejoicing trode,
And the air trembled with the breath of God ;
It lives in those soft accents, to the sky[7]
Borne from the lips of stainless infancy,
When holy strains, from life's pure fount which sprung,
Breathed with deep reverence, falter on its tongue.

And such shall be *thy* music, when the cells,
Where Guilt, the child of hopeless Misery, dwells,
(And, to wild strength by desperation wrought,
In silence broods o'er many a fearful thought,)
Resound to pity's voice ; and childhood thence,
Ere the cold blight hath reached its innocence,
Ere that soft rose-bloom of the soul be fled,
Which vice but breathes on, and its hues are dead,
Shall at the call press forward, to be made
A glorious offering, meet for him who said,
" Mercy, not sacrifice!" and when, of old,
Clouds of rich incense from his altars roll'd,
Dispersed the smoke of perfumes, and laid bare
The heart's deep folds, to read its homage there!

When some crown'd conqueror, o'er a trampled world
His banner, shadowing nations, hath unfurl'd,
And, like those visitations which deform
Nature for centuries, hath made the storm
His pathway to dominion's lonely sphere,
Silence behind—before him, flight and fear ;
When kingdoms rock beneath his rushing wheels,
Till each fair isle the mighty impulse feels,
And earth is moulded but by one proud will,
And sceptred realms wear fetters, and are still ;
Shall the free soul of song bow down to pay,
The earthquake homage on its baleful way?
Shall the glad harp send up exulting strains,
O'er burning cities and forsaken plains?
And shall no harmony of softer close
Attend the stream of mercy as it flows,
And, mingling with the murmur of its wave,
Bless the green shores its gentle currents lave?

Oh! there are loftier themes, for him whose eyes
Have search'd the depths of life's realities,
Than the red battle, or the trophied car,
Wheeling the monarch-victor fast and far ;
There are more noble strains than those which swell
The triumphs, ruin may suffice to tell!

Ye prophet-bards, who sat in elder days
Beneath the palms of Judah! Ye whose lays

With torrent rapture, from their source on high,
Burst in the strength of immortality !
Oh ! not alone, those haunted groves among,
Of conquering hosts, of empires crush'd, ye sung,
But of that spirit, destined to explore
With the bright day-spring every distant shore,
To dry the tear, to bind the broken reed,
To make the home of peace in hearts that bleed ;
With beams of hope to pierce the dungeon's gloom,
And pour eternal star-light o'er the tomb.

And bless'd and hallow'd be its haunts ! for there
Hath man's high soul been rescued from despair !
There hath the immortal spark for Heaven been nursed ;
There from the rock the springs of life have burst,
Quenchless and pure ! and holy thoughts, that rise,
Warm from the source of human sympathies—
Where'er its path of radiance may be traced,
Shall find their temples in the silent waste.

NOTES.

Note 1, page 583, line 27.
Still rise the cairns of yore, all rudely piled.

In some parts of Dartmoor, the surface is thickly strewed with stones, which, in many instances, appear to have been collected into piles, on the tops of prominent hillocks, as if in imitation of the natural Tors. The Stone-barrows of Dartmoor resemble the cairns of the Cheviot and Grampian hills, and those in Cornwall.—See COOKE's *Topographical Survey of Devonshire.*

Note 2, page 584, line 5.
And the rude arrow's barb remain to tell.

Flint arrow-heads have occasionally been found upon Dartmoor.

Note 3, page 584, line 8.
The chieftain's power—they had no bard, and died.

Vixere fortes ante Agamemnona
Multi ; sed omnes illachrymabiles
Urgentur, ignotique longa
Nocte, carent quia vate sacro.—*Horace.*

"They had no poet, and they died."—POPE's *Translation.*

Note 4, page 584, line 11.
There stands an altar of unsculptured stone.

On the east of Dartmoor are some Druidical remains, one of which is a Cromlech, whose three rough pillars of granite support a ponderous table-stone, and form a kind of large irregular tripod.

Note 5, page 584, line 24.
Bade the red cairn-fires blaze from every height.

In some of the Druid festivals, fires were lighted on all the cairns and eminences around, by priests, carrying sacred torches, All the household fires were previously extinguished, and those who were thought worthy of such a privilege, were allowed to relight them with a flaming brand, kindled at the consecrated cairn-fire.

Note 6, page 585, line 11.
'Twas then the captives of Britannia's war.

The French prisoners, taken in the wars with Napoleon, were confined in a depot on Dartmoor.

Note 7, page 588, line 7.
It lives in those soft accents to the sky.

In allusion to a plan for the erection of a great national school-house on Dartmoor, where it was proposed to educate the children of convicts.

WELCH MELODIES.

INTRODUCTORY STANZAS.—THE HARP OF WALES.

INSCRIBED TO THE RUTHIN WELSH LITERARY SOCIETY.

HARP of the mountain-land! sound forth again,
As when the foaming Hirlas horn was crown'd,
And warrior hearts beat proudly to the strain,
And the bright mead at Owain's feast went round:
Wake with the spirit and the power of yore!
Harp of the ancient hills! be heard once more!

Thy tones are not to cease! The Roman came
O'er the blue waters with his thousand oars:
Through Mona's oaks he sent the wasting flame;
The Druid shrines lay prostrate on our shores:
All gave their ashes to the wind and sea—
Ring out, thou harp he could not silence thee.

Thy tones are not to cease!—The Saxon pass'd,
His banners floated on Eryri's gales;
But thou wert heard above the trumpet's blast,
E'en when his towers rose loftiest o'er the vales!
Thine was the voice that cheer'd the brave and free;
They had their hills, their chainless hearts, and thee.

Those were dark years!—They saw the valiant fall,
The rank weeds gathering round the chieftain's board,

The hearth left lonely in the ruined hall—
Yet power was *thine*—a gift in every chord!
Call back that spirit to the days of peace,
Thou noble Harp!—thy tones are not to cease!

DRUID CHORUS ON THE LANDING OF THE ROMANS.

By the dread and viewless powers
  Whom the storms and seas obey,
From the Dark Isle's* mystic bowers,
  Romans! o'er the deep away!
Think ye, 'tis but nature's gloom
  O'er our shadowy coast which broods?
By the altar and the tomb,
  Shun these haunted solitudes!

Know ye Mona's awful spells?
  She the rolling orbs can stay!
She the mighty grave compels
  Back to yield its fetter'd prey!
Fear ye not the lightning-stroke?
  Mark ye not the fiery sky?
Hence!—around our central oak
  Gods are gathering—Romans, fly!

THE GREEN ISLES OF OCEAN.*

Where are they, those green fairy islands, reposing
  In sunlight and beauty, on ocean's calm breast?
What spirit, the things which are hidden disclosing,
  Shall point the bright way to their dwellings of rest?
Oh! lovely they rose on the dreams of past ages,
  The mighty have sought them, undaunted in faith;
But the land hath been sad for her warriors and sages,
  For the guide to those realms of the blessed, is death.

* *Ynys Dywyll*, or the Dark Island, an ancient name for Anglesey.

† The "Green Islands of Ocean," or "Green Spots of the Floods," called in the *Triads* "Gwerddonan Llion," (respecting which some remarkable superstitions have been preserved in Wales,) were supposed to be the abode of the Fair Family, or souls of the virtuous Druids, who could not enter the Christian heaven, but were permitted to enjoy this paradise of their own. Gafran, a distinguished British chieftain of the fifth century, went on a voyage, with his family, to discover these islands; but they were never heard of afterwards. This event, the voyage of Merddin Emrys with his twelve bards, and the expedition of Madog, were called the three losses by disappearance of the island of Britain.—Vide W. O. Pughe's *Cambrian Biography*, also *Cambro-Briton*, vol. i. p. 124.

Where are they, the high-minded children of glory
    Who steer'd for those distant green spots on the wave?
To the winds of the ocean they left their wild story,
    In the fields of their country they found not a grave.
Perchance they repose where the Summer-breeze gathers,
    From the flowers of each vale, immortality's breath;
But their steps shall be ne'er on the hills of their fathers—
    For the guide to those realms of the blessed, is death.

THE SEA-SONG OF GAFRAN.*

Watch ye well! The moon is shrouded
    On her bright throne;
Storms are gathering, stars are clouded,
    Waves make wild moan.
'Tis no night of hearth-fires glowing,
And gay songs and wine-cups flowing;
But of winds, in darkness blowing
    O'er seas unknown!

In the dwellings of our fathers,
    Round the glad blaze,
Now the festive circle gathers,
    With harps and lays;
Now the rush-strewn halls are ringing,
Steps are bounding, bards are singing,
—Ay! the hour to all is bringing
    Peace, joy, or praise:—

Save to us, our night-watch keeping,
    Storm-winds to brave,
While the very sea-bird sleeping,
    Rests in its cave!
Think of us when hearths are beaming,
Think of us when mead is streaming,
Ye, of whom our souls are dreaming
    On the dark wave!

THE HIRLAS HORN.

Fill high the blue *hirlas*,† that shines like the wave‡
    When sunbeams are bright on the spray of the sea;

---

* See note to the "Green Isles of Ocean."

† Hirlas, from *hir*, long, and *glas*, blue or azure.

‡ "Fetch the horn, that we may drink together, whose gloss is like the waves of the sea; whose green handles show the skill of the artist, and are tipped with gold."—From the Hirlas of Owain Cyfeiliog.

And bear thou the rich foaming mead to the brave,
 The dragons of battle, the sons of the free !
To those from whose spears, in the shock of the fight,
 A beam, like heaven's lightning,* flash'd over the field ;
To those who came rushing as storms in their might.
 Who have shiver'd the helmet, and cloven the shield ;
The sound of whose strife was like oceans afar,
When lances were red from the harvest of war.

Fill high the blue hirlas ! O cup-bearer, fill
 For the lords of the field, in their festival's hour,
And let the mead foam, like the stream of the hill,
 That bursts o'er the rock in the pride of its power :
Praise, praise to the mighty, fill high the smooth horn
 Of honor and mirth,† for the conflict is o'er ;
And round let the golden-tipp'd hirlas be borne,
 To the lion defenders of Gwynedd's fair shore,
Who rush'd to the field where the glory was won,
 As eagles that soar from their cliffs to the sun.

Fill higher the hirlas ! forgetting not those
 Who shared its bright draught in the days which are fled !
Though cold on their mountains the valiant repose,
 Their lot shall be lovely—renown to the dead !
While harps in the hall of the feast shall be strung,
 While regal *Eryri* with snow shall be crown'd—
So long by the bards shall their battles be sung,
 And the heart of the hero shall burn at the sound
The free winds of Maelor‡ shall swell with their name,
And Owain's rich hirlas be fill'd to their fame.

THE HALL OF CYNDDYLAN.

The Hall of Cynddylan is gloomy to-night ;§
I weep, for the grave has extinguish'd its light ;

---

  * "Heard ye in Maelor the noise of war, the horrid din of arms, their furious onset, loud as in the battle of Bangor, where fire flashed out of their spears."—From the Hirlas of Owain Cyfeilioo.

  † "Fill, then, the yellow-lipped horn—badge of honor and mirth.' —From the same.

  ‡ Maelor, part of the counties of Denbigh and Flint, according to the modern division.

  § " The Hall of Cynddylan is gloomy this night,
     Without fire, without bed—
     I must weep awhile, and then be silent.

     The Hall of Cynddylan is gloomy this night,
     Without fire, without being lighted—
     Be thou encircled with spreading silence !
         *   *   *   *   *   *   *   *
     The Hall of Cynddylan is without love this night,

The beam of the lamp from its summit is o'er,
The blaze of its hearth shall give welcome no more!

The Hall of Cynddylan is voiceless and still,
The sound of its harpings hath died on the hill!
Be silent forever, thou desolate scene,
Nor let e'en an echo recall what hath been!

The Hall of Cynddylan is lonely and bare,
No banquet, no guest, not a footstep is there!
Oh! where are the warriors who circled its board?
—The grass will soon wave where the mead-cup was pour'd!

The Hall of Cynddylan is loveless to night,
Since he is departed whose smile made it bright!
I mourn; but the sigh of my soul shall be brief,
The pathway is short to the grave of my chief!

THE LAMENT OF LLYWARCH HEN.

[Llywarch Hen, or Llywarch the Aged, a celebrated bard and chief of the times of Arthur, was prince of Argoed, supposed to be a part of the present Cumberland. Having sustained the loss of his patrimony, and witnessed the fall of most of his sons, in the unequal contest maintained by the North Britons against the growing power of the Saxons, Llywarch was compelled to fly from his country, and seek refuge in Wales. He there found an asylum for some time in the residence of Cynddylan, Prince of Powys, whose fall he pathetically laments in one of his poems. These are still extant, and his elegy on old age and the loss of his sons, is remarkable for its simplicity and beauty.—See *Cambrian Biography*, and Owen's *Heroic Elegies and other poems of Llywarch Hen*.]

The bright hours return, and the blue sky is ringing
With song, and the hills are all mantled with bloom;
But fairer than aught which the summer is bringing,
The beauty and youth gone to people the tomb!
Oh! why should I live to hear music resounding,
Which cannot awake ye, my lovely, my brave?
Why smile the waste flowers, my sad footsteps surrounding?
—My sons! they but clothe the green turf of your grave!

Alone on the rocks of the stranger I linger,
My spirit all wrapt in the past as a dream!
Mine ear hath no joy in the voice of the singer,*
Mine eye sparkles not to the sunlight's glad beam;

<blockquote>
Since he that own'd it is no more—
Ah Death! it will be but a short time he will leave me.

The Hall of Cynddylan it is not easy this night,
On the top of the rock of Hydwyth,
Without its lord, without company, without the circling feasts!'
  See Owen's *Heroic Elegies of Llywarch Hen*."
</blockquote>

* "What I loved when I was a youth is hateful to me now."
  *   *   *   *   *   *

Yet, yet I live on, though forsaken and weeping!
—Oh grave! why refuse to the aged thy bed,
When valor's high heart on thy bosom is sleeping,
When youth's glorious flower is gone down to the dead!

Fair were ye, my sons! and all-kingly your bearing,
As on to the fields of your glory ye trode!
Each prince of my race the bright golden chain wearing,
Each eye glancing fire, shrouded now by the sod!*
I weep when the blast of the trumpet is sounding,
Which rouses ye not! O, my lovely! my brave!
When warriors and chiefs to their proud steeds are bounding,
I turn from heaven's light, for it smiles on your grave!†

GRUFYDD'S FEAST.

["Grufydd ab Rhys ab Tewdwr, having resisted the English successfully in the time of Stephen, and at last obtained from them an honorable peace, made a great feast at his palace in *Ystrad Tywi* to celebrate this event. To this feast, which was continued for forty days, he invited all who would come in peace from *Gwynedd, Powys*, the *Deheubarth*, Glamorgan, and the marches. Against the appointed time he prepared all kinds of delicious viands and liquors; with every entertainment of vocal and instrumental song; thus patronising the poets and musicians. He encouraged, too, all sorts of representations and manly games, and afterwards sent away all those who had excelled in them with honorable gifts."]—*Vide Cambrian Biography.*

Let the yellow mead shine for the sons of the brave,
By the bright festal torches around us that wave!
Set open the gates of the prince's wide hall,
And hang up the chief's ruddy spear on the wall!
   There is peace in the land we have battled to save:
Then spread ye the feast, bid the wine-cup foam high,‡
That those may rejoice who have fear'd not to die!

Let the horn, whose loud blast gave the signal for fight,
With the bee's sunny nectar now sparkle in light,§

---

* " Four and twenty sons to me have been,
      Wearing the golden chain, and leading princes."
                              Elegies of Llywarch Hen.

The golden chain as a badge of honor, worn by heroes, is frequently alluded to in the works of the ancient British bards.

† " Hardly has the snow covered the vale,
    When the warriors are hastening to the battle;
    I do not go, I am hinder'd by infirmity."
                              Owen's *Elegies of Llwarch Hen.*

‡ Wine, as well as mead, is frequently mentioned in the poems of the ancient British bards.

§ The horn was used for two purposes, to sound the alarm in war, and to drink the mead at feasts.

Let the rich draught it offers with gladness be crown'd,
For the strong hearts, in combat that leap'd at its sound!
 Like the billow's dark swell, was the path of their might,
Red, red as their blood, fill the wine-cup on high,
That those may rejoice who have fear'd not to die!

And wake ye the children of song from their dreams,
On Maelor's wild hills, and by Dyfed's fair streams!*
Bid them haste with those strains of the lofty and free,
Which shall float down the waves of long ages to be.
 Sheath the sword which hath given them unperishing themes,
And pour the bright mead; let the wine cup foam high,
That those may rejoice who have fear'd not to die!

THE CAMBRIAN IN AMERICA.

When the last flush of eve is dying
 On boundless lakes, afar that shine;
When winds amidst the palms are sighing,
 And fragrance breathes from every pine:†
When stars through cypress-boughs are gleaming,
 And fire-flies wander bright and free,
Still of thy harps, thy mountains dreaming,
 My thoughts, wild Cambria! dwell with thee!

Alone o'er green savannas roving,
 Where some broad stream in silence flows,
Or through th' eternal forests moving,
 One only home my spirits knows!
Sweet land, whence memory ne'er hath parted!
 To thee on sleep's light wing I fly;
But happier, could the weary-hearted
 Look on his own blue hills, and die!

THE MONARCHY OF BRITAIN.

[The Bard of the Palace, under the ancient Welsh Princes, always accompanied the army when it marched into an enemy's country, and while it was preparing for battle, or dividing the spoils, he performed an ancient song, called *Unbennaeth Prydain*, the monarchy of Britain. It has been conjectured that this poem referred to the tradition of the Welsh, that the whole island had once been possessed by their ancestors, who were driven into a corner of it by their Saxon invaders. When the prince had received his share

---

* Maelor, part of the counties of Denbigh and Flint. Dyfed, (said to signify a land abounding with streams of water,) the modern Pembrokeshire.

† The aromatic odor of the pine has frequently been mentioned by travellers.

of the spoils, the bard, for the performance of this song, was rewarded with the most valuable beast that remained.—See JONES's *Historical Account of the Welsh Bards.*]

SONS of the Fair Isle!* forget not the time,
Ere spoilers had breath'd the free winds of your clime!
All that its eagles behold in their flight,
Was yours from the deep to each storm-mantled height!
Though from your race that proud birthright be torn,
Unquench'd is the spirit for monarchy born.
Darkly though clouds may hang o'er us awhile,
The crown shall not pass from the Beautiful Isle.

Ages may roll ere your children regain
The land for which heroes have perish'd in vain.
Yet in the sound of your name shall be power,
Around her still gathering till glory's full hour,
Strong in the fame of the mighty that sleep,
Your Britain shall sit on the throne of the deep!
Then shall their spirits rejoice in her smile,
Who died for the crown of the Beautiful Isle!

TALIESIN'S PROPHECY.

[A prophecy of Taliesin relating to the ancient Britons, is still extant, and has been strikingly verified. It is to the following effect:—
" Their God they shall worship,
Their language they shall retain,
Their land they shall lose,
Except wild Wales."]

A VOICE from time departed yet floats thy hills among,
O Cambria! thus thy prophet bard, thy Taliesin sung!
The path of unborn ages is traced upon my soul,
The clouds which mantle things unseen, away before me roll,
A light, the depths revealing, hath o'er my spirit pass'd,
A rushing sound from days to be, swells fitful in the blast,
And tells me that for ever shall live the lofty tongue,
To which the harp of Mona's woods by freedom's hand was strung.

Green island of the mighty!† I see thine ancient race
Driven from their fathers' realm, to make the rocks their dwelling-place!
I see from Uthyr's‡ kingdom the sceptre pass away,
And many a line of bards, and chiefs, and princely men decay.

* *Ynys Prydain,* the ancient name of Britain, signifies the Fair or Beautiful Island.
† *Ynys y Cedeirn,* or Isle of the Mighty, an ancient name given to Britain.
‡ Uther Pendragon, king of Britain, supposed to have been the father of Arthur.

But long as Arvon's mountains shall lift their sovereign forms,
And wear the crown to which is given dominion o'er the storms,
So long, their empire sharing, shall live the lofty tongue,
To which the harp of Mona's woods by freedom's hand was strung!

OWEN GLYNDWR'S WAR SONG.

Saw ye the blazing star?*
The heavens look down on freedom's war,
  And light her torch on high!
Bright on the dragon crest†
It tells that glory's wing shall rest,
  When warriors meet to die!

Let earth's pale tyrants read despair,
  And vengeance, in its flame;
Hail ye, my bards! the omen fair
  Of conquest and of fame,
And swell the rushing mountain-air
  With songs to Glyndwr's name.

At the dead hour of night,
Mark'd ye how each majestic height
  Burn'd in its awful beams?
Red shone th' eternal snows,
And all the land, as bright it rose,
  Was full of glorious dreams!

Oh! eagles of the battle!‡ rise!
  The hope of Gwynedd wakes!§
It is your banner in the skies,
  Through each dark cloud which breaks,
And mantles, with triumphal dyes,
  Your thousand hills and lakes!

A sound is on the breeze,
A murmur as of swelling seas!

---

* The year 1402 was ushered in with a comet or blazing star, which the bards interpreted as an omen favorable to the cause of Glyndwr. It served to infuse spirit into the minds of a superstitious people, the first success of their chieftain confirmed this belief, and gave new vigor to their actions.—*Vide* Pennant.

† *Owen Glyndwr* styled himself the *Dragon;* a name he assumed in imitation of *Uther*, whose victories over the Saxons were foretold by the appearance of a star with a dragon beneath, which Uther used as his badge; and on that account it became a favorite one with the Welsh.—Pennant.

‡ "Bring the horn to Tudwrou, *the Eagle of Battles.*"—Vide *The Hirlas Horn, a poem by* Owain Cyfeiliog. The eagle is a favorite image with the ancient Welsh poets.

§ Gwynedd (pronounced Gwyneth,) North Wales.

The Saxon on his way!
Lo! spear, and shield, and lance,
From Deva's waves, with lightning glance,
    Reflected to the day!
But who the torrent-wave compels
    A conqueror's chain to bear?
Let those who wake the soul that dwells
    On our free winds, beware!
The greenest and the loveliest dells
    May be the lion's lair!
Of us *they* told, the seers
And monarch-bards of elder years,
    Who walk'd on earth, as powers!
And in their burning strains,
A spell of might and mystery reigns,
    To guard our mountain-towers!
—In Snowdon's caves a prophet lay:*

    Before his gifted sight,
The march of ages pass'd away
    With hero-footsteps bright,
But proudest in that long array,
    Was Glyndwr's path of light!

PRINCE MADOC'S FAREWELL.

Why lingers my gaze where the last hues of day,
  On the hills of my country, in loveliness sleep?
Too fair is the sight for a wand'rer, whose way
  Lies far o'er the measureless worlds of the deep!
Fall, shadows of twilight! and veil the green shore,
That the heart of the mighty may waver no more!

Why rise on my thoughts, ye free songs of the land
  Where the harp's lofty soul on each wild wind is borne?
Be hush'd, be forgotten! for ne'er shall the hand
  Of minstrel with melody greet my return.
—No! no!—let your echoes still float on the breeze,
And my heart shall be strong for the conquest of seas!

'Tis not for the land of my sires, to give birth
  Unto bosoms that shrink when their trial is nigh;
Away! we will bear over ocean and earth
  A name and a spirit that never shall die.
My course to the winds, to the stars, I resign;
But my soul's quenchless fire, O my country! is thine.

---

* Merlin, or Merddin Emrys, is said to have composed his prophecies on the future lot of the Britons, amongst the mountains of Snowdon. Many of these, and other ancient prophecies, were applied by Glyndwr to his own cause, and assisted him greatly in animating the spirit of his followers.

CASWALLON'S TRIUMPH.

[Caswallon (or Cassivelaunus) was elected to the supreme command of the Britons, (as recorded in the Triads,) for the purpose of opposing Cæsar, under the title of Elected Chief of Battle. Whatever impression the disciplined legions of Rome might have made on the Britons in the first instance, the subsequent departure of Cæsar they considered as a cause of triumph; and it is stated that Caswallon proclaimed an assembly of the various states of the island, for the purpose of celebrating that event by feasting and public rejoicing.—*See the Cambrian Biography.*]

From the glowing southern regions,
  Where the sun-god makes his dwelling,
Came the Roman's crested legions,
  O'er the deep, round Britain swelling;
The wave grew dazzling as he pass'd,
With light from spear and helmet cast,
And sounds in every rushing blast
  Of a conqueror's march were telling.

But his eagle's royal pinion,
  Bowing earth beneath its glory,
Could not shadow with dominion
  Our wild seas and mountains hoary!
Back from their cloudy realm it flies,
To float in light through softer skies;
Oh! chainless winds of heaven arise!
  Bear a vanquish'd world the story!

Lords of earth! to Rome returning,
  Tell, how Britain combat wages,
How Caswallon's soul is burning
  When the storm of battle rages!
And ye that shrine high deeds in song,
O holy and immortal throng!
The brightness of his name prolong,
  As a torch to stream through ages!

HOWEL'S SONG.

[Howell ab Einiot Llygliw was a distinguished bard of the fourteenth century. A beautiful poem, addressed by him to Myfanwy Vychan, a celebrated beauty of those times, is still preserved amongst the remains of the Welsh bards. The ruins of Myfanwy's residence, Castle Dinas Brân, may yet be traced on a high hill near Llangollen.]

Press on, my steed! I hear the swell*
Of Valle Crucis' vesper-bell,

---

* "I have rode hard, mounted on a fine high-bred steed, upon thy account, O thou with the countenance of cherry-flower bloom. The

Sweet floating from the holy dell
   O'er woods and waters round.
Perchance the maid I love, e'en now,
From *Dinas Bran's* majestic brow,
Looks o'er the fairy world below,
   And listens to the sound!

I feel her presence on the scene!
The summer air is more serene,
The deep woods wave in richer green,
   The wave more gently flows!
O fair as Ocean's curling foam!*
Lo! with the balmy hour I come,
The hour that brings the wand'rer home,
   The weary to repose!

Haste! on each mountain's dark'ning crest,
The glow hath died, the shadows rest,
The twilight-star on Deva's breast,
   Gleams tremulously bright;
Speed for Myfanwy's bower on high!
Though scorn may wound me from her eye,
Oh! better by the sun to die,
   Than live in rayless night!

THE MOUNTAIN-FIRES.

["The custom retained in Wales of lighting fires (*Coelcerthi*) on November eve, is said to be a traditional memorial of the massacre of the British chiefs by Hengist, on Salisbury plain. The practice is, however, of older date, and had reference originally to the *Alban Elved*, or new year,"—*See the Cambro Briton.*
When these fires are kindled on the mountains, and seen through the darkness of a stormy night, casting a red and fitful glare over heath and rock, their effect is strikingly picturesque.]

Light the hills! till heaven is glowing
   As with some red meteor's rays!
Winds of night, though rudely glowing,
   Shall but fan the beacon-blaze.
Light the hills till flames are streaming,
   From† Yr Wyddfa's sovereign steep,

---

speed was with eagerness, and the strong long-hamm'd steed of Aban reached the summit of the high land of Brân."
* "My loving heart sinks with grief without thy support, O thou that hast the whiteness of the curling waves! * * * * * I know that this pain will avail me nothing towards obtaining thy love, O thou whose countenance is bright as the flowers of the hawthorn!"
—Howell's *Ode to Myfanwy.*
† Yr Wyddfa, the Welsh name of Snowdon, said to mean the *conspicuous place*, or *object.*

To the waves round Mona gleaming,
    Where the Roman track'd the deep!
Be the mountain watch-fires heighten'd,
    Pile them to the stormy sky!
Till each torrent-wave is brighten'd,
    Kindling as it rushes by.
Now each rock, the mist's high dwelling,
    Towers in reddening light sublime;
Heap the flames! around them telling
    Tales of Cambria's elder time.

Thus our sires, the fearless-hearted,
    Many a solemn vigil kept,
When, in ages long departed,
    O'er the noble dead they wept.
In the winds we hear their voices,
    "Sons! though yours a brighter lot,
When the mountain-land rejoices,
    Be her mighty unforgot!"

ERYRI WEN.

["SNOWDON was held as sacred by the ancient Britons as Parnassus was by the Greeks, and Ida by the Cretans. It is still said, that whosoever slept upon Snowdon would wake inspired, as much as if he had taken a nap on the hill of Apollo. The Welsh had always the strongest attachment to the tract of Snowdon. Our princes had, in addition to their title, that of Lord of Snowdon."]—PENNANT.

THEIRS was no dream, O Monarch-hill,
    With heaven's own azure crown'd!
Who call'd thee—what thou shalt be still,
    White Snowdon!—holy ground.

They fabled not, thy sons, who told
    Of the dread power, enshrined
Within thy cloudy mantle's fold,
    And on thy rushing wind!

It shadow'd o'er thy silent height,
    It fill'd thy chainless air,
Deep thoughts of majesty and might
    For ever breathing there.

Nor hath it fled! the awful spell
    Yet holds unbroken sway,
As when on that wild rock it fell,
    Where Merddin Emrys lay!*

---

* Dinas Emrys (the fortress of Ambrose,) a celebrated rock amongst the mountains of Snowdon, is said to be so called from having been

Though from their stormy haunts of yore,
　Thine eagles long have flown,*
As proud a flight the soul shall soar,
　Yet from thy mountain-throne!

Pierce then the heavens, thou hill of streams?
　And make the snows thy crest!
The sunlight of immortal dreams
　Around thee still shall rest.

Eryri! temple of the bard!
　And fortress of the free!
'Midst rocks, which heroes died to guard,
　Their spirit dwells with thee!

CHANT OF THE BARDS BEFORE THIER MASSACRE BY EDWARD I.†

Raise ye the sword! let the death-stroke be given:
O! swift may it fall as the lightning of heaven!
So shall our spirits be free as our strains:
The children of song may not languish in chains!

Have ye not trampled our country's bright crest?
Are heroes reposing in death on her breast?
Red with their blood do her mountain-streams flow,
And think ye that still we would linger below?

Rest, ye brave dead! 'midst the hills of your sires,
O! who would not slumber when freedom expires?
Lonely and voiceless your halls must remain—
The children of song may not breathe in the chain!

---

the residence of Merddin Emrys, called by the Latins Merlinus Ambrosius, the celebrated prophet and magician: and there, tradition says, he wrote his prophecies concerning the future state of the Britons.

There is another curious tradition respecting a large stone, on the ascent of Snowdon, called *Maen du yr Arddu*, the black stone of Arddu. It is said, that if two persons were to sleep a night on this stone, in the morning one would find himself endowed with the gift of poetry, and the other would become insane.—*See* Williams's *Observations on the Snowdon Mountains*.

* It is believed amongst the inhabitants of these mountains, that eagles have heretofore bred in the lofty clefts of their rocks. Some wandering ones are still seen at times, though very rarely, amongst the precipices.—*See* Williams's *Observations on the Snowdon Mountains*.

† This sanguinary deed is not attested by any historian of credit And it deserves to be also noticed, that none of the bardic productions since the time of Edward make any allusion to such an event.—*See the Cambro-Briton*, vol. I., p. 195.

THE DYING BARD'S PROPHECY.*

> "All is not lost—the unconquerable will
> And courage never to submit or yield." *Milton.*

The Hall of Harps is lone to-night,
   And cold the chieftain's hearth:
It hath no mead, it hath no light;
   No voice of melody, no sound of mirth.

The bow lies broken on the floor
   Whence the free step is gone;
The pilgrim turns him from the door
   Where minstrel-blood hath stain'd the threshold stone.

And I, too, go: my wound is deep,
   My brethren long have died;
Yet, ere my soul grow dark with sleep
   Winds! bear the spoiler one more tone of pride!

Bear it where, on his battle plain,
   Beneath the setting sun,
He counts my country's noble slain—
   Say to him—Saxon, think not *all* is won.

Thou hast laid low the warrior's head,
   The minstrel's chainless hand;
Dreamer! that numberest with the dead
   The burning spirit of the mountain land!

Think'st thou, because the song hath ceased,
   The soul of song is flown?
Think'st thou it woke to crown the feast,
   It lived beside the ruddy hearth alone?

No! by our wrongs, and by our blood,
   We leave it pure and free;
Though hush'd awhile, that sounding flood
   Shall roll in joy through ages yet to be.

We leave it 'midst our country's woe—
   The birthright of her breast;
We leave it as we leave the snow
   Bright and eternal on Eryri's† crest.

We leave it with our fame to dwell
   Upon our children's breath.
Our voice in their's through time shall swell—
   The bard hath gifts of prophecy from death.

---

* At the time of the supposed massacre of the Welsh bards by Edward the First.
† Eryri, Welsh name for the Snowdon mountains.

He dies; but yet the mountains stand,
　Yet sweeps the torrent's tide;
And this is yet *Aneurin's** land—
Winds! bear the spoiler one more tone of pride!

THE FAIR ISLE.†

(FOR THE MELODY CALLED THE "WELSH GROUND.")

Sons of the Fair Isle! forget not the time,
Ere spoilers had breathed the free air of your clime:
All that its eagles behold in their flight
Was yours, from the deep to each storm-mantled height.
Though from your race that proud birthright be torn,
Unquench'd is the spirit for monarchy born.
　　　　　　CHORUS.
Darkly though clouds may hang o'er us awhile,
The crown shall not pass from the Beautiful Isle.

Ages may roll ere your children regain
The land for which heroes have perish'd in vain;
Yet, in the sound of your names shall be power,
Around her still gathering in glory's full hour.
Strong in the fame of the mighty that sleep,
Your Britain shall sit on the throne of the deep.
　　　　　　CHORUS.
Then shall their spirits rejoice in her smile,
Who died for the crown of the Beautiful Isle.

THE ROCK OF CADER IDRIS.

[It is an old tradition of the Welsh bards, that on the summit of the mountain Cader Idris, is an excavation resembling a couch; and that whoever should pass a night in that hollow, would be found in the morning either dead, in a state of frenzy, or endowed with the highest poetical inspiration.]

I LAY on that rock where the storms have their dwelling,
　The birthplace of phantoms, the home of the cloud;
Around it for ever deep music is swelling,
　The voice of the mountain-wind, solemn and loud.
'Twas a midnight of shadows all fitfully streaming,
　Of wild waves and breezes, that mingled their moan;
Of dim shrouded stars, as from gulfs faintly gleaming;
　And I met the dread gloom of its grandeur alone.

* Aneurin, one of the noblest of the Welsh bards.
† Ynys Prydain was the ancient Welsh name of Britain, and signifies *fair* or *beautiful isle*.

I lay there in silence—a spirit came o'er me;
  Man's tongue hath no language to speak what I saw:
Things glorious, unearthly, pass'd floating before me,
  And my heart almost fainted with rapture and awe.
I view'd the dread beings, around us that hover,
  Though veil'd by the mists of mortality's breath;
And I call'd upon darkness the vision to cover,
  For a strife was within me of madness and death.

I saw them—the powers of the wind and the ocean,
  The rush of whose pinion bears onward the storms;
Like the sweep of the white-rolling wave was their motion,
  I *felt* their dim presence,—but knew not their forms!
I saw them—the mighty of ages departed—
  The dead were around me that night on the hill:
From their eyes, as they pass'd, a cold radiance they darted,—
  There was light on my soul, but my heart's blood was chill.

I saw what man looks on, and dies—but my spirit
  Was strong, and triumphantly lived through that hour;
And, as from the grave, I awoke to inherit
  A flame all immortal, a voice, and a power!
Day burst on that rock with the purple cloud crested,
  And high Cader Idris rejoiced in the sun:—
But O! what new glory all nature invested,
  When the sense which gives soul to her beauty was won!

HYMNS FOR CHILDHOOD.

INTRODUCTORY VERSES.

O! BLEST art thou whose steps may rove
Through the green paths of vale and grove,
Or, leaving all their charms below,
Climb the wild mountain's airy brow!

And gaze afar o'er cultur'd plains,
And cities with their stately fanes,
And forests, that beneath thee lie,
And ocean mingling with the sky.

For man can show thee nought so fair,
As Nature's varied marvels there;
And if thy pure and artless breast,
Can feel their grandeur, thou art blest!

For thee the stream in beauty flows,
For thee the gale of summer blows;
And, in deep glen and wood walk free,
Voices of joy still breathe for thee.

But happier far, if then thy soul
Can soar to Him who made the whole,
If to thine eye the simplest flower
Portray His bounty and His power:

If, in whate'er is bright or grand,
Thy mind can trace His viewless hand,
If Nature's music bid thee raise
Thy song of gratitude and praise ;

If heaven and earth, with beauty fraught,
Lead to His throne thy raptured thought ;
If there thou lovest *His* love to read ;
Then, wand'rer, thou art blest indeed !

THE RAINBOW.

"I do set my bow in the clouds, and it shall be for a token of a covenant between me and the earth."—*Genesis*, ix. 13.

SOFT falls the mild reviving shower
  From April's changeful skies,
And rain-drops bend each trembling flower
  They tinge with richer dies.

Soon shall their genial influence call
  A thousand buds to-day,
Which, waiting but that balmy fall,
  In hidden beauty lay.

E'en now full many a blossom's bell
  With fragrance fills the shade ;
And verdure clothes each grassy dell,
  In brighter tints array'd.

But mark ! what arch of varied hue
  From heaven to earth is bow'd ?
Haste ; ere it vanish, haste to view
  The rainbow in the cloud !

How bright its glory ! there behold
  The emerald's verdant rays,
The topaz blends its hue of gold
  With the deep ruby's blaze.

Yet not alone to charm thy sight
  Was given the vision fair—
Gaze on that arch of color'd light,
  And read God's mercy there.

It tells us that the mighty deep,
  Fast by the Eternal chain'd,
No more o'er earth's domain shall sweep,
  Awful and unrestrain'd.

It tells that seasons, heat and cold,
　　Fix'd by his sovereign will,
Shall, in their course, bid man behold
　　Seed-time and harvest still.

That still the flower shall deck the field,
　　When vernal zephyrs blow ;
That still the vine its fruit shall yield,
　　When autumn sunbeams glow.

Then, child of that fair earth ! which yet
　　Smiles with each charm endow'd,
Bless thou His name, whose mercy set
　　The rainbow in the cloud !

THE SUN.

The Sun comes forth ; each mountain height
　　Glows with a tinge of rosy light,
And flowers, that slumber'd through the night
　　Their dewy leaves unfold ;
A flood of splendor bursts on high,
And ocean's breast gives back a sky
　　All steep'd in molten gold.

Oh ! thou art glorious, orb of day ;
Exulting nations hail thy ray,
Creation swells a choral lay,
　　To welcome thy return ;
From thee all nature draws her hues,
Thy beams the insect's wing suffuse,
　　And in the diamond burn.

Yet must thou fade ;—when earth and heaven
By fire and tempest shall be riven,
Thou, from thy sphere of radiance driven,
　　Oh Sun ! must fall at last ;
Another heaven, another earth.
New power, new glory shall have birth,
　　When all we see is past.

But He who gave the word of might,
" Let there be light,"—and there *was* light.
Who bade thee chase the gloom of night,
　　And beam the world to bless ;
For ever bright, for ever pure,
Alone unchanging shall endure
　　The Sun of Righteousness !

THE RIVERS.

Go ! trace th' unnumber'd streams o'er earth
　　That wind their devious course,

THE STARS.

That draw from Alpine heights their birth,
   Deep vale, or cavern source.
Some by majestic cities glide,
   Proud scenes of man's renown,
Some lead their solitary tide,
   Where pathless forests frown.

Some calmly roll o'er golden sands,
   Where Afric's deserts lie;
Or spread, to clothe rejoicing lands
   With rich fertility.
These bear the bark, whose stately sail
   Exulting seems to swell;
While these, scarce rippled by a gale,
   Sleep in the lonely dell.

Yet on, alike, though swift or slow
   Their various waves may sweep,
Through cities or through shades they flow,
   To the same boundless deep.

Oh! thus, whate'er our path of life,
   Through sunshine or through gloom,
Through scenes of quiet or of strife,
   Its end is still the tomb.

The chief whose mighty deeds we hail,
   The monarch throned on high,
The peasant in his native vale—
   All journey on—to die!

But if *Thy* guardian care, my God!
   The pilgrim's course attend,
I will not fear the dark abode,
   To which my footsteps bend.

For thence thine all-redeeming Son,
   Who died the world to save,
In light, in triumph, rose, and won
   The victory from the grave!

THE STARS.

"The heavens declare the glory of God, and the firmament sheweth his handywork."
                                    Psalm xix. 1

No cloud obscures the summer sky,
The moon in brightness walks on high,
And, set in azure, every star
Shines, a pure gem of heaven, afar!

Child of the earth! oh! lift thy glance
To yon bright firmament's expanse;
The glories of its realm explore,
And gaze, and wonder, and adore!

Doth it not speak to every sense,
The marvels of Omnipotence?
Seest thou not there the Almighty name
Inscribed in characters of flame?

Count o'er those lamps of quenchless light,
That sparkle through the shades of night;
Behold them!—can a mortal boast
To number that celestial host?

Mark well each little star, whose rays
In distant splendor meet thy gaze:
Each is a world, by him sustain'd
Who from eternity hath reign'd.

Each, kindled not for earth alone,
Hath circling planets of its own,
And beings, whose existence springs
From Him, the all-powerful King of Kings.

Haply, those glorious beings know
No stain of guilt, or tear of woe;
But, raising still the adoring voice,
For ever in their God rejoice.

What then art *thou*, O child of clay!
Amid creation's grandeur, say?
E'en as an insect on the breeze,
E'en as a dew-drop, lost in seas!

Yet fear thou not!—the sovereign hand
Which spread the ocean and the land,
And hung the rolling spheres in air,
Hath, e'en for thee, a Father's care!

Be thou at peace! the all-seeing eye,
Pervading earth, and air, and sky—
The searching glance which none may flee,
Is still, in mercy, turned on thee.

THE OCEAN.

"They that go down to the sea in ships, that do business in great waters; these see the works of the Lord, and his wonders in the deep."—*Psalm*, cvii. 23, 24.

HE that in venturous barks hath been
  A wand'rer on the deep,
Can tell of many an awful scene,
  Where storms for ever sweep.

For many a fair, majestic sight
  Hath met his wand'ring eye,
Beneath the streaming northern light,
  Or blaze of Indian sky.

Go! ask him of the whirlpool's roar,
  Whose echoing thunder peals
Loud, as if rush'd along the shore
  An army's chariot wheels;

Of icebergs, floating o'er the main,
  Or fix'd upon the coast,
Like glitt'ring citadel or fane,
  'Mid the bright realms of frost;

Of coral rocks, from waves below
  In steep ascent that tower,
And fraught with peril, daily grow,
  Form'd by an insect's power;

Of sea-fires, which at dead of night
  Shine o'er the tides afar,
And make the expanse of ocean bright,
  As heaven, with many a star.

O God! thy name *they* well may praise,
  Who to the deep go down,
And trace the wonders of thy ways,
  Where rocks and billows frown!

If glorious be that awful deep
  No human power can bind,
What then art *Thou*, who bidd'st it keep
  Within its bounds confined!

Let heaven and earth in praise unite,
  Eternal praise to Thee,
Whose word can rouse the tempest's might,
  Or still the raging sea!

THE THUNDER-STORM.

Deep, fiery clouds o'ercast the sky,
  Dead stillness reigns in air,
There is not e'en a breeze, on high
  The gossamer to bear.

The woods are hush'd, the waves at rest
  The lake is dark and still,
Reflecting on its shadowy breast
  Each form of rock and hill.

The lime-leaf waves not in the grove,
  The rose-tree in the bower;
The birds have ceased their song of love,
  Awed by the threatening hour.

'Tis noon;—yet nature's calm profound
  Seems as at midnight deep;

But hark! what peal of awful sound
　Breaks on creation's sleep?
The thunder bursts!—its rolling might
　Seems the firm hills to shake;
And in terrific splendor bright,
　The gather'd lightnings break.

Yet fear not, shrink not thou, my child!
　Though by the bolt's descent
Were the tall cliffs in ruins piled,
　And the wide forest rent.

Doth not thy God behold thee still,
　With all-surveying eye?
Doth not his power all nature fill,
　Around, beneath, on high?

Know, hadst thou eagle-pinions free,
　To track the realms of air,
Thou could'st not reach a spot where He
　Would not be with thee there!

In the wide city's peopled towers,
　On the vast ocean's plains,
'Midst the deep woodland's loneliest bowers,
　Alike the Almighty reigns!

Then fear not, though the angry sky
　A thousand darts should cast;
Why should we tremble, e'en to die,
　And be with *Him* at last?

THE BIRDS.

"Are not five sparrows sold for two farthings; and not one of them is forgotten before God?"—*St. Luke*, xii. 6.

Tribes of the air! whose favor'd race
May wander through the realms of space,
　Free guests of earth and sky;
In form, in plumage, and in song,
What gifts of nature mark your throng
　With bright variety!

Nor differ less your forms, your flight,
Your dwellings hid from hostile sight,
　And the wild haunts ye love;
Birds of the gentle beak!* how dear
Your wood-note, to the wand'rer's ear,
　In shadowy vale or grove!

Far other scenes, remote, sublime,
Where swain or hunter may not climb,

---

* The Italians call all singing birds, *birds of the gentle beak*.

THE SKY-LARK.

The mountain-eagle seeks;
Alone he reigns a monarch there,
Scarce will the chamois' footstep dare
    Ascend his Alpine peaks.

Others there are, that make their home
Where the white billows roar and foam,
    Around the o'erhanging rock;
Fearless they skim the angry wave.
Or shelter'd in their sea-beat cave,
    The tempest's fury mock.

Where Afric's burning realm expands,
The ostrich haunts the desert sands,
    Parch'd by the blaze of day;
The swan, where northern rivers glide,
Through the tall reeds that fringe their tide,
    Floats graceful on her way.

The condor, where the Andes tower,
Spreads his broad wing of pride and power
    And many a storm defies;
Bright in the orient realms of morn,
All beauty's richest hues adorn
    The bird of paradise.

Some, amidst India's groves of palm,
And spicy forests breathing balm,
    Weave soft their pendant nest;
Some deep in Western wilds, display
Their fairy form and plumage gay,
    In rainbow colors drest.

Others no varied song may pour,
May boast no eagle-plume to soar,
    No tints of light may wear;
Yet, know, our Heavenly Father guides
The least of these, and well provides
    For each, with tenderest care.

Shall He not then *thy* guardian be?
Will not his aid extend to *thee?*
    Oh! safely may'st thou rest!—
Trust in his love, and e'en should pain,
Should sorrow tempt thee to complain,
    Know what He wills is best!

THE SKY-LARK.

CHILD'S MORNING HYMN.

THE Sky-lark, when the dews of morn,
Hang tremulous on flower and thorn,

And violets round his nest exhale
Their fragrance on the early gale,
To the first sunbeam spreads his wings,
Buoyant with joy, and soars and sings.

He rests not on the leafy spray,
To warble his exulting lay;
But high above the morning cloud
Mounts in triumphant freedom proud,
And swells, when nearest to the sky,
His notes of sweetest ecstasy.

Thus, my Creator? thus the more
My spirit's wing to Thee can soar,
The more she triumphs to behold
Thy love in all thy works unfold,
And bids her hymns of rapture be
Most glad, when rising most to Thee!

THE NIGHTINGALE.

CHILD'S EVENING HYMN.

When twilight's grey and pensive hour
Brings the low breeze, and shuts the flower,
And bids the solitary star
Shine in pale beauty from afar.

When gathering shades the landscape veil,
And peasants seek their village-dale,
And mists from river-wave arise,
And dew in every blossom lies.

When evening's primrose opes to shed
Soft fragrance round her grassy bed;
When glowworms in the wood-walk light
Their lamp, to cheer the traveller's sight;

At that calm hour, so still, so pale,
Awakes the lonely nightingale;
And from a hermitage of shade
Fills with her voice the forest-glade;

And sweeter far that melting voice,
Than all which through the day rejoice;
And still shall bard and wand'rer love
The twilight music of the grove.

Father in heaven! oh! thus when day
With all its cares hath pass'd away,
And silent hours waft peace on earth,
And hush the louder strains of mirth;

Thus may sweet songs of praise and prayer
To Thee my spirit's offering bear;

Yon star, my signal, set on high,
For vesper-hymns of piety.

So may thy mercy and thy power
Protect me through the midnight hour;
And balmy sleep and visions blest
Smile on thy servant's bed of rest.

THE NORTHERN SPRING.

When the soft breath of Spring goes forth
Far o'er the mountains of the North,
How soon those wastes of dazzling snow
With life, and bloom, and beauty glow!

Then bursts the verdure of the plains,
Then break the streams from icy chains;
And the glad reindeer seeks no more
Amidst deep snows his mossy store,

Then the dark pine-wood's boughs are seen
Fringed tenderly with living green;
And roses, in their brightest dyes,
By Lapland's founts and lakes arise.

Thus, in a moment, from the gloom
And the cold fetters of the tomb,
Thus shall the blest Redeemer's voice
Call forth his servants to rejoice.

For He, whose word is truth, hath said,
His power to life shall wake the dead,
And summon those he loves on high,
To " put on immortality !"

Then, all its transient sufferings o'er,
On wings of light the soul shall soar,
Exulting, to that blest abode,
Where tears of sorrow never flow'd.

PARAPHRASE OF PSALM CXLVIII.

" Praise ye the Lord. Praise ye the Lord from the heavens: **praise** him in the heights."

Praise ye the Lord! on every height
  Songs to his glory raise!
Ye angel-hosts, ye stars of night,
  Join in immortal praise!
Oh! heaven of heavens! let praise far-swelling
  From all thine orbs be sent!

Join in the strain, ye waters, dwelling
  Above the firmament!

For His the word which gave you birth,
  And majesty, and might;
Praise to the Highest from the earth,
  And let the deeps unite!

Oh! fire and vapor, hail and snow!
  Ye servants of His will!
O! stormy winds, that only blow
  His mandates to fulfil;

Mountains and rocks, to heaven that rise;
  Fair cedars of the wood!
Creatures of life that wing the skies,
  Or track the plains for food;

Judges of nations! kings, whose hand
  Waves the proud sceptre high!
O! youths and virgins of the land,
  O! age and infancy!

Praise ye His name, to whom alone
  All homage should be given;
Whose glory, from the eternal throne
  Spreads wide o'er earth and heaven!

DE CHATILLON; OR, THE CRUSADERS.
A TRAGEDY.
HITHERTO UNPUBLISHED.

DRAMATIS PERSONÆ.

RAIMER DE CHATILLON,	*A French Baron.*
AYMER,	*His Brother.*
MELECH,	*A Saracen Emir.*
HERMAN,	
DU MORNAY, }	*Knights.*
GASTON,	*A Vassal of Raimer's*
URBAN,	*A Priest.*
SADI,	
MORAIMA,	*Daughter of Melech.*

Knights, Arabs, Citizens, &c.

ACT I.

SCENE I.—*Before the gates of a City in Palestine.*
URBAN, PRIESTS, CITIZENS, *at the gates. Others looking from the walls above.*

  Urb. (*to a* CITIZEN *on the walls above.*) You see their lances glistening? You can tell
The way they take?

Cit.   Not yet. Their march is slow;
They have not reach'd the jutting cliff, where first
The mountain path divides.
    Urb.   And now?
    Cit.   The wood
Shuts o'er their track. Now spears are flashing out—
It is the banner of De Chatillon.
        (*Very slow and mournful military music without.*)
This way! they come this way!
    Urb.   All holy saints
Grant that they pass us not! Those martial sounds
Have a strange tone of sadness! Hark, they swell
Proudly, yet full of sorrow.
        [*Knights, Soldiers, &c., enter with* RAIMER DE CHATILLON.
                Welcome, knights!
Ye bring us timely aid! men's hearts were full
Of doubt and terror. Brave De Chatillon!
True soldier of the Cross! I welcome thee;
I greet thee with all blessing! Where thou art
There is deliverance!
    Rai. (*bending to receive the Priest's blessing.*)
                Holy man, I come
From a lost battle.
    Urb.   And thou bring'st the heart
Whose spirit yields not to defeat.
    Rai.   I bring
My father's bier.
    Urb.   His bier!—I marvel not
To see your brow thus darken'd!—And he died
As he had lived, in arms?
    Rai. (*gloomily.*)   Not, not in arms—
His war-cry had been silenced. Have ye place
Amidst your ancient knightly sepulchres
For a warrior with his sword?—He bade me bear
His dust to slumber here.
    Urb.   And it shall sleep
Beside our noblest, while we yet can call
One holy place our own!—Heard you, my lord,
That the fierce Kaled's host is on its march
Against our city?
    Rai. (*with sudden exultation.*) That were joy to know.
That were proud joy!—who told it?—there's a weight
That must be heaved from off my troubled heart
By the strong tide of battle!—Kaled!—Ay,
A gallant name!—how heard you?
    Urb.   Nay, it seem'd
As if a breeze first bore the rumor in.
I know not how it rose; but now it comes
Like fearful truth, and we were sad, thus left
Hopeless of aid or counsel—till we saw——
    Rai. (*hastily.*) You have my brother here?
    Urb. (*with embarrassment.*) We have—but he——

Rai. But he—but he!—Aymer de Chatillon.
The fiery knight—the very soul o' the field—
Rushing on danger with the joyous step
Of a hunter o'er the hills!—is *that* a tone
Wherewith to speak of *him!*—I heard a tale—
If it be true—nay, tell me!
 Urb.   He is here;
Ask him to tell thee——
 Rai.   ——If that tale be true—
    (*he turns suddenly to his companions.*)
—Follow me!—give the noble dead his rites,
And we will have our day of vengeance yet,
Soldiers and friends!   [*Exeunt omnes.*

Scene II.—*A Hall of Oriental architecture, opening upon gardens. A fountain in the centre.*

Aymer de Chatillon—Moraima.

Mor. (*bending over a couch on which her brother is sleeping.*) He sleeps so calmly now; the soft wind here
Brings in such lulling sounds!—Nay, think you not
This slumber will restore him? See you not
His cheek's faint glow?
 Aym. (*turning away.*) It was *my* sword which gave
The wound he dies from!
 Mor.   Dies from! say not so!
The brother of my childhood and my youth,
My heart's first friend!—Oh! I have been too weak,
I have delay'd too long!—*He* could not sue,
He bade *me* urge the prayer he would not speak,
And I withheld it!—Christian, set us free!
You have been gentle with us! 'tis the weight,
The bitter feeling, of captivity
Which preys upon his life!
 Aym.   You would go hence?
 Mor. For *his* sake!
 Aym.   You would leave me! 'tis too late.
You see it not—you know not, that your voice
Hath power in its low mournfulness to shake
Mine inmost soul?—That you but look on me,
With the soft darkness of your earnest eyes,
And bid the world fade from me, and call up
A thousand passionate dreams, which wrap my life
As with a troubled cloud?—The very sound
Of your light step hath made my heart o'erflow
Even unto aching with the sudden gush
Of its deep tenderness!—You know it not?
—Moraima!—speak to me!
 Mor. (*covering herself with a veil.*) I can but weep!
Is it even so?—this love was born for tears!
Aymer! I can but weep! (*going to leave him, he detains her.*)
 Aym. Hear me, yet hear me!—I was rear'd in arms

And the proud blast of trumpets, and the shouts
Of banner'd armies, these were joy to me,
Enough of joy! Till you—I look'd on you—
We met where swords were flashing, and the light
Of burning towers glared wildly on the slain—
And then——
    Mor. (*hurriedly.*) Yes! then you saved me!
    Aym.   Then I knew
At once, what springs of deeper happiness
Lay far within my soul—and they burst forth
Troubled and dash'd with fear—yet sweet!—I loved!
Moraima! leave me not!
    Mor.   For *us* to love!
Oh! is't not taking sorrow to our hearts,
Binding her there.—I know not what I say!
How shall I look upon my brother? Hark!
Did he not call? (*she goes up to the couch.*)
    Aym.   Am I beloved? She wept
With a full heart!—I am! and such deep joy
Is found on earth! If I should lose her now!
If aught——(*an attendant enters.*)
(*To attendant.*) You seek me! why is this?
    Att.   My Lord,
Your brother and his knights.
    Aym.   Here! are they here?
The knights—my brother—said'st thou?
    Att.   Yes, my Lord,
And he would speak with you.
    Aym.   I see—I know
(*To attendant.*) Leave me! I know why he is come—'tis vain,
They shall not part us! (*looking back on Moraima as he goes
      out.*)   What a silent grace
Floats round her form!—They shall not part us! no!
                                  [*Exit—Scene closes.*

SCENE III.—*A square of the city—a church in the back
    ground.*

RAIMER DE CHATILLON.

Raimer (*walking to and fro impatiently.*)
And now, too, now! My father unavenged,
Our holy places threaten'd, every heart
Task'd to its strength? A knight of Palestine
Now to turn dreamer, to melt down his soul
In love-lorn sighs; and for an infidel!
—Will he lift up his eyes to look on mine?
Will he not—hush!
    [AYMER *enters. They look on each other for a moment
      without speaking.*]
    Rai. (*suppressing his emotion.*) So brothers meet! you
      know
Wherefore I come?

Aym. It cannot be, 'tis vain.
Tell me not of it!
Rai. How! you have not heard?
(*turning from him.*)
He hath so shut the world out with his dreams,
The tidings have not reach'd him! or perchance
Have been forgotten! You have captives here?
Aym. (*hurriedly.*) Yes, mine! my own—won by the right of
 arms!
You dare not question it.
Rai. A prince, they say,
And his fair sister—*is* the maid so fair?
Aym. (*turning suddenly upon him.*) What, *you* would see
 her!
Rai. (*scornfully.*) I!—Oh, yes! to quell
My soul's deep yearnings!—Let *me* look on swords.
—Boy, boy! recall yourself!—I come to you
With the last blessing of our father!
Aym. Last!
His last!—how mean you?—Is he——
Rai. Dead?—yes! dead.
He died upon my breast.
Aym. (*with the deepest emotion.*) And I was *here!*
Dead!—and upon *your* breast!—*You* closed his eyes—
While I—he spoke of me?
Rai. With such deep love!
He ever loved you most!—his spirit seem'd
To linger for your coming.
Aym. What! he thought
That I was on my way!—He look'd for me?
And I——
Rai. You came not!—I had sent to you,
And told you he was wounded.
Aym. Yes—but not—
Not *mortally!*
Rai. 'Twas not that outward wound—
That might have closed; and yet he surely thought
That you would come to him! He call'd on you
When his thoughts wander'd!—Ay, the very night,
The very hour he died—some hasty step
Enter'd his chamber—and he raised his head,
With a faint lightning in his eyes, and ask'd
If it were yours!—That hope's brief moment pass'd—
He sank then.—
Aym. (*throwing himself upon his brother's neck.*)
Brother! take me to his grave,
That I may kneel there, till my burning tears,
With the strong passion of repentant love,
Wring forth a voice to pardon me!
Rai. You weep!
—*Tears* for the garlands on a maiden's grave!
You know not *how* he died!

Aym.   Not of his wound?
Rai. His wound!—it is the silent spirit's wound,
We cannot reach to heal!—One burning thought
Prey'd on his heart.
Aym.   Not—not—he had not heard—
He bless'd *me*, Raimer?
Rai.   Have you flung away
Your birthright?—Yes! he bless'd you!—but he died
—He whose name stood for Victory's—he believed
The ancient honor from his grey head fall'n,
And died—he died of *shame!*
Aym.   What feverish dream—
Rai. (*vehemently.*) Was it not lost, the warrior's latest field,
The noble city held for Palestine
Taken—the Cross laid low?—I came too late
To turn the tide of that disastrous fight,
But not to rescue him. We bore him thence
Wounded, upon his shield—
Aym.   And I was *here!*
Rai. He cast one look back on his burning towers,
Then threw the red sword of a hundred fields
To the earth—and hid his face!—I knew, I knew
His heart was broken!—Such a death for *him!*
—The wasting—the sick loathing of the sun—
Let the foe's charger trample out my life,
Let me not die of *shame!*—But we will have——
Aym. (*grasping his hand eagerly.*) Yes! vengeance!
Rai. Vengeance!—By the dying once,
And once before the dead, and yet once more
Alone with Heaven's bright stars, I took that vow
For *both* his sons!—Think of it, when the night
Is dark around you, and in festive halls
Keep your soul hush'd, and think of it!
(*A low chant of female voices, heard from behind the scenes.*)
       Fall'n is the flower of Islam's race,
         Break ye the lance he bore,
       And loose his war-steed from its place,
         He is no more—
(*Single voice.*)   No more!
       Weep for him mother, sister, bride!
       He died, with all his fame—
(*Single voice.*)   He died!
Aym. (*Pointing to a palace, and eagerly speaking to his attendant, who enters.*)
Came it not thence?—Rudolf, what sounds are these?
Att. The Moslem Prince—your captive—he is dead,
It is the mourner's wail for him.
Aym.   And she—
His sister—heard you—did they say she wept!
                                        [*Hurrying away.*

Rai. (*indignantly.*) All the deep-stirring tones of Honor's voice
In a moment silenced! [*Solemn military music.*
(*A funeral procession, with priests, &c., crosses the background to enter the church.*)
Rai. (*following* AYMER *and grasping his arm.*)
Aymer! there, look there!
It is your father's bier!
Aym. (*returning,*) He bless'd me, Raimer?
You heard him bless me?—Yes! *you* closed his eyes,
He look'd for me in vain!
[*He goes to the bier, and bends over it, covering his face.*

ACT II.

SCENE I.—*A room in the citadel.*

RAIMER, AYMER, *Knights, assembled in Council.*

A Knight. What! with our weary and distracted bands
To dare another field!—Nay, give them rest.
Rai. (*impatiently.*) Rest! and that sleepless thought—
Knight. These walls have strength
To baffle siege. Let the foe gird us in—
We must wait aid; our soldiers must forget
That last disastrous day. [press
Rai. (*coming forward.*) If they forget it, in the combat's
May their spears fail them!
Knight. Yet, think thee, chief.
Rai. When *I* forget it—how! you see not, knights!
Whence we must *now* draw strength. Send down your thoughts
Into the very depths of grief and shame,
And bring back courage *thence!* To talk of *rest!*
How do they rest, unburied on their field,
Our brethren slain by Gaza? Had we time
To give them funeral rites? and ask we now
Time to *forget* their fall! My father died—
I cannot speak of him! What! and *forget*
The infidel's fierce trampling o'er our dead?
Forget his scornful shout? Give battle now,
While the thought lives as fire lives!—*there* lies strength!
Hold the dark memory fast! Now, now—this hour!
Aymer, you do not speak.
Aym. (*starting.*) Have I not said?
Battle! yes, give us battle!—room to pour
The troubled spirit forth upon the winds,
With the trumpet's ringing blast! Way for remorse!
Free way for vengeance!
All the Knights. Arm! Heaven wills it so!
Rai. Gather your forces to the western gate!
Let none forget that day! Our field was lost,
Our city's strength laid low—one mighty heart
Broken! Let none forget it! [*Exeunt.*

SCENE II.—*Garden of a Palace.*
MORAIMA.

Mor. Yes! his last look—my brother's dying look
Reproach'd me as it faded from his face.
And I deserved it! Had I not given way
To the wild guilty pleadings of my heart,
I might have won his freedom! Now, 'tis past.
He *is* free now!
     [AYMER *enters, armed as for battle.*
Aymer! you look so changed!
 Aym. Changed!—it may be. A storm o' the soul goes by
Not like a breeze! There's such a fearful grasp
Fix'd on my heart! Speak to me—lull *remorse!*
Bid me farewell!
 Mor. Yes! it *must* be farewell!
No other word but that.
 Aym. No other word!
The passionate, burning words that I could pour
From my heart's depths! 'Tis madness! What have I
To do with love? I see it all—the mist
Is gone—the bright mist gone! I see the woe,
The ruin, the despair! And yet I love,
Love wildly, fatally!—But speak to me!
Fill all my soul once more with reckless joy!
That blessed voice again!
 Mor. Why, why is this?
Oh! send me to my father! We must part.
 Aym. Part!—yes, I know it all! I could not go
Till I had seen you!—Give me one farewell,
The last—perchance the last!—but one farewell,
Whose mournful music I may take with me
Through tumult, horror, death!
     [*A distant sound of trumpets.*
 Mor. (*starting.*) You go to battle!
 Aym. Hear you not that sound?
Yes! I go *there*, where dark and stormy thoughts
Find their free path!
 Mor. Aymer! who leads the foe?
(*Confused.*) I meant—I mean—my people!—Who is he,
My people's leader? [—you seem—
 Aym. Kaled. (*looking at her suspiciously.*) How!
The name disturbs you!
 Mor. My last brother's name.
 Aym. Fear not *my* sword for him!
 Mor. (*turning away.*) If they should meet!
I know the vow he made. (*To* AYMER)
     If thou—if *thou*
Should'st fall!
 Aym. Moraima! then your blessed tears
Would flow for me? then you would weep for me?
 Mor. I must weep tears of very shame—and yet—

If—if your words have been love's own true words,
Grant me one boon!   [*Trumpet sounds again.*
  Aym.   Hark! I must hence—a boon!
Ask it, and hold its memory to your heart,
As the last token, it may be, of love
So deep and sad.
  Mor.   Pledge me your knightly faith!
  Aym. My knightly faith, my life, my honor—all,
I pledge thee all to grant it!
  Mor.   Then, to-day,
Go not *this* day to battle!—He is there,
My brother Kaled!
  Aym. (*wildly.*) Have I flung my sword
Down to dishonor?   [*Going to leave her—she detains him*
  Mor.   Oh! your name hath stirr'd
His soul amidst his tents, and he had vow'd,
Long ere we met, to cross his sword with yours,
Till one or both should fall. There hath been *death*
Since then, amongst us; he will seek *revenge*,
And *his* revenge—forgive me!—oh! forgive!
—I could not bear *that* thought!
  Aym.   Now must the glance
Of a brave man strike me to the very dust!
Ay, this is *shame*.   [*Covering his face.*
(*Turning wildly to Moraima.*) You scorn me too?
    Away!—she does not know
What she hath done!   [*Rushes out.*

    Scene III.—*Before a gateway within the city.*

    Raimer, Herman, *Knights, Men-at-arms,* &c.

  Her. 'Tis past the hour.
  Rai. (*looking out anxiously.*) Away! 'tis *not* the hour!
Not yet!—When was the battle's hour delay'd
For a Chatillon? We must have come too soon!
All are not here.
  Her.   Yes, all!
  Rai.   They came too soon!   [all here!
(*Going up to the knights.*) Couci, De Foix, Du Mornay—here,
And *he* the last!—*my* brother!   (*To a Soldier.*)
    Where's your lord?
(*Turning away.*) Why should I ask, when that fair Infidel——
                                   [Aymer *enters.*
The Saracen at our gates—and *you* the last!
Come on, remember all your fame!
  Aym. (*coming forward in great agitation.*) My fame!
—Why did you save me from the Paynim's sword,
In my first battle?
  Rai.   What wild words are these?
  Aym. You should have let me perish *then*—yes *then!*
Go to your field and leave me!
  Knights. ('*thronging round him.*) Leave you!

DE CHATILLON.

Rai. Aymer!
Was it *your* voice?
  Aym.   *Now* talk to me of fame!
Tell me of all my warlike ancestors,
And of my father's death—that bitter death!
Never did pilgrim for the fountains thirst
As I for this day's vengeance!—To your field!
—I may not go!
  Rai. (*turning from him.*) The name his race hath borne
Through a thousand battles—lost!   [*Returning to* AYMER.
          A Chatillon!
Will you *live* and wed dishonor?
  Aym. (*covering his face.*)   Let the grave
Take me and cover me!—I must go down
To its rest without my sword!
  Rai. There's some dark spell upon him! Aymer, brother!
Let *me* not die of shame!—He that died so
Turn'd sickening from the sun!
  Aym.   Where should I turn?
          [*Going up abruptly to the knights.*
Herman, Du Mornay! ye have stood with me
I' the battle's front—ye know me!—ye have seen
The fiery joy of danger bear me on,
As a wind the arrow!—Leave me now—'tis past!   ·[*smiled,*
  Rai. (*with bitterness.*) He comes from *her!*—the infidel hath
Doubtless for this.
  Aym.   I should have been to-day
Where shafts fly thickest, and the crossing swords
Cannot flash out for blood!—hark! you are call'd!
    [*Wild Turkish music heard without. The background
    of the scene becomes more and more crowded with
    armed men.*
Lay lance in rest!—wave, noble banners, wave! •
          [*Throwing down his sword.*
Go from me!—leave the fallen!—
  Her.   Nay, but the cause?
Tell us the cause!   [crested helm
  Rai. (*approaching him indignantly.*) Your sword—your
And your knight's mantle—cast them down! your name
Is in the dust!—our father's name!—the cause?
—Tell it not, tell it not!
      [*Turning to the soldiers and waving his hand.*
Sound, trumpets, sound!
On, lances, for the Cross!   [*at* AYMER.
    [*Military music. As the knights march out, he looks back*
          I would not now
Call back my noble father from the dead,
If I could with but a breath!—Sound, trumpets, sound!
          [*Exeunt knights and soldiers.*
  Aym. Why should I bear this shame?—'tis not too late!
    [*Rushing after them—he suddenly checks himself.*
My faith!—my knightly faith pledged to my fall!   [*Exit*

DE CHATILLON.

Scene IV.—*Before a Church.*

Groups of citizens passing to and fro. Aymer *standing against one of the pillars of the Church in the background, and leaning on his sword.*

  1*st Cit.* (*to* 2*d.*) From the walls?—how goes the battle?
  2*d Cit.* Well, all well,
Praise to the Saints!—I saw De Chatillon
Fighting, as if upon his single arm
The fate o' the day were set.
  3*d Cit.*   Shame light on those
That strike not with him in their place!
  1*st Cit.*   You mean
His brother?—Ay, is't not a fearful thing
That one of such a race—a brave one too—
Should have thus fallen?
  2*d Cit.*   They say the captive girl
Whom he so loved, hath won him from his faith
To the vile Paynim creed.
  Aym. (*suddenly coming forward.*) Who dares say *that?*
Show me who dares say that!
            [*they shrink back—he laughs scornfully.*
                Ha! ha! ye thought
To play with a sleeper's name!—to make your mirth
As low-born men sit by a tomb, and jest
O'er a dead warrior! Where's the slanderer? Speak!

  A Citizen *enters hastily.*

  Cit. Haste to the walls!—De Chatillon hath slain
The Paynim chief!   [*They all go out.*
  Aym. Why should they shrink?—I, I should ask the night
To cover me!—I that have flung my name
Away to scorn!—Hush! am I not alone?
                [*Listening eagerly.*
There's a voice calling me—a voice i' the air—
My father's!—'Twas my father's! Are the dead
Unseen, yet with us?—fearful!
  [*Loud shouts without, he rushes forward exultingly.*
            'Tis the shout
Of victory!—We have triumph'd!
                We!—my place
Is 'midst the fallen!
  [*Music heard, which approaches, swelling into a triumphant march. Knights enter in procession, with banners, torch-bearers. &c. The gates of the church are thrown open, and the altar, tombs, &c., within, are seen illuminated. Knights pass over, and enter the church. One of them takes a torch, and lifts it to Aymer's face in passing. He strikes it down with a sword; then seeing* Raimer *approach, drops the sword, and covers his face.*
  Aym. (*grasping* Raimer *by the mantle, as he is about to pass.*) Brother! forsake me not!

DE CHATILLON.

Rai. (*suddenly drawing his sword, and showing it him.*)
                                My sword is red
With victory and revenge!—look—dyed to the hilt!
—We fought—and where were you?
  Aym.   Forsake me not!
  Rai. (*pointing with his sword to the tombs within the
      church.*) Those are proud tombs!—the dead, the glori-
    ous dead,
Think you they sleep, and know not of their sons
In the mysterious grave?—We laid *him* there!
—Before the ashes of your father, speak!
Have you abjured your faith?
  Aym. (*indignantly*) Your name is mine—your blood—and
    you ask *this!*
Wake *him* to hear me answer!—have you—No!
—You have not *dared* to think it.
                        [*Breaks from him and goes out.*
  Rai. (*entering the church, and bending over one of the
      tombs.*)   Not yet lost!
Not yet *all* lost!—He shall be thine again!
So shalt thou sleep in peace!
            [*Music, and chorus of voices from the church.*
          Praise, praise to Heaven!
Sing of the conquer'd field, the Paynim flying,
  Light up the shrines, and bid the banners wave!
Sing of the warrior, for the red-cross dying,
  Chant a proud requiem o'er his holy grave!
            Praise, praise to Heaven!
Praise!—lift the song through night's resounding sky!
Peace to the valiant for the Cross that die!
          Sleep soft, ye brave!

ACT III.

Scene I.—*A platform before the Citadel.—Knights entering.*
  Her. (*to one of the Knights.*) You would plead for him?
  Knight.   Nay, remember all
His past renown!
  Her.   I had a friend in youth—
This Aymer's father had *him* shamed for less
Than his son's fault—far less!—
We must accuse him—he must have his shield
Reversed—his name degraded.
  Knight.   He might yet—
  All the Knights. Must his shame cleave to *us?*—We cast
    him forth—
We will not bear it.

            Raimer *enters*
  Rai.   Knights! ye speak of *him*—
My brother—was't not so?—All silent!—**Nay,**
Give your thoughts breath!—What said ye?

Her. That his name
Must be degraded.
Rai. Silence! ye disturb
The dead—thou hear'st, my father!
　　　　　　　[*Going up indignantly to the Knights*
　　　　　　　　Which of ye
Shall first accuse him? He whose bold step won
The breach at Ascalon ere Aymer's step,
Let him speak first!
He that plunged deeper through the stormy fight,
Thence to redeem the banner of the Cross,
On Cairo's plain, let him speak first! or he
Whose sword burst swifter o'er the Saracen,
I the rescue of our king, by Jordan's waves.
I say, let him speak first!
Her. Is he not an apostate?
Rai. No, no, no!
If he were *that*, had my life's blood that taint,
This hand should pour it out!—he is not *that*.
Her. Not yet.
Rai. Not yet, nor ever!—Let me die
In a lost battle first!
Her. Hath he let go
Name—kindred—honor—for an infidel,
And will he grasp his faith?
Rai. (*after a gloomy pause.*) That which bears poison—
should it not be crush'd?
What though the weed look lovely?
　　　　　　　[*suddenly addressing one of the Knights.*
　　　　　　　　You have seen
My native halls, Du Mornay, far away
In Languedoc?
Knight. I was your father's friend—
I knew them well.
Rai. (*thoughtfully.*) The weight of gloom that hangs—
The very banners seem to droop with it—
O'er some of those old rooms!—Were we there now,
With a dull wind heaving the pale tapestries,
Why, I could tell you—
　　　　　　　[*coming closer to the Knight.*
　　　　　　　　There's a dark-red spot
Grain'd in the floor of one—you know the tale?
Knight. I may have heard it by the winter fires,
—Now 'tis of things gone by.
Rai. (*turning from him displeased.*) Such legends give
Some minds a deeper tone.
(*To* HERMAN.) If *you* had heard
That tale i' the shadowy tower——
Her. Nay, tell it now!
Rai. They say the place is haunted—moaning sounds
Come thence at midnight—sounds of woman's voice.
Her. And you believe—

Rai.   I but believe the deed
Done there of old. I had an ancestor—
Bertrand, the lion-chief—whose son went forth
(A younger son—I am not of *his* line)
To the wars of Palestine. He fought there well—
Ay, all his race were brave ; but he return'd,
And with a Paynim bride.
  Her.   The recreant!—say,
How bore your ancestor?
  Rai.   Well may you think
It chafed him—but he bore it—for the love
Of that fair son, the child of his old age.
He pined in heart, yet gave the infidel
A place in his own halls.
  Her.   But did this last?
  Rai. How *should* it last? Again the trumpet blew
And men were summon'd from their homes to guard
The city of the cross. But *he* seem'd cold—
That youth! he shunn'd his father's eye, and took
No armor from the walls.
  Her.   Had he then fallen?
Was his faith wavering?
  Rai.   So the father fear'd.
  Her. If *I* had been that father——
  Rai.   Ay, *you* come
Of an honor'd lineage. What would you have done?
  Her. Nay, what did *he?*
  Rai.   What did the lion-chief?
                [*Turning to* Du Mornay.
Why, thou hast seen the very spot of blood
On the dark floor!—He slew the Paynim bride ;
Was it not well? (*He looks at them attentively, and as he goes out exclaims—*)
            My brother must not fall!

Scene II.—*A deserted Turkish burying-ground in the city—tombs and stones overthrown—the whole shaded by dark cypress-trees.*

  Mor. (*leaning over a monumental pillar, which has been lately raised.*) *He* is at rest—and I—is there no power
In grief to win forgiveness from the dead?
When shall I rest? Hark! a step—Aymer's step!
The thrilling sound!
         [*She shrinks back as reproaching herself.*
          To feel *that* joy even *here!*
Brother! oh, pardon me!
  Rai. (*entering, and slowly looking round.*) A gloomy scene!
A place for—Is she not an infidel?
Who shall dare call it murder?
          [*He advances to her slowly, and looks at her*
              She is fair—

The deeper cause! Maid, have you thought of death
'Midst these old tombs? [grave
   Mor. (*shrinking from him fearfully.*) This is my brother's
   Rai. *Thy* brother's!—that a warrior's grave had closed
O'er *mine*—the free and noble knight he was!—
Ay, that the desert-sands had shrouded him
Before he look'd on thee!
   Mor.   If you are *his*—
If Aymer's brother—though your brow be dark,
I may not fear you!
   Rai.   No? why *thou* shouldst fear
The very dust o' the mouldering sepulchre,
If it had lived, and borne his name on earth!
Hear'st thou?—that dust hath stirr'd, and found a voice,
And said that thou must die!   [Heaven
   (*Mor* (*clinging to the pillar as he approaches.*) Be with me,
You will not *murder* me!
   Rai. (*turning away.*)   A goodly word
To join with a warrior's name!—a sound to make
Men's flesh creep. What!—for Paynim blood
Did *he* stand faltering thus—my ancestor—
In that old tower?
   [*He again approaches her—she falls on her knees.*
   Mor.   So young, and thus to die!
Mercy—have mercy! In your own far land
If there be love that weeps and watches for you,
And follows you with prayer—even by that love
Spare me—for it is woman's! If light steps
Have bounded there to meet you, clinging arms
Hung on your neck, fond tears o'erflow'd your cheek,
Think upon those that loved you thus, for thus
Doth woman love! and spare me!—think on them;
They, too, may yet need mercy! Aymer, Aymer!
Wilt *thou* not hear and aid me?
   Rai. (*starting.*)   There's a name
To bring back strength! Shall I not strike to save
His honor and his life? Were his *life* all——
   Mor. To save his life and honor!—will my death——
   [*She rises and stands before him, covering her face hur-*
      riedly.
Do it with one stroke! I may not *live* for him!
   Rai. (*with surprise.*) A woman meet death thus!
   Mor. (*uncovering her eyes.*) Yet one thing more—
I have sisters and a father. Christian knight!
Oh! by your mother's memory, let them know
I died with a name unstain'd.
   Rai. (*softened and surprised*) And such high thoughts from
      her!—an infidel!
And she named my mother!—Once in early youth
From the wild waves I snatch'd a woman's life;
My mother bless'd me for it (*slowly dropping his dagger,*)—
      even with tears

She bless'd me. Stay, are there no other means?
(*Suddenly recollecting himself.*) Follow me, maiden!
Fear not now.
Mor. But he—
But Aymer—
Rai. (*sternly.*) Would'st thou perish?—name him not!—
Look not as if thou would'st! Think'st thou dark thoughts
Are blown away like dewdrops, or I, like him,
A leaf to shake and turn i' the changing wind?
Follow me, and beware!
[*She bends over the tomb for a moment, and follows him.*
AYMER *enters, and slowly comes forward from the background.*
Aym. For the last time—yes! it must be the last!
Earth and heaven say—the last! The very dead
Rise up to part us!—But *one* look—and then
She must go hence for ever! Will she weep?
It had been little to have *died* for her—
I have borne shame.
She shall know all!—Moraima!—said they not
She would be found here at her brother's grave?
Where should she go?—Moraima!—there's the print
Of her step—what gleams beside it?
[*Seeing the dagger he takes it up.*
Ha! men work
Dark deeds with things like this!
[*Looking wildly and anxiously around.*
I see no——blood!
[*Looking at the dagger.*
Stain'd?—it may be from battle—'tis not—wet.
[*Looks round intently listening; then again examines the spot and suddenly exclaims—*
Ha!--what is this?--another step in the grass!--
Hers and another's step! [*He rushes into the cypress-grove.*

SCENE III.--*A Hall in the Citadel, hung with Arms and Banners.*
RAIMER—HERMAN—*Knights in the background, laying aside their Armor.*

Her. (*coming forward and speaking hurriedly.*) Is it done?--Have you done it?
Rai. (*with disgust.*) What! you thirst
For blood so deeply?
Her. (*indignantly.*) Have you struck, and saved
The honor of our house?
Rai. (*thoughtfully to himself.*) The light i' the soul
Is such a wavering thing!—Have I done well?—[*To* HERMAN.
Ask me not!—Never shall they meet again.
Is 't not enough?
[AYMER *enters hurriedly with the dagger, and goes up with it to several of the knights, who begin to gather round the front.*

Aym. Whose is this dagger?
Rai. (*coming forward and taking it.*) Mine.
Aym. Yours! yours!—and know you where——
Rai. (*about to sheath it, but stopping.*) Oh! you do well
So to remind me!—Yes! it must have lain
In the moslem burial-ground—and that vile dust—
Hence with it!—'tis defiled. [*Throws it from him.*
Aym. If such a deed—
—Brother! where is she?
Rai. Who?—what knight hath lost
A Ladye-love?
Aym. Could he speak thus, and wear
That scornful calm, if—no—he is not calm—
What have you done?
Rai. (*aside.*) Yes! she shall die to him!
Aym. (*grasping his arm.*) What have you done?—speak!
Rai. You should know the tale
Of our dark ancestor, the Lion-Chief,
And his son's bride.
Aym. Man! man! you *murder'd* her. [*Sinking back*
It grows so dark around me! She is dead!
(*Wildly.*) I'll not believe it!—No! she never look'd
Like what could die! [*Coming up to his brother.*
If you have done that deed—
Rai. (*sternly.*) If I have done it, I have flung off shame
From my brave father's house!
Aym. (*in a low voice to himself.*) So young, and dead!—
because I loved her—dead! *To* RAIMER.
Where is she, murderer? Let me see her face.
You think to hide it with the dust!—ha! ha!
The dust to cover *her!* We'll mock you still:
If I call her back, she'll come! Where is she?—speak!
Now, by my father's tomb, but I am calm.
Rai. Never more hope to see her!
Aym. Never more!
[*Sitting down on the ground.*
I loved her, so she perish'd.—All the earth
Hath not another voice to reach my soul,
Now hers is silent!—Never, never more!
If she had but said—farewell!—(*Bewildered.*) It grows so dark!
This is some fearful dream. When the morn comes, I shall
wake.—
—My life's bright hours are done!
Rai. I must be firm,
[*Takes a banner from the wall and brings it to* AYMER.
Have you forgotten *this?* We thought it lost,
But it rose proudly waving o'er the fight
In a warrior's hand again!—Yours, Aymer, yours!
Brother! redeem your fame!——
Aym. (*putting it from him.*) The worthless thing!
Fame?—*she* is dead!—give a king's robe to one
Stretch'd on the rack! Hence with your pageantries

Down to the dust!
 Her.   The banner of the Cross!
Shame on the recreant!—Cast him from us!
 Rai.   Boy!
Degenerate boy! *here*, with the trophies won
By the sainted chief of old in Paynim war
Above you and around; The very air,
When it but shakes their armor on the wall,
Murmuring of glorious deeds; to sit and weep
Here for an Infidel! My father's son,
Shame! shame! deep shame!
 Knights.   Aymer de Chatillon!
Go from us, leave us!
 Aym. (*starting up.*) Leave you! what! ye thought
That I would stay to breathe the air *you* breathe!—
And fight by you! Murderers! I burst all ties!
    [*Throws his sword on the ground before them.*
There's not a thing of the desert half so free! [*To* Raimer.
You have no brother! Live to need the love
Of a human heart, and steep your soul in fame
To still its restless yearnings! Die alone!
Midst all your pomps and trophies—die alone!—
    [*Going out he suddenly returns.*
Did she not call on me to succor her?
Kneel to you—plead for life?—The Voice of Blood
Follow you to your grave!—   [*Exit.*
 Rai. (*with emotion.*) Alas! my brother!
The time hath been, when in the face of Death
I have bid him leave me, and he would not!—
    [*Turning to the Knights.*
      Knights!
The Soldan marches for Jerusalem—
We'll meet him on the way.

ACT IV.

Scene I.—*Camp of* Melech, *the Saracen Emir.*

Melech—Sadi—*Soldiers.*

 Mel. Yes! he I mean—Raimer de Chatillon!
Go, send swift riders o'er the mountains forth,
And through the deserts, to proclaim the price
I set upon his life!
 Sadi.   Thou gav'st the word
Before; it hath been done—they are gone forth.
 Mel. Would that my soul could wing them! Didst thou heed
To say his *life?*—I'll have my own revenge!
Yes! I would *save* him from another's hand!
Thou said'st he must be brought alive?
 Sadi   I heard
Thy will, and I obey'd.
 Mel.   He slew my son—

That was in battle—but to shed *her* blood!
My child Moraima's! Could he see and strike her?
A Christian see her face, too! From my house
The crown is gone! Who brought the tale?
  Sadi.   A slave
Of your late son's, escaped.
  Mel.   Have I a son
Left? speak, the slave of which? Kaled is gone—
And Octar gone—both, both are fallen—
Both my young stately trees, and she my flower—
—No hand but mine shall be upon him, none!—
                    [*A sound of festive music without.*
What mean they there!   [*An attendant enters.*
  Att.   Tidings of joy, my chief!
  Mel. Joy!—is the Christian taken?
       [MORAIMA *enters, and throws herself into his arms.*
  Mor.   Father! Father!
I did not think this world had yet so much
Of aught like happiness!
  Mel.   My own fair child!
Is it on *thee* I look indeed, my child? [*Turning to attendants.*
Away, there!—gaze not on us!—Do I hold
Thee in my arms!—They told me thou wert slain.
Raimer de Chatillon, they said——
  Mor. (*hurriedly.*)   Oh, no!
Twas he that sent thee back thy child, my father.
  Mel. He! why, his brother Aymer still refused
A monarch's ransom for thee!
  Mor. (*with a momentary delight.*) Did he thus?
                             [*Suddenly checking herself.*
—Yes! I knew well!—Oh! do not speak of him! [much
  Mel. What! hath he wrong'd thee?—Thou hast suffer'd
Amongst these Christians! Thou art changed, my child.
There's a dim shadow in thine eye, where once—
—But they shall pay me back for all thy tears
With their best blood
  Mor. (*alarmed.*)   Father! not so, not so!
They still were gentle with me. But I sat
And watch'd beside my dying brother's couch
Through many days: and I have wept since then—
Wept much.
  Mel.   Thy dying brother's couch!—yes, thou
Wert ever true and kind
  Mor. (*covering her face.*) Oh! praise me not!
Look gently on me, or I sink to earth;
Not thus!
  Mel.   No praise! thou'rt faint my child, and worn:
The length of way hath——
  Mor. (*eagerly.*)   Yes! the way was long
The desert's wind breathed o'er me. Could I rest?
  Mel. Yes! thou shall rest within thy father's tent.
Follow me, gentle child! Thou look'st so changed.

Mor. (*hurriedly.*) The weary way,—the desert's burning
    wind—   [*Laying her hand on him as she goes out.*
Think thou no evil of those Christians, father!—
They were still kind.

SCENE II.—*Before a fortress amongst the Rocks, with a Desert beyond.—Military Music.*

RAIMER DE CHATILLON—*Knights—Soldiers.*

Rai. They speak of truce?
The Knights.   Even so. Of truce between
The Soldan and our King.
Rai.   Let him who fears
Lest the close helm should wear his locks away,
Cry "truce," and cast it off. I have no will
To change mine armor for a masquer's robe,
And sit at festivals. Halt, lances, there!
Warriors and brethren! hear.—I own no truce—
I hold my life but as a weapon now
Against the infidel! He shall not reap
His field, nor gather of his vine, nor pray
To his false gods—No! save by trembling stealth,
Whilst I can grasp a sword! Wherefore noble friends,
Think not of truce with me!—but think to quaff
Your wine to the sound of trumpets, and to rest
In your girt hauberks, and to hold your steeds
Barded in the hall beside you. Now turn back
    [*He throws a spear on the ground before them.*
Ye that are weary of your armor's load,
Pass o'er the spear, away!
They all shout.   A Chatillon!
We'll follow thee, all! all!
Rai.   A soldier's thanks!
    [*Turns away from them agitated.*
There's one face gone, and that a brother's! (*Aloud.*) War!—
War to the Paynim—war! March and set up
On our stronghold the banner of the Cross,
Never to sink!—
    [*Trumpets sound. They march on, winding through the rocks with military music.*

Enter GASTON, *an aged vassal of* RAIMER'S, *as an armed follower—*RAIMER *addresses him.*

You come at last!—And she—where left you her?
The Paynim maid?
Gas.   I found her guides, my lord,
Of her own race, and left her on the way
To reach her father's tents.
Rai.   Speak low!—the tale
Must rest with us. It must be thought she *died.*
I can trust *you.*
Gas.   Your father trusted me.
Rai. He did, he did!—my father! You have been

Long absent, and you bring a troubled eye
Back with you.—Gaston! heard you aught of *him?*
  Gas. Whom means my lord!
  Rai. (impatiently.) Old man, you know to well—
Aymer, my brother.
  Gas.   I have seen him.
  Rai.   How!
Seen him! Speak on.
  Gas.   Another than my chief
Should have my life before the shameful tale!
  Rai. Speak quickly.
  Gas.   In the desert as I journey'd back,
A band of Arabs met me on the way,
And I became their captive. Till last night—
  Rai. Go on!—Last night?
  Gas.   They slumber'd by their fires—
I could not sleep, when one—I thought him one
O' the tribe at first, came up and loosed my bonds,
And led me from the shadow of the tents,
Pointing my way in silence.
  Rai.   Well, and he—
You thought him one of the tribe.
  Gas.   Ay, till we stood
In the clear moonlight forth—and then, my lord——
  Rai. You dare not say 'twas Aymer?
  Gas.   Woe and shame!
It was, it was!
  Rai. In their vile garb too?
  Gas.   Yes,
Turban'd and robed like them.
  Rai. What!—did he speak?
  Gas.   No word, but waved his hand
Forbidding speech to me.
  Rai.   Tell me no more!—
Lost, lost—for ever lost!—He that was rear'd
Under my father's roof with me, and grew
Up by my side to glory!—lost—is this
My work?—who dares to call it mine? And yet,
Had I not dealt so sternly with his soul
In its deep anguish——What! he wears their garb
In the face of Heaven? You saw the turban on him?
You should have struck him to the earth, and so
Put out our shame forever!
  Gas.   Lift my sword
Against your father's son!
  Rai.   My father's son!
Ay, and so loved!—that yearning love for *him*
Was the last thing death conquer'd! see'st thou there?
    [*The banner of the Cross is raised on the fortress.*]
The very banner he redeem'd for us
I' the fight at Cairo! No! by yon bright sign
He shall not perish!—this way—follow me—

I'll tell thee of a thought. [*Suddenly stopping him.*
Take heed, old man!
Thou hast a fearful secret in thy grasp:
Let me not see thee wear mysterious looks—
But no! thou lov'st our name!—I'll trust thee, Gaston!
[*Exeunt.*

SCENE III. *An Arab encampment round a few palm-trees in the Desert.—Watch-fires in the background.—Night.*

Several Arabs enter with AYMER.

Arab Chief. Thou hast fought bravely, stranger; now come on
To share the spoil.
 Aym. I reck not of it. Go,
Leave me to rest.
 Arab. Well, thou hast earn'd thy rest
With a red sabre. Be it as thou wilt.
[*They go out.—He throws himself under a palm-tree.*
 Aym. This were an hour—if they would answer us.
—They from whose viewless world no answer comes—
To hear their whispering voices. Would they but
Speak once, and say they loved!
If I could hear thy thrilling voice once more,
It would be well with me. Moraima, speak!
[RAIMER *enters disguised as a dervise.*
Moraima, speak!—No! the dead cannot love!
 Rai. What doth the stranger here?—is there not mirth
Around the watch-fires yonder?
 Aym. Mirth?—away!
I've nought to do with mirth—begone!
 Rai. They tell
Wild tales by that red light;—would'st thou not hear
Of eastern marvels?
 Aym. Hence!—I heed them not.
 Rai. Nay then, hear *me!*
 Aym. Thee!
 Rai. Yes, I know a tale
Wilder than theirs.
 Aym. (raising himself in surprise.) Thou know'st!—
 Rai. (without minding, continues.) A tale of one,
Who flung in madness to the reckless deep
A gem beyond all price.
 Aym. My day is closed.
What is aught human unto me?
 Rai. Yet mark!
His name was of the noblest—dost thou heed?
Even in a land of princely chivalry;
Brightness was on it—but he cast it down.
 Aym. I will not hear—speak'st *thou* of chivalry?
 Rai. Yes! I have been upon thy native hills—
There's a grey cliff juts proudly from their woods,
Crown'd with baronial towers.—Rememberest thou?
And there's a chapel by the moaning sea—

Thou know'st it well—tall pines wave over it,
Darkening the heavy banners, and the tombs—
Is not the Cross upon thy fathers' tombs ?—
Christian ! what dost thou *here ?*
  Aym. (starting up indignantly.) Man ! who art thou ?
Thy voice disturbs my soul. Speak ! I will know
Thy right to question *me.*
  *Rai. (throwing off his disguise, stands before him in the
   full dress of a Crusader.)* My birthright !—look !
  Aym. (Retreating from him with horror.) Her blood is on
   your hands !—keep back !   [ing mine—
  Rai. (scornfully.) Nay, keep the Paynim's garb from touch-
Answer me *thence !*—what dost thou here ?
  Aym.   You shrink
From your own work !—you, that have made me thus '
Wherefore are you here ? Are you not afraid
To stand beneath the awful midnight sky,
And you a murderer ? Leave me.
  Rai.   I lift up
No murderer's brow to Heaven !
  Aym. You *dare* speak thus !—
Do not the bright stars, with their searching rays,
Strike through your guilty soul ? Oh, no :—'tis well,
Passing well ! Murder ! Make the earth's harvests grow
With Paynim blood !—*Heaven* wills it !—The free air,
The sunshine—I forgot—they were not made
For infidels. Blot out the race from day !
Who talks of *murder ?* Murder ! when you die
Claim your soul's place and happiness i' the name
Of that good deed !   [*In a tone of deep feeling.*
    If you had loved a flower
I would not have destroy'd it !
  Rai. (with emotion.)   Brother !
  Aym. (impetuously.)   No !—
No brother now !—she knelt to you in vain ;
And that hath set a gulf—a boundless gulf—
Between our souls. Your very face is changed—
There's a red cloud shadowing it : your forehead wears
The marks of blood—*her* blood ! [*In a triumphant tone.*
But you prevail not ! You have made the dead
The mighty—the victorious ! Yes ! you thought
To dash her image into fragments down,
And you have given it power—such deep sad power
I see nought else on earth !
  Rai. (aside.) I dare not say she lives.
      [*To* AYMER *holding up the cross of his sword.*
      You see not *this !*
Once by our father's grave I ask'd, and here,
I' the silence of the waste, I ask once more
Have you abjured your faith ?
  Aym.   Why are you come
To torture me ? No, no, I have not. No !

But you have sent the torrent through my soul,
And by their deep strong roots torn fiercely up
Things that were part of it—inborn feelings, thoughts—
I know not what I cling to!
   Rai.   Aymer! yet
Heaven hath not closed its gates! Return, return,
Before the shadow of the palm-tree fades
I' the waning moonlight. Heaven gives time. Return,
My brother! By our early days—the love
That nurtured us!—the holy dust of those
That sleep i' the tomb!—Sleep! no, they cannot sleep!
Doth the night bring no voices from the dead
Back on your soul?
   Aym. (*turning from him.*) Yes—*hers!*
   Rai. (*indignantly turning off.*) Why should I strive?
Why doth it cost me these deep throes to fling   [come
A weed off?—(*Checking himself.*) Brother, hath the stranger
Between our hearts for ever? Yet return—
Win back your fame, my brother!
   Aym.   Fame again!
Leave me the desert!—leave it me! I hate
Your false world's glittering draperies, that press down
The overlabor'd heart! They have crush'd mine. Your vain
And hollow-sounding words are wasted now:
You should adjure me by the name of *him*
That slew his son's young bride!—our ancestor—
That were a spell! Fame! fame!—your hand hath rent
The veil from off your world! To speak of fame,
When the soul is parch'd like mine! Away!
I have join'd these men because they war with man
And all his hollow pomp! Will you go hence?
(*Fiercely,*) Why do I talk thus with a *murderer?* Ay,
This is the desert, where *true* words may rise
Up unto Heaven i' the stillness! Leave it me!—
The free wild desert!   (*Arab Chief enters.*)
                Stranger, we have shared
The spoil, forgetting not——A Christian here!
Ho! sons of Kedar!—'tis De Chatillon!
This way!—surround him! There's an Emir's wealth
Set on his life! Come on!
     [*Several Arabs rush in and surround* RAIMER, *who, after vainly endeavoring to force his way through them, is made prisoner. As they are leading him away,* AYMER, *who has stood for a moment as if bewildered, rushes forward, and strikes down one of the Arabs.*
   Rai.   And he stands there
To see me bought and sold! Death, death!—not chains!
   Aym. Off from my brother, infidel!
                [*The others hurry* RAIMER *away.*
(*Recollecting himself.*)   Why, then, Heaven
Is just!—So! now I see it! Blood for blood!
                      [*Again rushing forward.*

No! he shall feel *remorse!*—I'll rescue him,
And make him weep for her! [*He goes out*

ACT V.

SCENE I.—*A Hall in the Fortress occupied by* DE CHATIL-
LON'S *followers.*

Knights listening to a Troubadour.

Her. No more soft strains of love. Good Vidal, sing
The imprison'd warrior's lay. There's a proud tone
Of lofty sadness in it.

(TROUBADOUR *sings.*)

" 'Twas a trumpet's pealing sound,
And the knight look'd down from the Paynim's tower,
And a Christian host in its pride and power,
 Through the pass beneath him wound.
Cease awhile, clarion! clarion, wild and shrill,
Cease! let them hear the captive's voice—be still.

" I knew 'twas a trumpet's note!
And see my brethren's lances gleam,
And their pennons wave by the mountain stream,
 And their plumes to the glad wind float.
Cease awhile clarion! clarion, wild and shrill,
Cease! let them hear the captive's voice—be still

" I am here with my heavy chain!
And I look on a torrent sweeping by,
And an eagle rushing to the sky,
 And a host to its battle-plain!
Cease awhile, clarion! &c., &c.

" Must I pine in my fetters here?
With the wild wave's foam, and the free bird's flight,
And the tall spears glancing on my sight,
 And the trumpet in mine ear?
Cease awhile, clarion!" &c., &c.

[AYMER *enters hurriedly.*

Aym. Silence, thou minstrel, silence!
Her. Aymer, here!
And in that garb! Seize on the renegade!
Knights, he must die!
Aym. (*scornfully.*) Die! die!—the fearful threat!
To be thurst out of this same blessed world,
Your world—all yours! (*Fiercely.*) But I will *not* be made
A thing to circle with your *pomps* of death,
Your chains, and guards, and scaffolds! Back! I'll die
As the free lion dies!— [*Drawing his sabre*
Her. What seek'st thou here?
Aym. Nought but to give your Christian swords a deed
Worthier than—where's your chief? in the Paynim's bonds!
Made the wild Arabs' prize!—Ay, Heaven is just!

If ye will rescue him, then follow me :
I know the way they bore him !
  Her.   Follow thee !
Recreant ! deserter of thy house and faith !
To think true knights would follow *thee* again !
'Tis all some snare—away !
  Aym.   Some snare !—Heaven ! Heaven !
Is my name sunk to this ? Must men first crush
My soul, then spurn the ruin they have made ?
—Why, let him perish !—blood for blood !—must earth cry out
In vain ?—Wine, wine, we'll revel here !
On, minstrel, with thy song !
         [*Minstrel continues the song.*

   " They are gone, they have all pass'd by !
 They in whose wars I had borne my part,
 They that I loved with a brother's heart,
   They have left me here to die !
 Sound again, clarion ! clarion, pour thy blast !
 Sound for the captive's dream of hope is past !"

  Aym. (*starting up.*) That was the lay he loved in our boyish
   days—
And he must die forsaken !—No, by Heaven
He shall not !—Follow me ! I say your chief
Is bought and sold !—Is there no generous trust
Left in your souls ? Du Foix, I saved your life
At Ascalon ! Du Mornay, you and I
On Jaffa's wall together set our breasts
Against a thousand spears ! What ! have I fought
Beside you, shared your cup, slept in your tents,
And ye can think— [*Dashing off his turban.*
     Look on my burning brow !
Read if there's falsehood branded on it—read
The marks of treachery there !
  Knights (*gathering round him, cry out.*) No, no, come on
To the rescue ! lead us on ! we'll trust thee still !
  Aym. Follow, then !—this way—If I die for him,
There will be vengeance !—He shall think of me
To his last hour !   [*Exeunt.*

  Scene II.—*A Pavillion in the Camp of Melech.*

     Melech *and* Sadi.

  Mel. It must be that these sounds and sights of war
Shake her too gentle nature. Yes, her cheek
Fades hourly in my sight ! What other cause—
None, none !—She must go hence ! Choose from thy band
The bravest, Sadi ! and the longest tried,
And I will send my child——
  Voice without.   Where is your chief ?
  [*Arab and Turkish Soldiers enter with* De Chatillon.
  Arab Chief. The sons of Kedar's tribe have brought to the
  son

Of the Prophet's house a prisoner!
 Mel. (half drawing his sword.) Chatillon!
That slew my boy! Thanks for the avenger's hour!
Sadi, their guerdon—give it them—the gold!
And me the vengeance!
  [*Looks at* RAIMER, *who holds the upper fragment of his sword, and seems lost in thought.*) This is he
That slew my firstborn!
 Rai. (to himself.) Surely there leap'd up
A brother's heart within him! Yes, he struck
To the earth a Paynim——
 Mel. (raising his voice.) Christian! thou hast been
Our nation's deadliest foe!
 Rai. (looking up and smiling proudly.) 'Tis joy to hear
I have not lived in vain!
 Mel.   Thou bear'st thyself
With a conqueror's mien! What is thy hope from me?
 Rai. A soldier's death.
 Mel. (hastily.) Then thou would'st *fear* a slave's?
 Rai. Fear!—As if man's own spirit had not power
To make his death a triumph! Waste not words;
Let my blood bathe thine own sword. Infidel!
I slew thy son! (*Looking at his broken sword.*) Ay, there's
  the red mark here!
 Mel. (approaching him.) Thou darest to tell me this!
  [*A tumult heard without, voices crying*—A Chatillon!
 Rai. My brother's voice! *He is saved!*
 Mel. (calling.) What, ho! my guards!
  [AYMER *enters with the knights fighting their way through* MELECH'S *soldiers, who are driven before them.*
 Aym. On with the war-cry of our ancient house,
For the Cross—De Chatillon!
 (*Knights shout.*) For the Cross—De Chatillon!
  [RAIMER *attempts to break from his guards.* SADI *enters with more soldiers to the assistance of* MELECH. AYMER *and the Knights are overpowered.* AYMER *is wounded and falls.*
 Mel. Bring fetters—bind the captives!
 Rai.   Lost—all lost!
No!—he is saved!
  [*Breaking from his guards, he goes up to* AYMER.
Brother, my brother! hast thou pardon'd me
That which I did to save thee? Speak!—forgive!
 Aym. (turning from him.) Thou see'st I die for thee!—She
  is avenged!
 Rai. I am no murderer!—hear me!—turn to me!
We are parting by the grave!
  [MORAIMA *enters veiled, and goes up to* MELECH.
 Mor. Father!—O! look not sternly on thy child,
I came to plead. They said thou hadst condemn'd
A Christian knight to die——

DE CHATILLON.

Mel.   Hence—to thy tent!
Away—begone!
   Aym. (*attempting to rise.*) Moraima!—hath her spirit come
To make death beautiful? Moraima!—speak.
   Mor. It was his voice!—Aymer!
                [*She rushes to him, throwing aside her veil.*
   Aym.   Thou livest—thou livest!
I knew thou could'st not die!—Look on me still.
Thou livest!—and makest this world so full of joy—
But I depart!
   Mel. (*approaching her.*) Moraima!—hence! is this
A place for thee?
   Mor.   Away! away!
There is no place but this for me on earth!
Where should I go? There is no place but this!
My soul is bound to it!
   Mel. (*to the guards.*) Back, slaves, and look not on her!
                [*They retreat to the background.*
              'Twas for this
She droop'd to the earth.
   Aym.   Moraima, fare thee well!
Think on me!—I have loved thee! I take hence
That deep love with my soul! for well I know
It must be deathless!
   Mor.   O! thou hast not known
What *woman's* love is! Aymer, Aymer, stay!
If I could die for thee! My heart is grown
So strong in its despair!
   Rai. (*turning from them.*) And all the past
Forgotten!—our young days!—His last thoughts *hers!*
The Infidel's!
   Aym. (*with a violent effort turning his head round.*)
            Thou art no murderer! Peace
Between us—peace, my brother!—In our deaths
We shall be join'd once more!
   Rai. (*holding the cross of the sword before him.*)
             Look yet on this!
   Aym. If thou hadst only told me that she lived!
—But our hearts meet at last! [*Presses the cross to his lips.*
Moraima! save my brother! Look on me!
Joy—there is joy in death! [*He dies on* RAIMER'S *arm.*
   Mor. Speak—speak once more!
Aymer! how is it that I call on thee,
And that thou answerest not? Have we not loved?
Death! death!—and this is—death!
   Rai.   So thou art gone,
Aymer! I never thought to weep again—
But now—farewell!—Thou wert the bravest knight
That e'er laid lance in rest—and thou didst wear
The noblest form that ever woman's eye
Dwelt on with love; and till that fatal dream
Came o'er thee!—Aymer! Aymer!—thou wert still

'The most true-hearted brother!—there thou art
Whose breast was once my shield!—I never thought
That foes should see me weep! but there thou art,
Aymer, my brother!—
   Mor. (*suddenly rising.*) With his last, last breath
He bade me save his brother!   [*Falling at her father's feet.*
                     Father, spare
The Christian—spare him!
   Mel.   For *thy* sake spare *him*
That slew thy father's son!—Shame to thy race!
                  [*To the Soldiers in the background.*
Soldiers! come nearer with your levell'd spears!
Yet nearer;—Gird him in!—my boy's young blood
Is on his sword.—Christian, abjure thy faith,
Or die—thine hour is come!
   Rai. (*Turning and throwing himself on the weapons of the
     Soldiers.*) Thou hast mine answer, Infidel!
          [*Calling aloud to the Knights as he falls back
                     Knights of France!
Herman! De Foix! Du Mornay! be ye strong!
Your hour will come!
                Must the old war-cry cease?
[*Half raising himself, and waving the Cross triumphantly.*
For the Cross—De Chatillon!
                                    [*He dies.*
              (*The Curtain falls.*)

ANNOTATIONS ON "DE CHATILLON."

"THE merits of the *Siege of Valencia* are more of a descriptive than of a strictly dramatic kind; and abounding as it does with fine passages of narrative beauty, and with striking scenes and situations, it is not only not adapted for representation, but on the contrary, the characters are developed by painting much more than by incident. Withal, it wants unity and entireness, and in several places is not only rhetorical but diffuse.

"From the previous writings of the same author, and until the appearance of the *Vespers of Palermo*, it seemed to be the prevalent opinion of critics, that the genius of Mrs Hemans was not of a dramatic cast—that it expatiated too much in the developement of sentiment, too much in the luxuriancy of description, to be ever brought under the trammels essentially necessary for the success of scenic dialogue.

"The merits of the *Vespers* are great, and have been acknowledged to be so, not only by the highest of contemporary literary authorities, but by the still more unequivocal testimony of theatrical applause. What 'has been, has been,' and we wish not to detract one iota from praise so fairly earned; but we must candidly confess, that before the perusal of *De Chatillon* (although that poem is probably not quite in the state in which it would have been submitted to the world by its writer,) we were somewhat infected with the prevailing opinion, that the most successful path of Mrs. Hemans did not lead her towards the drama. Our opinion on this subject is, however, now much altered; and we hesitate not to say, after minutely considering the characters of Raimer—so skilfully acted on, now by fraternal love, now by public duty—and of Aymer and Moraima, placed in situations where inclination is opposed to principle—that, by the cultivation of this species of composition, had health and prolonged years been the fate of the author of *De Chatillon*, that tragedy, noble as it is, which must now be placed at the head of her dramatic efforts, would in all probability have been even surpassed in excellence by ulterior efforts.

"Mrs. Hemans had at length struck the proper keys. It is quite evident that she had succeeded in imbibing new and more severe ideas of this class of compositions. She had passed from the narrative into what has been conventionally termed the dramatic poem—from the *Historic Scenes*, to *Sebastian* and the *Siege of Valencia*; but the *Vespers of Palermo* and *De Chatillon* can alone be said to be her legitimate dramas.

"The last, however, must be ranked first by many degrees of comparison. Without stripping her language of that richness and poetic beauty so characteristic of her genius, or condescending in a single passage to the mean baldness, so commonly mistaken by many modern writers for the stage as essentially necessary to the truth of dialogue, she has, in this attempt, preserved adherence to reality amid scenes allied with romance—brevity, and effect in situations strongly alluring to amplification; and, in her delineation of some of the strongest, as well as the finest emotions of the heart, there is exhibited a knowledge of nature's workings at once minute, faithful, and affecting."—*MS. Critique by* Δ.

MISCELLANEOUS PIECES.

I GO, SWEET FRIENDS!

I go sweet friends! yet think of me
   When spring's young voice awakes the flowers
For we have wandered far and free
   In those bright hours, the violet's hours.

I go; but when you pause to hear,
   From distant hills, the Sabbath-bell
On summer-winds float silvery clear,
   Think on me then—I loved it well!

Forget me not around your hearth,
   When cheerly smiles the ruddy blaze,
For dear hath been its evening mirth
   To me, sweet friends, in other days.

And oh! when music's voice is heard
   To melt in strains of parting woe,
When hearts to love and grief are stirr'd,
   Think of me then!—I go, I go!

ANGEL VISITS.

> "No more of talk where God or angel guest
> With man, as with his friend, familiar used
> To sit indulgent, and with him partake
> Rural repast."   *Milton.*

Are ye for ever to your skies departed?
 Oh! will ye visit this dim world no more?
Ye, whose bright wings a solemn splendor darted
 Through Eden's fresh and flowering shades of yore!
Now are the fountains dried on that sweet spot,
And ye—our faded earth beholds you not!

Yet, by your shining eyes not all forsaken,
 Man wander'd from his Paradise away;
Ye, from forgetfulness his heart to waken,
 Came down, high guests! in many a later day,
And with the patriarchs, under vine or oak,
'Midst noontide calm or hush of evening, spoke.

From you, the veil of midnight darkness rending
 Came the rich mysteries to the sleeper's eye,
That saw your hosts ascending and descending
 On those bright steps between the earth and sky:
Trembling he woke, and bow'd o'er glory's trace,
And worshipp'd awe-struck in that fearful place.

By Chebar's* brook ye pass'd, such radiance wearing
 As mortal vision might but ill endure;
Along the stream the living chariot bearing,
 With its high crystal arch, intensely pure!
And the dread rushing of your wings that hour,
Was like the noise of waters in their power.

But in the Olive-mount, by night appearing,
 'Midst the dim leaves, your holiest work was done!
Whose was the voice that came divinely cheering,
 Fraught with the breath of God, to aid his Son?
—Haply of those that, on the moonlit plains,
Wafted good tidings unto Syrian swains.

Yet one more task was yours! your heavenly dwelling
 Ye left, and by th' unseal'd sepulchral stone,
In glorious raiment, sat; the weepers telling,
 That *He* they sought had triumph'd, and was gone!
Now have ye left us for the brighter shore,
Your presence lights the lonely groves no more.

But may ye not, unseen, around us hover,
 With gentle promptings and sweet influence yet.
Though the fresh glory of those days be over,
 When, 'midst the palm-trees, man your footsteps met?

---
* Ezekial, chap. x.

Are ye not near when faith and hope rise high,
  When love, by strength, o'ermasters agony?
Are ye not near when sorrow, unrepining,
  Yields up life's treasures unto Him who gave?
When martyrs, all things for His sake resigning,
  Lead on the march of death, serenely brave?
Dreams!—but a deeper thought our souls may fill—
  One, One *is* near—a spirit holier still!

IVY SONG.

WRITTEN ON RECEIVING SOME IVY-LEAVES GATHERED FROM THE RUINED CASTLE OF RHEINFELS, ON THE RHINE.

O! HOW could Fancy crown with *thee*
  In ancient days the God of Wine,
And bid thee at the banquet be
  Companion of the vine?
Thy home, wild plant, is where each sound
  Of revelry hath long been o'er,
Where song's full notes once peal'd around,
  But now are heard no more.

The Roman on his battle-plains,
  Where kings before his eagles bent,
Entwined thee with exulting strains
  Around the victor's tent:
Yet there, though fresh in glossy green,
  Triumphantly thy boughs might wave,
Better thou lovest the silent scene
  Around the victor's grave.

Where sleep the sons of ages flown,
  The bards and heroes of the past;
Where, through the halls of glory gone,
  Murmurs the wintry blast;
Where years are hastening to efface
  Each record of the grand and fair;
Thou in thy solitary grace,
  Wreath of the tomb! art there.

O! many a temple, once sublime,
  Beneath a blue Italian sky,
Hath nought of beauty left by time,
  Save thy wild tapestry!
And, rear'd 'midst crags and clouds, 'tis thine
  To wave where banners waved of yore,
O'er towers that crest the noble Rhine,
  Along his rocky shore.

High from the fields of air look down
  Those eyries of a vanish'd race—

Homes of the mighty, whose renown
    Hath pass'd, and left no trace.
But there thou art!—thy foliage bright
    Unchanged the mountain storm can brave:
Thou, that wilt climb the loftiest height,
    Or deck the humblest grave!

'Tis still the same! where'er we tread
    The wrecks of human power we see—
The marvels of all ages fled,
    Left to decay and thee!
And still let man his fabrics rear,
    August in beauty, grace, and strength;
Days pass—thou ivy never sere!*—
    And all is thine at length!

TO ONE OF THE AUTHOR'S CHILDREN ON HIS BIRTHDAY.

WHERE sucks the bee now?—Summer is flying,
Leaves round the elm-tree faded are lying;
Violets are gone from their grassy dell,
With the cowslip cups, where the fairies dwell;
The rose from the garden hath pass'd away—
Yet happy, fair boy, is thy natal day!

For love bids it welcome, the love which hath smiled
Ever around thee, my gentle child!
Watching thy footsteps, and guarding thy bed,
And pouring out joy on thy sunny head.
Roses may vanish, but *this* will stay—
Happy and bright is thy natal day!

ON A SIMILAR OCCASION.

THOU wakest from rosy sleep, to play
    With bounding heart, my boy!
Before thee lies a long bright day
    Of summer and of joy.

Thou hast no heavy thought or dream
    To cloud thy fearless eye;
Long be it thus—life's early stream
    Should still reflect the sky.

Yet, ere the cares of life lie dim
    On thy young spirit's wings,
Now in thy morn forget not Him
    From whom each pure thought springs!

---

* "Ye myrtles brown, and ivy never sere."—*Lycidas.*

So, in the onward vale of tears,
  Where'er thy path may be,
When strength hath bow'd to evil years
  He will remember thee!

CHRIST STILLING THE TEMPEST.

FEAR was within the tossing bark
  When stormy winds grew loud,
And waves came rolling high and dark,
  And the tall mast was bow'd.

And men stood breathless in their dread,
  And baffled in their skill;
But One was there, who rose and said
  To the wild sea—*be still!*

And the wind ceased—it ceased!—that word
  Pass'd through the gloomy sky;
The troubled billows knew their Lord,
  And fell beneath His eye.

And slumber settled on the deep,
  And silence on the blast;
They sank, as flowers that fold to sleep
  When sultry day is past.

O Thou, that in its wildest hour
  Didst rule the tempest's mood,
Send thy meek spirit forth in power,
  Soft on our souls to brood!

Thou that didst bow the billow's pride
  Thy mandate to fulfil!
Oh, speak to passion's raging tide,
  Speak, and say, " *Peace, be still!*"

EPITAPH.

OVER THE GRAVE OF TWO BROTHERS, A CHILD AND A YOUTH.

THOU, that canst gaze upon thine own fair boy,
  And hear his prayer's low murmur at thy knee,
And o'er his slumber bend in breathless joy,
  Come to this tomb! it hath a voice for thee!
Pray!—thou art blest!—ask strength for sorrow's hour,
Love, deep as thine, lays here its broken flower.

Thou that art gathering from the smile of youth
  Thy thousand hopes; rejoicing to behold

All the heart's depths before thee bright with truth,
　All the mind's treasures silently unfold!
Look on this tomb!—for thee, too, speaks the grave,
Where God hath seal'd the fount of hope he gave.

MONUMENTAL INSCRIPTION.

Earth! guard what here we lay in holy trust,
　That which hath left our home a darken'd place,
Wanting the form, the smile, now veil'd with dust;
　The light departed with our loveliest face.
Yet from thy bonds our sorrow's hope is free—
We have but lent the beautiful to thee.

But thou, O Heaven! keep, keep what *thou* hast taken,
　And with our treasure keep our hearts on high;
The spirit meek, and yet by pain unshaken,
　The faith, the love, the lofty constancy—
Guide us where these are with our sister flown—
They were of Thee, and thou hast claim'd thine own.

THE SOUND OF THE SEA.

Thou art sounding on, thou mighty sea,
　For ever and the same!
The ancient rocks yet ring to thee;
　Those thunders nought can tame.

Oh! many a glorious voice is gone
　From the rich bowers of earth,
And hush'd is many a lovely one
　Of mournfulness or mirth.

The Dorian flute that sigh'd of yore.
　Along the wave, is still;
The harp of Judah peals no more
　On Zion's awful hill.

And Memnon's lyre hath lost the chord
　That breathed the mystic tone;
And the songs at Rome's high triumphs pour'd
　Are with her eagles flown.

And mute the Moorish horn that rang
　O'er stream and mountain free;
And the hymn the leagued Crusaders sang
　Hath died in Galilee.

But thou art swelling on, thou deep,
　Through many an olden clime,
Thy billowy anthem ne'er to sleep
　Until the close of time.

Thou liftest up thy solemn voice
  To every wind and sky,
And all our earth's green shores rejoice
  In that one harmony.

It fills the noontide's calm profound,
  The sunset's heaven of gold;
And the still midnight hears the sound,
  Even as first it roll'd.

Let there be silence, deep and strange,
  Where sceptred cities rose!
Thou speak'st of One who doth not change—
  So may our hearts repose.

THE CHILD AND DOVE.

SUGGESTED BY CHANTREY'S STATUE OF LADY LOUISA RUSSELL.

Thou art a thing on our dreams to rise,
'Midst the echoes of long-lost melodies,
And to fling bright dew from the morning back,
Fair form! on each image of childhood's track.

Thou art a thing to recall the hours
When the love of our souls was on leaves and flowers;
When a world was our own in some dim sweet grove,
And treasure untold in one captive dove.

Are they gone? can we think it, while *thou* art there,
Thou joyous child with the clustering hair?
Is it not spring that indeed breathes free
And fresh o'er each thought, while we gaze on thee?

No! never more may we smile as thou
Sheddest round smiles from thy sunny brow;
Yet something it is, in our hearts to shrine
A memory of beauty undimm'd as thine.

To have met the joy of thy speaking face,
To have felt the spell of thy breezy grace,
To have linger'd before thee, and turn'd, and borne
One vision away of the cloudless morn.

A DIRGE.

Calm on the bosom of thy God,
  Young spirit! rest thee now,
Even while with us thy footstep **trod,**
  His seal was on thy brow.

Dust, to its narrow house beneath!
Soul to its place on high!—
They that have seen thy look in death,
No more may fear to die.

Lone are the paths, and sad the bowers,
Whence thy meek smile is gone;
But oh!—a brighter home than ours,
In heaven is now thine own

SCENE IN A DALECARLIAN MINE.

"O! fondly, fervently, those two had loved,
Had mingled minds in Love's own perfect trust,
Had watch'd bright sunsets, dreamt of blissful years
——And thus they met."

"Haste, with your torches, haste! make firelight round!"
They speed, they press—what hath the miner found?
Relic or treasure—giant sword of old?
Gems bedded deep—rich veins of burning gold?
—Not so—the dead, the dead! An awstruck band,
In silence gathering round the silent stand,
Chain'd by one feeling, hushing e'en their breath,
Before the thing that, in the might of death,
Fearful, yet beautiful, amidst them lay—
A sleeper, dreaming not!—a youth with hair
Making a sunny gleam (how sadly fair!)
O'er his cold brow: no shadow of decay
Had touch'd those pale bright features—yet he wore
A mien of other days, a garb of yore.
Who could unfold that mystery? From the throng
A woman wildly broke; her eye was dim,
As if through many tears, through vigils long,
Through weary strainings:—all had been for him!
Those two had loved! And there he lay, the dead,
In his youth's flower—and she, the living, stood
With her grey hair, whence hue and gloss had fled—
And wasted form, and cheek, whose flushing blood
Had long since ebb'd—a meeting sad and strange!
—O! are not meetings in this world of change
Sadder than partings oft! She stood there, still,
And mute, and gazing—all her soul to fill
With the loved face once more—the young, fair face,
'Midst that rude cavern, touch'd with sculpture's grace,
By torchlight and by death:—until at last
From her deep heart the spirit of the past
Gush'd in low broken tones:—"And there thou art!
And thus we meet, that loved, and did but part
As for a few brief hours!—My friend, my friend!

First-love, and only one! Is this the end
Of hope deferr'd, youth blighted? Yet thy brow
Still wears its own proud beauty, and thy cheek
Smiles—how unchanged!—while I, the worn, and weak,
And faded—oh! thou wouldst but scorn me now,
If thou couldst look on me!—a wither'd leaf,
Sear'd—though for thy sake—by the blast of grief!
Better to see thee thus! For thou didst go,
Bearing my image on thy heart, I know,
Unto the dead. My Ulric! through the night
How have I call'd thee! With the morning light
How have I watch'd for thee!—wept, wander'd, pray'd,
Met the fierce mountain-tempest, undismay'd,
In search of thee!—bound my worn life to one—
One torturing hope! Now let me die! 'Tis gone.
Take thy betroth'd!"—and on his breast she fell,
—Oh! since their youth's last passionate farewell,
How changed in all but love!—the true, the strong,
Joining in death whom life had parted long!
—They had one grave—one lonely bridal bed,
No friend, no kinsman there a tear to shed!
His name had ceased—*her* heart outlived each tie,
Once more to look on that dead face, and die!

ENGLISH SOLDIER'S SONG OF MEMORY

TO THE AIR OF "AM RHEIN, AM RHEIN!"

SING, sing in memory of the brave departed,
  Let song and wine be pour'd!
Pledge to their fame, the free and fearless-hearted,
  Our brethren of the sword!

Oft at the feast, and in the fight, their voices
  Have mingled with our own;
Fill high the cup, but when the soul rejoices,
  Forget not who are gone!

They that stood with us, 'midst the dead and dying,
  On Albuera's plain;
They that beside us cheerly track'd the flying,
  Far o'er the hills of Spain;

They that amidst us, when the shells were showering
  From old Rodrigo's wall,
The rampart scaled, through clouds of battle towering,
  First, first at Victory's call!

They that upheld the banners, proudly waving,
  In Roncesvalles' dell;
With England's blood the southern vineyards laving,
  Forget not how they fell!

Sing, sing in memory of the brave departed,
   Let song and wine be pour'd!
Pledge to their fame, the free and fearless-hearted,
   Our brethren of the sword!

HAUNTED GROUND.

> "And slight, withal, may be the things which bring
> Back on the heart the weight which it would fling
> Aside for ever—it may be a sound,
> A tone of music, Summer eve, or Spring,
> A flower—the wind—the ocean—which shall wound,
> Striking the electric train, wherewith we are darkly bound."—*Byron.*

Yes, it *is* haunted, this quiet scene,
Fair as it looks, and all softly green;
Yet fear thou not—for the spell is thrown,
And the might of the shadow, on me alone.

Are thy thoughts wandering to elves and fays,
And spirits that dwell where the water plays?
Oh! in the heart there are stronger powers,
That sway, though viewless, this world of ours!

Have I not lived 'midst these lonely dells,
And loved, and sorrow'd, and heard farewells,
And learn'd in my own deep soul to look,
And tremble before that mysterious book?

Have I not, under these whispering leaves,
Woven such dreams as the young heart weaves?
Shadows—yet unto which life seem'd bound;
And is it not—is it not haunted ground?

Must I not hear what *thou* hearest not,
Troubling the air of the sunny spot?
Is there not something to rouse but me,
Told by the rustling of every tree?

Song hath been here—with its flow of thought,
Love—with its passionate visions fraught;
Death—breathing stillness and sadness round—
And is it not—is it not haunted ground?

Are there no phantoms, but such as come
By night from the darkness that wraps the tomb?
A sound, a scent, or a whispering breeze,
Can summon up mightier far than these!

But I may not linger amidst them here!
Lovely they are, and yet things to fear;
Passing and leaving a weight behind,
And a thrill on the chords of the stricken mind.

Away, away!—that my soul may soar
As a free bird of blue skies once more!

Here from its wing it may never cast
The chain by those spirits brought back from the past.

Doubt it not—smile not—but go thou, too,
Look on the scenes where thy childhood grew—
Where thou hast pray'd at thy mother's knee,
Where thou hast roved with thy brethren free ;

Go thou, when life unto thee is changed,
Friends thou hast loved as thy soul, estranged ;
When from the idols thy heart hath made,
Thou hast seen the colors of glory fade ;

Oh ! painfully then, by the wind's low sigh,
By the voice of the stream, by the flower-cup's dye,
By a thousand tokens of sight and sound,
Thou wilt feel thou art treading on haunted ground.

THE CHILD OF THE FORESTS

(WRITTEN AFTER READING THE MEMOIRS OF JOHN HUNTER)

Is not thy heart far off amidst the woods,
   Where the red Indian lays his father's dust,
And by the rushing of the torrent floods
   To the Great Spirit, bows in silent trust ?
Doth not thy soul o'ersweep the foaming main,
To pour itself upon the wilds again ?

They are gone forth, the desert's warrior-race,
   By stormy lakes to track the elk and roe ;
But where art thou, the swift one in the chase,
   With thy free footstep and unfailing bow ?
Their singing shafts have reach'd the panther's lair,
And where art thou ?—thine arrows are not there.

They rest beside their streams—the spoil is won—
   They hang their spears upon the cypress bough ;
The night-fires blaze, the hunter's work is done—
   They hear the tales of old—but where art thou ?
The night-fires blaze beneath the giant pine,
And there a place is fill'd that once was thine.

For thou art mingling with the city's throng,
   And thou hast thrown thine Indian bow aside ;
Child of the forests ! thou art borne along
   E'en as ourselves, by life's tempestuous tide.
But will this be ? and canst thou *here* find rest ?
Thou hadst thy nature on the desert's breast.

Comes not the sound of torrents to thine ear,
  From the savannah-land, the land of streams?
Hear'st thou not murmurs which none else may hear?
  Is not the forest's shadow on thy dreams?
They call—wild voices call thee o'er the main,
Back to thy free and boundless woods again.

Hear them not! hear them not!—thou canst not find
  In the far wilderness what once was thine!
Thou hast quaff'd knowledge from the founts of mind,
  And gather'd loftier aims and hopes divine.
Thou know'st the soaring thought, the immortal strain—
Seek not the deserts and the woods again!

STANZAS TO THE MEMORY OF * * *

In the full tide of melody and mirth—
  While joy's bright spirit beams from every eye,
Forget not him, whose soul, though fled from earth,
  Seems yet to speak in strains that cannot die.

Forget him not, for many a festal hour,
  Charm'd by those strains, for us has lightly flown,
And memory's visions, mingling with their power,
  Wake the heart's thrill at each familiar tone.

Blest be the harmonist, whose well-known lays
  Revive life's morning dreams when youth is fled,
And, fraught with images of other days,
  Recall the loved, the absent, and the dead.

His the dear art whose spells awhile renew
  Hope's first illusions in their tenderest bloom—
Oh! what were life, without such moments threw
  Bright gleams, "like angel-visits," o'er its gloom?

THE VAUDOIS VALLEYS.

Yes, thou hast met the sun's last smile
  From the haunted hills of Rome;
By many a bright Ægean isle
  Thou hast seen the billows foam.

From the silence of the Pyramid,
  Thou hast watch'd the solemn flow
Of the Nile, that with its waters hid
  The ancient realm below.

Thy heart hath burn'd, as shepherds sung
  Some wild and warlike strain,
Where the Moorish horn once proudly rung
  Through the pealing hills of Spain.

And o'er the lonely Grecian streams
  Thou hast heard the laurels moan,
With a sound yet murmuring in thy dreams
  Of the glory that is gone.

But go thou to the pastoral vales,
  Of the Alpine mountains old,
If thou wouldst hear immortal tales
  By the wind's deep whispers told!

Go, if thou lovest the soil to tread
  Where man hath nobly striven,
And life, like incense, hath been shed,
  An offering unto Heaven.

For o'er the snows, and round the pines,
  Hath swept a noble flood;
The nurture of the peasant's vines
  Hath been the martyr's blood!

A spirit, stronger than the sword,
  And loftier than despair,
Through all the heroic region pour'd,
  Breathes in the generous air.

A memory clings to every steep
  Of long-enduring faith,
And the sounding streams glad record keep
  Of courage unto death.

Ask of the peasant *where* his sires
  For truth and freedom bled?
Ask, where were lit the torturing fires,
  Where lay the holy dead?—

And he will tell thee, all around,
  On fount, and turf, and stone,
Far as the chamois' foot can bound,
  Their ashes have been sown!

Go, when the Sabbath-bell is heard,*
  Up through the wilds to float,
When the dark old woods and caves are stirr'd
  To gladness by the note.

---

* See *Gilly's Researches among the Mountains of Piedmont*, for an
nteresting account of a Sabbath-day among the upper regions of the

When forth, along their thousand rills,
   The mountain people come,
Join thou their worship on those hills
   Of glorious martyrdom.

And while the song of praise ascends,
   And while the torrent's voice,
Like the swell of many an organ, blends,
   Then let thy soul rejoice.

Rejoice, that human hearts, through scorn,
   Through shame, through death made strong,
Before the rocks and heavens have borne
   Witness of God so long!

SONG OF THE SPANISH WANDERER.

PILGRIM! O say, hath thy cheek been fann'd
By the sweet winds of my sunny land?
Know'st thou the sound of its mountain pines?
And hast thou rested beneath its vines?

Hast thou heard the music still wandering by,
A thing of the breezes, in Spain's blue sky,
Floating away o'er hill and heath,
With the myrtle's whisper, the citron's breath!

Then say, are there fairer vales than those
Where the warbling of fountains for ever flows?
Are there brighter flowers than mine own, which wave
O'er Moorish ruin and Christian grave?

O sunshine and song! they are lying far
By the streams that look to the western star;
My heart is fainting to hear once more
The water-voices of that sweet shore.

Vaudois. The inhabitants of these Protestant valleys, who, like the Swiss, repair with their flocks and herds to the summit of the hills during the summer, are followed thither by their pastors, and at that season of the year assemble on that sacred day to worship in the open air.

Many were they that have died for thee,
And brave, my Spain! though thou art not free;
But I call them blest—they have rent *their* chain—
They sleep in thy *valleys*, my sunny Spain!

THE CONTADINA.

WRITTEN FOR A PICTURE.

Not for the myrtle, and not for the vine,
Though its grape, like a gem, be the sunbeam's shrine;
And not for the rich blue heaven that showers
Joy on thy spirit, like light on the flowers;
And not for the scent of the citron trees—
Fair peasant! I call thee not blest for *these.*

Not for the beauty spread over thy brow,
Though round thee a gleam, as of spring, it throw;
And not from the lustre that laughs from thine eye,
Like a dark stream's flash to the sunny sky,
Though the south in its riches nought lovelier sees—
Fair peasant! I call thee not blest for *these:*

But for those breathing and loving things—
For the boy's fond arm that around thee clings,
For the smiling cheek on thy lap that glows,
In the peace of a trusting child's repose—
For the hearts whose home is thy gentle breast
Oh! richly I call thee, and deeply blest!

TROUBADOUR SONG.

The warrior cross'd the ocean's foam
  For the stormy fields of war;
The maid was left in a smiling home
  And a sunny land afar.

His voice was heard where javelin showers
  Pour'd on the steel-clad line;
Her step was 'midst the summer flowers,
  Her seat beneath the vine.

His shield was cleft, his lance was riven,
  And the red blood stain'd his crest;
While she—the gentlest wind of heaven,
  Might scarcely fan her breast

MISCELLANEOUS PIECES.

Yet a thousand arrows pass'd him by,
　And again he cross'd the seas;
But she had died as roses die
　That perish with a breeze.

As roses die, when the blast is come
　For all things bright and fair—
There was death within the smiling home—
　How had death found her there?

END OF THE FIRST VOLUME.

Printed in the United Kingdom
by Lightning Source UK Ltd.
122884UK00001B/3/A